TEMPEST OVER TEXAS

For my friends at the Houston, Austin, Baton Rouge,
and Shreveport Civil War Round Tables.

The hospitality, kindness, and congeniality
of their members knows no bounds.

TEMPEST OVER TEXAS

The Fall and Winter
Campaigns of 1863–1864

Donald S. Frazier

State House Press

State House Press
at Schreiner University
Kerrville, TX
325-660-1752
www.mcwhiney.org

Cataloging-in-Publication Data

Names: Frazier, Donald S. (Donald Shaw), 1965-, author.

Title: Tempest over Texas: the fall and winter campaigns of 1863-1864 / Donald S. Frazier.

Description: First edition. | Kerrville, TX: State House Press, 2020. | Includes
bibliographical references and index.

Identifiers: ISBN 9781649670182 (soft cover); ISBN 9781933337838 (cloth);
9781933337852 (ebook)

Subjects: LCSH: Louisiana – History – Civil War, 1861-1865 – Campaigns. | Louisiana –
History – Civil War, 1861-1865 – Naval operations. | Texas – History – Civil War, 1861-1865
– Campaigns. | Texas – History – Civil War, 1861-1865 – Naval Operations. | United States
– History – Civil War, 1861-1865 – Campaigns. | United States – History – Civil War,
1861-1865 – Naval Operations. | Mexico – History – European Intervention, 1861-1867.

Classification: LLC E475.4 (print) | DDC 973.7

First edition 2020
First paperback printing 2023

Cover and page design by Allen Griffith of Eye 4 Design

Distributed by Texas A&M University Press Consortium
800-826-8911
www.tamupress.com

CONTENTS

Preface and Acknowledgments   1

ONE   The French Intervention   5

TWO   The Next Campaign   24

THREE   Creating the Trans-Mississippi   52

FOUR   Restoring a Confederate Order   76

FIVE   Reconnaissance   97

SIX   Sabine Pass   107

SEVEN   Morganza   136

EIGHT   The Invasion of Louisiana   159

NINE   Hurricane at Botany Bay   176

TEN   Texas Overland   196

ELEVEN   The Battles for Opelousas   217

TWELVE   The Houston Campaign   241

THIRTEEN   Bayou Bourbeau   265

FOURTEEN   The Beaches of Texas   293

FIFTEEN   Retreat and Advance   307

SIXTEEN   Esperanza   324

SEVENTEEN   A Persistent Enemy   344

EIGHTEEN   Texas   369

NINETEEN   Allons au Texas   380

TWENTY   Matagorda   394

TWENTY ONE   1864   406

TWENTY TWO   A Confederate Nation   424

EPILOGUE   Again   443

Endnotes   452

Bibliography   481

Index   494

PREFACE AND ACKNOWLEDGMENTS

This is a complicated book. I had intended, when I launched my *Louisiana Quadrille* more than a decade ago, to finish the telling of the story of Texas's and Louisiana's Civil War in four books—hence the clever series title. That was before I dove headfirst into this remarkable rabbit hole. The Civil War in this part of the Trans-Mississippi seemed easy enough at first glance, and I plotted out how I would tell the tale. But, as any researcher can attest, broad outlines rarely survive contact with the sources.

Tempest Over Texas was written while on a one-year sabbatical from McMurry University. I also wrote *Blood on the Bayou* at that time, so this is literally the back half of that original manuscript. Of the two, this work is far and away the most complex, and yet still does not finish the *Quadrille*. There will have to be a fifth volume that will include a topic I think has been covered very well by other scholars—the Red River Campaign of 1864.

What makes this book so complex? Those with only a cursory knowledge of Texas and Louisiana's Civil War History (which, it turns out, is a sizable group even among fans of the period) often frame the story as being composed of two major episodes: The Fall of New Orleans in May 1862, and the Red River Campaign of 1864. The silent stretches before, in between, and after have remained opaque for decades. My life's work has been an attempt to tell the story as fully, and as interestingly, as possible.

When I started, the Civil War was a popular topic, as was American History in general. America, at least for the time being, now seems hostile to history. The up and coming generation seems more interested in comic book heroes than American heroes.

Be that as it may, I remain on a mission.

I always knew the story I was telling would end in 1864 and kind of dribble along into 1865. What I discovered about the Red River Campaign, the closing episode, is no one could adequately explain to me why one would invade Texas—from New Orleans—via Shreveport. At the same time, a spate of books on the campaigns along the Texas coast in 1863 seemed never to be adequately tied to the operations in Louisiana. Nothing seemed to add up. So, I decided to sort it out. The result is *Tempest Over Texas*.

I hope this resulting volume makes sense, because it ended up being a large task. The geographical scope ranges from the Mississippi River to the Rio Grande . . . all the way to Mexico City! It also involves scores of regiments, and officers, and ships, and places. There is international intrigue and geopolitical brinkmanship, there are diplomats, revolutionaries, deserters, and soldiers. There are French troops and ironclads. There are also the ever-present questions of race and the fate of emancipated slaves. There is a lot about Unionist dissent behind Confederate lines. Through it all, there remain Tom Green, Alfred Mouton, Richard Taylor, and Nathaniel P. Banks, all of whom have been with me since the beginning of the *Quadrille*.

I believe I have changed the historiography of the American Civil War and in the process raised some important and timeless observations on the national experience. I have not read much about Gettysburg, relatively speaking, and I do not fool myself by believing those interested in the primary and secondary theaters of the war—Virginia and Tennessee—will spend much time with my work. I would argue, however, that it would do them little harm. For citizens of the New England States, New York, Ohio, Indiana, Illinois, Wisconsin, Missouri, and Iowa, their understanding of where the men of their states served is incomplete without examining the *Louisiana Quadrille*.

I need to spend a sentence or two on Nathaniel P. Banks. I have grown to appreciate him more the longer I spend with him. He did what he could in a difficult arena, and as will come clear in this book, often with his bosses actively undermining him. Anyone who has had *that* boss may come to appreciate General Banks in new ways. I cannot fully rehabilitate his reputation, but at least I can sympathize with some of his challenges.

Books are grand collaborations. I extend sincere thanks to the many great librarians and archivists most mentioned in the previous volumes. Still, they bear repeating. My greatest allies have been Mary Linn Wernet at Northwestern State University in Natchitoches, Louisiana, and Germain Bienvenu at Hill Memorial Library at Louisiana State University. They epitomize professionalism and help make my time spent in Louisiana's research libraries among my favorite memories as a scholar.

Many organizations invited me to speak on the topic and helped me get to Louisiana to do research. I want to especially thank Shane K. Bernard of the McIlhenny Company archives on Avery Island, Louisiana for his generous support. Others including J. A. Rummler and Angélique Bergeron of Pointe Coupée Parish, Louisiana, and the Fort Butler Foundation regulars including Andrew Capone, Drew Capone, Craig Bauer, Jimmy Johnson, and Glenn Falgoust helped point me to sources or provided them outright. Thanks also to super sleuth Dee Dee DiBenedetto of Palo Alto Plantation—she has a gift for research.

Ladd and Maryll Thibodaux, and Bass Thibodaux, also provided support services that I found invaluable—mostly involving fishing, eating, drinking, or a general atmosphere of *fais do-do*. Thanks also to Steven Mayeux of Cottonport, Louisiana, and Richard Holloway of Alexandria, Louisiana for being there early on.

Together I hope to someday lay a wreath at the site of General Grant's horse wreck with all these fine folks.

The Reverend Robert F. Pace, Ph.D., in a previous iteration, suggested the *Louisiana Quadrille* as a series one afternoon sitting around a table in Buffalo Gap, Texas. It is all his fault—from the series outline to the overly dramatic titles.

I am glad he provided the push to get these stories out of my head and into print. Will there be a fifth book in the Louisiana Quadrille? I am planning for it, God willing. I feel like I have resurrected these campaigns, these people, from obscurity and know them better than perhaps anyone else on earth. They lived, they struggled, and they passed, as do we all. I feel like I owe it to them, and to the readers who have followed this story from the very beginning, to close the loop and finish the chore. Alas, life intervenes.

I began this journey many years ago as a young associate professor. I had summers off to pursue my scholarship and advance the narrative. It was a happy life. Yet, I was destined for other adventures. In 2020 we started The Texas Center at Schreiner University to engage in all the current issues swirling around the state. The Civil War shaped Texas—indelibly—and crafted a place that, in my opinion, represents what the original founders of the United States had in mind. The framers in Philadelphia were Texans in their philosophy, they just hadn't met the place yet! As might be imagined, defending an honest approach to history has attracted sniping from both the left and right of the political spectrum.

"Who controls the past controls the future: Who controls the present controls the past," George Orwell famously wrote in his dystopian novel *1984*. There is at present a real struggle to control the past in the telling of the American story, and as Orwell suggests, it is actually about controlling the present.

This new task, this fresh purpose, has taken me away from the halcyon days of a scholar-professor and into a much larger effort. I am still writing, of course, but now my pen is pointed toward new and very present battlefields. One day I will return to the days of 1864 and 1865 and finish the telling of that time and place.

But not just yet.

ONE **THE FRENCH INTERVENTION**

Mexico, thus regenerated, will ever be favorable.
—Napoleon III
Emperor of France

On May 5, 1862, General Ignacio Seguín Zaragoza surveyed the slopes of Guadalupe Hill overlooking Puebla, Mexico. Bespectacled, slight of stature, and well groomed, he looked more a lawyer than a warrior. Despite his appearance, he had shown his mettle. As he scanned the fresh battlefield beneath gloomy, dark, brooding skies, the cloud-heavy heavens finally released and dropped a steady mountain shower—like they always did on spring afternoons in the mountains of Mexico. The rain, though, compounded the suffering of his men, especially the wounded. Such was war, he must have mused.

Raindrops pattered on the bill of his kepi as he gazed in relief and amazement across the rugged fields and gullies. The enemy he had fought for several hours was falling back, beyond the range of his cannon. Would they assault the hill again? Would the rain keep them away until tomorrow, perhaps? Would they finally overwhelm the tattered garrison of the fortified convent the men of Mexico had held to the point of the bayonet? Would the gaudy French Zouaves who threatened his nation's independence ultimately prevail despite this minor reverse?

Slowly, a realization dawned upon Zaragoza. He may have actually defeated the enemy. The well-disciplined French veterans of battlefields ranging from Algeria, Italy, and the Crimea had tried, and nearly succeeded, to take the city of Puebla. Although they had aborted their attempt at storming the heights, they had not re-formed their attack columns. Once in retreat they continued until they were out of sight, abandoning their wounded. Now these wrecked European soldiers lay suffering from ghastly injuries, many lying in the mud within feet of their objective on Guadalupe Hill.

Sensing an opportunity for plunder, and now able to vent their boiling tension, Zaragoza's *soldados* leapt over their own parapets to poke and prod the fallen. Some of the stricken Frenchmen wept—not only from the pain of their injuries but also from their wounded pride—as the victors manhandled them, stripping them of their hard-won campaign medals. These strips of brass and ribbon had made an impressive display on the Zouaves' chests and had served to raise their fighting spirit. Now the battlefield booty would provide a bonus for the soldados who might traffic them in the town market.

As the retreating French army disappeared out of sight, the shower dissipated, allowing Zaragoza to reconsider the scene of his victory. Shafts of sunlight piercing the thinning clouds revealed dead men wearing deep blue coats and bright red pants littering the slope. Others groaned and flailed in agony. There must be several hundred of them, Zaragoza may have thought. Stunned and still unclear on what he had accomplished, the Mexican general made his way back to his headquarters under the brightening sky to compose and file his reports with the government of President Benito Juárez.

He took his place at his writing desk, dipped his pen into ink, and began scratching on paper. "After three hours of fierce combat, the honor of our arms was well made," Zaragoza reported. He knew he and his soldados had delivered a telling blow against the French. "The enemy was scarred by the multitude of dead, wounded, and prisoners." Even so, Zaragoza knew his *Cinco de Mayo* battle had been a near run. "The courage of both sides shone," he continued, "but victory favored the justice of our cause."[1]

This fight in the mountains of Mexico was just a slice of what had been a turbulent decade across much of North America. After the 1846–1848 war between the United States and Mexico, both republics had turned inward to sort through contentious, long-standing domestic issues and had tumbled into civil war. Parties in the United States debated issues surrounding slavery, a correct reading of the U.S. Constitution, states' rights, national federalism, and even-handed economics. Mexicans, meanwhile, dueled over the political identity of

Texas-born General Ignacio Zaragoza, hero of the Battle
of Puebla on the Cinco de Mayo. *Library of Congress.*

their nation. They renewed a fight as old as their independence from Spain, and conservative and liberal factions slashed at each other once again, plunging their country into open, destructive warfare.

The United States, despite its own troubles, lamented the Mexican imbroglio, which came to be called *La Guerra de la Reforma* (The War of the Reform). The liberals under President Benito Juárez fought well in the late 1850s, and he had consolidated their control of most of Mexico by 1861. His conservative enemies, though, remained deeply ensconced in Mexico City and turned to a Mexican specialty, guerilla warfare, to prolong the contest. Buying time with the blood and treasure of the nation, the defeated conservative faction made a play for foreign intervention from Europe, hoping to reverse the tide of war by mortgaging Mexican independence.

Juárez did not help his situation. With many of countrymen working against him, Juárez found few allies as he tried to untangle his nation's war-wrecked economy. Crippled by political bickering, he foolishly weakened his position abroad by suspending debt payments to Mexico's principal foreign investors: Great Britain, Spain, and France. There simply was not enough money to go around. Unsympathetic to the chaos in Mexico, and willing to exploit the

President Benito Juarez of Mexico. *Library of Congress.*

weakness of the United States—after all, how could the Americans enforce the Monroe Doctrine when they faced a civil war of their own—these European powers united. In October 1861 they signed the Convention of London and promised to send a joint task force of ships and troops to the principal port of Veracruz to force Juárez to give them their money.

Mexican conservatives leapt at the opportunity. In 1859—three years earlier, at the height of the War of the Reform—Mexican envoys had approached Ferdinand Maximilian Joseph, the younger brother of the Austrian emperor Franz Joseph I, with a plan to settle the political issues of their homeland. Believing their country was incapable of thriving as a republic, these messengers hoped this distinguished, unemployed, European royal might be convinced to become the monarch of Mexico. This autocrat, the Mexicans argued, would be defended by the best soldiers in the world, sent from the most powerful nations on earth, which would want to set the nation right, if for no other reason than to protect their investment. The British blanched at such a prospect, but the French did not. Three years had passed, though, and the conservatives' scheme remained stalled.[2]

As if God favored conservative prayers, in 1862 the coalition of European ships and troops arrived on the Mexican coast. Scheming Mexican monarchists met with the aggravated Europeans and promised them a repayment of all national debts in exchange for their support in toppling Juárez and the liberals and establishing a Mexican monarchy. At first most of the Europeans seemed

Archduke Ferdinand Maximilian Joseph, an Austrian of noble pedigree who Mexican Conservatives hoped would agree to become their emperor. *Library of Congress.*

disinterested in picking sides in this scruffy, interminable Latin American conflict. Instead, French, Spanish, and British forces would blockade the Mexican coast until silver and gold flowed back across the Atlantic. They did not need to choose favorites as long as the foreign commerce of Mexico flowed past their cannon.

Unlike their partners, however, the French smelled an opportunity. By backing the minority party and putting it back into power in Mexico, they might create a client state. They could direct its economy and its production, all to *la gloire de la France.* There would be an additional dividend: France would have a base from which to influence matters in the Gulf of Mexico and meddle in the affairs of the United States, perhaps permanently crippling the American Union by maintaining its split from a single mighty power into two diminished nations.

Like Mexico, the United States had a disgruntled minority faction that might prove susceptible to French manipulation. The Confederate States of America would need foreign intervention to succeed, but few nations dared tangle with even a distracted United States. Perhaps there was an indirect approach. French resources might make their way to the American insurgents by a surreptitious route through Mexico. After all, the grandparents of these same Americans had held French weapons in their triumph at Yorktown in 1781, so why shouldn't latter-day revolutionaries handle French steel in their own bid for independence? A divided nation north of the Rio Grande would remove one of the greatest obstacles to French schemes in the Americas.

At first, Emperor Napoleon III held his views close, but certain observers understood his game. "An empire in Mexico would not have entered into the views of the French government had not a most important event, the civil war in the United States, been inaugurated a few months previously," noted Adolphe Guéroult of the Paris-based L'Opinion Nationale. Complaints against Juárez and his liberal government accelerated in France, he noted, "a few months after the first cannon shots were exchanged at Charleston."[3]

The joint-European expedition made great headway. Veracruz fell to a six-thousand-man Spanish force while twenty-five hundred French troops took other cities along the coast. In March 1862 Napoleon III sent over a sizable expeditionary army, ostensibly to beef up the European presence. Britain and Spain, growing wise to French imperial ambitions, withdrew from the Convention of London and quickly recalled their troops and moved their ships out of Mexican waters. The French remained, encouraged by a report from their minister plenipotentiary in Mexico City, Alphonse Dubois de Saligny. "With each passing day, I am more inclined to believe that nothing could prevent a corps of 4,000 to 5,000 European soldiers from marching right to Mexico City without encountering the slightest resistance," the diplomat claimed. Napoleon III was willing to test this theory.[4]

Freed from pretense, the French pressed on alone, beguiled by the offer of domestic support from Mexican conservatives. Some four thousand additional French troops arrived under the command of General Charles Ferdinand Latrille, Comte de Lorencez. Napoleon III authorized this veteran officer to take the liberal stronghold of Puebla, the gateway to the Valley of Mexico, and then to march against the national capital. After capturing Mexico City, the French could install a government of their choosing and banish Juárez and his republican supporters, solving Mexico's recurring civil war. At the same time, French proxies could influence affairs in the newly founded Confederate States of America. If conditions proved favorable, France might even recognize, and align, with the southerners.

French minister plenipotentiary to Mexico, Alphonse Dubois de Saligny. He had also led the French mission to the Republic of Texas two decades earlier. *Library of Congress.*

The growing Franco-Confederate connection seemed obvious. "Whoever shall write the history of the Great Rebellion," predicted the *Chicago Tribune* a few years later, "will not complete it until he has traced to its final termination the effort of the Austrian Archduke to establish himself on the throne of a Mexican empire." For Southerners hungry for French recognition, the sacrifice of Mexico's republic was a small price to pay. "Monroe Doctrine is dead for all time to come," trumpeted the *Charleston Mercury.*[5]

The Confederate envoy to France, John Slidell, assured Napoleon III the fledgling nation's intentions were sincere. "While foreign occupation of that country would excite the most violent opposition at the North," he wrote, "we, far from sharing such a feeling, would be pleased to see a steady, respectable, responsible government established there soon."[6]

Indeed, in the early months of 1862, the signs for French success at putting the Austrian nobleman in power amid the Mexican political wreckage looked favorable. Then came the disaster of Cinco de Mayo, from which the reverberations shuddered across the continent. "Zaragoza defended in Puebla not only the integrity of his country but also that of the United States," declared Mexican historian Justo Sierra. "An involuntary service . . . but one of inestimable value."[7]

Emperor Napoleon III of France, notorious for launching military adventures across the globe. *Library of Congress*

Napoleon III fumed when he heard the reports of the battle, for he knew time was precious. At any moment, the United States might regain the initiative in its war against the secessionists; indeed, the signs pointed toward a Federal resurgence. Just before the debacle at Puebla, Union major general Benjamin Butler had marched U.S. troops through the streets of New Orleans, the Confederacy's largest city, effectively stoppering exports from the Mississippi Valley. Time was slipping away for a French coup de main.

Napoleon III realized the Federal capture of one of the most strategic cities in North America might cripple any chance for Confederate success. Most Europeans understood it was the New Orleans banks that created the instruments by which Confederate independence might be financed and won. Cotton, the mainstay the South had hoped to leverage with European powers, served as security for Confederate loans. The fall of New Orleans, however, portended that creditors would never actually put hands on this collateral in case of default. Confederate credit plummeted, and rampant inflation spiraled.

The news from the Western Hemisphere lashed at Napoleon III for other reasons as well. Mexico was only one of his adventures. He had stationed troops in China, and he had plans for further escapades in Southeast Asia

General Élie Frédéric Forey became the architect of French policy in Mexico. *Library of Congress.*

and, perhaps, Korea. He had hoped to create an unassailable French enclave in the Americas quickly and inexpensively. The potential gain was worth the national risk, he believed, because even without allying with the Confederates, cotton could flow south across the border from Texas and onto ships bound for Calais, Marseilles, Le Havre, and Bordeaux. The French would meanwhile facilitate the flow of weapons and munitions through Texas to fuel the civil war in the United States. But now, the news from Puebla and New Orleans jeopardized his schemes. To make matters worse for the emperor, these events inspired French opponents of these international escapades, and domestic support of his world ambitions suddenly seemed precarious.

Still, Napoleon III believed a chance remained if a new timetable could be kept. His troops might still clear the way for an appropriate European nobleman to assume the Cactus Throne of Mexico before the United States could oppose the move. By the time the Americans could react, the massive French presence in the Western Hemisphere could be a fait accompli.

Therefore, Napoleon III dispatched a new commander, General Élie Frédéric Forey, to retrieve French fortunes in Mexico. "There will be people to ask you why we waste so many men, and spend so much money, in establishing a regular government in Mexico," Napoleon III wrote to his general. The answer, simply stated, was to make the world a place that suited the French. The United States, the emperor hoped, could remain an important nation and trading partner but must be kept from extending its influence over all of the Gulf of Mexico.[8]

Cotton, too, played a role. The Union blockade had crippled French textile mills. As Napoleon III wrote, "We now see by sad experience how precarious an industry is which is compelled to seek its raw material in a single market." Mexico, perhaps, could supply the needs of French industry, in terms of both

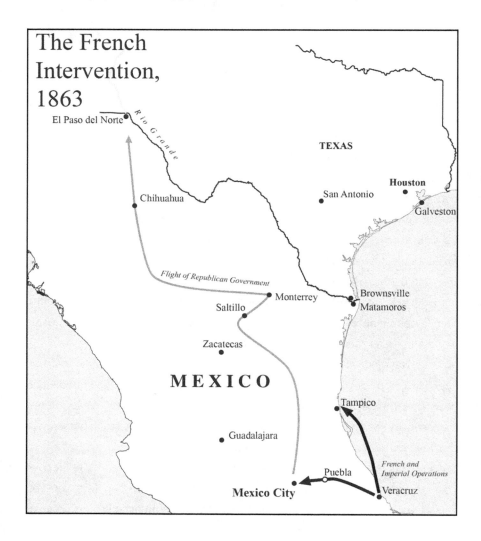

The French Intervention, 1863

El Paso del Norte

Rio Grande

TEXAS

Chihuahua

San Antonio

Houston

Galveston

Flight of Republican Government

Monterrey

Brownsville

Saltillo

Matamoros

Zacatecas

MEXICO

Tampico

Guadalajara

French and Imperial Operations

Puebla

Mexico City

Veracruz

supply and demand. "While it makes a market for our fabrics," he continued, the establishment of a friendly government in Latin America "secures us the material indispensable to our manufactures. Mexico, thus regenerated, will ever be favorable."[9]

Strategically, Mexico fell into five different theaters of operations. The easiest for the French to reach had been the eastern seaboard, centered on the port of Veracruz and stretching south to the Tabasco River and Campeche. The northern limits of this zone led to Tampico and the hinterlands of the Huasteca. In the tropical and disease-laden southeast lay Yucatan, Chiapas, and the wild country of Campeche and Tabasco—never completely controlled by officials in Mexico City and roiled by racial violence for decades. The French would ignore this second region and trust their Mexican puppets there to keep the peace.

The most important region to control was the interior, with gateways through the eastern towns of Jalapa and Orizaba and the prize being Mexico City. Roads led southeast through the garden region of Oaxaca, south through Guerrero all the way to the important port of Acapulco on the Pacific, and west and north into the highlands of Michoacán and Guanajuato.

The remaining two theaters were in the north Mexico. The troublesome border states of Coahuila, Nuevo Léon, and Tamaulipas had long been the domain of local strongmen—known colloquially as caudillos. From Mexico City, the gateway to this region was San Luis Potosi. In the northwest lay Guadalajara, Durango, and the vast deserts and mountains of Chihuahua and Sonora.

In the summer and fall of 1862 the French buildup continued, and reinforcements flowed into Veracruz. General Forey now commanded forty thousand French troops, nearly six percent of the entire national army, plus another ten thousand Mexican Imperialist auxiliaries. Despite their distractions, Americans took notice as the French presence expanded. The arrival of more Gallic legions coincided with a U.S. show of force on the Texas coast. In October 1862 a modest Union naval squadron captured Galveston and Indianola. A month later the French landed at Tampico, five hundred miles down the Gulf Coast, ostensibly to establish an outpost for collecting mules and beeves to supply the campaign for Central Mexico. The timing of these French and American maneuvers indicated each side was taking the measure of the other, like potential pugilists.

The French flexed their military muscle with a show of naval power. The freshly launched ironclad steam frigate *Normandie*, bristling with 6-inch rifled cannon in its broadsides, supported the Tampico expedition. The warship delivered two unmistakable messages to the United States: first, it had sailed across the Atlantic, not to overwhelm the non-existent Mexican navy, but rather to project unrivaled French power in the Gulf of Mexico by proving the voyage could be made. Second, even skeptics believed the *Normandie* alone could whip even the strongest Union vessel afloat and could sweep the western Gulf of Mexico. The Americans could not see that the French navy could dispatch two more ships, just as powerful, to the Gulf Coast if necessary.[10]

This international game of chicken took place on a remote and sparsely settled shore, but the gateway to Texas, Matamoros, and its saltwater boomtown port of Bagdad blossomed, nurtured by the contraband commerce of war. The two towns lay as a plump prize between the French at Tampico and the Americans at Indianola.

One of the greatest of American concerns in the Gulf of Mexico was the presence of a sizable French fleet, led by the formidable *Normandie*, a sistership to *Le Gloire*, pictured here. The French proved that iron-hulled warships could safely transit the Atlantic. *The French Battleship* La Gloire *by Francoise Geoffrey Roux* (1880), *Musee de la Marine.*

The Gulf Coast was controlled by cunning men, including local warlord Juan Nepomuceno "Cheno" Cortina. An illiterate Mexican *rico*, Cortina had troubled the United States before the Civil War, and he remained an important, and unpredictable, force on the border. He watched the movements of four great forces—the Imperialists, the Republicans, the Federals, and the Confederates—with a practiced eye, intent on backing winners wherever he could. For Cortina, self-interest often trumped patriotism.[11]

As the factions in Mexico and the American belligerents watched each other, favorites emerged on both sides. From his headquarters at Brownsville, Confederate brigadier general Hamilton P. Bee declared the liberals to be the South's enemy: "The tone of the Juarez government in Mexico has been hostile to our cause," Bee reported, "and at his dictation various measures have been initiated calculated to injure and annoy us." Meanwhile Governor Santiago Vidaurri, of Coahuila and Nuevo Léon, and others threatened to openly oppose Juárez if he persisted in his anti-Confederate declarations—not because of their love of the American South, but because they intended to remain El Jefe and see which way the political winds might blow. Like Cortina, they sought ways to benefit personally.[12]

The American vice-consul in Matamoros, M. M. Kimmey, embraced Juárez and his cause. Diplomats created a haven for Unionists and urged them to travel to New Orleans and join the U.S. Army while encouraging locals to remain loyal to Juárez and to plunder the Texan settlements across the river. American agents even teased the idea of returning the region from the Rio Grande to the Nueces River as a reward for Mexican support.[13]

Bee positioned his Confederates to snuff out any of these attempts and urged Mexican governors in bordering states to prevent such devilment. Bee believed Texas and the Confederacy could prosper in this unsettled atmosphere. Cotton was king on the Rio Grande. "With the glittering attraction of our cotton the whole available resources of Mexico are being brought to us," boasted Bee. "Shoes, blankets, cloth, powder, lead, saltpeter, sulphur . . . are now coming in quantity which will soon supply our wants." The trade was so brisk, Bee contended, San Antonio should become a great exchange hub with massive warehouse complexes where agents would swap cotton for items vital to sustain the Confederate war

Matías Romero Avendaño represented Mexican interests to Abraham Lincoln's government. *Library of Congress*.

effort. Access to cotton though Mexico could once again guarantee Confederate bonds and restore the value of the nation's currency. The fall of New Orleans might be erased. "I sincerely wish," Bee wrote, "that I could attract the attention of the government to the rich mine of wealth and power she has in this cotton."[14]

The new year, 1863, reversed Union fortunes in the Western Gulf. The Confederates recaptured Galveston, secured Sabine Pass and Matagorda Bay, and effectively swept the Texas coast of Federal forces. Forey used this opportunity to abandon his sickly northern outpost at Tampico. At the same time Juárez seemed to be losing his grip on the country, as the French prepared to launch a massive campaign to finish what they had started.[15]

Losing ground, Mexican liberals grew desperate. Mexican diplomat Matías Romero Avendaño lobbied passionately in Washington, D.C., on behalf of the flagging Republican cause, and his influence shaped the debate in the halls of government. President Abraham Lincoln was sympathetic to Romero's pleas. Congressmen, in a lather over the issue, split into two camps. Some, led by

General François Achille Bazaine led the French forces in the field and captured Mexico City in June 1863. *Library of Congress.*

Senator James A. McDougall of California, Representative Henry Winter Davis of Maryland, and Representative John Kasson of Iowa, flew under the nickname of Mexico "hawks" and favored confronting the French, even if it meant immediate war. Others, like Senator Charles Sumner, chairman of the Senate Foreign Relations Committee, were more pragmatic and urged caution until the Union had crippled the Confederacy and could face the French on more secure footing.[16]

While politicians strutted and postured, frustrated Americans who sensed a righteous cause began conversing about how volunteers might enter Mexico to join the Juaristas on their own. Republican promises of high pay and generous land bounties seeded groups like the Defenders of the Monroe Doctrine, the Mexican Aid Society, the Mexico Club, the Monroe Doctrine Committee, and the Monroe League to sprout in cities from California to New York. American fighting men, discharged from their service to the Union, might grow rich opposing the French and their Mexican toadies. Juan Cortina even advertised for recruits to join his 1st Mexican Volunteers from among Union soldiers absent from their commands—with or without leave—in the streets of New Orleans.[17]

By late spring 1863, with the United States growing more conscious of the threat, the French relaunched their Mexican adventure. Forey and his command swept into the interior from his base at Veracruz and besieged Puebla, forcing its capitulation on May 17 and undoing Zaragoza's brilliant defense of the previous year. As American armies slugged it out in the Mississippi Valley, the French army under General François Achille Bazaine pressed on, descending from the mountains into the Valley of Mexico.

Bazaine's campaign crumpled Juárez's flailing government. In early June 1863, while Confederates defended Vicksburg and Port Hudson, Bazaine's men captured Mexico City, and Forey installed General Juan Almonte, a conservative, as the new provisional president. Juárez fled to San Luis Potosi in northern Mexico to continue the struggle. "Adversity is not sufficient cause for fainting," Juárez

General Juan Almonte was a leading Conservative. In his colorful career, he helped capture the Alamo and had in turn become a prisoner at San Jacinto during the Texas Revolution. He served as Secretary of War under Antonio Lopez de Santa Anna in the US-Mexican War. The French installed him as regent of the Second Mexican Empire. *Library of Congress*.

proclaimed, for "Republicans who defend their native land and their rights." Despite this bluster, by mid-July, President Almonte and his *Junta Superior* declared the end of the Republic of Mexico and the emergence of a Catholic Mexican Empire backed by Napoleon III. French bayonets would insure the success of this new Mexican incarnation.[18]

Observers in the United States now understood what lay at stake in Mexico. "Casting all promises and pretexts to the winds," wrote Lieutenant Colonel Richard B. Irwin of the 19th Army Corps, "the French troops . . . marched into the capital of Mexico, made themselves masters of the country [and] vamped up a sham throne." Texas, or the entire Trans-Mississippi, might be next, the Union officer believed. "That Napoleon III nursed among his favorite dreams the vision of a Latin empire in America, built upon the ruins of Mexican liberty and taking in at least the fairest portion of Louisiana that his illustrious uncle had parted with so cheaply," Irwin sneered, "was well known."[19]

Despite this French success, Forey grew uneasy. He understood the risks Napoleon III was taking and saw in daily reports that the grand scheme could not be done as inexpensively, or as quickly, as hoped. Conquering Mexico City had been accomplished with a column of thirty thousand French troops, but subduing the rest of Mexcio would require tens of thousands more. Besides, Forey reasoned, not only had resistance in Mexico proven stubborn, but the Union had clearly regained the initiative in the U.S. Civil War that summer. While Bazaine and his Zouaves, *Voltiguers, Chasseurs-a-pied* and the *Légion Étrangère* routed Mexican Republicans, U.S. troops penned two large Confederate armies inside their Mississippi River forts. Federal armies had shoved Southern forces nearly out of Tennessee. Only Confederate general Robert E. Lee's Army of Northern Virginia appeared capable of holding its ground.

Supporting the Confederates would come with a steep price for the French. Great Britain would certainly oppose a French-Confederate alignment, widening a rift between the European nations. There remained, too, another delicate matter. Should they overtly assist the Confederacy, the French would also seem to support slavery, a cause they had worked against worldwide. The Americans had already made abolition central to their war aims; Abraham Lincoln had issued the Emancipation Proclamation effective January 1, 1863.

The battle of Puebla had an important, and often unappreciated, impact on the American Civil War. *Author's collection.*

Having liberated slaves, the United States had also militarized many black men, which would undoubtedly influence the course of the war. There were already signs these new troops would add combat strength to the Union. African American soldiers served at Port Hudson and fought well at Milliken's Bend, Fort Butler, and elsewhere in the Mississippi Valley and along the Atlantic coast, demonstrating their growing role in the conflict. Then, too, on June 11, 1863—a day after the French formed a new government in Mexico—black soldiers from the 54th Massachusetts and the 2nd South Carolina burned the town of Darien, Georgia, in a militarily worthless but politically startling gesture that sent a clear and terrifying signal to Southerners. At the very least, black soldiers could constitute a second American army and garrison strategic posts while President Lincoln's white army could oppose the French.

Overwhelming Union victories in the first two weeks of July 1863 cast a shade on French plans to support the Confederacy. The cataclysmic Battle of Gettysburg on July 1–3 mangled Lee's bold army, the only successful Confederate command, and crippled its offensive power in Virginia. The fall of Vicksburg on July 4 and

Port Hudson on July 9 completed the Union capture of the Mississippi River. Within days afterward, Federal troops fanned out on both banks of the river and scattered Rebel forces in the region.

After seeing these reverses, and with the obnoxious cause of slavery proving too bitter to swallow, Napoleon III grew cold on the Confederacy. "There had occurred in quick succession three events that must have sounded in his ears with tones that even his dull imagination could not easily misunderstand," crowed Lieutenant Colonel Irwin. "These were Gettysburg, Vicksburg, and Port Hudson. He had not the least notion of helping the unsuccessful."[20]

This crescendo of Union successes spoiled the timing of Napoleon III's Mexican adventure. His earlier hopes for a lightning campaign and a popular uprising in favor of his beneficence had lost their way. Nor could he count on the Confederacy to distract the United States from his advances. Still, the French pushed their plan. Even as the news of U.S. triumphs spread across the globe, the Second Mexican Empire sent a written invitation for Ferdinand Maximilian Joseph of Austria to assume the Cactus Throne and become its monarch. The young nobleman returned no immediate reply.

TWO

THE NEXT CAMPAIGN

There is no enemy of any force now in the department south of Alexandria.

—Major General Nathaniel P. Banks
Department of the Gulf

"**F**our great victories—Gettysburg, Helena, Vicksburg, Port Hudson—in eight days," trumpeted Secretary of War Edwin M. Stanton. "Every rebel army has been captured or is in flight." July 1863 would be forever historic. "Our success within so brief a period . . . is unexampled in military history," he gushed. "The rebel disasters are greater than ever befell a belligerent." The fall of the Confederacy seemed assured. The question remained: how to finish it?[1]

Major Generals Ulysses S. Grant and Nathaniel P. Banks had ripped off the arm of the Confederate Grendel. By cleaving the seceded states down the Mississippi, the stump remaining west of the river would surely wither. Grant and Banks could now set their armies to other tasks. Final victory in this civil war, these generals believed, lay to the east. Elements of Grant's Army of the Tennessee, the 9th, 13th, and 15th Army Corps, headed toward Jackson, Mississippi, under Major General William Tecumseh Sherman and by mid-month had driven the sluggish Confederate army under General Joseph E. Johnston from the state's capital. Having shooed away the Rebels, Sherman fell back. Then, Grant's great army began to break up, bound for service elsewhere.

Union general-in-chief Henry Halleck trusted Banks to destroy the remnant of Confederate forces in Louisiana. "I suppose the first thing done by your army after the fall of Port Hudson was to clean out the Teche and Atchafalaya countries," Halleck wrote to Banks. But Banks had not done so. Instead, the Confederates under Major General Richard Taylor had bloodied his disease-ridden, exhausted army at Kock's Plantation shorty after Banks shifted from Port Hudson to Donaldsonville. Taylor now held the interior, and much tedious work remained

Secretary of War Edwin M. Stanton. *Library of Congress.*

before Banks could sweep away the Rebel remnant. Why bother? Union troops—including the African American soldiers of his *Corps d'Afrique*—could mount a stout defense behind the Atchafalaya River, which the enemy could never hope to penetrate. Taylor and the Trans-Mississippi could simply rot away.[2]

Major General Grant agreed. He wanted no part in such trifling custodial work west of the Mississippi River. Instead, he wanted to launch his Army of the Tennessee eastward, onto its next great campaign. "Having cleaned up about Vicksburg and captured or routed all regular Confederate forces for more than a hundred miles in all directions, I felt that the troops that had done so much should be allowed to do more before the enemy could recover from the blow he had received," Grant wrote, "and while important points might be captured without bloodshed." One of these easy pickings, he held, was Mobile. He thoughtfully suggested to Halleck that portions of his and Banks's Mississippi Valley armies conduct a quick overland campaign against Mobile via Lake Pontchartrain, supplied by sea.[3]

To Halleck's generals, Mobile seemed like the logical, strategic step. Perhaps afterward the focus could move toward Tennessee and Georgia. While Grant had been reducing Vicksburg, Major General William Rosecrans had been

Major General Henry Halleck, the architect of Federal military strategy. *Library of Congress.*

maneuvering Lieutenant General Braxton Bragg's Confederates out of Tennessee. By the time Vicksburg and Port Hudson fell, Rosecrans had forced Bragg to retreat to Chattanooga. By July Rosecrans felt ready to pry the enemy out of its last toehold in Tennessee, and he thought the Mississippi Valley armies could lend a hand. To hasten the aid of additional troops, Rosecrans sent Grant information about the defenses of Mobile. Rosecrans felt enthusiastic about the prospect of cornering Bragg between the Union armies of the Tennessee and the Gulf to the southwest and his Army of the Cumberland and Army of the Ohio to the north. After snatching Mobile and clearing out Tennessee, Georgia would fall quickly as Rosecrans, Grant, and Banks converged. [4]

But what about the French? Halleck, no matter his personal views regarding a campaign to take Mobile, understood those of the president. In late July Abraham Lincoln, in his usual indirect way, demanded a move into Texas. "Can we not renew the effort to organize a force to go to Western Texas?" he asked Stanton. "Please think of it. I believe no local object is now more desirable." The armies and navies of the United States had relieved the president's worries about the ultimate outcome of the war by their victories at Gettysburg, Pennsylvania, and in the Mississippi Valley. Lincoln believed the time had arrived to counter the moves of Napoleon III in Mexico.[5]

Next Major General Banks weighed in. He, like Major General Grant, had other ambitions. To satisfy concerns in Washington, Banks reported that he had already effectively cleared southwestern Louisiana of Confederate troops and the job of securing the west bank of the Mississippi was, in essence, complete. "There is no enemy of any force now in the department south of Alexandria," he claimed. Brashear City, near the mouth of the Atchafalaya River, was again the bulwark of the Lafourche District. The Mississippi River, Banks asserted, remained secure from enemy field batteries and sharpshooters from at least Port Hudson to New Orleans. Brashear City's small garrison and several shallow draft gunboats could hold the Atchafalaya line.[6]

In addition, Banks hoped to put the quagmire of Louisiana behind him. "New Orleans is perfectly quiet, the people well disposed, and . . . the negro regiments are organizing rapidly." Let African American Louisianans, Banks argued, backed

A heroic image of Major General Nathaniel P. Banks, hero of Port Hudson. *Library of Congress.*

by a remnant force of white New York and New England regiments, hold Louisiana. This black-and-white army could dig in from Morganza to Brashear City. He, like Grant, wanted to turn immediately toward Mobile.[7]

Despite the consensus of his victorious Mississippi Valley generals, President Lincoln insisted on taking Texas. Major General Grant grew impatient. "It would have been an easy thing to capture Mobile at the time I proposed to go there," Grant later wrote. ". . . The troops from Mobile could have inflicted inestimable damage upon much of the country from which his army and Lee's were yet receiving their supplies." The president remained unconvinced. There were other enemies besides General Robert E. Lee.[8]

Other voices chimed in. "Texas had no military value at that moment," Lieutenant Colonel Richard B. Irwin grumbled from his post in New Orleans. "To have overrun the whole State would hardly have shortened the war by a single day." Mobile, Irwin argued, would "have taken from the Confederates their only remaining line of railway communication between the Atlantic seaboard and the States bordering on the Mississippi." That, he insisted, would shorten the war.[9]

Defeating the Confederacy quickly, though, would have to remain a lower priority for the moment. Whether Grant or Banks agreed, Lincoln believed that international concerns demanded action west of the Mississippi. The French and

Major General Ulysses S. Grant, the conqueror of Vicksburg. *Library of Congress.*

their Mexican Imperialist allies would certainly finish off the republicans that fall and secure the Rio Grande border. Texas already served as the Confederate gateway to Mexico. Instead of facing U.S. troops at Brownsville, victorious Franco-Mexican forces would be in contact with Rebels at war with the U.S. government. The potential combination of Napoleon III's troops with Confederates in Texas panicked Lincoln. Now that Vicksburg and Port Hudson had fallen, surely troops released from these campaigns could finish the job in the Trans-Mississippi and then move into Texas to serve as a counter-weight to French designs. The war against secession seemed nearly won; now was the time to play a few moves ahead internationally.

Lincoln may have remembered advice he had received a year and a half earlier. Leslie Combs, a leading Kentucky politician, suggested taking Texas in March 1862. "Allow me to make one suggestion on this subject— There are large German colonies & very few slaves west of the Colorado," he wrote. "A few regiments . . . landed at Matagorda Bay could easily penetrate the State to Austin and San Antonio & cut Texas in two parts." There would be much to gain, he wrote. "The whole country abounds in stock. This operation would checkmate all military movements against New Mexico & cut off the whole Rio Grande frontier from [foreign] intrigue. I know the Country well and you may rely on what I say."[10]

President Abraham Lincoln. *Library of Congress.*

Banks feared Lincoln's proposed campaign into Texas would swallow his small army. He simply lacked the troops for anything too ambitious in the vast expanses of the west. His army had dwindled. Twenty-two of his nine-months regiments had already served their terms and gone home, leaving him with only twelve thousand men of the once-sizable force that had conquered Port Hudson and defended New Orleans, Pensacola, and Key West. The troops left were exhausted, and many soldiers were sick. If, however, his army received an infusion of men from Grant's command, Banks believed he could make short work of the five thousand Confederates in and around Mobile. Texas, Banks thought, could wait.[11]

Though he did not agree with Lincoln, Grant understood his fretfulness, as he later wrote: "The President was very anxious to have a foothold in Texas, to stop the clamor of some of the foreign governments which seemed to be seeking a pretext to interfere in the war."[12] So Grant offered a partial solution. Landing a brigade or so of U.S. troops near Brownsville and controlling the lower Rio Grande Valley might serve as an appropriate check to the French threat "without wasting troops in western Louisiana and eastern Texas."[13]

No one in Washington was listening. "Halleck preferred another course," Grant wryly recalled. "The possession of the trans-Mississippi by the Union forces seemed to possess more importance in his mind than almost any campaign east of the Mississippi."[14]

Halleck wanted to proceed with caution. He had good reason to believe the capture of the Mississippi River Valley remained incomplete. Both Grant and Banks had overestimated the thoroughness of the jobs they had accomplished at Vicksburg and Port Hudson. The capture of the Mississippi had served usefully as propaganda, but the realities along its banks continued to trouble local commanders. Rebels west of the river menaced steamboat captains and commercial boats as they made their runs upstream and downstream. Sharpshooters played on passing steamers; more batteries, Halleck assumed, would certainly arrive soon and try their luck with shot and shell. Fearing for the safety of their property, owners argued for an aggressive policy to clear—and hold—the river's west bank from St. Louis to New Orleans.[15]

Admiral David Dixon Porter found himself with a powerful
gunboat fleet in search of a mission. *Library of Congress.*

This local clamoring further confused Federal strategy and delayed moves on Mobile and Texas as Union forces made an attempt to control the riverbank. Major General Frederick Steele, operating out of Helena, Arkansas, led the newly created Army of Arkansas and rendezvoused with a cavalry force from Southeast Missouri on the White River in late July, putting a broad swath of territory under Union control. Smaller forces from Natchez, Mississippi, crossed into eastern Louisiana and established a beachhead on the Mississippi River at Vidalia, adding to those at Young's Point, Milliken's Bend, Goodrich's Landing, and Lake Providence. Now the region between Bayou Macon and the Tensas River lay within striking distance of Union forces.

It soon became clear that the Mississippi Valley, tamped down for the moment, would require constant vigilance. Therefore, the U.S. Navy redistributed its gunboats to keep the shores clear of Rebels. "I placed 11 gunboats at the most dangerous points below Vicksburg," reported Rear Admiral David Dixon Porter.

"At present the river all the way through is unusually quiet, but from information obtained along the route, the Rebels are preparing for active guerilla warfare along the river." Although a rapid reaction force, the "Marine Brigade," was available to stamp out fires, the admiral believed it would be inadequate to the task. Porter instead wanted the west bank permanently occupied—and soon.[16]

Lincoln grew weary of the carping among his Mississippi Valley commanders and sought a solution to all of the problems bedeviling him in the region. He started by writing to Grant. "I see by a dispatch of yours that you incline quite strongly towards an expedition against Mobile," Lincoln acknowledged. While Lincoln stopped short of rebuking Grant, he did warn him that operations opposed to a Texas-first policy would be counterproductive. "This would appear tempting to me also, were it not that in view of recent events in Mexico, I am greatly impressed with the importance of re-establishing the national authority

Major General Francis J. Herron won the Medal of Honor at the Battle of Pea Ridge and was a hero again at Prairie Grove. He led a division of the 13th Army Corps during the Vicksburg campaign and afterward. *Library of Congress.*

in Western Texas as soon as possible," Lincoln explained. "I am not making an order, however. That I leave, for the present at least, to the General-in-Chief."[17]

Halleck, implementing Lincoln's veiled threat, retaliated against Grant by dividing his forces. The army that had taken Vicksburg was now scattered up and down the Mississippi. Troops headed for Kentucky, Arkansas, Missouri, and Natchez; Banks and his army would also be among the beneficiaries. Major General Francis J. Herron's Division had already moved into camps at Port Hudson; now the other divisions of the 13th Army Corps headed to New Orleans to join Banks in the Army of the Gulf, beefing it up by nearly fifteen thousand men.

"Halleck disapproved of my propositions to go against Mobile," Grant complained, "so that I was obliged to settle down and see myself put again on the defensive." Sherman and the four divisions of the 15th Army Corps spread

Major General James B. McPherson was associated with Ulysses S. Grant from early in the war. He led the 17th Army Corps in the Vicksburg Campaign. *Library of Congress.*

A friend of Abraham Lincoln, South Carolina native Major General Stephen A. Hurlbut was a politician turned soldier and led the 16th Army Corps from Memphis. *Library of Congress.*

out in an arc along the Big Black River east of Vicksburg to keep an eye on a Rebel cavalry division under General Frank Armstrong operating near Jackson. Major General James McPherson and the four divisions of the 17th Army Corps garrisoned Vicksburg and Natchez. Major General James Hurlbut and the 16th Army Corps occupied a swath from Memphis to Columbus, Kentucky, and eastward to LaGrange, Tennessee, and Corinth, Mississippi. These troops would also support operations in Arkansas.[18]

The final task—to make sure the Mississippi remained navigable for Union shipping—fell to Grant. "The troops that were left with me around Vicksburg were very busily and unpleasantly employed in making expeditions against guerilla bands and small detachments of cavalry which infested the interior," Grant recalled, "and in destroying mills, bridges and rolling stock on the railroads." This was a dismal use of the Army of the Tennessee he believed. "The guerillas and cavalry were not there to fight," he observed, "but to annoy, and therefore disappeared on the first approach of our troops." While tens of thousands of veteran Union troops swatted at these annoying pests in the Mississippi Valley, Major General Rosecrans and his sixty thousand Federals working their way through southeast Tennessee would have no help from Grant or Banks in rooting out Bragg's fifty thousand Confederates.[19]

Believing the Mobile issue settled, and a chastened Grant bedded down in Vicksburg, Lincoln turned to Banks, whom he wanted in position to address the issue in Mexico. The president had always favored the liberal cause as being most reflective of American ideals, and he believed Benito Juarez was the greatest hope for Mexico. Matías Romero Avendaño, serving in the Mexican Legation in Washington, made sure that his nation's republican cause remained compelling to Americans.

"Recent events in Mexico, I think, render early action in Texas more important than ever," Lincoln wrote Banks on August 5. "I expect, however, the General-in-Chief, will address you more fully upon this subject." Halleck did just that. "There are important reasons why our flag should be restored in some point of Texas with the least possible delay," he cabled Banks. "Do this by land at Galveston, at Indianola, or at any other point you may deem preferable."[20]

The arrival of the Europeans in Mexico clearly signaled a slide toward despotism in that country, resulting in an inevitable collision with the United States, Lincoln believed. French moves up the Mexican coast in August confirmed

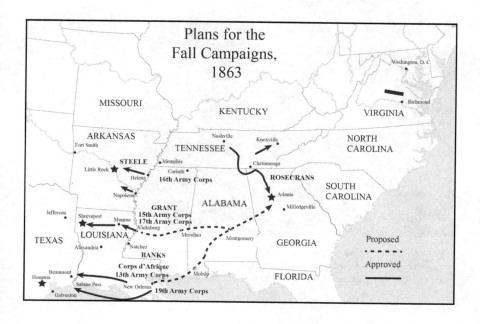

these fears and further fueled American anxiety. On August 8, 1863, four French steam frigates, three gunboats, and several transports arrived once again at the mouth of the Tampico river, anchored, and began a bombardment of the Mexican defenses that lasted for an afternoon. "The poor Mexicans are beginning to look for shelter from the storm, packing up and going in every direction," wrote a correspondent for the *New Orleans Era* whose story was picked up by the *New York Times*. "The Custom-House is left empty, and houses desolate, as well as many hearts, swept from all that is sacred and dear to them, and portions of this place, like the City of the Dead, are completely deserted." The republican garrison, commanded by Colonel Henry A. Mejia, fled into the mountains, "where the sons of the Gauls," the writer continued, "will not, at least for a time, reach them."[21]

The collapse of the Juarista defenses troubled the American journalist. "Mexico will make but little resistance to a grasping enemy who wishes to enlarge his bounds," he despaired, "and pay his expenses at the cost of the conquered."

French officers and a Zouave. These Algerian troops, with their exotic uniforms, were considered among the best in the world. Some American regiments on both sides of the Civil War adopted zouave style uniforms hoping it would lend them some of their legendary élan. *Library of Congress*.

Before long, eight hundred French marines, two hundred infantrymen, and a squadron of two hundred cavalry landed, marched up the river to Tampico, and completed the capture of the city. Within days the Europeans raised a garrison of sympathetic Mexicans to serve their purposes. "The French flag is flying in the fort, or entrance to the town," the American reported. "The company occupying it [is] commanded by a mulatto of this place, and composed of several Mexicans. This is the result of a nation divided against itself." The article finished with a flourish. "Take care that neither Prince nor Potentate shall have a foothold on this continent, for it is doubtless a war against liberty and Republicanism."[22]

Banks had to save the Union from the French. In addition, other chores needed his attention, as Halleck had pointed out in July. Banks needed to support efforts to reorganize Louisiana so that it could rejoin the Union. He might do the same in Texas, once he landed. Meanwhile, he should continue raising an army of black soldiers to hold the ground already won.[23]

Union enclaves could be garrisoned by African American troops to free up white troops for active campaigning. First, however, black regiments had to be raised and trained. Banks had hoped that widespread enlistment of liberated

A propaganda "before and after" photo of a drummer in the Corps d'Afrique identified simply as Taylor. *Center for Military History, Army War College.*

slaves would follow the suppression of the immediate Rebel threat along the Mississippi River. He had expected to raise eighteen regiments of infantry and cavalry along with engineers and several batteries of artillery. He envisioned his *Corps d'Afrique* as potentially mighty and certainly capable of holding the Atchafalaya line. So far, it was not.

Nevertheless, the mere raising of black regiments sapped Rebel morale. As Union authorities had suspected, the secessionist cause wilted in light of the militarization of Louisiana's freedmen. For example, Private Robert N. Pierce, a soldier in the 34th Texas Cavalry (Dismounted), believed the coming campaign would be spearheaded by black troops: "It is said they have boats and negroes to fight us," he wrote from a camp near Alexandria. "They put their negroes in front when they go in a fight. They don't care. I expect that [the Federals] have got near about as many negroes as we have men. If the negroes do get killed they make breastworks of them. To tell you the truth I don't want to get in any fight with them."[24]

To reenergize enlistments, Banks assigned Brigadier General George L. Andrews to take charge of the recruiting effort. This Massachusetts engineer pushed hard to complete the creation of the African American units. Banks assisted the effort by ordering "all able-bodied men of color" enrolled and liable for conscription. Government officials charged with managing the employment and education of freedmen could press as many of these men into the ranks as deemed militarily necessary. Andrews also ordered soldiers, firemen, and police officers to scour the streets of New Orleans to round up any loafers, vagrants, and vagabonds and press them into the ranks. Still, there were not enough black soldiers to conquer the rest of Louisiana alone. Major Harrison Soule of the 6th Michigan Heavy Artillery, stationed at Port Hudson, observed that the black regiments had grown in number, but the ranks had not swelled with eager volunteers. "They are not enlisting at all," he wrote his wife, "but as fast as our folks can catch them. They enlist them with the Bayonet for a persuader." Andrews ordered his troops to head into the countryside around Port Hudson "to collect negroes" and force them to join the U.S. army.[25]

Charles Prosper Fauconnet, the *gérat* (office manager) of the French consulate in New Orleans and a veteran diplomat, understood the Federal efforts. The

Corps d'Afrique "seems to me to be in reality a coerced conscription of all blacks, slaves, and free men alike," he reported to the government of Emperor Napoleon III. "It is racial exploitation by the abolitionists but under a different name; it will mean the downfall of the South . . . for the benefit of Americans in the North." In order to suppress the spirit of rebellion, Fauconnet wrote, Louisiana would have to be garrisoned by U.S. troops until its citizens agreed to form a government that forbade secession. At the same time, service in the army would employ and educate the former slaves. "The least costly method of achieving this result is clearly the government's policy," he observed, summarizing the New Orleans newspapers. "Louisiana will be guarded by these colored troops. The *Corps d'Afrique* will remain under arms as long as the government has need of its services."[26]

While President Lincoln believed one hundred thousand men could be raised in the Mississippi Valley, Banks knew otherwise. His press-gangs had exhausted the supply of the military aged African American males within his lines. Invading other slave-rich zones could rejuvenate the project, as Banks told Lincoln, clearly implying southern Alabama: "It is necessary to possess ourselves of other portions of country within the control of the enemy to increase this strength."

Troops of the Corps d'Afrique. The presence of liberated slaves in the ranks of the Federal Army caused distress among Confederates. *Library of Congress.*

Vast, remote Texas would provide few recruits for the African American military machine Lincoln envisioned. If the government wanted Banks to garrison Louisiana using black troops, he needed to head east toward Mobile, not west toward Texas.[27]

But Banks stepped lightly. Just over a week later, believing Grant may have overplayed his hand, Banks distanced himself from plans against Mobile, despite their obvious merits, for the time being. Instead he trimmed his sails in order to catch the prevailing political winds. "Independent of any political or diplomatic solutions," he wrote Halleck, "Texas presents an arena as important as any portion of the county." The capture of Galveston and the destruction of any steamers and railroads in the region would cripple Rebel forces and crimp the supply lines sustaining the armies east of the Sabine. "The rebellion in Louisiana," Banks conceded, "is kept alive only by Texas." All the energies of the Federal armies in the middle and lower Mississippi Valley, Banks now believed, should focus on crushing the Confederate Trans-Mississippi. This effort would have the secondary effect of threatening the French.[28]

Banks, clearly currying favor, expected to command these operations, of course. In the meantime, he rested and reorganized his command during the dry, sweltering days of August, sparing the men for the work ahead. Soldiers went into

Brigadier General George Shepley came to Louisiana with Major General Benjamin Butler, and stayed on as military governor of Louisiana. *Library of Congress.*

camps in Baton Rouge and New Orleans, where Banks remained at his St. Charles Hotel headquarters. Major General Godfrey Weitzel led a brigade to Thibodaux and established Camp Hubbard as an orderly garrison for the Lafourche District. Union provost officers returned to power, plantation guards returned to their old haunts, and conscription officers prowled towns and farms looking for young men, both white and black, to push into the Federal ranks.[29]

The time had arrived for Louisiana to rejoin the Union. Lincoln told Stanton that he anticipated bringing the state back into the fold that fall, which would advance two important causes—the reelection of his administration and support for the national abolition of slavery, perhaps even a Thirteenth Amendment to the U.S. Constitution. To work toward the president's goal, Stanton told military governor General George F. Shepley to make a register of the Unionists in every parish, "as soon as it can conveniently be done after the people are relieved from the presence of the rebel troops and included within the lines occupied by the armies of the United States." Shepley assured Stanton that his attorney general, Thomas J. Durant, was indeed registering all the loyal Louisianans he could and would soon call a convention to reorganize the state government. The army, Shepley urged, needed to finish off Confederate forces in Louisiana and extend Federal control throughout the state, if possible. Doing so would lay another burden on Banks.[30]

Lincoln's aspirations for the state were simple. He wanted a new state constitution that would recognize the Emancipation Proclamation and free all slaves in Union-held territory not covered in that document. "As an anti-slavery man," the president wrote to Banks, "I have a motive to desire emancipation." Overall, though, Lincoln hoped Louisiana could "adopt some practical system by which the two races could gradually live themselves out of their old relation to each other, and both come out better prepared for the new. Education for young blacks should be included in the plan." To make sure Shepley and his officials understood his wishes, Lincoln forwarded them a copy of his instructions to Banks.[31]

The bewildering buffet of strategic objectives confused Union commanders. Banks, while professing an appreciation for Halleck's strategic genius, dithered with a variety of excuses for not launching a summer campaign to finish Taylor.

His reinforcements from Grant had not arrived, he complained, and he had too few transports. Halleck, mistaking this inertia for lack of strategic insight, provided a blueprint for the upcoming campaign. He urged Banks to advance up the Red River to Alexandria and Shreveport before heading west into Texas. After all, Banks had made it look easy the previous spring during his drive up the Teche.[32]

Banks had indeed advanced nearly to Natchitoches the previous April and had almost destroyed Taylor's army. Because Shreveport was a long way away, and hard to get to, Banks had turned back toward his supply lines on the Mississippi. He had besieged Port Hudson, inadvertently allowing the enemy force to regenerate. The Confederates invasion of the Lafourche in June and Rebel penetration toward New Orleans had rattled Banks and left him wary of thrashing even farther into the Louisiana wilderness.

Despite Banks's wariness, the Red River plan had its attractions. Northeast Texas and the Red River Valley had high concentrations of former slaves, and the population of freedmen was bolstered by the flow of refugees. This corridor also contained tons of cotton and, by most reports, a sizable Unionist population. Perhaps Banks could achieve two of the desired outcomes—raising a black army

Major General Richard Taylor, the son of a US president and nemesis of the Union army in Louisiana. *Goelet and Buncombe Family Papers, #01112, Southern Historical Collection, University of North Carolina.*

and conquering Louisiana—though the true conquest of Texas would have to be postponed.

But Banks talked himself out of marching on Shreveport. He mentioned several objections in a letter to Halleck. First, Halleck's suggested line of invasion up the Red River would require too long of a supply line. Union columns converging from Vicksburg, Natchez, and Baton Rouge would eventually put the bulk of all the U.S. forces operating in the region into one large mass that would be difficult, if not impossible, to feed, arm, and equip in that remote area. This force would consume nearly four hundred tons of supplies a day.

An advance to Alexandria and beyond would allow the Rebels—Brigadier General Tom Green's Texas cavalry in particular—to sidestep the Union advance by moving behind the Sabine River then sallying out to "operate against the river and New Orleans," as they had in the past.[33]

Banks highlighted a physical limitation of the plan: the water was too low in the Red River to support transports and gunboats. With low water in the Red River ruling out a water-supplied invasion, a campaign into northern Louisiana would have to proceed overland, meaning thousands of wagons and tens of thousands of animals all jostling over the same inadequate wilderness roads.

The portion of the state Halleck wanted Banks to conquer was not the flat, easily accessible sugar parishes. Pine-studded, rolling hills would tangle the Union advance and offer few paths for a sizable army. "If the season were different," Banks hedged, "the northern line would be doubtless preferable on many grounds." In reality, the Massachusetts general would never agree to a Red River campaign if he could help it.[34]

In addition, Banks wanted to avoid hitting Taylor head on, if he could. He certainly did not need another bruising like the July 13 dustup at Kock's Plantation or a disaster like the June 23 assault on Brashear City.

Further, Halleck's plan was too risky and yielded little benefit, Banks believed. Even after the capture of Shreveport and subsequent invasion of the Lone Star State, the army would be too far from its base, too remotely placed in Texas, and not very menacing to the French. Emperor Napoleon III would have little to fear from an American army poised in Marshall, Texas. Banks could either invade Texas to intimidate the French, or he could take Shreveport and reconstruct

Louisiana, but he could not do both with the forces at hand. Banks concluded he should hold in Louisiana and focus on Texas.[35]

Banks identified Sabine City and nearby Beaumont, Texas, as "the very center of the circle upon which [the Confederates] operate," he explained to Halleck. Occupying this point would accommodate every goal of the campaign. "It executes your order by planting the flag in Texas," Banks pointed out. Besides, the move could be made by water instead of over land, and it could be accomplished with a comparatively small force. From the proposed stronghold, Union troops could march on Houston, Galveston, and Indianola. Southeast Texas, like Berwick Bay, would become a new forward base, "supported by the navy, whose light boats can run up to Orange or Beaumont." He would simply leapfrog along the coast, carving out enclaves. Driving in these wedges would make the portion of Louisiana below Alexandria militarily untenable for the Confederates.[36]

The commander of the Department of the Gulf adopted an even more expansive view of the Confederate Trans-Mississippi than Halleck's. Banks envisioned Confederate Houston as the hub of a wheel with a three-hundred-mile radius. One spoke stretched southwest from Houston toward the routes

Major General Frederick Steele was promoted to head the Army of Arkansas after leading a division in the 13th Army Corps. *Library of Congress*.

of international commerce and supply, from Brownsville to Eagle Pass, Texas. Another pointed northeast toward a complex of supply centers including Boggy Depot, Indian Territory, and Washington, Arkansas; Shreveport and Monroe, Louisiana; and Marshall, Texas. The final spoke connected to his headquarters at New Orleans and Grant's army at Vicksburg. Houston, Banks believed, was the true heart of the Confederate Trans-Mississippi theater. Take it, and the Rebel rim would collapse. "The occupation of Houston would place in our hands," he reflected, "the most populous and productive part of the state." Slaves could be liberated and pressed into the army, Texas would be occupied in a more meaningful way, and Confederate Louisiana would wither away, having been cut away from its military roots. Two states could be brought back into the Union instead of one.

Banks had a second motive he did not share with Halleck. If the occupation of Texas became unwieldy—it was huge—U.S. troops could fall back into Galveston and turn the island into a citadel. With some warships and a small garrison, holding Galveston against Confederate major general John B. Magruder would be easy. After Banks had established this and other fortified enclaves, his army would be a constant threat that tied the Texas forces close to the coast and away from Louisiana. Meanwhile, the bulk of the Army of the Gulf could easily slip away to take Mobile. Halleck, Lincoln, and Banks could each have their way.[37]

Halleck, viewing his maps in Washington, held a more limited assessment and did not see much merit in operating on the Gulf Coast. He remained convinced that Shreveport, Louisiana, was the Confederate hub. Houston, Galveston, Little Rock, and Alexandria were on the periphery—places to push to collapse the Confederate bubble. The Red River offered a channel straight into the heart of the enemy lair.

Although Union planners differed on the true center of gravity of the Confederate Department of the Trans-Mississippi, eventually they agreed *something* should be done to finish off Rebel resistance in the region. From Washington to New Orleans, a consensus slowly emerged that the armies of the United States would soon restore order and national control to Arkansas, Louisiana, and Texas with campaigns in autumn 1863. If the generals stationed there—Grant, Steele, and Banks—acted in concert and with alacrity, the French threat would work itself out. By the end of the year, there would be no Confederate strongholds left for Napoleon III to latch onto west of the Mississippi.

The compromise that emerged included elements of both Banks's and Halleck's plans—Mobile was off the table. Converging columns would destroy the enemy: General Steele would take Little Rock and clear northern Arkansas while a politically and militarily diminished Grant tackled the northern reaches of Louisiana and took Monroe. At the same time Banks and his reinforced army would overrun southern Louisiana and southeast Texas and cut off the Rebel armies from their source of supplies and sustenance. This plan would also place a sizable U.S. force between French assistance and Confederate troops. Having crimped the Confederate supply lines from Texas, the Union could watch the Rebel armies disintegrate.

Banks's troops were key to the overall success of the plan. The Army of the Gulf, organized into two corps, counted twenty-five thousand white troops that

Major General Edward O. C. Ord served in Virginia and Tennessee before assuming command of the 13th Army Corps at Vicksburg. *Library of Congress.*

could take the field against the twelve thousand Confederates in Louisiana south of the Red River and perhaps ten thousand still in Texas. Nearly ten thousand Union soldiers defended New Orleans while an additional ten thousand Federals held Baton Rouge and Port Hudson, should Taylor try another raid on the Mississippi Valley while Banks moved toward Texas. Meanwhile, the operations of Grant and Steele would force the Confederates to draw reinforcements away from Rebel commands in the Red River Valley and on the Texas coast.

This plan was a winner in Washington. Authorized to pursue the campaign, Banks gathered a new leadership team, and two new corps commanders arrived to assist him. Major General Edward Otho Cresap Ord led the four divisions of the 13th Army Corps that had been added to the Army of the Gulf. A forty-five-year-old Marylander, Ord was a West Point–trained engineer and a veteran of the pre–Civil War army. He had served in California and the Pacific Northwest and had been stationed at Fort Vancouver when the secession crisis broke. Ord had served with Grant since the battles of Corinth and Iuka in the fall of 1862. He

Major General William B. Franklin had been an important leader in the Army of the Potomac before his backing of George B. McClellan and political intrigue forced him into retirement. His leadership of the 19th Army Corps would be his comeback. *Library of Congress.*

had also taken command of the 13th Army Corps in the final days of the siege of Vicksburg. His unit would integrate a wave of Midwestern troops into Army of the Gulf, which was dominated by men from New York and New England.

Banks, now truly a theater commander, brought in Major General William B. Franklin to lead the 19th Army Corps. A Pennsylvanian, he had graduated first in the West Point class of 1843 and had a distinguished record in the Mexican War and a successful, if mundane, career supervising public works. Franklin fought in most of the major battles of the Army of the Potomac, from Bull Run to Fredericksburg. After a tempestuous tenure he resigned from that army, a casualty of infighting and intrigue. After sulking at home for half a year, Franklin was tapped to take charge of the three divisions of the 19th Army Corps.

Grant and the troops remaining at Vicksburg would cooperate with Banks and his Louisiana-Texas campaign in a subordinate role. Accepting the inevitable, Grant repaired his relationship with the president. "After the fall of Vicksburg I did incline very much to an immediate move on Mobile," he wrote Lincoln. "I see, however, the importance of a movement into Texas just at this time." Grant also commented on Lincoln's favorite Mississippi Valley project: "I have given the subject of arming the negro my hearty support," Grant boasted. "This, with the emancipation of the negro, is the heavyest blow yet given to the Confederacy."[38]

Grant headed for New Orleans to confer with Banks about the proposed movements. The generals needed to review logistical details and meticulous timing for the complicated campaign. Five columns, with nearly ninety thousand men, would drill into the heart of the Confederate Trans-Mississippi theater in a great double envelopment against fewer than thirty thousand Rebels. But roads were few, distances were great, and the enemy was tricky.

Multiple campaigns would be waged nearly simultaneously, but the blows had to fall in a certain sequence. Banks would strike first against the Confederate southern flank. Troops under generals Godfrey Weitzel and William H. Emory of the 19th Army Corps would wade ashore on the Texas coast and capture the supply and transportation hub of Beaumont as a preliminary move against Houston and Galveston. Around the same time, the Arkansas column under General Steele would smash the northern Confederate flank and take Little Rock, assisted by Brigadier General John Dunlap Stevenson's 3rd Division of the 17th Army

Major General William T. Sherman, a capable officer and close companion of Ulysses S. Grant, led the 15th Army Corps. *Library of Congress.*

Corps moving from Napoleon, Arkansas, on the Mississippi River. The 13th Army Corps would then move across Berwick Bay and, depending on circumstances, pivot toward Texas and capture Houston or move on to Alexandria and secure the lower Red River.

With the nerve center of Texas occupied and the supply lines to Mexico severed, the killing blow would then land in Louisiana. Grant's veterans—most of Major General Sherman's 15th Army Corps and Major General McPherson's 17th Army Corps—would leave Vicksburg and Natchez and push beyond the Ouachita River, capture Monroe along the way, and threaten the Rebel centers at Alexandria and Shreveport. Lieutenant General Edmund Kirby Smith's Confederate armies—cut off from help from Texas and Arkansas—would be alone to face this juggernaut.

With the makings of a plan settled by the end of August, the Federal armies stirred back to life. For Lieutenant William Fowler of the 173rd New York Infantry, the loss of his desk job at Port Hudson signaled the return of active campaigning. "The 19th Corps is being reorganized, for the purpose, I suppose, of active service," he lamented in late August. ". . . I do not fancy the prospect, for my present position suits me well. There is nothing so pleasant as staff service . . . it is vastly preferable to drilling and disciplining a lot of stubborn and stupid men." Captain Orton S. Clark of the 116th New York received orders to pack up his troops at Baton Rouge and board steamers bound for New Orleans. "Our comfortable tents were turned over to the post quartermaster," he sighed, "along with every thing not essentially necessary on a campaign."[39]

President Lincoln, having made his preferences known, prevailed without directly intervening. He believed that success in the Mississippi Valley would soon usher in a new era—certainly a new phase of the conflict—and that continued pursuit of his military ideas would bring victory. On August 26, 1863, he jotted a letter to an old Illinois friend, James C. Conkling, regretfully declining an invitation to speak at a political rally in Springfield. The president, though, wanted to send along an address for his friend to read to the assembly of "unconditional Union men." His missive gave his thoughts on the status of the war at the end of that bloody summer and revealed how optimistic Lincoln felt.[40]

Lincoln's letter addressed several points of contention held by Americans. He knew people in the North wanted peace and were impatient for it given the recent successes of Federal efforts. He saw three ways to achieve it. "First, to suppress the rebellion by force of arms," he wrote. "This I am trying to do." A second option would be to accept disunion which he considered unthinkable; a third, compromise. "I do not believe any compromise, embracing the maintenance of the Union, is now possible," Lincoln explained. "The strength of the rebellion, is its military—its army." The president and others viewed the Confederacy as little more than a military dictatorship. Even if politicians and civilians tried to broker a deal, who could make it binding on the Confederate forces in the field? How could civilians reach a treaty unless the enemy troops agreed to go home?[41]

The progress of the war seemed promising. "The signs look better," he wrote. "The Father of Waters again goes unvexed to the sea." Union victories bought by hard-fighting ar mies wrought this change. The navy, described by Lincoln as "Uncle Sam's web-feet," had done its part as well—"Not only on the deep sea, the broad bay, and the rapid river," he wrote, "but also up the narrow muddy bayou, and wherever the ground was a little damp."

Lincoln longed for peace: "I hope it will come soon, and come to stay." But first he believed an army of gallant, enthusiastic black troops—including the thousands of enthusiastic recruits from Louisiana who populated his imagination—would help create a new order in the South. When that day came, he believed, "there will be some black men who can remember that, with silent tongue, and clenched teeth, and steady eye, and well-poised bayonnet, they have helped mankind on to this great consummation."[42]

Peace would come, but only when its time had arrived.

THREE

CREATING THE TRANS-MISSISSIPPI

Without assistance from abroad, or an extraordinary
interposition of Providence, less than twelve months
will see this fair country irretrievably lost.

—Lieutenant General Edmund Kirby Smith
Confederate Department of the Trans-Mississippi

When word arrived in Texas of the fall of Vicksburg and Port Hudson, Major General John B. Magruder assumed his command would be next. He had already bolstered the works at Galveston and Sabine Pass. Everything down the coast, though, languished from two years of indifference and indecision by previous commanders. Taking the threat of a Union invasion seriously, Magruder assigned Confederate colonel William R. Bradfute to organize and lead the "Texas Coast Command."

Operating out of Indianola, Bradfute recognized the middle coast of Texas lay wide open to invasion, and believed, correctly, taking Matagorda Bay would be the key to conquering Texas. If the Federals controlled Matagorda Bay, they could sweep northwest to San Antonio and sever the supply arteries and cotton roads leading to Mexico. Union troops could then march on Houston or Galveston and complete the conquest of the state. To counteract that possibility, his engineers laid out an impressive earthwork, Fort *Esperanza*—Spanish for "hope"—on Matagorda Island, covering the bay entrance at Pass Cavallo.[1]

Magruder trusted Bradfute, in part, because he was a veteran of the old army and a seasoned officer. A native Tennessean, Bradfute had served in the Mexican War and in the 2nd U.S. Cavalry on the Texas frontier before secession. He joined the Confederate army, served as a staff officer in Missouri, worked on the staffs of Major Generals Benjamin McCulloch and Earl Van Dorn in Arkansas in 1862, then led a brigade in Mississippi. He had the necessary professional bona fides. A fellow officer describing him as having "great gallantry and energy."[2]

Major General John Bankhead Magruder had first commanded troops in Virginia but went to Texas to make his reputation. *Courtesy of Tom Pressly, Shreveport, Louisiana.*

Bradfute also had his detractors, and in many ways, he was typical of Confederate officers whose careers landed them in the Trans-Mississippi. One of his artillerymen described him as "the most vacillating man I ever saw, and as a commander he has my contempt." After a rough tenure leading troops in Mississippi, Bradfute returned to staff work under General Thomas C. Hindman in Arkansas in the fall of 1862. He then briefly commanded a scandal-plagued brigade of Texans. Lieutenant General Edmund Kirby Smith ordered the brigade broken up—two regiments eventually found their way to Louisiana—and gave Bradfute medical leave. Bradfute convalesced in Texas, joining Magruder's staff, and then moved into various administrative posts. The assignment to fortify the Texas coast was his moment of redemption. Bradfute brought energy to the task and spent the summer of 1863 transforming the paltry earthworks on the Texas coast into serious fortifications. He moved gangs of pressed slaves to the beaches to dig.[3]

Meanwhile in Shreveport, Lieutenant General Kirby Smith, with the whole of the Confederate Trans-Mississippi to fret over, had a legion of problems besides the defense of the Texas coast. He had to stabilize his demoralized department. Faced with a threadbare army, open insurrection in Louisiana, threats from every quarter, and tens of thousands of displaced people to contend with, his chores seemed to multiply daily. First, he had to establish, or in some cases reestablish, Confederate authority throughout his department. Next, he needed to recalibrate the relationship between the Confederate state governments in Texas, Louisiana, Arkansas, and Missouri to orient them toward his headquarters in Shreveport now that Richmond was remote and beyond the Union controlled Mississippi. Kirby Smith had much to repair, including recently wrecked magazines and depots. Of course, none of this would matter if Kirby Smith could not rationalize the finances and make governmental revenues predictable and stable to sustain the war effort.

In short, Kirby Smith had to make a mini-Confederacy complete with economy, law, order, army, and navy. Writing from Richmond, Major Josiah Gorgas, the Confederacy's Chief of Ordnance, understood the herculean task Kirby Smith

Lieutenant General Edmund Kirby Smith directed the Confederate armies of the Department of the Trans-Mississippi from his headquarters at Shreveport. *Goelet and Buncombe Family Papers, #01112, Southern Historical Collection, Wilson Library, University of North Carolina at Chapel Hill.*

faced. He predicted the Trans-Mississippi would require "some energetic genius to restore affairs in that quarter." The verdict had not yet been delivered on whether Kirby Smith was either.[4]

The commander of the Trans-Mississippi was a mathematics wizard, and he addressed his military situation by studying the numbers. The Confederate Army of the Trans-Mississippi looked impressive on paper with more than forty-two thousand men at arms. But the campaigns of April, May, June, and July had damaged his legions. To fill out his threadbare commands, Kirby Smith ordered his officers to push as many men into the ranks as possible. Deserters, those avoiding conscription, and even those simply dawdling while on detached assignment would all have to be brought in.

He also needed energy from his commanders. In Arkansas, Major General Sterling Price replaced ailing Major General Theophilus Holmes and took command of a sizable force headquartered in Little Rock. His army of eleven thousand included regiments from Arkansas, Missouri, and Texas divided into a sizable infantry division and two small divisions of cavalry. In the Indian Territory, three brigades of mounted Texans, Cherokees, Creeks, and Arkansans numbering

View of Indianola. Taken from the bay, on the Royal Yard, on board the barque Texana, Sept. 1860 / drawn from nature by Helmuth Holtz; Ed. Lang's lithographical establishment, Hamburg. *Library of Congress.*

nearly five thousand defended a line from Fort Smith to North Texas, but they lacked adequate leadership. Kirby Smith would need to look for candidates.

Kirby Smith's largest, and arguably best, army was the eighteen thousand men serving in Louisiana under the command of Major General Richard Taylor. Major General John G. Walker's robust Texas division moved from Monroe to Alexandria to guard the middle Red River while Taylor redeployed the rest of his command. Colonel James Harrison's reinforced brigade of Texas infantry and Brigadier General Tom Green's brigade of Texas cavalry watched the lower Red River while Brigadier General Jean Jacques Alfred Alexander Mouton's Louisianans and Colonel James P. Major's Texas and Arizona horsemen guarded the Teche. A small cavalry brigade remained in northeast Louisiana, and mounted battalions watched the Atchafalaya River and the Tensas River.

By contrast, only eight thousand men defended the coast of Texas. These included bloodied troops recently released from Louisiana, such as Captain William H. Nichols's and Captain Thomas Gonzales's batteries, Colonel Joseph Bates's 13th Texas Volunteers, and the scattered remnant of the 2nd Texas Cavalry. Most of the soldiers, though, had never smelled gunpowder. Major General Magruder positioned a small brigade near Sabine Pass, another at Galveston, and small garrisons at Liberty, Velasco, Saluria, Indianola, Mustang Island,

View of Matagorda. (*Taken from the Bay. Sept.* 1860). *Library of Congress.*

Corpus Christi, and Padre Island. Brigadier General Hamilton P. Bee commanded a few hundred Confederates at Brownsville and the Lower Rio Grande while San Antonio contained a small garrison as well. Magruder knew he had too few troops, spread too thinly, and he routinely reminded his commander of the fact. [5]

Lieutenant General Kirby Smith travelled to Rusk, Texas, to discuss Magruder's concerns, and learned much. Magruder had mobilized ten thousand state troops, the old and the young, as a temporary solution to guard his unprotected coast. To boost enthusiasm, he had issued a proclamation urging Texans "bearing the rifles that once repelled the Mexican invader," to "rush at a moment's warning from your prairies." The Federal troops he knew were on their way, he declared, "will yet learn that the spirit of the Alamo is the quick spirit of the land, and that Texas will not suffer her sons to be subjected to territorial vassalage, nor her daughters degraded to be associates of enfranchised slaves." Kirby Smith admired Magruder's enthusiasm but fretted over his independent streak. The Confederate commander of the Trans-Mississippi needed cooperation, and troops, closer to the *real* threat of Union invasion—from the Mississippi Valley—

The man pictured here is taken from a detail of the group picture of Trans-Mississippi Confederate officers. He is believed to be Colonel James P. Major, commander of the Second Cavalry Brigade. *McIlhenny Company Archives, McIlhenny Company, Avery Island, Louisiana.*

not sitting idly by against the *threat* of an invasion on a distant shore, and he pushed his subordinate to release troops to Louisiana. Magruder, convinced of the rightness of his views, did not yield but promised to do what he could. Frustrated, Kirby Smith returned to Shreveport.[6]

Kirby Smith's Confederacy needed to fill its larders. To do so, officials targeted personal property. The Impressment Act of March 26, 1863, allowed army officers to take virtually anything they needed—including slaves—to sustain the war in exchange for Confederate script or IOUs. Government bureaucrats set the prices. Kirby Smith warned leaders in Richmond the system would prove counterproductive and erode support for the cause, but instead the Confederate officials expanded their powers. The legislators passed a tax-in-kind in April 1863, authorizing that 10 percent of all farm produce be collected for use by the army.

Though he was cut off from Richmond, Kirby Smith would enforce these national laws in the Confederate Trans-Mississippi. Soon after the fall of Port Hudson and Vicksburg, he issued a call for a meeting of representatives all of the Trans-Mississippi state governments to be held in Marshall, Texas. Governor

Pre-war photo of Tom Green. He would become one of the most feared Confederates in the Trans-Mississippi. *Texas State Archives.*

Thomas O. Moore, his military aide Colonel T. C. Manning, and two state Supreme Court justices—Edwin Merrick and Albert Voorhies—represented Louisiana. Senators Robert W. Johnson and C. B. Mitchell came from Arkansas, as did Judge W. K. Patterson. Governor Thomas C. Reynolds represented Missouri. Texas sent its serving governor, Francis R. Lubbock, and its governor-elect, Pendleton Murrah, to Marshall, accompanied by Senator W. S. Oldham and Major Guy Morrison Bryan. These dozen men would set the tone for Kirby Smith's vision of the Department of the Trans-Mississippi.

The conference yielded interesting results. Cotton and conscription topped state concerns, as did foreign affairs. With the French actively intervening in Mexico, and with European merchants flocking to the Rio Grande to buy Confederate cotton, the civilian leaders recommended appointing commissioners to parley with authorities in Mexico and France to facilitate the trade. But Kirby Smith took the suggestion further. He drafted a letter to Emperor Napoleon III inviting French troops to occupy the Texas side of the Rio Grande to guarantee the uninterrupted flow of cotton.[7]

Major General John G. Walker whose Texas Division promised much. *Courtesy of Tom Pressly, Shreveport, Louisiana.*

As a reporter for the *Richmond Examiner* concluded, the destiny of Mexico lay at stake. Napoleon III *needed* the Confederacy. "France needs an ally as a shield to interpose between her new province of Mexico and the gigantic power of the United States."[8]

In addition to foreign assistance, Kirby Smith's government needed money. Confederate cash was plentiful, and worthless, so cotton would become the de facto currency of the Trans-Mississippi. Planters would be obligated to sell to the Confederate government up to one-half of their crops in exchange for interest-bearing bonds. Those who resisted would lose their cotton. The seized bales would then be sold to buyers along one of three routes: directly to agents of manufacturers, through the blockade to foreign buyers, or carried across the Mexican border to agents or buyers there.

Illicit trading cotton with Yankees had continued throughout the war. This trade had proven tricky, since the Federals could simply seize the staple as "contraband of war" instead of buying it. Kirby Smith would capitalize on this commerce by making it quasi-legal, licensing agents to conduct the business.

Brigadier General Alfred Mouton of Louisiana, a local hero.
Photo courtesy of the Acadian Museum, Erath, Louisiana.

These middlemen would also provide him deniability. By using brokers to facilitate the transfer, he could funnel the trade through Confederate hands, and the government could take its cut. Where the cotton went after the sale mattered little. More than one hundred thousand Confederate-owned bales waited at Louisiana landings and wharves, and Kirby Smith wanted to convert this treasure into powder and shot by whatever means possible.

Careful observers realized fortunes could be made under this new order. Two rivers—the Red and the Rio Grande—would mark the borders of this cotton kingdom. Two cities, Matamoros and New Orleans, would be the outlets. Two cotton bureaus, one in Shreveport and the other in Houston, would serve as the Confederate face of this great arrangement and would regulate the flow of the rivers of this precious commodity.

Kirby Smith's plans, though, rested on unstable foundations. Besides the potential for theft, graft, and corruption inherent in implementing the proposed system, instability in Mexico threatened this plan at the market end as well.

Early in the war, President Jefferson Davis had assigned José Agustín Quintero to the lower Rio Grande as his confidential agent. This Cuban-born journalist, diplomat, and one-time revolutionary had been in South Texas for years as a newspaper editor and maintained close contacts among the politicians, soldiers, and revolutionaries in strife-ridden Mexico. Davis trusted his judgment.[9]

Quintero had been remarkably successful in advancing the secessionist cause. By 1863 the wily Cuban had effectively navigated the perilous waters of caudillo politics involving warlords and strongmen like Santiago Vidaurri, José María Jesús Carbajal, and Juan Cortina. Quintero had established Brownsville, Matamoros, and the boomtown of Bagdad as the triangular outlet of the Confederate cotton trade. Upstream, Rio Grande City, Laredo, and Eagle Pass also served as minor gateways. Gun battles between Mexican factions may have flared in the region, but the volume of cotton heading for Brownsville continued to swell.

The effect of the cotton boom on the lower Rio Grande Valley had been tremendous. Matamoros and Brownsville blossomed from frontier garrison towns into thriving entrepôts for each nation. Fertilized by the cotton trade, Bagdad sprouted from a few board shacks on the south shore of the Rio Grande's mouth into a settlement of several thousand people serviced by dockyards, saloons, hotels, restaurants, and warehouses. Cotton lay in stacks everywhere. One northern observer described the boomtown as "an excrescence of war," a conflict-made carbuncle.[10]

Freighters stood to make a killing hauling goods up, down, and across the Rio Grande. Teamsters and muleskinners, whips cracking, kept up a steady routine of hauling goods twenty-five miles from Bagdad to Matamoros. Small paddle wheelers—fixtures on the river since the 1846 campaign in the Mexican War—wended their way from the waters of the Gulf of Mexico around the Rio Grande's torturous bends and turns. The trade employed more than fifteen thousand Northerners, Southerners, Mexicans, Englishmen, Scotsmen, and Frenchmen along this once-deserted stretch of beach. For the people of South Texas and Northeastern Mexico, is was the time of *Los Algodones*, "living in tall cotton."

Transportation hubs and new commercial centers erupted across the Texas prairies as sleepy settlements swelled with people involved with the cotton caravans. The journey from Shreveport to Matamoros spanned 600 miles. The railroad terminus at the tiny village of Alleyton—70 miles west of Houston and 125 east of San Antonio—became the gathering place for Arkansas, Louisiana, and East Texas convoys heading toward Brownsville, more than 300 miles away. San Antonio also blossomed with roads leading to Eagle Pass and Laredo and toward Victoria to catch the route to Brownsville. All roads heading south toward Matamoros and the Gulf of Mexico along the coastal prairies converged on Richard King's ranch at Santa Gertrudis Creek—the edge of civilization—before crossing the prickly pear, rattlesnake, scorpion, and tarantula infested 120-mile desolation known as "the sands."[11]

Formerly a South Texas wasteland, the sands became a highway of supplies. More than five thousand wagons routinely crossed this wilderness, those heading south loaded with cotton, and those heading north laden with merchandise, including rope, leather, blankets, lead, cigars, coffee, clothing, luxuries, delicacies, and army supplies. The mesquite trees bordering the road became festooned with white fiber torn from the passing loads of cotton. Carcasses of mules, oxen, and horses also marked the route, dried hides pasted to frameworks of bones in the arid wilderness.[12]

Back on the lush farms and plantations of the Trans-Mississippi, cotton producers howled over what they saw as government overreach. Food and livestock impressed for use of the army could be justified, these critics believed, but forcing growers to sell cotton to the government at suspicious prices appeared oppressive. The Confederate government, in effect, had entered into competition with private individuals, often wooing the same customers. In addition, frauds, charlatans, and imposters aggravated this anxiety by posing as government agents, sometimes taking away cotton—or anything else they fancied—in the name of the cause. Despite opposition from the planters, the Confederate government sent its minions across Kirby Smith's kingdom to support the cotton trade.

In mid-August, E. B. Cox, managing the salt mines at Petite Anse Island, Louisiana, watched as agents arrived at his place, seized his wagons, and headed toward Alexandria. They took a cargo of rock salt as well—an upending of Louisiana lagniappe. "They want all the teams to haul cotton from [Alexandria] and Natchitoches to Niblett's Bluff," he wrote. "It seems that they are going to take all cotton in this department and work it through to Brownsville to keep it out of the way of the enemy and to get supplies for our army." Cox had grown

Brownsville, Texas, viewed from Matamoros. *Harpers Weekly.*

frustrated in the salt business, already plagued by Confederate theft, unpaid bills, and outright seizure. "If I am driven off from here," he concluded, "I shall go out there and enter into the business."[13]

Other wagons also raised dust in the Trans-Mississippi. A mass exodus of refugees headed west into Texas and away from Union armies. Since the early days of the war, planters had moved tens of thousands of enslaved people from Louisiana into the Piney Woods and Grand Prairie regions of Texas. At first, owners intended these moves to keep their slaves from running toward Union armies. Now they moved their human property to keep them away from the approaching Federal armies. Some Louisiana and Arkansas neighborhoods dissolved as people abandoned their fields and homes in search of some stability in the sparsely settled counties west of the Sabine River. One sugar planter, William Frederick Weeks, fled New Iberia. As he boasted from Houston, "Negro property will be safe here when not one is left a slave in Louisiana." During the course of the war, owners herded an estimated one hundred thousand enslaved people into Texas.[14]

Among the refugees, the dislocation of war created a grim camaraderie. Black and white people, children and adults, horses, mules, wagons, dogs, baggage, and furniture crowded the streets, mingling with Confederate soldiers, "drunk and sober," as Louisiana teenager Kate Stone wrote. Everyone seemed to have a tale of hardship and narrow escape. Some had fled Federal soldiers, some feared vengeful slaves. "All have lost heavily," Stone observed. "Everyone was animated

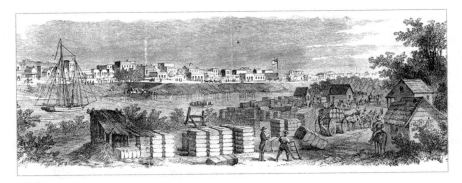

Brownsville viewed from the Mexican shore. Cotton is ready to be shipped. *Frank Leslie's Illustrated Newspaper.*

and excited. All were eager to tell their own stories . . . and everyone sympathized with everyone else. Nearly everyone," she added, "took his trials cheerfully, making a joke of them, and nearly all are bound for Texas."[15]

After reaching safety, many of the refugees tried to make the best of their predicament. Mary Eliza Avery McIlhenny, wife of Edmund McIlhenny, left their home and sugar plantations near New Iberia and finally settled in Galveston. "I am perfectly charmed," she wrote to her sister. "Its delicious sea breezes, splendid surf, delightful beach, [and] beautiful flowers would render a sojourn here very pleasant under any other circumstances. But ah! Refugees. Our pleasures here are almost pain."[16]

The threat of Federal invasion on the Texas coast kept these newcomers uneasy. McIlhenny, having found sanctuary in Galveston with her husband and her parents, Daniel Dudley and Sarah Marsh Avery, continued to worry about the family's future. In a letter to her sister, she wrote, "Papa does not consider the position safe from Yankee interference and Mama is terrified at the prospect of yellow fever in Houston, so that I fear we will soon again be wanderers." Her brother-in-law, Marshall McIlhenny, had a place in Bell County, Texas. Although far from the war, this home promised a harder, frontier life. "We have found the country so uncomfortable," she lamented. "Austin has been recommended, and if we can obtain accommodations we may go there."[17]

Having arrived safely in Tyler, Stone also feared invasion of her new home. She thought she and her mother might never be safe from the Union armies. "The

The levee at New Orleans. Cotton is ready to be shipped. *Frank Leslie's Illustrated Newspaper.*

Juan Cortina, the *patrón* and *caudillo* of the Lower Rio Grande Valley. *Library of Congress.*

fall of Vicksburg makes us tremble for Texas," she observed. "She can be invaded from so many points that Mamma knows not where to look for a place of greater safety."[18]

Many of these refugees fled a seemingly intractable problem. The Federals were demolishing the antebellum racial order. Texas major W. L. Robards reflected on his time in the Lafourche country between Thibodaux and Donaldsonville. If a plantation owner "whipped a negro," the Texan warned, "his testimony was sufficient to convict and send the master to Fort Jackson." White people, he reported, were kept under constant surveillance, and black people had become tools of the ruling authorities to tamp down support for secession or assistance to the Rebels. "A white man can go nowhere without a pass; a negro was permitted to go and come when he pleased," Robards noted. Once the enslaved had tasted liberty—and borne arms—they would never consent to a return to bondage.[19]

Many of Louisiana's planters who had remained loyal to the U.S. government in hopes of maintaining their property clearly chafed under northern occupation. Major Robards reveled in his schadenfreude, because loyal planters were not immune from abuses. Federal commissary officers pressed these loyal citizens for supplies, slaves, and livestock for the good of the army. "It is a remarkable fact," the Texan continued, "that Union men suffer most in loss of property. They respect the man who is ready to fight for his country or do all in his power to help the cause, while they detest the cringing sycophant." Neighbors heaped scorn on those who took the oath of loyalty. Robards wrote a warning to those who might choose this tactic in hopes of passing through the war unscathed. "You may tell Union men, if there be any in Texas, [that] Union sentiment will avail them nothing with Yankees."[20]

Louisiana citizens who pledged loyalty to the Union had another cause to regret their decision. Like their former slaves, white military-age men became subject to registration and potential conscription under The Enrollment Act of March 3, 1863. Starting that summer, provost marshals began pressing handfuls of white Louisianans into Federal service to complete the ranks of regiments forming in New Orleans. Vigorous, youthful fellows who had been praying to remain neutral in the blood-spattered war now had to choose sides. For some, this meant fleeing into the backcountry and joining the growing numbers of exiles in remote camps and secret hideouts. Others swallowed their pride and joined the Confederate army—an option many had resisted for two years—just ahead of the Union provosts.

Texans, far removed from the fighting, suffered less from this upheaval but faced challenges exacerbated by the newcomers as well as the vast, remote nature of their state. The country around Bastrop, Texas, one observer wrote in his

José Carvajal was born in San Antonio de Béxar and educated in the US but moved to Mexico during the Republic of Texas and led attempts at forming his own breakaway republic. He later became a supporter of Benito Juaréz. *Library of Congress.*

diary, seemed populated by hungry women and children dressed in homespun. Scarcity of imported goods, coupled with the grasping of Confederate tax-in-kind and conscription, made life difficult. "Schools and churches are closed," Private Fred Wade, a soldier on furlough from Green's Brigade, observed. "All men between 18 and 45 are in the army. A tenth of the bacon, wheat, and corn goes to the government and half the horses and cattle. Everyone is crying 'when will this cruel war end?'"[21]

Other Texans echoed the lament. At more than seventy years of age, naturalist Gideon Lincecum could tell things were going badly for the Confederacy. Writing from his farm, Mount Olympus, in Washington County, Texas, he grieved his sorry circumstances. "Until the war came, myself and my old lady were spending the evening of our protracted existence quite pleasantly," he wrote. "Our children settled all around us in good homes, and doing well. We had nothing to do but to go among them, receive their visits, and hear accounts of their successes." The conflict scattered his kin. Two grandsons fought with Green in Louisiana. "Those that are left behind," he lamented, "are the helpless women and children."[22]

Lincecum spent long, lonely days on his farm. "Almost everybody has gone to the war now," he wrote to a friend in the army. "I stay here by myself, having no associates, until I have almost forgotten the language." His neighbors had to work diligently to survive, leaving little time for social calls. Spinning and weaving occurred in most homes in the state. "People here are struggling hard,

Santiago Vidaurri, the powerful governor of Nuevo León and Coahuila. *Library of Congress.*

trying to clothe themselves," he wrote. "I find [the] community well enveloped in homespun." Lincecum was a man of education and letters and spent many of his hours in correspondence with friends and family far afield. Even this activity would soon cease, he feared. "Paper nearly all gone," he scrawled to a correspondent, adding sarcastically, "all's well."[23]

One Texan's wife insisted her suffering was too much to bear and demanded her soldier husband, fighting in Louisiana, come home. Officials had dragged thirty-seven-year-old Private William N. Corothers into the war from his cattle ranch northwest of Austin. While he served in the 2nd Arizona Cavalry, his wife Sarah and their three small children drifted into despair. "I think if they have nothing else to do they had better send the men home to their distressed families to make bread," she lamented. She did not trust the Confederate government and its management of the war. "If I was a man I would go to Mexico," she wrote. "I hope the Yanks will take the state. I would just as care [to] live under them as some we have to be under."[24]

The Trans-Mississippi Theater

◇ Key Fortifications
○ Cotton Export Point
● Supply Depot
★ Key Administrative Center

100 Miles

Unfortunately for women like Corothers, unless the French intervened or success on the battlefield earned the South its independence, the Confederate armies in the Trans-Mississippi continued to need troops. In many of the regiments, especially in Arkansas and the Indian Territory, more men were absent from the ranks than were present. Desertion in Louisiana was nearly as bad. Kirby Smith estimated around twenty-five thousand men needed to be rounded up and pushed back into the ranks. Conscription laws, already harsh and coercive, became tougher. Many exemptions from service disappeared and all recruiting in the Trans-Mississippi, which had often been done along rather informal lines, had to be channeled through the Bureau of Conscription in Shreveport or it would be deemed illegal. New orders circulated among the various commands. Recruits or conscripts who were not "regularly enrolled and assigned" with the proper authorities "will be deemed deserters and punished accordingly." Kirby Smith would have a regular army, not an armed band resembling little more than an organized militia.[25]

Confederate provosts and home guards enforced conscription throughout the region. Joseph Freeborn Rowley, a thirty-five-year-old teamster, returned from hauling cotton to the Rio Grande only to find a message from conscription

Refugees moving out. *Library of Congress.*

officers waiting for him at his farm on Onion Creek, south of Austin. He was to head into town and report to Colonel John Salmon "Rip" Ford, commander of all conscripts in Texas, and be enlisted into the Condeferate army. Being ill, Rowley ignored the order. Soon Confederate soldiers came hunting him. "I was sick in bed and my six shooter under the cover with the intent to kill if they had undertook to have taking me," Rowley wrote. "They asked me if I was sick. I told them that I was pretty damned sick and for them to go back and tell Ford that when I got able to ride I would come in and see him. If that did not suit him he could go to hell, God damn him."[26]

Ford was not amused. Rowley, recovered, fled his home, dodging conscription officers searching for him for two weeks before finally heading into Austin for a private audience with the Rebel colonel. He lingered near his office and aproached him as he was heading home. "On the street, I seen him," Rowley confessed. "When I spoke to him he appeared much excited and some short talk took place." Knowing his case to be hopeless, Rowley returned to his farm only to find that a party had come to arrest him and had just left. Grabbing some food, clothing, and a blanket, he saddled his horse and headed back toward Matamoros, Mexico, a marked man.[27]

The predicament of white southerners amused Abram Sells, an enslaved young man born and reared on the William A. Rimes Plantation near the Sabine River in Newton County, Texas. He remembered many would-be Confederates hiding in the dense East Texas forest. "Some of them march off in their uniforms, lookin' so grand," he recalled, "and . . . some of them hide out in the wood to keep from lookin' so grand."[28]

Kirby Smith set a heavy Confederate hand on his domain. He had held his meetings, issued his orders, and multiplied his bureaus. Kirby Smith's next move would be to turn Shreveport into an inland citadel, the last-stand redoubt of the Department of the Trans-Mississippi. By the time engineers had finished designing Fortress Shreveport, it would include a fan-shaped series of eighteen mutually supporting batteries facing south and west to defend from land attack.

First, though, he needed shovels. He also needed picks, axes, and carpenter's tools. Kirby Smith set Major H. T. Douglas to work gathering the implements and obtaining an inventory from each district. Spades, saws, and farm equipment would stream into depots at San Antonio and Houston, Texas; Fulton and Van Buren, Arkansas; and Shreveport and Grand Ecore, Louisiana.[29]

Kirby Smith also needed hands to work these tools. He urged his district commanders to impress slaves into Confederate service to free up white soldiers. "I believe a large number of men would by this measure be added to the effective force," Kirby Smith concluded. "The temper of the people is now favorable for such a step." Besides, the enslaved people of Texas, Louisiana, and Arkansas could see freedom coming. Owners were wary. "There is a feeling of distrust in the loyalty of their slaves," Kirby Smith observed. Sending their laborers to serve the government would yield a double benefit: black workers would be kept

Louisianan John R. Slidell, the Confederacy's representative in France. *Library of Congress.*

out of the hands of the Federals, and their supervised work would dampen any simmering ideas of revolt or insurrection.[30]

Union gunboats, of course, would be part of any invasion of Louisiana. To counteract the threat from the waterways, Kirby Smith ordered the construction of a naval base and foundry in Shreveport where an ironclad, CSS *Missouri*, would come to life armed with cannon taken from the wrecked USS *Indianola*. He created a submarine base nearby with plans for the construction of a half-dozen submersible war-engines along the lines of the CSS *Hunley*, just recently launched in Mobile, Alabama. There was also an underwater torpedo workshop where craftsmen built Singer contact mines. Union warships would ply the waters of Louisiana at their peril.

Shreveport, still a frontier city, had a curious relationship with the Red River. The watercourse had only been navigable that far up for fewer than twenty-five years. In 1841 Henry Shreve had cleared a massive log jam—the great raft—between the city and Natchitoches, allowing for the bulk of the water draining from the Red River basin to flow into the main river channel and fostering the settlement of the town. Prior to this engineering feat, nature had created a series of alternate channels and great catch basins to pass the water toward the Mississippi. Even though Shreve had opened the main channel, rises in the river often spilled over into these ancient bypasses, inundating the wilderness and pushing water toward the Gulf of Mexico through dozens of alternate paths. Therefore, navigation to Shreveport remained treacherous.

To baffle Union skippers, Confederate engineer William R. Boggs, who would become Kirby Smith's chief of staff, devised a series of traps that in essence made the perfidious Red River into a Confederate ally by artificially, and temporarily, reversing Shreve's great accomplishment. A dam near Shreveport equipped with a removable "stopper" allowed water levels to rise and fall downstream at the will of Rebel war planners. Plans also called for engineers to place obstructions at choke points downstream when danger neared; the effect of these blockages would be to recreate the great raft and force the Red River to overflow into a natural tangle of bayous and lakes, known collectively as Bayou Pierre to the west, and collect in a vast basin, known as Old Spanish Lake, near Natchitoches. If the

U.S. Navy tried to wend its way up the Red River, it would find itself stranded as the water spread through the low Louisiana wilderness and drained the riverbed.

The Confederates in the Trans-Mississippi needed time for all these plans to mature. War industries stirred to life in Texas. Meat-packing plants grew in Jefferson, quartermaster warehouses began to fill in Marshall, and powder mills fueled by niter harvested from Hill Country bat guano began churning out ammunition. European military supplies also started trickling in from Mexico.

Confederate officials divided these resources among the various commands. The sub-district of North Texas and the districts of Indian Territory and Arkansas would claim 40 percent and collect the supplies at Bonham and Jefferson, Texas. Depots at Houston and San Antonio would get 20 percent to distribute among the eastern, southern, and western sub-districts. Forces in Louisiana would draw 30 percent from items collected in Shreveport warehouses, and the Quartermaster Department would hold 10 percent in reserve.

Nevertheless, all of these efforts would come to nothing should the Union armies in the Mississippi Valley turn west. Kirby Smith needed the French to guarantee the success of his Confederate Trans-Mississippi. "The action of the French in Mexico and the erection of an empire under their auspices makes the establishment of the Confederacy the policy of the French Government," Kirby Smith wrote to John Slidell, the southern commissioner in Paris. "Without assistance from abroad, or an extraordinary interposition of Providence less than twelve months will see this fair country irretrievably lost and the French protectorate in Mexico will find a hostile power established on their frontier."[31]

Despite these grandiose plans, in reality the Trans-Mississippi Confederacy neared exhaustion. Most of its military-aged population served east of the Mississippi, leaving behind, Kirby Smith sighed, only "the aged, infirm, and the lukewarm." Invasion was imminent. "The preparations of the enemy and the disposition of his forces clearly shadow forth the policy of overrunning and conquering the States west of the Mississippi," he told Slidell. Once U.S. forces captured Louisiana, Arkansas, and Texas, they could easily make terms with the remaining eight seceded states east of the Mississippi should the need arise. The United States would then turn on the French.[32]

Kirby Smith also appealed to racial solidarity. The Yankees had resorted to "the forced impressment of our slaves into their army, to wage a ruthless war against their masters." The destiny of the Confederate nation, and the white race in North America, he argued, lay in the hands of Europeans. He pointed to the raising of African American troops under Major General Nathaniel P. Banks and Major General Ulysses S. Grant as proof of their intentions. "They have organized a force of over 100,000 negro troops," he revealed to Slidell, "which will be made available in their scheme of conquest this winter."[33]

Kirby Smith's message was clear. If the French wanted to avoid facing Union troops on the Rio Grande—many of whom were recently liberated slaves, who would surely foment a race war in Mexico—then the time to act had arrived.

FOUR

RESTORING A CONFEDERATE ORDER

We walked them out of stinking distance and shot them.
—Private John W. Watkins
Company B, 5th Texas Cavalry

The campaigns of 1863 had weakened Confederate control in the Trans-Mississippi. The passage and presence of Federal troops in April and May had also disrupted Rebel authority in south Louisiana. Lieutenant General Edmund Kirby Smith realized a renewed Union offensive would further energize a homespun opposition and might deliver a coup de grâce to Shreveport's efforts to control the state. The "lukewarm" residents of the region, as Kirby Smith had described them, had in reality begun turning stone cold toward the Confederacy. They needed to be chastened. If conscription was to work, it had to be enforced.[1]

Louisiana's population, though, had become a witch's brew of discontent. During the spring and summer of 1863, war had displaced, uprooted, scattered, or harmed nearly every family south of Alexandria. Black people who had spent their lives under strict controls and bounded within specific geographic limits found themselves herded by planters, soldiers, or circumstances to distant and unfamiliar points. Some simply bolted. Civilians fled the destruction of war. Civil liberties vanished, and lawlessness flourished. Demoralized Rebel armies leaked manpower in this environment, as disaffected and opportunistic soldiers quit the regular ranks to seek their fortunes amid this volatile human landscape.

In this political vacuum, some claimed trumped-up Unionist sympathies in hopes of attracting support from Federal authorities. A group in Winn Parish, located in the wooded hills between Alexandria and Monroe, sent a resolution to Union army commanders on the Mississippi River. These poor and middling farmers saw no common cause with Louisiana secessionists. "We have undoubted evidence that the Confederate States are designed to be very aristocratic and exceedingly oppressive in its form of government," their declaration read. The document also asserted "we believe the United States is the most democratic and best form of government now in existence." Secession, these anti-Confederates claimed, had been illegitimate and had not been achieved "by a vote of the people." Until Federal troops arrived, the Unionists of Winn County would arm and organize themselves in a state of semi-independence, pledging their "lives, property, and . . . sacred honor." Such blustery dissenters occupied a remote enclave of the state and caused little trouble, but they were a reminder that not all of Louisiana loved the Confederacy.[2]

Other more strategic regions had to be purified by fire and sword. Areas in Louisiana and Texas with long-standing reputations for being the haunts of common robbers and thieves now served as havens for the hunted and dispossessed. For many, the anarchy of war provided an occasion for a life of license and crime. Jayhawkers in these areas were another matter. These principled marauders actively targeted Confederate authority when possible. Jayhawkers ambushed conscription officers, promised protection to men who would leave the Confederate army, and did what they could to assist Union military efforts when possible.

For Confederate officials, the most troublesome domain lay in southwest Louisiana and southeast Texas. This hostile province stretched from the woods and swamps of Bayou Mallet west of Opelousas and the Pine Hills west of

Felix Pierre Poché, a lawyer before the war. *Diary of Felix Pierre Poché.*

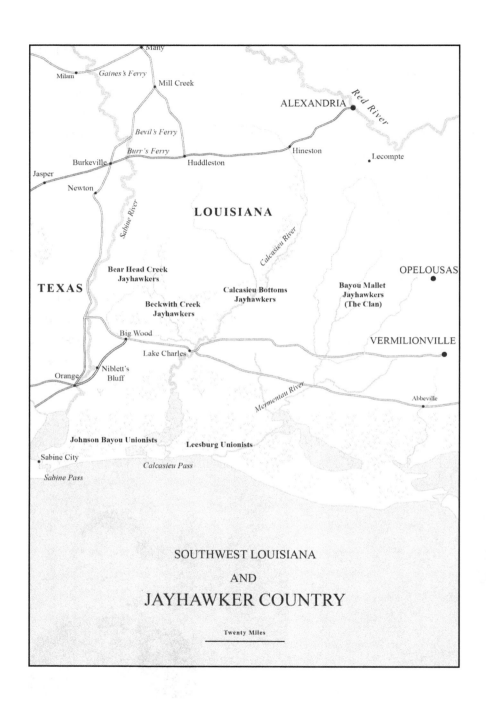

SOUTHWEST LOUISIANA

AND

JAYHAWKER COUNTRY

Twenty Miles

Alexandria to the tangles of the Big Thicket in Texas, a wilderness 150 miles east to west and more than 100 miles north to south. The Rebel supply corridor from Texas to Louisiana passed through this no-man's land; the roads west of Alexandria and Vermilionville became exceedingly dangerous.

Several discernable groups infested this bandit province. The marshy coast between the Texas line and the Teche country included mazes of *cheniers*— slight ridges covered in oak and cypress—and three major tidal lagoons. This complicated landscape provided havens for people beyond the law, clustered in settlements near the mouths of the Mermentau, Calcasieu, and Sabine rivers. Union blockaders called periodically on these villages, often to obtain fresh water, beef, and contraband cotton. Inland, the Sabine bottoms harbored gangs lurking around Bear Head Creek and other bands around Beckwith Creek. The Calcasieu river bottoms above Lake Charles provided hideouts as well.

Opelousas, the one-time capital of Confederate Louisiana, lay on this outlaw province's eastern edge. Teetering on the edge of civilization—a tenuous outpost of law and order—the town clung to a facade of prosperity and respectability. Confederate captain Felix Pierre Poché described Opelousas as "very neat, and from appearances, a pleasant little town and . . . the nicest inland town that I have seen in Louisiana." Captain Arthur W. Hyatt of the Confederate Guards Response Battalion could not believe the luxuries in the local stores he noticed as he passed through town. "We purchased real Havana cigars and French brandy, neither of which I had seen any of for eighteen months," he rejoiced. "It was a great treat, and I just everlastingly drank segars and smoked brandy all . . . afternoon." Somehow luxury items in short supply elsewhere seemed plentiful in Opelousas.[3]

The city had a dark side, too. Violent men lurked just beyond the edge of town. The irregular bands of desperados needed tools of war, and they stole horses, saddles, and livestock to equip and feed their partisans. Confederate troops feared moving far past their own picket lines without numbers. "Not long ago they caught some soldiers belonging to our regiment," Lieutenant John Coleman Sibley of the 2nd Louisiana Cavalry wrote his wife, "and killed them and then beat in their faces to pieces with their guns and committed several other deeds of atrocities." Besides smashing their faces beyond recognition, the ruffians piled moss around the corpses and attempted to burn them. Nervous citizens and soldiers alike identified the bandit chieftain as Ozémé Carrière and his followers as the "Clan."[4]

As Carrière's ruffians began to picket routinely within twenty miles of Opelousas, Rebel foragers and couriers disappeared. "I suppose they will swear vengeance against all Confederate soldiers," Sibley concluded, "and no doubt will kill everyone that falls into their hands." In response, Confederate officials formed "conscript hunters" from Louisiana's Home Guard, including a notorious squad from Rapides Parish under the command of Captain Robert M. "Bloody Bob" Martin and another, the "Prairie Rangers," from St. Landry Parish, under the command of Captain Samuel M. Todd. They would challenge Carrière and his followers by employing similar tactics as their adversaries.[5]

Intending to stamp out this insurgency, Major General Richard Taylor, the commander in West Louisiana, turned to his best troops to sweep Carrière from the prairie. He ordered two companies of veteran Texas cavalry from Brigadier General Tom Green's Brigade to flush out the ne'er-do-wells so that the local Home Guard might pursue them into the heart of the wilderness. "The outrageous acts of the conscripts, deserters, and free negroes who inhabit the region . . . came to the knowledge of the 'powers that be'," wrote Texan private William Randolph

John W. Watkins, 5th Texas Cavalry. *Courtesy Martha Hartzog, Austin, Texas.*

Howell of the 5th Texas Cavalry. "There is quite a number . . . who have taken to the woods and bottoms and evaded the enrolling officers, and declared it to be their intention not to fight for either Federal or Confederate governments." These same brigands, they believed, had served as guides to Major General Nathaniel P. Banks's troops a few months before in exchange for permission to plunder their neighbors. "This clan formed an alliance with the 'rail-splitters' minions," the Texan reported, "to murder alike citizen and soldier."[6]

The operation occurred on the night of August 8. At about sunset, seventy-five Texans moved west from Washington under the command of Captain Charles Shannon West of Kirby Smith's staff. When they arrived at Bayou Mallet, the troopers broke into three parties with lists of houses to search and persons to capture. At each targeted cabin, soldiers surrounded the building while a storming party broke in and searched the dwelling. "Thus we hunt conscripts," wrote Howell, "visiting a man's house at the hour of midnight and in some instances we took them away." Families witnessed the violence. "The women in some cases appeared much grieved, and cried and begged at an awful rate, when their husbands, fathers, and brothers were taken away," the Texan continued. Most, he contemptuously noted, spoke only French. "As we could not 'Parly Francais,' their wails amounted to nothing at all." By morning, the Texans rounded up a dozen

Charles Shannon West, an Austin attorney before the war and Judge Advocate General of the Confederate Trans-Mississippi Department. *Texas Jurists Collection, Rare Books and Special Collections, Tarleton Law Library, The University of Texas.*

men described as "deserters from the army" or "liable to conscription." Home Guards escorted the men to Opelousas for imprisonment and trial.[7]

The guerillas retaliated. In the early morning the next day, a party of around fifty mounted Clan members emerged from the woods and surprised one detachment of Texans at an abandoned farm. Many were sleeping off the night's weariness, and those scrounging for breakfast thought nothing of the approach of the riders, assuming they were friends. Several of the Texans mounted up to exchange greetings with the newcomers, only to be met by shotgun blasts. Private John W. Watkins of the 5th Texas Cavalry, snoozing at the time of the attack, started awake "when the firing commenced." Confusion and milling soldiers surrounded him. "Our officers were still calling out 'not to shoot, they are our men.' [So] I wasn't in a hurry." Not until a wounded comrade rode up did Watkins learn the gravity of the situation. "I . . . found his thigh broken just above the knee. They commenced a cross-fire on me about that time," he added, "I thought it best to get out of there."[8]

The Clan routed the veteran Texans, and Watkins and his comrades galloped into the open prairies, trusting their steeds to clear them from danger. Then the Clan melted away as other Confederates approached. When Captain West had collected his scattered troops, he ordered them to stand fast in the open country until the whereabouts of the enemy could be determined. That afternoon, the 2nd Louisiana Cavalry and the remainder of the 5th Texas Cavalry arrived to reinforce the mission with three hundred fresh troops. Now with a clear advantage, the horse soldiers received orders to, as Watkins wrote, "scour the woods and country for miles around, and to shoot every man connected with the clan."[9]

The following day, the Texas and Louisiana troops formed a long line of videttes and plunged into the woods, "driving for them as if for deer," according to Howell. On the evening of August 10, the Confederates surprised a large number of the Clan in their camps and immediately opened fire. "Most of them fled," Howell remembered, "while two or three stood up [and] fired." Two more Texans fell wounded, one mortally. The Confederates lunged ahead and rounded up four of the guerillas and marked them for death. "The family of one of them came to take leave of him a few minutes before he was led out to be shot, and it was truly an unpleasant scene," Howell wrote. "Methinks I can hear that woman and her children's cries to this moment." Private Watkins, who had experienced the whizz of pistol balls and buckshot the day before, was more callous. "As soon as we captured them," he wrote home to his wife, "we walked them out of stinking distance and shot them." One of the dead had been Carrière's brother and a career criminal. "Someone told me that he said he had been a robber fifteen years," Lieutenant Sibley recalled. "I could not understand him for he spoke in French."[10]

After the Confederate attacks, the Clan vanished. Four companies of the 2nd Louisiana swept the region a few days later but found no one. "It was a very dark and dangerous scout," Lieutenant Sibley wrote. "Rode all night and until nine the next day hunting and searching houses, but we did not get any."[11]

Texans, based on their recent experience battling the Clan, cautioned their countrymen traveling to Louisiana to come well-armed and to remain vigilant. "I am writing this for the purpose of informing the citizens of Texas, who may intend travelling from Niblett's Bluff to the eastward, of the state of affairs existing in this portion of the state," Howell wrote. "After the late punishment inflicted on the conscripts, consider it very unsafe for small parties to travel alone." Sibley said the same thing about travelers coming from north Louisiana. "I would advise persons coming down here to be very particular which way they come and not get too far west," he wrote.[12]

Instead of subduing the area, the bloody sweep inaugurated a vortex of violence. A Clan raiding party attempted to assassinate Captain Martin at his home. Unable to get a clear shot, they stole his horses. Bloody Bob Martin and

Southern Unionists. *Harpers Weekly*, August 4, 1866.

his conscript hunters, in turn, roared into the area around Hineston. At one homestead, the attackers kicked in the door of one cabin, shot a Rebel deserter inside, and then hanged the elderly homeowner for harboring the fugitive. "There was not a [more honest] or more inoffensive man in the country than this poor man," Unionist Dennis Haynes wrote. The pro-Confederates moved to the next farm and blasted two more men. One, shot through the bowels, cried out in agony. A raider responded by jumping off his horse and drawing a bowie knife. He "cursed him for a damned Tory, and stabbed the already dying man in several places," Haynes recorded, "till he was literally butchered in the most cruel and barbarous manner."[13]

The next day, Martin and his men encountered two more suspected Unionists. One agreed to give up all the known conspirators in the area in exchange for his life. The Rebels agreed. When the captive told all he knew, the riders decided to shoot him anyway. "He begged for heaven's sake to let him go and see his children (six in number)," Haynes wrote, "but no, no respite was given him." The other man confessed he was indeed a Unionist after being identified as such by a cousin riding with the Home Guard. The prisoner claimed, however, he was not involved in any depredations. He admitted he had warned conscripts in the area that Bloody Bob Martin and his men were on the hunt. "They shot him dead," Haynes wrote, "and left him and [the other man] to be devoured by vultures."[14]

Bloody Bob Martin's sweep through the Piney Woods of western Rapides Parish concluded near Lecompte. The secessionists pillaged and burned Jessamine Hill, the summer home of Unionist politician James Madison Wells, who had already fled west to the Calcasieu bottoms. "They robbed and plundered the Union men everywhere they went," Haynes claimed, "under the ostensible pretense of suppressing robbery and jayhawking . . . they robbed and out-jayhawked the worst jayhawkers in the country." This stroke in western Rapides Parish, and others like it across Louisiana, would reverberate for generations.[15]

Having addressed the problem with the Clan, at least temporarily, Major General Taylor's Confederate army in Louisiana needed rest. Surprisingly, the Federals obliged and put little pressure on their enemy. On the shores of Berwick Bay, scouts reported no indications of a Union advance up Bayou Teche. "There is no prospect of an engagement here," lawyer Thomas Jefferson League wrote to his wife in Galveston, warning her instead "there is more prospects of fighting in Texas than here."[16]

Others were not as certain. "Maybe the Yankees are coming . . . to give us another round," conceded Captain Keet McDade of the 13th Texas Cavalry Battalion to his wife, Ann, as he camped near Vermilionville. "For my part, I am 'plum' worn out, and today if I were at home, I would stay in the house one month. It would take that long to rest me sufficiently."[17]

Yet neither the Federal invasion of Louisiana nor Texas came. Confederates remained jumpy. Private Samuel Amsler of Company G, 4th Texas Cavalry, wrote his parents, "the feds are said to be coming up again in considerable force. I expect we will fall back by degrees to my beloved Texas which we will defend as Texians did in former days, and as true Texians know how to do yet."[18]

Like Amsler, few among the Confederates or the civilian population knew where the next blow would fall. "It is reported that Grant is going to or [has] gone to Mobile," salt mine manager E. B. Cox wrote from South Louisiana. If true, this left only the diminished Federal Army of the Gulf to worry about. "Banks' army seems to be lost in the fog," Cox continued. "No one knows where they are."[19]

Union commanders and politicians squandered nearly two months of active operations after the fall of Vicksburg and Port Hudson. In that time, Lieutenant General Kirby Smith reimagined and reorganized the Confederacy as a nearly sovereign Trans-Mississippi fiefdom. Civilian morale—still shaky—stabilized. "We have been in a great deal of excitement about the Yankees coming back up, but are getting over it now," Eliza Robertson of New Iberia wrote to her refugee friend, Sarah Marsh Avery, now living in Houston. "I most earnestly pray that we may never have another visit from those miserable wretches. I am sure I would almost as soon have a visit from the inhabitant of the *lower regions*."[20]

A heroic, nearly fantastic story helped buoy morale during the dog days of that dismal Confederate summer. Several officers captured during the Teche campaign returned—unexpectedly—with a stirring tale. They, and nearly another ninety Confederate officers, had successfully escaped from captivity and eluded their captors for nearly a week before reaching the safety of Rebel lines. This saga became known as the *Maple Leaf* affair after the name of the vessel that had nearly carried them to prison.

The tale started much the same for many of these repatriated soldiers. Most had been captured in April and May 1863 during the course of the Teche Campaign. Captain Julius Giesecke of the 4th Texas Cavalry became a prisoner at the Battle of Irish Bend. Captain Edward Wood Fuller, seriously wounded as skipper of the CSS *Cotton* in Bayou Teche, had recovered and then commanded the CSS *Queen of the West* during its last disastrous battle at Grand Lake. Yankee sailors pulled him from the water. Captain Oliver J. Semmes led the 1st Regular Battery during the Teche Campaign, but the Federals trapped him after he had scuttled the doomed CSS *Diana* near Franklin.

Others joined them in the rat-infested, makeshift prison at the New Orleans customs house. Officers taken on the retreat and at the capture of Fort Burton at Butte-la-Rose arrived, as did forty-two-year-old Lieutenant Z. M. Porter, who had joined the Rebel army at Pinos Altos, New Mexico Territory. Union troops picked him up near Opelousas. The Federal cavalry snagged Lieutenants William Jeter and Emile Carmouche, officers in Company F, 4th Louisiana Infantry, as they had rounded up cattle in Pointe Coupee for the troops across the river at Port Hudson. The last soldiers whom guards threw in the hole had been gathered in Mississippi during Brigadier General Benjamin Grierson's raid.[21]

The prisoners suffered weeks of horrible conditions. "Our entire little band of 25 of was put into a little hold but with one small window covered with iron bars," complained Captain Giesecke, a Texas German. "The place was so small that we could scarcely all find room to lie down and the odor was terrible. Rats were so bad they almost ate the hair from our heads." Within days fifty prisoners shared these same cramped quarters.[22]

On June 2 these men began a journey under guard toward northern prisons. After a short tugboat ride downriver, they boarded the ocean-going steamer *Cahawba*, already loaded with the discharged men of the 6th New York Infantry heading home. "The Federal officers on board treat us very well," Lieutenant Jeter wrote his sister. He hoped for a miracle. "We would all love to see the CSS Steamer *Alabama* heave into sight." Instead, the *Cahawba* arrived uneventfully in Virginia waters, dropping anchor off Fortress Monroe on June 8. Guards ushered the captives to the steamboat *Utica*.[23]

The following day, the New Orleans prisoners transferred from the *Utica* to the recently arrived steamer *Maple Leaf*, a vessel often employed as a truce ship between the Federals at Fortress Monroe and the Confederates at City Point, Virginia. On this trip only Union lieutenant William Dorsey, a sergeant, and twelve privates from the 3rd Pennsylvania Heavy Artillery guarded the men. "We began to hope we would be taken up the James River," Giesecke wrote, "and there exchanged." Instead, the *Maple Leaf* hove to in the Elizabeth River off the docks of Norfolk. "We were given more time," Giesecke added, "to brood our fate anew."[24]

On June 10, forty-seven additional Rebel officers boarded the ship, and the *Maple Leaf* returned across Hampton Roads to Fortress Monroe. Here the captured Confederates received bad news. Prisoner exchanges had been suspended, in part due to rumors of poor treatment of the captured Union officers of black regiments in Louisiana. The capture of so many Rebels at Port Hudson and Vicksburg, too, had also thrown off the equilibrium of the prisoner exchange cartel. "We were all to be sent to Fort Delaware and to be placed in close confinement to the end of the war," Giesecke wrote. The foreboding, star-shaped masonry citadel sat atop Pea Patch Island in the mouth of the Delaware River and already held thousands of prisoners from nearly every Confederate army and state. Jeter had a bad feeling about Fort Delaware. "We . . . did not relish the idea of going there at all," he wrote, "but saw no way to avoid it." A Federal gunboat escorted the prison-bound transport into the Chesapeake Bay.[25]

As the slower enemy warship fell far behind then slipped out of sight over the horizon, the prisoners aboard the *Maple Leaf* sensed an opportunity. Looking around the vessel, they found the Union lieutenant in his bunk, drunk and asleep. The other guards seemed bored. After an hour of whispers, glances, and preparations, a conspirator tapped the ship's bell three times, signaling twenty-five prepositioned Confederates to overpower the guards. The job was easy: the Pennsylvanian's weapons were not even loaded. "Only one man made any resistance at all," Jeter remembered. "He was a Dutchman who tried to get his gun, but one of our men knocked him down with the butt of a musket. That satisfied him." The Rebels now guarded the *Maple Leaf's* three-man crew and fourteen Pennsylvania soldiers. One southerner lowered the U.S. flag. "We were no longer prisoners," Jeter bragged. They were in the Atlantic Ocean, about fifteen miles northeast of Cape Henry, Virginia, in waters infested with Federal warships.[26]

Having captured the *Maple Leaf*, the Confederates faced a fresh dilemma. All agreed Captain Fuller, a former Confederate gunboat commander, should supervise the pilot of the vessel, but no one had any idea where to go. Few believed they could make a successful run to sea, since their coal was limited, and blockaders abounded. Instead, the Rebels turned the *Maple Leaf* about and headed south. When close to the beach near the Virginia and North Carolina line, Fuller ordered the skipper to stop the engines.

For most of the southerners aboard, the *Maple Leaf* was a ticket home. Seventy-one of the Confederates climbed into lifeboats, were lowered into the calm sea, and rowed away from the steamer. Fuller, still disabled from his battlefield injuries, waved farewell, and he and other sick and crippled Rebels remained on board, fearing they would not survive the escape. The embarrassed Union soldiers aboard agreed on their honor to proceed to Fort Delaware as though nothing had happened, providing the escapees with a head start from pursuit.

The Yankees lied. They overpowered their feeble guards and returned to Fortress Monroe to raise the alarm. Telegraph keys clattered from all along the Union-held Virginia and North Carolina coast, launching a ten-day manhunt for the Rebel ship-stealers turned escapees.

The Confederates landed on the beach near Knott's Island in Currituck Sound, North Carolina, and made their way into the Union-controlled interior. To improve their chances, the fugitives broke into small bands, and, with the assistance of local sympathizers and guerillas, slipped past enemy cavalry and gunboat patrols sent to recapture them. After managing to cross the wide Pasquotank River and easing between Federal positions at South Mills and Elizabeth City, North Carolina, the fugitives crossed the southern fringes of the Dismal Swamp. After days on the run, the Confederates crossed the broad Chowan River, entering friendlier territory near Murfreesboro, North Carolina. "Great was our joy since we found ourselves safe and sound within our own lines," Giesecke remembered. "We gave a thundering yell 'Hurrah for Dixie' and did not care whether the Yankees heard us or not." By June 21, most had encountered Confederate pickets and made their way to the Weldon and Southside Railroad for a trip into Richmond. The tattered but jubilant soldiers received back pay and a month's furlough to return to their units.[27]

The journey back to their regiments took nearly the entire month, and many of the officers once again passed dangerously close to Union forces along the way. Giesecke and three fellow officers made about a dozen stops on his way from Richmond to Alexandria, Louisiana. They traveled by rail to Wilmington, North Carolina; Kingsville, South Carolina; Augusta and Atlanta Georgia; and Montgomery, Alabama. He rode a steamboat down the Alabama River and up the Tombigbee to Demopolis before riding a stage to Meridian, Mississippi. Another train carried him to Jackson where he arrived on July 4, the day Vicksburg surrendered.

His way west blocked, Giesecke had headed down the New Orleans, Galveston, and Great Northern Railroad to Brookhaven, Mississippi, and then climbed aboard a stagecoach for Natchez, arriving at noon on July 6. "Right before the town lay two gunboats in the river," he recorded in his diary. "We were therefore compelled to lay over quietly . . . and await their convenient departure."

Giesecke pressed on. The Texan and three fellow officers crossed the Mississippi on a skiff the next morning and caught the stage at Vidalia for Trinity, Louisiana. When they arrived, they had just missed the regular steamboat to Alexandria. Cinching up their packs, they trudged for nearly thirty miles before hitching a ride on a wagon for the final fifteen.[28]

Other Trans-Mississippi officers who had been a part of the *Maple Leaf* adventure also drifted into town. All enjoyed the few days' rest before their furlough ended. At the same time his comrades fought the Battle of Kock's Plantation and retreated from the Lafourche country far to the south, Giesecke "passed a happy-go-lucky life." But soon enough the captain left his comfortable lodgings and headed toward Brigadier General Green's Brigade as it retreated up the Teche. "I reported for 'duty' on the march," he wrote. The following day Giesecke added, "It was my turn to stand on guard, and thus the old life was again at hand."[29]

The men of the *Maple Leaf* affair were celebrities. Civilians in South Louisiana loved hearing their story. Leila Robertson of New Iberia entertained several of the participants as they passed on their way back to their commands. "Heroes of the

Colonel Leopold L. Armant, 18th Louisiana Infantry.
Courtesy of Confederate Memorial Hall, New Orleans.

Maple Leaf, have been here," she bragged to her cousin Margaret Henshaw Avery, who was living as a refugee in Houston Texas. "I wish you could hear them tell their adventures." Some clamored for one of the men to write a book. "I think he prefers telling the story himself," Robertson observed. By the end of the summer, she didn't believe "anyone . . . had not heard of their escape from the *Maple Leaf*."[30]

For Confederate commanders, this boost in civilian morale seemed promising, coupled as it was with several weeks of respite from active campaigning. Major General Taylor used the reprieve from Union operations to rebuild his army. He had four cavalry commands holding northeast Louisiana: the 13th and 15th Louisiana Cavalry Battalions, the 12th Texas Cavalry, and the 19th Texas Cavalry, which was supported by Captain J. H. Pratt's Texas Battery. Two infantry regiments, the 22nd and 34th Texas Cavalry (Dismounted), built fortifications at Grand Ecore on the Red River near Natchitoches. The twelve regiments of Major General John G. Walker's Division camped in the pine hills southwest of

Alexandria. Part of Brigadier General Green's cavalry brigade, the 4th and 7th Texas and the 2nd Louisiana, lay near Opelousas and Washington. Its other elements—the 5th Texas and the 13th Texas Cavalry Battalions and Major Leonidas C. "Lee" Rountree's Cavalry Battalion—were twenty-five miles east, at Morgan's Ferry on the Atchafalaya River.[31]

Another cluster of infantry spread out around Vermilionville. These included two Texas regiments, the 15th Infantry and 31st Cavalry (Dismounted), and a small three-company battalion, the infantry of Lieutenant Colonel Ashley W. Spaight's 11th Texas Volunteers. Taylor had returned the infantry companies of the 13th Texas Volunteers and the tattered 2nd Texas Cavalry to Major General John B. Magruder in Texas. Taylor kept the four mounted companies of the 13th Texas volunteers—Major Rountree's Cavalry Battalion picketing the Atchafalaya—a while longer.

Taylor's Louisiana Infantry, formerly Mouton's Brigade and now commanded by Colonel Leopold L. Armant, camped at Vermilionville. This command had fallen on hard times. Desertion, disease, and casualties had reduced the regiments in this unit to the point that clearly consolidation was necessary. "The Crescent [24th], 18th and 28th Regiments are to be joined into Clack's [12th Battalion] and only 40 of the officers are to be retained in the regiment," reported Eliza Robertson from New Iberia. "The others are to be sent to the conscript camps to drill conscripts, and you may well imagine the state of anxiety the officers are in to know who is to be accepted and who rejected."[32]

Four other regiments served as pickets in the country between New Iberia and Berwick Bay. Colonel James P. Major, leading the 1st and 2nd Texas Partisan Rangers, and the 2nd and 3rd Arizona Cavalry, used his regiments to keep an eye on enemy movements from Brashear City and to report any gunboat activity on Grand Lake. Also serving here were the two mounted companies of Spaight's 11th Texas Volunteers and Captain William E. Gibson's Texas Battery.

The soldiers suffered as Louisiana broiled under the August sun. The rain had stopped, for the most part, in mid-July, and now every passage of troops churned up clouds of dust. Water sources soured or dried up completely. Bad water and bad air led to debilitating intestinal and respiratory illnesses. Regimental strengths dropped off by as much as 50 percent, and hospitals began to fill. Animals, too, suffered. In an age of horse-drawn armies, transportation became crippled as well. A bloom of flies and mosquitoes plagued the troops. Water levels in the rivers dropped. Sandbars effectively closed the mouth of the Red River to Union gunboats. The whole region fell into drought.

The unrelenting heat, dust, bugs, humidity, boredom, and illness drove the troops mad. One soldier in the 31st Texas Cavalry (Dismounted), camped near Vermilionville, suggested they name their bivouac "Camp Diarrhea," based on the most common complaint. A Louisianan agreed. "At this camp we were reminded of the gloomy and dismal days around Corinth in 1862," Major Silas T. Grisamore of the 18th Louisiana Infantry wrote near Vermilionville. "Our camp exhibited the appearance of a hospital rather than that of a warlike body." Colonel Armant moved his Louisianans to Abbeville hoping the proximity of sea breezes might improve their health. Making matters worse for the troops, Taylor ordered furloughs and leaves suspended, though it appeared the Federals had no intention of launching a renewed campaign.[33]

Lieutenant Colonel George Guess, 31st Texas Cavalry (Dismounted).
Guess (George W.) Letters (Mss. 793), *Louisiana and Lower Mississippi Valley Collections, Special Collections, Louisiana State University Libraries, Baton Rouge.*

One Texan officer hoped their misery mirrored that of the enemy. "We are doing nothing here but getting sick and trying to get better," Lieutenant Colonel George Guess wrote. "Banks army is all said to be sick in New Orleans and if they are there, I hope so and have no doubt of the truth of it."[34]

On August 21, around four hundred men, nearly half of the soldiers in Colonel Major's Brigade snapped. "Great excitement," Private William N. Corothers wrote. "Phillip's and Stone's mutinied and aim to start home to Texas and a good many of our regiment will join." Major ordered the men still loyal to stop the deserters. The next morning, officers formed the 2nd Arizona "exhorting the men not to join [the mutiny] but to stand by the colors," Corothers observed. "It was not well received for there is great dissatisfaction in this regiment. The cause . . . is short rations and strict discipline."[35]

Brigadier General Alfred Mouton took preventative measures to ensure compliance. Colonel Armant's Louisiana troops, on the move to Abbeville, received orders to shift their route if necessary to crush the Arizona insurrection if it were to get out of hand. On August 23, Colonel Major put the matter in simple terms. After assembling the men and passing by in inspection, he reasoned with them. Then, his mood darkened. "He gave them a very plain talk," Corothers remembered quoting his commander. "'God damn! You have to stay. If you go to Texas, Magruder will have the last one [of you] shot.'" That logic, and word that the Louisiana infantry might intervene, dampened the conspirators' ardor.[36]

At his headquarters, Taylor also disposed of some unfinished business. He had an officer to drive out of the army. Brigadier General Henry Hopkins Sibley, a native Louisianan, had led the campaign into New Mexico in 1861 and had commanded east of the Atchafalaya in 1862, but he had crossed Taylor during the Teche Campaign in 1863. Now he faced charges of "disobedience to orders" and "unofficer-like conduct." Green had taken over command of the brigade, and Taylor ordered a court-martial. General Sibley arrived at Opelousas on August 16 for his day of judgment, and the officers who would hear the case arrived soon thereafter. Major General Walker presided. The rest of the panel consisted of Green, William Read Scurry, Prince Camille de Polignac, and Captain J. W. West of Lieutenant General Kirby Smith's staff. Three weeks later, this panel declared

Sibley not guilty. The assembled officers—not including the accused—held a formal ball in Opelousas before returning to their commands. Sibley left for Richmond, shaken, and without a command.[37]

Some soldiers decried the proceedings. One Texan believed Taylor needed a scapegoat for the disastrous Teche Campaign and found one in Sibley. "Big fish eat little fish," sighed Private Theophilus Noel, 4th Texas Cavalry. "In bidding Sibley adieu, we do so under the full conviction that we have parted with a high-minded, noble, valorous and gifted officer, endowed with a principal too lofty and honorable to deign to any acts calculated to wrong any one. He was honorably acquitted, yet he was not restored to a command, greatly to the dislike of both citizens and soldiers." Another soldier agreed Taylor had been vindictive. "[Sibley] is accused of being a coward, of having been found drunk near the battlefield in a sugarhouse, and God knows what more," this soldier complained. "Everybody that saw him at the [Bisland] breastworks will cheerfully testify that the General behaved with the most conspicuous gallantry, and the accusation of drunkenness is a wicked, outrageous, lie. The charges against him are of quite a

Brigadier General Henry Hopkins Sibley, the luckless leader of many a Confederate misadventure. *Library of Congress.*

different character. . . . It must be very trying to the gallant General to be just at this moment deprived of his command, when his brigade is covering itself with immortal glory, and maintaining its reputation [as] a terror to the Yankees."[38]

After drumming out General Sibley, Taylor had to focus again on keeping his army fed and clothed. Believing the Federals would pursue his army into the interior, he had cached supplies along the line of his planned retreat and had set up a depot at Niblett's Bluff on the Sabine. Given the enemy's lack of energy, he now needed those supplies brought forward to Vermilionville. Lieutenant Sibley of the 2nd Louisiana Cavalry received orders to take twenty men and head to the Sabine and "hire or impress wagons and bring . . . all the bacon and coffee that could be got," he wrote. "The object in sending the escort was to guard the train from the Jayhawkers who were near the road." He returned, unmolested, with twenty wagons loaded with provisions.[39]

With the Clan suppressed for the time being, much of the clothing spun out of the Texas homesteads found its way to sons, husbands, fathers, and brothers in regiments serving in Louisiana. "The Louisianans have no love for any people of any state but their own, and as to money, they would much prefer to have Federal greenbacks to Confederate paper, so that it is wholly impossible to get any clothing for a Texan from here," complained Lieutenant Colonel Guess. Officers and men passing back to Louisiana from Texas brought welcome relief to some of the threadbare troops. Captain McDade, for one, admired his new homemade duds. "The pants fit very nice and I think a heap of them," he wrote his wife. "The shirt is bully, and the socks star."[40]

With no fighting imminent and the troops once again fed, clothed, and rested, morale among the Confederates improved. "If Banks had used any exertion he could have bagged all of us," reflected Private Watkins of the 5th Texas Cavalry. "I think he has had a hard time at Hudson and his army was too much reduced by sickness, bullets, and desertion, so that he was unable to move. We have heard nothing definite from him." Lieutenant Sibley shared this optimism. "It seems like we are preparing to stay here a while, perhaps some weeks or months," he wrote, "if the Yankees don't come after us again." Captain McDade believed the Trans-Mississippi was the least of the Federal's concern. He assured his wife, "I do not think there will be much fighting done here until Mobile and Charleston fall, and God grant they never may." Back in Texas, Sallie Patrick, a friend of Private Howell of the 5th Texas, yearned for the war to let up. "It is to be hoped that your noble brigade will have no more fighting to do for a time, for ever since you have been in Louisiana, you have been engaged in a succession of battles," she wrote, "and each one has had glory enough, honor enough, and fighting enough."[41]

FIVE

RECONNAISSANCE

Uncle Sam's nephews were in the neighborhood.

—Lieutenant Charles Furlong
Company F, 17th Wisconsin (Mounted) Infantry

The respite from Union pressure could not last. Although Major General Nathaniel P. Banks and his army had apparently vanished, troops from Major General Ulysses S. Grant's Army of the Tennessee seemed to be stirring and threated to renew the invasion of Louisiana. Major General Francis J. Herron's Division departed Port Hudson a few days in mid-August, heading downstream toward New Orleans. On August 19, Brigadier General Tom Green's Texans mounted up and headed toward the Mississippi River to provoke the enemy. "I don't know what the object is," wrote Private John W. Watkins of the 5th Texas Cavalry, "but I expect we will have a fight."[1]

Green and his troopers filtered unopposed to the west bank of the Mississippi. As intended, Federal commanders raised alarms about this Confederate activity, which conflicted with the government's stated gain of unfettered Union use of the great river. Green's advance, led by Major Leonidas C. "Lee" Rountree's three hundred Texans, probed as far as the outskirts of Plaquemine where its garrison, the 4th Wisconsin Cavalry and the 128th New York Infantry, presented tempting targets. "There are about two regiments of Yankees . . . they want to get rid of," Captain Keet McDade of the 13th Texas Cavalry Battalion wrote his wife, "yet it is very close to Port Hudson and the Yanks could reinforce in a very short time." His regiment and the 2nd Louisiana Cavalry stood by at Morgan's Ferry on the Atchafalaya River. Brigadier General Green arrived with the rest of his cavalry brigade a few days later.[2]

Green decided to let the Federals be for the time being. Instead, on August 21, his troops moved into camps at Morgan's Ferry, near where Bayou Rouge emptied into the Atchafalaya. Sergeant Alfred B. Petticolas of the 4th Texas Cavalry, a resident of Victoria, Texas, welcomed the potential return to action. "We have been lying idle too long," he penned in his journal. "I don't know what our Generals mean by not putting the army to work at their legitimate business—killing Yankees." In fact, Petticolas stood ready to cross the nearby Mississippi. "I am very much in hopes that we will go across the river before we are done," he added. "I don't think there is any use in keeping the 25 or 30,000 men on this side of the river. If the other side, where they are making their most strenuous efforts, is subdued, then we [too] are subdued."[3]

Green had hoped to uncover Federal intentions, and possibly a looming invasion across the Atchafalaya, but failed. Instead, the day after Green arrived at the Atchafalaya, Federal brigadier general John Dunlap Stevenson took command of the "Louisiana Expedition" at Vicksburg. He loaded four infantry brigades from the 17th Army Corps, three artillery batteries, and a cavalry battalion onto steamers and headed upriver toward Goodrich's Landing, away from the bulk of Major General Richard Taylor's army. Stevenson's goal was a reconnaissance in force to investigate the feasibility of a general advance toward Monroe. The Federals came ashore and pressed inland, fanning out and driving the few hundred nearby Rebel troops beyond the towns of Floyd, Monticello, and Delhi on Bayou Macon. Confederate couriers sounded the alarm across Louisiana.

On August 24, Stevenson continued to Monroe, marching through a region as yet untouched by war. "I found the country in a high state of cultivation, with immense crops of corn and cotton maturing, and vast numbers of cattle fattening in the canebrakes and swamps," Stevenson reported. "I have no doubt but that forage and beef could be secured from this country in sufficient quantities to supply the department for the ensuing winter." Two miles east of Monroe, the Texas and Louisiana cavalry led by Colonel William Henry Parsons tried to make a stand to protect the town, but they fell back. Parsons's men prepared another stand at Vienna, Louisiana, thirty miles west of Monroe and just sixty miles east of Shreveport. The Confederates let Stevenson take Monroe, hoping to trade territory for time.[4]

Surprisingly, the Federals only stayed overnight. Their reconnaissance complete, the Federals left. They reached Vicksburg by the beginning of September,

The Lower Mississippi

Fifty Miles

Memphis

Little Rock

Helena
STEELE

Pine Bluff

Napoleon

Mississippi River

Camden

ARKANSAS

Ouachita River

MISSISSIPPI

Shreveport

Monroe

Bayou Macon

STEVENSON

Vicksburg

LOUISIANA

Tensas River

Red River

Trinity

Natchez
Vidalia

CROCKER

Alexandria

Simmsport

Morganza

Morgan's Ferry

PORT HUDSON

GREEN

Opelousas

Port
Barré

Baton
Rouge

Atchafalaya River

Niblett's
Bluff

Lake Charles

Plaquemine

Vermilionville

Donaldsonville

HERRON

New Iberia

Thibodaux

New Orleans

Sabine Pass

FRANKLIN

Brashear City

having marched more than 150 miles. The Rebels, however, remained tense. "The Yankees have gone back to the Mississippi River but I suppose . . . that before a great while a larger force will try to go to Shreveport," observed Lieutenant George Ingram, 12th Texas Cavalry. "If they do . . . we will have one of the biggest fights that ever occurred on this side of the father of waters."[5]

Union commanders applauded Stevenson's reconnaissance. Major General Stephen A. Hurlbut, commanding the 16th Army Corps in Memphis, Tennessee, saw its success as a harbinger of a greater victory. He wrote Major General Frederick Steele, commanding in Arkansas, and reconfirmed the emerging plan for the fall campaign. "There is a strong expedition now on foot for Texas," he advised. While other Union forces moved in that direction, "a victory sharply followed up at or near Little Rock will clear Arkansas, send all the Missouri Confederate forces out of the war, and disband any resistance to our arms north of Red River." Stevenson's capture of Monroe and the unhindered Union penetration into the region between the Mississippi and Ouachita Rivers would keep Lieutenant General Edmund Kirby Smith from reinforcing Rebels in Arkansas with troops from Louisiana or Texas, lest he leave northern Louisiana, and his headquarters at Shreveport, exposed.[6]

Armed with this new information, Hurlbut sent Stevenson new orders. Realizing the richest acres in Arkansas remained to be harvested for the Union cause, he suggested Stevenson launch another raid, this time from Napoleon, Arkansas, to assist Steele's columns already driving across the state. Stevenson could lend a hand by approaching Little Rock from the south, turning any Confederate defenses of the capital, and pass through country untouched by war. Arkansas corn and cattle could feed the troops, and more slaves could be gathered for service in the army. "This movement will open the cotton-growing plantation country," he wrote General Henry W. Halleck, "the disloyal part of Arkansas, hitherto unpunished in this war."[7]

While the tide of war shifting against them in Arkansas, the Confederates in Louisiana struck back where they could, employing familiar forces and tactics. To ascertain Union plans to his front, Taylor again ordered his Texas cavalry to raid the west bank of the Mississippi in Louisiana. The threats of Brigadier General Green's men moving once again toward the outposts at Plaquemine

The ironclad gunboat USS Louisville. *Library of Congress.*

and Morganza would, with any luck, disrupt any Union operations. At least one Confederate Captain had complete confidence in his leader. "I guess General Green will have it all fixed right," commented McDade. "I am willing to go with him." As they had done the previous July, Colonel John L. Logan's Mississippi and Arkansas troops launched a cooperative raid on the east bank.[8]

The Confederates once again vexed the Mississippi. Commercial steamboats and gunboats alike reported gunfire zipping across their decks from both banks as they passed near Port Hudson. The crew of the transport *Iberville* arrived in New Orleans bearing tales of a serious encounter between Gunboat No. 24—the USS *Champion*—and Confederates in Morgan's Bend on August 30. Firing echoed near Port Hudson for the next three days.[9] Federal lieutenant commander E. K. Owen of the ironclad gunboat *Louisville* reported, "The guerillas . . . have been busily employed committing a series of depredations such as shooting negroes and stealing horses. The enemy are always mounted and armed with rifles and shotguns." He remained unimpressed. "A small force, say 500 men, would disperse this thieving gang."[10]

Yet, the Confederates rode unhindered and Union troops garrisoning the west bank suffered. In Point Coupee Parish, Major Rountree surprised an outpost of the *Corps d'Afrique* across the river from Port Hudson, killing a half dozen before riding away.[11]

While Steele conquered Arkansas and Green raided across the Atchafalaya, Brigadier General Marcellus Crocker launched a scouting expedition from Natchez, Mississippi, in preparation for the fall campaign. On September 1 he crossed a regiment of mounted troops over the Mississippi to Vidalia and quickly followed it with around four thousand men in two infantry brigades and two artillery batteries. Rebel pickets who had seen the movement rode to alert Confederates in Alexandria, including Major General John G. Walker's Texas Division. The pickets correctly predicted the target to be the important town of Trinity, where the confluence of the Ouachita, Tensas, and Little Rivers forms the Black River. They also warned Fort Beauregard at Harrisonburg, just upstream, might also be in peril, and Alexandria might be the ultimate target. A screen of mounted Union soldiers, galloping toward the Ouachita, guarded the size and scope of the Union invasion.[12]

The speed of the Union raiders surprised the few Confederate pickets from the 15th Louisiana Cavalry stationed west of Vidalia. The recently mounted Federals, veterans of every fight of the Army of the Tennessee since the Battle

Brigadier General Marcellus Crocker was a gifted leader in the campaigns of the Mississippi Valley but eventually left for Santa Fe to treat his tuberculosis. *Library of Congress.*

of Corinth, dashed thirty miles to Trinity that day, capturing enemy outposts en route. Union volunteers swam the Black River under fire, gathered any watercraft they could find, and returned to assist their comrades. The regiment crossed the watercourse in parcels on skiffs and cotton barges. "This was done under a heavy fire from the enemy, who did not abandon their position until two companies crossed," Lieutenant Charles Furlong reported. The Rebels took another position behind a thick hedge, but the Federals soon dislodged them, losing four men in the process.[13]

The Confederates fled the town, and the Federals pursued them for several miles before allowing them to leave and returning to Trinity. Just as the Federal troops arrived, the Confederate steamboat *Rinaldo*, loaded with supplies for the outpost, tied up to the landing, "the captain, I presume, not being aware that any of Uncle Sam's nephews were in the neighborhood," quipped Furlong. The Wisconsin troopers burned it. When Union pickets arrived, announcing Confederates were returning in larger numbers to retake the town, the Midwesterners prudently fell back across the Black River to rejoin the rest of the column.[14]

Two days later the Federals established a more substantial bridgehead west of the Ouachita River. The slower-moving infantry arrived opposite Trinity, created a pontoon bridge out of cotton barges, and secured the town. The 17th Wisconsin Mounted Infantry, once again in the lead, drove the eighty Confederate pickets from the 15th Louisiana Cavalry Battalion out of the area and established defensive positions on all the road junctions to the west, isolating Trinity.[15]

Colonel Horace Randal was a West Point graduate from Texas. *Huntington Library, San Marino, California.*

Two routes led from Alexandria to the Ouachita. The better one ran toward Harrisonburg, along the edge of the pine hills north of the swampy Catahoula Lake and Bayou Bushley bottoms. Another ran south toward Trinity, through the low country along the banks of the Little River. A lateral lane, the Hawthorn Road, ran from Trinity and bridged Bayou Bushley, connecting the southern route to the northern one at a junction about eight miles southwest of Harrsionburg. Union troops fortified their position at Trinity and sent the 17th Wisconsin on ahead to seize the important crossroads intersection at the edge of the pines. By the end of the day, Union troops had placed themselves between the Confederate garrison at Fort Beauregard and any reinforcements coming from Alexandria, two days' march away, isolating the post.[16]

A collision between the Confederates and Federals occurred just before midnight. Federal scouts reported some of Walker's Texans were coming from Alexandria along the northern route to rescue the troops at Harrisonburg. In the early minutes of September 4, the 17th Wisconsin trotted down the road in the darkness to slow the Rebel advance while Crocker's two brigades of Illinois and Indiana infantry, supported by two batteries of artillery, formed a line of battle,

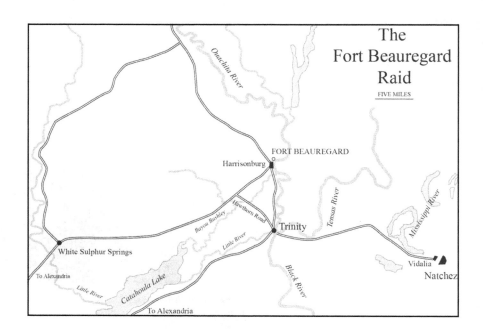

ready to receive the Rebel attack if the mounted troops fell back. Instead, the mounted Federals drove a screen of Louisiana cavalry back several miles down the road toward Alexandria, killing four in the night skirmish and losing five of their own. The Midwesterners, surprised at their own triumph, returned to the infantry line at around 8 AM to report the good news and no sign of the Texan infantry.[17]

Confederate colonel Horace Randal, leading just eleven hundred men without artillery or any cavalry beyond the skittish Louisianans, had played it safe. The enemy, whom he correctly believed greatly outnumbered him, would get to Fort Beauregard before he could. He sent a courier to advise the fort's commander—Lieutenant Colonel George Logan—to save what he could but to give up the fort and join him. The best Randal could do was draw the Federal attention away from the escaping garrison. The plan worked. In the darkness, while the 17th Wisconsin Mounted Infantry skirmished with the 15th Louisiana and probed for the oncoming Texans, Logan took Randal's advice and abandoned the earthwork and escaped with his horses, mules, and the rifled guns of Captain Thomas O. Benton's Louisiana battery. The Yankees had simply looked the wrong direction as the Rebels fled.[18]

After daybreak, the Texans fell back toward Alexandria, and the Federals turned toward Harrisonburg. They captured the abandoned Rebel earthwork, with its buildings now charred ruins, its casemates blown up, its heavy guns spiked, and their carriages burned. The Federal raiders inventoried four siege guns and four 6-pounders in the wreckage. After destroying the weapons, ammunition, and cannon that could not be carried off, Crocker's troops withdrew toward Natchez with two 6-pounders and the Rebel flag from Fort Beauregard as trophies.[19]

Major General Taylor pondered the meaning of the Federal moves. His commanders, Randal and Logan, reported the enemy strength to be at least fifteen thousand infantry in three brigades, two artillery batteries, and a regiment of cavalry. If so, this might be the beginning of a larger invasion into the heart of his command. Randal, fearing for the safety of Alexandria, asked for reinforcements, especially cavalry. Taylor ordered Colonel James P. Major to bring his restless—and mutinous—Texas and Arizona brigade north from the Teche country. The major general replaced them with Henry Gray's 28th Louisiana infantry and a screen of cavalry: the two mounted companies of Texans from Lieutenant Colonel Ashley Spaight's Battalion and the 2nd Louisiana, fresh from serving with Green along the Atchafalaya. Taylor also ordered another of Walker's brigades and a battery to find Randal and strengthen his line. If the Federals meant to strike Alexandria, Taylor reasoned, they would come down the roads from Trinity and Harrisonburg.[20]

Taylor readied his army for the fall campaign, but he had no idea where to make his stand. A month before he had planned on holding a line from Lafayette to the Sabine, but intelligence from freedmen captured from the Federals and enslaved by his soldiers indicated large numbers of troops were gathering at Brashear City. "This may be true, though no one here seems to pay any attention to it," Lieutenant Colonel George Guess wrote home to friends in Dallas. Was this a feint?[21] Something else, something big, seemed to be afoot, with Shreveport as the intended target. "We hear rumors of some kind of operation threatening northern Texas," Guess continued, "but know nothing of certainty."[22]

After the recent raids from Mississippi, Taylor pivoted his attention toward the east. "When we lost Vicksburg and Port Hudson," he admitted, "we lost not only control of the river, but of the valley." Based on what he had seen, Taylor believed the next Federal advance would be west from Vicksburg and Natchez, simultaneously, and up the Red River against Shreveport and Alexandria.[23]

Reports from Arkansas were grim as well. Steele was closing in on Little Rock. There could now be an advance on Shreveport from the north, as well. Kirby Smith, Price, and Taylor now knew the enemy intentions. Four sizable Union columns would march on Shreveport and Alexandria and converge on the two small Confederate armies in Arkansas and Louisiana.

When they did, there might be no stopping them.

SIX   SABINE PASS

Our loss was, strictly and positively, nobody hurt.

—Captain Frank H. Odlum
Company F, "The Davis Guards"
1st Texas Heavy Artillery

While Major General Ulysses S. Grant's commands threatened Little Rock, Shreveport, and Alexandria, Major General Nathaniel P. Banks aimed his killing blow at Houston. As Union troops from Vicksburg and Natchez fixed the Rebels' attention on the Mississippi Valley, Banks planned to send a water-borne column to initiate the final destruction of the Trans-Mississippi Confederacy by seizing key points on the upper Texas coast. Major General William B. Franklin would take most of the 19th Army Corps and land at Sabine Pass, "if it could be done without serious resistance," as Banks directed. Otherwise, Franklin would put the troops ashore a dozen miles or so down the coast. From there, the Union troops would dash for Beaumont, Liberty, or Houston, which, as Banks pointed out, "would have been nearly in the center of the forces in and about Louisiana and Texas, commanding the principal communications, and would [give] us ultimately the possession of the state." Galveston Island would fall next, taken from the mainland, and Banks would be the conqueror of Texas in a lightning campaign of a few short weeks. Louisiana, cut off from supplies and reinforcements, would wither while Grant launched his slashing moves across the state and into the Red River Valley. First, though, Franklin had to get his troops ashore.[1]

The bold plan for the Sabine Pass expedition required secrecy and delicate, precise cooperation across hundreds of miles of land and sea. Union gunboats would have to shoot their way past light opposition from shore batteries, allowing Major General Godfrey Weitzel to land his division from the 19th Army Corps and

Major General Nathaniel P. Banks, powerful politician and commander of the Department of the Gulf. *Library of Congress.*

capture Beaumont. Within days Brigadier General William H. Emory would follow with reinforcements. The result would be an indirect blow from an unexpected quarter—a left hook—to the Confederates. The Federals would catch them unaware.

The hour for launching the expedition was fast approaching. On September 2, while the Union raid on Fort Beauregard drew Major General Richard Taylor's attention to the Ouachita River and Lieutenant General Edmund Kirby Smith fretted over Arkansas, Major General Grant, along with U.S. adjutant general Lorenzo Thomas, traveled down the Mississippi from Vicksburg to the Union headquarters in New Orleans. Grant went to coordinate his part of the coming campaign, and Thomas went to learn what progress Banks had made in raising the *Corps d'Afrique.*

Two days later, their plans in place, the commanders celebrated the launch of the fall campaign by riding to the Champ d'Mars in Carrollton to review the troops of the Army of the Gulf. Banks took his reserve horse, a black mare. He loaned his bay warhorse, Charlie—purchased in Virginia and veteran of several battles there—to his guest. Grant, an excellent horseman, outpaced his companions even on an unfamiliar mount. The mood was lively and light for these conquering heroes, and the generals reviewed the troops with their horses in a fast walk.[2]

For the Union soldiers, however, the mood was less sanguine. That late summer afternoon near New Orleans was "intensively hot," Lieutenant Colonel Joseph B. Leake of the 20th Iowa Infantry remembered, standing in the ranks with his regiment under a broiling Louisiana sun as tempers simmered. The review was the first time most of these troops, Midwesterners from the 13th Army Corps and easterners from the 19th Army Corps, had stood together on the same field. Corporal Carlos Colby of the 97th Illinois Infantry did not believe this this new combination would work well. "We are now in the department of the Gulf," he grumbled in a letter home. "If Gen. Banks intends to bring the western troops under as strict a discipline as the eastern troops are, he had better to begin now to build more prisons, and send to the War Department for more troops to guard the 13th Army Corps."[3]

There had already been trouble. "Fights are of a frequent occurrence," continued Colby. "Some of the Maine troops are doing provost duty in the city and they are rather set up because they have the authority, this is the cause of a great deal of contention generaly ending in a fight, and a complete cleaning out of the eastern boys."[4]

Major General Godfrey "Dutch" Weitzel was an engineer by training but took the field to good effect in Louisiana. *Library of Congress.*

Brigadier General William Emory was famous for surveying the US-Mexican border and served capably in the Louisiana campaigns. *Library of Congress.*

The generals may not have appreciated the tension among the ranks. After passing the lines, Grant spurred Charlie into a dead run in a mischievous, showy dash of bravado. "The brilliant cavalcade of generals and staff officers was left behind by the hero of Vicksburg," observed a journalist. Banks at first had a hard time managing his mare, but she soon charged after her stable mate. Leake watched the "race between Grant and Banks—both splendid riders." The generals, satisfied with the ceremonies, moved on to other social obligations to find shade—and a drink—while the troops broke ranks.[5]

As the paraded troops broke formation, Weitzel's three Union brigades from the 19th Army Corps reached the Mississippi and loaded onto transports heading downriver for Texas. Meanwhile, two brigades from the 13th Army Corps received surprise orders. As they marched back to camp after the review, the men of Major General Francis J. Herron's Division were told to draw six days rations and be ready to load onto steamers at 5 AM. While Weitzel landed in Texas, Herron's men would whip Brigadier General Tom Green's Rebels on the Atchafalaya River and keep the enemy convinced of an imminent ascent up the Red River. This move would have the added benefit of sweeping away the enemy from both banks of the Mississippi and keeping the river open for commercial navigation. After accomplishing this quick raid, Herron's Midwesterners would reinforce Weitzel for the decisive blow against Houston. "General Herron will be able to accomplish this object and return in time to take part in the Texas expedition," Banks assured General-in-Chief Henry W. Halleck.[6]

A Mexican observer lurking along the docks of New Orleans watched all of these movements with keen interest. He brought hopeful news to the consulate, which immediately dispatched an encouraging note to President Benito Juárez at San Luis Potosi. The memorandum claimed twenty thousand Federal troops would be headed toward Texas by an overland march and another ten thousand would land at the mouth of the Rio Grande. "The president must be informed that these troops have the best feelings for his cause," the message read, "and will do what they can to aid him."[7]

For the Federals, a near calamity threatened to change the course of the campaign even before it started. After the review, Grant, Banks, and their high-ranking entourage headed to a lunch party at the home of a nearby Unionist planter. Already in high spirits, the officers enjoyed good whiskey and excellent food. The heat heightened the potency of the planter's punch. The officers were soon deep in their cups. Cocky guests, no doubt inspired by Grant's grandstanding

Major General Ulysses S. Grant came close to an abbreviated Civil War career in the streets of New Orleans. *Library of Congress.*

display at the review, goaded him to race a young cavalry officer the few miles back to the St. Charles Hotel. Thus challenged, Grant agreed.

The pair spurred into a gallop from their starting point, navigating the crowded road as a thrilling obstacle course and showing off their tipsy equestrian skills. Early in the race, the pair neared a railroad crossing in Carrollton. Grant's borrowed horse Charlie—he later described him as "vicious and but little used"— bolted at the hissing and chuffing of a locomotive. The spooked animal bucked and galloped out of control until it lost its footing. Some accounts reported Grant was thrown, others he crashed into an ambulance or wagon as well before the horse fell on him. Adjutant General Thomas watched the accident and reported Charlie "threw [Grant] over with great violence. The General, who is a splendid rider, maintained his seat in the saddle."[8]

The crazed horse nearly killed Grant. "When I regained consciousness, I found myself in a hotel nearby with several doctors attending me," Grant recalled. "My leg was swollen from the knee to the thigh, and the swelling, almost to the point of bursting, extended along the body up to the arm-pit. The pain was almost

Adjutant General of the Army Lorenzo Thomas is credited with orchestrating an extensive coverup regarding Grant's accident. *Library of Congress.*

beyond endurance." Grant, grievously injured would be debilitated for weeks. His part in the coming campaign would have to be delegated to other officers.[9]

Many felt relieved fate had benched Grant. Banks believed he had been drunk and irresponsible, leading to his wreck. The hero of Vicksburg, Banks and others whispered, had a potentially fatal flaw that might jeopardize the complicated movements of the coming months aimed at ending the Confederacy in the Trans-Mississippi. "I am frightened when I think that he is a drunkard," Banks wrote his wife. "His accident was caused by this, which was too manifest to all who saw him." Franklin agreed, reporting Grant had already been on a two-day bender before his smashup. Perverse mercy, Franklin concluded: the injury had been providential. Otherwise, he observed, Grant would have "frolicked for a fortnight" in New Orleans with potentially toxic results. Fortunately for the morale of the army, this drama played out beyond the sight of the Union soldiers heading back to war.[10]

Banks departed from Grant's sickbed to launch his campaign to finish off the Confederates west of the river. First, he reported to Halleck that he had dispatched an initial invasion force of five thousand men, three field batteries, and two batteries of heavy Parrott Rifles for the Sabine Pass expedition. His transports, escorted by the USS *Arizona*, would enter the Gulf of Mexico and rendezvous in Texas waters with the additional light draft gunboats USS *Sachem* and USS *Clifton*, which were coming from Berwick Bay.[11]

The newly arrived USS *Granite City*, a Rebel blockade-runner captured in the Bahamas a few months before and converted into a light draft gunboat, had already gone on ahead with a pilot familiar with Sabine Pass. Due to arrive on September 6 under the cover of darkness, the USS *Granite City*'s crew had two important tasks to accomplish that night. First, they would mark the entrance to Sabine Pass with a beacon to guide in the gunboat flotilla. Second, they would clearly mark the channels so that the skippers on the invasion ships could be sure of the depth and avoid going aground. Until they handled those chores, the invasion fleet would stay well clear of the shore and out of sight. With these navigation aids in place, the Union gunboats would dash in at first light on September 7 and paste the defenders before they could prepare a response.[12]

Banks envisioned a swift and daring naval attack. Just minutes behind the gunboats, General Weitzel would land a brigade of troops and clear out the remaining opposition, overrunning the enemy batteries. Confronted by four Union gunboats entering Sabine Lake, the Confederates would not be able to send reinforcements before the balance of the invasion force, led by General Franklin, had leapfrogged through the Sabine Pass, into Sabine Lake, and landed and secured Beaumont, thus isolating and defending the beachhead. Banks remained confident the enemy suspected nothing. "I have reliable information today from Galveston," Banks confided to Halleck, "which gives the force . . . at that point as 2,300 men, in a very demoralized condition. Our attack on Texas is expected in the direction of Vermilionville, Louisiana, or Niblett's Bluff." Not Sabine Pass.[13]

The expedition, though, already had some complications. Banks had too few light draft gunboats or transports, so he improvised. Weitzel's men floated on a hodgepodge invasion fleet. Many aboard doubted success. This mismatched menagerie somehow "was to sweep from the coast of Texas every vestige of rebellion," sneered Captain Orton S. Clark of the 116th New York, aboard the *Alexandria*. In all, some ten ocean steamers and sailing vessels, aided by a half

Union transports. Francis H. Schell, "Scene on the levee at Baton Rouge, La. Contrabands discharge the ammunition from the U.S. Transport *North Star* [?], Capt. S____ over the Mississippi steamer '*Iberville*.' *Courtesy of the Becker Collection, Boston, Massachusetts.*

dozen river paddle wheelers, transported three brigades of the 19th Army Corps. Many of the vessels needed repair. "The man who secured the vessels upon which the troops were now setting out on the treacherous waters of the Gulf, should have been dismissed from the service," complained Clark. "One of the steamers was minus a wheel . . . while most of our artillery with their horses were on board river steamers, about as fit for service in the Gulf as eggshells."[14]

Another challenge was that Banks and his advisors knew little about the Sabine Pass—other than its location on the map. Even naval officers in the gunboat detachment, tasked with clearing a way for the landing, had only a sketchy idea of the Confederate defenses or even the geography of the place. In October the year before, a smaller flotilla made easy work of a small Confederate earthwork there, but since then, the Rebels built the better-designed Fort Griffin to replace it. Small Union landing parties had put ashore on the nearby beaches against light opposition in the past, but the Union skippers feared at least two cottonclad gunboats—the *Uncle Ben* and the *Josiah H. Bell*—prowled the waters of Sabine Lake. These crude warships had drawn blood before, sallying out the previous January to capture and burn the blockaders USS *Morning Light* and USS *Velocity*. Unbeknownst to the Federals, the Rebels had also collected a number of transports in the Neches and Sabine Rivers that might rush reinforcements against any landings. Banks was wrong, the Confederates believed an invasion by sea was coming.

Lieutenant Richard "Dick" Dowling, an Irish Texan barkeep from Houston before the war. *Library of Congress.*

The invasion of Texas required precision, dash, and daring, but the geography of Sabine Pass argued against a bold stroke. The waterway could be tricky to navigate even in perfect peace, all agreed, and any passage meant proceeding by its two shallow channels, the Texas and Louisiana, which were separated by shoal water. The bar at the mouth of Sabine Pass also proved to be tough to cross. The Union skippers would have no time to gingerly pick their way through the underwater labyrinth of sandbars and oyster reefs. Once the shooting started, they would have to steam in fast.

The plan began to unravel early. The USS *Granite City*, despite having its guiding pilot aboard, had missed the Sabine Pass entirely in the darkness. It had to double back, putting the crew a day behind on their critical tasks. The other

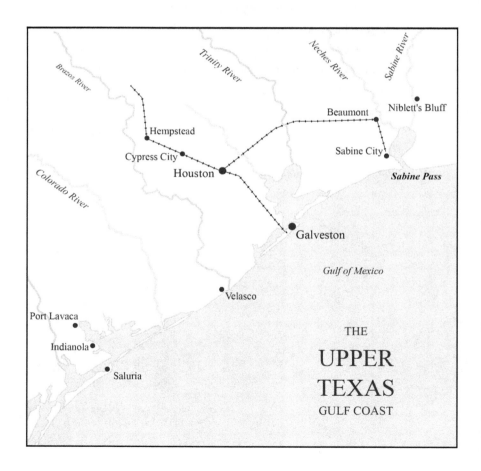

gunboats and part of the invasion fleet, led by Lieutenant Frederick Crocker, mistook the Calcasieu Pass for the Sabine Pass, and, fearing they had passed their rendezvous because the USS *Granite City* was missing, doubled back down the Louisiana coast toward Berwick Bay before realizing their mistake. These navigation errors by the gunboats and the landing force meant the transports carrying Franklin and his reinforcements arrived off the Sabine Pass first; some of the vessels came within sight of land before realizing their error. Sharp-eyed Texans sighted them. The arrival of transports, and not just gunboat blockaders, heralded the long-anticipated invasion was likely at hand. [15]

The USS *Granite City* finally arrived in the waning hours of September 6, and its crew tried to make up for losing half the night by immediately sounding the depth of the pass and its channels. At 2 AM on September 7, Confederate lookouts spied the lantern signals of careless surveying crews, and at Fort Griffin, Lieutenant Richard Dowling grew suspicious. He ordered his men to their guns in case the vessel tried to sneak past in the darkness. As the sun rose, bleary-eyed Confederates still stood atop the parapet, watching, as now two Federal vessels continued the work. The enemy ships slipped away about midmorning. Then, around noon, the Texans stood amazed as nearly twenty additional ships began to dot the horizon. Any element of surprise the Federals thought they had held vaporized along that hot Texas coastline.[16]

The invasion fleet lumbered into view like a team of oxen instead of dancing the carefully orchestrated saltwater minuet Banks had fantasized. As the ships came to anchor, the smoke from their funnels made a smudge on the southern horizon, making them even more visible to the watching Texans. Major General Franklin, assuming all remained on schedule and the enemy had already been pounded into submission by gunboats and swamped by Weitzel's assaults, ordered his reinforcement-laden transports toward the opening of the Sabine Pass. "I arrived," he reported, "crossed the bar, and was about to run in, when seeing nothing to indicate the presence of our people, I recrossed the bar." In the early afternoon, Crocker arrived and explained the problem to Franklin. The navy lieutenant correctly guessed the Confederates might have been startled by the fleet's arrival and that the element of surprise had been lost but believed the Texans would still pose little challenge. Crocker believed he could safely delay the attack until the next day, September 8. "By this series of misfortunes," Franklin grumbled, "the enemy . . . had two nights' warning that a fleet was off the harbor, and . . . a full view of most of the vessels composing it."[17]

Officers aboard each Yankee transport announced the troops had arrived at their destination. "Toward night," noted Captain Clark of the 116th New York aboard the transport *Alexandria*, "we reached the designated point, and were told that the long sandy beach was Texas, and that Sabine Pass was before us." Landing on a hostile coast would be new duty for the New Yorkers and New Englanders aboard the ships. What they could not see was the vast coastal marsh behind the beach that would make any advance nearly impossible.[18]

Only a handful of Rebels defended this difficult terrain. Captain Frank H. Odlum of Company F, 1st Texas Heavy Artillery commanded perhaps two hundred men at the post from his headquarters at Sabine City. Two companies of mounted infantry, one from Colonel W. H. Griffin's 21st Texas Infantry Battalion and one from Lieutenant Colonel Ashley W. Spaight's 11th Battalion, Texas Volunteers, could do little to affect the outcome, he realized but they might harass any landing. The burden of defense would fall to Lieutenant Dowling and his forty-six-man artillery company that served the fort's six guns—two long 32-pounders, two 32-pound howitzers, and two 24-pounders. Colonel Leon Smith, the hero of the Battle of Galveston, commanded the gunboats of the Texas Marine Department from his headquarters in Beaumont. Even fully alerted as they were, Smith's defensive mix of cottonclads and the mud fort at the Sabine Pass would be hard pressed to resist a skillful Federal invasion.

The U.S. Navy, demonstrating little such skill, proceeded cautiously. At daylight on September 8, Crocker edged the USS *Clifton* forward to get a closer look at the fort and to count the Rebel steamers hovering nearby. The Union gunboat anchored opposite the lighthouse on the Louisiana shore, and Crocker signaled for the Weitzel's assault force transports to cross the bar at the mouth of the Sabine Pass and prepare their troops for a landing. Through his telescope, the Yankee skipper spied nothing unexpected. "I found a cottonclad gunboat," Crocker reported, "and a very strong looking battery situated where I expected to find it." He needed to know the size and number of guns inside the redoubt, so he ordered his sailors and marines into action. They needed to shell the fort to see

USS *Clifton*, a pre-war ferry boat. U.S. *Navy Historical Center.*

how the Confederates would answer. The guns of USS *Clifton* fired the first shots of the invasion of Texas at 6:30 AM, September 8, 1863, a day that had dawned clear and beautiful.[19]

The USS *Clifton* lay two miles up the Sabine Pass and about a mile and a half away from Fort Griffin. Its big 9-inch Dahlgrens and 32-pounders bucked and roared over the course of an hour, firing more than two-dozen rounds in a steady, but unhurried bombardment. Despite the shells screaming past his position, Lieutenant Dowling refused the bait; his men held their fire. If the Federals wanted to know what defended the Sabine Pass, they would have to come closer to find out. "Their shots are all good," Odlum admitted, "but doing no damage." The post commander dispatched a courier to the telegraph station in Beaumont, thirty miles away with news that the long-anticipated invasion was at hand. The telegram heading for Major General John Bankhead Magruder in Houston accurately reported six steamers past the bar in Sabine Pass and estimated a total of twenty-one ships, including those still in the Gulf of Mexico.[20]

Despite the odds, Captain Odlum declared his intention to make a fight of it. "I have only three companies to keep the enemy at bay," he wrote. "I am under the impression they will try to take us by sea and land." Realizing that the Federal dawdling provided him time to arrange a creditable defense, Odlum sent word to the *Uncle Ben* to come nearer to the fort but to remain out of range of the USS *Clifton's* guns. Odlum also sent word to Beaumont for transports to bring down any troops manning the works there to repel a landing on the coast. Only timely reinforcements from farther away, he believed, would give him a chance of success. "If possible," he prodded, "I hope the commanding general will send troops here at once."[21]

When Odlum's plea for assistance arrived at Colonel Smith's Beaumont headquarters, he forwarded them to Confederate outposts at Orange, Beaumont, and Niblett's Bluff, urging the troops there to converge on Sabine City and Fort Griffin. The steamboat *Florilda* would transport these troops to the battle. Smith mounted his horse for the thirty-mile ride to see what disaster might be unfolding at the Sabine Pass and what, if anything, he could still do to help.[22]

With these efforts in motion, Oldlum's message to Magruder finally arrived in Houston later that day. The officers there, with no way of knowing what was happening at the Sabine Pass and Beaumont, anticipated the Federals had struck swiftly and assumed Odlum and his fort were already lost. In reality, however, the battle had yet to be joined. When Magruder, who had been away from his headquarters, finally received word, he penned a dispatch of his own, breaking the bad news to Lieutenant General Edmund Kirby Smith in Shreveport. After making excuses for being surprised and defeated, Magruder reassured headquarters of the Confederate Department of the Trans-Mississippi all would be right in the end.

With the gloomy news, albeit prematurely, delivered, Magruder rounded up the makings of a brigade and ordered them to southeast Texas "to prevent the enemy, if possible, from ascending the Sabine River, or from occupying the important position of Beaumont and thus securing the railroad," he wrote. The 3rd Texas Infantry, the 1st Texas Cavalry, the 23rd Texas Cavalry, the balance of the 21st Texas Battalion, and three Texas artillery batteries—including Captain O. G. Jones's "Dixie Grays" and the Louisiana Campaign veterans under Captains William H. Nichols and Thomas Gonzales—would cauterize the invasion wound by fighting for Beaumont.[23]

Magruder, however, had underestimated Dowling and the Texans at Sabine Pass. All morning on September 8, the gunners had remained in their fort, silent, while the Federal invasion force clumsily contemplated its next move. Having learned nothing from his hour-long shelling of Fort Griffin, Lieutenant Crocker ordered the USS *Clifton* back to the bar so that he could consult with Generals Franklin and Weitzel about their options. Although the Confederate strength remained unknown, it could not amount to much. The plan that emerged from the Union council of war called for a tardy execution of what was nearly the original plan: a closely timed assault by the four gunboats followed by an assault landing near Fort Griffin by a picked storming party that would charge over the works to carry the position.

With only a portion of Weitzel's command going ashore, moving the right vessels into position and loading the correct troops onto the appropriate steamers consumed much of the day. Troops crowded tightly into the transports yearned to be ashore. "As the morning wore on, the question began to be asked, 'why don't we land?'" remembered Major Elias P. Pellet of the 114th New York, who was crammed aboard the transport *Cahawba* along with the men of the 8th Vermont and 160th New York. The shuttling of boats and troops seemed to take forever. Then one vessel, the *Crescent*, went aground beyond the reach of tugboats sent to retrieve it. Meanwhile a blockader, the ninety-day gunboat USS *Cayuga*,

The transport *Cahawba*, one of the workhorses supporting the Department of the Gulf. Alfred Rudolph Waud, artist. *Library of Congress.*

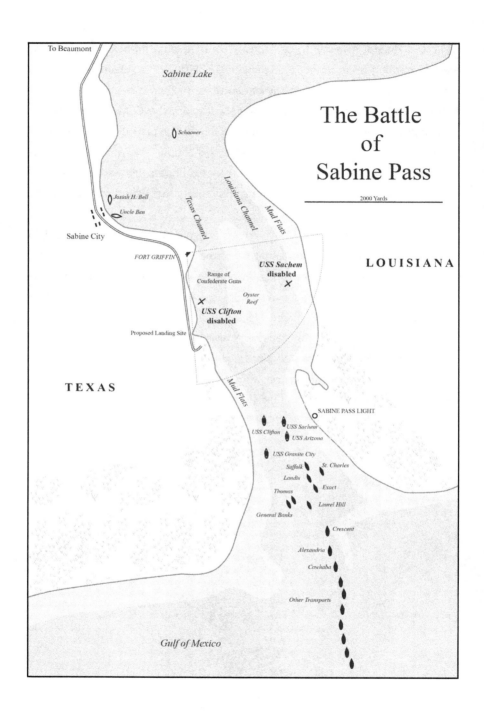

To Beaumont

Sabine Lake

Schooner

The Battle of Sabine Pass

2000 Yards

Josiah H. Bell
Uncle Ben

Sabine City

Texas Channel

Louisiana Channel

Mud Flats

LOUISIANA

FORT GRIFFIN

Range of
Confederate Guns

USS Sachem
disabled

Oyster
Reef

USS Clifton
disabled

Proposed Landing Site

TEXAS

Mud Flats

SABINE PASS LIGHT

USS Clifton
USS Sachem
USS Arizona

USS Granite City

Suffolk
St. Charles
Landis
Exact
Thomas
Laurel Hill

General Banks

Crescent

Alexandria

Cawhaba

Other Transports

Gulf of Mexico

arrived and paced offshore, ready to lend a hand with the invasion but drawing too much water to come in close.[24]

While the vessels shoved about in the murky waters off the Sabine Pass, Generals Franklin and Weitzel, along with Lieutenant Crocker, scouted the proposed landing site. Their conclusions pointed to a potential disaster. "Small boats grounded in mud about 125 feet from the shore," Franklin reported. Sailors jumped over the side to approach the shore but sank up to their knees in the mire. After struggling to the beach, they found "the shore itself is a soft marsh," Franklin groaned. Heavily laden troops might be bogged down, waist high in the water, only to struggle ashore at this miserable site. Once ashore, only a narrow road offered solid passage toward the Confederate fort, which "completely commands the road and the channels," Franklin reported. He argued against the landing.[25]

Crocker persisted. His boats had not the heft in armor or guns to do it alone. Instead of floundering through the mudflats, Crocker suggested the Army should beach the assault steamers in close to the landing site and, with luck, unload troops onto, or closer to, dry ground. "A landing of troops could only be affected

The Battle of Sabine Pass. *Harper's Weekly.*

. . . where the bank was nearly perpendicular and the water of sufficient depth," Crocker wrote. The spot chosen, though, lay within range of Fort Griffin's guns, which most understood might massacre the men packed aboard the steamers. Reluctantly, Franklin ordered the *General Banks* and the *Thomas*, loaded with assault forces, brought forward to make the attempt. Lieutenant Crocker readied his navy crews for "a close engagement."[26]

One other issue compounded Crocker's worry. The Texans appeared to have pre-sighted their guns and marked the pass with ranging stakes. "It being evident from the appearance of the enemy's guns that they were elevated and pointed to command one particular place in the Texas channel," he reported. To thwart this Rebel trick, Crocker would launch the attack up the eastern, or Louisiana, channel to force the Rebels to retrain their guns and throw off their aim.[27]

The careful choreography of this land and sea ballet remained critical. The USS *Sachem*, loaded with twenty-six sharpshooter from the 161st New York, and the USS *Arizona* would steam up the Louisiana channel and dash quickly past the Rebel guns. When the Texans turned their cannon to fire at these vessels, the USS *Clifton* would move close to Fort Griffin to engage its defenders at near point-blank. When the USS *Clifton* approached within a few hundred yards, the rifles of seventy-seven soldiers from the 75th New York and the big guns of the USS *Clifton* would rake the fort with grapeshot and small arms and suppress the defenders. With this fight raging, the USS *Granite City* would cover Weitzel's landing of a force of picked men from the *Thomas* and the *General Banks*; these five hundred veterans would finish the work by rushing over Fort Griffin's walls with bayonets. Meanwhile, the USS *Sachem* and the USS *Arizona* would push into Sabine Lake and make short work of *Uncle Ben* or any other Rebel cottonclads there.[28]

While the Federals schemed, the Confederates at Fort Griffin received their first reinforcements. Captain Odlum, Colonel Smith, and an ordnance officer, Captain W. Spaulding Good, rode into Fort Griffin. The *Uncle Ben* arrived shortly afterwards bearing several dozen riflemen from Spaight's 11th Texas Volunteers Battalion and made a feint toward the Union gunboats, but prudently withdrew after the USS *Sachem* sent three rifled shells whirring past. About one hundred men of the 21st Texas Infantry Battalion positioned themselves outside the fort, preparing to fight off any landing parties as they struggled ashore. Other

Texans were coming, these arrivals declared. Three companies from the 20th Texas Infantry left their Sabine River posts more than thirty miles away aboard the steamer *Florilda*. These few troops would do what they could to slow the juggernaut gathered in the Sabine Pass.[29]

The Federal invasion finally rolled forward at 3 PM on September 8, 1863, a day and a half behind schedule. As planned, the USS *Clifton* churned slowly toward Fort Griffin, opening the Federal assault with a steady thumping of its guns, followed by the USS *Sachem* and, far astern, the USS *Arizona*. "The movement of the gunboats," Franklin observed, "progressed according to the plan for about thirty minutes." Private Henry O. Gusley, a marine aboard the *Clifton* and a veteran of naval fighting at New Orleans, Port Lavaca, Galveston, and the Teche Campaign, reported, "all hands were glad for the opportunity of showing the troops that sailors could fight as well as soldiers."[30]

Gunners aboard the *Clifton* found the range and began hurling their shells with some precision over the Rebel battery. Inside, Lieutenant Dowling still ordered his men to hold their fire. Soldiers aboard the Union transports out in the gulf crowded the railings to watch the show. "Field glasses were instantly brought into use . . . to witness the engagement," wrote Dr. Harris Beecher, assistant surgeon from the 114th New York aboard the *Cahawba*. "The fort was silent, while shells were exploding over it, and the opinion began to increase among spectators that the work was evacuated."[31]

Relieved at the lack of Confederate response, the U.S. Navy's time had come to finish off the fort. While his gunners continued pounding the enemy battery, Crocker signaled for the USS *Sachem* and the USS *Arizona* to make their run up the Louisiana channel into Sabine Lake with a full head of steam. The gunboats obeyed, their 30-pounder and 20-pounder Parrot Rifles firing at the fort as they gathered speed. Crocker wigwagged to the USS *Granite City*, the *General Banks*, and the *Thomas* to close up and prepare for their landing. All seemed to be proceeding as he and Franklin had planned.[32]

Lieutenant Dowling watched as the USS *Sachem* led the way up the Louisiana channel and ordered his men to bring their guns to cover this threat, just as Crocker had hoped. The ranging posts positioned on the Louisiana shore now proved their usefulness. As the Yankee steamer came opposite a white piling driven into the shore opposite Fort Griffin, some twelve hundred yards away, Dowling personally fired the first shot, then signaled for the rest of his gunners to open fire, knowing these men had practiced this action many times and every cannon had preregistered the range. "I opened with the whole of my battery on the foremost boat," Dowling reported. This rippling salvo surprised the Federals watching from out to sea. "It was not until the Sachem started boldly up the channel," Dr. Beecher noted, watching through his binoculars from aboard the Cahawba, "that a column of smoke shot up from the fort, indicating the presence of the enemy."[33]

Halfway through this first salvo, Private Michael McKernan of Houston sighted down the tube of his gun inside Fort Griffin then drew away, clutched the lanyard hard, then snapped the lock, firing his cannon. The weapon roared and lurched backward amid a cloud of smoke as its heavy round from the 32-pounder skimmed across the water before smashing through the wooden hull and deep into the heart of the USS Sachem. The gunboat immediately erupted into a scalding cloud of superheated, high-pressure steam. The crippled ship, streaming billows of smoke and scalding vapor, lost its momentum and, canting slightly to port, glided to a stop within easy range of the Confederate cannons, even then reloading to finish it off.[34]

Aboard the USS Sachem, Acting Master Amos Johnson acted fast to save his ship. He ordered the anchors dropped to keep the injured vessel from drifting aground then signaled to the USS Arizona to come and tow his ship to safety. Now firing without the aid of a targeting stake, the adjusted Rebel fire flew wide of its mark with their second volley, churning up the water but missing the USS Sachem for the time being; with luck, Johnson believed, the vessel might be rescued from its predicament. Even from miles away, observers realized some tragedy had struck the venerable old boat but could not know how badly the ship had been injured. "The poor Sachem," Beecher sighed, "was seen enveloped in a cloud greater than her guns could make."[35]

Lieutenant Crocker and the USS Clifton pressed the fight, hoping to draw fire away from the USS Sachem. The gunboat moved steadily ahead up the Texas channel, assuming the setback would prove temporary. "We hastened to get between the disabled ship and the battery, and thus draw the fire upon ourselves," reported Marine private Gusley, "until she was drawn off." To the stern of USS *Sachem*, the USS *Arizona* realized its consort's trouble, and its crew watched as sailors leapt overboard to escape the deadly scalding. Instead of heading to the rescue, Acting Master Howard Tibbits ordered his engines reversed, believing the USS *Sachem* now blocked the way ahead. Once out of range of the fort's shelling, Tibbets ordered the USS *Arizona*'s boats lowered so that his officers might come aboard the USS *Sachem*, bring off the wounded, and appraise the damage.[36]

Inside Fort Griffin, Dowling—almost too late—saw the next Federal gunboat barreling ahead and ordered his crews to traverse their guns toward this new threat. These shots would not be pre-planned, but he trusted his troops to drive away the USS *Clifton* before it came close enough to rake the fort with grapeshot. Most of the Texan's shots missed as the USS *Clifton* closed the distance. "Their aim," reported Crocker, "had, as I expected, become . . . deranged." At just past five hundred yards away, the USS *Clifton*'s luck ran out as one of the Rebel guns managed to score a hit that sliced through the ropes controlling the ship's rudders. Now at the mercy of its forward momentum and bucking a strong ebb tide, the ship plowed forward and glided slightly to starboard into the mid-channel shoal, keeling slightly to port, "in such a position that only three of her guns could bear," Crocker groaned. Dowling ordered every gun concentrated on this closer—and now grounded—target.[37]

The Federal sailors fought from where they stood. "She used grape," Dowling observed, "and her sharpshooters poured an incessant shower of Minie balls into the works." As Colonel Smith strode the parapet, waving a Rebel flag and cheering on the gunners, the Texans inflicted damage on the USS *Clifton* at close range. One shot splintered the ship's hull and deck before knocking its way through the machinery and cracking the steam drum. Now a second Yankee gunboat filled with scalding vapor. The furnace-hot gasses drove Federal soldiers off the top deck. "Many, thinking the vessel was about to blow up, jumped overboard," Crocker reported. Another solid shot careened through the USS *Clifton*, sending splinters through the crew and grievously wounding Crocker's executive officer. Even with this punishment, many of the Union sailors stuck to their guns.[38]

The Texans outshot Crocker. In response, the Yankee skipper ordered the bow pivot gun commander to run back the gun, load it with solid shot, and blow a hole through the deck and gunwale. "This he did," bragged Crocker, "and that gun was thus brought into use."[39]

Marine private Gusley fought on, proud of the ship's crew. "We have been in several battles since our enlistment, but never have we been in one where we saw displayed so much coolness and calm courage," he wrote. "From the captain to the powder boys . . . every one stood by his quarters."[40]

Of course, not everyone aboard the USS *Clifton* maintained his composure. Crocker ordered Acting Master Benjamin S. Weeks, the captain of the useless aft pivot gun, to serve as his new executive officer. Instead, Weeks "replied that 'he did not see anything to do,'" Crocker seethed. The Confederates soon provided a chore. An exploding shell started a fire. "I directed him to have the fire extinguished," Crocker continued. "He asked me if I expected him to do it himself, saying that he did not know where the buckets were and could not control the men." Crocker turned to a nearby engineer who promptly had the blaze under control. Another man's desire to save himself had direct consequences for the rest of men. Though splinters and shell fragments began to whittle away Crocker's

USS Clifton, foreground, and USS Sachem, rear, in trouble under the Confederate guns. *Harper's Weekly.*

crew, no one tended their injuries. The ship's surgeon, Dr. Daniel D. T. Nestell, had scrambled over the side of the ship and stood in shallow water, hidden in the relative safety of a rudder well.[41]

Across the Sabine Pass, the situation in the Louisiana channel also deteriorated. The plight of the disabled USS *Sachem* had not improved. Boats from the USS *Arizona* arrived to carry away some of the wounded, but in the course of floundering backwards, the USS *Arizona* had also run aground. With the USS *Arizona* now in peril, no rescue would be coming for the USS *Sachem*. Three of the four union gunboats were aground, two of which were crippled. Adding to the Federals' misery, the Confederate cottonclad *Uncle Ben* reappeared, heading downstream from Sabine Lake to finish off the stranded trio of Yankee warships.

Acting Master Johnson gave up hope of saving the USS *Sachem*. He ordered his crew to spike the 20-pounder Parrot Rifle in the bow and to flood the magazines. Another sailor raised a white flag from the stern. In the meantime, the crew of the USS *Arizona* worked their vessel off the shoals, but they abandoned the fight. The gunboat backed toward the Gulf of Mexico with the 30-pounder rifle in its bow still firing at Fort Griffin.[42]

Alone, the men aboard the USS *Clifton* faced a losing battle. "The enemy's fire was becoming hot and deadly," Crocker admitted. A shot struck the muzzle of one of the 9-inch Dahlgrens, spraying iron fragments among its crew. With casualties mounting and the USS *Sachem* silenced, more crewmen left their posts and went overboard to escape the mayhem. "Enough of them remained," Crocker maintained, "to keep up a very effectual fire, which was being done with the faint hope that we might yet be supported." Then word arrived that his principal cannon, the 9-inch pivot gun firing though the USS *Clifton's* bow, had lost its firing mechanism. When Crocker went to investigate, he watched as the determined crew fired the gun by striking a hammer on the primer. Braced by such examples of bravery, Crocker determined to fight until the army made its way ashore.[43]

He did not know, however, that the army was no longer coming. Amid the cannon melee, the landing force held its position out of range, fearful of joining what appeared to be a deteriorating Union attack. Instead of sheering in and depositing the men on the Texas shore as planned, the *Granite City* and the *General*

Banks kept their distance. "The *Clifton* was aground, and, unfortunately, in exact range of my proposed point of landing," Weitzel explained. If he had brought up his troop-laden boat, the heavy guns of Fort Griffin would simply traverse and cut it to pieces. The veteran soldier believed he must at least *try* to accomplish his mission but hesitated to compound the Union disaster. He prudently ordered his command to stand by and await developments.[44]

Despite the grit of its crew, the USS *Clifton* clearly lay doomed. On board the gunboat, Acting Master Weeks lowered the Stars and Stripes without orders then informed the skipper of his decision. "The officer," Crocker fumed, "came to me and entreated me to surrender and save a useless sacrifice of life, adding that he had already hauled down the flag!" Crocker ordered the flag back up, but the signal of surrender had already been given. The remaining crewmen left their pieces and headed overboard, hoping somehow to reach the safety of the Union transports. Weitzel, from the deck of the *General Banks*, saw the flag on the sternpost of the USS *Clifton* go down. He canceled his landing orders and instead directed the steamboat and the USS *Granite City* to head down Sabine Pass and out of danger. "Thus, my last hope left me," Crocker lamented, "and I surrendered, immediately destroying all signal books and public papers." The battle of Sabine Pass had lasted less than an hour.[45]

The afternoon victory shocked and thrilled the Texans. They had captured 2 gunboats, killed around 20 of the enemy, wounded as many more, and captured around 180 sailors and nearly 100 soldiers. The forty-six men of the Davis Guards, Company F, 1st Texas Heavy Artillery, had borne the brunt of the fight. "Our loss was, strictly and positively, nobody hurt. Not a single man received even a scratch," crowed Captain Odlum. "On the whole, it is a glorious and honorable little affair," he boasted from his headquarters. "The men are in high spirits and elated with the result, and eager for another attack. It does really seem that Providence has kindly favored us in this affair." Praise poured in for Dowling's scrappy gunners. "The Davis Guards, one and all, God Bless them," gushed Colonel Smith of the Texas Marine Department. "The honor of the country was in their hands, and they nobly sustained it."[46]

The outcome of the fight also surprised the gallery of onlookers aboard the Union transports. "The distance . . . was too great to allow the troops to see the details of the fight," observed Major Pellet of the 114th New York. "The most that could be discerned with the naked eye was the continuous puff of smoke from the guns of both gunboats and battery, and the glass, at first, revealed nothing more." The soldiers wondered who had prevailed when the firing faded. "When the smoke cleared away," wrote Captain Clark of the 116th New York on board the *Alexandria*, "two of the gunboats . . . were seen entirely disabled and flying white flags in token of surrender while the third slowly retired towards the fleet." The Federal soldiers watched as a Rebel steamer arrived to haul off the USS *Sachem* and the USS *Clifton* around sunset. "These vessels, with their brave crews, heretofore so well known to our men, were never seen again," lamented Dr. Beecher, aboard the *Cahawba* with the 114th New York. "An unexpected turn was given to events."[47]

General Franklin had no idea how to proceed. His instructions were to land somewhere in the vicinity if he could not come ashore at the Sabine Pass, but the first forty miles of the Texas coast was a wasteland. Good beaches fronted a five-mile belt of sea marshes, backed by miles of coastal prairies. Without docks, all their supplies would have to be landed in the surf and hauled by wagon. This would be terrible country for a campaign, Franklin realized. Having anticipated being ashore well before now, the men of the 19th Army Corps ran short of fresh water. Their horses and mules whinnied and brayed from thirst. Franklin could not go forward and landing anywhere else amounted to marooning his command on a deserted beach. "Short rations had been experienced before and we had been days with nothing to eat," observed Captain Clark, "but never in our previous service had we been deprived of water."[48]

The troops who were crowded aboard the transports worried about their future. "As the men retired to rest that night, they discussed the question, 'What can be done now, since the only available gunboats are destroyed?'" noted Dr. Beecher. Others feared a darker fate. "Nobody had such a knowledge of the coast as to make it safe to attempt a landing," Major Pellet of the 114th observed. Beecher agreed. "How could the men avoid the reflection that if they . . . succeeded in landing on the barren coast of Texas, they would have starved?" The Texans, too, might counterattack. If they made speedy repairs to the USS *Sachem* and the USS *Clifton*, they might add them to their flotilla of cottonclads and take a run at the troop ships. They had a good record of wrecking Union vessels in Texas waters. "The whole fleet would have been at their mercy," Pellet concluded. Franklin decided to cut his losses and ordered the expedition returned immediately to New Orleans. "When we turned out the next morning," Captain Clark remembered, "we found our ship already underway."[49]

Other Federal troops worried about their future, too. Marine private Gusley, now a prisoner along with the surviving crew of the USS *Clifton*, rode aboard a Confederate steamer and landed in Beaumont. He ate and rested from the ordeal he had just survived. "We got tolerably good rations thus far, though not as substantial as Uncle Sam's, yet we are thankful we have an appetite for it," he wrote in his diary. "May the appetite long continue, as there is no doubt we shall long need it." He would remain a prisoner for the next nineteen months.[50]

Shocked his men had won, General Magruder remained nervous, assuming the Federals would certainly try again. The day of the battle he issued general orders describing it to all of the Confederate forces in the District of Texas, New Mexico, and Arizona in order to buck up their courage. Beyond the immediate results and the matériel and men captured, he declared that the victory exhibited the fighting qualities of Texans. "The result . . ." he trumpeted, "proves that true pluck and resolution are qualities which make up for disparity of metal and numbers, and that no position defended with determination can be carried by the enemy's gunboats alone." He believed Franklin's invasion force remained in Texas waters. "Should any of the forts on the coast or the forces on land be attacked," he added, "the troops need but remember the success of their comrades at Sabine, emulate their courage and skill, and victory will be the result." Magruder hurried to Beaumont to see what he could do in person.[51]

What Magruder saw convinced him the Federals would soon return to Sabine Pass with a vengeance—perhaps within days. This had not been a probe, but a full-scale attempted invasion. He issued a dramatic call to Texans everywhere to assemble as a great militia to turn back the invasion. "Form yourselves into companies, and assemble at Beaumont with your arms," he urged. Volunteers passing through Houston would receive rations, ammunition, and transportation from his headquarters. "Shall it be said that your State was invaded and you

Troops from the Army of the Gulf aboard their transports. *Harper's Weekly*.

hastened not to the aid of your brethren in the field?" Magruder asked. He called on the "mothers, wives, and daughters of Texas" to urge "every man to do his duty and tarry no longer from the field." Even the old folks should prepare to defend their homes against the Yankee hordes or suffer the fate of Louisiana's citizens. "Business men and planters, the time has come for you to turn aside from your daily pursuits and rally to the defense of your country," Magruder urged.[52]

He also appealed to the veterans—and the heroic ego—of the Lone Star State. "Old Texans, men of the days of '36, men of the Republic, you have grasped the rifle and trusty knife before at the call of danger," Magruder declared. Heroes of these by-gone days, including Brigadier General Tom Green and Colonel Walter P. Lane, already served in the army, he noted, and their old comrades-in-arms should now serve as well. "Come now . . ." Magruder called. "Form with them a wall of fire and steel against which the foe will press in vain."[53]

The attack at the Sabine Pass led to another flurry of orders among the troops in Texas. Two weeks before, Magruder had summoned the 1st Texas Cavalry away from South Texas to reinforce the position, but they were late. They finally arrived at Sabine City two days after the fight. The bloated corpses of Yankee casualties washing ashore gave many of these troops the first sense of what they might soon face. The 20th Texas Infantry and two companies of the 1st Texas Heavy Artillery joined them, as did elements of the badly scattered and demoralized 23rd Texas Cavalry. Lieutenant Colonel Reuben Brown brought in his small 12th Texas Cavalry Battalion as well. The next time the Federals came, they would have to face a more formidable foe.[54]

Martin, a young man enslaved to twenty-two-year-old private Joseph Fitzpatrick of the 1st Texas Cavalry, was among the throng heading toward Beaumont. He had grown up with Fitzpatrick—who had owned Martin since he was five and living in Macon, Georgia—and only three years of age separated the two men. The enslaved man felt conflicted about his presence with the regiment. "I knew the Yankees were going to win, from the beginning," he confessed. "I wanted them to win and lick us southerners, but I hoped they was going to do it without wiping [us] out." Martin was not a soldier, but a servant, usually employed helping his enslaved father prepare meals or caring for the sick and wounded. "I was official lugger in of men that got wounded," Martin remarked. "I never wore a uniform— grey coat or khaki coat—or carried a gun."[55]

As the regiment moved east, away from his home on the Fitzpatricks' one-thousand-acre ranch northeast of Victoria, Martin thought about running away. He could head to Mexico, as many had, or perhaps escape to the Union army if his owner's regiment went to Louisiana. "I spent most of my time planning and thinking of running away," he continued, "but my old father used to say, 'no use running from bad to worse, hunting better. Every man has to serve God under his own vine and fig tree.'" The elder slave also argued in favor of loyalty, telling his son these Texans would "stand flatfooted and fight for the blacks the same as for members of their own family," Martin continued. Besides, his father counseled, "the war ain't gonna last forever, but . . . our forever was going to be spent living among Southerners, after they got licked." Martin followed this counsel. He stayed with his owner and dutifully headed toward Beaumont.[56]

In the end, Magruder's histrionics and troop concentrations served no purpose. The Federals had gone. On September 11, the various elements of the invasion force began disembarking at New Orleans and continued to do so for the next three days. "This was the *finale* of the 'Sabine Pass Expedition,'" noted Dr. Beecher. "While rebellious citizens quietly laughed over the 'grand fizzle,' our men said nothing, but experienced some sad reflections." Tent cities sprang up at New Orleans as the 19th Army Corps returned to Louisiana.[57]

The mission to plant the flag in Texas still remained, and the troops knew their time in camp would be limited. "The next morning," Major Pellet wrote, "each individual soldier rose from his hard bed, dried out his blankets, and asked his neighbor the question, 'what next?'"[58]

SEVEN **MORGANZA**

"The heat is killing to men and horses."

—Rear Admiral David Dixon Porter
United States Navy

ajor General Nathaniel P. Banks's early September efforts to conquer Texas had barely avoided outright disaster, but victory crowned Federal armies elsewhere. On September 2, Major General Ambrose Burnside captured Knoxville, Tennessee. A week later, on September 9, Major General William Rosecrans finally captured Chattanooga, Tennessee, while Major General Frederick Steele's troops marched into Little Rock, Arkansas. Confederate forces were on the run nearly nationwide. Only the Federal armies on the lower Mississippi seemed unable to launch a successful offensive—Grant was crippled and his role in the fall campaign thrown into confusion, and Banks had nearly lost a chunk of his army on the Texas coast. During these same first two weeks of September, the only high point for the Army of the Gulf was that Major General Francis J. Herron's raid up the Mississippi River had proceeded as planned.

Here, on the great river, the rhythms and tactics were familiar, and the enemy well-known. Union gunboat commanders, reinforced by Herron's infusion

USS Lafayette, ironclad. U.S. *Naval History and Heritage Command.*

of infantry, would address the bothersome Rebel snipers on the banks of the Mississippi. Three Union warships already patrolled between Donaldsonville and the Red River, looking for elusive Confederate raiders. The ironclad USS *Lafayette* and the tinclad USS *Signal* prowled between Bayou Sara and the mouth of the Red River. Downstream, the tinclad USS *Kenwood* operated between Port Hudson and Donaldsonville. Herron's flotilla was a welcomed addition to the neighborhood.

There was another impressive stranger arriving as well. The Union's most sophisticated gunboat, the river monitor USS *Neosho*, entered the mix of warships on the Mississippi. Lieutenant Commander James P. Foster, the naval commander of this stretch of the river, loved the newcomer. "Her turret works admirably, revolves in thirteen seconds, and can be made to revolve so slowly that you barely perceived the motion," he wrote. Its monstrous 11-inch Dahlgrens could cover a 240-degree arc and rapidly target any enemy threat on the riverbank. "In training the guns I found no difficulty in stopping her on any object I thought proper to aim at, and even when revolving fast I could stop her so that the slightest turn either way would bring the guns to bear where I wished." The USS *Neosho*'s sister ship, USS *Osage*, patrolled from the mouth of the Red River to Natchez. Rebel raiders on horseback stood little chance against modern war engines like these. If the Rebels rolled out field pieces, their rounds would bounce off while USS *Neosho*'s big bores would blow the enemy cannons to flinders. Even so, these Yankee behemoths would not be nimble enough to scare the snipers away for long.[1]

USS Signal, tinclad. *Library of Congress.*

The Federals needed this infantry and cavalry infusion to end such Confederate harassment. The reinforcements were coming, in the shape of a column of transports splashing upriver from New Orleans. The 2nd Division, 13th Army Corps, crowded the transports *Iberville*, *Sallie Robinson*, *Dan G. Taylor*, *Arago*, and *Empire Parish*. First, Herron and his men had to secure the area where the Texans had last been spotted. At daybreak on September 6, Herron put troops ashore on the west bank of the Mississippi about a mile below Springfield Landing, in the vicinity of where Texans had jumped the *Corps d'Afrique* camp a week before. They marched through New Roads before crossing back over to Port Hudson that afternoon, empty handed.[2]

The Rebels had vanished. Herron went aboard the USS *Neosho* and asked Commander John C. Febiger, in charge of the gunboat division south of Port Hudson, for recommendations. He had few to offer. Low water in the mouth of the Red River and a growing sandbar prevented the gunboats from entering and penetrating deep into enemy territory. Simmesport and the Atchafalaya River crossings remained in Rebel hands, allowing Confederates to cross into Pointe Coupee unhindered to strike again. The best the Federals could hope for was to establish a garrison and react to any Rebel moves. In essence, surrender the initiative and rely on rapid reaction.

Herron ordered his command back aboard their transports and continued another ten miles upriver, landing at McCallum's plantation, four miles down-stream from Morganza and nine miles above and opposite Bayou Sara. Herron's

USS Neosho, river monitor. U.S. *Naval History and Heritage Command.*

five thousand soldiers—nine infantry regiments, four companies of cavalry, and three batteries of artillery fielding eighteen guns—spread out among the fields.[3]

The Yankees had just missed their target. "Major Rountree's command . . . started out into Federal lines to see what they could discover and bring in what plunder they might find," wrote Texas captain Keet McDade. The night before, the Texans had been riding toward Plaquemine and had marched away from the Mississippi, toward Bayou Gross Tête. The Federals had simply arrived a few hours too late. Instead, Herron placed his command potentially between Major Leonidas C. "Lee" Rountree and his line of retreat to Morgan's Ferry. The Texans realized the danger and reversed directions while gallopers streaked north to spread the alarm to the troops guarding the crossing of the Atchafalaya River. Brigadier General Tom Green ordered Major Hannibal Honestus Boone to lead about one hundred men of the 13th Texas Cavalry Battalion across the river that night, locate Rountree, and then locate the Yankees. The 4th, 5th, and 7th Texas cavalries; the five cannons of the Val Verde Battery; and the six guns of Captain Oliver Semmes's 1st Regulars would take a position behind the west bank levee to defend Morgan's Ferry. Green asked Brigadier General Alfred Mouton, commanding south of the Red River, for reinforcements to counter the Union threat.[4]

Herron knew that Confederates were prowling about, and on September 7 ordered a reconnaissance of the country between the Mississippi and Atchafalaya Rivers on. At sunrise Colonel Henry Day, hoping to collide with the Confederates,

USS Osage, river monitor. U.S. *Naval History and Heritage Command.*

took a third of the division toward the Atchafalaya. Cavalry companies from the 6th Missouri and a company of mounted infantry screened the advance of three infantry regiments—the 20th Wisconsin and the 91st and 94th Illinois. Two 12-pounders would add some muscle to the column. The rest of the command, and Major General Herron, remained near the Mississippi, "and made ourselves as comfortable as the state of the weather, which was hot, and the poultry yards, which were well stocked, would permit," commented Sergeant Irvine Dungan of the 19th Iowa.[5]

The Federal patrol moved up the Mississippi road from McCallum's plantation to Morganza, turned left, west, and took the Opelousas road to the west as it followed Bayou Fordoche, an ancient outlet of the Mississippi that had filled with silt and debris until it became a stagnant channel, just a dozen yards wide. The road ran along the south bank, between the wooded margin of the bayou on its right and a low levee on its left protecting cultivated fields and farms. About four miles farther along, the patrol continued as their route curved southward and fronted the luxuriant sugarcane fields of M. C. Sterling's Botany Bay Plantation. Bayou Fordoche, on their right, made a horseshoe bend toward the west a little more than two miles beyond. In this bulge lay the Norwood Plantation and the intersection where the road to Opelousas headed west, bridged Bayou Fordoche and continued on toward the Atchafalaya River, while the bayou road headed south toward the junction with Bayou Gross Tête, more than a dozen miles away. The Union patrol made their turn west and followed the road toward the Atchafalaya, five miles away.

Day's Midwesterners entered difficult terrain. The march would take them through perfectly flat country broken by tree lines and cane fields, which created poor visibility. Patches of dense woods were jungle-like and vine entwined, perfect for ambushes. After crossing the Fordoche bridge, the Federals faced more than three miles of muddy and fetid bottomlands before reaching the Atchafalaya levee. Morgan's Ferry, where the Opelousas Road cross the river, lay three miles upstream from there.

The Confederates, aware of the enemy expedition, moved to harass them. Confederate pickets watched as the Federals moved out of their camps on the Mississippi and began their trek. Eager couriers on lathered mounts reported

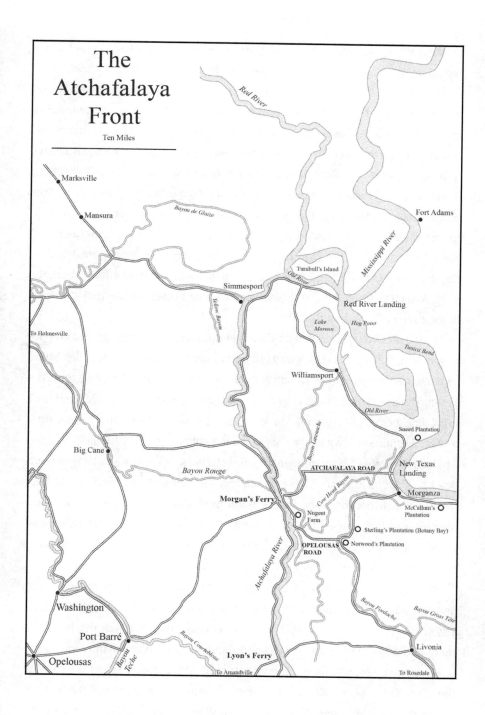

The Atchafalaya Front

Ten Miles

Marksville

Mansura

Red River

Bayou de Glaize

Fort Adams

Mississippi River

Simmesport

Turnbull's Island

Old River

Red River Landing

Yellow Bayou

To Holmesville

Lake Moreau

Hog Point

Tunica Bend

Williamsport

Old River

Bayou Latenache

Sneed Plantation

Big Cane

Bayou Rouge

ATCHAFALAYA ROAD

New Texas Landing

Cow Head Bayou

Morgan's Ferry

Nugent Farm

Morganza

McCallum's Plantation

Sterling's Plantation (Botany Bay)

OPELOUSAS ROAD

Norwood's Plantation

Atchafalaya River

Washington

Bayou Fordoche

Bayou Gross Tête

Port Barré

Bayou Courtableau

Lyon's Ferry

Livonia

Bayou Teche

Opelousas

To Arnaudville

To Rosedale

to Major Boone and Major Rountree who had arrayed their cavalry battalions at the road junction near Norwood Plantation. The two Texans led their commands up the road toward Morganza to toy with the Union column. When the Texans neared a point at the northwestern edge of the Botany Bay Plantation cane fields, additional scouts arrived, announcing the Federals had been sighted in the road just ahead. The road's curve and the cane's height prevented Boone and Rountree from seeing what the riders reported, so they halted their troops. The officers and their staffs would scout on ahead without them. As they rounded the curve of the bayou a mile farther along, the two Texan officers had a clear view down the road toward the Mississippi. What they saw, though, shook them: through the rising, wavy, heat mirage of the road they could see 250 troopers of the 6th Missouri Cavalry trotting toward them. The heavy blue column was just a few hundred yards away. The Confederate officers wheeled their horses around galloped back to the safety of their battalions.[6]

Boone and Rountree yelled for their men to shake out of column and prepare an ambush. "They hurried back and ordered us to go into the woods, to dismount, to hitch, and to form a line of battle in an instant," Captain McDade wrote. The Texans did as ordered but they had not concealed themselves or organized their firing line before the Federal Missourians were upon them. The Texans fired a ragged, unfocused volley. "We gave them a round, and the cowardly scamps wheeled and broke like deer," remembered McDade. "We did not kill any of them dead but wounded some. One of them lost his gun and another his hat." This failed ambush occurred just before noon. Boone and Rountree ordered their men to send their horses to the rear and deploy as skirmishers, the element of surprise lost. The Rebels spread out in the trees, along the levee, and in drainage ditches to challenge the Union advance in a more conventional fashion.[7]

Back toward Morganza, Union infantrymen had just broken ranks to rest and eat their lunch in the shade of the trees along the road, waiting for the cavalry to scout the way forward. The shooting down the road had not bothered them and was somewhat expected and they remained nonchalantly munching their rations. As the Union couriers returned, the soldiers stood up to hear the news. The spooked Missourians ignored them, riding to Colonel Day's headquarters before delivering the news that the Rebels were close. After hearing the report, Day spread the word to his officers and drummers to beat the assembly as his mounted troopers re-formed as a reserve while the infantry continued the contest.

Spreading infantry skirmishers to their front, the blue lines fanned out across the fields of Sterling's plantation, heading toward the its buildings while guiding on Bayou Fordoche. As they advanced in the punishing heat, they began to see blossoms of smoke dotting the line of cane fields and along the Fordoche levee an instant before the sound of Confederate small arms popping in the distance made it across the fields.

The Federal skirmishers returned fire; then the line of battle opened up, sending hundreds of bullets whizzing through the Confederate positions. "That day we had the heaviest picket skirmish that we have ever had in Louisiana," claimed Captain McDade. A Texan near him fell to earth, gasping and twitching, startling the officer. A bullet had grazed the trooper, cutting his shirt and raising a large purple welt; he was lucky. "It knocked the breath out of him," McDade noted. As the afternoon wore on, the outnumbered Texans fell back.[8]

The Union skirmish line advanced steadily all afternoon. The Texans continued to take shots at the Yankees but continued to yield ground. The Federals kept pushing, finally moving past Sterling Plantation, across the Fordoche road, over the bayou, and into the bottomland. "We drive them . . . through swamps and undergrowth," Private Ed Hartley of the 94th Illinois wrote home. "It is dreadfully hot." By sunset, the Federals had skirmished more than ten miles under the brassy Louisiana sky and had been under sporadic fire for six hours. Only a few men on each side had been hit.[9]

Night fell fast, and the men panted from the hard day's work. Canteens among the Federal troops had long since run dry. The stifling heat abated little after sunset, and the darkness seemed impenetrable. The moon would not rise until much later, and even then, it glowed as a mere sliver. Colonel Day, despite fighting all day, had not yet reached the Atchafalaya River. It still lay somewhere in the distance, in the darkness—how far he could not say. He ordered his two cannons to fire into the blackness, hoping to send 12-pound iron scouts into the underbrush and canebrakes instead of flesh and blood. The Texans did not answer. The infantry moved forward once again. Rebel muskets flashed in the trees and thickets, and Yankee muzzles answered, but these sudden strobes failed to illuminate much. Occasionally the Union artillery would buck and roar in a brilliant burst of light and sparks, the gunners aiming at the enemy rifles, but this tedious advance into the gloom whittled away several more hours without gaining much ground or learning much new. The Union skirmishers groped their way forward while behind them regiments shuffled out of battle lines and into road columns. Around midnight, Day and his troops finally neared their objective, the east bank of the Atchafalaya.[10]

"It is very dark, we do not know anything about the country, and are afraid we are getting into a trap," Hartley wrote. Day guessed otherwise, believing instead the troops he had chased all day might be crossing the river at that very moment. If so, now was the time to corner and kill them. He called up his artillery and ordered them to send a salvo across the river to see what happened. "No sooner was the first shot fired than the Rebels opened on us with 12 cannon," Hartley gasped. "We are completely surprised. We are marching in column and never suspected the enemy being near." The west bank of the Atchafalaya flashed fire and white light as the Confederates, with knowledge of the ground and the ranges to their targets, pounded the Federal column mercilessly.

The Federal formation fell apart. Stunned, Day ordered his guns out of action while his shocked infantry scattered amid the chaos. Most of his soldiers fell to the ground where they were and crawled behind cover in the darkness.

Colonel John McNulta, 94th Illinois. *McLean County Museum of History.*

Texan slugs zipped and whirred overhead as Colonel John McNulta of the 94th Illinois attempted to rally his broken regiment. In a flare of fire and smoke a shell fragment shattered his hip, and McNulta tumbled from his horse.[11]

The Confederate ambush pinned the Federals to the earth. "Everything is in dreadful confusion on our side," Hartley admitted. "There was no commander to be found just then, and no two men knew where his company was." For thirty minutes the Confederates raked the road, fields, swamps, and trees with canister, shell, and bullets. The Federal soldiers who could broke and ran away. Flashes of fire studded the clouds of smoke roiling from the west bank of the Atchafalaya. "Vicksburg was nothing beside it," Hartley decided. "It seemed impossible for man to live there at all." The veteran lay still until the firing slackened.[12]

After quaking in the darkness for an hour, Hartley hustled to get away. "I went to find our terror-stricken men," he wrote. He made his way through the tangles, feeling his way. "I never felt so queer before," he continued. "All alone in such a dreadful place expecting every moment to meet a host of Rebels and knowing not but what our men were all gobbled up." After bushwhacking for two miles, he began to stumble across fellow soldiers making their way back across Bayou Fordoche and down the road in front of Sterling's plantation. Colonel Day re-formed as much of his command as he could locate, and led it back to Morganza, arriving in the black hours before sunrise, his men thirsty, tired, and beaten.[13]

The Confederates had been located. Major General Herron listened to Colonel Day's report and, combined with the revelations of captured Confederates understood that enemy blocked the only nearby way into the interior. The prisoners said Simmesport, about eighteen road miles north of Morgan's Ferry, would also certainly be contested, and the water remained too low for gunboats to be of much use. Herron decided he would lead the whole division back to the Atchafalaya River the next day and see if he could dislodge Green and his Texas troublemakers. "He shows fight, and says he will meet us at Morgan's Ferry," Herron reported, "and I propose to accommodate him." At 4 AM he briefed his officers. By 8 AM he had the bulk of his division in road columns heading toward the Atchafalaya. He would waste no time dislodging the Rebels.[14]

Despite the early start, Herron and his men learned nothing new on September 8. Another hot day broke upon the Federal regiments as they trudged back down the Opelousas road toward the Atchafalaya. After fifteen miles, the troops arrived at the scene of the ambush of the night before. The Confederates had gone; none appeared on the Atchafalaya's west levee. The Federals fell back about a mile from the river, made camps without fires, and waited. Perhaps the Confederates would cross that night, and blunder into the waiting Union troops.

Instead, the night passed peacefully. At 4 AM on September 9, the regiments quietly fell into their columns and slipped as noiselessly as possible back to Sterling's Botany Bay Plantation, the levee providing a natural breastwork. With the sun rising, the soldiers fell out, cooked breakfast, then after a brief respite, retraced their steps to Morganza and the Mississippi. Their transports carried the footsore troops the last few miles downstream to McCallum's plantation.[15]

The enemy had been wily, and Herron reviewed what he had learned. The Confederates under Green—he estimated them as 3,000 strong and well equipped with artillery—would probably contest any attempted crossing of the Atchafalaya. Meanwhile, gunboat skippers at the mouth of the Red River reported that two small steamboats operating on the Atchafalaya and the lower Red River increased the Rebels' mobility and kept them in communication with their forces farther inland from whom they could draw supplies and reinforcements. Herron leaned little more from interrogating the few Texans his men had swept up in the skirmishing.

There was also bad news across the Mississippi. "On the east side of the river, 4,000 cavalry under Logan . . . are annoying the planters and firing upon boats," Herron reported. These troops roamed from the outskirts of Port Hudson and along Morgan and Tunica Bend to opposite the mouth of Red River at the hamlet of Fort Adams, Mississippi.[16]

Herron could not decide where to strike—east toward Colonel John L. Logan or west toward Green. The Union troops at McCallum's plantation in Morgan's Bend knew enemies infested both banks of the Mississippi, but they could not figure out how to drive them off permanently.

As the Federals dithered, the Rebels watched the enemy for any sign of their intentions. They seemed stuck near Morganza. "Our Yank is home," confirmed Private William Randolph Howell of Company C, 5th Texas Cavalry, into a shirt pocket diary on September 9. Texas captain Leander McNelly's scouts also played along the periphery of the Union camps, harassing the pickets. The Union expedition had stalled.[17]

Sympathetic civilians from Bayou Sara across the Mississippi rowed over to Herron's camp and reported a small brigade of Confederate cavalry belonging to Logan's Division had taken a position about fifteen miles away. Herron, they hoped, would drive them away. Unless, of course, the tales these well-intentioned citizens was a ruse to lure Herron into an ambush.[18]

It did not matter either way. Indecision, heat, and fatigue clearly dulled the fighting edge of the Yankees at McCallum's plantation. "The division . . . seemed in a half-disorganized state," Sergeant Dungan complained, "part of the troops remaining on the boats and many straggling out on shore whenever a convenient shade could be found. A spirit of carelessness prevailed." The dry conditions also made for bad water. Herron's Division began to leak soldiers too sick from stomach cramps and diarrhea to fight. Transports arriving with rations routinely carried ill soldiers back to New Orleans.[19]

After two days, Herron decided once again locate the threat on the west bank and discover if the Confederates had come back across the Atchafalaya River. He organized a company of mounted infantry of picked men drawn from every regiment to back up his carbine-armed cavalry, and on September 10 he sent out all his mounted troops to learn where Green had gone. Starting at New Texas

Union camps at Morganza, Louisiana. *Library of Congress.*

Landing, the Federals took a lesser used but more direct route to the north of the Opelousas Road that also led to Morgan's Ferry. These troopers crossed the wooded Fordoche bottoms unopposed. Herron's instincts had been correct, and the Federals arrived on the heels of Green's pickets returning to the Atchafalaya. The Yankee horsemen watched the enemy pickets ferrying back and forth across the river toward Green's Brigade, visible behind the far levee.[20]

The Confederates took notice of the enemy arrival. "A small party of Yanks . . . fired into some of our stragglers but hurt no one," Howell noted. "We . . . are sent to entertain our 'guests.'" A sizable force of Texans recrossed the river to drive the Federals away.[21]

Amid intermittent rain, the Union scouts rode back to Herron's headquarters to report their discovery. Green's presence a day's march to the west convinced Herron to remain vigilant. Both armies remained close to their camps the following day, September 11, each believing an attack might be imminent. That night thunderstorms drenched Federal and Confederate alike.

At 5 AM Lieutenant Colonel Joseph B. Leake led another reconnaissance patrol, this one composed of the 19th Iowa, the 26th Indiana, a section of guns from Battery B, 1st Missouri Light Artillery, and all of the cavalry and mounted infantry, toward the Atchafalaya to once again make contact with the Confederates. Herron also wanted Leake to establish an observation post near the Fordoche crossing and keep the Rebels from observing the Union camps on the Mississippi. Leake and his men might also serve as bait to lure the Confederates across the Atchafalaya. If Leake's command could hold its position long enough, Herron could come to the rescue with the balance of the division and crush the Confederates.[22]

The Texans proved elusive. Lieutenant Colonel Leake's patrol skirmished with Rebel horsemen all the way to the crossing of Bayou Fordoche at Norwood Plantation before he halted his expedition for the night. He had lost three men— snatched by McNelly's Texans within rifle shot of the Union infantry camps— and was irritated by his inability to gain an advantage on the Rebels. Leake established his headquarters at the plantation's big house in the bulge of the Bayou Fordoche road. The next morning, he held the 19th Iowa in reserve but ordered the 26th Indiana and the Missouri cavalry to sweep away any Rebel pickets in the bottoms and push them back as far as possible. When the Federals came near the Atchafalaya, they encountered fire from the Val Verde Battery across the river.[23]

Having sent his troops to shoo away the Texans, Leake personally scouted the region, looking for some geographical element that might give him an edge. What he found troubled him. Beside the main roads heading west to Opelousas and south to the crossing of Bayou Grosse Tête, numerous other trails and farm paths cut through the surrounding jungle-like woods and the swamps of the Atchafalaya bottoms. One muddy and poorly defined drover's road headed northeast from Morgan's Ferry toward New Texas Landing on the Mississippi and intersected the Opelousas road at the northwest corner of the Sterling Plantation. Another trail followed the berm of an unfinished railroad from below Morgan's Ferry in a straight southeastern line toward Baton Rouge, providing a potential path for Confederates to infiltrate the woods to the south and west of his position and come in on his left and rear. Other paths edged around to the north, but most seemed impractical for the movement of hundreds of mud-churning boots and hooves. Even so, enterprising Rebel pickets could easily slip between his outpost at Norwood Plantation and Herron at McCallum's plantation. Leake realized he was too exposed and had too few men. [24]

USS Rattler, tinclad. U.S. *Naval History and Heritage Command.*

While Leake assembled his misgivings in a report to Herron, Confederates struck on the east bank of the Mississippi. On September 13, Logan's Rebels snatched twenty-four devout officers and sailors of the tinclad USS *Rattler* while they attended church in Rodney, Mississippi, a village between Fort Adams and Natchez. As the raiders hustled off their prisoners, a covering force fired small arms at the gunboat in the river before fading back into the interior. The less saintly crewmembers of the USS *Rattler* retaliated by shelling the town, hitting the church and some houses but not the Confederates.[25]

As Herron digested this latest affront, Leake's report arrived. Though the lieutenant colonel argued his Norwood Plantation outpost was too exposed, Herron returned orders for Leake to hold in place. There were too many Confederates causing too much mischief, and Herron needed to study the problem and find a solution.

The next day Major Bacon Montgomery led his 6th Missouri Cavalry down the road toward Grosse Tête and came back with more troubling news. Rough roads intersected this route from the west, toward the Atchafalaya, which would allow the enemy to cross a force to the south beyond the range of Leake's pickets. Rebels could mass to Herron's left and rear undetected. Leake again explained his uneasiness to Herron, fearing the enemy might surround him and cut him to pieces before help could arrive. Taking into account Montgomery's corroborating report, Herron relented, but only slightly. He allowed the infantry to fall back to Botany Bay Plantation, a mile closer to the Mississippi. The Union cavalry would hold a separate position at the Norwood Plantation to cover the intersection of the the Opelousas Road and the Grosse Tête Road.[26]

The soldiers of Herron's Division understood they had been sent up the Mississippi River to drive away Rebel partisans on its banks but wondered why they seemed to be lingering so long in Pointe Coupee Parish. Perhaps there was another, grander strategy at work. "I think we are waiting for a force to get in the rear of the Rebs, and we will remain here to hold them where they are," speculated Private William Henry Harrison Clayton of the 19th Iowa. Until his regiment heard otherwise, he would make the best of his situation while camped at Sterling's plantation. "We have all the sweet potatoes here that we can eat and have plenty of sugar and molasses which we get from a sugar house," Clayton boasted. "We have a great old time making candy and eating it."[27]

On the river, Captain William P. Black, an officer in the 37th Illinois, speculated about Herron's next move. Had the plans changed? After two weeks in Pointe Coupee, amid rumors arriving with every supply boat, he hoped to be heading downriver soon, away from the Confederate-infested cane fields. "The news is that [the 13th Army Corps] has left New Orleans, destination unknown," he wrote his parents. Perhaps the Mobile expedition was happening after all. This, he believed, might lead to a cushy outcome for him. "I think Herron's policy is to remain here until all the troops have been sent out of New Orleans on expeditions, and then go down and garrison the city during the winter," Black wrote. "Very pleasant if it can only be carried into execution."[28]

As the hot days dragged on at Botany Bay Plantation, Leake remained active. As part of his mission, he tried to keep the enemy away from the McCallum plantation. Believing Rebels routinely follow the road to New Texas Landing to spy on Union positions, he ordered two infantry companies to head northeast of Botany Bay, beat their way through the woods north of where Bayou Fordoche

A Confederate drawing of the banks of the Atchafalaya. *Morgan Wolfe Merrick Papers, Daughters of the Republic of Texas Library, The Alamo, San Antonio, Texas.*

bent east toward the Mississippi, then angle toward the river and surprise any Confederates lurking north of Morganza. This patrol came back empty handed, reporting no enemy activity. Meanwhile, Leake fortified his position. He ordered his artillery to cut the levee at the southwest corner of Sterling's cane fields so that their guns could target any Texans coming up on the cow path from the Atchafalaya. Despite their best efforts to remain vigilant, the various Federal commands between the Mississippi River and Bayou Fordoche wilted in the Louisiana heat.[29]

While the Federals fumbled around in Pointe Coupee, Rebel theater commanders struggled to decipher their enemy's strategic objectives from their headquarters at Alexandria and Shreveport. What, they debated, had been the Union intent at Sabine Pass? What did Herron's presence at Morganza indicate? What did the scouting raids from Vicksburg and Natchez mean? Since the Confederates knew none of the answers, Major General Richard Taylor wanted to take General John H. Walker's Texas Division and Colonel James P. Major's cavalry brigade out of Alexandria and strike east against Vidalia, Louisiana, to create havoc along that stretch of the Mississippi and smoke out enemy intentions. He would also avenge the attack on Fort Beauregard by wiping out the men who had captured it.

Lieutenant General Edmund Kirby Smith thought Taylor should reconsider. "Let me caution you against being too far influenced by the desire of retaliation," he lectured. The weather was too hot and the swamps malarial. Let the enemy traverse these stretches of Louisiana made nasty by heat and drought. "We cannot afford unnecessarily to lose a man from duty," Kirby Smith continued. "When the frosts come, you will have occupation for twice their number."[30]

Taking Kirby Smith's advice, Taylor settled on a cavalry raid instead. He sent Colonel Major out from his position east of Pineville. Major crossed his brigade over the Ouachita River at Trinity, dropped off the 1st and 2nd Texas Partisan Rangers to hold the bridgehead, and picked up the 15th Louisiana Cavalry Battalion as guides. At dawn on September 14, he struck Union forces camped at Vidalia, Louisiana, with the 2nd and 3rd Arizona. One company of the 30th Missouri infantry and some partially organized African American troops destined for the 2nd Mississippi Artillery (African Descent)—armed largely with shotguns—and a company of pontoon engineers composed the startled garrison. The 250 Rebel riders swept through the poorly armed pickets and surprised and overran the pontoon train camp, shooting down the workers, cutting loose the mules, and pillaging the tents.[31]

While the Rebels ransacked the camp, some of the Federals recovered and moved to stop the destruction. Colonel Bernard G. Farrar rallied his 30th Missouri and counterattacked, causing the Confederates to fall back and regroup under the cover of a hedge. After a hot skirmish the raiders fell back toward Trinity. By 8 AM two regiments of Union infantry and some mounted troops from the garrison at Natchez crossed the river in parcels to reinforce the positions at Vidalia. By midmorning portions of four Union regiments formed into line of battle. Elements of the 17th Wisconsin Mounted Infantry pursued the retreating Rebels, catching up with them and trading shots as they crossed the Ouachita. The Federals had chased off their attackers, but the raid had panicked the black recruits, killed several, trashed their camp and pontoon train, and had killed two and wounded four Missourians. The Federals killed six Arizonans, wounded another eleven, and captured two prisoners, including an officer of the 3rd Arizona.[32]

The Third Minnesota Regiment Entering Little Rock by
Stanley M. Arthurs (1910). *Minnesota Historical Society Collections.*

The Federals fully understood the two-fold purpose of the Rebel raid. Raising black troops remained critically obnoxious to the enemy. In addition, pontoon bridges were one of the most important tools of war in Louisiana, and anytime they could be destroyed, they must. Orders arrived for Colonel Farrar to move the inexperienced African American soldiers and the surviving pontoon crews to the Mississippi side of the river. The navy and veterans of the Vicksburg campaign would defend Vidalia.[33]

Returning from their raid, the Confederates concluded the presence of bridging equipment indicated a Union offensive toward Alexandria. They assumed Union troops would no doubt be heading back to Trinity, and soon. Crossing there, they would probably pass north of the Catahoula Basin and threaten Pineville, some forty miles to the southwest. If so, Alexandria, on the other side of the Red River, would be under the Union guns.

Confederate planners in the Trans-Mississippi received more bad news around this same time. Union major general Frederick Steele had outmaneuvered, outthought, and outfought Confederate major general Sterling Price in Arkansas. Little Rock had fallen to the Federals the week before, and the Confederates had fallen back into the southwestern portion of the state. The Arkansas River Valley was largely in Federal hands and they were still pursuing Price. Lieutenant General Kirby Smith sensed Shreveport would be the next target for the Army of Arkansas while Major General Ulysses S. Grant and the Army of the Tennessee would move against Alexandria.

Confederate soldiers in Louisiana became jittery. Lieutenant John Coleman Sibley of the 2nd Louisiana Cavalry, escorting a wagon train of provisions from Texas to General Green's camps near Morgan's Ferry, passed through much of Taylor's army en route. Something was stirring. "I think from what I see and hear that we will all soon leave this country," he wrote his wife. "Everything shows it. All the stores, ammunition, troops, and in fact the whole army seems to be preparing to move and everything has an up the country direction."[34]

Vidalia fell under the jurisdiction of the 17th Army Corps, which was operating out of Vicksburg. While Major General Grant remained in New Orleans, secretly recovering from his injuries, Major General William T. Sherman served as the de facto commander of the Army of the Tennessee. Tired of lying idle at Vicksburg, he longed to put an end to the incessant raids and skirmishes west of the Mississippi. In preparation, he asked Brigadier Generals John Dunlap Stevenson and Marcellus Crocker to provide sketches, based on their recent raids, of the region east of the Ouachita River. Sherman also wanted to make sure the Rebels did not rebuild Fort Beauregard at Harrisonburg.[35]

The navy would have a part to play as well. When the rivers rose in the coming months, Rear Admiral David Dixon Porter could send ironclads up the Ouachita and Red Rivers to support Sherman's invasion. In the meantime, he would content himself with keeping the banks of the Mississippi River clear of Rebel pests while hoping for cooler weather. "I want to begin to strike at the cavalry scattered in my front as soon as the weather permits," Sherman wrote to Major General James McPherson, commander of the 17th Army Corps. "The heat is killing to men and horses. All ponds and cisterns have dried up."[36]

The signs of a change in weather seemed promising. While the once-formidable Army of the Tennessee lay panting in the shade, a wind from the west and towering clouds flashing on the horizon gave Sherman hope. Heavy thunderstorms swept through the Mississippi River Valley on September 15 ahead of the first cool front of fall. Rain fell for the next few days, then frequently for the next two weeks. Sherman would soon have the weather he craved and the water in the Red River would rise.

Not all the news arriving in Vicksburg was positive. As the rains fell, Sherman received word from New Orleans of the debacle at Sabine Pass. The grand strategy to cut off Confederate reinforcements and supplies from Texas had collapsed. General staffs wondered: could Major General Nathaniel P. Banks execute such an important, and complicated, campaign? Could he finish the job in the Trans-Mississippi? Grant's injury and now this Texas coast disaster gnawed at the foundations of the Union strategy in the Mississippi Valley.

Despite the setbacks, Major General Banks remained self-confident and believed he knew a way to restart Federal efforts in the Mississippi Valley. The various columns would suffer a lack of coordination unless they were under a unified command. He floated an idea which had simmered in his head for months.

He asked General-in-Chief Henry W. Halleck to let him control and coordinate the movements of all the troops from Memphis to New Orleans. He wanted a new theater-level command.

The Vicksburg and Port Hudson Campaigns had both showed some weaknesses in Union command and coordination in the Mississippi Valley. Grant had always pledged cooperation with Banks but had never delivered on his promises. Instead, Grant had hoarded a larger army than Banks thought he needed to reduce Vicksburg, while the Army of the Gulf constantly teetered on the brink of failure from having too few troops. Tired of these complications, Banks wanted sole control over the next campaign. With the Mississippi in Union hands, the old vexations of communications no longer troubled the armies. Messages could pass freely between columns. Besides, Banks argued, he outranked both Grant and Sherman. And, Grant was unstable and now sidelined after nearly killing himself in a drunken horse wreck.

Banks believed he delivered a solid argument to Halleck. Only the absence of more soldiers prevented him from completing all of President Abraham Lincoln's Texas projects, Banks argued, while also finishing off Louisiana as Halleck wanted. The *Corps d'Afrique* numbered twelve thousand in early September but would eventually have thirty thousand men in its ranks, Banks assured. Until then, he would use the thirty thousand to forty thousand men from Grant's Army of the Tennessee to advance the cause in the Trans-Mississippi. He promised to send Grant's troops back to him after the invasion succeeded, the Confederates were scattered, and the black troops were in garrisons. "I think we present a very just and strong claim to the temporary assistance we ask at your hands," Banks argued.

Besides, Grant was incapacitated, and Banks suspected he was suffering, too, from a diminished reputation. Banks was prepared to finish the Hero of Vicksburg professionally. The commander of the Department of the Gulf simply did not trust Grant—or his weakness for whiskey—to conduct any future campaigns or cooperate according to his liking.[37]

The Army of the Gulf, meantime, moved into position for the next phase of the great fall campaign. Major General William B. Franklin, having recovered from the humiliation at the Sabine Pass on the Texas coast, ordered both the 13th and 19th Army Corps to converge by riverboat and rail on Brashear City. The new plan was for the Army of the Gulf to move up Bayou Teche while troops from the Mississippi River severed the Red River Valley. Herron's command could cross the Atchafalaya River and fall on the Rebel left. Taylor would either have to fall back toward Alexandria to counter these threats and avoid being crushed between two Union armies or give up Louisiana and head to Texas. Franklin would stick to Taylor's Rebels, wherever they went, while Sherman's army finished off whatever Confederates Kirby Smith might rally.

Banks's timing proved unfortunate.

Large events in northwest Georgia now commanded Halleck's attention and complicated Banks's ambitious design to become the master of Union troops in Louisiana and Texas. Major General William Rosecrans had driven the Confederate Army of Tennessee out of Chattanooga and into Georgia during the first two weeks of September. Rebel leaders in Richmond had responded by reinforcing General Braxton Bragg's beleaguered army with Lieutenant General James Longstreet's lethal corps, which was detached from General Robert E. Lee's Army of Northern Virginia. The move justifiably panicked Union planners. Halleck scrambled to beef up Rosecrans's army and looked to the west for help. The ripple of troop movements would reach beyond the Mississippi.

The massive campaign in the Trans-Mississippi might have to wait.

Union operations in Arkansas felt the first pinch. At nearly the same time Banks had been scheming to divest Grant of his army, Halleck ordered troops in the Mississippi Valley readied for transfer. Major General McPherson, commanding the 17th Army Corps, recalled Stevenson's Division from operations in southeast Arkansas and instead shuttled them toward Chattanooga, Tennessee. Steele, instead of having enough men to pursue his defeated enemy into Southwest Arkansas and, perhaps, into Louisiana and Texas, instead fell back to Little Rock and dug in.

Confederate commanders in the Department of the Trans-Mississippi, ignorant of these Union troop movements, remained clenched for the invasion of Louisiana. Then, Major General Taylor, still trying to discern Federal intentions, received disturbing news. The Federals had crossed over Berwick Bay in force on September 16. Rebel forces in Louisiana would be pinched between four heavy columns, they believed—one under Steele from Arkansas aimed at Shreveport, one under Sherman launching out of Vicksburg also converging on Shreveport, one launching out of Natchez under McPherson cutting the Red River at Alexandria supported by Herron, and Banks driving up Bayou Teche to clear the rest of the Confederates out of Louisiana.

Believing they knew, at last, Union intentions, Taylor understood his position was untenable. His two brigades of Confederate infantry at Vermilionville were no match for the enemy force gathering at Brashear City. One of his officers heartily agreed. "The Brigade of Louisiana troops who were on picket down there . . . came up on 'double quick' last night and report thirty thousand Feds at the Bay and on the Bayou Teche this side," gasped Lieutenant Colonel George Guess of the 31st Texas Cavalry (Dismounted). "If this is so, we will have to leave here, in a 'whoop,' not many days instant." He assumed the Federals would converge from every side, even from Kansas. "The truth is, the storm is now rising to burst upon the devoted head of Texas," he despaired. "The Federal army is advancing, one column by this route, one up Red River, one from Helena, and one through the Indian Nation, all pointing toward a concentration about Shreveport or Jefferson and Marshall." Guess believed the Confederate army would fight a cataclysmic battle within a few weeks to determine the fate of the Department of the Trans-Mississippi. The result would show whether northeast Texas would face invasion. "It will be a fearful and momentous struggle," he predicted.[38]

EIGHT

THE INVASION OF LOUISIANA

Old Tom Green won't willingly leave without first giving them a fight.

—Private John W. Watkins
5th Texas Cavalry

onfederate couriers galloped all across Louisiana, from Niblett's Bluff to Morgan's Ferry, from Shreveport to Vermilionville, spreading word of the three Union columns. The cataclysmic battle for the Trans-Mississippi had arrived. "The darkest frown of God Almighty must certainly now be upon us," sighed Lieutenant Colonel George Guess, a Texan. "If he is smiling behind this frown, it is much to be hoped that his smile may soon become visible to us."[1]

While the mood among the Confederates turned dark, Major General Nathaniel P. Banks looked forward to the coming campaign. Assuming General-in-Chief Henry W. Halleck would add most, if not all, of the 15th and 17th Army Corps to his command, Banks stayed in New Orleans, where he could coordinate the various armies of the Mississippi River Valley. The Army of the Gulf had commenced the tedious crossing of Berwick Bay preparatory to its move into the interior of Louisiana, and its regiments gathered on Tiger Island, waiting for their turn to cross. "A railroad running from Algiers to Brashear City was employed night and day in transporting troops and the necessary supplies and ammunition for them, which was evidence enough that we would soon proceed there," observed Captain Orton S. Clark of the 116th New York, a few days after his return from Sabine Pass. When he finally arrived at Brashear City, he saw the small Union outpost had once again blossomed into a canvas city.[2]

This new army differed from the command Banks led up the Teche the previous spring. Gone were the nine-months men, now safely back home in New England, resuming their lives as bank tellers and shop clerks. Instead he had hardened veterans from nearly every Union state. Many of the New Yorkers and

The Union depot and encampment at Brashear City. *David Hunter Strother, Drawings and Sketches, The West Virginia and Regional History Holdings, West Virginia University Libraries, Acc. No. p.95.30.68.*

New Englanders of the 19th Army Corps had never served alongside men from Ohio, Indiana, Illinois, Missouri, and Iowa like those in the 13th Army Corps. The easterners were not sure they liked their new comrades. "We soon found it impossible to live with these western men as they were constantly telling of their prowess, and what they would now do in this department if we paper collar soldiers would only let them alone," grumbled Captain Clark.[3]

Brawls between the westerners and the easterners broke out as officers tried to get the two corps to cooperate. "I think they would rather shoot at each other than 'Johnnies,'" observed Private Henry Whipple of the 29th Wisconsin. He had already been in a particularly nasty scuffle back in New Orleans. This time he watched the scrap develop and tried his best to stay out of it. "I did not intend to do anything but look on until a fellow of the 165th New York struck me on the head with a 10-inch navy revolver," Whipple claimed. "I suppose the reason he hit me is that he saw the number and letters '29 Wis' on my cap and knew I was from the West, and considered that reason enough." Thus provoked, Whipple joined the fray, punching and beating his way through the easterners alongside men from the 11th and 47th Indiana. "We cleaned them out all right and sent nine to the hospital," he boasted.[4]

In addition to the combative and rowdy western infantry, Banks also had the luxury of more mounted troops. Some, including the 1st Texas (Union) and the

1st Louisiana (Union), had plenty of experience in the region. Various companies from Illinois and Indiana regiments brought in from garrisons in Tennessee were also bona fide cavalry; Banks planned to augment this force with infantry regiments mounted for the campaign. This added horsepower would help counter any threats posed by Major General Richard Taylor's Texans and Louisianans.

These mounted Federals led the way, crossing over Berwick Bay and moving unopposed as far as the abandoned Rebel encampments at Bisland. The 19th Army Corps followed, glad to be away from the Vicksburg blowhards of the 13th Army Corps.

The cavalry pressed on, but the following infantry did not advance far. The Rebels had left obstructions in the lower Teche: a number of torpedoes as well as pilings, sunken hulks, and destroyed gunboats. Work parties would have to clear the way so that supply boats—and gunboats—could proceed up the bayou. Banks recommended Major General William B. Franklin take his time moving up the country until the much-larger 13th Army Corps could cross Berwick Bay. If the 19th Army Corps got too far ahead, Taylor might concentrate against it and thrash it. "While rapidity is desirable, the movement should be secure," Banks advised through his chief of staff, Brigadier General Charles Pomeroy Stone.[5]

This invasion lacked the crispness of Banks's Teche Campaign the previous spring. Low water in the Mississippi and elsewhere had delayed the arrival of

Wreck of the C.S.S. Cotton, still snarling navigation on lower Bayou Teche. *Becker Collection.*

transports to catapult the troops across Berwick Bay, and the 13th Army Corps, hobbled by having only two steamboats, spent days moving troops across. Once over, this large force had more supplies and ammunition than its vehicles could haul. Major General Edward Otho Cresap Ord, commanding, needed more wheels, and he believed Banks and Franklin favored the easterners by giving them everything they needed while starving his command of the tools for making war. The 19th Army Corps had 350 wagons and only 6,000 men in its ranks. Ord's command numbered 15,000 men and had only 400 wagons. He wanted Franklin to give up one hundred vehicles to his men.[6]

Ord's men needed the transportation. As he pointed out to his superiors, he did not know how Franklin's men fought, but his soldiers from Ohio, Indiana, Illinois, Kentucky, Missouri, and Wisconsin liked to shoot. "My men have been accustomed in the sieges to fire away much ammunition," he argued, "and I should like to carry 240 rounds of ammunition [per man] in wagons." These bullets would be in addition to forty rounds in the cartridge boxes and forty in each man's pockets. His cannons needed four hundred extra rounds per gun besides what they carried in limbers and caissons. "To do this will take nearly all my wagons," he pointed out. Even after the transfer of conveyances from the 19th Army Corps, he would have only 500 wagons for his large command while 250 would easily support the New Yorkers and New Englanders. Based on these ratios, he grumbled, Banks should actually assign 625 wagons to the 13th Army Corps.[7]

Sergeant Leonard K. Andrews, Company C, 12th Connecticut Infantry, an easterner in the 19th Army Corps. *Courtesy of Denis Gaubert, Thibodaux, Louisiana.*

While the Federals bickered and their logistics imbroglios delayed their advance, Taylor took the opportunity to order most of his troops out of the lower Teche region and away from danger. On September 17, Colonel Henry Gray led his eight-hundred-man Louisiana Brigade through the rain and mud into camps at Bayou Carencro, north of Vermilionville. The 2nd Louisiana and the Texas squadron, Companies A and F, 11th Texas Volunteers, remained behind to provide updates on the enemy progress. As the Federal cavalry advanced, the Rebels hurriedly fell back over two sleepless days, giving up Franklin but reestablishing a picket line south of New Iberia. "Found a soft place on the roadside and soon slept finely, rain or no rain, Yankees or no Yankees," admitted Texas sergeant H. N. Connor. "So ended this grand retreat, noted in the annals of our squadron as 'Mudwall Jackson's grand strategic movement.'"[8]

Back at Morgan's Ferry on the Atchafalaya River, Texan private John W. Watkins sat beneath his dripping canvas tent, anticipating the army would soon abandon this part of Louisiana as well, given the Yankee advance up the Teche. Rebel steamboats, probably the little *Argus* and more substantial *Robert Fulton*, had arrived bringing in cotton and sugar to be hauled by wagons to Texas. They had brought no reinforcements.

Private Thomas Daley, Company C, 12th Connecticut Infantry an easterner in the 19th Army Corps. *Courtesy of Denis Gaubert, Thibodaux, Louisiana.*

Across the Atchafalaya, Major General Francis J. Herron's Federal Division showed little activity or inclination to fight. Other than some sloppy skirmishes, alarms, and probes on September 17 and 18, the enemy showed little aggression. This certainly meant trouble, Watkins believed. "When we think everything the most quiet is the time we may look for a battle," he wrote to his wife. He had heard about the pontoon train at Vidalia and he, like most others, believed Alexandria would be the target of the converging enemy columns. Herron's men had been quiet, he reasoned, because they must be heading north to the Red River to assist, "marching up the north side."[9]

Major General Taylor ordered all of his regiments to fall back, but the men in the ranks remained unaware of where he would rally his army. Watkins speculated the Confederates would leave the Atchafalaya soon and "make our way toward Niblett's Bluff," he wrote his wife. "Such I understand are our orders." The Texas infantry of Colonel James Harrison's Brigade left Vermilionville and leapfrogged past Gray's Louisianans at Bayou Carencro to take up positions at Washington on September 19 under blue skies, the first in days. A retreat north, though, would once again place Brigadier General Tom Green and his Texans as the rearguard of Taylor's army as they came in from the Atchafalaya. "Old Tom Green won't willingly leave without first giving them a fight," Watkins predicted. "Though I can't see what advantage can be gained by it. But old Tom's love of fighting and his hatred of the Yankees will cause him to go to extreme measures to give them a whipping."[10]

Brigadier General Mouton, commanding Taylor's troops south of Red River, left his headquarters in Opelousas, Louisiana, to concentrate his brigades near Washington. The rain had gone, at least, and the weather had turned "almost disagreeably cool," according to captain George W. O'Brien of Spaight's 11th Texas Volunteers. Mouton, with troops coming in on roads from Pointe Coupee to Alexandria, was unsure where this campaign would end. That, he believed, lay entirely at the discretion of the enemy.[11]

Louisiana captain Arthur W. Hyatt, a veteran of the Teche Campaign, was once again tired of the marching and counter-marching in reaction to a Union invasion. He came to a witty conclusion about Federal intentions. "Banks never

This unidentified officer of the 8th Indiana would have been busy keeping his westerners of the 13th Army Corps from scrapping with the easterners of the 19th Army Corps. *Courtesy of Denis Gaubert, Thibodaux, Louisiana.*

found but one army he could whip (meaning this one)," Hyatt quipped, "and . . . he was everlasting pelting away at [it] out of spite."[12]

Mouton knew he faced long odds. Nearly thirty thousand Federals had started across Berwick Bay; the advanced elements of this army occupied the town of Franklin, just fifteen miles from the Confederate pickets south of New Iberia. Mouton had fewer than four thousand men. Once his troops began gathering at Washington, he ordered them to continue on to Alexandria; by the evening of September 19 the lead elements of his infantry division marched up parallel roads, fifteen miles apart, to within forty miles of their destination.

An exchange with Brigadier General Green perplexed Mouton, though. The Texan reported he believed Major General Herron's outposts near Morganza could be surprised and, with enough men, overwhelmed. The venture would be risky, since it involved a crossing of the Atchafalaya River—and Confederate arms would have to prevail or risk a nearly impossible retreat. Even so, the Texan badgered the Louisianan with several dispatches. Mouton reluctantly agreed but left the actual execution up to his subordinate. "I instructed General Green to make every preparation for such a movement," Mouton reported. Unlike the bungled

A 13th Army Corps Zouave in the 11th Indiana. *Library of Congress.*

attack at Fort Butler ten weeks before, there would be no miscommunications or delinquent recalls. Green would be solely responsible for the outcome. What he hoped to achieve by this risky venture seemed a mystery to Mounton.[13]

Yet another issue confused Confederate planning. Mouton had ordered a general retreat upon learning the Federals had crossed Berwick Bay in strength, but since then the enemy cavalry had advanced like a blue ripple to within only eight miles of New Iberia before ebbing back to Franklin. There they remained. The Federals' two thousand cavalry and mounted infantry might have made short work of the 2nd Louisiana and the Texas Squadron and rumbled through New Iberia to Vermilionville, but they had not. The Union advance seemed to have fizzled.

Major General Taylor, monitoring all of these movements, also puzzled over the Union movements. He had three fronts to watch—Alexandria and an advance by McPherson from Natchez, the Atchafalaya River and Herron's command, and New Iberia and the massive column under Franklin and Ord. He had Major General John G. Walker's Division holding the line at the Red River, and Mouton's infantry was retreating there to rally on Walker. Together these two Rebel divisions could muster some five thousand troops and, positioned behind defensible terrain, might blunt efforts to take Alexandria. Should Major General William Tecumseh Sherman and the 15th Army Corps march on Shreveport from Vicksburg, there would be few troops to oppose him. Taylor had Green watching Herron on the Atchafalaya, but only a mere cavalry screen facing the Army of the Gulf. Colonel James C. Major's cavalry brigade, Taylor's only mobile reserve, had fallen back from Trinity and the Ouachita River line after its raid on Vidalia, and it now hovered east of the Red River, screening the infantry buildup at Alexandria.

Remarkably, nothing more happened. The Federal columns—from Little Rock to Vicksburg, from Natchez to Morganza, and from Berwick Bay to Franklin—seemed suddenly frozen. The enemy had launched a massive campaign then, just as quickly, halted it.

Taylor believed that this was the moment when he should strike: but where? Green seemed to have the best idea. Herron's inert division seemed irrelevant to the coming campaign, but Green considered them a potential threat. He needed to thrash them before leaving the region. If he could neutralize this Federal force, Green would not have to worry about pursuit as he fell back beyond the Atchafalaya. Bloodying the Yankees in Point Coupee at best might destroy them or at least drive them off, allowing Green to remove his troops to join the Rebel concentration against either Sherman or Franklin. Taylor liked the concept but wanted to make sure he knew what he was facing on other fronts. He ordered Mouton to turn his infantry around. He also ordered Colonel Major to take most

A 19th Army Corps soldier in Company A, 165th New York, Duryee's Second Zouaves. *Author's Collection.*

of his brigade to Big Cane, halfway between Morgan's Ferry and Washington, and to send one regiment to New Iberia.[14]

Couriers delivered the orders. The first to receive them was Gray's Louisiana Brigade at Bayou Chicot; the column halted, turned, and countermarched southward. Colonel Harrison's Texas Brigade received the word about the same time. Harrison's men had been marching since sunrise on September 20 and had fallen out for a noontime rest on the road between Washington and Holmesville, alongside Bayou Beouf. Captain O'Brien had nodded off on the roadside when "Lo! Awakened from a very pleasant nap . . . by the most impolite of all musical instruments, the drum, and the woe-returning cry of 'Fall in!'" The soldiers filed around and headed back down the road they had just come up. "All were very much chagrined by the occurrence," O'Brien observed, "for there was a hope with many that our destination was Texas."[15]

Between the Atchafalaya and the Mississippi, while Green grew bold, Herron and his Federal commanders grew careless. In a recent brush they had allowed the Texans to move between Lieutenant Colonel Joseph B. Leake's skirmishers and reserves in the "bottoms" between the Atchafalaya and the Fordoche, and the Rebels had come close to capturing the lot of them. One of Herron's brigadiers, Iowa politician-turned-general William Vandever, warned him the Confederates could do the same thing—on a grander scale—to the entire outpost detachment

The camp and officers of the 19th Kentucky Infantry, veteran soldiers of the 13th Army Corps. *Courtesy of Tom Pressly, Shreveport, Louisiana.*

at Botany Bay Plantation. Herron disagreed. He believed Lieutenant Colonel Leake and his cluster of troops at Bayou Fordoche could handle Green, but as a concession he moved his division camps from McCallum's Plantation to the hamlet of Morganza, four miles upstream. Even so, his division seemed inert. So did its commander.[16]

Herron's principal concern lay with the Rebels on the east bank of the Mississippi and he cared little for operations west of the river. He believed that while Green had been attracting Union attention, Confederate colonel John L. Logan had put four thousand men and artillery into position to disrupt shipping. Logan's men had captured and burned a steamer loaded with provisions just above Donaldsonville, prompting troops from New Orleans to move out and hunt for the perpetrators. For Herron, this threat to the supply line far outweighed that of Green's one thousand Texans to his west. Even so, his infantry remained poised to react to events as they might unfold, sending scouts as far as the mouth of the Red River while others served as landing parties for gunboats patrolling the river.

Herron lacked focus; to compound the problem he and was falling ill like so many of his men. And sensing this, Lieutenant Colonel Leake rode to Morganza on September 24 to learn what he could about his commander's intentions. He found Herron ailing in his stateroom aboard one of the transports. "Went to the river," Leake scrawled into his diary. "Had a long talk with General Heron—said we would stay about a week." By October 1, Herron and his men would leave Point Coupee, bound for some other destination.[17]

The Confederates, meanwhile, grew impatient. Green strained at the leash to hit these Federals soon, and Taylor was inclined to let him. First, though, he wanted to be sure of his lines on Bayou Teche. Federal cavalry inexplicably remained fixed at Jeanerette and Taylor wanted to know what they were hiding. On October 2, Colonel Walter P. Lane arrived with his 1st Texas Partisan Rangers to stiffen the cavalry line. Rebels rode forward to find answers to these mysterious enemy movements only to learn the Yankee cavalry had fallen back toward Franklin, driving all the livestock they could capture toward the infantry camps below that town. From all appearances, this was not an army on the advance but an army merely stripping the Teche country of anything useful. For Taylor, this seemed a curious way to use thirty thousand veteran troops.[18]

Although he could not explain it, Taylor became convinced the Federals seemed disinclined to advance. So he confirmed Mouton's blessing for Green to hit Herron but at the same time ordered his small infantry division toward Morgan's Ferry—in case Green got in over his head. The steamboats *Argus* and *Robert Fulton* would bring up ammunition and rations. Meanwhile, Couriers arrived at the camps of Major General Walker's Texas Division, in the piney hills southwest of Alexandria, with orders to roust the men out of their comfortable camps and back into the war. They were bound for Washington. There Taylor would decide if they should head east toward Simmesport and join Green's efforts against Herron or south to oppose Major General Franklin. Taylor would ignore the threat to Alexandria from the direction of Natchez—there seemed to be no immediate movement from that direction for some reason. So, if the Federals would not assume the offensive, Taylor would.[19]

Pleased to have been unleashed, Green planned his attack. On September 26, he wrote to Colonel Major and told him to leave the area east of Alexandria and bring forward most of his brigade. Green wanted Major's best regiment—Major George M. Frazer's 3rd Arizona—to continue another dozen miles south and cross the Atchafalaya at Lyon's Ferry, then take the Bayou Gross Tête road near the village of Livonia. This critical mission would provide security for the Confederate right flank in case any Federals might be coming up from Plaquemine or Baton Rouge to save Herron.[20]

While Green put his strike force into place, Taylor received confirmation he had correctly guessed enemy intentions. Early in the morning, Confederates prowling near Franklin picked up a brightly uniformed soldier from the 165th New York—Duryea's Zouaves—and brought him in for interrogation. The exotically clothed soldier admitted his division of the 19th Army Corps, led by Brigadier General James W. McMillan, composed the vanguard of a larger invasion that had advanced no farther than Bisland. The rest of the army remained around Berwick Bay; some had not even made it across. Armed with this information, Taylor believed Mouton could supervise the situation on the lower Teche with the scant forces at hand. Green had the time, and now the men, he needed.[21]

Unknown to most of these soldiers maneuvering in Louisiana, the peculiar behavior of the Union forces on the lower Mississippi had good cause. Events

475 miles to the east had changed the trajectory of the Federal Trans-Mississippi campaign. Lieutenant General Braxton Bragg's reinforced Confederate Army of Tennessee crushed Union major general William Rosecrans at the Battle of Chickamauga on September 19 and 20. Halleck's urgent requests for reinforcements from the Mississippi Valley now ballooned into outright demands as news of the scope of the defeat flooded into Washington. "The whole country seemed paralyzed by this unhappy event," Major General Sherman remembered. "The authorities in Washington were thoroughly stampeded." Within a week, Sherman led three of his four 15th Army Corps divisions out of Mississippi toward Chattanooga. There would be no advance from Vicksburg or Natchez.[22]

The Union disaster at Chickamauga, the loss of Sherman and his troops, and the freezing of the Arkansas Campaign caused Major General Banks to rethink his plan. Four divisions had left for southeast Tennessee. He alone—with the 13th and 19th Army Corps—would have to conquer Louisiana and Texas. Banks doubted he had enough troops to succeed. Major General Grant, still crippled but sufficiently recovered to leave New Orleans, headed upriver to Vicksburg to resume command of what was left of the Army of the Tennessee, but even he would probably remain on the defensive now.

Banks halted his operations while he mulled his other options. The destruction of the Confederate Army of the Trans-Mississippi now seemed out of reach. With no columns coming from Arkansas, Vicksburg, or Natchez, the Army of the Gulf could do little but butt up against the same troops it had fought, round after round, for months. Taylor would retreat to Alexandria, and the Union supply line would stretch to the breaking point. It would be the Teche Campaign all over, but against more Confederates this time. Certainly, hopes of conquering Texas faded as well.

Or had they? As Banks reflected on the bad news from Georgia, he quickly changed his mind and his objective. He would not, could not, conquer Louisiana. But he might be able to accomplish his mission against Texas. "I bear in mind constantly the instructions of the Government as to Texas," he wrote Halleck, "and shall lose no time in doing all that is required of me so far as the means in my hands render it possible." Leaders in Washington, Banks believed, had asked him to accomplish the impossible. Instead, he would deliver the possible.[23]

The Confederates in Louisiana could not have known how profoundly events in Georgia had affected their fate—in essence, Lieutenant General Bragg had saved the Trans-Mississippi. Instead, they saw before them another round of hard fighting and risky operations with little to gain. The footsore Louisiana infantry arrived at Morgan's Ferry on September 26. "This little march . . . was the most fatiguing of any that I have made during the war," groused Captain Hyatt. "The

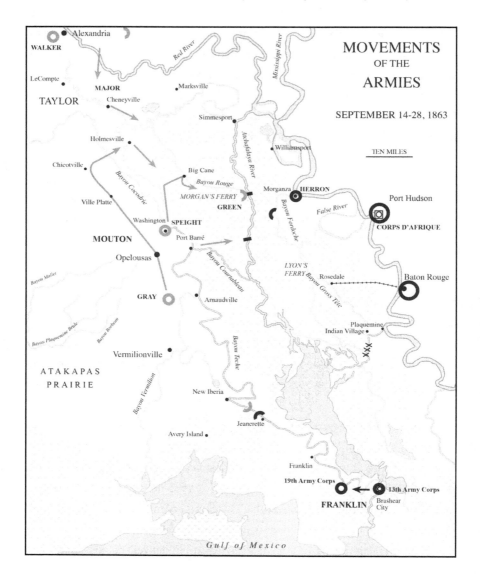

road was exceedingly dusty and water very scarce." Furthermore, the Louisianan doubted the wisdom of the move. "It is said that we are to cross the Atchafalaya . . . for the purpose of attacking the enemy on the other side," he continued. "I cannot think the move a good one . . . in case of defeat, we would lose our whole force."[24]

The Federals, still paralyzed by the implications of the Battle of Chickamauga, had little inkling of Green's approach. At this critical point, an ashen-faced Major General Herron left on a transport heading for New Orleans. Illness had finally cratered him. He left his division in the care of a new arrival bearing a string of war-like names: Major General Napoleon Jackson Tecumseh Dana. Rebels had nearly killed this Army of the Potomac warhorse at Antietam, and he had only recently returned to duty—a year later. He would manage the sleepy Pointe Coupee command while Herron recovered his health. As Herron's steamboat paddled its way into the current of the Mississippi, heading south, Major General Dana went to his new headquarters to begin his tenure minding what had become a castaway division. He needed a little time to familiarize himself with this strange command in this alien land.

Far to the south, storms both man-made and natural were brewing in the Gulf of Mexico. The steamer *Love Bird* anchored off Matamoros, Mexico, after a nearly two-month voyage from Liverpool. Onboard were 10,000 Enfield rifle-muskets and 156 pistols as well as two million rounds of ammunition and five million percussion caps—all bound for Lieutenant General Edmund Kirby Smith's armies. On September 26, the delighted Confederate commander on the Rio Grande, Brigadier General Hamilton P. Bee, began the process of unloading the vessel and brought ashore 210 crates of firearms—more then 4,200 weapons— before disaster struck. While the dumbfounded Confederates looked on from the beach near Boca Chica, the French warship *Panama* came alongside the British merchantman and seized it in the name of Napoleon III and the French Empire. The next morning, the *Love Bird* winged its way over the southern horizon, hauled away by its Gallic captor.[25]

The French, while professing sympathy for the southern cause, were also determined to keep weapons out of the hands of the Juaristas opposing them in

Mexico. The *Love Bird* and two other vessels they had seized carried more than seventeen thousand Enfield rifle-muskets that had possibly been bound for Mexico. These zealous French skippers reminded U.S. diplomats, war-planners, and politicians what a threat an open border between Mexico and Texas posed. French authorities impounded the weapons. They could have just as easily allowed them to pass, but they wanted the send the United States a clear message that that French intentions in Mexico did not *have* to concern the civil war north of the Rio Grande. Perhaps an accommodation, a reconciliation, could be made between Union and Imperial interests. These signals warned that the western Gulf of Mexico would soon be tempestuous, indeed. Confederate officials remained gobsmacked by what seemed like French perfidy.[26]

There were more natural storms brewing elsewhere in the Gulf. On September 28, a bright cobalt sky spanned the dome of heaven over the Sabine Pass. Such clear air provided a good opportunity for ship captains to see a long way with good field glasses. But what was there to see? From ten miles out to sea, the scenery at the Sabine Pass appeared as nothing more than a hairline-thin buff-colored smudge. This featureless, flat, and uninteresting coast held little allure for the Cape Cod sailors of the schooner-rigged collier *Manhasset*. Like the view, duty for the small crew of the Union-contracted supply vessel was dull. Anchored by bow and stern in about six fathoms of water, the crew tended to mundane chores. The *Manhasset* would rock on its cables while waiting for the next warship to appear on the horizon, looking for coal. The ship was nothing special, just a simple refueling station for Union blockaders.

The schooner carried a cargo of life's blood for the Federal warships—three hundred tons of anthracite. Warships like the USS *Cayuga* or the larger USS *Seminole* would occasionally visit the *Manhasset* to take on a mountain of black nuggets before resuming their patrol of Texas waters. Working the coast made these war-monsters hungry. The twin 200-horsepower engines on the USS *Cayuga*, for instance, gobbled a ton of coal an hour. When cruising, stokers banked their ships' fires, and deck crews unfurled the sails. If the deck crews went to quarters to cut out some nimble blockade-runner, heavers fed the fires that heated the water—that created the steam—that drove the ship. A burst of smoke from the funnels let every observer know when a Yankee blockader was firing up and heading out on the chase.

Once the warships had emptied the schooner's hold, its civilian sailors would spread the Manhasset's sails and glide back to New Orleans for another load. These routine shuttles passed mostly without incident, with one exception. The schooner had fed coal to the United States gunboats Arizona, Clifton, and Sachem during the Sabine Pass expedition earlier in the month, and that had been an unlucky affair. Since then, the Manhasset had gone back to New Orleans, taken on a new load of coal, and returned to its regular station ten miles off the lonely Texas coast.[27]

For the past few days the crew of the Manhasset had been enjoying cool weather. Gentle breezes from the northwest made for flat seas. On the morning of September 28, though, the watch noticed the winds shifting to the south and east and becoming gusty after what had started as such a promising day. The barometer fell, too. The sky over the Gulf of Mexico remained a deceptive blue, but keen eyes spied a squall line on the eastern horizon. As the day wore on, the wind fairly whistled through the rigging. Should they make sail and leave their station? Should they try to outrun the coming storm?

The ship's skipper, Acting Master Richard D. Ryder of Chatham, Massachusetts, thought moving the ship would create too many complications. He would have to communicate his new whereabouts to the ships he tended, and they, in the meantime, might run short of fuel. That meant a lot of sailing—and a lot of work—for every Union sailor along the eastern Texas coast. Better to ride out the storm out if possible. The seven crewmen trusted the skipper, but all hands aboard the Manhasset knew a squall was coming. They could not be sure how bad it might be.

The skies over Morgan's Ferry, 150 miles northeast of the coal schooner's anchorage and 75 miles into the Louisiana interior, also grew dark and ominous; this would not be just a routine storm, many feared. Brigadier General Green, battle fever upon him, paid little heed to the weather. As he ordered his Confederate army across the Atchafalaya River, the first drops of what promised to be a tropical deluge began to fall.

NINE

HURRICANE AT BOTANY BAY

Who likes war?

—Captain Arthur W. Hyatt
Confederate Guards Response Battalion

Under a pattering rain, the soldiers of two Rebel divisions queued up for their turn to cross the dark waters of the Atchafalaya River. Teams of grunting men pulled ropes that hauled troop-laden barges eastward in the late afternoon of September 28. The mood, like the atmosphere, lay heavy. Brigadier General Tom Green planned a desperate gamble. Should he and his men succeed, he would cripple one of the Union forces threatening Louisiana. If they failed, he could lose his army.

The crossing took hours. First across were the scrappy Texas cavalry led by the warrior-named majors Leonidas C. "Lee" Rountree and Hannibal Honestus Boone, shuttled across on two large ferry flats, their horses swimming alongside. Next Captain Oliver J. Semmes brought over his guns. Early into this hours' long crossing, the rain turned heavy, lightning arced across the sky, and the wind rose; by evening the rain fell in sheets. Two brigades of drenched foot soldiers crossed next, shouting to be heard above the storm and stumbling their way into the boats amid the deepening darkness. Three regiments of Texas cavalry dismounted and crossed last, leaving their mounts under guard on the west bank. Just after midnight, Brigadier General Green had three bedraggled, waterlogged brigades and a battery east of the Atchafalaya.

Behind Green, two regiments from Colonel James P. Major's Brigade and the Pelican Artillery guarded the crossing. Gallopers arrived to report the 3rd Arizona had also gotten across at Lyon's Ferry and now held the road to Gross Tête twenty miles to the south. The sodden Confederates, now in position to launch Green's raid, tried to rest as best they could under the unrelenting rain and gusty winds of a tropical storm coming ashore from the Gulf of Mexico.[1]

The men spent the balance of that miserable night hunting dry ground—and failed. "Of course, there was no sleep for the troops, there being a great deal of water in the road," noted Captain Arthur Hewitt, a Louisianan of the Confederate Guards Response Battalion. He refused to lie in the mud. "We wrapped ourselves in our blankets and pulled down some rails from a fence and endeavored to sleep on them." Texan captain George W. O'Brien could not get comfortable. He spent the dark and stormy hours "lying, sitting, and standing, but [doing] very little sleeping from the rain all night."[2]

The Confederates had come to eliminate Major General Francis J. Herron's Division if they could. Green's men had scouted the Union outpost at M. C. Sterling's Botany Bay Plantation for nearly three weeks. They had daily traded shots with the Midwesterners positioned there. Rountree's and Boone's Texans knew every lane, cow path, and byway in the region and every approach to Morgan's Ferry, the only useful crossing of the Atchafalaya below Simmesport that could allow a Union army to threaten Opelousas or allow a Rebel army to prowl the Mississippi. The Texan scouts believed slipping around and behind the Federals outpost would be easy. After disposing of the Union detachment holed up at Sterling's plantation, Green hoped, they could hit the enemy camps at Morganza and drive the Yankees into the river.

Green planned a double envelopment to start as soon as the morning of September 29 grew light enough to see. The plan was straightforward. First the Confederates would fix the Federals' attention toward the front. Green's Brigade would advance across the bottoms in a strong skirmish line backed by artillery. The enemy would probably mistake the attack for just another picket skirmish. Meanwhile, Rountree and Boone would keep their horsemen ready but out of sight on the Opelousas Road. When the enemy skirmishers fell back to their reserves, these troopers would dash forward, take the bridge over Bayou Fordoche, and overrun the camps of the 6th Missouri Cavalry at Norwood Plantation beyond. Green's Brigade and Semmes's artillery would press forward out of the Cow Head Bayou bottoms and emerge along Bayou Fordoche in front of the Union position at Botany Bay Plantation. The Yankees would respond by facing their infantry and artillery west and south toward these threats.

They would not suspect that to their north two thousand Confederate Infantry would be moving into position to cascade down upon them. Green would send Colonel Henry Gray and his brigade of three small regiments—the 18th, 24th, and 28th Louisiana—to the north, guided through the swampy forests by Lieutenant Emile Carmouche, a native of Pointe Coupee Parish and one of the heroes of the Maple Leaf affair. The eight hundred Louisianans would provide security for Green's attack by blocking the road to Morganza and preventing Union reinforcements from intervening. Once the Union outpost fell, the Louisiana Brigade would lead the advance to the Mississippi during the second phase of the attack.[3]

Once Gray had isolated the battlefield, Green would drop the hammer. With the enemy's focus to his front, Boone and Rountree would stand ready to dash up the Opelousas Road from the Norwood Plantation but the killing blow would come from Colonel James Harrison's infantry brigade crashing in on the Yankee right and rear from the cover of dense sugar cane. To get into position these foot soldiers would march along a drover's road, which was "wide enough for one man," according to Captain O'Brien. They would follow the winding road through the swampy bottoms of Cow Head Bayou until they emerged at the long curve of the road to Opelousas, near the northwest corner of Sterling's cane fields. Lieutenant Reed Weisinger and other riders from Boone's Battalion would guide these men to their positions.[4]

Harrison's four units would advance in a double file led by the 15th Texas Infantry, which would be followed by the 31st Texas Cavalry (Dismounted), the three infantry companies of Lieutenant Colonel Ashley W. Spaight's 11th Texas Volunteers, and Lieutenant Colonel Franklin Clack's four-company "Confederate Guards Response Battalion" borrowed from the Louisiana Brigade. Once out of the quagmire of the bottoms and onto the northern margins of Sterling's cane fields, these troops would form into assault columns and sweep in from the north and east to complete the encirclement of the Union positions.

The battle should be short and nearly bloodless, Green hoped. These Federal troops would skirmish for an hour to their fronts but realize all hope lost when the

Rebel infantry showed up behind them and Texas cavalry romped on their flanks. Rational men would surrender, Green believed, before casualties mounted.

The Confederate army stepped off to perform this intricate dance as the leaden skies grew slightly lighter, signaling dawn. Dull gray skies and thick blowing mists replaced the sheets of rain from the night before, but everything remained slick and every movement felt cumbersome. The roads crossing the bottoms turned to brown batter as hundreds of shoes and hooves cut and churned the sodden soil of Louisiana.

As the Confederates made their move, at Botany Bay Plantation and Norwood Plantation, the Federals had done what they could to stay warm and dry. Union troops filled sugarhouses, slave quarters, barns, sheds, and houses. For the lonely cavalry videttes forced to stand in the slashing rain, the night had seemed endless. Visibility in these camps had always been terrible. For nearly three weeks the tall crops and swampy woods in the bottoms between the Mississippi and the Atchafalaya Rivers had provided limitless concealment for Confederate infiltration. Only constant vigilance and aggressive patrolling had kept the Yankee

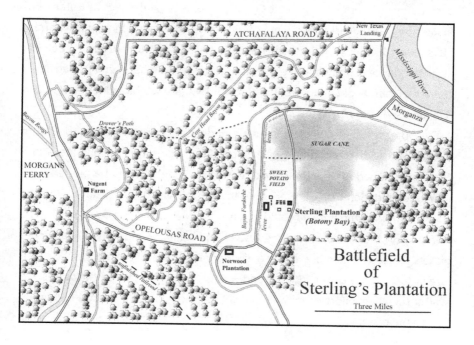

Battlefield
of
Sterling's Plantation

Three Miles

outpost safe. Now pickets could see nothing in the heavy mists of the morning. It seemed unlikely the Rebels would be out in weather like this.

Around 11 AM on September 29, listeners at the Norwood Plantation and Botany Bay Plantation noted scattered shooting near the Union picket line a mile beyond Bayou Fordoche. The alarm shots had been answered by a much heavier volume of return fire. It sounded like the beginning of yet another skirmish. For men trying to stay dry and warm, it also sounded inconvenient.

The commander of the outpost line sent a courier to Major Bacon Montgomery at the 6th Missouri cavalry camps two miles away at Norwood Plantation. The officer listened to the messenger's tale and quickly understood that if the shooting lasted for more than a few minutes, the rest of the battalion might have to turn out and investigate the disturbance. He waited, and the firing continued.

Therefore, Montgomery put the rest of his men on notice. Bugles blew *Boots and Saddles* as the firing grew in intensity and the sound drifted closer to Bayou Fordoche. Within minutes the troopers at Norwood's heard *Stand to Horse.* While alarming, the shooting still seemed routine. Until he knew more, Montgomery decided not to bother Lieutenant Colonel Joseph B. Leake over at Botany Bay Plantation. Neither did the commotion seem important enough to warrant his sending a rider to Morganza. The 150 Missourians turned out of their dry accommodations, formed a line of battle in the fog and haze, and waited. Then came the sounds of cannon rolling through the gloom. This added a new, and dangerous, dimension to the affair.

Yet, the skirmish failed to intensify; indeed, it barely seemed to sputter along, even with the addition of artillery. The aggressive Confederate attack Green had hoped for literally bogged down in the deep mire of a plowed field, now saturated. Semmes's Battery fired toward the Union skirmishers with little effect. Its horses and limbers could barely move the guns in the deep mud, made worse by the arrival of yet another wave of torrential rain. Unhurried, the Yankee pickets refused to yield in the face of so inert a threat. Since the firing had yet to lure in the Federal cavalry, Boone and Rountree could not make their sweep to scatter the enemy horsemen, who had yet to emerge from Norwood Plantation to take the bait.

Green, not wanting to reveal his mounted column prematurely, ordered the dismounted 4th and 5th Texas cavalries to redouble their efforts to clear out the stubborn enemy skirmishers. His veterans complied, but the efforts nearly ruined them. "We were then ordered to charge . . . about three miles through the deepest mud I ever saw," wrote Texas private John W. Watkins, "and I was completely broken down."[5]

This wallowing advance caused Green's timetable to slip. Impatient, Green ordered the dismounted 7th Texas cavalry and some of Semmes's guns to come up the road and use its firmer footing to launch directly at the Bayou Fordoche bridge. This did the trick.

The Missourians, seeing a Confederate column approaching through the rain, realized the day's skirmish had taken a serious turn. They had been flanked—and nearly cut off. The Federal pickets collapsed back on their reserve, which in turn mounted up and fell back to the rest of their command at Norwood Plantation.

Having removed the obstacle at last, the Texans re-formed on the wooded banks of the Fordoche while the artillery reassembled at the bridge. The attack had become confused and his command jumbled; Green sent a courier with orders for Boone and Rountree to come up, but the battle plan had clearly fallen apart. "In the meantime, the forces that were sent in the rear got around sooner than we expected," Watkins panted.[6]

While the Confederate diversion had foundered in front of Norwood Plantation, the infantrymen who would launch the main assault had arrived at their designated locations punctually and were in position. The Louisiana Brigade, dressed in the Yankee blue *Corps d'Afrique* uniforms captured at Brashear City in June, had advanced, emerged onto the road to Morganza as planned, and formed into a brigade column facing east. The crops on their right masked their position from the Union pickets at Botany Bay, and the curve of the road concealed them from Union troops that might come from Morganza, several miles away. With the stopper in place, Harrison's blue-clad troops followed, debouching from the woods down the narrow cow path to Colonel Gray's right. They hustled across the road, over the levee, and into the cane field to their front before re-forming into columns.[7]

Once reorganized, the infantry advanced. Gray headed up the road toward Morganza, parallel with Harrison's command which was thrashing its way forward through the sugarcane. Using the field roads and turning rows, the columns zig-zagged east, then south, then east again through the dense crop, closing the distance to the clusters of buildings on the grounds of Botany Bay Plantation. The infantry commanders, though, seemed confused. This portion of the battle was supposed to be the encirclement and cleanup. Amid the thrashing of cane, the crackle of rain, peals of thunder, and mud-caked tramp of brogans, the foot soldiers could hear the occasional thumping of artillery and the faint popping of small arms, but they heard nothing to indicate the Yankee infantry had yet engaged.[8]

The security of the Confederate plan also risked detection from another quarter. Two days before, on September 27, the steamboat A.G. *Brown* had arrived at Morganza bearing the Federal's heavy camp equipment and extra clothing. When Major General Nathaniel P. Banks had sent Herron's Division up the river, the men had gone in light marching order, expecting a short stay. The division

Major General Napoleon Dana was a veteran of many a hard battle in Mexico and with the Army of the Potomac in Virginia and Maryland. Wounds received at Antietam kept him out of the war until his transfer to the Army of the Gulf. *Library of Congress.*

baggage had remained with the convalescents and a guard regiment near New Orleans. The arrival of the division baggage upriver meant clean clothes and, therefore, improved morale. That morning, Major General Napoleon J. T. Dana had dispatched the usual courier bearing daily orders for Lieutenant Colonel Leake along with a surprise—two wagons loaded with the knapsacks and other camp gear belonging to the 19th Iowa and 26th Indiana. The dispatch rider, instead of dashing ahead, accompanied these wagons and their small infantry escort at a leisurely pace in the drizzle. The muddy roads did not allow haste, and these men saw no urgency to their errand. They plodded directly toward Gray's Louisianans.[9]

Meanwhile, keen Union sentries near Botany Bay Plantation eventually discovered the Rebel infantry thrashing about in the cane. Like most of his comrades, Sergeant Irvine Dungan of the 19th Iowa had spent the morning finding something to eat and a place to keep dry, but around 11:30 a new sound caught his attention. "A shot was heard at the picket post north of camp, then three or four shots in quick succession all from our picket posts," he wrote. Firing had been going on all morning down by Norwood Plantation, but this was different—and closer. An eruption of gunfire from the cane fields answered these warning shots, sending bullets buzzing and whistling though the slave cabins where he and his

Private Cornelius Comegy, 19th Iowa. *Trans-Mississippi Photo Archives.*

men were quartered. Drummers beat the long roll, announcing the emergency, and the troops from Iowa as well as the men of the 26th Indiana hustled to grab their weapons and accoutrements and turned out in line of battle.[10]

At the Sterling house, Lieutenant Colonel Leake heard the firing and belted on his sword before heading onto the porch to investigate. Seeing the gun smoke at the north edge of the cane field, he issued orders to turn out the two 10-pounder Parrott rifles and position the guns in the levee gap, facing northeast, where they could sweep the cane. An orderly brought him his horse, and Leake rode back to the slave cabins, where he found the 19th Iowa in line, awaiting orders in the rain. He "commanded the line himself to 'About face!'" The Yankees spun around. "Advance to the fence and commence firing!'" he ordered. The Hawkeyes surged forward to the rails and, taking aim, "our regiment fired the first volley at the advancing line of infantry," Dungan boasted. Leake hurried back to the 26th Indiana, led them to a position to the left and forward of the Iowans, and directed them to fire toward the right oblique. Leake now realized this would be no ordinary skirmish. The Rebels had come for his command, as he long suspected they would.[11]

Leake, having established his line of battle facing north, scampered back to check on his cannons, which he hoped to find on the left of his line. Instead of limbering the guns and moving them down the road to the levee gap, where they could enfilade any Rebel advance had manhandled them into the yard behind the Sterling house. Here outbuildings, trees, and other obstructions limited their fields of fire and their ability to pivot toward threats. Leake saw that one caisson with ammunition had made it to the gap, but the cannon had not. No time remained to correct the error.[12]

The brisk Federal fire at first surprised and confused the Confederates thrashing though the sugarcane. They had been discovered, in march columns, and now must fight this battle—apparently alone. Some of the soldiers lost their composure. "The command to [move] forward and to charge, with an occasional cry to retreat, were comingled together in dreadful confusion," Captain O'Brien wrote, "while the enemy rained among us and the cane around us a terrible shower of whistling, wounding, and killing bullets." One soldier in the 11th Texas

Volunteers, the son of one of the unit's officers, fell dead near his father. Officers and sergeants stepped forward and knocked the wavering troops into a ragged line of battle headed once again toward the enemy. When the Confederates came upon an irrigation ditch, they jumped in and took cover "against the whirlwind of bullets around us," O'Brien continued. The Rebels, pinned down, returned fire blindly, unable to see through the cane and the rain.[13]

The volume of fire had an effect. The Federals, taking a few casualties themselves, realized they had enemy fire coming from both their front *and* right. The Rebel line overlapped theirs, and the 19th Iowa slowly faded back toward the village of slave cabins of Botany Bay Plantation. The Hoosiers, their flank now uncovered, gave ground as well, falling back to the cover of the sugarhouse, and then the Sterling house and outbuildings. While directing these maneuvers, Lieutenant Colonel Leake took a glancing hit that knocked him from his horse; he remounted, bleeding badly, and rushed on to his regiments to try to keep them formed—and fighting.[14]

A third firefight erupted to join those crackling at the Fordoche Bridge and among the buildings at Botany Bay Plantation. The supply wagons Major General Dana had sent out that morning ran headlong into the Louisiana Brigade about three miles north and east of the Sterling House and about three miles from the Union camps at Morganza. The surprised Federal infantry escort deployed,

Colonel John C. Black, 37th Illinois. He won the Medal of Honor at the Battle of Prairie Grove the previous year. *Author's Colleciton.*

skirmishing with Gray's Louisianans. The Confederates did not press the fight, but the Yankees could plainly hear the sounds of heavy battle coming from the direction of Sterling's plantation. The Union courier, his original mission now forgotten, dashed back to Morganza. He reported Rebels held the road to Sterling's plantation but Lieutenant Colonel Leake seemed to be holding his own. Dana ordered Colonel John C. Black to take his 37th Illinois infantry and make sure all was well. Once he reached Leake, Dana directed, Black—noted for heroism and cool leadership at the Battle of Prairie Grove nine months before— was to take command. Dana next sent riders up and down the Mississippi levee to flag down any gunboats patrolling nearby. This battle, he believed, had the potential to become serious.[15]

It certainly appeared serious to the southern soldiers in the cane fields. The Confederates rallied, and cries of "Charge, Charge!" rippled down the line as officers watched the enemy line break apart. The Texas and Louisiana troops, tangled and mingled by the confused opening of the battle, surged forward in clumps and squads, tearing through the cane until reaching another irrigation ditch closer to the enemy. The line did not stop at this cover but instead emerged into open grounds of a sizable sweet potato field. Federal bullets cut down several of the attackers, but the Rebels pressed on.[16]

The Federal regiments took cover in three building clusters at the Botany Bay Plantation agricultural complex. The easternmost, or right, was a sugarhouse and its associated structures. The center cluster was an extensive village of slave cabins, workshops, barns, and sheds. The Sterling house and outbuildings composed the leftmost cluster, behind the other two and closest to the levee alongside the Bayou Fordoche road. The Iowans occupied the sugarhouse, the Indianans occupied the cabins and sheds, and a small collection of picket squads, orderlies, and the headquarters staff held the Sterling house. Creative Union soldiers made "the most of every house, fence, and tree," wrote one participant.[17]

Confederate colonel James Harrison moved to break up the enemy strongholds. He ordered the 15th Texas Infantry and the 31st Texas Cavalry (Dismounted) to overrun the slave cabins and break the enemy center. As his ragged line moved forward to the attack, shots coming from the sugarhouse led Harrison to command Lieutenant Colonel Spaight to take his 11th Texas Battalion and Lieutenant

Colonel Clack and the Confederate Guards Response Battalion and clear out the Hawkeyes on the Union right. These soldiers overran the sugarhouse, forcing the 19th Iowa to fall back to their left and join the Hoosiers among the slave cabins.

Colonel Harrison, seeing Spaight and Clack uproot the Iowans, led his line of battle forward. The troops who had captured the sugarhouse turned to their right and pitched in as well. "We fought from house to house, and street to street, desperately," Harrison reported. Some of the Yankee defenders took cover beneath the structures and shot some Texans in their backs, and Harrison ordered squads to clear each building. "By a vigorous attack," Louisiana Captain Arthur W. Hyatt remembered, we "drove them from cabin to cabin."[18]

It was a very tight battle. "We were close together, and knocked them down with our guns," claimed Private Edwin Hartley, one of the pickets from the 94th Illinois. "In one instance I saw one of our men and one of theirs fighting with their fists."[19]

The Union soldiers, their right flank turned, fell back toward the Sterling House and the levee, their front now facing east. The two 10-pounder Parrot Rifles, largely useless in the battle, now lay between the Rebel and Federal lines. The battle had been raging for an hour.[20]

Back at the Fordoche Bridge, Brigadier General Green tried to reinstate his battle plan. The four hundred mounted troops under Majors Boone and Rountree sped across the bridge and angled toward their right, heading directly for the camps of the 6th Missouri. The Federal horse soldiers, distracted by the heavy firing coming from the north, had turned their attention away from the Fordoche, and the Texan cavalry charge struck Major Montgomery, his baffled officers, and his 160 troopers hard on the flank. "Majors Boone and Rountree made a dashing charge upon the enemy's cavalry, drawn up in line of battle near the house," Green reported, "and scattered them with such effect that they were not seen afterwards."[21]

The Missourians fled through the fields east toward the Mississippi. As they scampered toward safety, they actually passed around the left and then behind the advancing Texas infantry, each side mistaking foes for friends.

Lieutenant Colonel Leake, unaware he now fought alone, ordered his scattered men to fall back behind the cover of the levee and re-form their ranks. The Union battle line now faced east, the 26th Indiana on the left, the 19th Iowa on the right. These seasoned troops regained their composure and began to deliver disciplined volleys from behind their earthen rampart and into the Confederate troops.

"They poured a destructive fire into us," admitted Captain Hyatt, "and for a short time, we were checked, or, rather, we were not quite so impetuous."[22]

One clump of wet and winded Texans took cover behind a substantial brick building just fifty yards ahead of the Union firing line. Bullets smacked into its walls and whizzed by; one Texas soldier spun violently backward and dropped dead. Amid this violence, Lieutenant John B. Jones, adjutant of the 15th Texas, turned to some of the others trapped behind the structure and told them he believed they had botched the attack and driven the Federals into a nearly impregnable position. He "remarked that it was perfectly useless to try and dislodge them by a charge in front with the men we had." If, however, the Yankees surged forward in a disciplined attack, they would sweep the grounds of Botany Bay Plantation, recapture their cannons, and probably make their way toward safety, killing and capturing Rebels as they went. Green's cavalry had somehow missed the battle. Jones and the others, realizing their danger, used the building as cover and dodged and wove their way back toward the cabins and sheds a hundred yards away, the heavy rain and billowing gun smoke helping to cover them.[23]

Jones and his party found Lieutenant Colonel Harrison sheltering among the cabins with about half of his brigade. The Texan remained hopeful. Although hopelessly mingled, his command still held these buildings and had plenty of fight left. If Leake and his men attempted to escape by pushing east toward Morganza, they would have to do it over these troops, he assured Jones. The other half of the brigade, though, had broken and headed back toward the north, seeking the cover of the cane fields and the irrigation ditch. Harrison commanded Jones and others to find and rally those troops, and others lurking in the fields, and move around the left of the Union line.[24]

Jones took Captain O'Brien and ran across the sweet potato field toward the shaken Confederates in the cane. When the Texans arrived, they noted a lot of Louisianans had not advanced. "Too many of Clack's Battalion remained in the ditches," O'Brien scolded. The officers began the task of gathering men and forming them once again into a useful force.[25]

Seeing the Confederate attack had stalled, Leake took the opportunity to consolidate his command and find a way to escape. He ordered the 26th Indiana to pick up and slide to the right, passing south down the road behind the 19th Iowa and giving up the levee to the north—left—of the gap where he had at one time hoped to place his now-useless cannon. Perhaps his Missouri cavalry, a mile away to the right, remained intact. He might have to run his command by the right flank along the levee all the way to the Norwood Plantation before running around the left flank of Harrison's Texans to get away.

Perhaps the enemy had already fallen back to the cane fields. Leake ordered his line forward to find out. Within a few paces of the levee, ragged firing by Colonel Harrison's Rebels convinced Leake that escape through the cabins would be too costly. He searched for a second solution but found new trouble on his left. The Confederates in the cane had rallied, and bullets began to zip down his entire line. Leake noticed a wide swath of unguarded ground—the sweet potato field—separated the two wings of the Rebel brigade. Some of the troops in the 19th Iowa, seeing this three-hundred-yard-wide span of open country, contemplated making a run northeast through the field to the cane beyond. This gauntlet, Leake believed, would be too risky, and his regiments would be enfiladed from both right and left. He hoped he could avoid a mad dash. Perhaps reinforcements might arrive if his two regiments held out long enough. By now, he hoped, news of the fight had surely reached Morganza.[26]

It had. And in response, Colonel Black's 37th Illinois had moved to the skirmish line of the baggage guard to assess the situation. The rumble of the gun battle at Sterling's plantation convinced Black that Leake might have the advantage, but some of the panic-stricken Missouri cavalrymen who clustered to his line thought otherwise. The Rebels had surrounded Leake, these horsemen reported, and he and his regiments were lost. Black fell back a short distance, formed a line of battle, and held his ground. If he advanced to the rescue, he might only be adding his men to the disaster. Black and the 37th Illinois would not be going to Botany Bay Plantation. Leake, the 19th Iowa, and 26th Indiana would have to come to him.[27]

While Leake and his Yankees looked for a way out of the trap, the Texans and Louisianans in the cane looked to finish off their enemies. Captain O'Brien, Lieutenant Jones, and others had seen the 26th Indiana make its shift to the right through the opening in the levee and, assuming they had broken and run, and gathered some troops to pursue. "I ran down along the levee . . . on the enemy's side of it toward and past a portion of their battery," O'Brien wrote, noting the abandoned caisson. Waving his sword over his head, he declared victory when he saw an approaching cluster of troops, their sodden banner stuck to the staff. Green's dismounted cavalry, he believed, had finally arrived. He turned toward his troops and urged them on, then, turning back to face the road, realized his error.[28]

The approaching soldiers were men of the 19th Iowa. Leake, despairing of rescue, had decided to fight his way to freedom. He readied his men for a dash across the sweet potato field. Then they saw the Rebels coming in from the left and hesitated.

O'Brien, seeing the Federals turn toward him, ordered his followers to dive over the levee and blaze away at the Iowans. "I retreated," the Texan recalled, "and saw several of my men fire upon them with effect."[29]

The sniping derailed the Federals' bolt for freedom and revealed to the Hoosiers and Hawkeyes that they had one more obstacle to surmount if they were to escape. The 19th Iowa turned, faced this new threat, and delivered a volley.

"I jumped down the other side of the levee, just as the bullets whistled over," O'Brien remembered, "trimming the weeds and grass on the top of it and throwing them in every direction." One of his soldiers lay writhing, clutching a serious wound in the thigh. Amid the buzzing bullets, Lieutenant Jones arrived at O'Brien's precarious position, huffing and puffing. "He told me to remain with the men while he went to get more," the Texan recalled. O'Brien looked over the levee and watched as the Iowans readied to deliver another round. The Texans fled. "Looking around, I saw only two or three men with me and retired rather hastily," O'Brien admitted. He jumped down from the levee into the safety of the drainage ditch at the cane field's edge.[30]

The shaken Confederates in the cane field once again wavered in the face of disciplined Federal volleys. O'Brien looked down the length of the trench and saw men quitting the position and running away. "This is the only time that I thought of being whipped," the officer lamented, "if the men could not be stopped and brought back." O'Brien leapt from his place of safety and hurried toward his men as the Iowa regiment rippled another line of shots, shredding the stalks all around him.[31]

After beating the cane with hundreds of hot bullets, the Iowans once more screwed up their courage for a dash to freedom. This time their strength failed them. Sergeant Dungan watched as his comrades withered. They had hoped "to cut through the cane and gain the woods," he wrote, "but the men were so fatigued, it was impossible." Leake ordered his men to hold tight and await events.[32]

Soon after, it appeared salvation was on the horizon. To their right, through blowing rain, the Federal soldiers could see a large clump of cavalry trotting beyond the right flank of the 26th Indiana. The 6th Missouri had arrived, Leake believed, and they might clear a path to freedom. Then he saw the Hoosiers fire into the cavalry, unhorsing two, before collapsing into panic-stricken squads. Leake realized these riders were Texans—and they had just rolled up on the Federal right flank.[33]

Brigadier General Green's trap had closed; Leake was whipped. "Our commander, seeing he could do nothing more, told us to take care of ourselves as best we could," Private Ed Hartley wrote. "At the same time he waved his handkerchief and rode up to them and told them he surrendered." Some of the Iowa Federals stood dumbfounded. Others, shaking off the shock, made a dash for the cane field or woods.[34]

Amid the confusion, the Texans continued to take casualties from Yankees in fence corners or in concealment. Green, arriving at the battlefield, rode to Colonel Leake and implored, "Why don't you stop this firing?" He could not. "Colonel Leake surrendered merely himself, not his command," Sergeant Dungan pointed out. Texans swarmed across Sterling's plantation, even though a few Union holdouts fired "till their guns were wrenched from their hands."[35]

The disorganized Confederates searched the area for the Yankees who had scattered. Private Hartley, among others, had made it to the cane field then lay flat. "I could see them passing by, hunting us, but they did not see me," he wrote. "They stayed out but for a few moments." Private Augustine Robinette of Company C, 19th Iowa, along with a friend, had broken for the timber as soon as his officers had started surrendering. Once sheltered in the trees, he found others from the lost regiments. "Came across 20 of the 19th Iowa and 26th Indiana," Robinette recorded in his diary. A slave guided the squad of fugitives through the surrounding swamps and forests to safety.[36]

Although Green had taken Botany Bay, his battle plan had miscarried. The fight should have been over quickly. His dismounted cavalry should have engaged Leake's detachment long enough for Harrison to fall on the rear. This should have been a fight between skirmishers that ended with the Federals being surprised and surrendering. Instead of a quick coup de main, it had become a line-of-battle slugging match, a muddy house-to-house and hand-to-hand battle in the pouring rain. The clock now read 1:30 PM and Green believed he had another fight ahead at Morganza. The troops there, though, would be ready, rested, and waiting. His army, which had not slept in twenty-four hours and was exhausted from marching and fighting in a tropical storm, had to reorganize itself as Major W. L. Robards and his ordnance officers gathered the plunder.[37]

The take disappointed the Rebels. The Confederates captured the section of 10-pound Parrotts with limbers and caissons, as well as two ambulances, a hospital wagon with medicines, and two stands of colors. The southerners with inferior weapons would swap for better ones from the captures. They took a small number of prisoners, too. Green's men rounded up fewer than five hundred Federal soldiers who, Captain Hyatt admitted, "fought very bravely, and are a tolerable good-looking set of fellows, but . . . fighting on the wrong side." Confederate bullets and bayonets had killed or wounded more than sixty Federals.[38]

The toll in Southern blood outweighed the gain. "In the whole, I do not think the expedition paid," grumbled Captain Hyatt. Colonel Harrison reported more than one hundred men killed, wounded, or missing. Colonel Gray numbered eleven casualties, including men lost skirmishing near Morganza and men from the Confederate Guards Response Battalion hit in the attack on Botany Bay

Plantation. The Texas mounted cavalry lost six. Major Boone had been shot high in his right arm and in his left hand; most believed he would not live. Somehow the dismounted Texas cavalry that was supposed to have started the battle emerged without a scratch.[39]

Precious time slipped away as Green gathered together his troops. By the time he had reorganized, he knew the Federals at Morganza had been aware of the attack on Sterling's plantation for nearly three hours. Conditions were worse than ever. The rain had often slackened but never relented the whole day, adding to the messiness of the terrain. It would take several more hours to ready his command to attack the garrison on the Mississippi, Green must have realized.

These fatal hours, he knew, would play toward the Federal advantage. Dana had already moved his men to the river side of the levee and ordered them to dig in. When the tinclad USS *Kenwood* steamed up from the south the Union soldiers cheered wildly. Before long the tinclad *Signal* and the fearsome river monitor USS *Neosho* would add their guns to the defense. The ironclad USS *Lafayette* was nearby and steaming toward Morganza as well. Even if Green attacked, he would lack the firepower to counter this naval threat.

When scouts reported Dana's new position, Green abandoned his hopes of catching the rest of the Yankee command. His Confederates had done all they could.

Green sent a flag of truce to Dana so that the dead could be buried, and the wounded tended. He proposed, and the Federals accepted, a twenty-four-hour armistice. Dana rejoiced, believing he had been granted more time to ready his position for the Rebel attack. Green breathed easier as well, knowing he could perform the tricky maneuver of crossing his men back across the Atchafalaya River unmolested.[40]

The Confederates slipped away that afternoon. The troopers of the 3rd Arizona, having come up from Livonia and Bayou Gross Tête, covered the retreat. It was a miserable withdrawal. The roads had been quagmires coming up that morning; the passage of troops and several more inches of rain—and still more rain falling—had made them feel bottomless. "I never suffered so much on a march in my life," complained Captain Hyatt. "The roads are so slippery that it is impossible to take ten steps without falling down." The officer fell a half-dozen times in the nine hours it took the men to travel the six miles to Morgan's Ferry. Private Joseph Faust, a young German from New Braunfels serving in the 7th Texas Cavalry described "mud up to our knees." This veteran of the New Mexico Campaign, Galveston, the Teche Campaign, and the Lafourche Campaign declared this his worst journey of the war: "It was the hardest trip any of us had yet experienced," Faust declared. "We arrived in camp by midnight tired and battered."[41]

Once across the Atchafalaya, the weary Confederates had to sleep without tents, in the mud. The rain slackened, but the temperature fell. The soldiers had not eaten. "The man who can undergo these hardships, and keep his temper as well," observed Hyatt, "he's a devilish nice fellow. I wish somebody would say 'Take a drink.'"[42]

That night, the battleground fell quiet. Union survivors who remained hidden in the fields around Botany Bay Plantation made their way back to the Union camps on the Mississippi. Gunboats rocked reassuringly at anchor in the river. "I have been in some hard fights," Hartley mused, glad to be out of the fix, "but this was by far the hardest."[43]

For Major General Dana, the battle at Bayou Fordoche had been an introduction to war in the Trans-Mississippi. He admired the pluck of these 13th Army Corps westerners. "Of one thing I feel sure—that, after being surprised, they fought as officers and men gallantly," he reported. "They sustained the high reputation of veteran soldiers."[44]

The day's battle had added to Confederate brigadier general Green's reputation for surprise and audacity, and the Federals remained on edge. "We are expecting an attack every hour day and night," admitted Private Hartley. He had been in the very eye of the storm and did not want a repeat of what he had endured. "Why we are not reinforced I cannot tell," he complained. He believed, as did many on the muddy bank of the Mississippi, Green fielded a force of ten thousand men. Even so, Hartley mused, "we sleep on our arms every night and are ready. If they attack us, we will do all in our power and that is all that is expected of us." Green may have fallen short of his own expectations, but he had scared the Federals into mortification.[45]

At Morgan's Ferry the Confederate troops faced a tedious day as the tropical storm slowly rained itself out. Captain Hyatt, covered in filth, had not been dry in days. "Well, now, I am a sweet looking object in daylight," he wrote into his diary on September 30. "I supposed I had better go and soak myself in the Atchafalaya River, and get some of the mud off." Then he thought of a better remedy. "I would rather soak myself in whiskey, ten to one." During the summer campaign, he had acquired an African American slave as war booty, but he could not find the man. Oh well, he thought, just another inconvenience among many. He wrote, "I have got no one to put up my tent, it is too wet to make a fire, and altogether, I am in a hell of a fix. Who likes war?"[46]

Far away to the southwest, September 30 dawned bright and clear, and Confederate troops walking the beach at Sabine Pass made a remarkable discovery. The violent tropical storm had driven the coaling schooner *Manhasset* ashore. The ship's masts were broken, revealing the crew had evidently tried to raise sail, too late, in the teeth of the storm. At that point all the sailors could have done was to drop anchor and hope for escape. The crew had survived the storm's pounding and sat forlorn on the beach, but their vessel had not. The howling winds from the south-southeast had forced *Manhasset* toward shore, its anchors furrowing the sea bottom in vain. Storm surges the previous night had finished it off, tossing the vessel and its cargo of coal onto the beach, where it heeled over.

The New England sea captain had gambled but lost. The commander of the collier *Manhasset*, like the commander at Botany Bay Plantation, had waited too long, and the storm that broke upon them had ruined them.

TEN

TEXAS OVERLAND

That stopped the "gents" for the day.

—Private William Randolph Howell
5th Texas Cavalry

I t finally quit raining in southern Louisiana on the first day of October 1863. Captain Arthur W. Hyatt cheered. "Bully!" he wrote. "The sun is shining, and things begin to look a little more cheerful this morning." The weather had become a little chilly, too. These farmers-turned-soldiers believed they would have a frost soon. The men of the little Confederate army on the Atchafalaya River enjoyed the respite from the brutal and schizophrenic atmosphere of the previous two months. They had gone from heat, drought, and dust to chill, rain, and mud. Well, they mused, perhaps the sun would dry their blankets and firm up the roads.[1]

The news of the Battle of Sterling's plantation ran like a bolt of electricity through the Confederate commands in Louisiana and soon buoyed attitudes even in faraway Texas. "The gallant Green and his brave men have . . . again encountered, and as usual, defeated the enemy," gushed Texan Sallie Patrick. "What praises do Green and his men deserve for the *inestimable* service they have been and are still rendering their country. I feel proud to know that I have one friend in that noble band."[2]

Brigadier General Tom Green reported to his wife he had survived yet another battle—and he had been amazing. "I am yet in the land of the living, after another brilliant victory near the banks of the Mississippi," he crowed. "We have again given the enemy a wholesome lesson, and I have so far been exceedingly fortunate as commander, beginning with Val Verde." He had an enviable record, he believed, and Louisiana had made him a hero. He happily recited it for the folks at home. "The last *four* battles fought in Louisiana have been under my command, three of which are splendid victories, and the other one of the most desperate fights on record, for the numbers engaged, and one where there was more *fruitless* courage displayed than any other, perhaps, during the war."[3]

The Federals may yet try to root him out of his position on the Atchafalaya, Green allowed, but he doubted it. Confident of his assessment, Green ordered Colonel James P. Major to take his troopers back toward Washington. Other work remained to be done in south Louisiana. "The Yankees are to-day making demonstrations as though they intended to advance upon us; but if they do, it will be after *very* heavy reinforcement," he opined, "as we gave those now here such a terrible basting day before yesterday that they will not again voluntarily engage us."[4]

He admitted to his wife his destruction of Lieutenant Colonel Joseph B. Leake's outpost had come at a price. His best infantry, the 15th Texas, lost at least seventy-five killed and wounded, more than a third of the men in the fight. But he had also lost a reliable subordinate. "The loss which was greater to me than all the others put together, was the desperate wounding of the best cavalry officer in the army—Major [Hannibal] Boone of my brigade," he lamented. "The Major's right arm was torn to atoms and amputated in the socket of the shoulder. His left hand was also torn up and two-thirds of it amputated, leaving him only his little finger and one next to it, having lost the thumb and two fingers of that hand and over half the hand itself."[5]

Besides the loss of this reliable soldier, a slight fever dampened Green's mood. "I have had a dumb chill to-day—the first one I have had in Louisiana," he whined to his wife. Green worried, with the cool snap upon them now, he would not be alone in his suffering. "I fear," he wrote, "we will have serious sickness as the winter approaches." Green had a prescription for what ailed him, but he could not get the medicine. "If I had a little good brandy or whisky, or even (Louisiana lightning) rum I could break my dumb chill in a minute," he claimed, "but there is nothing of that kind in the wilderness of the Atchafalaya."[6]

Over the next three days, as the Confederates enjoyed the boost to their morale, the Union troops reorganized and sought out the enemy's intentions. Major General Napoleon Jackson Tecumseh Dana ordered Federal troops to nose around past the battlefield and sniff out the Confederates while the men of the 6th Missouri did their best to discourage enemy snoopers. Dana abandoned the battle-scarred Botany Bay Plantation and established a new outpost closer to Morganza, but he hoped to either leave Pointe Coupee soon or receive reinforcements so that he could pursue Green. He feared he did not have enough men to ensure there would not be a repeat of the disaster at Sterling's plantation. With only one hundred cavalry left in the saddle, he could not adequately cover all of the approaches to his position. "The country here is so difficult to patrol and affords so much cover that it would require five times that number to keep it properly reconnoitered," Dana pointed out.[7]

It would not matter. Green would soon leave to confront the Union army on Bayou Teche. The Rebels may have blunted the invasion of Texas at Sabine Pass and bloodied the invaders at Morganza, but Confederate officers agreed the Union army gathering in the fields from Berwick Bay to Franklin presented the greatest threat yet. Lieutenant General Edmund Kirby Smith believed the Federals would be relentless in this invasion and warned the people of his Department of the Trans-Mississippi to brace for the collision. "Your homes are in peril," he wrote in a proclamation to be published in Louisiana, Arkansas, and Texas. "Vigorous efforts on your part can alone save portions of your state from invasion. You should contest the advance of the enemy, thicket, gully and stream." He warned the citizens that only their determination and energy would save them from the destruction visited upon South Louisiana. "By a vigorous and united effort you

Bayou Teche, near Franklin, Louisiana. Arlington plantation stands to the right, and a sugar mill on the left. *Harper's Weekly, December 8, 1866.*

preserve your property, you secure independence for your-selves and children—all that renders life desirable," he promised. "Time is our best friend. Endure awhile longer; victory and peace must crown our efforts."[8]

But what was the ultimate target of this Federal invasion, Shreveport or Houston? It made no difference to Sallie Patrick, who wrote her soldier friend she felt no anxiety for the Lone Star State. "I feel more hopeful than usual," she admitted. "I have never yet thought . . . that our loved state will be overrun by the Yankees this fall. It is true they have made demonstrations on our coast but it is hardly probable they will effect a landing." If they did come ashore, she assured him, "they will meet with as warm a reception here from the Texians as they have met elsewhere."[9]

Kirby Smith and other Trans-Mississippi Confederates had no idea what complications confounded the larger strategic picture for Major General Nathaniel P. Banks. Even Banks did not know what his ultimate target should be. On October 3, Major General Ulysses S. Grant wrote the commander of the Department of the Gulf to confirm he could not help him conquer Louisiana or Texas. Any extra troops he had were bound for Georgia, and he would have to cease all offensive operations along the Mississippi River. "Orders to me from Headquarters of the Army prevent me entirely from keeping any portion of my promises to you in regard to furnishing you with further aid," Grant wrote. He only had sixteen thousand men to hold his positions from Helena, Arkansas, to Natchez, Mississippi. He faced four brigades of Rebel cavalry in Mississippi that were supported by more than twenty artillery pieces. Grant apologized. "I assure you, general, this is no less a disappointment to you than to me," he claimed. "I was anxious to give you the aid to make your expedition a certain success."[10]

Banks was about to lose Grant himself. Major General Henry W. Halleck summoned the hero of Vicksburg to Cairo, Illinois, to receive instructions on how to handle the occupation of the Mississippi Valley and the raising of African American soldiers in the region. Still on crutches after his horse wreck, Grant complied. Once he was there, however, Secretary of War Edwin M. Stanton buttonholed him with an entirely different mission. The secretary asked Grant to leave the Father of Waters behind and retrieve the situation at Chattanooga.

General Braxton Bragg's victory not only blunted the Union invasion of the Confederate Department of the Trans-Mississippi but also ended Grant's work in the Mississippi Valley.

Grant's new job left Rear Admiral David Dixon Porter as Banks's only high-ranking ally in Louisiana—but the navy officer abandoned him as well. Banks wanted to operate on Bayou Teche as he had in the spring and overrun the region in a swift campaign north to Alexandria. Then, he would nose his army overland toward Texas—provided he could get a healthy complement of gunboats protecting Berwick Bay and the Atchafalaya River line.

Banks asked Rear Admiral Porter to send some of his light draft tinclads. Porter declined. He simply would not risk them in the Gulf of Mexico. "These vessels would not live ten minutes in a seaway," Porter explained. "They are fragile vessels with one-quarter and three-quarter inch iron on them and drawing only 30 inches of water. The first roll—everything on them above deck would go overboard, and the first time they pitched they would break in two." In addition, the Atchafalaya and Bayou Sorrel remained too low to be navigable, removing the option of bringing the gunboats in through the Atchafalaya Basin's interior tangle of bayous.[11]

Banks absorbed the drumbeat of bad news. He alone would have to defeat Taylor and his army, invade Texas, and help keep the lower Mississippi flowing unvexed to the sea.

The commander of the Department of the Gulf still had his orders: counter the French threat, invade Texas, pacify and restore Louisiana to the Union, and raise an army from the thousands of liberated slaves. He had once, for a brief moment, been the master of nearly ninety thousand U.S. troops. The goal of ending the Confederacy west of the Mississippi had seemed within reach. Now Banks had fewer than thirty thousand soldiers—just the Army of the Gulf. Clearly, he did not have enough men to accomplish all of the ambitious tasks his government had assigned to him.

On October 3, the Confederates holding the line below New Iberia scouted toward the Union positions near Franklin to learn what was taking the enemy so long to advance. Colonel William G. Vincent led forward the 2nd Louisiana Cavalry, the 1st Texas Partisan Rangers, and the Texas Squadron but collided with the 1st Texas Cavalry (Union) below Jeanerette. The Rebels fell back when the Texas Unionists charged in a disciplined line but rallied and made a stand, deploying a "skirmish gun" to keep the Federals at a distance. Sergeant H. N. Connor described it as "a small rifle, firing a 1 ¼ pound [ball] a distance of four miles"; he and his fellow Texans nicknamed the piece "Aunt Jane."[12]

The little gun bucked and roared. Hundreds of yards away, the bolt, smaller than a cupped palm, lifted a Texas Unionist out of his saddle in a puff of dust and blood before slinging him to the sod several feet away. His shocked mount bucked and cantered from the violence and the sudden loss of weight on its back. Unnerved, the other Union horseman reined their mounts around and loped away, wanting to put more distance between them and this mystery weapon.[13]

Invigorated by the spectacle, the Rebels advanced, but the enemy kept just out of reach. The troopers serving Aunt Jane could not get a bead on the elusive horsemen weaving about in the distance. When the Rebel line edged too close, the Federals made another stand. The Confederates once again wheeled Aunt Jane into position in the middle of the bayou road, but their action proved to be a reckless mistake. "We found we were being drawn into a trap," gasped Sergeant Connor, "as their infantry began to open on us from front and flanks, keeping the air perfectly alive with their screechings." Bullets clipped branches and leaves over the Texan's head, but none struck flesh. The Rebels dropped the trail of their bantam cannon and prepared to play upon the Union infantry, a much fatter target.[14]

New Iberia. *Frank Leslie's Illustrated Newspaper*, Nov. 14, 1863.

As the makeshift gunners readied their piece, they noticed a Federal battery rumbling into position 500 yards away down the road. These cannon would smother them with shot and shell. "To say that we were surprised does not express the emotion," Connor continued. "It might not have been 'scared,' but it was close to it. I thought to myself, 'Here's the last of you.'" Connor finished priming "Aunt Jane" and fired one more round—perhaps his last act on earth.

The earth around him erupted in clods of sod, earth, and splinters as the enemy's return salvo shredded the Confederate line. A shot sliced off the leg and tunneled through the horse of Captain M. T. Squires, Chief of Artillery on Brigadier General Alfred Mouton's staff, "throwing his blood all over us and our gun," Connor wrote. The shocked officer lay beneath his horse, bleeding to death; the stunned Texans dove to the ground as successive rounds roared in, ripping apart Aunt Jane's wheel, splintering its limber, and eviscerated its horses. The Texans leapt to their feet on the run. "A general skedaddle took place," Connor admitted. "A bad day's work for us. Farewell, 'Aunt Jane.'"[15]

The Confederates meanwhile used their interior lines to nimbly shift their focus away from the Atchafalaya River to the Union army moving up Bayou Teche. Green ordered his four brigades to head west. The infantry followed Colonel Major and his cavalry toward Washington on Sunday, October 4. The Texas cavalry serving as the rearguard on the Atchafalaya watched them leave, many hoping

The Army of the Gulf crossing Vermillion Bayou. *Frank Leslie's Illustrated Newspaper.*

this move would ultimately take them west of the Sabine River. Private William Randolph Howell, 5th Texas Cavalry, felt homesick and needed a little spiritual encouragement. To elevate his mood, he went to hear "the first sermon since we have been in the state," as he recorded in his diary. "Could almost imagine myself at church [at home] in Plantersville."[16]

While Green abandoned his position on the Atchafalaya in stages, skirmishing continued throughout the day along Bayou Teche. The Federal cavalry again traded carbine shots with the chastened Confederates as they moved along the bayou road between Jeanerette and New Iberia. Around 11 AM, an overconfident Colonel Edmund J. Davis of the 1st Texas Cavalry (Union) had a horse shot out from under him in one of these mounted dustups and found himself surrounded by Rebels, a prisoner. As they held him at gunpoint, the Unionist Texans nearby surged toward the Confederate skirmishers. Davis's captors fled. The colonel resumed his place at the head of his regiment, and the rolling gun battle continued. By late afternoon the northerners had driven the Confederate line almost to New Iberia.[17]

Colonel Vincent, taking advantage of time purchased with sweat, smoke, and shot by his skirmishers, prepared an ambush just south of New Iberia. Troopers from the 2nd Louisiana Cavalry, 1st Texas Partisan Rangers, and the Texas Squadron concealed themselves in a sizable drainage trench called Nelson's Canal, which ran from an unfinished railroad grade to their right to the bayou on their left, with a bridge where the road crossed the ditch. The hedge- and fence-bordered canal emptied into the Teche near the half-submerged wreck of the twice-scuttled, would-be ironclad, CSS *Stevens*.

Colonel Edmund J Davis, 1st Texas Cavalry (US). *Courtesy of Tom Pressly, Shreveport, Louisiana.*

With his positions set, Vincent ordered forward a squad of Rebels to engage the approaching enemy and lure them into the trap. After making contact, the southerners galloped back down the road in feigned flight. "The last scout passed over the bridge, his horse limping badly, being wounded," observed Connor. Union cavalry, smelling blood, rode after him, pistols and carbines blazing.[18]

When the pursuing Federals crossed the bridge, Vincent's bugler sounded the attack. "We opened a crossfire at them from ten feet to 150 yards, which . . . hushed up their racket very suddenly," Connor continued. The Unionist Texans, ambushed from front and both flanks, struggled to back up and get away. "For 10 or 15 minutes the lane presented a grand scene of confusion, men without horses, horses without riders, dead, wounded men and beasts, men shouting, horses screaming with pain, officers giving orders, and the continuous rattle of musketry," Connor added. "All combined made it a grim and fearful scene."[19]

Other Federals hurried forward to help the trapped regiment. Cavalry charged toward the Confederate right but reined in and retreated when a volley from the cover of Nelson's Canal tore through their ranks at close range. Their distraction allowed their comrades to escape the ambush. As their enemy retreated, Rebels climbed out of the ditch to fire at them but did not tarry long. The Union artillery once again came to the rescue.

Satisfied with their work, the Louisiana and Texas Confederates fell back to their horses. "In doing that, we were placed in direct range of their batteries, which were planted by this time on and near the bridge," Connor remembered,

Centreville, Louisiana. A battery of Union artillery deployed across the main street. *Becker Collection.*

"but we ran the gauntlet of shot and shell tearing up the earth around us." Vincent and his men sustained few losses and punished the Federals into ending their pursuit for the day.[20]

Down the road from the ugly little cavalry battle, the Union army under Major General William B. Franklin continued trudging along Bayou Teche. His was the second major Union army to pass through this region in four months, and many of the men of the 19th Army Corps had traveled this way the previous April, during the Teche Campaign. The newcomers of the 1st, 3rd, and 4th Divisions of the 13th Army Corps put on a show for the dazed citizens of the town of Franklin. "On coming near this nice little city, we straitened up, dressed our files, and put on the best of soldierly appearances," remembered Private Reuben B. Scott, Company A, 67th Indiana. The Union bands struck up "Rally 'Round the Flag" and "The Star-Spangled Banner" as the regiments passed. "We made a grand appearance," Scott boasted, "while the citizens looked on in apparent astonishment." The column of enemy soldiers, animals, and wagons seemed endless.[21]

Aware of Franklin's movements, Brigadier General Mouton knew he could not stop this Yankee juggernaut. He ordered a retreat to Vermilionville, leaving behind only pickets. Colonel Major's Brigade would join him there, he believed, before nightfall on October 5. The enemy, according to one of the Union prisoners pinched in the Nelson Canal ambush, was heading for Texas. The Yankee captive told Mouton that Franklin commanded seventy-five thousand men—about fifty thousand more than he actually had. Incredulous, Mouton hurried along his infantry from the Atchafalaya River and directed them to positions at Evergreen and Holmesville, where they could watch for enemy movements by way of the Red River and Bayou Teche with equal felicity.[22]

Taylor seemed baffled. Major General Dana's Federals remained in Pointe Coupee and gunboats blockaded the mouth of the Red River while Franklin threatened from the south. Reacting to these multiple threats, Taylor had marched his most potent weapon, Major General John G. Walker's Texas Division, from Alexandria to Washington, then from Washington to nearly Simmesport, and then back toward Washington again. Walker's scouts reported seeing Union gunboats on the Atchafalaya but reported the Federals under Dana were not advancing across Morgan's Ferry toward Washington. Yet, the enemy concentration of infan-

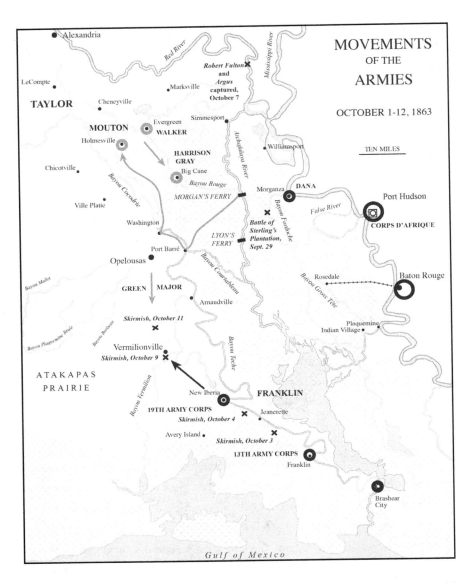

MOVEMENTS
OF THE
ARMIES

OCTOBER 1-12, 1863

TEN MILES

Alexandria

Red River

LeCompte

Marksville

Robert Fulton and **Argus** captured, October 7

Mississippi River

TAYLOR
Cheneyville

Simmesport

MOUTON Evergreen
WALKER

Holmesville

HARRISON GRAY

Atchafalaya River

Williamsport

Chicotville

Big Cane

Bayou Rouge

MORGAN'S FERRY

Morganza **DANA**

Port Hudson

Bayou Cocodrie

Ville Platte

False River

CORPS D'AFRIQUE

Washington

LYON'S FERRY

Battle of Sterling's Plantation, Sept. 29

Bayou Fordoche

Port Barré

GREEN | **MAJOR**

Bayou Courtableau

Opelousas

Bayou Mallet

Rosedale

Baton Rouge

Bayou Grass Tête

Arnaudville

Skirmish, October 11

Bayou Plaquemine Brule

Bayou Borbeau

Plaquemine Indian Village

Bayou Teche

Vermilionville
Skirmish, October 9

A T A K A P A S
P R A I R I E

Bayou Vermilion

New Iberia
19TH ARMY CORPS
Skirmish, October 4

FRANKLIN
Jeanerette

Avery Island

Skirmish, October 3

13TH ARMY CORPS
Franklin

Brashear City

Gulf of Mexico

try and artillery from the 13th and 19th Army Corps loitered at New Iberia. Would they strike west toward Abbeville and push to cross the Mermentau River, the Calcasieu River, and the Sabine River? Taylor wondered: was this an invasion of Louisiana . . . or Texas?

Taylor's lack of clarity and the confused movements of the Confederate army exhausted the men for little return on their efforts. He made a few more adjustments to his dispositions, and Walker's Division spread out at Evergreen while Mouton's infantry division held positions Big Cane. "I certainly do object to this way they have got of eternally marching our brigade from point to point," complained Louisiana captain Hyatt. "Last month we marched over 290 miles, and we have been on the go every day, so far, this month." The Confederate cavalry, meanwhile, warily concentrated near Vermilionville, which Mouton held tentatively. Brigadier General Green's mounted men moved from the Atchafalaya toward positions along Bayou Carencro, a dozen miles north of the town, preparing to cover the retreat.[23]

Just before noon on October 7, three days after the head of the Union column moved into Franklin, the army's last wagons moved through the town. Corporal Carlos Colby of the 97th Illinois, detailed as a guard, realized he had family in Franklin. As he ambled through the business district alongside the slow, creaking, rattling wagons, he decided to take a detour to see if he could locate his kinsman. "I took the trouble to hunt up Cousin Warren," he wrote his sister. "I found him keeping a drug store. He was well, but a rank sesech. His first words when I made myself known to him were, 'I am glad to see you, but sorry to see you enlisted in the cause that you are in.'" Colby was stunned by this frosty reception. "He expressed his sentiments so strongly that it made me almost mad."[24]

Colby's cousin turned rude. Although it was about lunchtime, Warren "did not as much as ask me to stop to dinner," Corporal Colby sputtered. "I was treated so coolly that I did not make a stop of more than ten minutes. He pointed out his son to me, a growing man of about 18, but did not introduce him. Otherwise than [saying] that his family were well, he said nothing about his affairs." Colby resolved to have nothing more to do with this cousin. "When I left he told me that if I camped in the vicinity to call again." Colby knew better. "I would not call on him again," Colby assured his sister, even "if I were encamped in the town."[25]

The slow pace of this Federal invasion continued to baffle the Confederates. Mouton had recalled Green away from Morgan's Ferry fearing an imminent battle but had not coordinated the move with his superiors. Major General Taylor, in Alexandria and ignorant of Green's move, ordered the steamboats *Argus* and *Robert Fulton* down the Red River under the direction of one of his young aides, Lieutenant John Marsh Avery, to cooperate with Green's command on the

Atchafalaya. Taylor directed Avery to remain on board until he had communicated directly with Green. But by the time the vessels had cleared the Red River and turned into the Atchafalaya near Simmesport, Green had left, headed toward Vermilionville. The inexperienced lieutenant tied up his boats at the landing and attempted to find out where the Texans had gone, and during the pause his crews rolled cotton aboard to take back to Alexandria.

While Avery shillyshallied, a slave from one of the boats used the opportunity to make a dash for freedom. After a ten-mile jog to the Mississippi River, he flagged down a Union gunboat at the mouth of the Red River and gave news of the Rebel vessels being near.

Reacting quickly, crewmen aboard the river monitor USS *Osage* who were unable to clear the sandbar into the Atchafalaya lowered boats, rowed to battle, and put ashore a landing party of sailors and marines. These nimble raiders captured and burned the *Argus* and *Robert Fulton* without firing a shot and took the dilatory Avery prisoner.[26]

The pointless loss of important transports, coupled with the inscrutable Confederate strategy and constant fumbling, caused the English-born Captain Hyatt to lose his temper. Camped in "a perfect swamp, damp, and covered in rank weeds" at Big Cane, he questioned the competency of the Rebel high command. "If there was any good reason for it, I should say, 'all right,'" he wrote. Instead he saw an infantry brigade slowly unraveling from desertion and disease and being marched to exhaustion. He cast the blame at the generals of the Confederate Department of the Trans-Mississippi. "Our 'big He,' Lieutenant General E. Kirby Smith, is a most gifted gentleman with a mind sufficiently large to cover the states of Louisiana, Arkansas, and Texas," Hyatt scribbled sarcastically, "at the same time it is occupied with picnic, blackberry and crawfish parties, and his young wife. Most men could only attend to one of these at a time and do them justice."[27]

The feisty captain also complained about Major General Taylor. "'He No. 2' . . . is a quiet, unassuming little fellow, except on a retreat, when he is really noisy," Hyatt continued. "On these occasions he had been known to curse and swear at mules and wagons, but this is overlooked as it is only done for affect." Hyatt blamed Taylor for the loose discipline in the army. "He is celebrated for having never punished a deserter, the number of them he has, his evident encouragement of desertion, and the quality of his staff."[28]

Hyatt reserved most of his venom, though, for Mouton. "'He No. 3' . . . is called, not inaptly, the Creole General," he sneered. "Like No. 1 and No. 2, he possesses no administrative qualities. His brigade numbers about 800 for duty. The number of deserters from this brigade in the last twelve months will sum up to 2,500!" Hyatt believed Mouton had willingly let his command dwindle away. "It is said that [he] feared to shoot a conscript, lest it should make him unpopular in his state," the captain continued, "and affect his chances for the gubernatorial chair."[29]

The frustrations of the Rebel army were understandable, but the strategic picture clarified as the hours passed. The next contest, it appeared, would come near Vermilionville. On Bayou Teche south of the town, Colonel Major and his Texas and Arizona cavalry arrived to reinforce Vincent and his hard-pressed horsemen hovering near New Iberia. Reenergized by this assistance, the mounted Confederates braced for several more days of skirmishing. On October 6, the troops fell back, maneuvering north of New Iberia and the margins of Spanish Lake. The next day, October 7, the Rebels again retreated, crossing the prairies, thundering across the Bayou Vermilion bridge, and taking positions on the nearby bluffs. Pickets on the other side of the stream would warn of the enemy approach.[30]

The Federals, however, were in no hurry to pursue. Behind a skirmish line and screen, commissary and quartermaster officers began transforming New Iberia into a permanent garrison. The wreck of the gunboat CSS *Stevens*, once the paddle wheeler *Hart*, blocked Bayou Teche downstream at the intersection with Nelson's Canal. Union officers pressed gangs of local African American laborers to dismantle the vessel and clear the stream. Transports *St. Charles*, *Red Chief*, and *Hancox* unloaded their supplies at Olivier's Landing, about a mile below the wreck, requiring relays of wagons to haul the goods the final three miles overland into town.[31]

The Federal cavalry spread out across the region and gathered in anything of military value. "Those places where the army camped have suffered very much," complained sugar planter William Frederick Weeks of New Iberia. Livestock, vehicles, and food flowed into army depots. The Union harvest also included people. "Many negroes have been conscripted," Weeks added.[32]

Another steamboat paddling up Bayou Teche, the A. G. *Brown*, bore important cargo. Major General Banks, his staff, and Major General Edward Otho Cresap Ord—commander of the 13th Army Corps—traveled from New Orleans by rail and Brashear City by steamboat, then pressed up the bayou toward the sharp end of his army. On the morning of October 9, they arrived at Olivier's Landing below New Iberia. Engineers had prepared a special treat for him. About noon, Banks watched demolition charges crack the CSS *Stevens*'s carcass into two parts. Though impressed, Banks did not tarry and headed for New Iberia. He paused in town only long enough to telegram Major General Dana to take his men out of Pointe Coupee and return them to Camp Carrollton for their next assignment. Banks pressed on, bound for the front.[33]

Banks could hear occasional gunshots in the distance as he made his way north along the Federal column. Once again at the head of the Army of the Gulf, he ordered the advance to resume. On the evening of October 9, the Union army fought its way across Bayou Vermilion against light opposition. The 1st Texas Cavalry (Union) skirmished with the 2nd Louisiana but could not save the Pinhook Bridge from fiery destruction by the Confederates. The Union cavalry, unfazed, splashed across at a ford near Ile Copal, the plantation home of former governor Alexandre Mouton—the father of Confederate brigadier general Mouton—and

Ile Copal Plantation. *Author's collection.*

continued the fight, forcing the Rebel cavalry to give ground. These Federals reported the Rebels were retiring from Vermilionville and urged the infantry to come up and secure the prize.

Major General Godfrey Weitzel's Division moved toward the burned Pinhook Bridge and ordered up the pontoon train while Brigadier General Cuvier Grover's troops splashed across at the ford. Engineers from the *Corp d'Afrique* assembled two pontoon bridges amid the burned pilings while most of the 19th Army Corps, having waded across Bayou Vermilion, deployed in line of battle to hold the north bank and cover the laborers.[34]

The next morning, October 10, the Federals advanced through Vermilionville and headed north to maintain contact with the enemy. The Easterners of the 19th Army Corps pushed steadily northward behind a screen of skirmishers from the 1st Texas Cavalry (Union), driving the Rebels more than five miles toward the wooded margins of Bayou Carencro. Using signal flags, Union spotters in the town's church steeples relayed to their commanders Confederate troop movements among the fields and farms north of Vermilionville.[35]

The Confederates, outnumbered and hard pressed, were retreating behind cover to mask their strength. Riders from Colonel Major's retreating Rebels met Brigadier General Green and his cavalry brigade coming in from the Atchafalaya and alerted him to the presence of the Federals. The Texans deployed along the banks of Bayou Carencro to await their enemy's arrival. Yet the Yankees stopped well short. The Federals in the 19th Army Corps instead paused just north of town, miles from the Carencro. Behind them, the 13th Army Corps crossed Bayou Vermilion on freshly built pontoon bridges.

Green, with his cavalry division concentrated and concealed by the terrain, watched for an opportunity to strike. Ten miles of open prairie separated the two picket lines. But once again the Union army compressed, accordion-like, this time in Vermilionville.

Satisfied all was secure, Banks ordered the advance to resume. On the morning of October 11, a force of Union cavalry under Colonel John J. Mudd pressed forward to uncover the enemy. But the Rebels, who needed to keep the enemy from seeing across the wide-open spaces of Buzzard Prairie beyond Bayou Carencro, boiled out of the tree line and formed in the open ground, determined to brush back the Federals. The Union cavalry and mounted infantry, thus checked, deployed as well.

The Northerners soon learned the Southern horsemen, armed with rifles and at home in the saddle, would be troublesome. "Their arms were superior to ours and they knew it," observed Private Samuel H. Fletcher of Company A, 2nd Illinois Cavalry. "They would stand off and shoot indefinitely . . . which is the true way to fight with cavalry. They would throw a ball a mile with great force and accuracy and at three quarters of a mile would often go over our lines, while ours only served to kick up dust a quarter of a mile ahead of the enemy, who would shout, 'A little more powder.'"[36]

The folly of pitting unsteady mounted infantry and carbine-armed cavalry against these Texas veterans became apparent. "A successful cavalry force cannot be improvised," observed Private Fletcher. Under the constant pattering and whirr of small arms fire, the poorly drilled Yankee regiments broke formation and scattered; Green's men took advantage of the confusion to ride around the enemy line and envelop its flanks. Under this pressure, the mounted infantry on either end of the formation broke for the rear, leaving the Union cavalrymen to fend for themselves in the center of the line. "It was a hot place," Fletcher noted. "The bullets zipped past our ears like a flight of hornets."[37]

The carbine-armed Union cavalry saw their position dissolving and prudently headed toward the rear. As the columns turned, Private George Crosby, a trooper next to Private Fletcher, took a round through his right arm that passed completely through his body and exited out his left arm. He was dead instantly, slumped in the saddle. "I did not know that anything unusual had occurred until [a soldier in] the next file behind me, cried 'Fletch, Crosby is killed!'"[38]

The day's brawl passed with few additional casualties, but it innaugurated a new pattern for the near-daily dustups between the Union and Confederate mounted troops. "A skirmish of half a day was a common occurrence," recalled Fletcher. "The enemy continued to annoy us in about the same way as long as we remained."[39] The Union army seemed suspended, unwilling to move forward without knowing what lay beyond Bayou Carencro.

Confederate major general Richard Taylor had watched the day's cavalry fight from a distance and began to formulate a theory about the enemy's intentions.

George Boutwell, US Commissioner of Internal Revenues. *United States Archives.*

Upon his return to his quarters at Opelousas that evening, Taylor learned a priest had reported Union troops were moving a pontoon train west, out of New Iberia and toward Abbeville, clearly indicating a move in the direction of Texas. Was the push to Vermilionville a feint? Taylor wondered. Was this Union cavalry action merely a screen? Did Franklin mean to pin down the Confederates at Opelousas with the 19th Army Corps while the 13th Army Corps made a left turn toward Texas? Taylor believed so. He wrote to Lieutenant General Kirby Smith's chief of staff, Brigadier General William R. Boggs, that he suspected a move for Texas along the lower coast road and that the next day or two would probably settle the question.[40]

On the evening of October 10, in the safety of Vermilionville, Franklin appropriated the lawn of Ile Copal for his headquarters while Banks bedded down less than a mile away nearer the pontoon bridges at the Basil Crow Plantation. At both spots, locals streamed in to pledge their allegiance to the United States. "The people of this parish represent that they are heartily tired of Texan rule, and it is indicated that if the Government will furnish a basis of protection, a mere point of support, they will make armed resistance to another invasion by the Confederates," a staff officer reported.[41]

Major General Cadwallader C. Washburn, commanding the advanced elements of the 13th Army Corps, cautioned his men about their relations with the locals. He doubted their professions of loyalty. "We must take nothing from

Congressman, and future Louisiana governor, Michael Hahn.
Courtesy of Tom Pressly, Shreveport, Louisiana.

a Union man," Private Henry Whipple of the 29th Wisconsin heard the general admonish. "At the same time, [he] told us that there was not a Union resident within 300 miles."[42]

On October 11 the Federals continued to grind forward. The 19th Army Corps moved behind its cavalry screen and arrived unopposed at Bayou Carencro, occupying the former Rebel position around noon. Behind them, elements of the 13th Army Corps already across Bayou Vermilion moved to reinforce the 19th Army Corps while cavalry and mounted infantry scouted eastward, chasing rumors the 2nd Louisiana Cavalry and a band of newly raised partisans might be operating near Breaux Bridge and St. Martinville, slipping around the right of the army and heading toward its supply lines.[43]

Banks watched the progress and complications of his invasion. The Rebels were many, and wily. Yet he wanted to make the shift toward Texas. What he needed were other troops to pin Taylor to the dirt, but the men he had in mind were already in southeast Tennessee. If the Rebels brought up their infantry and concentrated on either of his corps on its own, he would be in dire trouble. How could he bluff Taylor and still gain Texas? Banks left Major General Franklin with orders to go as far north as Washington—but no farther.

These tedious little scrapes in this burned-over part of Louisiana held little charm for Banks, and by October 12 he headed back to New Orleans and to political business, confident his field commanders could manhandle Taylor's

Interior of the St. Charles Hotel in New Orleans,
headquarters of the Army of the Gulf. *Library of Congress.*

army. At his St. Charles Hotel headquarters, Banks issued orders intended to speedily readmit Louisiana to the Union. He detailed his plans to Massachusetts congressional representative George Boutwell, a friend and highly experienced political operative whose résumé included service as governor of the Bay State and as the first U.S. commissioner of internal revenues. This important Washington ally, Banks believed, would be the perfect liaison with the White House. After gauging Boutwell's response, the general next directed the military governor, George Shepley, and his state officials—Attorney General Thomas J. Durant and Congressman Michael Hahn—as well as Louisiana's Federal officials—including the Treasury Department's agent, Benjamin F. Flanders, and Federal judge John Smith Whitaker—to advance his agenda.

Banks met surprising resistance: "I found most of these gentlemen so interested in topics that seemed to me disconnected with the general subject, and so slightly disposed to encourage my participation in the affair, that I retained the letter I had written." He would save Boutwell and his connections

Treasury Department agent and future Louisiana governor,
Benjamin Flanders. *Louisiana Digital Archives.*

for future use. Banks needed proof of what he had directed, and what these administrators had ignored. Shepley and the other state officials, having already been in direct communication with Lincoln, told Banks to mind his own business. Banks understood bringing Louisiana back into the Union *was* his business, and he feared the repercussions that might ensue should their efforts miscarry.[44]

Banks tired of the political machinations. If the political leadership in Louisiana were truly working directly with the president, then they should follow Lincoln's wishes. Banks would focus on Texas. "[I] turned my attention," he wrote, "to matters more likely to be accomplished."[45]

ELEVEN **THE BATTLES FOR OPELOUSAS**

Shall be very glad to get definite instructions.

—Major General William B. Franklin
The Army of the Gulf

On October 12, 1863, Brigadier General Tom Green's cavalry division, tired and in need of rest, ammunition, and provisions, yielded the prairies on either side of Bayou Carencro to the Yankees and fell back several miles. His brigade, now commanded by Colonel Arthur Pendleton Bagby, passed through Opelousas. Colonel James P. Major's men provided the rearguard.

The Federals, of course, followed. The 1st Texas Cavalry (Union) and 1st Louisiana Cavalry (Union) maintained contact with the retreating Rebels, swapping shots with them as they went. Major's Texans turned and laid an ambush three miles north of Opelousas, just around a bend on the Washington road. The eager Federals recoiled when they realized their mistake and reined around, then it was their turn to be pursued back through town. The Rebels broke off after a few miles, and Green continued northward beyond Washington to the hamlet of Moundville, putting the wide and deep Bayou Courtableau between themselves and the enemy.[1]

The Federals, having caught their breath, set out vedettes on the thickly wooded banks of Bayou Bourbeau, but the bulk of the cavalry returned to the prairies around Bayou Carencro, three miles away.

Confederate major general Richard Taylor rode with a scouting detachment of Major's men to within field-glass range of the enemy picket line at Bayou Bourbeau. He could also see the bulk of the enemy cavalry trotting back across Buzzard Prairie between Bayous Bourbeau and Carencro. Was his old nemesis, the 19th Army Corps, beyond those far woods?[2]

These enemy still seemed to be in no hurry, and Taylor pondered the situation. He believed the Federals had no intention of bringing on a battle; they just wanted to know where Green was heading. Since the Federal infantry, artillery, and wagons had not crossed the Carencro, they could very well be going to Texas, Taylor thought. The force that had dogged his retreat today was probably merely a feeler to determine *his* intentions.

After mulling over the question, Taylor arrived at his conclusion. Major General Nathaniel P. Banks intended to invade Texas. The commander of the District of West Louisiana returned to his headquarters to write his report to the commander of the Department of the Trans-Mississippi, Lieutenant General Edmund Kirby Smith.

Taylor feared that beyond his vision, and beyond Bayou Vermilion, the Yankees planned to simply sidle—crab like—one hundred miles along the coast of Louisiana until they reached the Sabine River. They could turn Brashear City into a major depot, garrisoned with troops and gunboats, but give up all the country between there and Alexandria. Instead, each estuary and inlet along the Louisiana coast would provide a potential victualing base that could not be cut by Green's cavalry. Light draft transports coming up Bayou Vermilion, the Mermentau River, and the Calcasieu River could renew and refresh the Federal army in its westward invasion.

Taylor also realized the five divisions of the 13th and 19th Army Corps would be tough to beat. Certainly, the enemy would never be foolish enough to split his army. "He may then move his masses well together and render it impossible for me to bring him to action without encountering an overwhelming force," he warned Kirby Smith. Taylor suggested Major General John Bankhead Magruder assemble a mobile force in Texas and send it on a reconnaissance eastward as far as the Calcasieu and Lake Charles to confirm his suspicions. "He could not only materially delay the enemy's movements," Taylor hoped, "but might very likely capture a fleet of supplies or destroy a pontoon train."[3]

Magruder understood. He had already gathered a sizable force of about twenty-five hundred men around Beaumont in response to the Battle of Sabine Pass and sent scouts across the Sabine to make contact with the Yankees, as Taylor suggested. Troopers from the 1st Texas Cavalry even scouted beyond Lake

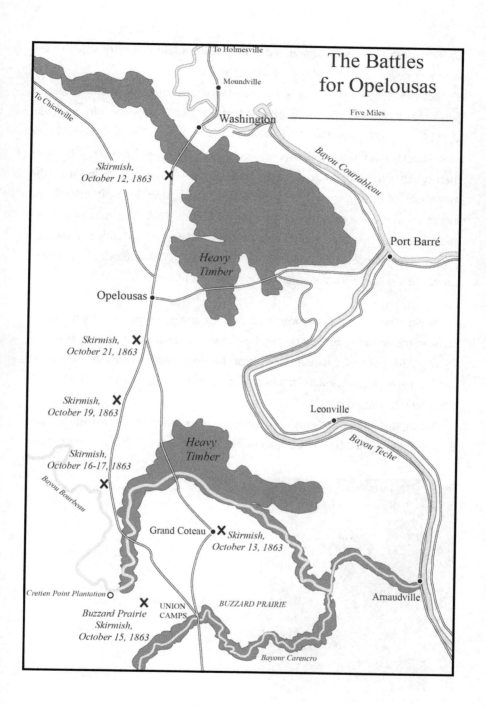

The Battles
for Opelousas

Five Miles

To Holmesville

Moundville

Washington

To Chicotville

Bayou Courtableau

Skirmish,
October 12, 1863 ✘

Port Barré

*Heavy
Timber*

Opelousas

Skirmish, ✘
October 21, 1863

Skirmish, ✘
October 19, 1863

Leonville

*Heavy
Timber*

Bayou Teche

Skirmish, ✘
October 16-17, 1863

Bayou Bourbeau

Grand Coteau ✘ Skirmish,
October 13, 1863

Cretien Point Plantation ○

Arnaudville

✘
Buzzard Prairie
Skirmish,
October 15, 1863

UNION
CAMPS

BUZZARD PRAIRIE

Bayour Carencro

Charles when no Federals appeared and rode an additional forty miles to the Mermentau River, still without contacting the enemy.

Meanwhile, Colonel Augustus Buchel, Magruder's commander in the Eastern Sub-District of Texas, went to work. His first act was to engineer a ferry system at Niblett's Bluff using the small steamer *Dime*. Men and matériel could now pass quickly and reliably between Texas and Louisiana. Enslaved laborers then constructed a plank road in the swampy Sabine bottoms to facilitate the movement of troops to and from the new ferry crossing. He next established a courier line to the telegraph station at Beaumont. To keep any Yankee spies guessing, Buchel ordered commanders at Sabine Pass to constantly parade their troops along the coast so that observers aboard the Union blockading vessels could see the Confederates remained vigilant and in force.[4]

At Vermilionville, a heavy rain soaked both armies overnight. When the sun rose on the morning of October 13, both commands could see standing water all over the prairies between the Bayou Carencro and Opelousas. Certainly, conditions were unfavorable for a heavy advance. Nothing new would be learned until the roads dried out.

During this lull, Banks's major generals Edward Otho Cresap Ord and William B. Franklin realigned the various pieces of the Army of the Gulf according to their

B. W. Varnell, Company B, 1st Texas Cavalry. Library of Congress.

present scheme. The Rebels would probably not make a stand south of Alexandria, especially given that Green had fallen back beyond Bayou Courtableau. The only offensive actions that soggy day were foraging expeditions by Union cavalrymen, and they drove in livestock, poultry, and hay stolen from the farms between Opelousas and Vermilionville. They also quit their positions on Bayou Bourbeau.[5]

To the watching Texans, the Federals seemed to be pulling out. The withdrawal of the Union horsemen and the vanished Federal infantry seemed to confirm Taylor's belief that this invasion, so far, was merely a preamble to a bolder move toward Texas. "Enemy appears to be leaving still," Private William Randolph Howell of the 5th Texas Cavalry scrawled in his diary at the muddy Confederate camp.

The Texan cavalry, intrigued by what they were seeing, moved up and occupied the heavily wooded banks of Bayou Bourbeau where they could watch the Yankees across the wide-open expanse of Buzzard Prairie. The question remained, were the Federals still along the Carencro, or did the trees and the Federal cavalry hide Banks's army slipping away, heading west?[6]

When Taylor's reports arrived in Shreveport, Lieutenant General Kirby Smith considered this possibility. If Banks intended to make a move for Texas, then Kirby Smith advised Taylor to "spare no efforts with the disposable force at your command in retarding his march and in co-operating with General Magruder in the defense of his district." This might mean taking his army into Texas and leaving the Red River Valley open to invasion from the Mississippi Valley. Kirby Smith did not worry much about this possibility. Having learned the particulars and scope of General Braxton Bragg's victory at Chickamauga, Kirby Smith felt convinced this danger had passed. Events in North Georgia had so upset the Union war plans that all available troops would leave the Mississippi Valley and head to eastern Tennessee—as they had. "This result . . . if confirmed, will relieve the department in Louisiana and Arkansas," he wrote Taylor. "You will, I know, exert yourself to co-operate with General Magruder. His district is in all probability to be made the theater of operations this winter."[7]

While Confederate commanders edged toward a consensus about enemy intentions, Union commanders found the evolving plan for Louisiana and Texas agonizingly fluid. With Banks back in New Orleans, the command of the expedition once again shuffled upwards. Franklin held overall command of the expedition while Ord took charge of troops in the field. Banks telegraphed Major General Franklin to ask if he should send Dana's Division to him and to request the hard-fighting troopers of the 1st Texas Cavalry (Union) return to his headquarters. Franklin would comply with the order as soon as he could, but he advised against sending Dana's foot soldiers across Berwick Bay. "I do not think I need another division of infantry," he replied. The Texas Union troops, though, he could not give up. Franklin noted, "This is an uncomfortable place, as the enemy is continually trying to find a weak point in our lines with his cavalry." If Banks wanted to send reinforcements, he should send more cavalry, Franklin advised. Banks could keep Dana and his chewed-up infantry.[8]

As the Union presence sank roots in southern Louisiana, signs indicated local support for the Confederacy seemed to be ebbing away while resentment against Green's Texans flowed. Rebel deserters drifted into the Union positions at Carencro, Vermilionville, and New Iberia daily, as did civilians and Unionists seeking protection. "The prisoners report the Texans in good spirits and determined to fight to the last," wrote a New York reporter. "The Rebel deserters are principally French Creoles, or Arcadians, whom the people of Texas and Louisiana despise for their cowardice and treachery." The presence of Ozémé Carrière and his gangs around Opelousas also terrorized the citizens, who desperately wanted protection from such brigands, outlaws, and ruffians from whichever army—from whichever government—could provide it. If the Federal army would persist in the region, the inhabitants would welcome them enthusiastically, or so they professed.[9]

Brigadier General Green meanwhile resolved to discover Federal intentions. On the evening of October 13, he launched a raid around the Union army. He dispatched Colonel Henry C. McNeil to take the 5th Texas Cavalry, his trustiest regiment, to overrun the enemy outpost at the Jesuit College at Grand Coteau, scatter the Union pickets, and open a path through the Union outposts. He would then fling the 2nd Louisiana, including many men familiar with this part of their state, through the hole to learn what they could of Union movements deep behind the Union right at Bayou Carencro. He sent along a section of Captain Oliver J. Semmes's well-drilled battery to make a stand in case they ran into serious opposition and needed to affect an escape.

The raid succeeded brilliantly. The Texans surprised the Federal cavalry at Grand Coteau as expected. Private Howell boasted matter-of-factly, "we run them out of town and camp about two miles above." With the enemy scattered, Colonel William G. Vincent and his Louisianans barreled through.[10]

The audacious Rebels encountered no serious resistance that evening and reaped a windfall in the dark morning hours of October 14. More than seven miles beyond Bayou Carencro and about three miles from Vermilionville, the Louisianans spied a Union signal station wigwagging messages with a torch from the top cupola of a large plantation home. This was a relay station maintaining communications between the 19th and 13th Army Corps; they were surely chattering about the dustup at Grand Coteau. The Confederates crept into position and, with a flash of artillery, scared away the guards while the cavalry swarmed over the position. The Louisianans snatched up the unsuspecting Union signal corps troops, their equipment, and most importantly their papers. After snipping the telegraph line leading to Franklin's headquarters in Vermilionville, the troops of the 2nd Louisiana and Semmes's Battery hurried off into the remaining darkness with their prizes. They had made enough noise to alert the Federals something was amiss in the gap between their two corps.[11]

Safely away from the Union army, the Rebels examined their prizes. Thumbing through the captured notebooks and folios, Confederate officers discovered all of

Signals being sent at night. *Library of Congress.*

the enemy's ciphers, maps, signals, and codes. They also interrogated prisoners. The captives confirmed Taylor's suspicions that Texas was indeed the object of the campaign, but they made clear this was not the immediate target. Instead, the Federals intended to resume the advance north on two fronts with the entire Army of the Gulf to capture Opelousas and Port Barré simultaneously. Having driven back the Rebels beyond Bayou Courtableau, Franklin would *then* lead the army west.

Couriers carried this news back to Brigadier General Green. Based on this windfall, he could do what he did best: he ordered his men to organize an ambush to buy time for Taylor to formulate a reaction. Huddled behind the screen of the heavily wooded margins of Bayou Bourbeau, the Texans plotted for a chance to waylay the western column when it marched toward Opelousas in the coming daylight hours.

As the sun rose on October 14, the Federals remained in their Carencro bivouac. "All quiet on both roads this morning," Private Howell confided to his journal. He relaxed. "Get a haversack of pork and bread from camp which is quite acceptable, we having eaten nothing for 24 hours."[12]

Frustrated, Green advanced his skirmishers toward the enemy positions hoping to find the enemy pickets and perhaps draw out the enemy cavalry.

Chretien Point Plantation. *Library of Congress.*

Instead, the Federals delivered a bold responded by deploying rifled artillery across the open prairie. It was his answer: the Yankees were still there in force. After the artillery came the supporting Union cavalry. "The skirmish . . . all along the lines, continues sharply until dark when General Green falls back a short distance and camps in a skirt of timber," Howell noted from the banks of Bayou Bourbeau. "Nothing but a horse hunt on our side." That night, Green had a section of rifled cannon of his own shell the Union camps hoping the harassment might precipitate a useful response. It did not.[13]

The next morning, October 15, the Union troops finally began to move. Major General Godfrey Weitzel led the 19th Army Corps beyond Bayou Carencro with his division in front, supported by Brigadier General Cuvier Grover's Division. Major General Stephen Burbridge's division of the 13th Army Corps lay well to the rear with orders to close up on the advance and provide the reserve. The troops advanced on an angle toward Hypolite Chretien's plantation, three miles to the northwest, determined to drive the troublesome Green from his cover by flanking the Texans on their right. Rebel skirmishers dogged Weitzel's advance but fell back steadily, luring the Federals on. The Union advance crossed Buzzard Prairie at a steady pace, bulldozing the Texan skirmish line ahead of it, while constantly sidling to the left. Casualties began mounting as the skirmishing intensified and the outnumbered Texans gave way.

The Battle of Buzzard Prairie. *Frank Leslies Illustrated Newspaper.*

It was all by design. Most of Green's Texans remained hidden on the grounds of the plantation and in the nearby woods, with the Val Verde Battery on the right of their line with the balance of Semmes's Battery on the left.

Weitzel, believing the outnumbered Texans were only covering the retreat of the rest of Green's division, ordered his Federals to advance with gusto toward the Chretien Point Plantation.

Then Green struck. Bagby's Brigade sprang the ambush by boiling out of the woods and rushing the right side of the Union line. Colonel George M. Love's First Brigade of Weitzel's First Division, 19th Army Corps, had seen these ruffians before—many of these same eastern regiments had been roughed up at the Battle of Kock's plantation the previous July. As at that battle, the Federals again took to their heels in the face of the Texan onslaught, hurried along by surprisingly accurate shelling from Semmes's Battery.

The Union reserves, westerners all, held. A countercharge by the ferocious 1st Texas Cavalry (Union) blunted Bagby's advance, then Federal artillery finished the job. "We had another tussle with the Yankees and a little before noon we had to retreat as the Yankees were moving up and making it hot for us," admitted Captain Julius Giesecke of the 4th Texas Cavalry. Federal shells savaged the retreating Texans, one round wounding seven in a single burst. Gunners in the 2nd Massachusetts Battery punished Semmes's Battery as well. "We dismounted one gun and exploded their ammunition chest forcing them to retreat," wrote a Bay State gunner. "A piece of one of our shells cut off the head of one, passed through another, and killed his horse—deadly work."[14]

Weitzel rallied his troops and ordered his unsteady soldiers to stand their ground and advance no farther. He could not be sure what lay beyond Bayou Bourbeau and he would not be goaded into yet another Texan ambush. The Rebels, he believed, seemed too eager for a fight. What were they hiding? Perhaps Taylor had run up his infantry and prepared to pounce just beyond the trees. Weitzel grew uneasy. While he studied the situation, his division lay prone in the open fields. "We did not have a chance to fight," grumbled a soldier in the 28th Massachusetts. "We were under fire from both batteries. We laid in a corn field all day." The prairie stalemate, "a hard fight" one soldier described it, had already killed or wounded nearly twenty Federals.[15]

Weitzel ordered Burbridge to bring up his division of the 13th Army Corps. Since the Rebels had hit the Federal right, perhaps sending the reserves around the left would unhinge their position and force them from their cover. Burbridge needed little urging. "We heard the artillery of the Rebels and prepared to march immediately to the support of the Nineteenth Corps," wrote a soldier in the 96th Ohio. The westerners moved through the ranks of the easterners, determined to press the Rebels and clear the woods.[16]

The Confederates had planned for this. As Burbridge's newcomers rumbled across the grounds of the Chretien Point Plantation, Texans concealed in a creek bottom running perpendicular to Bayou Bourbeau fired a volley at close range that ripped through the ranks of these impetuous Federals. The Rebels saw some prudent Federal officers order their regiments to halt, then fall back to the easterners in the prairie. "That stopped the 'gents' for the day," Howell noted.[17]

The Battle of Buzzard Prairie had been a heavy skirmish. Dozens on both sides had been killed and wounded. But it confirmed that the intelligence gathered from the raid two days before was reliable. Green had done his best to act on it, but the Yankees had in effect spit out the bait and wriggled off the hook. He ordered his Texans back toward Opelousas, yielding the field to his enemies.

The Federals spent the rest of the day making sure the threat had passed. Once again, the Federals halted. They moved no farther than the belt of woods and the big loop of Bayou Bourbeau covering the Opelousas Road and its bridge crossing over the deep ravine. They had advanced perhaps a half dozen miles. Then, the 1st Texas Cavalry (Union), who had done much to save the day for the Federals, bid their comrades farewell. They turned their mounts back toward the south, bound for New Orleans on orders of Major General Banks—despite Franklin's objections.[18]

The plodding Federal advance had not pushed very far into Rebel Louisiana, had not brought Major General Taylor to battle, and had accomplished little of strategic value. Instead, the army continued to shrink, as detachments lay spread out along the line of invasion, garrisoning various towns, protecting supply lines, and remaining in position for the inevitable turn west. The Army of the Gulf barely had enough troops concentrated in one place to challenge the Confederates operating below Alexandria.

As Green had learned, the objective of this slow advance was a triangle of villages—Opelousas, Washington, and Port Barré on Bayou Courtableau—and the reopening of water communications via the bayou to the Upper Teche and Atchafalaya and on to Berwick Bay. Banks had conquered this region the previous April and May, and it had proven good ground then. It would serve as a useful base this time as well. Capturing these towns would provide the Army of the Gulf with options.

Some in the Union army lost patience with the sluggish pace. Major General Ord, West Pointer, friend of Major General Ulysses S. Grant, and veteran of many fast, hard-hitting campaigns, grew tired of what he considered a clumsy, pointless operation run by amateur generals. On October 16, claiming illness, he turned over command of the 13th Army Corps to Major General Cadwallader C. Washburn and headed home to Maryland. His replacement, a Maine native, had moved to Wisconsin and made a fortune in timber before the Civil War. Washburn's wealth and prestige had earned him election to Congress. At the war's outbreak he, like Ord, had risen to a position of importance within Grant's Army of the Tennessee. He distinguished himself in the Vicksburg Campaign. The new commander also had connections: his brother, Elihu Washburn, was a friend of President Abraham Lincoln and one of Grant's strongest supporters.

Major General Cadwallader Colden Washburn was a wealthy industrialist, entrepreneur, and congressman before the war and a gifted administrator. *Library of Congress.*

Brigadier General Camille Armand Jules Marie, Prince de Polignac. A French nobleman and veteran of the Crimean War, he commanded Texans in Louisiana, who lovingly referred to him as "Prince Polecat." *Wikicommons*

Like Ord, the Texans wondered why the Federals did not prosecute the campaign with more vigor. On October 16, troops from the 5th Texas Cavalry picked a fight with the Union pickets around the Rogers Plantation, several miles south of Opelousas, once again trying to bring on a battle or at least learn a little about the enemy positions. After three hours of swapping shots, the Texans decided to see how game the enemy really was. "We . . . send two companies back to a bunch of oaks, dismount," wrote Private Howell. "The remainder of us get 'badly frightened' <u>all at once</u> and run, seemingly for life, up the road, but our 'Yanks' smell a ruse, and won't follow." Even so, Howell noted, Texans captured three of the enemy riders. The prisoners "say they are bound for Texas <u>at dark</u>."[19]

The information gleaned from the captured troopers was not true. Sounds of gunfire started up at first light the next day and rarely abated, so the Texans kept probing. "The enemy made an attack on our pickets this morning about 10 o'clock, but without any result," Major General Franklin reported to Banks back in New Orleans: "We may expect such attacks as long as we stay here." The Rebels were determined to maintain contact. "The theory of the attack, I think, is that they thought we were a rear guard protecting a movement to the westward and thought they could easily beat us and probably take us," Franklin observed. "As soon as they saw infantry, they left, and our artillery helped to send them off."[20]

Based on all Green and his troopers had learned, Taylor changed his mind. The threatened invasion of Texas was mere ruffle and bluff. If it were going to happen, it would have occurred by now. No, the Yankees would head toward Alexandria, he believed, not Houston. Taylor ordered his infantry divisions—those of Brigadier General Alfred Mouton and Major General John G. Walker—to concentrate at Moundville, near Washington.

Taylor also ordered the two Texas regiments at Grand Ecore under Prince Camille de Polignac to head south and join the army. "On account of his foreign and illustrious birth," Captain Felix Pierre Poché observed, the French nobleman and brigadier general "excited a great deal of interest among the troops. He is a light complected man, with blue eyes, sandy hair, rosy cheeks, and almost red whiskers, his size is rather under medium height, and is rather slim." His uniform, consisting of "a small loose grey cloth coat, blue pants and plain boots" seemed unimpressive to the clothes-conscious Louisianan. His chapeau, though, was "a two-cornered hat, 'a la Napoleon,'" and, for Poché, helped to make up for the lack of a spiffy uniform. Taylor commanded him to combine his two regiments of Texans with those of Colonel James Harrison and to command the whole brigade. His Lone Star warriors, skeptical of this fancy newcomer, simply dubbed him "Prince Polecat."[21]

Try as he might, Green had not definitely determined the enemy's true intentions. So, Taylor planned for a battle on ground of his choosing between Washington and Alexandria. His men braced for a fight. "My opinion," speculated Captain George W. O'Brien in the 11th Texas Volunteer Battalion, "is that the enemy are rather occupying General Taylor here intending a demonstration against his rear, or that they have a larger force than is supposed and intend to advance further." The Texas captain shrewdly believed they would take Opelousas, Washington, and Port Barré, fortify them, and *then* decide between Alexandria and Houston.[22]

As had become the custom, Brigadier General Green and his men prepared to precipitate the battle. Colonel R. B. Hubbard of the 22nd Texas Infantry attended a meeting of the army's officers and met Green for the first time. Hubbard had believed the rumors Green was impetuous and often picked a fight for no good purpose. The men of Harrison's Brigade had been shot up at Sterling's plantation for very little gain on the enemy; they resented the cavalry for not doing its part. After meeting Green, Hubbard changed his mind. "It is said [Green] was mad and reckless, but such criticism is most unjust," he concluded. "I met him . . . near the city of Washington, in Louisiana. How cool and calm he was then in counsel. How calmly he talked, seeking council with his officers in the weary vigils of night." The Texas cavalry chief was no madman. If anything, he was a careful planner.[23]

Taylor relied on Green to organize and execute, his usual tactic when the Yankees came. First, Taylor would place the Confederate infantry and artillery on ground of his liking and form a battle line. Then, the plan went, Green would lure the enemy into the ambush.

Learning the Union threat from Pointe Coupee had vanished and the Federals there had headed to New Orleans, Taylor ordered his army to move about fifteen miles north, up Bayou Beouf, secure in the knowledge this enemy force would not ascend the Red River and drop in on his rear. His troops dug fieldworks facing south on the east bank of the Beouf, a span of open ground providing excellent fields of fire. His army was now between Holmesville and Washington, where he could react to a Federal push toward Alexandria via the Teche, the most likely threat, or one along Bayou des Glaises and the Red River to the east.

The Yankees might choose to come straight at him. Taylor protected his flanks in a swath of swamps and canebreaks on his left while Bayou Beouf protected his right. A side road to his rear traversed this difficult terrain and connected to Big Cane in the east. The tangles of the Cocodrie Swamp would discourage any Union attempts to bypass the position west of his line. In front of his chosen ground, drainage ditches and fences crossed open fields, providing cover for the eleven thousand Rebel infantry and creating impediments to a Union assault. The narrowness of the field also constricted the approach, meaning the Rebels could grind up each Yankee Division in turn as it advanced. The weight of Confederate artillery, seven batteries mounting more than thirty guns, would riddle their ranks with shell and canister. Taylor directed the 13th Texas Cavalry (Dismounted) to support Green near Opelousas and stiffen their line in case the enemy pushed too hard.[24]

If the enemy headed toward Texas, Taylor concluded, there would be little his army could do to oppose them. If they instead were bound for the heart of

Louisiana, he would not yield his home state without a fight. On October 18, Taylor passed through his infantry on his way to the front. "He is a son of old 'Rough and Ready,'" observed Private J. P. Blessington of the 16th Texas Infantry. "He has a good record of past services under Stonewall Jackson in Virginia. Owing to his arrival in camp," Blessington pointed out, "the troops anticipated being brought into action every day."[25]

Much lay at stake. The country from Washington to Alexandria that bordered Bayou Beouf remained largely unspoiled by war. When Banks had passed that way twice the previous spring—once heading north, the other heading back toward the Mississippi—his men had been too fatigued and too hurried to spend much time plundering. The Federals had also not been as deliberate in gathering slaves as they had farther south. As a result, crops, houses, and tools remained largely intact, and many slaves remained on the area plantations. "There are a great many large and beautiful sugar and cotton plantations on Bayou Boeuf, and the traveling is in consequence more agreeable than in the Attakapas region, I think," Poché noted. "I think, upon the whole that, after Lafourche, the Bayou Boeuf region is the prettiest interior country that I have seen in Louisiana."[26]

Taylor arrived in Opelousas to check his pickets and seek news of the Federal army. On October 19, Taylor learned the enemy was clearly heading for the Red River Valley, not Texas. Patrols sent to the Mermentau to link up with those coming from Texas returned, reporting no Yankees in sight. "They report all quiet on the Texas roads," reported one scout to Lieutenant General Kirby Smith. "The enemy's whole army," Taylor concluded, "was in my immediate front."[27]

Taylor was mostly correct in his latest assessment of the Union position, but the true answer remained far more complicated. In actuality, Banks and the Army of the Gulf lay strewn from Opelousas to New Orleans, overwhelmed by the trinity of their orders: "plant the flag in Texas," raise African American regiments, and secure Louisiana. Between Franklin's field army and Banks's headquarters, outposts of quartermasters, commissary officers, provosts marshals, signal stations, and recruiters raising troops for the Corps d'Afrique operated in busy nodes along the tracks of the New Orleans, Opelousas, and Great Western Railroad, along Berwick Bay, along Bayou Teche, and across Bayou Vermilion.

Curiously, Dana and his 2nd Division, 13th Army Corps, had returned to New Orleans and now lay idle. True to his exchange with Franklin, Banks kept them in the city. He had other plans for them.

Major General Franklin, meanwhile, labored under opaque orders. He had sent Weitzel out from his camps on Bayou Carencro while believing Opelousas to be the next objective and Port Barré to be a forward base of supply. But a dispatch arrived at his headquarters indicating Banks no longer cared about Port Barré; New Iberia would remain the logistics hub for the campaign. Franklin fumed at the news. The steamer *Red Chief* had already started for Port Barré via the Atchafalaya and Bayou Courtebleau and could not be recalled. It was heading straight into Rebel hands. Then messages arrived directing Franklin to proceed as planned to Opelousas and Port Barré.[28]

Released from the tension of trying to ascertain his orders, Franklin prepared to uncoil his army. On the afternoon of October 19, he ordered Colonel John G. Fonda to take his mounted brigade, including the 1st Louisiana (Union), portions of the 6th Missouri and 14th New York Cavalries, and the newly converted 118th Illinois Mounted Infantry, toward Opelousas to find the enemy. Franklin would support them with two infantry regiments, the 23rd Wisconsin and the 32nd Indiana, and a pair of artillery batteries.

Colonel John G. Fonda, 118th Illinois. *The Zouave Archives.*

The Confederates opened fire within minutes of their enemy's leaving their camps at the crossing of Bayou Bourbeau. While the Rebels could not fully appreciate the complexity of the Yankee invasion, Taylor, conferring with Green in a camp south of Opelousas, could clearly see the enemy before him. Heavy skirmishing the rest of the afternoon reinforced Taylor's conviction that Louisiana, not Texas, was the true objective of this campaign. He ordered three infantry regiments to leave their outpost at Moundville and rotate up to Green's lines to lend a hand.[29]

The developing skirmish centered on the road near the sugarhouse at the Hudson Plantation. Colonel James P. Major's Texas horsemen continued to work around the Union left flank, unanchored as they were on the prairies to the west. "After a pretty warm engagement for some two hours," wrote Sergeant H. N. Connor, we "succeeded in forcing their support back upon the batteries." Dismounted cavalry and the rifled muskets of the 13th Texas Infantry presented a beefy appearance to the Federals. "This rather dampened their ardor," Connor continued, "and fearing perhaps that we had been reinforced, their batteries fell back to their old position that they had occupied the day before."[30]

Isaac Yost, Company C, 118th Illinois. *Library of Congress.*

For Private Thomas E. Mix of the 118th Illinois Mounted Infantry, this was his first taste of mounted service. "Came near to being surrounded," he wrote in his diary, "but got out of the scrape."[31]

Rebels crowed that the Federals had gained no ground. "We made a stand and succeeded in checking the advance of the Yankees," boasted Captain Julius Giesecke, 4th Texas Cavalry. After the fight, which had killed or wounded about forty men on each side, the victorious Texans swept the field for enemy stragglers. "Found a Yankee squad in a potato patch," Connor added, "and after a lively chase, our squadron captured 1 captain, 1 sergeant and 6 privates."[32]

Once again, the Federals became inert, spending October 20 in their camps along Bayou Bourbeau. They outnumbered Green's cavalry twice over and deployed far more artillery. Why did they not fight? Their cavalry had been adequate, sometimes skillful, but the Yankees seemed uninterested in renewing the contest.

Little transpired that Tuesday, as some Confederates commented in their writings. "Went into camps and laid down to sleep," noted Captain Giesecke. "The day passed very quietly, only a few shots were heard from the outposts." Colonel Major ordered some of his troopers to swing far out to the west of Opelousas to make sure the Federals had not communicated with Carrière and his bandits. "Sent to catch jayhawkers," Connor scribbled into his journal. "Found their nest, but no birds in it."[33]

The people of Opelousas, though, feared a battle would be fought in the streets of their town. While the armies eyed each other five miles to the south, news of the nearby presence of the Union army prompted many residents to move their property—including their slaves—out of the way. "The town is like a small sea, swept by a storm," noted a local minister. Caravans of civilians headed northwest toward Ville Platte, seeking safety.[34]

The Federals had good reasons for remaining quiet that day. Major General Franklin took time to meet with his officers to plot the destruction of Green's Texans and thus eliminate the greatest challenge to moving freely across the prairies of south Louisiana. Franklin wanted the troops around Opelousas to continue to keep Green's attention. Meanwhile, he positioned a fast strike force of his best-mounted troopers to try to cut off Green's men from the rest of Taylor's army by pushing to the east, through Port Barré, and then northwest along Bayou Courtableu to Washington. Franklin's heavy infantry columns would take Opelousas and trap Green between these forces. The pesky Texans would have to skedaddle up the Ville Platte road to survive, putting an impassible swamp between him and the rest of the Confederate forces. Taylor's command would be sundered, and his army blind. He would have to abandon his works and retreat to Cheneyville to reunite his forces or face overwhelming odds—two infantry divisions to five.

On October 21, the Federals emerged from an early morning fog and fell on Green in a massive blue avalanche. "Enemy advancing in force," Sergeant Connor wrote near Opelousas. "Had a very sharp little skirmish fight with them but 'tis no use. They outnumber us two to one and more." As the northerners advanced, soldiers from the *Corps d'Afrique* formed into line as well, "singing at the tops of their voices," observed a soldier in the 83rd Ohio, "'John Brown's body lies moldering in the grave.'" Under heavy fire from small arms and artillery, the Texans attempted to defend a line along Bayou Tesson three miles south of Opelousas. Then, word arrived that Yankee cavalry had been spotted near Port Barré. Taylor understood his peril and ordered his troops to fall back toward Moundville in a hurry, but not in a panic.[35]

Couriers arrived in the Confederate infantry camps along Bayou Beouf and spread the alarm that the Federals were pressing Green and his cavalry. "Everything in commotion," wrote Louisiana captain Arthur W. Hyatt of the Confederate Guards Response Battalion. "Tents struck and we await the order to move." The news sent a ripple through the various camps, and men and animals scurried about. "A fight or a footrace," Hyatt continued, "I don't know which yet." Just down the battle line, Colonel George Flournoy received orders to take his 16th Texas Infantry to Green's assistance.[36]

The fighting escalated that afternoon as the Federals fed reinforcements into the drive through Opelousas. Union and Confederate battle lines crisscrossed the farms and fields between the armies in an intricate but deadly dance. "The Federals began marching slowly toward us and we constantly retreated slowly [away]," wrote Private Joseph Faust, 7th Texas Cavalry. "We exchanged shots constantly with the enemy on long distances until they brought up their cannons."[37]

Constant harassment also kept the Union army on edge. "We had to be practically in line of battle the whole time," observed Sergeant T. B. Marshall of Company K, 83rd Ohio. "On this day we marched in column by division, thus enabling the whole brigade to form a line of battle in a moment."[38]

The Confederates found the Union troops grinding forward the entire day, pushing through Opelousas hard on the Texans' heels. Colonel Major and his brigade, to make room on the road, headed northwest up the Ville Platte road to Chicot, "a collection of four or five miserable huts, a tavern, and a store." Bagby's Brigade and the two Texas infantry regiments scampered through Washington and across Bayou Courtableau, just ahead of the Yankee mounted column coming from Port Barré. "Green's Brigade went up the Moundville road," Sergeant Connor reported. "Here a party of 2,000 men (Yankees) came near cutting that brigade off." Lieutenant Colonel Edwin Waller's Texas Battalion, arriving late, found their way to safety blocked. They turned their horses toward the Ville Platt road to get away.[39]

Franklin's forces had neither bagged the Texas horsemen nor completely cut them off from the main Confederate army but his troops had moved swiftly and split them up. Federal cavalry followed them as far as the enemy outposts north of Moundville before falling back.

"Just as I suspected," groused Captain Hyatt, "a foot race! We left camp today in a devil of a hurry." The men of the 4th, 5th, and 7th Texas cavalry had fought and retreated twenty miles that day, ending their exhausting journey at Big Cane around midnight. Surely the battle for south Louisiana would occur soon, the Confederates believed. "Every minute seemed an hour to us, till the ball should be opened," Private Blessington of the 16th Texas Infantry wrote. Green's cavalry division, spent and split as it was, would have to leave the fighting to Walker's and Mouton's foot soldiers.[40]

After the fighting on October 21, Taylor believed he had finally teased out the enemy's intentions. Texas may have been the original aim of the campaign, Taylor conceded, but plans had clearly changed. The attack at Sabine Pass was to have been the first step in a two pronged-invasion. The troops landed in Pointe Coupee were to have moved between Taylor and his line of retreat toward Alexandria. Banks had intended to hem Green and Mouton between these three forces and drive Taylor's Rebels into the inhospitable Calcasieu country. The Confederate victories at Sabine Pass and Sterling's plantation had upended the Yankee plan, Taylor supposed, forcing the enemy to change his campaign.

His intelligence revealed another development that might impact the strategic balance in Louisiana. The withdrawal of Confederate cavalry from Mississippi to serve in Georgia and Tennessee freed up the Union troops at Natchez, and especially Vicksburg, to operate west of the Mississippi River. He now looked for danger from three directions. "I shall watch the Texas road closely, as well as Simmesport and the Atchafalaya," he wrote Kirby Smith.[41]

Taylor expected the decisive battle for Louisiana to occur soon. In preparation, he led a march to maintain contact with the Federals lest they surprise him with another sudden rush. He accompanied Colonel Oran M. Roberts and a provisional brigade composed of the 11th, 15th, and 18th Texas Infantry in a reconnaissance in force back to Washington. What he saw worried him. The Federals appeared to be bridging Bayou Courtableau at Barré's Landing with the intention of bypassing his ambush above Moundville and moving around his left flank along the Big Cane road. Meanwhile, a second force would move through Ville Platte and bypass his position around his right flank. These two wings of the Union army would concentrate behind him with supply lines running along the Red River to the Mississippi. "I think that all thought of the enemy moving to Texas now may be dismissed," he assured Kirby Smith, "unless after first marching up the valley of Red River to Shreveport." Taylor sent orders for officers to move his hospitals and supplies from Alexandria to Natchitoches. He believed he had been outfoxed.[42]

For the time being, though, the Federals did little to vindicate such a lofty belief in their prowess. For the next two days, the Army of the Gulf camped in two parts, forming a seven-mile line from Opelousas in the west to Port Barré in the east. A thunderstorm and cold front whipped through on October 23, and once again the Federal army waited for the roads to dry.

Taylor took this reprieve to move his army up Bayou Beouf toward Holmesville and from there to Evergreen on Bayou Huffpower. From this new position, Taylor could pivot west and cover the Ville Platt road to Alexandria, face south to

Union columns crossing the prairies north of Vermilionville. *Frank Leslies Illustrated Newspaper.*

confront a direct approach by Franklin up Bayou Beouf or turn east and counter an invasion via Big Cane or the Red River.[43]

At this critical point in the campaign, Franklin was just as flumoxed as Taylor, and asked for clear directions from Union headquarters. Should he press on until he made contact with the enemy and bring on a battle, or should he fall back to a point where he could feed his horses and keep the wagons carrying the food for his troops safe? Were his men operating in the cold rain to destroy the Confederate army in Louisiana, or was this all an elaborate show meant to confound the enemy and buy time to face left and invade Texas? He wrote to Banks's chief of staff, Brigadier General Charles Pomeroy Stone: "Shall be very glad to get definite instructions."[44]

Franklin thought moving against Taylor would bring nothing but trouble. His lines of supplies would get longer, and he would have to detach troops to guard it, leaving little clumps of isolated outposts that might easily fall prey to any marauding cavalry that worked their way around his army. The Confederates, meanwhile, drew nearer to their base of supplies. A move toward Texas now would uncover the Union line of communications and potentially open the Teche country—Vermilionville, New Iberia, and Franklin—to recapture by Taylor. If Banks envisioned a move overland toward Texas now, it would be a delicate and intricate matter.[45]

Franklin and his twenty-five thousand troops had taken thirteen days to cover the forty miles between Vermilionville and Opelousas, but now they could not easily move forward or backward. As rain drenched the Federal troops, they settled in for what they believed would be a long stay. The troops foraged and plundered throughout the neighborhood. "We exercised our enterprise by gathering together a vast supply of sugar, molasses, and corn," wrote Surgeon J. T. Woods of the 96th Ohio. Nearby, another Buckeye regiment made itself at home. "We went into camp in a pecan grove and we used all the nuts we could club from the numerous trees," Sergeant Marshall of the 83rd Ohio wrote. The Midwesterners had outpaced their camp equipment and had no canvas to protect them from the showers. The soldiers raided a nearby shed holding great piles of dried cowhides to make roofs over their blankets. "These were all right and afforded us a good shelter," Marshall continued, "but when water soaked, our olfactories were compelled to do extra duty."[46]

Then Franklin's army grew peckish. Commissary officers had hoped the transport *Red Chief* would soon arrive with provisions. After all, this was one of the reasons Franklin had pressed on to Port Barré instead of falling back to Bayou Carencro. The water route to Berwick Bay, he learned, remained too low and the vessel had instead turned around. Franklin, now tethered to a wagon supply line, knew without a doubt he could go no further until the roads dried out. In fact, he preferred heading no farther north, ever, if it could be helped. He had two week's rations for the men, but forage for his army of animals remained problematic, and the swampy country he would have to pass through promised no solution. Better grass could be found at New Iberia or by moving back toward the Mississippi. He sent out his mounted troops to gather in what food they could and extend the time he could spend in the region. "Get plenty of sweet potatoes," wrote Private Mix of the 118th Illinois Mounted Infantry. "We live on them nearly."[47]

Any position in south Louisiana would be better than the one his forces occupied, Franklin believed. Now he was stuck.

TWELVE   **THE HOUSTON CAMPAIGN**

It is desirable that the enemy should still regard
the movement in your direction as the real one.

—Brigadier General Charles Pomeroy Stone
Chief of Staff, Department of the Gulf

ajor General Nathaniel P. Banks was not worried about Major General
William B. Franklin or his conundrum. Banks worried about Texas.

In mid-October the troopers of the 1st Texas Cavalry (Union), which had done excellent service in the campaign so far, arrived in New Orleans. There, these men learned Colonel Edmund J. Davis would be leading them back to their home state to rally Unionists to the flag. "Won't some of my Texans friends and enemies get waked up," crowed a Lone Star loyalist serving as an official with the U.S. Treasury Department in New Orleans. "I have already contracted to have one man . . . hanged and whether I ask it, or try and prevent it, I think it will be done anyhow. We have a regiment of refugee Texans here, and when they get back, won't they make the fur fly." There would be other troops heading to Texas as well. Major General Napoleon J. T. Dana's 2nd Division, 13th Army Corps, which had relocated to New Orleans after the bruising at Sterling's plantation, would go.[1]

Banks would attempt another landing on Texas soil. While Franklin pinned Major General Richard Taylor to the Red River, Banks would put Dana's Division ashore at the mouth of the Rio Grande and reoccupy the old U.S. base at Brazos Santiago Island. Davis and his Texans would provide the sabers and saddles needed for an effective showing in south Texas.

At Camp Carrollton, Banks organized a dress parade and review of the 2nd Division, then Dana followed with an address revealing this secret scheme to the rank and file. "After dress parade, three cheers for General Dana and the Rio

Grande' gave us to know what was before us," remembered Private Henry Carl Ketzle of the 37th Illinois.[2]

Banks's surprise plan simply reprised his campaign outline of September. Dana's two brigades would "plant the flag in Texas" as directed, but at a point where Banks thought they might have the greatest immediate impact in intimidating the French in Mexico. In addition, these troops could sever the Confederate Trans-Mississippi cotton trade and begin the strangulation of Lieutenant General Edmund Kirby Smith's wartime economy by effectively controlling the Rio Grande. Confederate war matériel would once again have to sneak past the Union blockaders. The French—the great boogeyman who had worried President Abraham Lincoln and General-in-Chief Henry W. Halleck the

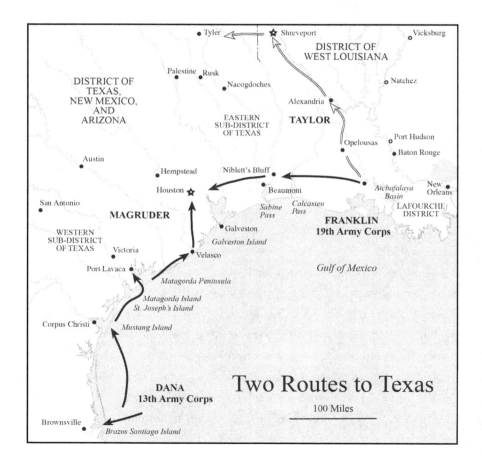

past summer—would see thousands of U.S. troops on the Mexican border and be inclined to mind their meddling.

Having established a toehold, Banks would then implement a second phase. He would take Houston. Reinforcing Dana's Division from Louisiana with other elements of the 13th Army Corps, his troops would hopscotch up the Texas coast, seizing the rough frontier hamlets and muddy inlets that sustained the Confederate traffic on the western Gulf of Mexico. These moves would probably provoke a battle somewhere near the mouth of the Colorado River at Matagorda Bay or the mouth of the Brazos River at Velasco. Once the Rebels had been driven from this defensive line, Banks would create a magazine of supplies on the Texas coast and link it by sea to New Orleans. Franklin's army, having kept the Rebels busy in Louisiana, would establish similar bases on Bayou Teche—either at Vermilionville or New Iberia—and as the Rebels had long feared, crab-walk west along the Louisiana coast toward Houston, establishing new bases as they went.

If Franklin could not force a battle, perhaps Taylor could be defeated without a fight. The Confederates in Texas and Louisiana, faced with threats east and west, would face few good choices. One possibility was that Taylor might reoccupy the Teche region as Banks and Franklin feared, and as had been done the previous June, but this would be a hollow victory. The region, stripped of supplies by months of Union occupation, could not sustain his forces. Another dash across Berwick Bay, as Taylor had done the previous June, would be unlikely since the U.S. Navy promised plenty of gunboat protection for Brashear City. The post had been heavily fortified since the summer's disaster and remained strongly garrisoned, in part by regiments of the *Corps d'Afrique*. The other option open to the Rebels, and the one Taylor long believed he would have to take, would be a retreat into Texas in preparation for a decisive battle for Houston—and the Trans-Mississippi.

Word of Banks's ambitions traveled fast. In Texas, Major General John Bankhead Magruder believed he had parsed together what was about to happen from the scraps of information trickling in from Louisiana. He felt squeezed. "With a force on the coast threatening Houston, and my movable troops available to meet Banks on the Sabine not being more than 6,000 or 7,000 men at the most," he wrote, "should I fall back before Banks, he will reach Houston. Should I not

Brigadier General Albert Lee was a justice of the
Kansas Supreme Court before the war. *Library of Congress.*

do so, the force from the coast will reach Houston." The Confederates gave the
Federals too much credit for being able to conduct such a coordinated campaign
over hundreds of miles of land and sea.[3]

On the day Banks announced his plan to the men who would be landing in
Texas, Franklin seemed oblivious to anything other than the 2nd Division, 13th
Army Corps, was heading toward Brownsville, Texas. He proceeded with his
orders as though Taylor's army remained the only Union priority and Franklin
figured he would eventually fight the three threadbare Rebel divisions with his
five Federal divisions. On the frosty morning of October 24, Franklin ordered
Brigadier General Albert Lee to take his small cavalry division, make contact with
the Rebels, and see how far up Bayou Beouf they had gone. The horse soldiers
found an enemy screen nine miles beyond Washington, Louisiana. "It is the
opinion of General Lee . . . that the whole force is retreating as fast as it can
toward Alexandria," Franklin reported to Banks's chief of staff, Brigadier General
Charles Pomeroy Stone. "It consists of cavalry and infantry." Franklin concluded
the chance for landing a damaging blow to Taylor and his Confederates had
passed. "It is useless," he admitted, "to march this large force any farther with
any expectation of getting a fight from the enemy. There is absolutely nothing
within reach." He recalled his cavalry to Opelousas and Port Barré.[4]

Taylor, however, was not through with Franklin. The scuffle with Lee's Union cavalry, coupled with the testimony of prisoners taken near Opelousas, convinced Taylor he understood the murky Union war plan well enough to see an opportunity. Since the Red River was clearly the key, Magruder should send his best troops from Texas to Louisiana so that Taylor could use the combined army to crush Franklin that fall or winter—before the spring rise in the Red and Mississippi Rivers brought the U.S. Navy and possible reinforcements into play. Anticipating Magruder's objections, Taylor explained to Kirby this plan would protect Texas best: Franklin would not dare weaken his front to send troops to reinforce Dana; if he did, so much the better, as Taylor's reinforced army would demolish Franklin's shrinking forces.[5]

Taylor suggested the time for a decisive battle had arrived and his views were correct. "We have beaten the enemy is several skirmishes, taking prisoners. He, however, declines any serious engagement unless he has his whole force in hand." Taylor reported no movement overland toward Texas. "All the recent prisoners say the expedition is going to Alexandria and Shreveport." Magruder sent word to Kirby Smith arguing otherwise and wrote Taylor he believed an amphibious expedition to Texas was imminent. Taylor dismissed Magruder's objection, telling Kirby Smith, "I think no movement to Texas is possible."[6]

Lieutenant General Kirby Smith was inclined to agree with his Louisiana subordinate. If Taylor was right and the Red River would be the Federal invasion route, Kirby Smith would concentrate the entire Confederate Army of the Trans-Mississippi somewhere near Natchitoches, drawing troops from Major General Sterling Price in Arkansas and Magruder in Texas to give Taylor some heft in the fight. He directed Magruder to weaken his coastal garrisons, concentrate at Niblett's Bluff, and send troops through the East Texas piney woods toward Natchitoches.

Should Taylor be wrong—if Texas remained in peril by an overland movement along the coast road from New Iberia—Magruder's breakaway force could oppose the Federal advance by defending the Calcasieu and the Sabine. Kirby Smith flattered Magruder, directing him to command this force in the field. "Under your command," Kirby Smith wrote, "your Texans will fight to the death, and that with Taylor's force and the re-enforcements from [Arkansas] and those you can bring or send, we will not only destroy the enemy column venturing up Red River, but will decide the fate of the department for the next twelve months."[7]

Still, Kirby Smith hedged a bit, realizing Franklin and Banks might have bamboozled Taylor. "The movements of the enemy in your front make it probable that Alexandria is their objective point, but they have not sufficiently developed their plans to decide certainly upon their true lines of intentions," he chided Taylor. After all, Magruder's cavalry scouts had recently spied a pontoon bridge heading for the Mermentau River. Despite Taylor's convictions he knew what Banks was thinking, might Franklin have simply pushed the Rebels as far north as possible to ensure the success of a dash west, involving crossing three major streams and the relocation of the Federal base of supplies? In any event, Kirby Smith had taken stock of Franklin and declared him so sluggish that the Confederates would probably have time to respond, no matter what the plan of invasion turned out to be. If the enemy advanced up the Red River, he lectured Taylor, they would never be so foolish as to do so before the spring rise. Even so, Kirby Smith issued orders to assemble an appropriate army.[8]

Franklin, though, had no intention of moving up the Red River. The weather had turned cold and wet, and the roads upon which his supply wagon depended began to fail. He believed he could stay in his current positions and feed his men by relays of wagons from New Iberia, but he also faced an acute shortage of forage for his animals. No grass—no horses. No horses—no wagons. No wagons—no supplies. "A move somewhere must be made soon," Franklin insisted. Either south or east, but not north or west. "I think we must get nearer to New Iberia or the Mississippi River."[9]

Franklin worked the problem over in his head, and he reached his own conclusion. "There is difficulty in sweeping the country between the Teche and Mississippi from this point as a base," he decided. "The bayous are hard to cross and a rain makes the road impracticable." If Texas remained the true objective, then it made no sense to fall back across the Atchafalaya River at Morganza and Simmesport. "New Iberia," he declared, "would be a better point to start from than any point farther to the front." Not only were the Rebels confused, but so were Franklin's own men. Was this campaign to be an advance to battle, which

Franklin thought impractical? Or was it a defense of the Atchafalaya Line so that some of the Army of the Gulf troops could be fed into a Texas campaign?[10]

Taylor convinced himself he knew Franklin's plans better than the enemy did. He moved his skittish army to new camps and rested, believing the Yankee flood had crested for the time being. Many of his men rejoiced, assuming the campaign might be drawing to a conclusion for the season. "The weather is a little better," observed Texas Captain Julius Giesecke. "Our regiment was placed in the Negro quarters of an old deserted farm, and we began to hope that it was to be our winter quarters." Another German, seventeen-year-old Private Joseph Faust of the 7th Texas Cavalry, imbibed with his friends, relieved the grinding campaign of endless picket fights had ended. "We are quite merry," he wrote home. Captain Arthur W. Hyatt turned thirty-one years old in his new camp near Holmesville on October 26. "A very sorry day it is too—cold, cloudy, and dismal indeed," he groused. "No birthday dinner for me—no turkey, no wine, no nothing but corn bread and old beef, of which I am heartily tired of." At least they had quit marching.[11]

Franklin's Union army ended its invasion at Bayou Courtableau. His cavalry scouted and scoured the country around Opelousas to make sure the Rebels remained on the defensive, to encourage local Unionists, and to strip the land of food and fodder to fuel their army. On October 26 troopers from the 1st Louisiana Cavalry (Union) skirmished with troops from the 2nd Louisiana Cavalry near Ville Platt. These Confederates, a mere rearguard, easily gave way. Now the region lay open and unprotected and Federal foragers went to work gathering what they could instead of pursuing the enemy.

The lackluster Yankee invasion of Louisiana grew inert in the cold, wet days of late October, allowing Taylor to double-check his theory about Federal intentions. Texan and Louisianan scouts, operating from Washington and Ville Platt, kept the enemy camps at Opelousas and Port Barré under observation, but revealed the Federals at Morganza had disappeared. Taylor worried they might be heading for a rendezvous with Franklin's command. Green sent Captain Leander McNelly and a detachment of picked troops to scour the road leading from Port Barré to Morgan's Ferry and Simmesport. "Find no Yankees either!"

Foraging. *Harper's Weekly*.

cheered Private William Randolph Howell of the 5th Texas. The Texas cavalrymen lingered there for the next two damp days to make sure. It became clear
the imminent threat of an attack up the Red River Valley had faded.[12]

Finally, Franklin ordered his army to retrace its steps. He still did not know
the scope of Banks's Texas expedition, or his role in it, but he started to move
portions of his army back toward the south. He decided that, given the length
of his supply lines and the poor roads, he would reestablish his line at Bayou
Carencro with his headquarters and reserves at Vermilionville. The telegraph line
would reconnect him to New Orleans so he could get better instructions from
Banks. He also learned the 13th Army Corps would have its third commander in
as many weeks. Dispatches announced Major General Dana would assume that
role in a few days with his headquarters in Texas.

This news, perhaps intended to confuse the Rebels, also confused Franklin.
Major General Cadwallader C. Washburn, miffed at this turn of events and his
perceived demotion, returned to command the forces of the 3rd Division and
4th Division, 13th Army Corps, and the cavalry brigade around Port Barré,
Washington, and Opelousas. He had once led the vanguard of the Army of the

Gulf into the interior of Louisiana, and he would now lead them as the rear guard as the army fell back to Carencro. The men of the Army of the Gulf, a bit at a time, left their camps and plodded back the way they had come. Starting on October 29, two days of cold rains soaked the columns, turning the prairies and roads to mud, adding to their misery.[13]

To stretch their supplies, the Federals continued to ransack the farms and fields in the area. "Our boys continue to forage and come into camp loaded down with poultry, pigs, hogs, sugar and honey," trumpeted a newspaper reporter. At one residence west of Opelousas, soldiers from the 1st Louisiana Cavalry (Union) "began a pillage that the Devil himself would blush at," one local observed. "Everything fell before them. They loaded 10 wagons and any number of horses. I had rather be [dead] than linked to such devils."[14]

Colonel John G. Fonda's Union cavalry continued to scoop up anything useful, but their wanderings left these horsemen scattered among the area's farms and plantations. Soldiers from the 2nd Louisiana Cavalry responded, overrunning a detachment of foragers on the Ville Platt road on October 30 and collaring thirteen of the Federals as prisoners. Infantrymen pausing in Opelousas turned out to keep the Rebels at a distance and to provide cover for the scattered mounted detachments to assemble safely in town. The Confederates shied away, pursued by the rallied Union horse soldiers, who came away empty-handed. "Could not find any rebs," complained Captain Samuel Gordon of the 118th Illinois Mounted Infantry. "The scamps . . . crawled into their hiding places. We returned to camp about sunset, tired, wet, cold, and hungry." The following day, the Union horsemen struck back, pushing up the road to Washington, driving a body of Confederate infantry under Colonel Oran M. Roberts across Bayou Courtableau to Moundville. Clearly the Rebels would not let the Yankees leave peacefully.[15]

By November 1, having purchased a little breathing room, General Franklin continued to collapse his army southward toward his base at Vermilionville. The 1st Division, 13th Army Corps, left Opelousas and marched straight to New Iberia. The two divisions of the 19th Army Corps, along with a brigade of cavalry and the heavy siege guns, reoccupied Vermilionville about a dozen miles south of the Carencro. The two brigades of Brigadier General George McGinnis's 3rd Division, 13th Army Corps, finally left Port Barré, covered by a screen of cavalry

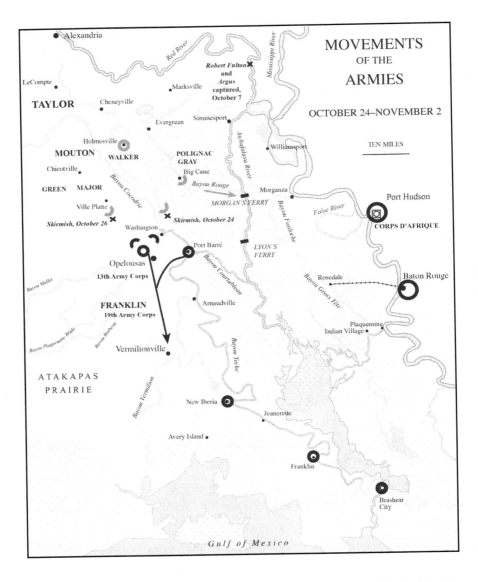

and mounted infantry commanded by Colonel Fonda. The infantry headed for the old camps at Bayou Carencro, and the horsemen fanned out to cover the retreat.

The last Federals to leave Opelousas were the infantry of the 2nd Brigade, 4th Division, commanded by Major General Stephen Burbridge. These troops would serve as the reserve for the cavalry rearguard and mind the road crossing at Bayou Bourbeau. Should the Rebels pursue, which they might, this command could come to the rescue of the Union cavalry, fend off the Confederates, and call for reinforcements from the two infantry brigades positioned at Bayou Carencro.[16]

The Confederates, having been clubbed back from following too close, remained ignorant of the Federal movements for several days. The cold rains that ruined the roads for the Federals also kept the Confederates in camp. "Remained in camp, mud and water," wrote Private Howell at Evergreen. The weather did not break until October 31. "Remained in our quarters all day," noted Captain Giesecke. "The weather was beautifully clear but very cold. We received molasses and, as we had plenty of appropriated sugar, had a grand candy pulling and eating at night." Officers took advantage of the break in the weather to order men from the various regiments to head to Alexandria to fetch the camp equipage for their commands. Taylor clearly believed the Federals would spend the winter in Opelousas. He was wrong. They had gone, and he did not know it.[17]

General Franklin had engineered a successful retreat. He and his staff reestablished their headquarters at Ile Copal on the banks of Bayou Vermilion, intending to leave the Opelousas country between Bayou Carencro and Bayou Courtebleau as something of a disputed zone between U.S. and Confederate authority. Perhaps the Rebels would busy themselves hunting Ozémé Carrière's people and forgo harassing his army. Franklin would maintain his position in Lafayette Parish until he received further instructions from Banks.

The true sentiments of the Louisianans Franklin encountered remained mysterious. While the Federal troops slogged back to Vermilionville, officers tried to interpret the political leanings of the local population. Union officers reported a sizable portion of the inhabitants of South Louisiana was ready to rise up and resist the secessionists. Some believed Franklin could raise one thousand men from the citizens of Vermilionville, Opelousas, and the region with the assistance of key leaders like Carrière. This vision seemed to harmonize with Banks's views and what General Franklin had reported earlier, on his march up to Opelousas. Carrière and the Clan should be the nucleus of a brigade of mounted Louisiana partisans. "Offer commissions to men who are leaders, and those who enlist may be assured that their services shall be only in their own state, and habitually west of Berwick Bay," came word from New Orleans.[18]

Franklin had his doubts about Carrière. He did not believe him to be an ardent Union man, per se; Franklin thought he was just a local bandit chieftain who knew how to capitalize on the chaos of war. "I have sent for him three times, and while our force was at Opelousas he had ample time to come in," Franklin explained to Union headquarters. "But neither he nor any of his men came." Carrière's reaction to the summons did not surprise Franklin given the circumstances. Rebel cavalry prowled the countryside and, Franklin pointed out, "these people did not believe that we intended to hold the country." Without Union military muscle to ensure success, why would men like Carrière gamble with their lives?[19]

Franklin's views proved prescient. Carrière had not answered his summonses because the Confederates were hunting him and all like-minded dissenters. Once again conscript hunters and the Home Guard scoured the piney woods of western Louisiana. One command led by Captain Patrick Keary of Cheneyville— President Jefferson Davis's nephew by marriage—included three other Louisiana officers furloughed from the Army of Northern Virginia to gather a battalion of backwoods sharpshooters from Louisiana. They had hoped to reinforce General Robert E. Lee's army with new conscripts but had failed. Instead, they only assembled a threadbare patrol of reluctant soldiers systematically searching the homes of the proscribed.

Among the Unionists on the lists in western Louisiana was Dennis Haynes, living on a small farm in the woods west of Hineston. In late October, the Confederates arrived unexpectedly at Haynes's gate. "I was, with my two little sons, in the horse lot, attending to some fattening hogs, when the cavalry charged upon the house," he remembered. A non-combatant, Haynes believed he was in no danger. "I went to the house and met them in the yard, when a sergeant asked me if my name was Haynes," he continued. "I told him yes." The Confederates informed the luckless Unionists they had orders to arrest him and his seventeen-year old son for opposing the secessionist cause.[20]

The Rebels escorted Haynes and his son to Hineston. Before being locked in the guardhouse with three men brought in the day before, Haynes sent a note to his wife. She arrived and begged for her husband's release. "Nothing could be done in my behalf," Haynes wrote. He and his son were liable for conscription into the Confederate army, and neither had complied. Besides, several of his neighbors had fingered Haynes as an avowed Unionist. "Orders were from General Dick Taylor to kill every man who did not come in," Haynes wrote. He believed he and his boy would soon be dead. Seeing some nearby Rebel officers, he made the Masonic sign of distress. The Southerners acknowledged a fellow member of the craft and ordered him protected and sent to Shreveport for trial. They showed mercy by releasing his son.[21]

The other three prisoners were not as lucky. "On the following morning," Haynes observed, Rebels ordered the men out of the guardhouse, "tied with their hands behind their backs with rawhide strings, their spurs and knives taken from them, and sent under guard to 'Bloody Bob' Martin," captain of a Home Guard company. They never returned. Haynes, under close guard, headed on the road north through Carol Jones's store instead, bound toward Many, Louisiana. From there he would head to Shreveport to face charges of high treason and the possibility of a hangman's knot.[22]

He shared the road with a column of refugees heading for Texas. Hugh Keary, and his brother, W. E. Keary, abandoned their plantation near Cheneyville believing Louisiana was lost to the Union. "He had along all of his stock, cattle, and sheep, about twenty wagons, about a dozen carriages, and three hundred negroes, three or four of whom were handcuffed and tied together with a log-chain, and a negro guard over them with old muskets and bayonets," wrote Haynes. "Keary's property had to be guarded, lest the 'Jayhawkers,' as they called all the Union men, might pounce upon him and capture his negroes and concubines." The Kearys also brought a pack of bloodhounds to chase any slaves who might make a break for freedom. This column of misery, stretching more than a mile, also headed toward Many, where they would take the left-hand road toward the crossing of the Sabine and on to Nacogdoches, Texas.[23]

When Haynes arrived at Many, his captors shoved him in the local jail. Once inside, they threw him into a seven-by-five-foot cage with a runaway slave and a Cajun deserter from Avoyelles Parish. Haynes protested to his guard. "I asked him to take the negro out of the cage," he wrote. The cell was too small for three men, Haynes argued, and he did not want to be held alongside a black man. The Rebels should at least "have some respect for his color."[24]

After languishing under this close confinement for a week, Haynes and the other prisoners were hauled out of the jail. Once again, the column of the damned got underway. After a hard day's march, the party made camp at an abandoned plantation on the road to Shreveport. This evening Haynes found himself locked inside a smokehouse. The Confederates in the escorting battalion, which Haynes described as "backwoods Americans, Creoles, Frenchmen, Spaniards, [and] half-breed Indians" busied themselves by tending to their mounts, making camp, issuing rations, and chopping wood. Haynes and another of the condemned used the opportunity to begin digging under the log walls of the building, hoping to make a break during the night.[25]

When the prisoners heard their guards snoring, they made their move. Haynes went last, and felt his ribs dislocate as he wiggled and squeezed through the narrow trough they had scooped; at last he was free. Haynes stumbled through the darkness, found a mount, and, using a blanket for a saddle and a rope for a bridle, dashed off into the woods. No one pursued. The next morning Haynes emerged on the main Natchitoches-to-Shreveport road. Bluffing his way south to travelers he encountered, and avoiding towns, he reached the main road heading from Alexandria to Texas.

Trying a dead reckoning cross-country toward his home in Hineston, Haynes ran into trouble. While crossing a field at a rude plantation in the pines, he stopped a local man to ask for directions. When informed he was nearly on the correct route home—just eight miles to the east—Haynes returned to the main road to complete his journey. The plantation owner, watching the conversation and alarmed that Haynes had been trespassing on his place, hollered for his wife to fetch his shotgun. His neighbor, who had provided Haynes with directions, caught the spirit and drew a derringer on Haynes before he could turn his horse onto the road. "I believed they aimed at killing me," he wrote. He spurred his horse, but the exhausted animal only stumbled. One assailant unloaded his small pistol and broke Haynes's right arm three inches below the shoulder. The fugitive fell from his horse but landed on his feet and ran toward the underbrush. The plantation owner, by now armed, set his bloodhounds after Haynes, and the baying, snarling dogs cornered him. The hopeless Unionist gave up, uncertain of his future.[26]

Instead of killing the prowler, the planter took him back to the house and bound up his wound. "He appeared very sorry for what he had done," Haynes recalled. Even so, the two men escorted the unlucky traveler toward Hineston. With dislocated ribs and a broken arm, Haynes found every footfall of his horse agonizing. When they arrived at the village, the local Home Guard took custody. "It was proposed by some of the company to kill me right off," Haynes wrote, while others thought, "it was not necessary to kill me then, that I would die anyhow." Instead, the Home Guard commander sent a rider to find any nearby Confederates so that this suffering intruder could become someone else's problem.[27]

Nearly helpless yet agonizingly close to home, Haynes plotted his next escape. With the aid of sympathetic guards, he slipped away into the night. Haynes ran as far away from civilization as he could, passing into the Calcasieu swamp, where he could not be tracked. After splashing through the maze of trees and water, he emerged at the cabin of a friend, who loaned him a horse. Mounted once again, the tortured man made his way home. Haynes reunited with his family, and they made a hiding place for him in the swamp. Two of his older sons stayed undercover with him. All around their swampy refuge, search parties scoured the region. After recovering his breath, Haynes, worried about his festering gunshot wound, headed toward the home of a known Unionist who treated him. "Under my arm was a tablespoon of worms," Haynes noted. "In fact, I stunk like carrion." With his wound drained and dressed, Haynes began to heal and regain his strength.[28]

The neighborhood, though, had clearly become dangerous. Everyone—Unionists and Secessionist alike—had been ordered into the Home Guard. "All but a few of the Union men joined," Haynes observed, "to keep from being torn up. I could scarcely trust anybody." The bedraggled fugitive headed back to his hideout near home. Where could he go to escape the vengeance of the Confederacy?[29]

Unbeknownst to Haynes, the answer to this question remained cloudy at best. On November 2, while he shivered in the swamp, a new set of Union troop movements only confused things. For a week, General Franklin had been sending dispatches to New Orleans in what had been, in effect, a one-sided conversation.

From Banks's lack of detailed response, it seemed clear he was distracted, and did not seem to care about road conditions or the availability of fodder around Bayou Carencro. Banks had little to say about arming, protecting, or rescuing local Unionists. Franklin appeared to be on his own. Then, Banks disappeared.

Now Banks's chief of staff, Brigadier General Stone, sent news to Franklin. "The major-general commanding sailed from the Southwest Pass of the Mississippi River, with the troops under command of Major General Dana," the newly arrived dispatch read. "Should he be successful in effecting a lodgment, as he desires, he will immediately dispatch steamers to Berwick Bay, to receive troops as re-enforcements to the coast expedition." Franklin now understood he had been a mere actor in an elaborate ruse designed to pin down Confederate troops in Louisiana and keep them from reinforcing Texas. Next, his army would be siphoned off, bound for the Lone Star State.[30]

Stone acted as Banks's proxy during his absence. A Massachusetts officer, Stone was already notorious, having run afoul of Republican radicals early in the war after the debacle at Ball's Bluff, Virginia. The U.S. Congress Joint Committee

Brigadier General Charles Pomeroy Stone, the scapegoat for the Union disaster at the Battle of Ball's Bluff. Service in Louisiana would provide him a chance to regain his reputation. *Library of Congress.*

on the Conduct of the War had sentenced him to prison for six months. Eventually exonerated in early 1863, Stone had come to Louisiana to restore his fortunes and his reputation. Banks took him in, and now Stone called the shots on behalf of his commander.

In the same dispatch, Stone advised Franklin to continue the charade however he wished. New Iberia could be the new pivot point for Franklin's army, as he had suggested. Troops could be massed there and threaten a move overland to the west while being in place for an easy march to Berwick Bay and transport to the Texas coast. By posting at New Iberia, Stone agreed, Franklin would keep the Confederates off balance and uncertain if the invasion of Texas would come by land or sea. Franklin, however, had also to maintain the appearance of hostile intent in Louisiana. "It is desirable," Stone instructed, "that the enemy should still regard the movement in your direction as the real one, and as much show as possible should be made of an intended push westward toward the Sabine, or northwesterly toward Alexandria."[31]

Banks had left Franklin in a fix. The officers of his army had already abandoned any hopes of going north because of the lack of fodder and the headaches of keeping the command fed. At the same time, the Confederates had abandoned the country south of Alexandria and showed little interest in renewing hostile contact. Franklin, burdened by intentionally vague orders, had prudently fallen back to better ground. Now, Banks wanted him to continue to look threatening, but retreats are rarely intimidating. To make the task even more difficult, Banks wanted the largest of the 13th Army Corps divisions readied to reinforce his operations on the Texas coast. When they departed, Franklin would have to appear ever more dangerous, but with fewer troops.[32]

Franklin has missed a signal. The news General Dana would not be coming to Vermilionville to take command of the 13th Army Corps but would headquarter in Texas instead had been a clue. He could not know it, but the expedition to capture Brownsville was already at sea and anchored off the mouth of the Rio Grande. Banks had slipped away to personally plant the flag in Texas, leaving Stone to bring his field commanders into the larger picture. The chief of staff would answer any question or provide any necessary clarifications while the commander of the Department of the Gulf remained incommunicado in the western Gulf, personally seeing to the invasion of the most remote corner of the Confederacy. Franklin and his commanders would have to rely on their own judgment to handle any emergencies in Louisiana. No one could be certain when Banks would be back in his New Orleans office.

Stone's dispatch had relieved Franklin from one worry: He no longer had to protect the west bank of the Mississippi River from Rebel marauders. This assignment now fell to the garrisons in the district of Baton Rouge, which had to defend the region from Bayou Grosse Tête and Plaquemine to the mouth of the Red River. The new commander there, Brigadier General Philip St. George Cooke, was yet another veteran of the Army of the Potomac sent to Louisiana after a lackluster performance in the East. He had been outfoxed during the 1862 Virginia Peninsula campaign by his Confederate son-in-law, General James Ewell Brown "Jeb" Stuart, and he had held mostly administrative posts since then.

Brigadier General Henry Birge, a veteran campaigner in Louisiana.
Cartes de visite, Lincoln's Army Civil War Virtual Museum.

Cooke would now inherit the task of keeping the Mississippi River flowing unvexed to the sea. "There are indications of the assembling of bands of guerillas in that region," Stone warned Cooke from the headquarters of the Department of the Gulf. "The major general commanding deems it proper that you should . . . guard the passage down the country." Brigadier General Henry Birge, commanding in the Lafourche District, would be responsible for the region from Plaquemine to Brashear City. At nearly the same instance, Rear Admiral David Dixon Porter read a dispatch from Stone claiming, "all was quiet along the banks of the Mississippi River within the limits of this military department."[33]

Now enlightened, Franklin dutifully moved to maintain his sham invasion. "I shall send out a cavalry force in the direction of the Mermentau as soon as possible, and, if I consider it feasible or safe, shall send a division of infantry there with bridge train, or at any rate with materials for building a bridge," he reported to Stone. The rains and the passage of his troops had rendered the roads between Opelousas and Taylor's camps at Holmesville impassable, he believed, and he did not fear any trouble from the Confederates. "I think the impression is strong," Franklin wrote confidently, "that we are going to Texas."[34]

Banks's real invasion was already underway. The voyage had proven to be more challenging than expected. After forming into a convoy with gunboat protection, the invasion force headed southwest "in regular line across the heaving bosom of

The transport *George Peabody* carried Federal troops during the invasion of Texas. Alfred Rudolph Waud, artist. *Library of Congress.*

the Gulf of Mexico," noted Private Ketzle of the 37th Illinois aboard the transport *George Peabody*. Out at sea in the Gulf of Mexico, rolling swells made many of the troops sick. Then, blustery and chilling gales lashed the expedition with rain for the next five days. Many of the poorly maintained transports reported distress. "It was quite stormy and rough, so much so that our rudder chain snapped and thus left the boat unmanageable," Ketzle remembered. "Boat hands with the assistance of our boys (most of Company D being old lake sailors) soon fixed the steering apparatus with ropes, block and tackle [and] thereby we were able to keep in our course but soon we noticed other boats having apparently worse trouble than we, as on some we could see white flags hoisted."[35]

While the elements punished their enemies, Confederate forces in Texas were unprepared for the storm of Federals about to hit the shores. Events in Louisiana had baffled these defenders, and most assumed the threat lay no nearer than Alexandria, hundreds of miles away. About 7,000 men served in the Eastern and Western sub-districts of Texas, the areas that would bear the brunt of the Union invasion, but they were parceled out in weak garrisons. The largest concentration of troops, around 2,000 men, protected Galveston. The second largest post, Sabine Pass, counted 1,500 men on duty. The balance laid strewn in packets of a few hundred men each, from Niblett's Bluff on the Louisiana bank of the Sabine to the depots at Beaumont, Houston, Velasco, Saluria, Port Lavaca, and Corpus Christi. Most telling was that a mere 500 Confederate troops operated along the line of the Rio Grande from Brownsville to Laredo.

The Rebel troops in these wildly scattered places held confused notions of the grander picture. "I do not know how long we will stay here," Private Augustus V. Ball of the 23rd Texas Cavalry wrote from Beaumont. "We were ordered to this place en route to Niblett's bluff . . . but some think we will be ordered back to Houston as there is no Federals in the direction that we were ordered. They have been defeated by General Green and changed their route for Alexandria."[36]

With no threat of immediate danger and with winter on its way, these lonely garrisons leaked soldiers. Around Beaumont, regimental strength dwindled as demoralized soldiers slipped away to escape the threat of fighting in Louisiana. Private Ball, serving in a recently dismounted cavalry regiment, grew impatient as he watched comrades and messmates vanish. "About 60 has left within the past

3 nights," he wrote his wife. "Nine left our company night before last, carrying their clothes, guns, and 40 rounds of ammunition with them. Fifty of them are at home, 35 are here for duty."[37]

With more men absent from his company than present, Ball could sympathize only so far. "The boys say that they do not intend to desert but they are determined to go [home and] get their horses," he continued, "but they go off in the night and it cannot be called anything else but desertion, and the leaders of them if they can be found out will be punished as such." Officers serving at Beaumont tried to check this growing flood of deserters by ordering their troops to shoot anyone leaving without permission. Ball took the hint. "I expect to stay with the command as long as there is a man in it," he scrawled, "expect to do what I think is wright [sic] and nothing else."[38]

Confusion and demoralization seeped up the chains of command and reached Major General Magruder's headquarters in Houston. He felt conflicted, as Lieutenant General Kirby Smith had ordered him to bring troops east to Louisiana and lend a hand at keeping the Yankees out of Alexandria. Magruder hedged. "I leave Texas not only open to attack by sea, but also the railroads at Houston exposed to attack by Niblett's Bluff," he wrote back. Still, he could see the urgency of smashing the Federals in Louisiana. Yet, he could not shake the feeling that Texas would soon be invaded.[39]

So, Magruder dragged his feet. Getting his scattered Texas army to Louisiana, he argued, would require a herculean effort of logistics. "The difficulties are almost insurmountable within the time expected," Magruder professed. Corn had to be gathered, wagons collected, and commands mustered, equipped, and moved over long distances. "I am making every exertion, and will continue to do so, to overcome these difficulties," he claimed. "I will command the troops in the field myself, and I think I can induce them to follow me." Meanwhile, he ordered Colonel Augustus Buchel to continue caching supplies at Niblett's Bluff. Within a few weeks, if all went well, Magruder believed he could position four thousand mounted troops and five batteries of artillery on the Sabine River for service in Louisiana.[40]

As he sent his men off to the Sabine, Magruder thought he might assuage his anxieties about leaving Texas undefended by replacing the Louisiana-bound troops on the coast with militia leavened with troops drawn from the Northern Sub-District of Texas. The threat to Texans from Union armies in Arkansas and Indian Territory seemed less grave at the moment.

Brigadier General Henry McCulloch, commanding at Bonham, Texas, did not agree. "I am not willing to see them go without informing the major-general of the effect that their withdrawal may have upon the country," he wrote to Magruder's headquarters. The Confederacy would lose north Texas, McCulloch declared; the Rebel army in the Indian Territory was "simply an outpost" where Brigadier General William S. Steele commanded a lackluster force of Indians and Texans. The Creeks and Cherokees in his army could only be counted on "when rations are issued, and pay-day comes."[41]

Having registered his complaints, McCulloch dutifully readied a mounted brigade to send toward Houston. It included the 1st and 4th Arizona and the 20th, 29th, and 30th Texas cavalries, along with three poorly equipped batteries. Desertions and detachments had whittled these commands down to a muster of only 1,500 men. McCulloch would be left with only the 5th Texas Partisan Rangers, a few hundred state troops, and no artillery to protect north Texas. Colonel James Bourland's "Border Regiment" would also remain, but they spent all of their time patrolling the Comanche and Kiowa frontier in northwest Texas. McCulloch admitted there were perhaps 800 repentant deserters in the Northern Sub-District of Texas he had cajoled back into service, but they would likely backslide if given the chance.[42]

McCulloch conceded the immediate threat to north Texas was minimal, but he assured Magruder that once the Federals caught wind of the move, they would arrive like an avalanche from Kansas and Arkansas. "What will there be to hold them in check and keep them out of this country?" McCulloch asked. Some of his officers suggested the Missouri guerillas under William Clark Quantrill— heading to Texas for the winter—might help, but McCulloch remained skeptical. "I have but little confidence in men who fight for booty," he wrote, "and whose mode of warfare is but little, if any, above the uncivilized Indian."[43]

These protests did not bother Magruder. He remained convinced of the lurking menace off the Texas coast. Although Banks had been humiliated at Sabine Pass, Magruder suspected he had not abandoned his plans to invade

Mexican Conservatives inviting Maximilian to become their emperor and to ascend the Cactus Throne. *The Mexican Delegation appoints Ferdinand Maximilian of Austria as Emperor of Mexico* (1864) by Cesare Dell'Acqua. *Historical Museum of Castello di Miramare.*

Texas by sea. The questions remained: Where would the Yankees land? Where should he concentrate his troops? Logically, given the movements of Franklin's men in Louisiana, Confederate officials anticipated another fight along the coast of southeast Texas aimed at Houston and Galveston, the most important points in the state. Feeling a hunch the Federals might try Sabine Pass a second time, Magruder ordered Colonel Philip N. Luckett's Brigade to leave their rendezvous point at Beaumont and redirect south to reinforce the dismal post, notorious for its mud, disease, and lack of creature comforts, instead of east to Niblett's Bluff.

This change brought no joy to the Texans who had been ordered to the hovels of Sabine City. Private Ball wondered if Magruder was disciplining the troops for their lack of patriotic ardor. "I do not know why they were sent there unless it was to keep them from all leaving and going home. I see no other cause for our going," he speculated, other than "to secure what few that is left of us." Ball hated his new assignment. "Sabine Pass is said to be one of the meanest places in the state of Texas to live at. It is a perfect mud hole, and when it rains the water stands shoe mouth deep all over the place and besides there is not a stick of wood to be had without shipping it down the river 30 or 40 miles." Clearly it would be an uncomfortable place to spend what promised to be a hard winter.[44]

Meanwhile, In Mexico City, it promised to be a hard winter as well. General Forey, worried over events in Mexico and the almost comic opera of who would govern the unruly nation, had become disillusioned. Where was the popular rising in favor of monarchy? He now believed the French intervention in Mexico had been based on fatally flawed assumptions. It appeared to him the United States might now be powerful enough to suppress their rebellion and also oppose the French. Forey feared an American intervention in Mexico, perhaps before the end of the year, and he told L'Empereur so.

On October 1, 1863, with a new gambit in mind, Napoleon III had recalled his chief architect of the Mexican adventure to Paris. Forey obeyed and had headed back on France on October 24, passing along the command of the Mexican enterprise to General Bazaine. Forey would not be going directly home, though. He had some stops to make on the way.As the French general headed home across the Atlantic, he followed in the wake of men who continued to press for an emperor in Mexico. They had left Veracruz while affairs appeared to favor the conservatives, and imperialists. Armed with optimism these envoys intended to present their case in person before thirty-one-year-old Maximillian.

At his castle Miramar, near Trieste, the young nobleman granted the Mexicans an audience and considered their appeal; still Maximillian offered no reply.

THIRTEEN

BAYOU BOURBEAU

Brave boys, to stay is death, fall back as best you can.
—Lieutenant Colonel Albert H. Brown
96th Ohio Infantry

A s Major General Nathaniel P. Banks, Major General Napoleon J. T. Dana, and the 2nd Division, 13th Army Corps, neared Brazos Santiago at the southern tip of Texas, Rebel scouts rode into Confederate major general Richard Taylor's lines at Holmesville and Evergreen to report the Federal army in Louisiana had pulled out, heading south. Taylor, surprised, sent for Brigadier General Tom Green to give him his next orders. "It was said that the Yankees had left Washington and Opelousas and were on their way to [Berwick] Bay," recorded Captain Julius Giesecke of the 4th Texas Cavalry. The German officer knew his regiment would soon be on the chase. "Our chances of again seeing the Yankees was good."[1]

Taylor reported the intelligence to Lieutenant General Edmund Kirby Smith. "Reports from my pickets render it probable the enemy is retreating to Berwick Bay," Taylor wrote to Kirby Smith's chief of staff, Brigadier General William R. Boggs. He could not be sure, though, and proceeded cautiously. "I shall not move the main body of my forces until further developments," Taylor continued. "The country will enable the enemy to move without endangering his rear, unless I bring on a general action, which I do not deem advisable."[2]

Why was Major General William B. Franklin retreating? The Union threat to the Red River had clearly played out. Where Franklin and his men went next, Taylor could only speculate. "Banks does not wish to move on Niblett's Bluff with me on his rear," Taylor conceded. Perhaps Major General Ulysses S. Grant had called for the 13th Army Corps to return to his army, this time to help retrieve

Federal fortunes at Chattanooga. Maybe, Taylor hoped, Confederate successes elsewhere had come to the relief of Louisiana.[3]

Taylor ordered Green to find Franklin's retreating army. On the morning of November 2, Colonel James P. Major's men converged on Washington from Ville Platte to the northwest while Green arrived from Evergreen and Big Cane from the northeast. The rearguard of Franklin's army, fewer than twenty miles down the road from Washington, retreated much as it had advanced—slowly and deliberately.[4]

Green and his reunited division headed down the road to Opelousas that morning, with his scouts trying to make contact with the enemy. Once in town, a detachment headed east along the road to Port Barré, while the balance continued in the most likely direction of the Federal retreat. About two and a half miles south of town, the road forked. The left lane headed more directly toward Grand Coteau six miles away. The right—the Belleview Road—had been skirmished over for the last week and eventually curved to its crossing of Bayou Bourbeau and across Buzzard Prairie to Bayou Carencro three miles beyond. The Confederate column split again as the 2nd Louisiana peeled off toward Grand Coteau.

Colonel Arthur Pendleton Bagby's Brigade continued due south. "We were right on the Yankee's heels," observed Captain Giesecke. They found a screen of Federal cavalry near the scene of the previous weeks skirmishes and, after emptying some saddles, pushed the detachments from the 4th Indiana, 1st Louisiana (Union), and the 14th New York cavalries across Bayou Bourbeau and onto the prairie beyond. One detachment continued south down the lane toward the Chretien Point Plantation from the intersection with the main road as it curved toward the east.[5]

Some of the Federals were surprised by the sudden Rebel reappearance. Union foragers, digging up sweet potatoes at a farm north of Bayou Carencro on the road to Grand Coteau, looked up to see a line of blue-coated cavalry approaching. Assuming them to be friendly, the officer of the detail mounted up and trotted up to greet the newcomers and swap news; he gave a salute when about fifty yards away. The horsemen, though, were from the 2nd Louisiana, still wearing their captured uniforms from Brashear City. One of the troopers shot the Yankee officer through the heart. He then spurred his horse forward, dismounted, and, as he put it, "skinned" the dead Iowan of his clothing and personal effects.[6]

With Rebels back on the prowl, Major General Stephen G. Burbridge ordered his drummers to beat the long roll and brought his five Union infantry regiments and two sections of artillery into formation. They would have to rescue the cavalry and check the Confederate advance. This scuffle on Buzzard Prairie appeared more annoying than threatening. "They were driven away and took refuge in the woods," reported Major General Cadwallader C. Washburn, commander of the rear guard, after arriving to investigate the firing. Burbridge ordered his infantry to advance up the road to Opelousas, but the Texas horsemen stayed out of range of the infantry's rifles. The Federals attempted to maneuver the nimble Rebels into a more substantial fight but failed, and they eventually advanced just to the wood line along Bayou Bourbeau. Burbridge ordered out skirmishers to investigate, with some heading over to Chretien Point Plantation to make sure it was clear of Texans as well.

Runners came back reporting the southerners had darted onto the prairies west of the bayou and then, surprisingly, turned and formed a line of battle. Burbridge, lured on, followed with his brigade, splashing across Bayou Bourbeau and forming a line of battle on the western edge of the woods, facing the

Major General Stephen G. Burbridge would later earn the nickname "The Butcher of Kentucky" for his suppression of guerillas in his home state. *Courtesy of Tom Pressly, Shreveport, Louisiana.*

enemy. Union gunners with the 17th Ohio and 2nd Massachusetts rolled across the bridge, went into battery, and began shelling the enemy line. The enemy horsemen slipped away out of range, and by 3 PM the Rebels had gone. Burbridge reported his findings.[7]

Washburn, at his post on Bayou Carencro, believed he knew the Confederates' game. "I think their move today was to endeavor to develop our strength," he reported to Major Wickham Hoffman, the assistant adjutant-general at headquarters. "I directed as little to be exposed to view as possible."[8]

Washburn had failed; Green's scouts saw all of the Federal brigades through their weak screen of cavalry. They knew about the entire disposition of the portion of the Union army now camped at Bourbeau, in the open expanse of Buzzard Prairie, and back at Carencro—everything between the two bayous. Prisoners taken, too, gave details of troop strengths and positions. The Confederates now knew three infantry brigades and a cavalry brigade—a quarter of the Union Army of the Gulf—lay precariously exposed.

The Rebels maneuvers had drawn out Burbridge's command, and his men now occupied an advanced position three miles beyond Bayou Carencro, the main Federal line. Washburn told them to stand fast. The outpost was the same campsite that had changed hands several times in the course of the campaign. It was an ideal spot from which to observe enemy movements on the prairies to the west and to picket the Opelousas road, providing ample time to raise a warning if the Confederates brought up the rest of their army. "I shall expect fighting every day that I remain here, and probably we will have to meet their entire force if we stay long enough for them to concentrate it," Washburn warned his superior, Major General Franklin, who was back at Vermilionville. "I do not apprehend that we shall need any help, though I wish we had more cavalry," he continued. The Union horsemen of Colonel John G. Fonda's Brigade were few in number, exhausted from a month of constant skirmishing, and now rode underfed horses.[9]

In the late afternoon, unaware that Green's scouts were watching, Burbridge's 1,500 men erected a village of tents in the woods south of the intersection of the main road to Opelousas and the byway to Chretien Point Plantation. The bridge crossing Bayou Bourbeau was the Federal lifeline to Bayou Carencro. The soldiers occupied a shady, orderly encampment defined by roads to the right (north) and front (west). A prairie stretched before them. They lived in the shade of large, widely spaced trees, with the densely wooded ravine of Bayou Bourbeau behind them and dense woods along the watercourse to the north. These soldiers, men of the 23rd Wisconsin, 83rd and 96th Ohio, and 60th and 67th Indiana, guarded the crossing with the assistance of the six guns of the 17th Ohio Battery and two more from the 2nd Massachusetts Battery. This brigade of infantry supporting Fonda's hard-working cavalry screen served as the extreme end of the Union army in southern Louisiana.[10]

The terrain seemed favorable for defense. Bayou Bourbeau formed a bulbous, pear-shaped cul-de-sac about two and a half miles north to south. A half-mile wide neck opened on its northern end, but the base of the loop was three times as wide at its southern end. At Burbridge's camp, the road to Opelousas cut the east side of the great twist nearly in the middle, about a mile south of its most narrow opening, then curved around to the north to pass through the neck onto more open ground beyond. The thick, wooded eastern margins, scalloped and uneven in places where farmers had gathered timber, offered concealment. The forest also hid three deep ravines radiating west from the eastern side of the Bayou Bourbeau twist. The terrain to the west was relatively open, with only thin skirts of brushy trees and high grass.

A fence-enclosed fallow field lay near the northwest corner of the camp and across the curving road to Opelousas. Sentinels stationed there had clear visibility along the edge of the tree line looking north for several miles. Surmising any heavy enemy advance would have to come from the north, Burbridge also ordered his pickets to deploy into the woods and take up positions along a lateral ravine about a mile north of camp—the farthest of the three that ribbed the eastern side of this bayou twist. Fonda's cavalry pickets deployed well out onto the prairie to cover any enemy advances from the west.

Washburn rode in from his headquarters on Bayou Carencro to inspect the position. He approved. The Rebels might harass this outpost but could not make a serious advance with their infantry without ample warning given by Burbridge's command. The fact that three miles of open prairie lay between his main line at

Bayou Carencro and these troops at Bayou Bourbeau seemed of little concern to Washburn. Burbridge could certainly hold his own long enough for reinforcements to cover this short distance.

Confederates eyed the Yankee position through field glasses, gaining a rough idea of how the enemy camp lay. That night, six deserters from the 1st Louisiana Cavalry (Union) rode into the Confederate lines and revealed all they knew. The Union rearguard, three brigades of the 13th Army Corps, lay nearly ten miles from the Vermillionville camps of the two divisions of the 19th Army Corps, their closest reinforcements.

From this windfall of intelligence, Green believed both Federal commands lay exposed—Burbridge's dangerously so. He might snap up this isolated band of infantry before Washburn could come to the rescue. It would be a reprise of Sterling's plantation. If Taylor advanced all of his infantry, the Confederates might destroy Washburn's entire division. To make the most of the opportunity, Green would have to make masterful use of the terrain and his timing would have to be precise.[11]

Yet, Taylor had shown no interest in provoking a major battle that far south. Changing tack, Green argued he might at least rough up Washburn's command and materially diminish their strength at little cost to the Confederates. Taylor agreed, but he held the main body of the Confederate army at Holmesville, more than forty miles away. He agreed to commit Colonel Oran M. Roberts's outpost—three regiments of infantry at Moundville, a dozen miles away—to the fight. Green sent gallopers with orders for the one thousand Texan foot soldiers to come forward.

On Bayou Bourbeau, Burbridge began to have doubts about his position and spent a fitful night. At 2 AM on November 3, he summoned the colonels of his regiments and outlined his fears. He believed his command lay too far forward. When his commander had inspected the outpost, Burbridge had asked Washburn to either come up with the other two brigades or call him back to Bayou Carencro, but neither option had occurred. He repeated the requests in dispatches. Instead, Burbridge "received at last, in reply, a refusal, concluding with laconic sarcasm, to the effect that apprehensions of danger arose from nothing but 'a scare,'" recorded Dr. J. T. Woods, the regimental surgeon of the 96th Ohio.[12]

Burbridge felt otherwise; he believed the Rebel cavalry would be back in the morning. He told his regimental officers to make the troops ready, and in the darkness, field officers returned to their regiments to pass the news along. Line officers roused their men early and told them to clear their pieces and load their cartridge boxes with forty rounds. At 4 AM the troops fell into lines of battle, ready for whatever the dawn might bring.[13]

Sunrise came, but Green and his Texans did not. Relieved, the Federal soldiers broke ranks and prepared breakfast. Besides eating fresh meat brought in from the local farms, "the boys were anticipating a splendid combination of luxuries," wrote a soldier in the 23rd Wisconsin: state elections for some and payday for all. Paymasters would be passing out two months' pay for every soldier.[14]

The Wisconsin men would be voting absentee in races held in their home state. "One feature in soldier's voting struck me with particular force," a journalist in camp wrote. "They use, generally, cartridge boxes for ballot boxes. How suggestive a picture! The cartridge box emptied of its load of death dealing missiles to receive a gentle ballot. War putting aside the sword," the writer marveled, "to take up a mightier weapon."[15]

As the morning progressed, the soldiers of the 83rd Ohio received orders to escort a train of empty wagons heading toward Chretien Point Plantation in search of food and fodder. The regiment formed up, and trudged down the road, their day off interrupted by this fatigue detail.

Just out of sight, Brigadier General Green studied his prey. After a few hours, he formulated a simple plan of attack. He convened his commanders at Opelousas. Green wanted Colonel Roberts to lead the 11th, 15th, and 18th Texas infantries through the woods bordering Bayou Bourbeau along the eastern edge of its long loop and to fall on the Federal right. Detachments from a mounted regiment—the 7th Texas Cavalry—would cover Roberts's left in the direction of Grand Coteau in case the enemy had forces there, particularly cavalry, that rushed to the sound of the guns once the firing started. The Federals would naturally form to face this threat, perhaps believing it to be a screen covering the general advance by Taylor's entire Confederate army. Both Burbridge and Washburn, alert to a possibility of a Rebel advance, would spend valuable time ascertaining the level and direction of the threat. They would expect cavalry. Instead, Green would bring infantry.

While the footsoldiers tangled in the woods, Major's and Bagby's Brigades, mounted, would pass wide around the Union left then fall on their flank and rear with eight regiments. Major, on the Rebel right, would continue the sweep to the south and come around through Chretien Point Plantation to face Buzzard Prairie. The 4th, 5th, and the 13th Texas Cavalry Battalion, now the center of the great "C"-shaped Confederate line, would dismount, face east, and support the Val Verde Battery and a section of rifled artillery from Captain James M. Daniel's battery. They would collapse the unanchored left flank of the Union line.

Colonel Roberts understood the need for deception and stealth. He pulled two companies from the 11th Texas and a third from the 15th Texas to form a one-hundred-man skirmishing detail. These sharpshooters, led by Major Nathaniel Jackson Caraway, would be all the enemy would see of his brigade until he could get his main line of battle into lethal range. Roberts knew his troops were tired. They had already marched nearly ten miles by daybreak. These Texans, from three different brigades, were also strangers to each other, having only recently served as the advance guard of Taylor's army near Moundville. Even so, he believed this thrown-together force would advance into the very muzzles of a veteran Yankee brigade. He ordered his surgeons to prepare for casualties.[16]

As agreed, Roberts advanced his troops out of Opelousas about midmorning. The Union pickets posted nearest to town watched as a thin line of Rebel skirmishers came across the rolling terrain, emerged from the cover of trees, and cut across a curve in the road a half-mile away. The Confederate line then advanced boldly in their direction, down the road and across the broad fields of a farm. The Yankees fired warning shots to alert the pickets along the ravine in the woods a few hundred yards away, as well as the rest of their brigade, which lay a mile to their rear, but simmering stews, surly paymasters, and proxy politics distracted their comrades.[17]

Confederate colonel Roberts heard the shots and rode forward to make sure his skirmishers were working together. As he approached, bullets kicked up puffs of dust in the road and buzzed overhead. If these Federals had cannons near, which they must, they could easily rake the road, he observed. He returned and ordered his densely packed formations to move into the woods to their left while Major Caraway spread out his skirmishers for one hundred yards on either side of the road and continued the advance. Roberts also ordered the squadron from the 7th Texas Cavalry to head toward the left and scout the banks of Bayou Bourbeau and Buzzard Prairie beyond. He wanted no surprises popping up behind from the direction of Grand Coteau.[18]

The weather had warmed up, and this day would get hotter still. Having raised the alarm, the Yankee sentinels, still firing, gave ground. They accurately reported seeing about one hundred enemy soldiers. They had not seen the 900 just behind.[19]

At first their comrades did not understand the danger. "While our fresh pork . . . was lazily boiling," wrote Corporal Reuben B. Scott, 67th Indiana, "suddenly we heard the pickets firing off in front, and thinking we had another day's skirmishing on our hands we, without putting on our coats, buckled on our cartridge boxes and grabbed our faithful rifles, and were in ranks in a few minutes." Officers called every regiment in Burbridge's command into line. "When ordered, the men

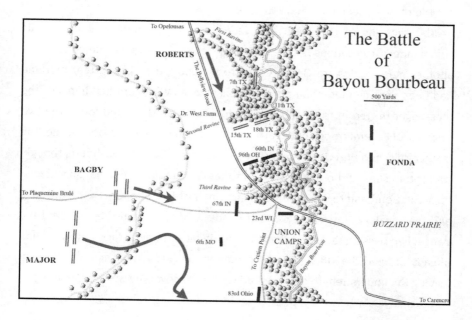

fell into line laughing, some . . . suggesting that the Rebels 'were trying to get into camp to vote,'" a soldier in the 23rd Wisconsin noted. "Others wondered if the 'butternuts knew that the statute penalty was for disturbing an election.'" The 83rd Ohio, having just started out on their foraging mission, paused about a mile away and formed up. "We piled out of the wagons and took our places in line of battle," noted Sergeant T. B. Marshall. [20]

Burbridge sent a galloper to the Carencro camps at the first hint of trouble, but the couriers returned around 10:30 AM with perfunctory orders to send a few companies of the 60th Indiana north to strengthen the picket line and make sure all was well. Clearly Washburn had few concerns that the Confederates were in earnest. [21]

The 118th Illinois Mounted Infantry, scattered across the prairie to the west, was completely unready. When no early attack had occurred, company and regimental officers used the morning to drill the troops. Now, though, the men could see Rebel cavalry skirting to the west in heavy columns. Guns from the 2nd Massachusetts Battery rumbled up and deployed as the Illinois men scrambled to reassemble their regiment. The rifled guns boomed and bucked, and the Rebels faded away across the grassy plain. The gunners reloaded their pieces, but their targets seemed to have vanished. [22]

The shooting to the north also faded. Burbridge, perhaps stung by his commander's accusations that he had been "scared," changed his mind and sent another message toward Bayou Carencro to report the fighting that morning had been nothing more than picket skirmishing, as Washburn had implied. The messenger trotted in to Washburn's camps just after 11 AM and found the two brigades of Federal troops under arms and preparing to march to the rescue. The courier delivered Burbridge's report of a false alarm. General Washburn, though, was not so sure, and ordered his men to remain in place while he hurried over to Bayou Bourbeau to see for himself, arriving just before noon. Both Burbridge and the cavalry commander, Colonel Fonda, told Washburn they believed the danger had passed; the enemy had once again faded away. In fact, Burbridge had already ordered the 118th Illinois to come in, unsaddle their horses, and rest, leaving the understrength 6th Missouri Cavalry to cover the western approaches to his camps. Washburn, perturbed by the disturbance, rode back toward his division. The 83rd Ohio, resting easy, returned to its foraging expedition.[23]

Yet, the Confederates had not gone.

Shortly after Washburn crossed Bayou Bourbeau on his way back to his headquarters, firing once again erupted behind him. The Union pickets had rediscovered the advancing line of Major Caraway's Texans and opened up. The Indianans fanned out, taking cover in the buildings of a farm and the ravine leading away from the homestead and began the steady, rhythmic firing of a well-drilled skirmish line.[24]

Behind the Confederate skirmishers, Colonel Roberts decided the time for muscle had arrived and deployed his entire brigade to push these new Federals out of the way. The 15th Texas, armed with Enfields, formed with its right on the road to command better fields of fire. The smoothbore-armed 18th Texas fell into line on their left to form the center of Roberts's Brigade. The 11th Texas attempted to deploy on the far left, but the ravine and woods of Bayou Bourbeau broke up their formation.[25]

The detachment of the 60th Indiana focused on Caraway's skirmishers hiding in the trees to their immediate front, but they lost their nerve as hundreds of additional Confederates spread out in the woods and along the far edge of the farm fields. The Hoosiers left their buildings and ravine, heading back in a hurry and sending runners ahead to report what they had seen.

Caraway's Texans bounded after the Indianans likes hounds after rabbits. Roberts, meanwhile, ordered his line of battle to keep steady and to follow at a regular pace, marching across the farm to another swale beyond and then back into the woods.[26]

For the Federals in camp, the volume of firing coming from the north indicated something new. Then, more evidence of danger arrived. Union cavalrymen, astride lathered horses, rode into Burbridge's camps and reported large numbers of Confederate cavalry advancing across the prairies to the west. "The Philistines were upon us," Surgeon Woods declared. Drummers beat the long roll, and the soldiers once again abandoned their kettles and ballots and fell into line of battle. This time the Confederate cavalry appeared to be sincere. None of these

Federals realized Rebel infantry was also near, nor that their camps were in the jaws of a vice.[27]

Officers in the Union camp responded first to the approaching threat from the north and ordered the regiments to wheel around to face that direction. The troops dutifully moved into position across the road to Opelousas, their camps behind them, the ravine of Bayou Bourbeau to their right. The rest of the 60th Indiana—whose skirmishers were already engaged and begging for help—took the lead, their rifles all facing the trees to their font. The 96th Ohio took position to the Hoosiers' left, where the road to their front emerged from the trees and bent gently toward the north. The 67th Indiana, backed by a section each of the 17th Ohio and 2nd Massachusetts Batteries, held the Federal left flank. They were completely exposed on the prairie but supported by 150 Missouri cavalrymen who would keep an eye toward the west. Burbridge ordered Colonel Fonda to take the rest of his mounted troops east, down the Opelousas road and back toward Buzzard Prairie, and keep open his line of communications with Major General Washburn's regiments nearer to Bayou Carencro. The remaining four guns of the 17th Ohio Battery would deploy near the camp where they could sweep the road to the north. Burbridge also ordered a rider to find his recently departed foraging expedition, the 83rd Ohio, and bring it back. With these decisions made, the general released Colonel Richard Owen to take the rest of his 60th Indiana to join their skirmishers. The 96th Ohio would move north and into the woods as well. Burbridge's reserve, the 23rd Wisconsin, deployed in front of the camps in the road to the Chretien Point Plantation, facing the prairies to the west.[28]

The Confederates moved to strike a heavy blow against Burbridge's isolated, and now spread out, Union brigade. Caraway's Texans, advancing through the woods, could see the Hoosier reinforcements coming, and the major ordered all of his men to take cover in the second ravine and play on these new arrivals. The 60th Indiana, reunited with its skirmishers, returned fire. Behind Caraway, Colonel Roberts kept his battle line well to the rear and out of sight until he could determine the strength of the enemy before him. After several minutes of a deep-woods firefight, Roberts decided to break the deadlock and ordered a general advance by the entire brigade of nine hundred men.

The noise of this collision rolled back across the Union camps. Surgeon Woods looked up from his work with a start. "The quick crack of the skirmish rifle is followed by the sharp, rattling volley," he wrote later. Deep in the trees, the men of the 60th Indiana realized they were swamped by nearly three to one.[29]

"Very soon," Roberts reported with understated satisfaction, "the enemy gave way."[30]

Burbridge urged a second Federal regiment to hurry up and fire into the enemy formation, covering the retreat of the demoralized Indianans. The command of "'Forward 96th Ohio,' sends them to meet the solid lines of gray, and full in each other's faces the deadly volleys are exchanged," Woods remembered. The new regiment did not stay for long. Both the Buckeyes and the 60th Indiana fell back several hundred yards under the punishing Rebel fire. Each regiment had gone in against the Texans alone and had been shivered by volleys, and now a steady stream of wounded trickled into camp, searching for the surgeon's tent. The Yankees established a new line of battle six hundred yards away from the Texans, stretching their line from the bayou on its right to the Opelousas road on its left.[31]

With his artillery and the 67th Indiana covering the approaches from the west, Burbridge had two more regiments he could commit to this deep-woods battle. His couriers had located the 83rd Ohio, and these troops were on their way back to join the fight. In the meantime, he turned to the 160 men in the 23rd Wisconsin. This regiment deployed facing west in anticipation of another day of heavy cavalry skirmishing. Compact infantry formations usually made short work of mounted regiments if they ever caught one in a volley. Against enemy infantry, the army with the tightest brigades usually won in these brutal slug matches. Burbridge and his officers realized they were fighting the wrong kind of battle. "Up to this time no one supposed that the enemy had any infantry within striking distance of us," explained Colonel Joshua James Guppey, 23rd Wisconsin. Burbridge ordered his regiments to close up and tighten their lines, facing north.[32]

A little after 1 PM, the Texan attack paused. Colonel Roberts ordered his men to rest, drink water, and realign themselves. Advancing through rough terrain had made a tangle of their formations. "The marching in line had been very difficult on account of the weeds, ditches, and briars in the field, and the deep gullies, logs, brush, branches, and curves of the bayou in the woods," Roberts wrote. The men of the 11th Texas had tried to navigate the swampy course of the bayou but had foundered in mud and waist-deep water. They gave up and formed a column behind the left rear of the 18th Texas. Major Caraway's skirmishers, too, were exhausted. Roberts ordered the companies back to their regiments and brought forward a relatively fresh unit, Company B, 15th Texas Infantry, to take their place. After ten minutes, Roberts ordered his brigade back to its feet.[33]

Meanwhile Burbridge faced other trouble. Colonel Major's Confederate cavalry galloped onto the prairie to the left of the Union line, "scattering like wild Comanches." Union officers with binoculars could see columns of what appeared to be Confederate infantry and artillery deploying into line of battle far beyond these darting horsemen. Burbridge's left regiment, the 67th Indiana, stood exposed on the prairie, as did the guns they supported.

The Confederates saw this and seized the opportunity. The Texas and Arizona cavalry surged toward the 67th Indiana, aiming for its left flank and rear. The regiment's well-drilled companies wheeled their battle line to their left to face this threat. From the camps, one observer believed they had formed into a Napoleonic-era hollow square to defend against cavalry. Whether pivoting on their left to face west—or forming a square—the Hoosiers had now opened up a significant gap in the Federal firing line. Major General Burbridge, more worried about the infantry to his north than the "wild Comanches" to his west, sent an aide to Lieutenant Colonel Theodore Buehler with orders for him to re-form his line and close up on the left of the 96th Ohio.[34]

But Buehler froze. The Prussian-born Indiana officer could not decide which way to turn. He feared the mounted Texans on his left might overrun his regiment while his men complied with these new orders. If he remained facing west to confront the enemy cavalry, the Rebel infantry on his right, the Enfield-armed 15th Texas, would rake the length of his line with volleys. Burbridge could not believe it when the Hoosiers failed to move. He reiterated the command twice more. Then, sensing Buehler's dilemma, he sent orders for the sections of the 17th Ohio and 2nd Massachusetts batteries to keep the Rebel cavalry away from the Indianans.[35]

With rounds now spinning across the prairies in their direction, the mounted Rebels trotted out of range and beyond the bottom of the loop in Bayou Bourbeau and south toward the Chretien Point Plantation.

The soldiers of the 83rd Ohio, hurrying back to camp, now lay in the path of Colonel Major's loping marauders. The Buckeyes abandoned their forage train and formed up to face the new cavalry threat. "As the field was level, we could see the whole movement and knew what to do without being told," Sergeant T. B. Marshall wrote. "The only thing to do was to get back and do it quick." The Texas and Arizona cavalry swarmed past the left of the Ohioans and out of small arms range without pausing. Surprised, the Federals resumed their hustle toward camp. As they moved up, though, the Ohioans could see even more Confederates to the west coming to join the attack.[36]

Green had ordered forward his veteran brigade. Colonel Bagby led his dismounted regiments in line of battle behind Major's horsemen, and with their screen removed, emerged from the smoke and dust and into clear view. Gunners from the Val Verde and Daniel's Batteries fired into the Union flank, sending shell fragments and solid shot rattling through the trees beyond. Federal cannon fired back; this drew Bagby's attention, and he saw two guns of the 17th Ohio had been left exposed by the shift of the 67th Indiana. He directed Captain Keet McDade to take the men of the 13th Texas Battalion back to their horses to remount. As they had done a month before at Sterling's plantation, these Texans would charge these Yankees, sabers drawn.[37]

Back in the Union camps, quartermasters, commissary officers, artificers, paymasters, and other support troops sensed an impending disaster. This was no skirmish, as the cannon shot ricocheting through camp proved. They knew Confederate cavalry had already passed south of the camps and moved beyond the Bourbeau onto Buzzard Prairie. The road to safety must surely now be severed. Burbridge's command lay surrounded, these rear echelon Yankees feared.[38]

They would not wait around to find out. "At the summons of the long-roll, the stores of the brigade had been promptly loaded, and started pell-mell for the rear," Surgeon Woods observed. "In mad haste some dashed into the deep ravine, to find their wagons instantly mired." Other wagons and caissons moved down the road three hundred yards behind the Union infantry battle line, crossed the

The 60th Indiana fighting in the woods. *Becker Collection*.

bridge, and spurred their teams toward Bayou Carencro. They were followed by Colonel Major's Texas and Arizona horsemen now prowling Buzzard Prairie, who quickly gave chase.[39]

Focused on the infantry battle to the north, which he believed to be the greatest threat, Burbridge was unaware the enemy had gained his left and rear. In this fog of battle, he commanded the 60th Indiana to advance once again, find the enemy, and hold them while the 96th Ohio came up on their left. Colonel Guppey moved his Wisconsin men into line near the road to Opelousas, facing north, in reserve.

The 60th Indiana found Roberts's skirmishers pushing out of the second ravine and up a slight rise. Then, peering into the trees beyond, the soldiers could see the rest of Roberts's Brigade, a hundred yards behind the skirmishers. Each side raked the other with volleys and then clawed at each other with clouds of musket fire. The collision occurred near the crest of a slight ridge between the second and third ravines. Colonel Roberts directed his officers to advance the Confederate line steadily, moving forward a few paces with every volley. The Texans gained ground and passed over their own skirmishers to gain the rise, three hundred yards from where they had started this rolling gun battle.[40]

The outnumbered Hoosiers could not hold without help. "It is a host against which a handful of stout-hearted men are battling," fretted Surgeon Woods, "and which it is impossible for them to withstand." Frightened men began to leave the ranks and head to the rear. Burbridge, seeing a growing stream of fugitives emerging from the woods, once more ordered the 67th Indiana, now isolated behind the left of the Union line, to wheel away from their threat to the west, and to make a right oblique into the woods to lend a hand. Waving his hat as he dashed up to his reserve regiment, Burbridge ordered in the 23rd Wisconsin to stiffen the line. "Pointing to a hollow between two rises of ground, [he] ordered [Guppey] to form his regiment there," a soldier reported, "adding 'and it's a damned hot place, too.'"[41]

The Wisconsin men complied. "I put my regiment in the designated position as quickly as possible, and ordered my men to lie down," Colonel Guppey reported. He feared the 96th Ohio and 60th Indiana would soon break. His Badgers might check the enemy pursuit, but they could not hold them long. Some of the Ohio officers, seeing Guppey's line, convinced some of their shaken soldiers to fall in with the 23rd Wisconsin. Guppey remained cool. "I ordered my men not to fire a gun till I gave the command."[42]

Meanwhile the men of the 83rd Ohio continued to move smartly toward their camps and the sound of battle. As their column approached the fight, the Buckeyes looked left and saw mounted Confederates forming to rush the guns of the 17th Ohio, unimpeded, across the prairie. The regiment lurched to a halt, faced left into line of battle, and then move toward the 17th Ohio on the double quick, causing McDade and the Texans, already gathering momentum in their charge, to swerve away. The rescued gunners prudently limbered up and headed to the rear, escorted by the remains of the 6th Missouri Cavalry, not stopping until they were beyond Bayou Bourbeau and onto Buzzard Prairie. Having rescued the guns from being overrun, the 83rd Ohio fell back and resumed their trek toward the fight in the woods.[43]

The 13th Texas Cavalry Battalion overruns the 67th
Indiana and the Union camps. *Becker Collection.*

North of the 83rd Ohio, Lieutenant Colonel Buehler and the 67th Indiana
struggled to obey Burbridge's orders to close up on the left of the 96th Ohio.
Hearing the crescendo of firing from the woods, Buehler—a veteran of the
Prussian Army as well as most of the battles of the Vicksburg Campaign, believed
this was the point of decision. Racked by indecision, he finally ordered his men
to shift their formation again, turn toward the northeast, and head toward the
sound of the guns. If he was correct, Buehler would put the 67th Indiana upon
the right flank of the Confederate infantry, drive them back, and allow Burbridge
time to draw his entire brigade back to Bayou Bourbeau and realign it to face
toward the west.[44]

Buehler's gamble failed. As the Federals changed their facing, McDade's
mounted 13th Texas Cavalry Battalion, denied the chance to capture the cannon of the 17th Ohio battery, instead pounced on the backs of the 67th Indiana.
The Texans charged into the midst of the distracted Hoosiers, striking them
on the left and rear. The Rebels shattered the disorganized infantry formation.

"Both forces became all mixed, and a pandemonium of sticking with bayonets, clubbing of muskets, and shooting with revolvers," remembered Private Scott. Many of the Yankees bolted for their camps and the woods; the majority of the regiment surrendered.[45]

Major General Washburn, returning to his headquarters, was about halfway between Burbridge's camp and his own when the volume of firing reached this crescendo. He turned to see panicked quartermasters and paymasters bolting out of the trees. Once again, he turned around and rode back to Bayou Bourbeau to see to the matter, but not before he dispatched two aides with orders for his colonels to form the rest of his division and bring it forward. "I soon discovered we were assailed with terrible energy by an overwhelming force in front and on both flanks," he reported. "Many of the troops had broken and were scattered over the field, and the utter destruction of capture of the whole force seemed imminent." Wheeling his horse, he spurred the animal back toward Bayou Carencro to personally fetch his troops.[46]

Burbridge's isolated brigade faced disaster. To its front, the Texan infantry was steadily advancing. These well-disciplined Rebels stood firm, reloading and delivering accurate and devastating blows to the Union line. Each advancing Union regiment, committed piecemeal, moved up to fire only to be smothered in return by a blaze of bullets from the three Texan regiments. The 60th Indiana and the 96th Ohio bent into semi-circles, their well-dressed lines becoming mobs as Texans overlapped each flank. "All are under a most galling fire, and writhe as if in a final death struggle," wrote Woods. The smoke, noise, and confusion of the battle further isolated the newly arrived 23rd Wisconsin, and the two shaken Union regiments, into pockets beset by enemies to their front and, now, slipping around their flanks. "The gallant 60th cannot for another moment endure the storm of balls that beats upon them," Woods reported from camp. "They break."[47]

The rest of the Federal line collapsed as well. Colonel Owens rallied some of the 60th Indiana in their camps beyond the road to Opelousas whiled the soldiers in the 96th Ohio, with fight still left in them, fell back to this new line and re-formed. Behind them, the 23rd Wisconsin, alone in the woods, bought time, "making havoc in the enemy ranks," wrote one soldier. Colonel Guppey's

Colonel Joshua Guppey, 23rd Wisconsin, had been a country
judge in Columbia County, Wisconsin. *Author's collection.*

Badgers punished the advancing 18th Texas Infantry for ten minutes—precious
moments that allowed the 60th Indiana and 96th Ohio to regroup. The 11th and
15th Texas, though, began to curl around his flanks, "giving me a heavier fire
than I could return," Guppey admitted. He sent a runner asking Burbridge to
hurry forward the fresh 83rd Ohio. Shortly afterward, Guppey spun and fell to
the ground, shot below the left knee. Many of his men thought him slain, and
they lost heart. Guppey gave up the fight. As he hobbled to the rear, his regiment
streamed toward the trees and tents of their camps, where the rest of the brigade
seemed to be re-forming.[48]

The Confederates, meanwhile, had been tripped up. Colonel Roberts readied
his men to pursue his defeated adversaries just to watch Union cavalry and
mounted infantry smash into his left flank from across Bayou Bourbeau, just
as he had feared might happen. Where was the 7th Texas Cavalry, which was
supposed to prevent this? The perturbed colonel sent a staff officer out to the
prairies to find more cavalry, but few horsemen came. In frustration, he turned
the 11th Texas Infantry to face to its left and punish its assailants. Precious
minutes ticked away.[49]

The timing of this attack was fortuitous for the Federals. It provided a distraction at just the moment Burbidge feared he was about to lose his colors, his
guns, and his command. His cannon he could save. Realizing enemy rifles could

easily shoot down his gunners and horses and knowing the Texan cavalry could outride them in a chase, Burbridge ordered the Federal artillerymen to escape his collapsing position. They red legs needed little prodding. The guns of the 2nd Massachusetts Battery, near the road, shredded the trees harboring the Texas infantry with one last blast of canister while the 17th Ohio Battery rattled toward the bridge and out of the fight. At last limbers arrived to take the Massachusetts guns away.[50]

This chore underway, Major General Burbridge rode among the men of the 96th Ohio and 60th Indiana and ordered them to withdraw by swinging away and to the rear and re-form in the woods at the back of their camps—the high bank of Bayou Bourbeau serving as useful cover. "The gallant Burbridge [rode] up and down the tattered fragments of his brigade, directing and encouraging men who every instant proved themselves hero-hearted," Woods recorded. The general grabbed one of the regimental flags and began to belt out the song "The Battle Cry of Freedom": "Rally round the flag, boys, rally once again," he sang over the noise of the battle. The remnants of the three regiments joined the singing

Colonel George Wythe Baylor was a Texas frontiersman. After the war he would lead Texas Rangers in El Paso. *Edward Clifton Wharton Family Papers, Louisiana and Lower Mississippi Valley Collections, LSU Libraries, Baton Rouge, Louisiana.*

and, heartened, fell back into the trees along Bayou Bourbeau in good order, now facing toward the west. The Union cavalry, Burbridge believed, would secure his flanks.[51]

The unharmed 83rd Ohio joined them, retreating through the camps to this new position. "We knew there was plenty of assistance if we could only reach it," Sergeant Marshall wrote. Several of his troops broke ranks to rescue items from their tents—including payday money. The cohesion of the regiment fell apart as the momentum of the retreat swept it toward Bayou Bourbeau. Many kept going in the confusion and emerged onto Buzzard Prairie beyond.[52]

Seeing the Federals retreating, the mounted Texans swarmed forward. Riders tore through the Union camps and, ignoring the enemy infantry, snapped at the column of limbered artillery as it rumbled its way across the Bayou Bourbeau bridge. The Texans could not stop Lieutenant William Marland from safeguarding the two guns from the 2nd Massachusetts Battery, but they mobbed the Federals' last gun, a 10-pounder Parrott from the 17th Ohio, as it crossed the bridge. They shot down the horses to bring the limber and gun to a crashing halt, and they also captured the caisson.

Major's Brigade, already on Buzzard Prairie, spotted the stream of escaping artillery and surged up from the south as the enemy broke out onto the prairies. While most of the Texans chased the fleeing Federals, Colonel George Wythe Baylor kept his regiment in hand. He led the 2nd Arizona Cavalry all the way around the Union left and into the Union camps at Bayou Carencro. There he found the enemy preparing to advance. Faced down by troops from the 11th Indiana, 29th Wisconsin, 24th Iowa and a section of artillery, Baylor prudently fell back.[53]

Some of the Confederates on Buzzard Prairie appeared overwhelmed by the swarm of Yankee fugitives and confused to find so many Federals still had some fight in them. One Rebel horseman confronted an artilleryman who happened to be a German from Ohio. "Halt! Halt! You Yankee vagabond!" the Texan yelled, his pistol drawn. To his surprise, the German spun around and knocked him on the head with his rammer. The Texan toppled off his horse. "You go to hell," the gunner responded.[54]

Back in the Union camps where what was left of the 60th Indiana, 23rd Wisconsin, 83rd and 96th Ohio rallied, the respite ended, and the battle devolved into a general melee and hundreds of individual gunfights. At one point the colors of the 96th Ohio fell to the ground; one of the soldiers dashed in "among the reeling, swaying combatants," and carried the flag to safety. The Union brigade did not hold long. "Not an organized command remains," lamented Surgeon Woods as he made his way across Bayou Bourbeau.[55]

Lieutenant Colonel Albert H. Brown of the 96th Ohio mounted his horse and ordered his men to disperse, head across the ravine, and form beyond the Bourbeau. "Brave boys, to stay is death," he bellowed, "fall back, as best you can, to the other side of the woods, we will rally there." The troops obeyed. Further south, the scattered soldiers of the 83rd Ohio swept up the shot-up remnant of the 23rd Wisconsin, saving their regimental colors from capture. Burbridge rode over to his last intact regiment, "hat in hand, face pale, though . . . quite cool and collected," noted an Ohio soldier, to convince them to re-form across the bayou. The general turned to these retreating troops, calling out to them, "I rely on the eighty third Ohio." He would re-form his battered brigade around the 83rd.[56]

The Confederates rounded up hundreds of Federals who simply gave up. Corporal Charles Hankamer of the Texas Squadron, riding with Major's Brigade,

Brigadier General Robert A. Cameron had been an Indiana newspaper publisher before the war and soon proved fearless in battle. *Courtesy of Tom Pressly, Shreveport, Louisiana.*

found himself in a desperate situation. This bold twenty-six-year-old miller from Jefferson County, Texas had ridden alone into a clump of Yankees, who turned on him. Brandishing his pistol, he demanded they all surrender. Instead, they threatened to overwhelm him. When they hesitated, however, Hankamer shot one dead and wounded another. The frightened troops, described as "all foreigners," surrendered. He marched his prisoners back into Rebel lines, "having to shoot and kill one to get . . . twenty-two," noted his sergeant, H. N. Connor.[57]

The Texas infantry, delayed by the annoying Union cavalry on their flank, once again ground forward to finish the fight. Roberts's Brigade charged through the trees and into the northern periphery of the camp in time to see the enemy in flight and McDade's, Bagby's, and Major's men following on their heels. With nothing left to accomplish against the Union infantry, "Our men were halted, faced to the rear, and marched back to attack the enemy's cavalry who had forced their way to our rear," Roberts reported. "They were immediately repulsed and scattered, and some few of our men rescued whom they had taken prisoner."[58]

The Federal cavalry and mounted infantry, chastened, fell back beyond Bayou Bourbeau and re-formed to cover the retreat of Burbridge's survivors. They had save the brigade from annihilation.

Major's Brigade, unable to catch the Union guns as they fled across Buzzard Prairie, had become badly scattered and was now sandwiched between Burbridge's battered but intact brigade to their left, and Washburn's reinforcements on their right. Now Texan officers struggled to re-form the command. Major ordered those he could muster to systematically saber and shoot down as many of the fleeing Yankees as they could as they retreated out of danger. As the Texans cantered back across the prairies toward Bayou Bourbeau, Baylor's couriers reported the oncoming Federal reinforcements. They also saw Burbridge's troops starting to coalesce into a new line. Ignoring the threat to their rear, the Texans believed they might still finish off the stricken Union brigade. Major ordered what men he could to dash in amongst them.

"They ride rapidly on, when, as if by magic, there rises from the thick grass a line of men, till this moment unseen, who with level muskets pour into their ranks a volley that sends them reeling back with many an empty saddle," cheered Woods. The 46th Indiana, the advance regiment from Brigadier General Robert A.

Cameron's Brigade, had saved Burbridge's rattled command from being overrun from the rear. The newly arrived Hoosiers watched as Major lead his surprised men back toward Chretien Point Plantation and out of the fight. Buzzard Prairie was once again completely Federal territory.[59]

Three hours after pickets first announced the presence of the Rebels, Washburn's Division deployed into line out on Buzzard Prairie, while Burbridge's remnant rallied, relieved. Colonel Fonda's cavalry formed a line of skirmishers in advance. "The whole brigade was now lined up under protection of the cavalry and a sorry sight it presented," admitted Sergeant Marshall of the 83rd Ohio. "The whole of the Sixty-Seventh Indiana was gone except the adjutant and major. A few of the Sixtieth Indiana were left, and about a third of the Twenty-Third Wisconsin, a few of the Ninety-Sixth Ohio, and nearly all of our regiment." Only two guns from the 17th Ohio deployed nearby.[60]

Brigadier General Green arrived in the captured enemy camps and reorganized his men to continue the battle. Roberts's infantry deployed along the tree line east of Bayou Bourbeau while the Rebel artillery fired over their heads and kept Washburn's Division at a distance in the prairie beyond. Even so, the Federals prepared to advance, also eager to continue the fight, now on better terms. Green knew he was outmatched, and his Confederates did not tarry. They hurriedly pillaged what they could from Burbridge's camps and attempted to burn the rest before the momentum of Washburn's advance convinced them to leave. "If there would have been even a half-hour cessation," wrote a soldier in the 5th Texas Cavalry, "we would have taken every piece of the captured artillery off of the field instead of leaving it there." They captured only a single 10-pound Parrot. "Deeming it imprudent to fight this large additional force," Green drolly reported, "I withdrew . . . the enemy not attempting to follow me." He stationed the straight-shooting 15th Texas Infantry as a rear guard in order to discourage close pursuit by the enemy cavalry.[61]

The Federals crossed Bayou Bourbeau and picked through the remains of their camp. "What was not taken away was piled up and burned," Sergeant Marshall remembered. The Rebels had even dumped over their pots of pork stew. The army payroll was gone. A soldier in the 5th Texas Cavalry remembered seeing it in the captured camp before skedaddling. "The table in the pay tent was piled up with money," he wrote. "I don't know what became of this money," he claimed, "whether it was destroyed or whether it was recaptured by the enemy. We did not get it. It may have been burned, too."[62]

Green's attack had savaged but not completely destroyed Burbridge's command. His Confederates had killed or wounded 200 of the 1,040 men in the brigade and captured more than 500. Only about 300 of the Yankee infantry that had fought that day now stood in line of battle beside Washburn's Division. The 67th Indiana had suffered the worst with 211 men killed, wounded, or captured. The 23rd Wisconsin lost its popular commander, Colonel Guppey, who survived the fight but, hobbled by his wound, fell prisoner. His regiment lost 128 men of the 160 in the fight—80 percent. The regiments in the fight the longest also lost heavily, the 60th Indiana numbering 131 of its men among those lost, followed by 116 from the 96th Ohio. Even the lightly engaged 83rd Ohio had nearly 60 men captured. The cavalry brigade, having skirmished since nearly sunup, lost around 50 men. The 17th Ohio lost a gun, limber, and caisson, and 25 of its gunners. The Federals had saved most of their heavy camp gear, ammunition, and vehicles, though, thanks to their skittish teamsters.[63]

Green's troops paid a toll in their attempt to destroy the Federal brigade. Colonel Roberts reported 145 of his 900 infantry slain, injured, or captured. The 18th Texas in the center of his line—the troops that had tangled with the 23rd Wisconsin—lost 60 killed, wounded, or missing. On their left, the 11th Texas, which had to fight off the counterattack by the Federal cavalry slipping around the flank, lost 19 men to gunfire and had another 32 captured. The 15th Texas fought on the right of the infantry line and lost 34 killed, wounded, or missing. Losses were remarkably light among Major's Texas and Arizona cavalry; he reported around 20 casualties. Bagby's Brigade lost just 3 men, all wounded among the mounted daredevils of the 13th Texas Cavalry battalion. Yankee shells wounded only 1 Rebel artilleryman. The exhausted Confederates declared victory and marched into Opelousas just after dark.[64]

The Yankees fell back to Bayou Carencro. Although punished that day on Bayou Bourbeau, back in their camps along the Carencro they counted the scores of Green's men snatched up over the last few weeks of fighting. Officers ordered a section of artillery as well as an infantry lieutenant, sergeant, and 20 men of the

29th Wisconsin, along with others to guard some 185 Rebel captives held inside a makeshift rope corral on the edge of their camps. "The prisoners are all Texans," wrote Private Henry Whipple, "and are a very fine looking lot of men." Chances were good in the coming weeks these Lone Star Rebels would be swapped for the Midwesterners just recently taken.[65]

On November 4, the war in Louisiana paused for a day. Brigadier General Green forwarded a flag of truce so that his men could recover the bodies of their fallen comrades. "No one thought of anything else," Captain Giesecke of the 4th Texas Cavalry wrote in his diary.[66]

Elsewhere that day, Major General Taylor arrived at Green's headquarters in Opelousas to think through his next move. Taylor brought rumors a Union naval expedition had departed New Orleans as well as a stack of Magruder's dispatches, filled with anxiety about Texas. After visiting with his most-trusted lieutenant, Taylor penned a response in which he conceded the existence of a Union amphibious expedition but doubted it was going to Texas. "I have just received positive information from New Orleans that an expedition of some 5,000 men is . . . in the river with Banks in person in command," Taylor wrote. "The last rumors point to Mobile as the objective point . . . but I have nothing but rumors."[67]

It started raining again that night as the conference broke up. The next morning Texas scouts rode into Opelousas to report the Yankees once again on the move, but still heading away. Washburn had left Bayou Carencro and was heading toward Vermilionville. Taylor, convinced the Yankees had abandoned their campaign altogether, headed toward Holmesville to decide where next to send his army.

As his ambulance headed north, Taylor passed another bunch of Federals on the move. Yankee prisoners taken at Bayou Bourbeau composed this soggy collection of troops that slopped along the muddy road, heading for Alexandria and an uncertain future. Colonel Guppey of the 23rd Wisconsin hobbled along with the aid of a crutch, determined to stay with his troops. He had plenty of time to review the battle, and he chatted with men who had fought it with him. "Our disposition at first was against a cavalry attack," he pointed out, "and I think we could have driven the cavalry if it had been unaided by infantry." That had not been the case, all agreed, but Major General Burbridge had also mismanaged the fight. "As it was, three of our regiments were used against the rebel infantry," Guppey reflected, "unfortunately one at a time."[68]

As Major General Taylor's horses and vehicle splashed alongside this forlorn and mud-splattered blue column, "I observed an officer, in the uniform of a colonel, limping along with his leg bandaged," Taylor wrote. The general ordered his driver to pull over so he could ask why this wounded officer was being marched along with the enlisted men. The colonel had refused to be separated from his soldiers, came the reply. Taylor admired the man's grit.

The Confederate commander got out of his carriage and stepped into the same mud as his adversaries, walking over to the Yankee officer. "I approached him, and, as gently as possible, remonstrated against the folly of walking on a wounded leg," Taylor continued. Guppey said his wound was not serious or painful and he could keep up. "His regiment was from Wisconsin, recruited among his neighbors and friends, and he was very unwilling to leave it," Taylor wrote. Moved by the fellow's care for his men, Taylor invited him to at least ride with him in his ambulance for part of the way to rest his leg. Guppey reluctantly agreed.

The two soldiers rode on in silence until, uncomfortable with the tension, Taylor engaged the colonel in small talk. Eventually, after several hours, the two had struck up a lively conversation. "Impressed by his bearing and demeanor," Taylor remembered, "I asked him in what way I could serve him." Guppey wanted Taylor to ensure a letter got home to his wife in Columbus, Wisconsin. She had been ill, and the colonel wanted to allay her fears as to his safety.

Taylor paroled Guppey on the spot. "You shall go to the river tonight," the general replied, "catch one of your steamers, and take home the assurance of your safety. Remain on parole until you can send me an officer of equal rank, and I will look to the comfort of your men and have them exchanged at the earliest moment."[69]

FOURTEEN

THE BEACHES OF TEXAS

I am certain that in New England and the West men will readily volunteer for service in Texas, if it is permitted.

—Major General Nathaniel P. Banks
Department of the Gulf

A t the far end of the Texas coast, more than 425 miles to the southwest of Vermilionville and even farther away from the mud and blood of Sterling's plantation and Bayou Bourbeau, Union soldiers crowded the railings of an invasion fleet, eager to catch a glimpse of land and glad to be in calm waters. "The unclouded, noon-day sun, shone from a sky of as brilliant a blue as poet or painter ever gave to the sky of Italy," wrote Private Edwin B. Lufkin, far from his Weld, Maine, home. "On the right, the low, sandy shore of Padre Island extended farther than the eye could reach; on the left, the high; roundtopped sand-hills of Brazos Island hid the distant mainland from view; and a little farther away, beyond the mouth of the Rio Grande, lay the chapparel-fringed Mexican coast, with the dark blue wall of the Guadaloupe mountains in the background." Directly ahead, and seemingly a little inland, stood the white lighthouse of Point Isabel.[1]

Yankee tars in ships' boats rowed soldiers from the 19th Iowa Infantry, or at least the pitiful remnant of the battle at Sterling's plantation, toward the low dunes of the distant shore. On November 2 the boats' keels crunched into the sand, and the soldiers vaulted overboard into the knee-high surf of Brazos Santiago Island, just north of the mouth of the Rio Grande. They waded in as the vanguard of Major General Banks's long-anticipated invasion of Texas. After forming into line of battle, the Vicksburg veterans marched four miles down the barren island to the shore of Boca Chica, a shallow outlet of the Laguna Madre that separated the barrier island from the dunes of mainland Texas. This expedition, these soldiers agreed, would be very different than their time in Pointe Coupee Parish.[2]

While the Hawkeyes tended to business, Private James Oliver of Company B, 15th Maine—a veteran of the hectic defense of New Orleans the previous June—claimed honors as the first to "plant the flag in Texas" in obedience to General-in-Chief Henry W. Halleck's orders. The soldier ran with a company flag to one of the abandoned government buildings, climbed onto its roof, and waved the Stars and Stripes for the invading army "amidst the tumultuous cheers of the soldiers on the vessels within view of the very romantic and inspiring spectacle," as Lieutenant Henry A. Shorey recounted. "The men from Maine—the extreme northeastern state of the Union—had restored the country's flag to a point upon the extreme southwestern portion of the territory so long held by the Confederate forces, and almost within sight of the inhabitants of a foreign nationality."[3]

With these honors completed, the Union army began the laborious chore of unloading thousands of men, hundreds of horses, heavy equipment, vehicles, and supplies upon the Texas shore. Heavy surf and rolling seas made putting the troops ashore difficult. It would be several days before the navy finished the task, but the slow pace would not matter because few enemies were about. The men of the 19th Iowa surveyed their surroundings as they provided security for the landings. "Brazos Santiago is a sand bar with no vegetable life and nothing good about it," wrote Sergeant Irvine Dungan, "except the sea breezes." To the northwest, soldiers could see Point Isabel, the location of the U.S. Army depot

Major General Nathaniel P. Banks led the invasion of Texas from the stateroom of the transport *McClellan*. Alfred Rudolph Waud, artist. *Library of Congress*.

in the opening campaign of the Mexican War. To the south and east, the troops could see French and British warships just off the coast of Mexico. The nefarious trading port of Playa Bagdad lay just out of sight, just half a dozen miles away.[4]

Other than a few Texan scouts who watched the Yankees come ashore, no Rebels appeared. "The landing of United States troops upon Texas soil seems to have been . . . a "surprise party" to the Rebel commanders," Lieutenant Shorey declared. "The Sabine affair and the subsequent continued occupation of the Teche by the army under Franklin . . . had so completely absorbed the attention of the enemy on the Louisiana border, that no tidings of the departure from New Orleans of a separate expedition seems to have reached them."[5]

One of the Rebel observers, Captain Henry T. Davis of the 33rd Texas Cavalry, could not believe what he was seeing from his perch atop the Point Isabel Lighthouse. Twenty-four ships of various sizes, he estimated, had emerged from the haze of the Gulf of Mexico. He and his nineteen-man detachment hid five miles back in the chaparral overnight but returned on the morning of November 3 to take another look. More ships had come in, and thousands of troops camped in hundreds of tents amid huge piles of supplies covering the barren sands of Brazos Santiago Island. Some of these invaders had landed to the north on Padre Island as well. Davis also saw the horses of the 1st Texas Cavalry (Union). "Fearing that cavalry might be landed at Boca Chica to cut us off," the captain wrote, "I left."[6]

The mere arrival of the Union fleet off the coast had already triggered chaos in the Rio Grande Valley. Several companies of Tejano Confederates had dissolved when the first Federal sails appeared on the horizon, and one officer, Captain Adrían J. Vidal, led his men on a looting spree. These mutineers, many nursing grudges that predated the current war, threatened to overrun Brownsville in advance of the Union landings, but they veered off at the last minute in the face of Confederate resolve. A number of Texas Unionists and filibustering American volunteers in Matamoros had encouraged the Tejanos to break ranks, but the main agitator was the caudillo "Cheno" Cortina. Vidal and his men would eventually filter into Federal service or cross the river and lend their hearts and pistols to Cortina, but first they would plunder ranches and settlements for nearly a dozen miles up the Rio Grande from Brownsville.[7]

The shockwaves from the Union presences in South Texas rolled into the interior over the course of the next few days. Captain Richard Taylor of Company A, 33rd Texas Cavalry—and no relation to the commander of the Confederate army in Louisiana—resumed observation of the Union army landing in Texas. As he and five of his soldiers watched, some of the Union cavalry splashed across the shallow Laguna Madre. Only a company of Federals herded several hundred horses across the shallow bay to let them graze on the mainland. Taylor wished he had more men, for he might have been able to steal the herd. "Being unable to fight with the few men under me, I very quietly withdrew to the river to watch their movements," he wrote. He and his men set up their observation post at the dusty cabins of the Palmetto Ranch. The next afternoon, November 4, Taylor and his men ran for their lives. "At 1:10 o'clock I discovered about one-half mile below, coming up the road, about 200 cavalry in full-charge," he continued. He and his men scattered into the brush, watching as the 1st Texas Cavalry (Union) thundered past on their way to Brownsville.[8]

That very day, while burial details cleaned up the human wreckage along Bayou Bourbeau in far-away Louisiana, Union major general Nathaniel P. Banks occupied a stateroom aboard the transport *McClellan* off the mouth of the Rio Grande. The commander of the Department of the Gulf took great pride in his landing in Texas. He had deceived the Confederates about his intentions and had fixed the enemy's attention on Louisiana. It appeared as though Confederate major general John Bankhead Magruder may have stripped this region of its defenders in response to the threat east of the Sabine River. Banks had stolen a march on his enemies and, he expected, would soon sever the Trans-Mississippi Confederacy's cotton lifeline to Mexico.

Banks penned a celebratory dispatch to Halleck. "I have the honor to report that on November 2, at meridian, the flag of the Union was raised on Brazos Island," he trumpeted, then amplified his triumph. "It was occupied by a small force of rebel cavalry which fled at our disembarkation."[9]

Banks established his headquarters at Brazos Santiago. He had come with a sizable force of around four thousand men. He had nine regiments of Midwesterners from the 2nd Division, 13th Army Corps, plus the 13th and 15th Maine transferred from the 19th Army Corps in the defenses of New Orleans to make up for losses suffered at Sterling's plantation. In addition, the 1st Regiment of Engineers, *Corps d'Afrique*—the same men who had handled much of the digging at Port Hudson—were now in Texas, as was the freshly mustered 16th Infantry, *Corps d'Afrique*, from New Orleans. These African American soldiers would handle the chores associated with managing the Brazos Santiago supply base in South Texas.[10]

Empty transports returned to Louisiana to fetch more men. At Vermilionville, Brigadier General Michael K. Lawler's 1st Division, 13th Army Corps, received word to continue marching south toward the transports that would meet them in New Orleans and take them to Texas. Major General Cadwallader C. Washburn, still smarting from the rough treatment his men had received at Bayou Bourbeau, learned that he too would leave Louisiana behind to command the advance up the Texas coast.[11]

Banks asked Halleck if any reinforcement could be had for this next push. He also wanted draftees to bring his regiments to full strength. "I am certain that in New England and the West men will readily volunteer for service in Texas, if it is permitted," he suggested to Halleck. Success, Banks believed, hinged on ever-

Brigadier General Hamilton P. Bee was a Texas politician and veteran of the various wars of the Republic of Texas. *Lawrence T. Jones III Texas photography collection, DeGolyer Library, Southern Methodist University.*

more Union troops being committed to his Texas expedition. He also knew the Rebels in Louisiana could be lethal. "Unless we are strengthened," he warned Halleck, "we may have to abandon the great advantage we have gained." Ever the politician, he feared Halleck would oppose such a creative and unconventional campaign in Texas, so Banks enlisted political allies in Washington to advocate his position. He penned a letter to his ally, Massachusetts representative George S. Boutwell, a luminary among Republicans, asking him to lobby President Abraham Lincoln for New England troops to be dispatched to Texas.[12]

Meanwhile, the Confederates responded to the landings by making a hasty retreat. Brigadier General Hamilton P. Bee, Confederate commander on the Rio Grande, ordered the evacuation of Brownsville on November 3. His few hundred jangled and nervous troops, already on edge from the machinations of Cortina and the Matamoros Unionists, set fire to thousands of bales of cotton and then did what they could to destroy the munitions stored at Fort Brown, on the edge of town. In a mighty flash, more than four tons of gunpowder exploded in the magazine, shattering windows throughout the settlement and showering it with bricks and flaming debris. Some nearby stores and homes began to burn, and marauders turned out to ransack what they could. Around midnight, Bee and a ten-man escort were the last Confederates to leave the former hub of the Trans-Mississippi cotton trade. Looters took advantage of the Confederate soldiers'

Elizabeth Street, 1865, the main thoroughfare in Brownsville. *Library of Congress.*

Typical landing at Brownsville, 1865. *Library of Congress.*

departure to pillage Brownsville, but they would have to work fast. Word arrived that the town would soon be reoccupied by troops, this time Federal, as part of the systematic dismantling of the Confederacy's Rio Grande trade network. [13]

Major General Napoleon J. T. Dana, now commander of the 13th Army Corps, moved his headquarters inland while his men carried on with the mission. On November 5 the quick-riding, hard-hitting 1st Texas Cavalry (Union) captured Brownsville without a fight and moved upriver from there, driving Confederates from the 33rd Texas Cavalry before them. Soldiers of the 94th Illinois arrived that evening to occupy the town, and to tamp down the chaos.[14]

The Illinois troops would soon be reinforced. Additional infantry marched toward the smoky smudge on the clear, blue, Texas horizon. "Started for the mainland by fording Boca Chica, an inlet over one-half mile wide and over four feet deep," wrote Private Henry Carl Ketzle of the 37th Illinois. "Most all the boys had to make two trips to bring arms, clothing, and accouterments across, a trip long to be remembered by many." That night, the men slept on the battleground of Palo Alto. On November 6 Union troops passed through the field of Resaca de la Palma and occupied Brownsville in strength. The stump of the 19th Iowa occupied empty warehouses—once full of cotton—on the bank of the Rio Grande. "Here we were as far away from home as we could get and stay in the United States," noted Sergeant Dungan. "We were on the very outskirts of Uncle Sam's wide-spread domain."[15]

Some of the troops who crossed the Boca Chica as part of the invasion force removed their shoes before they waded into the saltwater. "The bottom was thickly covered with oysters, so the sixty rods of the ford became a real 'Via Dolorosa' to our naked feet," complained Private Lufkin of the 13th Maine. Lufkin and his regiment reached the mouth of the Rio Grande that evening and then to a spot along the river and opposite Playa Bagdad. The Texan shore was home to a settlement called Clarksville, which "consisted of three old wooden houses," Lufkin remembered. Across the river, though, lay bustling Playa Bagdad, which "looked like quite a thriving place."[16]

Some of the Union quartermasters, eager to feed their troops, crossed the river. On the Mexican side of the Rio Grande they bought bread from merchants in Playa Bagdad, which remained a cotton boomtown.[17]

As his men overran Brownsville, Banks sought to implement the next phase of his invasion. He wrote a dispatch to Brigadier General James Henry Carleton, who was commanding U.S. forces in New Mexico. Carleton's headquarters was near Fort Bliss, Texas, about seven hundred direct miles away or twelve hundred miles up the Rio Grande. Banks let the Far West commander know he had landed. "It is our expectation that the flag will be permanently maintained here," he wrote. With that being the case, Banks wondered, could Carleton invade Texas from New Mexico and move on San Antonio from the west? Any coordination of the efforts from the coast and from Fort Bliss would have to be made by sending dispatches through Mexico via Monterrey and Chihuahua, but a pincher movement would help reclaim Texas for the Union. Because of the distance between the generals, Carlton did not receive the dispatch until Christmas Eve, nearly six weeks later. With these chores complete Major General Banks followed his command ashore and shifted his headquarters to Brownsville.[18]

Banks's arrival had already spread political pandemonium along the Mexican frontier. The sudden change in authority in the Rio Grande Valley violently realigned factions trying to maneuver the shoals of the French invasion of that country, the American Civil War, and a civil war within the government of President Benito Juárez. One of these players, former Imperialist General de Division José Maria Cobos, had been plotting a local coup for almost a year—with the avowed support of Cortina—from the sanctuary of Confederate Brownsville. He had fled

Mexico City after the French reverses of 1862 and had gathered two hundred followers to his cause on the Texas side of the Rio Grande. The change of flags now forced his hand. As the vanguard of the Union army swept into Brownsville, Cobos and his men raced across the Rio Grande into Matamoros, drove out the Republican governor, Manuel Ruiz, and started a *pronunciamiento* against Juárez. This bold revolution unleashed days of gun battles between competing factions, including one led by Cobos's erstwhile ally, Cortina.[19]

Major General Banks arranged his headquarters to a backdrop of Mexican battles echoing from across the Rio Grande. The Union troops were astonished at this alien land they had conquered. "Between the 5th and 9th of November there were three revolutions in Matamoros, just across the river," noted Private Lufkin. Banks prepared to involve troops from the United States if needed to sustain their faction against the French puppet. He put his artillery in position to shell the Mexican town and issued orders to his infantry to be ready for action. "During one of these revolutions, when the office of the United States Consul in Matamoros was threatened, the troops in Brownsville were held in readiness to cross the river to protect it," Lufkin continued, "but as it was not actually molested we were not called upon to invade Mexico."[20]

The U.S. authorities clearly had their favorites in the fight across the river. As the smoke cleared from all of the turmoil, "the successful party was hostile to Maximilian's French army," Lufkin concluded, "and friendly to the United States."

Matamoros beckoned just across the narrow Rio Grande, 1865. *Library of Congress.*

Cobos died in front of a firing squad, and Banks felt relieved. "My most sanguine expectations have been realized," he wrote to President Abraham Lincoln. "Everything is now favorable as could be desired." The victorious authorities in Matamoros loaned three shallow draft steamers to the victorious *norteamericanos* in Brownsville to help them move additional troops and supplies to and from the Gulf of Mexico. Juárez's men could also shuttle U.S. troops across the border if another crisis came.[21]

In Paris, Confederate diplomat John Slidell blamed the French for the loss of Matamoros and urged Napoleon III to send troops and retake the important town. "The failure to occupy it has already been productive of the most mischievous consequences," Slidell pointed out. Earlier that year the French warship *Panama* seized weapons from the *Caroline Goodyear* and the steamer *Love Bird* off the mouth of the Rio Grande. French skippers claimed they believed the weapons on the Confederate ships were headed for Juárez and his Republicans. Had the French held Matamoros, there would have been no misunderstanding, Slidell explained, and the sixteen thousand firearms might have equipped sixteen thousand Texans eager to repel the Yankee invaders.[22]

Instead, the French and the Confederates now shared a problem. "The Texas bank of the Rio Grande will now be the point of departure of Federal emissaries to excite the population of northern Mexico in favor of Juárez, furnishing subsidies of money and munitions of war," Slidell fumed. American mercenaries would now have a pathway to join the Republican armies. Slidell felt vindicated by his Excellency's response. "The Emperor too readily appreciates the immense consequences which may result from the occupation of the Rio Grande by hostile instead of friendly armies."[23]

The French, though, proved to be enigmatic. In Washington, the Mexican minister to the United States, Matías Romero Avendaño, pumped Robert M. McLane, former ambassador Mexico, for information. Would there be collusion between the French and the Confederates? What he learned gave little hope for the Mexican Republicans. McLane told Romero he believed the French would never establish a permanent foothold in Mexico, but the emperor's advisors disagreed, believing the venture would take root, "provided that they had the perseverance to carry it to the end and were skillful in the mode of developing it." The conversion of some of Juárez's warlords to the Imperialist cause—like Santiago Vidaurri, the governor of Coahuila and Nuevo Léon, or some of the squabblers in Matamoros—would help the French project, McLane warned. Given the circumstances, McLane advised Romero to maintain the status quo and not to urge an American intervention in the Mexican civil war. "If by our actions war breaks out between France and this [U.S.] government," McLane advised, "France will immediately ally itself with the South and this alliance would produce two lamentable results for Mexico. First, instead of having only one enemy as we do now, we would have two." Neither McLane nor Romero believed the United States would defeat a Franco-Confederate alignment.[24]

The key to French success, according to McLane, lay in making Napoleon III's intervention on the side of Mexican Conservatives seem popular with the Mexican people. The Archduke Maximillian of Austria had made this a requirement of his ascending the Cactus Throne; he would only cross the Atlantic if he could be certain of popular support. Napoleon III needed to "make it appear in Europe that the Mexican people really desire monarchy, or would accept it with pleasure," McLane reported. If this desire was demonstrated, England, Spain, and other powers on the continent would probably recognize the imperial regime, "and the fate of Mexico would be sealed," McLane wrote. Romero agreed. The French, he observed, were careful to stage demonstrations of Mexican support so that "the intervention is anxiously desired as the remedy for all the evils."[25]

Robert Milligan McLean by George Peter Alexander Healy (1858). *State of Maryland.*

Now that Banks had planted the American flag once again in Texas, the long-term implications remained murky. Not only had an anti-Juárez coup been precipitated—and suppressed—in Matamoros, but U.S. bayonets in the region implied a Federal willingness to aid the Republican cause, sending a warning to any Mexican border chiefs who might be leaning toward the Imperialists. This show of force ordered by Lincoln in August and endorsed by Halleck was international brinkmanship wrapped in a gauzy covering of Trans-Mississippi grand strategy.

Banks's grand invasion had worked as planned. Confederate resistance in the Rio Grande Valley collapsed with shocking rapidity. The men of the 1st Texas Cavalry (Union) fanned out across South Texas, scouting the cotton roads away from the Rio Grande into the interior and upriver toward Laredo. Troopers ransacked the Rebel salt works at El Sal del Rey, about fifty miles northwest of Brownsville. The Federal horsemen returned from their hunt reporting the region lay wide open and subject to whatever Union authorities willed.

The Rebels would take days to recover from their shock. Confederate forces in South Texas regrouped at Richard King's ranch on Santa Gertrudis Creek, 115 miles north of Brownsville and about the same distance east across the South Texas scrub from Laredo. On November 8 Brigadier General Bee reported his dire

The main house at the King Ranch at the time of the war. *King Ranch Archives.*

situation to Major General Magruder. Vindicated, because he had warned about the possibility of a Federal naval invasion in October, Magruder forwarded this news to Lieutenant General Edmund Kirby Smith in Shreveport. The Confederate dream of a Franco-Texan enclave in northern Mexico and South Texas faded.[26]

Bee had little at hand with which to fight. Affairs in Louisiana had pulled most of the Confederate forces in Texas toward the Sabine River, leaving Bee with fewer than three hundred men of the 33rd Texas Cavalry. They were strewn from the coast to Laredo. His artillery? One cannon. Bee imagined the situation was more dire than he could see. The invaders on the Rio Grande, Bee believed, had come from the East Coast as the vanguard of a completely new army, not from Banks's command in Louisiana. "My impression is that the expedition is from the Atlantic coast," he reported, "and intended to occupy the line of the Rio Grande as a demonstration against the French in Mexico." If Bee had been right, then the Confederate Trans-Mississippi would have faced a serious, and simultaneous, threat in Texas and Louisiana, and Union armies could envelop Texas from the Sabine and the Gulf Coast. Bee told Magruder he would remain at King's ranch as long as the position remained tenable.[27]

Bee did not know if the locals would rally to the cause. The popularity of the Confederacy among the local Tejano population had crumbled with the arrival of the Yankees. "The news from the river is distressing," he wrote to Magruder. "Bands of robbers are prowling around, doing all the damage possible." There was an exception to this gloomy report. "Major Santos Benevides . . . told his men that the enemy had landed, and that those who did not wish to fight for the Confederacy would receive a discharge," Bee explained. "The answer was 'Viva la Confederacion, viva Major Benavides!'" The major's portion of the regiment had retreated to Laredo.[28]

In other good news, Bee reported during the retreat his men had successfully carried away from Brownsville about one million dollars' worth of clothes, blankets, and other goods of value to the army in the Trans-Mississippi.

These bright spots notwithstanding, Bee had to report on the possible far-reaching consequences of the Federal invasion. The loss of Brownsville and the scattering of Confederate troops might permanently destroy the important cotton trade that had been sustaining the Confederate Trans-Mississippi. To do what he could, Bee ordered all salvageable bales in South Texas be shipped to Laredo and Eagle Pass. He believed Vidaurri remained sympathetic to the Confederate cause and would welcome the trade through his state and away from his rivals in Tamaulipas and on the coast.[29]

Bee clearly needed troops. He asked Magruder for two thousand. Without them, he feared, he would lose all of South Texas. At King's ranch alone this would mean twenty thousand beef cattle and three thousand horses would fall into Federal hands. Of course, tens of thousands more such assets lay all across the region. "The more I contemplate the value of this stock country to us, the more valuable is seems to the enemy," he sighed. "A strong force (which I hope can be spared, as the danger of invasion from Louisiana does not seem imminent) can check these predatory bands and protect the trade to Eagle Pass until spring." He proposed holding a line from Corpus Christi to Laredo, with a fallback line stretching from Eagle Pass in the west to Saluria on Matagorda Island in the east.[30]

Despite Bee's plea, Magruder refused to be stampeded by the Federals' sudden appearance. He had no intention of sending troops to Bee piecemeal. Instead, he moved energetically to create a strategic tourniquet to the wound. He believed Banks invaded not only to capture the Rio Grande but also, potentially, to aim an offensive at the state's population centers, such as San Antonio, Austin, and Houston. With this in mind, Magruder envisioned three natural lines of defense for Texas. He disregarded Bee's suggestion of the Nueces River line from Corpus Christi to Laredo and instead focused first on the Guadalupe River line from Victoria and Fort Esperanza at Saluria on Matagorda Island. Failing this, the Colorado River would be the fallback position, though it effectively surrendered all of South Texas to the enemy. The Brazos River was the last line between an enemy advance and Houston. It must hold.[31]

FIFTEEN   **RETREAT AND ADVANCE**

Positions of vital importance may be lost.

—Major General John Bankhead Magruder
Commander, District of Texas, New Mexico, and Arizona

On November 8, 1863, the French gunboat *Panama* arrived in New York harbor, fresh from Mexico via Cuba, with General Élie Frédéric Forey aboard. Newspaper reporters speculated on the nature of his visit to the United States but assured their readers the architect of the French adventure in Mexico's stay "will be brief, as he intends to reach France with the least possible delay." His arrival, though, was coincidental to the planting of the Stars and Stripes on the banks of the Rio Grande opposite Matamoros. Undoubtedly there would be official conversations regarding French and American interests during his short visit.[1]

Meanwhile, when Major General Nathaniel P. Banks had stepped ashore in South Texas under a bright blue sky and mild weather, he believed he had left stormy Louisiana well enough protected. While Colonel Edmund J. Davis led the 1st Texas Cavalry (Union) banging about Brownsville, Banks's old chief, Major General William B. Franklin, dragged his battered rearguard to Vermilionville during a cold drizzle. At least Franklin's army was once again consolidated. The 13th Army Corps troops moved into camps alongside the 19th Army Corps, and all the soldiers prepared to hold their ground.

The Confederates let them go. "The Yanks are taking advantage of this weather to make their way back," observed Captain Julius Giesecke of the 4th Texas Cavalry. He did not care. He was safe, warm, and dry in a deserted slave cabin on the Lastrappes Plantation near Arnaudville, well east of the retreating Yankees.

Some of Giesecke's comrades were more ambitious. They noticed foragers and ne'er-do-wells from the Federal army nabbed what they could as they left.

Confederates followed, taking dozens of the looters' wagons and some three hundred liberated slaves who were running toward the protection of the retreating Union army.[2]

Major General Richard Taylor, commander of the District of West Louisiana, believed he had bested his opponent and wanted to give credit where it was due. Brigadier General Tom Green should be promoted to major general, he urged Lieutenant General Edmund Kirby Smith. "The exact moment when a heavy blow could be given was seized in a masterly manner," Taylor wrote. "He has surpassed my expectations, which I did not think possible. This officer has within the past few months commanded in three successful engagements—on the Lafourche, on the Fordoche, and near Opelousas—two of which were won against heavy odds." Since Green commanded a division of cavalry, Taylor argued his rank should be increased: "His sphere of usefulness should be enlarged." Taylor also recommended the government elevate Colonel James P. Major to brigadier general in reward for his "marked energy and zeal." This team of officers and their Texans had done most of the fighting in Louisiana in 1863 and had earned promotions. Kirby Smith concurred and forwarded the recommendations to Richmond.[3]

At Vermilionville, as the Federal soldiers settled in, Franklin reported his successful retrograde move to Department of the Gulf headquarters in New Orleans, including the news about the attack on his rearguard. "Who commands on the part of the enemy?" came Brigadier General Charles Pomeroy Stone's reply. "How strong do you consider him?" If Major General Taylor and his Confederates were pursuing Franklin in force, there might be more trouble.[4]

Union affairs remained in a delicate state. Banks planned to sustain his invasion of Texas with reinforcements from back east while Franklin held his ground in Louisiana. If no new troops could be found for the Texas adventure, Banks would cannibalize the army in Louisiana, and Franklin would have to make do. If Taylor received reinforcements from Texas or Arkansas, then Franklin's command might be in jeopardy. If, however, the attack on the rearguard at Bayou Bourbeau had been Taylor's parting shot, then the Confederates might be in the process of reinforcing Texas to crush the invasion force there with overwhelming numbers. Brigadier General Stone worried Banks had set his army up to be defeated in detail.[5]

For his part, Major General Franklin did not worry about the Rebels trailing him to Vermilionville. "I have brought all my force to this place and will give them a fight here if they will accept," he reported to Stone, "which I do not believe." His three Federal infantry divisions and one brigade occupied a strong position backed by plenty of heavy artillery. Was he now on the defensive, he asked, or should he press back against the Rebels if they came at him?[6]

Word from New Orleans was vague. "It is important to retain as large a force of the enemy as possible in your front," Franklin's orders read. "Keep him amused." The Confederates in Texas, Stone relayed, had concentrated in eastern Texas away from the Rio Grande, giving Major General Napoleon J. T. Dana a chance to consolidate his position. If Major General John Bankhead Magruder sent troops to Louisiana to back Taylor and made an attempt to take Vermilionville, Franklin could tie up the bulk of the Rebel army while Dana and Banks conquered Texas without much trouble.[7]

Franklin doubted Magruder would surge across the Sabine, but he believed in being prudent. On November 9, Franklin ordered his men, suffering from the arrival of yet another wet cold front, to dig in. Engineers laid out a compact line on the crest of the high northern bank of Bayou Vermilion to protect the bridges. Entrenchments and abatis took shape along the northern margin of his camp while details scavenged building materials by dismantling structures in the village of Vermilionville, just a half mile to the north, opening up clear fields of fire. The Federals also built huts, figuring the stay might last through the winter. Let the Confederates come, Franklin figured. "My position here is good against double my number," he boasted.[8]

The Confederates, of course, kept pickets nearby. Private William Randolph Howell of the 5th Texas Cavalry watched the northerners burrow in. "Find plenty Yanks in and around town," he jotted in his diary.[9]

By the next day, Franklin had modified his views. Perhaps Magruder might be coming to Louisiana after all. Federal cavalry scouting toward the Mermentau River captured five troopers from the 1st Texas Cavalry, a "regiment that I had not heard before," Franklin reported. These prisoners shared disturbing news. Confederate blockade-runners, including the Derby and the Antelope, had run in supplies for an army gathering on the Sabine River. The absence of troops on the

Rio Grande might mean Magruder was indeed heading toward Vermilionville in cooperation with Taylor. In addition, Confederate irregulars had begun prowling around his supply depot at New Iberia, and his scouts reported the Rebels could potentially throw a cavalry force into his rear.[10]

Franklin ordered out his patrols on November 11. The Federal cavalry scouted toward the Confederates at Bayou Carencro that afternoon to see if their numbers had grown. Brigadier General Albert Lee's horsemen made contact with the enemy pickets and drove an estimated three hundred Rebels back to their supports. They did not press too close, staying out of cannon range of the bayou. Of course, Lee returned with a vague report, since he was uncertain how many Rebels might lay hidden along Bayou Carencro.

This vague account, however, proved unacceptable. The following morning, November 12, Franklin ordered Lee back out—this time with enough men to complete the task. With fifteen hundred mounted troops and a section of artillery, Lee barreled north toward the enemy. Troopers from the 2nd and 3rd Illinois Cavalry and the 118th Illinois Mounted Infantry drove in the Rebel pickets once again, but this time they kept riding toward the tree line marking Bayou Carencro.

The Confederates found this aggressiveness surprising. "They were in one mile of camp before we could saddle up," wrote Private John W. Watkins of the 5th Texas Cavalry.[11]

The Midwesterners reined in after catching a glimpse of the enemy forces milling about and coming into formation. When the Confederate cavalry under Brigadier General Green emerged from the woods in full battle array, the Federals fell back. The Texans spurred after them.[12]

The contest ebbed and flowed as the lines of mounted troops maneuvered for advantage while officers made notes about enemy strengths. After a while, the Federal horsemen attempted to make a stand, but Rebel artillery rolled up and pounded them. The superior numbers of Texas cavalry threatened to overwhelm the Yankees. Brigadier General Lee had all the information he came for, but he had to commit all of his mounted regiments into a fight to get it.

The Confederates tumbled the northerners back several miles, killing or capturing a dozen of them in the chaotic brawl. The Texans, in their enthusiasm, had followed too closely, riding to within a mile of the Union fortifications.

Then Texans began to fall. Union artillery—including the heavy 20-pounders of the 1st Indiana Heavy Artillery—bloodied them. "As soon as we came in range of their guns they opened an awful hot fire on our troops, killing and wounding about 20," Watkins wrote. Captain Giesecke ordered his 4th Texas Cavalry to turn about—and run. "They unexpectedly bombarded us so terribly," he wrote, "that we were forced to beat a hasty retreat."[13]

Major General Franklin, finally satisfied he knew what he was facing, reported the fight to headquarters in New Orleans, noting his losses but pointing out "we damaged them with our artillery more than they did us."[14]

Both sides reflected on what they had learned. Each had a good look at the other. Brigadier General Lee reported the Rebels in force with artillery, cavalry, and infantry about seven thousand strong. "The enemy," he reported to New Orleans, "is waiting for something—what, I cannot tell." Perhaps, he feared, reinforcements from Texas or elsewhere.[15]

Along the Carencro, tired and rattled Rebels thought they faced a mere enemy rear guard, especially given the sighting of enemy forces approaching the Mermentau. Instead they had been pasted by artillery indicating the presence of the Army of the Gulf in force. "I don't think the enemy are falling back to the [Berwick] bay as was first supposed," concluded Watkins. "I believe they are

The skirmish near Bayou Carencro, north of Vermilionville. *Becker Collection.*

waiting for the waters to rise so that they can transport supplies. Time will tell what they are up to."[16]

Had Taylor brought up his infantry? Franklin could not be sure. Lee may have reported accurately, but Taylor was tricky.

While the Federals were gaining ground in Texas, they were losing turf in Louisiana. The siphoning off of so many troops had left Major General William B. Franklin with a dwindling command and ended all thoughts of an advance. His new challenge in Louisiana was how to use his army to keep the very active Confederates from cutting the Union supply lines between Brashear City and New Iberia.

The Federals—Banks—had created two complicated fronts. Confederate generals in Louisiana could not believe their luck. Major General Richard Taylor now got busy creating a third complication.

Franklin's retreat into prepared positions on Bayou Vermillion indicated his command would no longer present a threat to the Red River Valley. Now, Brigadier General Tom Green could make Franklin's life miserable and keep him blind as to Confederate intentions. Taylor, based on news from Texas, believed the remnant of the Army of the Gulf was largely abandoning Louisiana. He expected them to head for the easily defended Berwick Bay by the end of the year, giving up the lower Bayou Teche region as well. With the Red River Valley no longer in danger, what should he do with his infantry? Major General John G. Walker's Division and Brigadier General Jean Jacques Alfred Alexander Mouton's Division remained idle.

Taylor and his generals agreed he should jab this force into the hole Major General Nathaniel P. Banks had left in Louisiana. While Green screened the movement, Taylor ordered Walker to take the two infantry divisions and their artillery across the Atchafalaya River to raid the Mississippi River south of the Red River as far as Donaldsonville and Bayou Lafourche. These troops could probably do better work there, Taylor believed, than just about anywhere else. Their pressure might force Banks to choose between reinforcing Texas from Franklin's command or keeping it in Louisiana to safeguard Union gains. Confederate couriers paddled across the Mississippi to inform troops on the east bank of the offensive plan and to request they coordinate their efforts.[17]

While the Union army reorganized and dug in at Vermilionville, the bulk of the Confederate army in Louisiana infantry was on the move. A small mounted force composed of a company from the 5th Texas Cavalry and the 13th Texas Cavalry battalion led the way back into Pointe Coupee Parish. On November 12, while Green and his cavalry demonstrated against the Union works at Vermilionville, the men of Walker's and Mouton's Divisions, with five batteries of artillery, headed east, away from the battle, and crossed the Atchafalaya River at Simmesport and moved into several positions in northern Pointe Coupee Parish. If the Confederate infantry had ever been spotted on Buzzard Prairie, as Major General Franklin's scouts had suggested, they certainly were not there now.[18]

Served by such sketchy intelligence by his cavalry chief, Franklin did not like being in Vermilionville, even with his stout earthworks. He had a wide stream behind him and Confederates hovering nearby and no real understanding of enemy intentions. His gunners may have pounded the Rebels on November 12, but the enemy reappeared fresh the following morning with what Franklin called "a large observing force" but none of the infantry Lee reported. Franklin lost faith in his cavalry chief's report. "I think it is a rear guard, and that we have ceased to amuse him," he reported to Stone. The Confederates were on the move. But to where?[19]

The next day, a running gun battle behind his lines gave Major General Franklin cause to compound his worries. Major St. Leon Duperier and his Mounted Zouaves, a recently collected gaggle of deserters and dodgers who had been pushed back into the Rebel ranks, fired on the A. G. Brown as it steamed down Bayou Teche to Brashear City. When it passed beyond their range, the squadron of mounted Confederates turned their muskets on the Southerner. They dogged the Southerner as it headed upstream, between the Olivier Plantation and New Iberia, splintering wood and shattering glass but causing no casualties. On board, a company from the 22nd Regiment Corps d'Afrique blazed away at the Rebel rabble for more than three hours. The Southerner arrived at the Union camps nicked and scarred, but intact.[20]

The 75th New York, recently transformed into mounted infantry, received orders to run these offenders to ground. The men and horses clattered aboard the Southerner, crossed Bayou Teche in several trips, formed their column, and picked up the Rebel trail. The Confederates, with a large head start, had faded into the Grand Bois, the deep forest bordering a lobe of the Atchafalaya Basin known as Lake Fausse Pointe, ten miles east of St. Martinville and ten miles northeast of New Iberia. The Federals followed into the woods as far as Bayou Portage then turned around, unable to cross. They settled for scattering the enemy but not defeating them.[21]

Franklin heard the news and feared correctly that the Confederates might be moving to threaten his communications with Berwick Bay. If so, they might spark a bushwhacking battle that would be difficult for him to manage. "It will embarrass me much to fight them," he pointed out, noting the potential of having to beat his way through the Rebels to his base of supplies. Now he had a great excuse for continuing his retreat. Franklin gladly gave up the line at Bayou Vermilion and ordered his officers to relocate the army to New Iberia. His troops abandoned their elaborate camp and headed out of town, burning the Pinhook Bridge behind them as they left.[22]

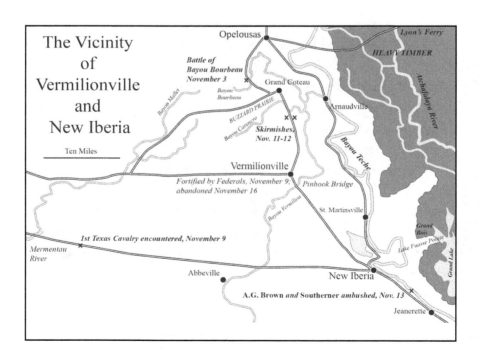

On the evening of November 16, Green's pickets moved gingerly into the deserted Yankee works. The Union campaign for Louisiana appeared to be over for the season.

The expedition to Pointe Coupee Parish proved to be the first time many of the veterans of the Louisiana campaigns actually saw Major General Walker in the field. They had fought whole campaigns predicated on his bringing forward his division, only to be disappointed. This time, though, he was in the field, heading toward the enemy, and in charge. "I saw General Walker for the first time," admitted Captain Felix Pierre Poché. "A most ordinary and simple man in appearance, but a very good general, so they say," adding, "though he had accomplished nothing since his arrival in Louisiana."[23]

Taylor wanted to repeat the tactics he had employed below Donaldsonville in July during the waning days of the Port Hudson campaign. His men complied, and after a week's work Confederate field artillery pieces once again pointed their muzzles across the Father of Waters. Battery Number 1 lay at Hog Point, a mile below Red River Landing and the river's mouth. Louisianans equipped with a 12-pounder Napoleon from the St. Mary's Cannoneers and two 3-inch rifles from the Pelican Artillery stood alongside Texas crews who had two 10-pounder Parrot rifles from Captain James M. Daniel's Lamar Artillery. Crews created two other batteries at intervals along the Mississippi River, one twenty miles downriver on the Sneed and Cottier Plantations, above Morganza, and the other eleven miles farther along at the Claiborne Plantation, near New Roads and Bayou Sara. On the morning of November 18, a heavy fog settled over the river, masking Rebel designs.[24]

Later that day the fog's lifting revealed a fat target: the transport *Emerald*, loaded with about five hundred soldiers from the 13th Army Corps, including the recently recruited Company M, 1st Indiana Heavy Artillery, along with dozens of convalescents released for duty. The steamboat's prudent skipper had tied up on the opposite bank until navigation improved and they could continue downstream. Acting quickly, riflemen from the 16th Texas infantry climbed to the top of the levee and put the vessel in their sights while artillerymen quietly

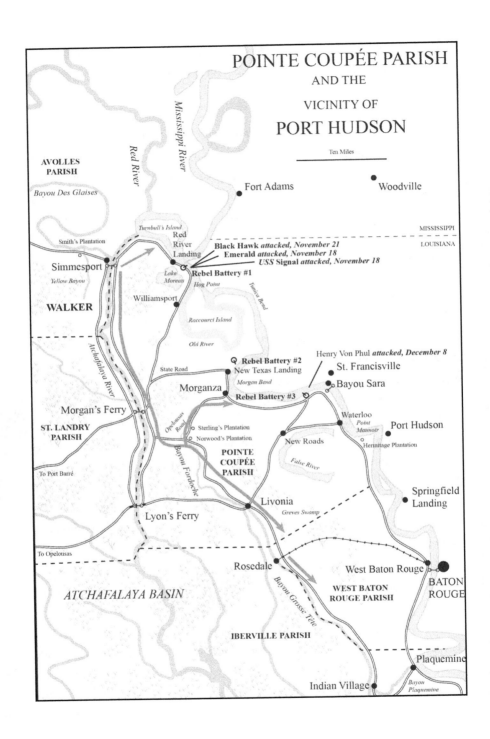

POINTE COUPÉE PARISH

AND THE

VICINITY OF

PORT HUDSON

Ten Miles

Mississippi River

Red River

AVOLLES PARISH

Bayou Des Glaises

Fort Adams

Woodville

Turnbull's Island

Smith's Plantation

Red River Landing

Black Hawk attacked, November 21
Emerald attacked, November 18
USS Signal attacked, November 18

MISSISSIPPI

LOUISIANA

Simmesport

Yellow Bayou

Lake Moreau

Rebel Battery #1

Hog Point

Tunica Bend

WALKER

Williamsport

Raccourci Island

Old River

Henry Von Phul attacked, December 8

Rebel Battery #2
New Texas Landing

St. Francisville

State Road

Morgan Bend

Bayou Sara

Morganza

Rebel Battery #3

Atchafalaya River

Morgan's Ferry

ST. LANDRY PARISH

Opelousas Road

Sterling's Plantation

Norwood's Plantation

Waterloo
Point Mannoir

Port Hudson

New Roads

Hermitage Plantation

To Port Barré

Bayou Fordoche

POINTE COUPÉE PARISH

False River

Lyon's Ferry

Livonia

Greves Swamp

Springfield Landing

To Opelousas

Rosedale

West Baton Rouge

BATON ROUGE

ATCHAFALAYA BASIN

Bayou Grosse Tête

WEST BATON ROUGE PARISH

IBERVILLE PARISH

Plaquemine

Indian Village

Bayou Plaquemine

turned their pieces. When Rebel spotters saw the vessel's crew casting off its moorings, the artillery opened up.[25]

The firing caught the men aboard the *Emerald* unawares. "The captain had the anchor weighed, preparatory to moving ahead, and just at this time the opposite shore was discovered to be alive with gray-backs," wrote one passenger, journalist George C. Harding.[26]

The salvos from the Texas and Louisiana guns were joined by small arms fire from the infantry. The Confederates punished the vessel, "tearing her from stem to stern," wrote Private J. P. Blessington of the 16th Texas Infantry.[27]

Projectiles tore away one wheelhouse and crashed through the main cabin. A 12-pounder shell exploded in the pilothouse. "In exploding," Harding remembered, it "tore it to pieces and knocked over the pilot, who, considerably stunned and bewildered, ran below."[28]

The vessel spun to port, facing downstream, and ran ashore on the east bank. The Rebel riflemen continued to tear open and ram home their cartridges, firing away nearly all the ammunition in their boxes at the vessel, which was now lying at extreme range.

A quick-thinking Union soldier in the 17th Kentucky saved the situation. He confronted the panicked skipper "and threatened to blow the pilot's brains out, and drove him to his post," one soldier explained. The *Emerald* heaved, sighed, and huffed backed to life. It chuffed away downstream, shredded but afloat.[29]

That same afternoon, Confederates gunners saw another target: The USS *Signal* was splashing upstream, responding to the report of Rebels on the levee. The tinclad was towing a barge loaded with a 9-inch Dahlgren cannon. The Louisiana and Texas troops at Hog Point ambushed the vessel. Their opening salvo sent rounds crashing through the gunboat's thin armor. Nine shots hit the target. One cannonball hit the base of the cabin on the port side, peeling up the iron sheeting; another hit careened up through the ship, creasing—but not cutting—the ship's steam pipes before spinning through the steering controls and exiting through the top deck and smokestack. A solid shot from a Louisiana 3-inch rifle hit the armor covering the vessel's boilers but ricocheted off. The lucky gunboat remained fully functional. Other shots exploded in the galley, turning pots, pans,

USS Choctaw, ironclad. U.S. *Naval History and Heritage Command.*

and cutlery into missiles below decks. By the time the USS *Signal* pulled out of range, shot and shell had demolished the crew quarters located above the boilers. Four sailors were left cut and bleeding, and another had a mangled leg.[30]

The powerful ironclad USS *Choctaw*, on station at the mouth of the Red River about a mile upstream, came down to rescue the tinclad. The vessels passed each other as the warship's big guns raked the west bank of the Mississippi. The Texans had seen the gunboat coming and had prudently withdrawn their field pieces. The infantry also slipped back under cover. "It was impossible to see the effect of our shell, but we succeeded in driving the enemy away," reported Union lieutenant commander Frank Ramsay. For the next few hours his gunners pumped dozens of heavy 100-pounder and 9-inch projectiles in the direction of the invisible enemy, aiming at and hitting nothing.[31]

While the USS *Signal* had been enduring the fire of the Rebel guns, the shot-up *Emerald* tied up at Bayou Sara under the guardianship of the USS *Lafayette*. The ironclad's skipper, Lieutenant Commander James P. Foster, grew nervous. Not only were there Rebels on the west bank, but couriers now alerted him to the presence of an estimated two thousand enemy soldiers east of the Mississippi, apparently taking positions to make a rush against Port Hudson and its largely *Corps d'Afrique* garrison. Foster sent the *Emerald* on its way, bearing dispatches and warnings for Baton Rouge and Donaldsonville. Troops at both posts needed to be vigilant. Meanwhile, he would take the USS *Lafayette* and the tinclad USS *Kenwood* upstream as far as the mouth of the Red River to see what he could do.[32]

On November 19, the river remained quiet. The USS *Choctaw* escorted the steamboats *White Cloud* and *Nebraska* downstream, passing the USS *Lafayette* and the USS *Kenwood* on their way up.

The Confederates prudently remained quiet. After the enemy vessels had passed, the 19th Texas Infantry and Captain Daniel's Texas Battery moved through the ruins of the village of Morganza to take their turn on the river. They saw nothing promising. "The enemy seemed to be aware of their movements, as all of their transports were escorted," Blessington recalled.[33]

The next morning, all of Walker's Division fell back from the river, their primary goal of rattling the enemy accomplished. Now Walker would move south. Lieutenant Colonel Lee Rountree's Texas cavalry battalion, familiar with this region, scouted south down Bayou Grosse Tête and headed toward the river town of Plaquemine.

Reports of this move, coupled with news of the ambush of the USS *Signal* and the *Emerald*, spread panic down the river. Telegraph wires hummed from Port Hudson to Baton Rouge, signal flags snapped and fluttered, and the wires from Donaldsonville to Thibodaux carried breathless requests for assistance.

USS St. Claire, tinclad. U.S. *Naval History and Heritage Command.*

USS Essex, ironclad. U.S. *Naval History and Heritage Command.*

Brigadier General Michael K. Lawler's three brigades of the 1st Division, 13th Army Corps, lying in camps at Berwick Bay awaiting transportation to Texas, were the closest Federal reinforcements. The new threat on the Mississippi River forced Lawler to release his 1st Brigade so that it could reinforce the garrison at Fort Butler and Donaldsonville. If the Rebels meant to come down the west bank of the Mississippi, as they had in June, the men of the 7th and 22nd Kentucky, the 42nd and 120th Ohio, and the 1st Indiana Battery of Light Artillery would be waiting and, Lawler believed, would be adequate for the task. The tinclad USS *St. Clair* started for Plaquemine to join the USS *Argosy*, which was already on station.[34]

Until these troops and vessels could move into position, officers dispatched a detachment to picket Plaquemine. Commander Robert Townsend, aboard the doughty, slab-sided ironclad USS *Essex* as it heaved to off Donaldsonville, believed this to be a mistake. "I do not know what bright thought induced the military authorities to stick down 200 troops at Plaquemine where there should be either a strong force, or none at all," he queried. "Of course, the navy would be expected to cover such a blunder should the Rebels attack." Townsend believed this was typical army behavior. "In their placid, self-congratulatory moments, [they] are somewhat inclined to make light of the goings of the Navy," he observed. "But when an alarm comes their first thought and cry is for a gunboat, and many a scrape have the gunboats helped them out of, often saving them from utter destruction."[35]

The identity of the leader of this Confederate raiding force remained unclear, troubling the Federals. Most naval officers agreed it seemed like infantry and artillery, likely including Walker's Texas Infantry Division. But were they alone? Had Brigadier General Green brought all or part of his command east of the Atchafalaya while Franklin retreated to New Iberia? Was Green in command? If so, this might mean another slashing attack into the Lafourche District, a repeat of Colonel James P. Major's raid in June, but this time backed by five brigades of infantry and upwards of ten batteries of artillery. A huge battle for the Lafourche District might be in the offing if this was true.

As the days passed, the Confederates on the Mississippi continued to make transiting the river risky. They kept a sharp lookout for possible targets. On the morning of November 21, USS *Lafayette* and USS *Signal* convoyed the coal-laden transport *Ike Hammit* downstream, past the batteries. The Rebels let them pass.

Meanwhile the steamer *Black Hawk* arrived at the mouth of the Red River. Aboard, agents of the U.S. Revenue service and others supervised the deckhands who rolled 150 bales of confiscated cotton onto the transport. This chore done, the government officials wanted to press on for New Orleans and their payday. They were advised to wait. The escorts had already gone, and the only remaining warship, the USS *Choctaw*, had to stay on station. Other escorts would certainly arrive overnight, and the *Black Hawk* could continue its journey in the morning under guard. Impatient with the answer, the Treasury Department employees ordered the vessel to proceed despite the dire warnings of the naval officers.[36]

Confederate lookouts soon spied the lone transport—a juicy target. Artillerymen in Captain William Edgar's Alamo City Guards punished the revenue men for their impatience. Although they rushed their guns back into position, the *Black Hawk* had passed nearly beyond range before they could open fire at its stern. Smoothbore 6-pounders drilled the vessel with solid shot while 12-pounder howitzers firing shell, case, and canister dismantled the upper works. One blast of canister shredded the pilothouse and splattered its occupant; bursting shells set the upper decks on fire. The wounded *Black Hawk* paddled toward the east bank and splashed to a halt, ablaze. The surviving passengers scrambled to shore and scattered into the shelter of the woods. Shots by Rebel riflemen kept the ship's crew from fighting the fire. The noise and smoke in turn summoned the USS *Choctaw*, which arrived with its cannon blazing. The Confederates pulled back from the river, giving up their quarry, but not before most of the *Black Hawk's* upper decks had burned.[37]

Within hours other gunboats converged on the site. The crew of the USS *Choctaw* put out the fire and tied the wreck of the *Black Hawk*—amazingly still afloat—alongside. The USS *Signal* reappeared from downstream along with the river monitor USS *Neosho*. This armada pounded the vacant west bank with heavy guns. Their fury did not matter. The Confederates were already miles away, out of range of even the heaviest of the Union cannon.[38]

Survivors of these attacks painted a lurid picture. The *Black Hawk* had run a gauntlet with rounds coming in from front, flank, and rear, its survivors reported. "In addition to this, there was a perfect storm of Minie balls from squads of sharpshooters," the vessel's commander told an eager reporter for the *New York Herald*. The intensity of the Rebel ambush, he added, "rending into fragments the saloons of the boat." The reporter had a chance to see the wreck later and walked away dumbfounded. "She is splintered and scarred in all parts," he wrote.[39]

Downriver in New Orleans, businessmen who had enjoyed the commerce of an unvexed Father of Waters for nearly ten weeks understood the implications. If these attacks could not be halted, their city would suffer as business dried up. Charles Prosper Fauconnet, the Secretary for the French Legation in New Orleans, described the suffering in a dispatch to the court of Emperor Napoleon III. "Along the river, things do not appear to be any better," he wrote. "A day does not pass without some boat being attacked, riddled with bullets, or burned. . . . Already in these attacks and boat fires, numerous passengers, particularly women and children, have met a terrible death."[40]

Near the Confederate batteries, property owners paid the price when the Federals retaliated. Captain Poché had left Pointe Coupee Parish on July 8 to take his family to safety in Thibodaux. Upon his return, he found the war had ravaged the region. Morganza lay in ashes. Bullets scarred most of the buildings that remained intact, and heavy artillery had cut furrows through the crops. Most of the homes had been plundered by troops from both armies. "Families had to retreat further inland," he observed. During their absence, "demons like perfect vandals pillaged their homes carrying away all they could use and destroying everything else." Poché's extended family faced danger daily. When sharp-eyed lookouts on Union gunboats spied Captain Daniel's Lamar Artillery taking position on the Cottier Plantation, a few miles above the ruins of Morganza, they shelled the area mercilessly. Poché arrived to find his in-laws huddled at the base of the levee in a makeshift bomb shelter. Innocents on both sides suffered.[41]

Stories of the bloody harassment on the Mississippi and its human toll made for sensational stories in newspapers across the nation. The Father of Waters, which President Abraham Lincoln had assured the public national forces controlled—and supposedly flowed unvexed to the sea—now seemed to be a death trap.

Where, people muttered, was General Banks?

SIXTEEN **ESPERANZA**

It was a funny fight.
—Private Albert Marshall
33rd Illinois Infantry

In Brownsville, Texas, more than 500 miles by sea from New Orleans, Banks received delayed word of Franklin's retrograde move—and declared victory. The two-state strategy was working.

After all, Banks's Texas expedition had already provided robust diplomatic leverage. Secretary of State William H. Seward wrote the commander of the Department of the Gulf a warm letter, noting "I have great pleasure in congratulating you upon the successful landing and occupation upon the Rio Grande which is all the more gratifying because it was effected at a moment of apparently critical interest to the national cause." The presence of U.S. troops sent a clear message to the French and their Mexican puppets. Seward confirmed the United States backed the Juárez regime and considered Mexico "as a theater of a foreign war, mingled with civil strife." Banks, his officers, and his troops should not meddle in Mexican affairs. "But at the same time you will be expected to observe military and political events as they occur in Mexico, and communicate all that shall be important for this Government to understand concerning them." Seward trusted Banks and his officers to be the eyes of the nation on the border.[1]

The Union flag had been planted in Texas, as requested.

When the news of Banks's expedition reached the offices of the War Department, the triumphs in Texas lost their luster. General-in-Chief Henry W. Halleck had been blindsided by the invasion of Texas, and he was not happy. He also did not care for Banks's dispatches hounding him for reinforcements while a military crisis loomed at Chattanooga. "The concentration of Rebel forces in Northern

Secretary of State William Seward was pleased with Banks and his Texas operation. *Library of Congress.*

Georgia had compelled us to send there everything available," Halleck explained in a return dispatch.[2]

Halleck scolded Banks for bad timing and poor judgment. Banks had withdrawn Dana's Division from Pointe Coupee Parish and flung them upon the Texas shore, leaving the west bank of the Mississippi River open to the Rebels—which Taylor had exploited. Now that Banks had split his army, neither part could support the other. If Kirby Smith, Taylor, and Magruder coordinated efforts, Halleck fumed, "the enemy can defeat you . . . by concentrating all his forces against your separate and isolated columns." Banks had made his Army of the Gulf vulnerable to defeat in detail. Sooner or later, Halleck feared, the Confederates would catch on.[3]

This danger would only grow more acute. Franklin's contraction of his lines squeezed more of the Army of the Gulf away from Louisiana and into the operations in Texas. As the number of troops in New Iberia grew smaller, new reinforcements arrived at Brownsville from New Orleans.

One of the new arrivals in Texas was the 3rd Brigade, 2nd Division, 13th Army Corps, led by the highly regarded Brigadier General Thomas E. G. Ransom. "I saw [him] during the assault of the 22nd of May 1863," during the Vicksburg Campaign, Major General William Tecumseh Sherman observed. "I then marked him as of the kind of whom heroes are made." One of Ransom's officers agreed with the assessment. "Ransom shone, as usual, above all the others. There are none like him in this battle . . . always where the danger was greatest, always cool and confident."[4]

On November 16, soon after his arrival in Brownsville, Ransom received orders from Banks to load five infantry regiments—the 13th and 15th Maine, the 20th and 34th Iowa, and the 8th Indiana—along with a battery of artillery and the 1st Engineers of the *Corps d'Afrique*, onto the transports *McClellan*, *Planter*, and *Matamoros*. Under escort of the USS *Monongahela*, they were to steam along the Texas coast toward Corpus Christi Bay. Ransom had planned to use the light draft steamer *Matamoros* to ferry troops across the bar of Corpus Christi Pass, at the south end of Mustang Island, and conduct a surprise attack on Fort Semmes, an earthen outpost on the island's northern shore that guarded Aransas Pass. Ransom wanted to approach from behind, on the sheltered and unprotected bay side. This plan proved impossible, however, because the wind had pushed away so much water in the pass even a light draft vessel could not cross it.

The landings would have to be made on the open beach, amid pounding surf and rolling breakers. At sunset, Brigadier General Ransom disembarked his troops near the southern tip of Mustang Island to wade or ride small boats to shore. The unopposed landings were not completed until nearly dawn, but the first units ashore, the 13th and 15th Maine Regiments and the 20th Iowa, immediately formed up and, with a powerful line of skirmishers in advance, began

USS Monongahela. US *Navy History and Heritage Command.*

Brigadier General Thomas E. G. Ransom, the beau ideal of a soldier. *Library of Congress.*

a difficult twenty-two-mile trek through loose sand toward the Rebel garrison. Sailors from the USS *Monongahela* made the difficult journey as well, dragging two boat howitzers. At 4:00 AM on November 17, after trudging eighteen miles without seeing any sign of the enemy, Ransom halted his column and rested his men for two hours until daylight. The Federals re-formed their columns at sunrise and advanced to within one mile of Fort Semmes.[5]

The Federals greatly outmatched the tiny Rebel garrison. Fewer than one hundred men from the 8th Texas Infantry and 3rd State Troops manned the three heavy guns that pointed out to sea, which would be of no use against infantry approaching by land. The 15th Maine deployed into line of battle while the 13th Maine shook out skirmishers, and both regiments advanced toward Fort Semmes. Ransom held the balance of his brigade in reserve. Some of the Texan pickets fired at the Federals before falling back to the fort. The Mainers answered with a ripple of fire from the skirmishers followed by the steady staccato popping of men firing at will. Cannon aboard the gunboat added their deep booming to the noise. "Our advance at once opened fire," remembered Lieutenant Henry A. Shorey of the 15th Maine, "and the gunboat *Monongahela* ran up to an eligible position and tossed a few shells into the enemy's works." The steady pelting of small arms continued for about an hour until the New England regiments paused and formed into assault columns. Ransom rode forward, prepared to personally lead them over the works.[6]

The capture of Fort Semmes proved easy. The hour's worth of shooting at the post had pinned the defenders behind their ramparts and prevented their escape in small boats lying on shore for that purpose. The Confederates—surrounded, outnumbered more than ten-to-one, under a heavy artillery barrage and without hope of escape—had little choice but to run up a white flag. Despite the intimidating shelling and small arms fire, there was only one Southern casualty: an old man of the State Troops, eager to extend a friendly greeting to the Union soldiers, took a bullet in the arm as he rushed outside the defenses, his intentions misunderstood.[7]

Colonel Isaac Dyer of the 15th Maine supervised the capitulation. "Nearly one hundred stalwart Texas Rangers—tall, stout, robust looking fellows—fell into our hands as prisoners," Lieutenant Storey bragged. Those captured included the post commander, Captain William "Captain Jeff" Maltby, eight other officers, and eighty-nine men. The Federals also took 3 heavy guns, 100 small arms, 1 small schooner, 10 boats, 140 horses, and 125 beef cattle. Ransom awarded the flag of Fort Semmes to the State of Maine as a trophy.[8]

Word had reached the Confederates in the town of Corpus Christi that Fort Semmes was under attack, and the echoes of cannon fire rolling across the wide bay like distant thunder confirmed it. The fort's defenders were local people whose families now feared the worst. Colonel William R. Bradfute, commander

Colonel Isaac Dyer, 15th Maine. *Center for Military History, Carlisle Barracks.*

of the Texas coastal defenses, loaded around one hundred men aboard the steamboat *Cora* hoping to reinforce, or evacuate, the garrison. Drawing within sight of the fort, he spied the Stars and Stripes already waving above its ramparts. A few long-range shots from the USS *Monongahela* convinced him he was too late, and he ordered the vessel about. Instead of returning to Corpus Christi, though, Bradfute continued up the coast through Aransas Bay and Espiritu Santo Bay to Matagorda Bay without sending word back to Corpus Christi. There was no time: he rushed to arrive at Fort Esperanza before the Federals.[9]

Back in Corpus Christi, Confederate defenders sensed a battle was coming. The sound of big naval guns, then silence, made the Rebels fear for the fate of Bradfute and his men. That evening Major Edwin E. Hobby of the 8th Texas Infantry, having still received no word of the fate of the *Cora*, sent a delegation in a schooner flying a flag of truce to seek out Union forces and learn what had happened. The next day, November 18, news arrived that raised tensions: Fort Semmes had fallen, its garrison was taken prisoner, Bradfute had disappeared, and the size of the Union invasion force was substantial.[10]

The daytime arrival of Brigadier General Hamilton P. Bee with his small force from King's Ranch restored little confidence at Corpus Christi. Bee was not impressed with what he found, either. The militia Magruder had mobilized to defend the Texas coast had proven to be unstable. "No reliance can be placed on the state troops from this vicinity should I be obliged to fall back toward Goliad or farther east," Bee reported. "They will not leave their families in the rear." So, if he left Corpus Christi, he would probably take only the troops he came in with.[11]

In Houston, Magruder found himself embarrassed by this rapid advance up the coast by Union troops. He had been following the orders of Lieutenant General Kirby Smith and making efforts to substitute militia on the coast for the regular Confederate regiments he would send east into Louisiana. Now that the Federals had arrived in Texas—and fallen back in Louisiana—the militia was left bearing the brunt of the invasion while his steadier troops had gathered in the wrong end of the very large state. "Nevertheless, I hope to be able to get troops west in time to save, if not Saluria, at least Velasco at the mouth of the Brazos," Magruder wrote to headquarters in Shreveport. "It is highly probable, from the information received, that the enemy will attempt to take both these places."[12]

Magruder's scouts east of the Mermentau River in Louisiana fueled his worries but confirmed his plans. More Federal troops were leaving Vermilionville and heading south toward Brashear City, and Magruder suspected they would soon pop up on the Texas coast. He asked Kirby Smith to have Taylor send him troops. "Unless reinforcements are sent me with the utmost dispatch," Magruder warned, "positions of vital importance may be lost. Upon the issue of the impending attack depends the fate of the heart of Texas."[13]

The Confederates did not want to yield Matagorda Bay without a fight. Magruder ordered Colonel Leon Smith to leave Beaumont and head to Indianola to outfit a cottonclad flotilla capable of threatening Union transports. Perhaps the swashbuckling naval officer could turn the *Cora, Lucy Gwin, John F. Carr,* and *Lady of the Lake* into cottonclad gunboats as he had done with the *Neptune* and *Bayou City* at Galveston or the *Uncle Ben* and *Josiah* H. *Bell* at Sabine Pass. Magruder hoped for yet another stunning naval victory.[14]

The Texas weather slowed the Federals, buying the Rebels valuable time. Ransom had to hold his command at Mustang Island for five days because of pounding surf and wicked winds. "A norther came up without warning and almost

Leon Smith never held official rank in Confederate service, but it did not stop him from leading several bold naval operations. *Rosenberg Library, Galveston, Texas.*

the violence of a hurricane and causing the soldiers much suffering," wrote Private Lufkin of the 13th Maine.[15]

On November 21, as the storm abated, Major General Cadwallader C. Washburn arrived fresh from Bayou Carencro aboard the transport *Clinton*, bringing with him the 33rd Illinois and the 18th Indiana. He landed these troops on St. Joseph Island, the next barrier island to the north across Aransas Pass. Satisfied with his progress, Banks turned over the management of the Texas expedition to Major General Dana on the Rio Grande and Major General Washburn on the coast and, on November 22, sailed for New Orleans to resume overall command of the Department of the Gulf.[16]

Washburn resumed the pace. On November 23, sailors ferried Ransom's Brigade from Mustang Island across Aransas Pass to St. Joseph's Island, where they joined the newly arrived Midwesterners. One Illinois soldier described their new battleground as a sandy, desolate place, crawling with vast herds of deer and cattle—very different from Louisiana. The combined army marched north to Cedar Bayou, a three-hundred-yard-wide tidal cut in the barrier islands separating eighteen-mile-long Saint Joseph's Island from Matagorda Island. Captain Charles S. Ilsley of Company C, 15th Maine, and an ersatz band of sixty infantry mounted on Captain Maltby's captured mustangs led the advance.[17]

These riders traveled for several miles before spotting a truce party under Major Charles Hill of Colonel Bradfute's staff waiting for them on Cedar Bayou. Rumors had been circulating among the Texans that two of the prisoners had been hanged aboard a Federal warship, and the Rebels boldly demanded to know the fate of "Captain Jeff" Maltby and the Fort Semmes garrison. Ilsley sent Sergeant James Saunders wading across the bayou to talk to the enemy. The sergeant refused to answer any of their inquiries, and an agitated standoff ensued; Major Hill drew his pistol and shot the Maine soldier, wounding him badly and violating the truce. The Yankees across Cedar Bayou opened up, hitting Hill, who was "seen to limp away." He dropped and slowly bled out a few hundred yards away. His men never knew it. Panicked, they left him to die where he lay and frantically rode away to carry the news of the approaching Federals to Fort Esperanza.[18]

Word also came to Corpus Christi that the enemy had moved on. Since the Federals had marched up the coast, Bee concluded Corpus Christi had been bypassed and was untenable or irrelevant. On November 25, he gathered all his available troops, no more than five hundred including the company from the 8th Texas Infantry, and departed for the San Antonio River. From his new camp he could better oppose any Federal advance along the coastal road while remaining in communication with the forces at Matagorda Bay. Corpus Christi, deserted by its defenders, was an open town.[19]

In Shreveport, Lieutenant General Kirby Smith received Magruder's dispatches in amazement. Banks had surprised him. Kirby Smith's Louisiana major general, Richard Taylor, had been adamant the Federals aimed for the Red River Valley and then, when faced with evidence of an amphibious operation in the offing, Taylor held that Mobile, not Texas, would be attacked. Taylor had been wrong, and Magruder, as it turned out, had been right.

News from Corpus Christi and Houston caused Kirby Smith to fear a dark outcome: Banks would strangle his department and drive a wedge between the Confederates and any hope of French intervention or supplies by placing an army in South Texas. Kirby Smith assumed the Federals would try to take Victoria and then conquer San Antonio, cutting off both principal cotton roads to Mexico. "His true base of operations is Matagorda Bay," he concluded. Kirby Smith and his staff studied their maps. After taking the Alamo City, Union engineers would get the primitive railroad between there and Victoria up and running, assuring a supply line to the coast. "He would control a productive country," Kirby Smith confessed, "and his base for ulterior operations would be in striking distance of Houston and railroad system of Texas."[20]

It appeared the decisive battle for Texas was close at hand and the news of the Federal invasion of the Texas coast ran like an electric jolt throughout the rest of the state. Within two weeks of the sound of the first Federal boots on the south Texas shore, Confederate troops massed near the Sabine River reversed direction and headed southwest to oppose them.

Major General John Bankhead Magruder put his energy into reorganizing all of his troops in Texas to halt the Yankee invaders. To do so, he created a mounted division, initially commanded by Brigadier General James E. Slaughter, his chief of artillery. Magruder planned to center the new division on the lower Brazos River as his strategic reserve.

Magruder had many units available to fill Slaughter's 2nd Cavalry Division. He ordered Colonel Xavier Debray to build a brigade of mounted troops crafted from cavalry units previously dismounted and assigned to duty afoot. These men rejoiced at once again serving from the saddle and included Colonel Charles Pyron's 2nd Texas Cavalry, Colonel N. P. Gould's 23rd Texas Cavalry, Debray's own 26th Texas Cavalry, and Colonel Peter C. Woods's 36th Texas Cavalry. The Austin Light Artillery and a new battery forming under the command of Captain M. V. McMahan would support the brigade. Colonel Augustus Buchel commanded the other brigade of Slaughter's 2nd Cavalry Division, including his own 1st Texas Cavalry, Lieutenant Colonel Rueben Brown's 35th Texas Cavalry—recently cobbled together by adding Major Leonidas C. "Lee" Rountree's Battalion fresh from Louisiana—Colonel Alexander Terrell's 37th Texas Cavalry, and Captain W. G. Moseley's Texas Battery.[21]

Private Rudolph Coreth, an Austrian immigrant serving in the dismounted 36th Texas Cavalry under Colonel Woods, described how his unit left Beaumont aboard flat cars. They traveled on the dilapidated Texas and New Orleans railroad toward Houston and a reunion with their horses. "We had ten cars such as are used in Germany for transporting wood," he wrote his father. "We think our march is related to the Yankee attack at Brownsville."[22]

Colonel Gould's 23rd Texas Cavalry headed west toward Houston from Sabine Pass. One of his men expressed his uncertainty in a letter to his wife. "I do not know where we will be ordered to from there, though some think we will be ordered to San Antonio in western Texas," Private Augustus V. Ball wrote. "It is reported that the Yankees has taken Brownsville at the mouth of the Rio Grande River, but I do not know the truth of it."[23]

The truth was the Federal army had already raced up the coast and now lay poised to invade the Texas heartland. The last weeks in November promised to determine the fate of Confederate fortunes in the Lone Star State. If the Confederate positions around Matagorda Bay did not hold, then the roads to San Antonio, Austin, and Houston would indeed fall into Union hands, as Lieutenant General Edmund Kirby Smith had feared. Most of the Texans streaming down the roads and railways of the coastal bend did not know exactly where they were bound; neither did Major General Magruder. Their destination depended largely on the Federals.

Much faith was put in Confederate defenses at Fort Esperanza, which locals thought of as an impregnable "second Gibraltar," on Matagorda Island. This sandy barrier island ran generally southwest to northeast for thirty-eight miles and averaged about two miles across. At its eastern tip, the island broadened as it made a five-mile long bend to the left—north—and nearly connects to the mainland of Texas, separated only by McHenry Bayou and a sand bar called Bayucos Island. The hamlet of Saluria occupied the northern edge of this curve, near the fort. The Matagorda Island Lighthouse lay at the southern edge. Pass Cavallo, an inlet of the Gulf of Mexico and the gateway to Matagorda Bay, ran along the island's blunt eastern margin. Across Pass Cavallo lay Decros Point and the fifty-mile-long Matagorda Peninsula, a half-mile-wide strip of sand heading northeast and connecting to the mainland.

Could Fort Esperanza hold long enough for Slaughter's 2nd Cavalry Division to coalesce? The earthworks, rifle pits, and trenches of the post projected power and suggested the answer would be *yes*. The walls were stout—fifteen feet thick in places—and twelve feet high. The triangular fort formed a right angle in its north-west corner. There, arrowhead-shaped Salient Number 1 and its lone 24-pounder howitzer covered the McHenry Bayou ferry connection from Fort Esperanza and the nearby village of Saluria to Bayucos Island. Another bastion on the opposite side of the ferry also covered the crossing. Fort Esperanza's main battery lined the hypotenuse facing Pass Cavallo to the southeast but could pivot and cover the land approaches from the south. In the fort's northeast corner, a large 10-inch Columbiad occupied Salient Number 2, a sizable platform, and seven 24-pounders jutted out from the stair-step Salients 3 through 9. Seven separate earthen magazines fed ammunition to these guns. Rifle pits made an irregular string of outworks eight hundred yards away from the fort, spanning in an arc from Pass Cavallo to a stagnant lagoon protecting the rear. There were also mines, "torpedoes" in the parliance of the day, planted on the approaches.[24]

Fort Esperanza's garrison was small but adequate. Five companies of the 8th Texas Infantry manned the eight heavy guns. Several units of state troops raised

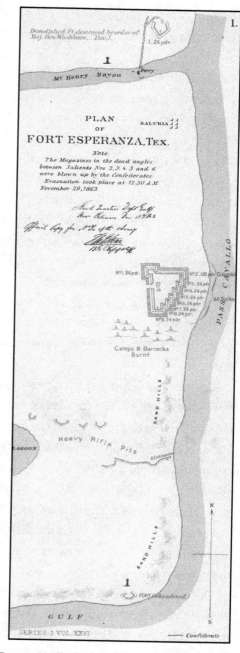

Diagram of Fort Esperanza. *Official Records of the War of the Rebellion Atlas.*

the fort's complement to about five hundred men. Major John Ireland had been commanding the post, but Colonel William R. Bradfute took charge after arriving on the steamer *Cora*. He had beaten the enemy to Matagorda Bay; would the Texan reinforcements do the same?[25]

Meanwhile, the weather again hobbled the Union advance. Stranded on St. Joseph's Island, the Federals attempted to traverse Cedar Bayou on the northern end of the barrier island. "The crossing of the bayou was found to be a more difficult task than had been anticipated," Lieutenant Henry A. Shorey of the 15th Maine admitted. Another storm had blown in without warning. "The presence of one of those terrific gales, termed 'Texas Northers,' rendered any effort . . . practically unavailing". Nevertheless, the innovative Federals persevered. They lashed together four small boats, creating a makeshift ferry, to transport the army across the bayou. The entire army arrived on the southern tip of Matagorda Island on the morning of November 26.[26]

Late on November 26, Major General Washburn received another brigade, the 1st Brigade, 1st Division, 13th Army Corps fresh from Louisiana, this one under the command of the unrelated, but similarly named, Colonel Henry D. Washburn.[27]

Colonel Washburn's weary soldiers marched twenty miles up the island on November 26 and halted at an abandoned ranch for the night. The next morning, the two Union brigades, Brigadier General Ransom's advancing up the middle of Matagorda Island and Colonel Washburn's slogging up the beach, pressed on, nearing Matagorda Lighthouse and spotting Fort Esperanza in the distance. At about 11 AM a line of Texan pickets contested the Union advance. In the brief skirmish that followed, Lieutenant George Fifer of the 33rd Illinois fell, grievously wounded, with a bullet through his chest. He was the first to fall of what most assumed would be many. Having drawn first blood in the battle for Fort Esperanza, the Rebels retreated to their outworks.[28]

Once behind cover, the Texans responded defiantly to the approaching Federals, firing their largest cannon and sending a huge 128-pounder round from the 10-inch Columbiad over the Yankees' heads. Less impressive salvos from the fort's 24-pounders followed.

Brigadier General Henry Dana Washburn was an Indiana lawyer. *Rutila-Washburn Ancestry.com.*

The Union infantry wisely scuttled out of range, taking shelter behind a line of dunes seven hundred yards from the outer works of the fort. They commenced digging in. Ransom held the left of the line, anchored on the waters separating Matagorda Island from the mainland. Colonel Washburn held the right, with his flank on the beach.[29]

The Federal regiments were well suited for the job ahead. Mostly Vicksburg veterans, the troops and their officers knew well the business of attacking a fort and laying a siege. Spying out the best approaches to the Rebel post, they constructed trenches, rifle pits, gun emplacements, and lines of circumvallation, little troubled by the poorly aimed Confederate artillery. Major General Washburn examined the objective with his field glasses. The impressive earthwork lay close to Saluria and had an excellent field of fire. "I soon discovered that the fort was a large and complete work, mounting heavy guns, and that all approaches were well guarded," Washburn reported.[30]

Although some Confederate soldiers and local citizens imagined the fort was unconquerable—and to an untrained eye, the works looked formidable—Private Albert Marshall of the 33rd Illinois thought he knew better. "They must have been a simple class of home guards," he wrote, "to practice soldiering in this fort." He conceded it "was very strong in some respects but built more with reference to

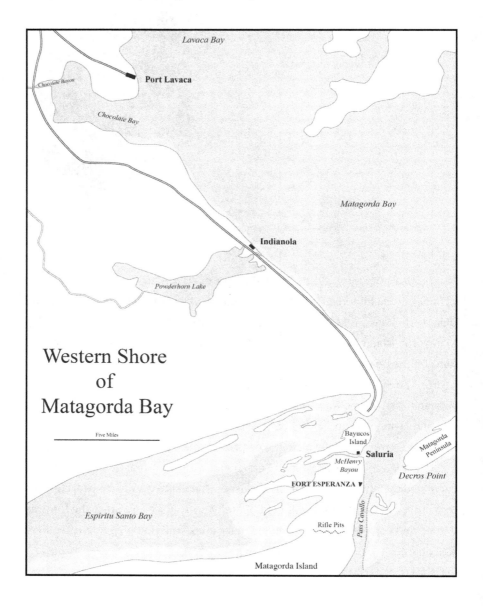

Western Shore
of
Matagorda Bay

Five Miles

Lavaca Bay

Chocolate Bayou

Port Lavaca

Chocolate Bay

Matagorda Bay

Indianola

Powderhorn Lake

Espiritu Santo Bay

Bayucos Island

Saluria

Matagorda Peninsula

McHenry Bayou

Decros Point

FORT ESPERANZA ▼

Pass Cavallo

Rifle Pits

Matagorda Island

attack by water than by land." In his estimation, the real weakness was "there were frame buildings in the fort . . . ready to burn."[31]

The five hundred Texans looked over the fort's parapet and saw they faced long odds. The enemy outnumbered them five times over. Lookouts watched the two gunboats in the gulf, expecting then to open fire at any moment. Bradfute sent riders to see if help was on its way. "I can hold this place with a few more men if you can prevent it from being flanked, and keep me supplied with provisions," his dispatches read. If the Federals crossed the lagoon, he would be cut off—and lost. Troops were on the way, his returning riders reported. The 2nd and 36th Texas Cavalries from Debray's Brigade might be as close as Victoria, about forty miles away. Still, Bradfute needed about twice that many regiments if he were to hold the fort.[32]

Overnight, wicked weather returned. A severe storm—another "blue norther" —came crashing through, starting with rain and high winds. Private Marshall remembered "rain turned to snow and covered the ground [and] in still water . . . ice of considerable thickness formed." At sunup on November 28, it became clear the howling northern winds would prevent Union gunboats from moving within range of the fort. Major General Washburn asked the navy for boats to cross the lagoon and cut off the fort from reinforcements coming from the mainland, but the boats could not maneuver through the whitecaps. Instead, both sides sniped at each other while the Texan guns played upon the dug-in Federal infantry.[33]

The Yankees did not allow the stormy day to keep them from working their way closer to the walls of Fort Esperanza. At dawn an infiltration party composed of picked men from each of the regiments in Colonel Washburn's Brigade rushed the Confederate outworks. Their position was quickly secured by the arrival of the 8th Indiana and the 33rd Illinois, which scared away a feeble Rebel counterattack. Brigadier General Ransom sent forward Battery F, 1st Missouri Artillery, and supplied covering fire from the left of the Union line. At the same time, crews brought up a section of guns from the 7th Michigan Battery, "under a heavy fire from the fort, fortunately not very accurate," as Colonel Washburn attested, on the right. The field pieces supplied covering fire while the 18th Indiana moved up in turn. In the course of the morning's maneuvering, the Texan artillery and small arms only managed to kill one of the advancing Federals. The Union field pieces, now repositioned, lobbed shells into the fort for the rest of the day.[34]

Despite earlier fears about a bloody struggle, both sides must have sensed the siege would not be a battle to the death. They spent the afternoon in what one Federal called "good natured" skirmishing. "It was a funny fight," wrote Private Marshall. The Confederate batteries only had solid shot and apparently their powder was poor, for the cannon balls that did not fall short of the Union lines simply rolled by.[35]

Both sides could plainly see each other, and "all kinds of bantering motions were made," as Marshall put it. Union troops stood up and mimicked the Confederates as they laboriously loaded and reloaded their large guns. As the Confederate soldiers rammed their shots home, the Yankees motioned with hats and hands to hurry up and shoot. When a Rebel rifleman fired, there was loud laughter and cheers as the soldiers threw themselves on the ground as if they had been hit. It appeared the Confederates caught on to the spirit of the occasion, and "as if wishing to amuse," they turned their 10-inch Columbiad away from the Union lines and toward the water, skipping a few shots out to sea toward the gunboats. "It was a splendid sight," wrote Marshall, and "our boys were not slow in showing the enemy they appreciated the entertainment."[36]

Despite the hijinks, many Union soldiers had been preparing for real combat. By the time the day faded into another freezing night, detachments of Vicksburg veterans from both Federal brigades had improved on the Texan trenches and had constructed a new line of trenches, two hundred yards long, just three hundred yards from the enemy parapets. If Major General Washburn's troops could not reduce Fort Esperanza by siege craft, they were now in position to carry it by storm.

That evening, Union commanders met to coordinate the assault planned for the next morning. The wind had died down during the day, allowing the guns of USS *Granite City* and USS *Monongahela* to come into play at last. Crews had improved the position of the two field batteries during the afternoon, and they had largely silenced the Rebel guns. The Texans had yielded their outworks, and the Federals had turned them into saps and approaches. All of this progress came at the light cost of one Union soldier dead and ten wounded. At first light on November 29, Colonel Washburn planned to lead his five regiments over the walls of the fort itself. If needed, Ransom would follow with his brigade.[37]

The Confederates held their own conference inside Fort Esperanza. The five hundred Texans were not eager to prove their mettle in close combat and instead advised Bradfute to give up hope for the fort. The small garrison could not resist a determined assault under covering fire from two field batteries and two gunboats. Bradfute agreed. He ordered his men to spike the guns, wreck the fort, and leave. His troops piled cotton bales around the seven magazines and spread gunpowder throughout the works. The last men out set fires to the trails of powder. The escaping Rebels scurried across the rope ferry to the Texan mainland, and eight men remained behind to slice the cables and deny its use to the enemy. As the last Confederates pulled their way across McHenry Bayou a few minutes past midnight, the detonation of Fort Esperanza's powder magazines flashed in the night sky and echoed across the beaches of Texas.[38]

Federal private Marshall, startled awake, remembered the explosions as a "wonderful display. A mountain of earth, iron, and timber all mingled together, darkened with immense clouds of smoke and brightened with the fierce flame of fire was, with one huge burst thrown high above us . . . creating one of the wildest and grandest scenes mortal man ever witnessed."[39]

As the detonations boomed across the sands of Matagorda Island, Union officers ordered their drummers to beat the long roll and their troops to form a line. With luck, quick action might trap the fleeing Rebels, but it soon became apparent Bradfute had escaped. Six of the eight men left behind surrendered to the oncoming Yankees. "We . . . captured the little hencoop of a fort," wrote Colonel Isaac Elliott of the 33rd Illinois, "but the garrison all escaped . . . [but] would have been perfectly harmless had we left them where they were."[40]

As with the other battles along the Texas coast, the short-lived siege of Fort Esperanza had been nearly bloodless on both sides. Colonel Washburn reported his losses remained at one man killed and ten men wounded, while Colonel Bradfute had lost one man killed and the six captured. The attack was also completely lacking in spoils. The powder magazine explosion and subsequent fire had consumed the equipment and supplies abandoned by the fleeing Rebels and burned the battery's gun carriages.

Colonel Isaac Elliot, 33rd Illinois. *Findagrave.com.*

Yankee engineers immediately went to work repairing and improving the fort to their liking. With the fall of Fort Esperanza, Federal troops were uncontested on the lower half of the Texas coast. Now Major General Washburn could set about establishing a firm base for continuing his Texas operations against Houston and Galveston—or San Antonio and Austin.[41]

Though denied his chance to gloriously storm over the fort's ramparts, Colonel Washburn nevertheless praised his veterans. "My officers and men behaved gallantly," he wrote, "showing that they had lost none of that coolness and bravery evinced by them upon the battlefields of Pea Ridge, Fredericktown, Port Gibson, Champion's Hill, Black River Bridge, Vicksburg, and Jackson." Lieutenant Shorey, less impressed, remembered the campaign for its cold wind and sandy discomfort. "The capture of Fort Esperanza cost but little in the way of bloodshed," he noted, "yet nevertheless the campaign was one of very great privation."[42]

On the morning of on November 29, Texan reinforcements arrived in time to see the smoke still rising from Fort Esperanza. The first troops from Debray's Brigade to approach were the veterans of Colonel Pyron's 2nd Texas Cavalry. As they rode into Indianola later that morning, they met Colonel Bradfute and his demoralized garrison retreating from the opposite direction. Bradfute ordered these mounted Rebels to follow him back to Chocolate Bayou and prepare to defend the town of Port Lavaca. He also sent couriers to advise all reinforcements to rally there.

Across the bay at almost the same time, Colonel Woods's 36th Texas Cavalry arrived at the hamlet of Matagorda after a forced march from Houston. Armed with freshly issued Enfield rifled muskets, they were ready for a fight. So was Colonel Leon Smith, who had gathered the steamers *John F. Carr* and *Cora* and eleven smaller sailing vessels to transport these reinforcements to Fort Esperanza. "Then the news came that our troops had left Saluria the night before, and that thus the entire bay had come into possession of the Yankees," Private Coreth wrote, "and we could not risk going over." Therefore, Colonel Woods ordered his men to Port Lavaca to help Bradfute and his ersatz brigade block the road. He left detachments at Matagorda to burn the bales of cotton stacked on the landing if the Yankees came.[43]

Colonel Smith repurposed his Matagorda Bay gunboat flotilla to oppose any Union attempts to land troops on the mainland. His flagship, the *John F. Carr*, mounted a 12-pounder and 18-pounder howitzer, and his sharpshooters and gunners were assisted by a smattering of militia provided by Colonel Bradfute. "They cannot speak a word of English" and "cannot tell their nostrils from a double-barrel shotgun," Smith complained. Even so, on November 30, he ordered the *John F. Carr* to head toward Pass Cavallo and look for enemy transports carrying troops for another landing. The move brought out the Union gunboats, but the two forces stood three miles away from each other. The Federals, not knowing the channel, feared grounding and refused to be baited into the muddy waters of Matagorda Bay. They steamed back to the deep, rolling water of the Gulf of Mexico, where the Rebel gunboats dare not go.[44]

The rim of Matagorda Bay was now largely at the mercy of the Federal army. The next move, however, remained a mystery.

SEVENTEEN

A PERSISTENT ENEMY

They have never met any troops they dread so much as Texians.

—Private John W. Watkins
5th Texas Cavalry

s Major General John B. Magruder studied the strategic situation. Union objectives in Texas remained murky. The geography of the Matagorda Bay region suggested San Antonio would be the likeliest target. The path to San Antonio from Indianola and Port Lavaca was dry, clear, and level—with decent roads. The distance, though, would be daunting. Union troops would have to cover 150 miles to reach San Antonio, creating a tediously long supply line behind them that the Texans could harass with their cavalry. Yet, if the Federals took the Alamo City, south Texas would be lost to the Confederacy. All pathways to Mexico would be sealed.

If the enemy persisted up the coast, the Matagorda Peninsula would be a poor approach. That windswept, glorified sand bar would compress the Union army and negate any numerical superiority. The Union navy could keep the army supplied, but the coast was treacherous along that stretch and had no natural harbors. Only a successful crossing of the wide Brazos River would allow the Federals to proceed deep into Southeast Texas. If the enemy made the attempt near its mouth, the US navy might prove decisive in getting the army across. Attempts at crossing farther inland would be unsupported and beset by Confederate attacks on flank and rear.

Magruder planned for any contingency. He ordered a part of his army to defend the roads to San Antonio and other troops to deploy along the Brazos. Fortifications at Quitana and Velasco would contest any landings at the river's mouth, while cavalry guarded every crossing for miles inland. Magruder bottled up the Matagorda Peninsula; the safest route of advance for the enemy was also the easiest for the Confederates to contain. If the Yankees moved up that natural causeway, which separated the mainland from the gulf, they would eventually smash into a line of Confederate fortifications and troops along the banks of Caney Creek, where the long sandy spit connected to the mainland. Even if Federal troops carried those works, they would have twenty-five miles of open country to traverse as they advanced to the Brazos.

If the Yankees received sizable reinforcements, Magruder realized, he might not hold them off. More troops would allow the enemy to pursue several approaches simultaneously. Reports indicated Major General Nathaniel P. Banks had most, if not all, of the 13th Army Corps already in Texas. Magruder believed he might have adequate troops to handle this threat, but if more Federals arrived, he would definitely need Confederate reinforcements from somewhere.

On November 28 he penned a letter to Brigadier General Tom Green. He wanted the veterans of his cavalry division to come home. Then Texas would be secure.[1]

While he waited for a response, Magruder tacked together his army of Texans and set them to their tasks. Brigadier General Hamilton P. Bee, relying mostly on Colonel James Duff's Brigade—including his 33rd Texas Cavalry and Colonel James Liken's recently created 35th Texas Cavalry, would protect the lines to Laredo and Eagle Pass, picket Chocolate Bayou between Port Lavaca and Indianola, and defend the road to San Antonio. At Velasco, Magruder posted a tiny infantry division of two brigades. Colonel Philip N. Luckett led one composed of the 3rd and 13th Texas, supported by Gibson's Battery. Its partner was Colonel Thomas Waul's Brigade, which included the Vicksburg veterans of the 2nd Texas Infantry, Waul's Legion, as well as the reassembled 8th Texas Infantry and the Austin Light Artillery. Around Houston and Galveston, Colonel Alexis T. Rainey, detailed from Magruder's staff, took command of a small brigade that was watching the eastern approaches to the state. His command included the 4th Cavalry Texas State Troops, 20th Texas Infantry, 21st Texas Infantry Battalion, and Captain Patrick Fox's Battery. Magruder recalled Lieutenant Colonel Ashley W. Spaight's 11th Texas Volunteers, serving as separate infantry and cavalry battalions in Louisiana, to Beaumont.

In addition, Magruder organized a reserve he could rush toward any threatened point. He had plenty of cannon. He designated four batteries—Captain Robert

Private Stephen Parks Allen of Waul's Texas Legion
was just a kid during the war. *Author's Collection.*

Hughs's, Captain Edmund Creuzbaur's, Captain William H. Nichols's, and the Dixie Grays—as the artillery reserve and positioned them on the rail line between Beaumont and Galveston. Magruder counted three brigades of state troops as part of his Texas order of battle, and he distributed these militia regiments among his Confederate commands to swell his army to around ten thousand men. Elsewhere, Confederate commanders in the Trans-Mississippi believed the Union forces in Louisiana no longer posed a threat, except as a source of reinforcements for Texas. Therefore, the shift of emphasis should be west of the Sabine River.

Magruder's troops and scouts had, however, picked up many Texas Unionists trying to reach the Federal lines at New Iberia. Colonel Augustus Buchel described one of them, Joseph Ritchie, as "a very dangerous character." Ritchie had been a pilot along the Texas coast before the war, and Confederates believed he now worked for the Federals. He had been captured along with some Calcasieu jayhawkers in Southwest Louisiana. In general, anti-Confederate subversives among the population seemed to be a growing problem.[2]

There were other concerns for the Rebels in Texas. Federal forces in the Rio Grande Valley had erased the Confederacy from the region, and their presence there continued to yield international dividends. "I have . . . received a message," Major General Napoleon Jackson Tecumseh Dana wrote to Banks, "that the French advance was falling back on Tampico, and preparations were making

Colonel Alexis T. Rainey. As an officer in the 1st Texas Infantry, he had been severely wounded early in the war at the Battle of Gaines Mill in Virginia. He returned to Texas to recuperate and lend a hand closer to home. *Findagrave.com.*

for the evacuation of Tamaulipas." The Imperial forces Dana believed had been heading to northeast Mexico seemed to be falling back. The arrival of the U.S. troops seemed to have bolstered the Juaristas' cause. For Magruder and his men, there would be no French intervention in Texas. The flag of the United States had been planted, indeed.[3]

While Texas seemed closer to being restored to Federal control, Louisiana continued to bedevil Union commanders. While Major General John G. Walker and his Pointe Coupee Parish expedition vexed the Mississippi River, Brigadier General Green's horsemen troubled the remnants of the Army of the Gulf as it settled into New Iberia.

The Yankees intended the town to be their forward line of operations and Major General William B. Franklin's men dug in. For a week soldiers from the locally raised 25th Infantry, *Corps d'Afrique*, worked with shovels instead of muskets and, using the long berm of the unfinished New Orleans, Opelousas, and Great

Western Railroad as a natural breastwork, constructed fortifications connecting this embankment to the Bayou Teche levee on the northwest end of town. Union officers rounded up townspeople and pressed them into labor alongside the African American soldiers. These crews dug another earthen wall along the edge of Nelson's Canal, at the southeast end of town, to seal a six-mile long enclosure. The troops of the 19th Army Corps, the remaining men of the 13th Army Corps, and all their animals and various staff detachments would camp in this neat rectangle all winter unless otherwise ordered.[4]

Franklin moved his headquarters into the ground floor of Judge John Moore's spacious mansion, The Shadows, its well-clipped lawn sloping down to Bayou Teche, on the main street in town. Before long, Judge Moore's landmark home resembled an army bivouac. The fence disappeared, providing fuel for Union campfires. The carefully manicured grounds gave way to the needs of the army. "Nothing . . . was sacred to the polluting touch of the barbarians," complained sugar planter William Frederick Weeks to his stepfather. "Even the garden and tender plants . . . was destroyed by being converted into a mule lot." Weeks's mother, Mary Moore, remained in her home; she lived upstairs while Major General Franklin maintained his office downstairs.[5]

Susan Smith, a teenaged enslaved girl owned by Charles Conrad Weeks of New Iberia, remembered when the Yankees came. "I seed de sojers in Iberia . . . dey take anythin' they wants," she remembered. She visited the bivouacs of

The home of Judge John Moore in New Iberia, appropriated by the Federal army. *Author's photo.*

these Federal troops regularly, "'cause dey give me crackers and sardines," she said. The Union troops told her she had her liberty. "I didn't know I'm free till a man say to me, 'Sissy, ain't you know you ain't got no more massa or missus?' I say, 'No, suh.'" It did not matter. Smith stayed with the Weeks family and tended their children.[6]

Franklin and his soldiers increased the comforts of their winter encampment. The Federal troops bivouacked there harvested what they needed—and wanted—from the neighborhood. Different waves of Federals ransacked Napoleone Geneviève "Appoline" Fournier's Patout Plantation, about six miles outside of the lines toward Jeanerette. "Bands of soldiers belonging to the infantry . . . came into her house and into her and her daughter's bedrooms, in fact everywhere," testified Fournier's son and business manager, Hippolyte Patout. "After the above acts were done by whites, the negroes . . . appeared on the scene. These colored troops stayed some hours upon the place." The *Corps d'Afrique* troops busted through locked doors and plundered freely. "They said they had a right to the property," Patout continued, "and also a right to burn up the place." Businesses and homes in town had fences torn down, siding carried away, and fixtures and furniture ransacked. The hand of war lay hard on New Iberia.[7]

Green and his Texans orbited nearby. They established camps along the Bayou Vermilion but put a picket post at Camp Pratt on the shores of Spanish Lake, a mere four miles north of the ramparts of fortified New Iberia. From here, Rebel horsemen from Green's old brigade rotated duties that included watching the Federals for any sign of a move toward Texas. They also harassed enemy scouts and foragers. Private William Randolph Howell, 5th Texas Cavalry, was among those who found a gap in the Union pickets. "Captured two US wagons and teams and 24 live Yankees," he crowed, "and get safely back to camp with them." Others of his regiment pinched another seven wagons and teams. When Texans drifted too close to the works, however, artillery from behind the berm brushed them back.[8]

The two armies would face off here for the next month. Despite the presence of the Texans around New Iberia, the Federals continued to fear that Brigadier General Green had led the raid into Pointe Coupee Parish. If so, there would soon be bold and deadly action along the Mississippi.[9]

At New Iberia, Major General Franklin received orders from Banks's chief of staff, Brigadier General Charles Pomeroy Stone, to "make such a strong demonstration as to ascertain whether he has a mere shell or a solid force in front." Franklin obeyed. He ordered his cavalry—three brigades—to make a wide loop out to the prairies west of New Iberia before slashing back toward Spanish Lake. Brigadier General Robert A. Cameron's 1st Brigade, 3rd Division, 13th Army Corps, would act as beaters, marching directly out of New Iberia toward Camp Pratt to drive the Rebels into the Federal cavalry's net. Two regiments with a long history of fighting the Texans—the 1st Louisiana (Union) and the 6th Missouri—would get the honor of charging their lines. On the drizzling morning of November 20, Franklin got his answer: His Union soldiers surprised the enemy and captured nearly half of the 7th Texas Cavalry. The Federals paraded their prisoners into New Iberia.[10]

Franklin continued to bruise the Rebels closest to his camps. The Texans quickly learned to keep their distance, and their pickets fell back to a position closer to Bayou Vermilion. The Federal cavalry next turned their attention to

Private Simeon J. Crews, 7th Texas Cavalry, was a veteran campaigner, but still managed to get captured by the Federals near Spanish Lake. *Library of Congress.*

irregulars operating near St. Martinville. On the drizzling, foggy night of November 22, Franklin sent seven hundred cavalry toward the Grand Bois and swamps of Lake Fausse Pointe, east of the Bayou Teche, guided by emancipated people from local plantations. At dawn the following morning, the Federal horsemen overran the camp of the Louisiana troops under Major St. Leon Duperier—fewer than one hundred unsteady partisans who had been forced into Confederate ranks by Major General Richard Taylor's conscript catchers. Many had deserted from the 10th Louisiana Yellow Jacket Battalion but returned when promised service as cavalry and had renewed their mischief by annoying steamboat traffic on Bayou Teche for weeks. Federals rode through their camps, scattering these unready Rebels, killing two and rounding up thirty prisoners.[11]

The south Louisiana standoff affected the civilians in the seventeen-mile region between Vermilionville and New Iberia. When the Confederates had retreated weeks before, many residents of the area had pledged their loyalty to the United States. Now that the Texans had returned, Confederates found plenty of hospitality despite the predilection for Federal protection among the locals.

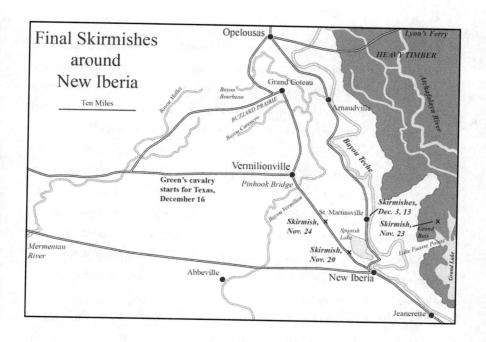

Final Skirmishes around New Iberia

Ten Miles

Opelousas

Lyon's Ferry

HEAVY TIMBER

Atchafalaya River

Bayou Mallet

Bayou Bourbeau

Grand Coteau

BUZZARD PRAIRIE

Bayou Carencro

Arnaudville

Bayou Teche

Vermilionville

Green's cavalry starts for Texas, December 16

Pinhook Bridge

Bayou Vermilion

St. Martinville

Skirmishes, Dec. 3, 13

Skirmish, Nov. 24

Spanish Lake

Skirmish, Nov. 23

Grand Bois

Mermentau River

Skirmish, Nov. 20

Lake Fausse Pointe

Grand Lake

Abbeville

New Iberia

Jeanerette

"We got plenty to eat once more from the citizen 'Kajans,'" Howell scribbled in his diary. The next day, while on picket, a family brought him three meals. The next day, "get dinner with some nice French girls," he wrote.[12]

Howell's replacements, a detachment of one hundred men from the 4th Texas Cavalry, crossed Bayou Vermilion amid a steady rain on an improvised span made from a cotton barge and the wreckage of the often-burned Pinhook Bridge. For twenty-two-year old Private Henry C. Wright, this was an invitation to visit familiar haunts, get fed, and dry off. He had served in the Teche Campaign the previous spring and had spent time getting to know people during the respite of the late summer. "We were up and down through that country," he wrote. "Sometimes the Yankees had possession, sometimes we. The people were harassed and impoverished with their resources exhausted." Even so, these Louisianans fed the Texans. Now, when homeowners welcomed him warmly or children ran out to greet him, his officers seemed surprised.[13]

"Wright, how do you manage to know so many people?" they asked. "Did you ever live in this country?"

"No," he replied, "I just got acquainted with them when we first came down here before times got so hard."[14]

On the morning of November 25, which dawned bright and clear, the Federals once again sallied forth to test the enemy strength. Although the rain had quit, the rise in Bayou Vermilion had carried away the makeshift bridge. A freedman informed the Federals in New Iberia the 4th Texas picket line, three miles north of Spanish Lake, had no way to cross to the safety of their reserves.[15]

The Confederates, scattered and relaxed, did not realize their peril. When the Texans saw a brigade of infantry advancing from New Iberia, "our fool lieutenants allowed the men to skirmish and exchange shots with them, which was exactly what they wished us to do," Private Wright remembered. Union cavalry, meanwhile, once again passed around the Texan picket line unseen, much as they had against the 7th Texas a week before. This time, Captain William Lee Alexander sniffed out the Federal trap and ordered his men to mount up and hustle back toward the Vermilion.[16]

Wright, astride a small mule, lumbered over to a nearby home and begged the owner to swap him a horse. "The Yanks will be here in fifteen minutes," the

Texan pleaded. "If you have a good horse they will take him, but if you let me have him, and keep my mule, they will not trouble the mule—or capture me—and I will bring him back in a few days." The Louisianan consented, bringing out a fine bay horse a little more than fourteen hands high. Wright put his saddle on the animal, turned his mule out into a pasture, and went on his way. "I knew as soon as I started that I had a horse among horses," he wrote, adding sheepishly, "and I will say now that for the twelve years he remained mine, I have seen but few of his equals, and no superiors." He rejoined his command only to find them falling back ahead of the Federal infantry.[17]

The Union cavalry moved to intercept the Rebels. "Our withdrawal, which first started out as a walk, soon became a trot, and then a gallop," Wright attested, "and at last a hard run to the tune of 'The devil take the hindmost.'" The mounted Federals thundered down an intersecting road in a column of fours. "It was a gallant sight to see," Wright admitted. "With pistol or sabre in one hand and their reins in the other, they came at full speed." The head of the Yankee column smashed into the rear of the fleeing Texans in an explosion of whirling horses, slashing blades, and snapping pistols.[18]

A bullet nicked Private Wright's new horse. "He gave a great spring and, getting the bit in his mouth, settled down to hard running," he recalled. The sudden lurch and subsequent dash caught the Texan by surprise, and his feet lost both stirrups, and his hat sailed from his head. "I held onto my gun—a long Enfield—useless on horseback, and clinching him with my knees let him run," Wright continued. The horse could not be slowed, nor steered, by reining in. "I was far from wanting to stop, and any place away from there looked good to me," he conceded. The Federals scooped up around sixty men before turning back, a mile short of Bayou Vermilion.[19]

Green ordered out the rest of his troops, thinking the Federals meant to bring on a general engagement, but instead the enemy horsemen faded away to the south. Texan prisoners once again shuffled into New Iberia. "The Yankees will brag a great deal over the capture of Texians as they are afraid of them," Private John W. Watkins of the 5th Texas Cavalry wrote his wife. Union prisoners he had talked to admitted as much. They "say they have fought Rebels from every state—but they have never met any troops they dread so much as Texians."[20]

Wright, pleased with his flight to safety, credited his horse. The next morning, an officer in the 7th Texas Cavalry, noticing the animal, identified it as the mount of one of his men, Sharp R. Whitley of Company F, who had been captured f ive days before. Wright realized he owed the Louisianan nothing, as the farmer had merely caught an abandoned Confederate mount. Wright paid the value of the horse to the officer, "thus becoming the owner of the finest animal that ever belonged to me," he remembered. The 7th Texas officer held the money for the captured soldier so that Whitley could procure another mount, should he return to the army. Wright rode to the Louisiana farm a few days later to recover his mule.[21]

Brigadier General Green knew his command could not sustain these careless losses. Colonel Arthur Pendleton Bagby's Brigade numbered maybe one thousand men. He had lost about 175 in the last week. Green ordered all of the Confederates to pull back beyond Bayou Vermilion while details rebuilt the Pinhook Bridge to avoid pickets being trapped again. The next morning, he addressed Captain Julius Giesecke and told him to take just thirty men out on picket. "Do not expose yourself and men too much," Green admonished. "All we want you to do is to give us fair notice of what is going on out there in the prairie." The German captain understood.[22]

The Federals remained in their lines, and Giesecke and his pickets spent pleasant days. "The citizens, through bad treatment by the Yankees, had become very southerly in their views, giving us every attention," he noticed. "We therefore lived like kings; nearly every house we passed invited us to take either breakfast, dinner, or supper, all having plenty for a Confederate soldier." When the 4th Texas Cavalry had been there the previous March—and May—and July—the residents had been far from generous. "Before the Yankees had been there," he scoffed, "we could get nothing for love or money."[23]

Around the same time Lieutenant John Coleman Sibley of the 2nd Louisiana Cavalry took a squad of men on a long scout to the west and south of New Iberia. From a church steeple, he could see the Federal lines seven miles away, over the open country, and he gave them a wide berth. About twelve miles from New Iberia, he observed several hundred Federal horsemen, men from the 2nd and

3rd Illinois Cavalry and the 118th Illinois Mounted Infantry, on a scout toward the salt works on Petite Anse Island. With so many Yankees about, Sibley and his men hid in the woods without fires as the weather turned cold and rainy. When they approached a known sympathizer for food and warmth the next day, he refused. "The old man was too uneasy to give it to us," Sibley wrote. "He said the enemy came to his house . . . looking for us and told him if he fed any more rebels they would burn him out of house and home."[24]

As Sibley watched, the Federal expedition returned to New Iberia. "Did not get any Rebs," noted Private Thomas E. Mix of the 118th Illinois Mounted Infantry in his journal.[25]

By the end of November, as both sides suffered from the rain and cold that swept into the area, the Federal lethargy in Louisiana seemed to confirm Texas was their principal target. In a final flourish, the Federal cavalry made a rush at the rebuilt Pinhook Bridge on the last day of the month, but nothing came of it.

"Yanks advanced to within range of our artillery at the bridge," Private Howell scribbled in his diary that day. "A few shots are exchanged, when the enemy fall back and we go to our quarters."[26]

From that point on, Federal and Rebel horsemen routinely brought in food from the countryside unmolested. "We went on a foraging out to the salt works," noted Private Mix. "Got plenty of salt, potatoes, and corn. All quiet on the Teche."[27]

Things were not so quiet on the Mississippi. Confederate attacks in Pointe Coupee Parish and the coverage in the papers reflected poorly on the Department of the Gulf and its commander. Major General Banks, still onboard ship and returning from his Texas escapade, had so far escaped the brunt of the criticism. His respite would not last.

On December 1, Banks arrived back in New Orleans to face a barrage of bad news. Sick, tired, and in need of rest, he was in no mood to endure the criticism. "The General arrived here . . . I am sorry to say, in poor health," wrote a *New York Times* reporter. "He was prostrated by fever, not of a serious nature, but necessitating a short time for recruiting his strength. He is a man of iron constitution; but the strongest must at last give way under the accumulation of mental and bodily labor." Perhaps a little rest would restore Banks, and he could finish the job in Louisiana, the newspaper suggested. "It is to be hoped that a little nursing in the bosom of his family here will speedily restore him again to health and usefulness."[28]

This Banks booster also noted his return to New Orleans coincided with an important anniversary. "Precisely one year ago, the North Star, in company with a fleet of transports, left the port of New-York amid the cheers of assembled thousands, who had gathered to see the great Banks' Expedition set out on its important and mysterious career." Since then, the newspaper crowed, Banks and others had wrestled the region away from the Rebels. "Baton Rouge, Vicksburgh, Port Hudson, and all intermediate points have been wrested from the rebels, the Mississippi River once again restored to commerce, and the so-called Confederacy cut completely in twain. Louisiana has been completely overrun by the victorious National forces, all the way between this and Alexandria, the rebel armies whipped and disorganized, and millions of treasure taken from them to enrich the national Treasury." Of course, this story mixed fantasy with fact.[29]

This admirer claimed Banks had recovered Texas. He "has once again planted the good old flag," the reporter wrote, "where it will now remain—by God's blessing—until every foot of its soil is wrested from pollution." Reality, though, was more complicated and had jagged edges.[30]

Banks was ill, and so was the Department of the Gulf. Despite all Banks had accomplished, the Rebels continued to embarrass the United States on the Mississippi by shelling passenger steamers. Major General Franklin remained fixed in New Iberia, unable to mount an adequate response to this Confederate threat. New Orleans caught the contagion, too, with many rumors swirling. One said Taylor would make another attempt to take the city.

Many of its citizens hoped Taylor would do so. As a sailor from the USS Richmond wrote, "I have spent considerable time rambling around N.O, secesh is as strong here, I think, as ever, but keep hid."[31]

As the New Orleans gossips whispered of Confederate ascendancy, the rheumy-eyed Banks steadily slogged through the pile of dispatches waiting at his headquarters. Mostly he faced a cascade of bad news about deteriorating conditions in Louisiana. Passenger steamers heading up the Mississippi had come under fire from Confederate artillery on both side of the river. Tinclads, too, had been shot up in the exchanges, showing just how feeble a weapon they were.

Deeper in his pile, Banks learned efforts to raise black troops in Louisiana had also run into numerous snags—recruitment was slow, desertions were brisk. Many of his white officers, unused to working with black soldiers, found command of these units to be difficult. Many were physically unfit for service, others were quick to slip away from camp, while others did not even speak English. One of the oldest of these new commands, the 4th Infantry, *Corps d'Afrique*, mutinied at Fort Jackson in protest over offenders being whipped.[32]

Banks also found messages from General-in-Chief Henry Halleck that were particularly ungracious. Planting the national flag in Texas had been the burning desire of the national government just four months ago—in August. Now Halleck called Banks's accomplishment a mistake.

Reading reports on the progress of the war elsewhere, Banks also realized he had been professionally eclipsed. As he reviewed the latest national news, he learned what he had missed while he had been on the coast of Texas. Major General Ulysses S. Grant, the "Hero of Vicksburg" and his one-time partner in securing the Mississippi River, had now become the "Savior of Chattanooga." Not only had the man who had nearly killed himself in a drunken riding accident in New Orleans become *the* national hero, but Grant had also introduced Major General William Tecumseh Sherman to the nation as his most capable lieutenant. While Banks had pursued his distant but innovative Rio Grande Expedition, Grant had crafted a solution to the military problems in southeast Tennessee and northwest Georgia that dominated the nation's attention. By the end of November Grant had forged a mighty army, composed of troops from the East and West, and routed General Braxton Bragg's winded and dysfunctional Army of Tennessee. Banks meanwhile had gone around in circles in Louisiana while conquering miles of sand dunes in Texas.

Nevertheless, Banks believed he had succeeded in delivering everything President Abraham Lincoln had asked of him and expected a reward. Even if the Confederates were harassing shipping *on* the Mississippi, he had nearly settled affairs *west* of the Mississippi, as were his orders. His regiments had conquered

Brazos Santiago, Padre, Mustang, St. Joseph's, and Matagorda Islands and established a secure and sizable beachhead on the Texas coast. In addition, his troops had captured Brownsville and disrupted the cotton trade into Mexico, which promised to starve the Confederacy of revenues and supplies from that quarter.

He had also stuck a finger in the eye of the French and their Mexican stooges. He would now thumb his nose at Halleck. Matagorda Bay was now a Federal lake, Banks claimed, "which enables us to control the State at our pleasure, and the occupation of every important point on the Coast except Galveston." Even so, Halleck still insisted on an ascent up the Red River.[33]

Banks thought otherwise. "It has been impossible within any reasonable time to gain a foothold in Texas, except by the sea at this season," he reasoned. An inland campaign through Louisiana would court disaster. The march by Louisiana, either via the Teche and overland to the Sabine, or by Alexandria or Shreveport, would require a five-hundred-mile slog to any important point in Texas. Water and supplies would be scarce, and all logistics would be wagon-bound. The Texans, too, would be wily. "The constantly retreating, but steadily concentrating forces of the enemy, who could not fail, by their superiority in numbers of their mounted troops, [would] inflict upon our columns, trains and communications serious and irreparable injury."[34]

If only the landings at Sabine Pass had worked. Banks believed, it "would have enabled me to place a force of from 15,000 to 17,000 men at Houston, in the very center of all the Rebel forces of Louisiana and Texas." One more push, on the Texas coast and not overland from Louisiana, was all he lacked. He just needed men. Just bringing his regiments up to strength, he argued, would win the day. "Appreciating the great exigencies of the Government, I am ashamed to ask for increased forces — but it seems to me, that our regiments from the East and the Northwest — depleted by constant and perilous service on sea and land — ought to be filled up, by drafted men or volunteers— I would be satisfied with this."[35]

Banks felt confident that in just a few weeks, perhaps a little longer, all would be set right. The commander of the Department of the Gulf had laid the foundations for a decisive winter campaign to finish off Texas. In the process he would weaken Louisiana to the point that a spring 1864 campaign would return

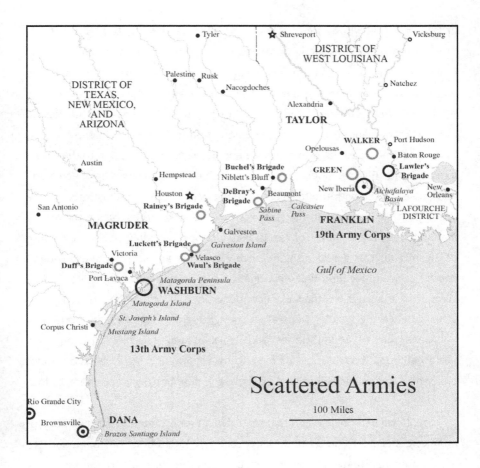

the Trans-Mississippi to the Union. This would be done while keeping the French in Mexico off balance and away from the Rio Grande. To further burnish the victor's diadem he placed on his own head, Banks had thus far accomplished these great strides at a minimal loss of blood and treasure.

He quickly learned few people in power cared about his Texas exploits. Since the fall of Vicksburg, the American public's attention had shifted away from the Mississippi Valley and toward affairs farther east.

To his credit, Banks had, with fewer troops than he thought he had needed, neatly rearranged affairs in the western Gulf of Mexico to suit the national interests, just as General-in-Chief Halleck and President Lincoln had instructed. However, foreign policy moves and grand strategies on a distant shore meant little to a nation whose sons, fathers, and brothers were fighting and dying in Virginia and Tennessee. While Grant was receiving accolades and laurels, Banks returned to New Orleans to face criticisms and unrealistic expectations. Banks realized his star had faded while Grant's glowed like Polaris.

President Lincoln added to Banks's growing funk. The president had waded into the conversation on political reconstruction in Louisiana. In early August Lincoln had believed Louisiana was well on its way to readmission to the Union as a free state. By November, the president learned little progress had been made and those trusted with the task were feuding. Most of the administrators of the Union political authority in the state blamed the lack of progress on the army's inability to conquer more of Louisiana, perhaps including everything south of Alexandria. This would bring staunchly Unionist areas firmly under Federal control. Lincoln, facing rough elections the next year, needed the state, and its electors, readmitted. So, the lack of cooperation—especially that created by the schism between Brigadier General George F. Shepley, his military governor of Louisiana, the civilian authorities, and Banks, his military chief in the region—perturbed him. "This disappoints me bitterly; yet I do not throw blame on you or on them," Lincoln wrote Banks. "I do, however, urge both you and them, to lose no more time."[36]

Lincoln wanted Shepley to organize a civilian government without waiting for more of Louisiana to be captured and occupied. "I wish him," Lincoln urged, "to go to work and give me a tangible nucleus which the remainder of the State may rally around as fast as it can, and which I can at once recognize and sustain as the true State government." Banks and his army, Lincoln coached, were to give them "hearty sympathy and support" in this endeavor. Texas, which had been the centerpiece of Lincoln's views in July and August, was no longer of much interest.[37]

Yet, the president's meddling had also added to the confusion in Louisiana. He had sent Shepley and his civilian authorities copies of his instructions to Banks on how Louisiana should be restored to the Union. Banks believed he was in charge of the process, but Shepley claimed authority based on receiving orders directly from the White House. Amid this argument, Banks had gone to Texas while Shepley dawdled.

Lincoln wanted to know why, and he wanted to hear what Banks had to say. Banks turned it back on the president. "Governor Shepley and the Honorable [Thomas Jefferson] Durant both notified me by official letters, that the subject of an election or state organization had been exclusively committed to him [Shepley], the military Governor," Banks explained. They had showed him Lincoln's orders. "I so understood it myself," Banks admitted. "I have had neither authority, influence, nor recognition as an officer entrusted with this duty. My suggestions are respectfully, but silently received by the Governor and his associates." Simply stated, Banks declared that it was not his job.[38]

If Lincoln had stayed out of the issue, they would be having a completely different conversation. "Had the organization of a *free* state in Louisiana been committed to me under general instructions only," Banks fumed, "it would have been complete before this day."[39]

Banks, resentful of the president's rebuke and the second-guessing of his policies, defended himself. He had done the most good in the arena where he had the most control. He had urged Governor Shepley and the political leadership of Louisiana to work diligently toward organizing a Unionist civilian government, but they had not been interested in considering his advice. So, "I . . . turned my attention, not unwillingly, to matters more likely to be accomplished, though not more important," Banks wrote. "The restoration of our Flag in Texas from Ringgold Barracks on the Rio Grande to the Brasos on the coast, rewarded my change in purpose." Shepley and his minions had been tasked with restoring Louisiana, not him. "How then," he asked, "can I be held responsible for the failure to satisfy your expectations?"[40]

Lincoln apologized. "I deeply regret to have said or done anything which could give you pain, or uneasiness," he wrote Banks. "I have all the while intended you to be *master*, as well in regard to re-organizing a State government for Louisiana, as in regard to the military matters of the Department; and hence my letters on reconstruction have nearly if not quite all been addressed to you." The president had no idea Shepley would cut Banks out of the process. "I now tell you that in every dispute, with whomsoever, you are master. . . . Instructions have been given directly to [Shepley] merely to spare you detail labor, and not to supersede your authority."[41]

Lincoln muddied the waters in Louisiana in other ways. On December 8, 1863, the president issued the Proclamation of Amnesty and Reconstruction, which became known as the Ten-Percent Plan, to facilitate the speedy reunion of the nation and to provide a rubric upon which the political life of the nation could proceed. Among its tenets was an oath of allegiance. Those wishing to return to the embrace of the United States would need to swear to "faithfully support, protect, and defend the Constitution of the United States and the Union of the States thereunder." In addition, former secessionists would need to promise to "support all acts of congress passed during the existing rebellion with reference to slaves, so long and so far as not repealed, modified, or held void by congress, or by decision of the supreme court." The oath takers would furthermore affirm that they would "abide by and faithfully support all proclamations of the President made during the existing rebellion having reference to slaves, so long and so far as not modified or declared void by decision of the supreme court." Many Louisianans balked at this broad stroke of government intervention and its anti-states' rights language, reinvigorating a bloc of pro-slavery Unionists.[42]

Banks learned he had other troubles, too. General-in-Chief Halleck, clearly influenced by political conversations circulating around Washington, opened yet another line of criticism of Banks, adding to the scorn against him. Halleck scolded the commander of the Department of the Gulf by declaring his strategy incompetent. Simply stated, Halleck told Banks he had blundered by planting the flag in Texas. Instead, he should have maintained his focus on Louisiana, as President Lincoln *now* wanted.[43]

Banks felt dumbfounded, and betrayed.

The Confederates were certainly making a mess of things as well and adding to Banks's headaches. Major General John G. Walker continued his devilment on the banks of the Mississippi. The burned and splintered steamers under repair on the New Orleans docks gave testimony to the Rebel campaign to spread terror and uncertainty on the river. Walker, though, was not through with his troublemaking. He would march his small army toward Plaquemine, the gateway to the Lafourche country, taking the same route Rebel cavalry had the previous summer.

Walker's and Brigadier General Jean Jacques Alfred Alexander Mouton's Divisions marched out of their camps in early December, following the Atchafalaya River, Bayou Fordoche, and Bayou Grosse Tête—a well-worn invasion route toward the Lafourche District. On December 3, the command camped on the battleground of Sterling's plantation. Most of Walker's Division remained unacquainted with these fields but, as Private J. P. Blessington noted, they saw "several corpses exposed to the rays of the sun, some of them only half buried." Walker's Texans kept going while Mouton's Division, held in reserve, camped on these haunted acres for several days. For many, especially the men of Prince Camille de Polignac's Texas Brigade, Sterling's plantation held troubling memories.[44]

Captain George W. O'Brian of the 11th Texas Infantry Battalion tried to reconstruct the battle. At the time of the fight, there had been torrential rain and the chaos of battle to contend with. Now he could investigate the place at his leisure. "Not as much sign as I anticipated," he wrote in his diary. He and fellow veterans paced off the distances they had charged on that fateful day—837 yards from the cover of the sugarcane to the Union position on the levee; 250 yards from the sugarhouse to the levee; the sweet potato field did not seem nearly so wide now. The soldiers tried to cement the fight in their minds. These military tourists helped themselves to syrup as sugar production had resumed after the battle. The following day, local slaves led them to a grave they believed to be that of one of their companions who had gone missing. They dug up the body and positively identified the soldier. "Poor fellow," O'Brien lamented. "Another martyr for self-government. He was a good soldier, a good friend and messmate, and would have made a good citizen." The men reburied the corpse.[45]

South of Mouton's Division, Walker's Confederates passed through devastated country. The Texans kept marching until they reached Livonia. "This section of country might have been termed the 'Paradise' of Louisiana before the war," noted Blessington, "but alas, what a change had befallen it now." Only a few African Americans, subsisting in the strange twilight of slavery the war had brought, lingered around mile after mile of homes, plantations, and farms that had been abandoned by their owners. "Mansion after mansion including costly sugarhouses," he continued, "now going to decay." The Texans resumed their course, with Bayou Gross Tête on their right, as they moved toward Rosedale.[46]

Pickets from Mouton's Division, meanwhile, moved into the ruins of Morganza to watch the Mississippi River and the monitor USS *Neosho* on patrol. Captain O'Brien beheld a forest of chimneys in the town. "Another memento of the base, cowardly, wickedness of our enemies," he wrote. The village's inhabitants had been "left roofless to roam and tell the tale of wrongs."[47]

Ahead of Walker's Division, the 13th Texas Cavalry Battalion pushed on to Plaquemine. When the Texans found Brigadier General Michael Lawler's Union brigade in position and ready, backed by gunboats, the horsemen turned around. There would be no easy way back into the Lafourche country, they reported to Walker. Their scouts urged caution.

Major General Walker received the bad news at his headquarters in Livonia. He had hoped to surprise the Federal garrison at Plaquemine, gobble them up in a lightning raid like Brigadier General Tom Green had done elsewhere, and then terrorize the Lafourche District. Clearly, however, the Yankees knew he was coming, and Walker and Mouton were certainly not Green.

Walker paused his army to consult Mouton and various brigade commanders. They all agreed the prize would not be worth the cost. "The circumstances of my position and the great necessity to preserve from useless sacrifice the only force left us for the defense of Western Louisiana, compelled me to abandon the attempt," he explained to Major General Richard Taylor. Green may have been the master at picking off isolated garrisons, but Walker refused to batter his command against a garrison that, in the end, would prove of little value. Walker ordered his column about and retreated toward Morgan's Ferry.[48]

While Confederates marched back through Pointe Coupee Parish, the 16th Texas Infantry and a collection of the best cannons and crews from every battery in the army dropped back to the Mississippi to intercept traffic and bid the river a macabre farewell. They moved into position at L. F. Claiborne's plantation above the crossing at Bayou Sara. On December 8, the Confederates spied the *Henry Von Phul* making its way upriver.

Bound for St. Louis, the *Henry Von Phul* carried passengers and a cargo of salt and sugar. The steamboat had passed the ironclad USS *Lafayette* at Bayou Sara

Henry Von Phul tormented by Confederate artillery. Thomas W. Knox, *Camp-Fire and Cotton-Field: Southern Adventure in Time of War, Life with the Union Armies, and Residence on a Louisiana Plantation* (New York: Blelock, 1865).

and expected to reach the safety of the next gunboat in line, the USS *Neosho*, near Morganza. The USS *Neosho* would escort the steamer past Sneed's and Cottier's plantations at Morgan Bend and Hog Point, and, then, presumably out of the Confederate danger zone.[49]

Instead, the steamboat's passengers and crew were caught by surprise as it traveled between the waiting ironclads. Thomas W. Knox, a newspaper correspondent for the *New York Herald*, as well as the operator of a government-run plantation at Waterloo, Louisiana, was among the passengers on the *Henry Von Phul* that afternoon. "Seated at a table in the cabin, and busily engaged in writing, I head a heavy crash over my head, almost instantly followed by another," he remembered. At first he thought the vessel had some mechanical trouble, but then he noticed the roof caving in.[50]

"The guerillas are firing on us," shouted a panicked passenger. The journalist shook off the shock, gathered his pen and papers, and dashed for his stateroom to see to the welfare of his traveling companion. The two men then helped other passengers hustle several women to the relative safety of the starboard wheelhouse, putting the boat between the ladies and the Rebels. The cannonade continued. The next flashes of Rebel guns hurled light artillery projectiles through the port side of the boat. "A sheet of wet paper would afford as much resistance to a paving stone as the walls of a steamboat cabin to a six-pound shot," Knox wrote. Two rounds punched completely through the hull and splintered the planking just inches from his head.[51]

The *Henry Von Phul* continued upriver and skips and splashes behind the steamer indicated it had moved beyond the Rebels' range. Passengers checked for damage and were relieved to find the steamboat's machinery was intact. "No one can express in words the anxiety with which we listened, after each shot, for the puffing of the engines," Knox remembered. "So long as the machinery was uninjured, there was no danger of our falling into Rebel hands." Smoke filled the boat, but Knox discovered a shell had crashed through a stateroom, exploded on a pillow, and scattered its feathery innards across a hot stove. He extinguished the smoldering stuffing and sheets before a serious blaze broke out.[52]

There had been casualties. The pilothouse had taken a direct hit. The helmsman continued to steer the vessel, but the boat skipper lay dead at his feet. "The first gun from the Rebels threw a shell which entered the side of the pilothouse and struck the captain, who was sitting just behind the pilot," Knox continued. The second round hit near the same spot. "A moment later a 'spherical case shot' followed the shell," Knox explained. "It exploded as it struck the woodwork." The barkeep had also been in the pilothouse and now lay dying atop a litter of "blood, splinters, glass, and the fragments of a shattered stove." Uninjured but in shock from his miraculous escape, the pilot continued managing the *Henry Von Phul*. The stricken steamboat reached the USS *Neosho* while the USS *Lafayette* steamed to the ambush site to drive off the assailants who, as usual, had vanished.[53]

Under escort, the passengers of the *Henry Von Phul* believed themselves to be safe. They were wrong. A half hour after the steamboat resumed its journey, cannon from the 1st Regular Battery and the Pelican Artillery fired at it from Sneed's plantation. "The first shell passed through the cabin, wounding a person near me," Knox wrote. The cannonball had also grazed a post behind his chair. More rounds passed through the cabin, and a shell exploded a deck below, knocking over Knox's table and knocking his chair off balance. He ran from the cabin, preferring death by iron projectiles rather than by splinters, and sheltered on the lower deck. As the steamer moved away from the Confederate guns, their shots tended to skip into the hull. "A loose plank on which I stood was split for more than half its length," he wrote. The lumber smacked into Knox's foot, bruising it badly. He lay prone on the deck, as did others. A shell burst above the deck, killing two men lying near him. "The right leg of one was completely severed below the knee," he wrote. The steamboat pulled away from its assailants while the USS *Neosho* rotated its turret, searching for the Rebel guns.[54]

Having survived its second assault, the *Henry Von Phul* was a wreck and its survivors terrorized. The ambushes had killed or injured twelve of the fifty passengers aboard, all civilians. Shell fragments had cut a pipe, filling the main cabin with scalding steam; another round had smashed the ship's safe; another smashed a trunk, turning it into a hive of splinters. Fragments of wood and glass lay everywhere. "I can hardly imagine a situation of greater helplessness than a place aboard a Western passenger steamer under the guns of a hostile battery," Knox concluded. "On a Mississippi transport, you are . . . in danger of being shot. You may be struck by splinters, scalded by steam, burned by fire, or drowned. You cannot fight, you cannot run away, and you cannot find shelter. With no power for resistance or escape, the sense of danger and helplessness cannot be set aside."[55]

The Union navy retaliated. Not finding any military targets to strike, sailors turned their big guns on any structure in sight. Indiscriminate shelling wrecked houses and outbuildings in Morgan's Bend. Captain Felix Pierre Poché arrived at his sister-in-law's home the following day to find it damaged even more that it had been. A second sister-in-law had suffered even more, her home taking a direct hit from a 9-inch Dahlgren. "Eugène Tircuit's house was hit," he observed. The heavy shell penetrated one end the house and exited the other end, "going through five walls, shattering two armoires, and ruining the house."[56]

The torment of the *Henry Von Phul* proved to be the last act of Walker's excursion in Pointe Coupee Parish. He and his two divisions crossed the Atchafalaya River and on December 10 the rains returned. Captain Arthur W. Hyatt, now a member of the Consolidated Crescent Regiment after a reorganization of the Louisiana Infantry, labored on through the horrible weather, slopping along in the same muck as he had marched through the night before the Battle of Sterling's Plantation. "It has been raining off and on for two days, and the roads are quite muddy," he again complained. "Our mules are worn out . . . cracking of whips, bellowing, etc., never was seen before. Everyone is covered with mud and cold and wet." Then the rain worsened. "We experienced a regular hailstorm . . . and such roads, they are past description. Nothing but mud, mud mud." It reminded him of another time—near this same place—where he had been miserable. "It almost come up to [rival] Fordoche."[57]

Taylor had done all he could, and now he bedded down his army for the winter. He left Walker near Simmesport; the Texans dug a line of earthworks near Yellow Bayou and went into camps near Bayou Des Glaize. Mouton's men were fated to march for several more weeks. Rumors of a major descent by Union brigadier general Frederick Steele's army in Little Rock, Arkansas, toward the Red River concerned Lieutenant General Edmund Kirby Smith enough that he moved troops into position to react.

Mouton's Louisiana and Texas infantry passed back through Alexandria before traveling on poor roads through Winnfield. "I never thought that there was a place as poor and miserable as this in the state of Louisiana," Poché complained, describing Winnfield as "an ugly little town of about six or seven ugly houses and two or three stores." The valley of the Ouachita River, though, met with his approval. "The surrounding country looks very good," he continued. "The village of Monroe is situated on the River and had a population of about twelve hundred people and many stores and very pretty houses and is a pretty little village." The last of Taylor's infantry entered their winter quarters in more wet, freezing weather. The campaign in Louisiana was over—for the moment. The battle for Texas would soon begin anew.[58]

EIGHTEEN **TEXAS**

"Learn the force, positions, and intentions
of the enemy, and the natural and artificial
difficulties to be met and overcome."

—Brigadier General Charles Pomeroy Stone
Chief of Staff, Army of the Gulf

A s the Confederates raided Pointe Coupee, and played their game of cat-and-mouse near New Iberia, Major General Cadwallader C. Washburn believed his efforts to conquer Texas had reached a critical stage. Scanning his maps, he understood that he could certainly press inland from Saluria on good roads and level terrain, but he had no interest in heading west. He wanted Houston, not Victoria and San Antonio, and he thought the best route there led along the coast, down the narrow Matagorda Peninsula, across Pass Cavallo.

Washburn wrote Major General Nathaniel P. Banks with his plans. Although some of his troops on a reconnaissance through Indianola had brushed away some Texan pickets and the way seemed clear, he wanted to head northeast, not northwest. "I have determined to move up the Matagorda Peninsula to the mouth of the Brazos River," he wrote. "There are two forts there which must be taken. If I have good luck, I will have that pass in one week."[1]

Therefore, Washburn began crossing troops across Pass Cavallo from Fort Esperanza to Decros Point at the peninsula's western end. Soon, he would have his command snake up the peninsula for fifty miles to the mainland and press on another twenty-five miles across the coastal prairie. He would attack the two forts guarding the mouth of the deep Brazos River at Quitana and Velasco from behind. Then, on to Houston.

Washburn expected the long march to be rugged but probably unopposed. He counted on Federal gunboats to keep the dunes clear until his troops were off the Matagorda Peninsula and ready to attack. In two weeks, he believed, he would have a new base of operations at Velasco that could be easily supplied and reinforced by sea. From the new base, he would head to Houston, which lay sixty miles away, before taking Galveston, which lay just forty miles up the coast.

Meanwhile, some of his troops crafted a permanent base on Matagorda Bay. His *Corps d'Afrique* engineers turned Fort Esperanza into an impressive headquarters; Washburn planned to leave the 23rd Iowa to hold the fort. The African American soldiers also transformed Decros Point into a supply depot. When even more reinforcements arrived from Louisiana, aboard the transports *Hussar* and *St. Mary's*, Major General Washburn had them land directly at Decros Point.[2]

Federal scouts explored what lay ahead and found the Matagorda Peninsula sandy, grassy, and nearly uninhabited. About halfway up the three-mile-wide sand spit, a "Dutch Settlement"—with two-dozen buildings and a handful of poor inhabitants—passed for the most notable village. Smith's Landing, about seven miles from where the peninsula joined the mainland, was another cluster of houses and outbuildings, mostly abandoned. Hardscrabble ranches, though, abounded.

The Union encampment quickly appropriated the ranch of Thomas DeCrow, son of one of the original Anglo settlers to Texas but who had family roots in Maine. The hungry Yankee invaders stripped the holdings of its livestock. "We had plenty of meat, but other rations were short," remembered Sergeant John M. Follett of the 33rd Illinois. They set up earthworks facing east toward the only land approach. Other Union Soldiers landed at Indianola, where they dismantled a long pier and several houses, and then they carried the lumber back to Decros Point. There they hammered together a new pier and warehouses, and soon the post assumed the appearance of a typical Federal encampment, complete with a growing canvas city laid out in regular streets.[3]

After capturing Velasco, Washburn believed he would need some heavy guns to complete the conquest of Texas. "Please do not forget to send me a battery of 20 or 30 pounder Parrotts. The First Wisconsin Battery at Brashear City— four 30-pounders—I should like," he wrote to Banks. "They will be wanted at Galveston."[4]

Banks, in a stunning change of mood, no longer seemed to share Washburn's confidence, and did not return a sunny response. Instead, he ordered Washburn to wait. Something in Louisiana had clearly given Banks pause.

Washburn was stunned. His suffering troops shivered on the windswept Matagorda Peninsula ready to press on to victory. He had few wagons making logistics a headache, and even his lightest draft vessels had trouble navigating the treacherous Texas coast, and time would only exacerbate this problem. Despite these conditions, Washburn's command had conquered the Texas coast in a month. He had momentum. He held the strategic initiative. His men could reach the mouth of the Brazos River with one more great effort and secure an excellent deep-water base perfectly located for further campaigns. He could be in Houston by Christmas. Astounded by Banks's orders, Washburn dutifully obeyed. "Hoping more troops may soon arrive," he signed in a dispatch to Banks, "and that I may receive orders to advance." His chance, Washburn believed, was slipping away.[5]

Even with the delay, Banks believed time remained to complete the conquest of Texas—which would create conditions for the subsequent collapse of Confederate Louisiana. The next orders Major General Washburn received from New Orleans indicated his campaign might come back to life. "The commanding general desires that you scout actively all the country in your front and make such demonstrations in the direction of Indianola and Palacios as your means may allow," wrote Brigadier General Charles Pomeroy Stone, Banks's chief of staff. Like Franklin in Louisiana, Washburn was to "amuse and confuse the enemy as to your intentions" while reconnoitering the area. This would be a feint in the direction of Victoria.[6]

The orders suggested Washburn should not draw too much attention to his command, and that he should not give away his intended line of march up the peninsula. "An advance of your forces will bring down upon you the concentrated forces of the enemy," the dispatch continued. "You must be largely re-enforced before such advance is made." In the meantime, Washburn should make as warm a camp as possible for the winter. The 2nd Engineers, *Corps d'Afrique*, would arrive soon to help with the heavy labor.[7]

While Louisiana cooled from its long simmer, Confederate authorities in Texas expected their region to be the next to boil. The campaign up the coast, if unchecked, would lead to the fall of Galveston and Houston. If the Yankee troops controlled these key points, they would be able to establish communications with Major General Franklin's army on the Teche. Most of Texas, and Louisiana below Alexandria, might soon be in Union hands. Trade across the Rio Grande would dry up. The Confederate Trans-Mississippi would have a Federal axe at its root.

The taproot, of course, was the long white cotton trail to Mexico. While Washburn planned his next move at Matagorda Bay, operations in the Rio Grande Valley had also picked up as Union forces continued to seal the border. In early December the 1st Texas Cavalry (Union) left Brownsville and headed west on a protracted scout. They patrolled up the Rio Grande to Fort Ringgold and beyond for nearly two weeks, looking for any signs of Rebel troops. Meanwhile Major General Dana outfitted an expedition to sever all cotton trade between the Confederacy and European and Mexican agents south of the border. An infantry regiment, the 37th Illinois, aboard light steamboats, followed the route of the 1st Texas Cavalry, steamed upriver to Fort Ringgold and Rio Grande City. This command netted hundreds of bales of cotton and slaughtered and salted scores of beeves.

The expedition also brought in Unionist recruits, swelling the ranks of Colonel Edmund J. Davis's regiment. "Many men from the Southern States had entered Mexico," remembered August Santleben, a German immigrant to Texas who had crossed over to Piedras Negras to avoid the war. "Some were refugees who fled the country because of their opposition to secession and sympathy for the Union cause, but many were skulkers seeking to avoid military service, and a large number were deserters from the Confederate army." He travelled more than three hundred miles on the Mexican side of the border from Eagle Pass to Matamoros before crossing over to Brownsville to enlist.[8]

Others had similar stories. Teamster Joseph Freeborn Rowley and his teenaged stepson, Fred, had fled Hays County, south of Austin, and taken refuge in Matamoros. When the Federals arrived in Brownsville, the two Unionists crossed back over the Rio Grande to resume their allegiance to the U.S. flag. Rowley's constitution, though, crumbled. Illness left him bed-ridden for a month. Once he recovered, he had no interest in enlisting himself or his stepson in the army. He did not want to fight the Rebels; he wanted to avoid them. He then attempted to book passage on a New Orleans–bound steamer, but profiteering boat captains charged outrageous prices. "They charged me one hundred dollars for me and stepson," Rowley complained. "It made me angry." Unable to pay so much money, he lingered in Brownsville, yearning for better fortune.[9]

In December, Rowley, who longed for the restoration of Union government in Texas, found himself frustrated when Brigadier General Andrew Jackson Hamilton arrived in Brownsville. "There are some hundreds of refugees from the interior of the state, most of who have traveled hundreds of miles, and have arrived destitute," Hamilton reported to Secretary of War Edwin M. Stanton. "To all whom are able-bodied, I say, 'If you are not willing to fight to reclaim your home, then you deserve no aid, and will get none.'" Hamilton also reported the Confederates had abandoned any hope of defending Texas below the Colorado River. Rowley would have to enlist—or starve.[10]

Some military authorities who had been making arrangements in the area for the past month also grumbled about Governor Hamilton and his sweeping pronouncements. Who was he, anyway?

Hamilton, a native of Alabama and a resident of Austin before the war, had served as a congressman from Texas and had tried to defuse the sectional crisis in 1861, before he had returned to Texas to serve in the state government. Hamilton fled the Lone Star State in the summer of 1862, just ahead of assassins determined to make him pay for his Unionist stance. Northerners lauded the exile, and his popularity with the Yankee social elite earned him a brigadier's commission and President Abraham Lincoln's appointment as the person who *was* Texas. Now, back on his home turf, Hamilton used his position to make several proclamations while assuming the air of a potentate.

Many in the army, especially Major General Dana, cared little for the Texan satrap. When Hamilton announced the United States was unequivocally in favor of the Juárez regime—which it was—officials in Washington sent notes

Brigadier General Andrew Jackson Hamilton, military governor
of Texas. *Courtesy of Tom Pressly, Shreveport, Louisiana.*

requesting the governor to watch what he was saying. The French might easily
take offence, and relations between the two nations were at a delicate stage.
Hamilton, nonplussed, set up his government as he saw fit and then waited for
the army to deliver him his kingdom.[11]

Meanwhile Major General Nathaniel P. Banks tried to put off General-in-Chief
Henry W. Halleck and pushed hard to finish his Texas project. In defiance of the
tone of his instructions from Washington, if not the actual wording, Banks sent
the remaining two brigades of the 4th Division, 13th Army Corps, from Brashear
City, Louisiana, to Matagorda Bay, Texas. They carried orders to feint toward San
Antonio via Victoria to give the impression that the campaign was once again
live and would veer to the west. Major General Cadwallader C. Washburn, in the
meantime, was to secure the rest of the Matagorda Peninsula and assess its
usefulness as an approach to Velasco.

A shipment of other vital equipment, key to breaking the Brazos River line,
followed the 4th Division troops. "The necessary material for bridging rivers is
being rapidly prepared," Banks's chief of staff, Brigadier General Stone wrote.

"Proper trains of artillery are also prepared for shipment, and by the time the necessary troops can be concentrated with you, this materiál can also be sent to you." While waiting for his army to assemble, Stone admonished, Washburn should make every effort "to learn the force, positions, and intentions of the enemy, and the natural and artificial difficulties to be met and overcome."[12]

The campaign in Texas was heading for a grand finale. The promise of more troops indicated Washburn's offensive would press on after all. The orders to reconnoiter the Matagorda Peninsula revealed the proposed line of attack. Pontoon bridges and heavy cannon would allow Washburn to cross the Brazos River, reduce any Confederate forts, and put Galveston under his guns. The fall of Texas would only be a matter of weeks.

Washburn, however, had no way of knowing how precious little time actually remained for him to succeed. The Federal indecision had afforded Confederate major general John Bankhead Magruder time to whip his lackluster command into a legitimate army capable of contesting the Union advance. He now claimed two robust mounted brigades, Colonel August Buchel's and Colonel Xavier DeBray's, and two small infantry brigades ready to defend the Brazos River line. Magruder had also amassed an impressive array of artillery. Heavy guns salvaged from the USS *Sachem* and the USS *Clifton*, captured at Sabine Pass, now poked out from the parapets of Velasco, and Quitana, at the mouth of the Brazos and from Virginia Point guarding the land approaches to Galveston. Magruder's officers pulled the light pieces that had once served in these forts and formed them into field batteries to add weight to his prairie army facing Washburn.

Georgia-born private, Augustus V. Ball, found himself in the crew of one of Magruder's new batteries. He had moved to Bowie County in Northeast Texas in 1861, when the sectional crisis had seemed to be just a heated political fuss. Then he watched the war turn into a raging fire that began to consume his friends and former classmates from Georgia, but the flames barely licked the edges of his western retreat. They finally singed his Boston, Texas, homestead in early 1862, when Confederate conscription laws forced him from his home and new wife. Ball joined the 23rd Texas Cavalry but left the mounted service—he had not liked the desertion that plagued that regiment—and transferred to Captain M. V. McMahan's Battery.

One of his new officers was Lieutenant Sam Houston Jr., son of the "Sword of San Jacinto." The young officer, who had served in the 2nd Texas Infantry, had been wounded and captured at Shiloh and had returned to Texas to recuperate at his Huntsville home. After his famous father died in July 1863, young Sam returned to Confederate service, this time as an artilleryman. Ball, a reluctant warrior, would drive one of his artillery limbers. "The officers in the battery are said to be clever men," he wrote to his wife from Richmond, Texas. "I have nothing to do but drive and take care of two horses. I will have no guard duty to do, nor hard work."[13]

Ball and the rest of McMahan's Battery were bound for the brigade rendezvous at Port Lavaca to oppose a Federal advance on Victoria. Beyond that, he had no idea what might happen. "I understand that the Feds have taken Powderhorn [the town of Indianola] down on the coast and that 6 thousand are advancing up this way. I have seen nor heard nothing positive," Ball continued. "I have no papers to read unless I give fifty cents for one, and I cannot do that often."[14]

For Private Rudolph Coreth of the 36th Texas Cavalry, the rumors of a Union advance on San Antonio meant his New Braunfels home could be in danger. "I thought that it would probably be a good idea to deposit a supply of flour in safe places, for example in the cave above Merz's stone creek," he wrote home. "One could keep a couple of barrels quite dry and safe and fetch them away quite unnoticed when one needed them."[15]

A Federal capture of San Antonio and reestablishment of Union forces in the Hill Country made sense to Coreth. "It might occur to the Yankees someday to go from Brownsville to San Antonio and the upper counties, where they will find like-minded people," he warned. The largely German Hill Country had voted against secession, and men from there had fled to Mexico. Many had found their way into the Unionist 1st Texas Cavalry. The way might now be open, he feared, for these exiles to return home. "Then [New] Braunfels wouldn't be safe anymore either."[16]

A week later, Magruder's Texas army assembled on the Brazos River. Officers reviewed and reorganized their commands. Brigadier General Hamilton P. Bee took over the cavalry division, relieving Brigadier General James E. Slaughter, who returned to Magruder's staff. Brigade reviews commenced. "There does not seem to be much confidence in the western troops here," Private Coreth wrote his family. His regiment was an exception. "General Bee was quite pleased with us."[17]

Magruder had crafted a highly mobile force of about thirty-five hundred men from the regiments he had rushed to the coast. Washburn's days of unopposed advances were over. Writing from Brazoria, Private Ball believed the army would "run up and down the coast, from point to point wherever there is the greatest prospect of the Yankees trying to land."[18]

In the meantime, things were looking up for the twenty-three-year-old artilleryman. "We are living just as high as any soldier could wish to live," he bragged to his wife. "We are getting plenty of good beef, corn meal, and flour and pork, and have sugar and pork aplenty. We have men detailed to cook for us, and we have a woman in the company to wash for us, and there is nothing to keep us from living perfectly at our ease. We have nothing to do but lie in camp and fatten."[19]

Meanwhile, an officer from the 1st Arizona Cavalry had arrived in Vermilionville, Louisiana, bearing a letter from Major General Magruder directly to Brigadier General Tom Green, bypassing the Confederate Trans-Mississippi chain-of-command. Major General Taylor and Lieutenant General Edmund Kirby Smith had no knowledge of the dispatch—yet. Magruder asked Green to bring his Texans home to defend their state against Washburn and his invaders. Green, of course, wanted nothing more. "I have been watching with great interest . . . the movements of the enemy in Texas since the invasion by Banks, and I assure you I am exceedingly anxious to be ordered there with my division of cavalry," Green wrote back. Even so, he feared this communication might be seen as irregular—and dutifully sent a copy of Magruder's letter to Taylor.[20]

Even while following military protocol, Green responded enthusiastically to the prospect. Not only did Green want to lend a hand back home, but also he believed fully half his command was already there without leave. He would come home and round them up, writing, "if I were in Texas I would be able to gather up my stragglers." He also bragged about his soldiers. "The troops which I have with me, about 2,000 effective and present for duty, are now veterans, and can be depended on under any circumstances," he wrote, adding they "have been under fire a great many times, many of them, as you know, beginning with the New Mexican campaign. They would certainly be worth more to you than any troops west of the Mississippi." His old brigade, he believed, had no peer. "The *esprit de corps*" Green gushed, ". . . is about as 'toploftical' as you would find in our army." He declared Colonel James P. Major's Brigade, which was near mutiny the previous August, to be "fine troops" under good leadership. Taken together, Green argued, these Confederate stalwarts "would form a nucleus around whom the new troops would rally and stand." He had already thrashed part of Washburn's command on Bayou Bourbeau. He would flog them again on the Brazos.[21]

Green knew his opponents. "The division which Banks took to Brownsville, Dana's (formerly Herron's), I whipped a part of badly on the Fordoche," he boasted. He told Magruder even though he had advanced his command on the Union works at Morganza, "Dana did not have the 'sand' to come out and fight." He would have no trouble evicting this timid Yankee from the sands of the Texas coast. "My fight at the Fordoche scared him nearly to death," Green claimed.[22]

While the Confederate general clearly hoped to return to Texas, he did not want to seem ungrateful to his military patron, and in his note to Magruder he noted the kindnesses Major General Taylor had shown him. Green credited him with his promotion to brigadier general, a hope he had "long since abandoned" due to the fallout from the New Mexico Campaign. Even so, Green wanted to go home. "Since I have been placed in command of all General Taylor's cavalry, I have led an active life," he declared, "and have done a great deal of work, and I hope some of it for the benefit of the cause." He worried, though, his enthusiasm to reinforce Magruder seemed disloyal. "It might look to General Taylor ungrateful in me to desire to leave his command and go to Texas," Green pointed out.[23]

Taylor read the copy of Magruder's letter Green had forwarded, and, surprisingly, gave his blessing. The Federal threat clearly had shifted to Texas, and Taylor knew Kirby Smith would order him to send troops there anyway, since "an active campaign in Texas would preclude the possibility of an offensive campaign here at the same time." He warned Magruder, though, not to communicate with one of his subordinates directly. "I . . . beg to suggest that communications to the commanders of Texas organizations in this district in regard to their return to Texas tend to impair their efficiency while here."[24]

Green started wrapping up his affairs in Louisiana. Taylor ordered him to seek a prisoner exchange with Franklin before he left. Even with his recent losses, Green boasted, "I am more than 20 to 1 ahead of them yet." Not only would his Texans be released from captivity, but many of the Louisiana troops paroled from Vicksburg and Port Hudson might be allowed to rejoin the Confederate army as well. Over the winter, Taylor believed, he could refashion these returnees into a mounted force capable of harassing the enemy and keeping the Yankees off balance.[25]

Green could go home.

NINETEEN **ALLONS AU TEXAS**

War showed us his wrinkled front, although we did not want to see it.

—Private A. E. Sweet
33rd Texas Cavalry

Unionists in both Texas and Louisiana longed for an escape from Confederate tyranny and grew inpatient to be behind Union lines. In South Texas, the presence of Federal troops in Brownsville as well as on Matagorda Bay offered hope, but not much. The Union advance in Louisiana followed by Franklin's retreat to New Iberia had inflated, then burst, Unionists dreams there. In the more remote districts of each state, turmoil often turned to murder. Unionists who had hoped for succor found themselves once again abandoned and at the mercy of the Secessionist next door.

An east Texas Unionist, Dennis Haynes had first come to Louisiana in May hoping to reach Federal lines during Banks's Teche Campaign. He now remained on a painful odyssey. He had fallen into and escaped Confederate clutches twice, received a small caliber wound to his upper arm, and lived like an animal in the Calcasieu swamps as he evaded the patrols of the Home Guards and Rebel conscript hunters.[1]

Increasingly desperate, and with patrols closing in, Haynes emerged from the swamps and headed toward the wilderness hamlet of Sugartown, close to the Texas border. "There was no chance for me to remain in this sector of the country," Haynes knew, "crippled as I was." Friends near Sugartown discouraged his plan of crossing the Sabine River and heading west. Haynes should instead reverse course and head southeast toward Opelousas, they suggested, and find there either the Union army or the bandit chieftain Ozémé Carrière and his followers, the Clan. Haynes heeded this advice and headed back across the Calcasieu bottoms.[2]

During December 1863, the crippled refugee dodged Rebels and trusted men who, for little incentive, might betray him. With the help of a network of Unionist handlers who passed him between safe houses and hideouts, Haynes eventually emerged on the prairies west of Opelousas. This region appeared largely clear of Confederates, but every farm here seemed to be inhabited by suspicious, French-speaking families who were vigilant and well-armed. These ruffians, though, turned friendly. "I was questioned very closely by every man who could speak English," Haynes remembered. "After satisfying themselves that I was all right," they allowed him into the shadow world of Carrière's Clan.[3]

Faint, failing, hungry, and horseless, Haynes threw himself upon the mercy of the Clan to shelter him until he could make a new plan. He soon discovered he was not alone in his troubles. Unionists from all over southwest Louisiana had taken refuge among the homesteads of these prairies. "I saw Captain Carrière," Haynes wrote. "He is a pure-blooded Creole Frenchman; speaks no language but broken French; had he had a good education he might have been a man of note and made his mark on the world." Haynes boarded with a mulatto woman— an associate of Carrière's—to bide his time until he could make it into Federal lines at New Iberia. If the Federals were all going to Texas, he reasoned, the Confederates, at least the Texans, would as well. When the enemy thinned out, Haynes believed, he could finish his flight to freedom.[4]

The Confederate army in Louisiana, too, was tired. The weather continued cold and rainy. For the weary and homesick Texans on the Vermilion, the grand scheme of the war seemed less important than finding someplace dry and warm to wait out this latest storm. Along with his comrades camped on the grounds of Ile Copal, Private William Randolph Howell of the 5th Texas endured the sodden days. "Tremendous rain," he wrote on December 11. He had tried to sleep, but water ran through his tent and flowed over his blankets.[5]

In the growing light Howell got up and looked outside toward the Pinhook Bridge. He had crossed that span many, many times. The first time had been March, when he had been heading toward the Yankee invaders, led by Major General Nathaniel P. Banks during his Teche Campaign. Howell's regiment had retreated across the bridge a month later—and helped burn it. He next rode across the rebuilt bridge in May heading south, and crossed it once again in

July, heading north. Brigadier General Alfred Mouton's men fired the bridge again in October. The Yankees rebuilt the third incarnation of the Pinhook Bridge soon after, but then in November they set it ablaze before he could tread its timbers. Howell had ridden back and forth on picket duty many times across the fourth bridge—this one built by Confederates—before flood waters took it. Then the Federals bushwhacked the 4th Texas Cavalry. The Rebels partially rebuilt it, again.

Private Howell stepped out into the wet, chilly morning. The bridge was gone. Once more floodwaters had carried it away. Perhaps it was a sign. They should quit tangling with the enemy.

One of his comrades stopped by and reported interesting news. The Federals, at least some of them, had left New Iberia, heading south. "Going to Texas I suppose," Howell wrote. He was correct. Banks was continuing to reinforce Major General Cadwallader C. Washburn.[6]

December 12, cold but clear, seemed as if it would pass peacefully. "All quiet below," Howell noted. Paymasters arrived and settled up with the soldiers, paying them through the previous October. In the late afternoon, runners spread news through the camps: "Orders tonight to leave for Texas in the morning," Howell scribbled. Major General John Bankhead Magruder, the commander of the District of Texas, Arizona, and New Mexico, needed reinforcements. Brigadier General Tom Green's Texans were finally going home to fight what most believed would be the decisive battle for the Lone Star State.[7]

The 5th Texas left behind an enviable record. They had come to Louisiana under General Henry Hopkins Sibley. After the Teche Campaign, Green took over the brigade but still answered to Brigadier General Mouton. Soon, however, Green eclipsed the Acadian general in reputation and became Major General Richard Taylor's favorite. It was easy to see why: In the time Green had operated in Louisiana after the Teche Campaign, his troops had captured nearly 3,000 Federal soldiers and had killed or wounded around 500. The Confederates under his command had lost as many killed and wounded on the battlefields of Brashear City, Fort Butler, Kock's plantation, Sterling's plantation, and Bayou Bourbeau but had yielded only about 500 prisoners of their own. The totals were lopsided—1,000 Confederates and 3,500 Federals lost in action—showing

Green's battlefield prowess. More than any other leader in the Department of the Trans-Mississippi, Green had provided good news and hope during the Confederacy's darkest hours. "If those fields were the only evidence upon which to rest the foundation of his fame," Major Joseph Draper Sayers would write later, "they would be more than sufficient to rank him with the greatest cavalry officers of any war."[8]

Now Green and his men readied for a return to Texas for what would arguably be their greatest contest. Taylor hated losing his aggressive general. "Upright, modest, and with the simplicity of a child, danger seemed to be his element, and he rejoiced in combat," Taylor wrote. "The great Commonwealth . . . will never send forth a bolder warrior, a better citizen, nor a more upright man than Thomas Green."[9]

The Texas warrior was at the pinnacle of his fame. When Green had come to Louisiana, many of his troops had referred to him as "Daddy Green." Nearly fifty, he had cared for his troops and seemed to be a likable, paternalistic, figure. To many of his young soldiers, he had even become a surrogate. Private Howell declared him the "Father of the Trans-Mississippi Department." By the end of the year, Green had become much more. From a Federal perspective, he had become the most dangerous Confederate west of the Mississippi.[10]

On December 16, near the battle-scarred remains of Vermilionville, Green formed his division of cavalry. Wearing riding gauntlets, a wide-brimmed hat, and a gray overcoat, he reviewed his troops. The fight to defend Texas had kept these men in Louisiana for most of 1863. Now that the Federals had invaded their home state, Green and his veterans would return to defend it and stiffen the ranks of the inexperienced troops on the Texas coast. Lieutenant Colonel Edwin Waller's 13th Texas Cavalry Battalion, still on the Atchafalaya River where it supported the operations of Major General John G. Walker's Division, would also head back to Texas, replaced by regiments of Louisiana cavalry, newly forming.[11]

As Green assembled his command, some of Colonel William G. Vincent's 2nd Louisiana Cavalry stood in formation, watching the Texans prepare to leave. While Green's troopers fought the great battle for Texas, Vincent's veterans would continue to operate along Bayou Teche and keep an eye on Major General William B. Franklin's Yankees.

After a casual salute to these comrades staying behind, Green ordered his bugler to signal the advance. Green turned his horse's head and spurred the animal westward. Then, he paused. With a flourish no doubt influenced by his days among his Francophone allies, he yelled to his command: *"Allons! Allons au Texas!"*[12]

Texas reached a crisis point. At Brownsville, Major General Napoleon Jackson Tecumseh Dana made good on his promise to sever all of the Confederate cotton roads leading to Mexico and to finish gleaning the cotton already within reach of his troops. The Rio Grande trade, he proudly wrote Banks, "is about stopped this side of Larado." New routes had emerged as the Rebels shifted the trade upriver to Eagle Pass but just as Banks had done in southern Louisiana, Dana would employ irregulars, bandits, and scofflaws to serve as Union auxiliaries in the region. "I desire to make the road from San Antonio to Eagle Pass and Laredo so perilous that neither Jew nor Gentile will wish to travel it," he boasted, asking Banks for "good, true, and daring men" to lead the effort. "I wish to kill, burn, and destroy all that cannot be taken and secured."[13]

At Fort Esperanza, Brigadier General Fitz Henry Warren arrived to replace the furloughed Colonel Henry D. Washburn in command of the 1st Brigade, 1st Division, 13th Army Corps. The newcomer kept his command busy. Described as "an excellent officer, well on in years, a severe disciplinarian, punctilious in the extreme, and irascible to the last degree," by a 33rd Illinois soldier, Warren quickly led his first outing to scout the shores of Matagorda Bay. On December 13 a regiment from his brigade boarded the gunboat USS *Alabama*, landed near Indianola, brushed aside a Confederate picket line from the 33rd Texas Cavalry, and took control of the town. These Federals, having bedded down in abandoned buildings, "waged unrelenting war on the fleas, which were all Confederate fleas" according to one Confederate wag.[14]

After raising, then lowering, the U.S. flag, the regiment returned to the gunboat and Fort Esperanza. Union troops would return periodically to the town aboard the steamers *Matamoros* and *Planter* and dismantle its piers and warehouses for use as raw materials in the expansion of the Union camp on Decros Point.[15]

It seemed clear to the Confederates their enemy intended to use Matagorda Bay as a permanent base for future operations, so Major General Magruder dug in for the fight. He ordered his men to strengthen Velasco against an amphibious assault and to construct batteries at other points along the coast. Troops excavated trench lines at the mouth of Caney Creek, a sizable bayou at the northeastern head of Matagorda Bay where Matagorda Peninsula joined the mainland. Troops and enslaved workers also dug in at Cedar Lake, a boggy collection of estuaries and shallow tidal bays eight miles farther northeast up the coast. Other picks and shovels broke ground at the mouth of the San Bernard River, another seven miles up the coast. The enemy's trick of bypassing strong positions would be tough to achieve here.[16]

Magruder had already seen to Galveston. During the spring and summer of 1863, the island city had become a fortress. It was no Gibraltar, and far less imposing than Vicksburg or Port Hudson, but it held a stout defensive position, nonetheless. The largest city in Texas was now ringed by redoubts and would not be a pushover as it had been in the fall of 1862. Brigadier General Green and his division, once they arrived from Louisiana, would post at Virginia Point, the principal mainland supply depot and communications point with the island. From here, the veterans could react to a Federal attempt on Galveston and could easily reinforce troops at Velasco or any other threatened point.

The Confederates considered their defensive arrangements. If the Federals forced a crossing of the Brazos River at Brazoria, some twenty miles by road upstream from Velasco, Major General Washburn could move his army between

Brigadier General Fitz Henry Warren, a politically connected Iowan. *Library of Congress.*

Galveston and Houston. Or, Washburn might capture Victoria first and cross the Brazos at Richmond, another forty miles by road upstream from Brazoria and on the direct road to Houston. Or, the Federals might continue the advance along the coast as they had the previous few months. Either way, the Confederates could fight them on nearly equal terms on the coastal prairies. Their two well-mounted Texas cavalry divisions would be able to operate with impunity against Federal lines of communications.

For his part, Washburn still placed his faith in a swift campaign that would catch the Confederates off balance. While the Confederates attempted to defend Houston, Galveston, and San Antonio simultaneously, the Federal army—with the aid of the navy—could quickly reduce Quintana and Velasco before the Rebels could concentrate their forces. The Union column would be across the Brazos River before the Texans could react. Banks agreed. "My desire is to occupy Galveston Island, if it can be done within reasonable time," Banks explained to General-in-Chief Henry W. Halleck, remembering well the scolding he had received for not being forthcoming about his previous plans in Texas. "This will give us the entire coast, and relieve the blockading squadron, which numbers now over thirty war vessels. . . . I shall concentrate on the Brazos all the disposable force at my command for a decisive and very short campaign."[17]

Galveston, instead of Houston, would serve as the center of Union-controlled Texas. After taking the city, Banks planned to shift his entire army west of the Sabine River into eastern Texas. He needed to replenish his command. Over the past year Federal and Confederate armies had stripped Louisiana of anything useful for conducting another campaign. "Eastern Texas offers us recruits, horses, forage, and supplies of every kind," he wrote to Halleck. Brownsville would be given up in favor of Brazos Santiago Island as a U.S. outpost on the Rio Grande. Banks would hold Fort Esperanza as a future entrepôt for an expedition into the interior, should it be needed. "So far as the occupation of the State is concerned," Banks bragged, "Matagorda Bay, which is now in our possession, gives us the key to the greater part of it, which we can occupy whenever we please."[18]

These were bold plans for Washburn and his current army. The commander at Matagorda Bay figured he needed twice as many men as the Confederates in order get across the Brazos, since the Rebels had been allowed enough time to concentrate their forces. He asked Banks for more troops. This message, with Banks's endorsement, traveled on to Halleck. At least one more division was needed to join the Texas effort. Perhaps these troops might come from the Vicksburg veterans of the 16th Army Corps who had been left behind when Major General William Tecumseh Sherman rushed with reinforcements to Chattanooga. This orphaned command could move into Louisiana while Banks shifted more 13th Army Corps or 19th Army Corps troops to Texas.[19]

Washburn waited impatiently. He was keen to move away from the sandy wastes of Matagorda Island, down the length of Matagorda Peninsula, and onto the bottomlands of Caney Creek, but he also expected to face about three thousand of Magruder's Texans along the way. The risk of moving with just the forces at hand would be worth the gain, he told Banks's chief of staff. The delay was losing him the advantage. "On the Caney are large plantations, plenty of corn, sugar, and mules," he reported. His draft animals were starving, he added, with losses of ten a day on the sterile wastes where he camped his army. "The importance of reaching a country where we can obtain forage you will readily see."[20]

As Washburn shivered on Matagorda Island and Decros Point, Union commanders in far south Texas operated with a great deal of creativity and local discretion. Major General Dana operated against targets of opportunity around Brownsville and ordered a detachment of the 91st Illinois to revisit the modest saltworks at El Sal del Rey to keep it out of operation. The greatest plum for Dana, though, lay just beyond his prudent reach. Richard King's sprawling ranch on Santa Gertrudis Creek, more than one hundred miles north of Brownsville, was the hub of Confederate activity—really, any activity—in the rugged country between Corpus Christi and the Rio Grande. He tapped Captain James Speed to lead about sixty men of the 1st and 2nd Texas Cavalries (Union) on a long-ranged scout toward the ranch.[21]

On December 23 the Federal riders from Brownsville reached the limit of their orders—an eighty-mile scout—but continued on another forty miles to Santa Gertrudis Creek. In a final dash, the Federals crashed onto the grounds of the King Ranch headquarters. Pistol- and carbine-wielding troopers fanned out to capture the proprietor and end his role in the cotton trade. A quick but deliberate search turned up cotton bales stacked and ready for transport, but King, warned of the enemy approach, had already fled, leaving his family in the care of his fiercely loyal *kineño* ranch hands.

One King loyalist, Francisco Alvarado, barred the Federals from entering the family home for only a minute before he was shot dead. The troopers ransacked the house while Captain Speed corralled the family members present. He roared at Hiram Chamberlin, King's father-in-law: "You tell King that if one bale of cotton is carried away from here or burned, I will hold him responsible with his life." He ended his threat with a warning. "Colonel [Edmund J.] Davis will be paying you a visit soon. When they do, you will think all hell has broke loose." The Federals did not tarry long. Word arrived Rebel cavalry was heading their direction, prompting the invaders to leave King's ranch on Christmas Eve.[22]

Meanwhile, in the Rebel camps at Velasco, Christmas presents arrived in the form of crates full of Enfields. Private Augustus V. Ball reported twenty-five hundred rifles and five thousand pounds of gunpowder had come through the blockade. "We have plenty of men and artillery in this neighborhood now to make a pretty good fight," Ball wrote to his wife. He estimated the Texan strength to be nearly eighteen thousand men on the Brazos, opposing, he believed, some twenty thousand Federals at the entrance to Matagorda Bay. "We are ready for them," he boasted, "and no one is afraid but them."[23]

Richard King, the cattle and cotton baron of South Texas. *King Ranch Archives.*

The presence of the Union army on the Texas Coast signaled monumental changes were surely coming to this remote part of the country. For residents, holiday merrymaking proved a welcome distraction. "Today being Christmas, all order of business was suspended, and we all went in for a regular jollification," wrote James Madison Hall. His plantation home was near Liberty, Texas, on the Trinity River some 140 miles northeast of Matagorda Bay and just 40 miles from Houston. "The egg nogg flowed freely and all went off as merry as a marriage bell. To close the scene at night the negroes had a ball in the yard by moonlight, they touched the light fantastic toe and were as happy as happy could be." Hall, who owned nine enslaved people at one time, believed this might be one of the last carefree Christmases his hands might have. "If Lincoln should succeed in his mad project and for which he is now prosecuting his unholy war, for their emancipation," Hall continued, "he will only plunge them into abject missery [misery] from their now happy condition."[24]

The last days of 1863 saw the Federals at Matagorda Bay move toward Port Lavaca and the interior. Brigadier General Warren ordered his command—the 33rd and 99th Illinois, the 8th and 18th Indiana, and the 7th Michigan Battery—to reoccupy Indianola, declaring the knocked-about village to be his brigade headquarters. From here, Warren prepared his troops for a reconnaissance in force into the interior and along the shores of Matagorda Bay. With luck, he might convince the Rebels that Victoria and San Antonio were the true targets of the Texas Campaign.

The Confederates responded by reinforcing their picket line on Chocolate Bayou, three miles beyond Port Lavaca and within ten miles of the Union camps at Indianola. For the next week, pickets from both armies patrolled toward the opposing lines.

Texan horsemen were posted where they could spy Indianola in the distance. On Christmas night, Private Alexander Edwin Sweet, Company A, 33rd Texas Cavalry found himself alone with Jim Neal, a veteran soldier. The Rebels suffered from the cold, wet weather. "We . . . could not have come nearer freezing to death that winter, on the bald prairies, than we did," remembered Private Sweet. "War showed us his wrinkled front, although we did not want to see it. I never knew anything about the horrors of war until I stood guard in a wet norther." This from a man who had yet to see combat.[25]

Sweet believed his companion was suffering psychological damage from the war. "He was a very peculiar sort of fellow," Sweet recalled. "He was a kind of military hermit. There were strange rumors in camps about Jim." The stories mostly involved his bloody murder, early in the war, of Texas Unionists; the deeds apparently haunted him. Neal often shattered a peaceful night by shrieking in his sleep, often pointing at a phantom, "an old German with his throat cut, whom nobody but himself could see," Sweet noted. Sweet had been assigned to guard the prairie against Union prowlers with this lunatic, and Neal's bizarre behavior continued unabated. Early in the morning of December 26, Neal—on watch—shook Sweet awake, whispering the enemy was at hand. "Jim laid his clammy hand on mine, and pointing in another direction, whispered through his clenched teeth, 'Now you see him, don't you?'"[26]

"Never did I see such mortal terror," Sweet confided, remembering Neal's expression. Even so, the soldier could not be sure if this was one of his comrade's hallucinations or a real threat. He looked at their horses; both animals had their ears perked and looked in the same direction. After coming fully awake, Sweet concluded the alarm was over a nearby coyote, nothing more. Neal, however, could not be convinced. "Perhaps it was the old white-bearded German whose throat Jim had cut who was prowling about," Sweet concluded.[27]

Sweet replaced his comrade on watch, and the night returned to a frosty stillness. The troubled Neal eventually fell asleep, only to begin murmuring and twitching. Sweet looked on as his sleeping companion muttered, "there was no need of cutting his throat, he would have died anyhow." The nightmare-plagued soldier then threw off his blankets and leapt to his feet. Sweet, terrorized, looked on dumbfounded. "There he comes again!" Neal shrieked, stabbing the darkness with his finger. "See his red beard! It is blood that makes it red! He's never laughed as he does tonight."[28]

Eventually, Sweet got Neal settled down. The first blush of dawn seemed to end the nightmares, but new frights took their place. Both men could hear drummers beating in the Union camps and, soon, mounted Federals appeared on the horizon a few hundred yards off. The two Texans hurried to their horses and bolted westward across the prairie, away from Indianola and toward Norris's Bridge over Chocolate Bayou, about three miles from Port Lavaca. "We were bounding over the grassy prairie toward our picket station," Sweet wrote. "Nevertheless, the Yankees gained on us; and as the bridge appeared in sight, they were not far behind us."[29]

"Throw off your overcoat, or some of our own men will shoot us," urged Neal. The prudent soldiers flung away their light-blue mantles and clattered across the bridge to safety.[30]

Brigadier General Warren, eager to prove his mettle in this new theater of operations, had launched a reconnaissance in force. About three thousand Union troops tramped out of the village of Indianola heading for the town of Port Lavaca, eight miles away. Three miles short of their goal, the Federals discovered the band of Rebel pickets from the 33nd Texas Cavalry defending the crossing of Chocolate Bayou at Norris's Bridge.

Confederate captain Richard Taylor, commanding the detachment, "rode a large horse, and was dressed in an attractive buckskin suit, in the breast pocket of which was exposed a plug of flat tobacco," Sweet remembered.[31]

The Texan officer, instead of ordering his men to retreat, stood tall in his stirrups, looked at the approaching enemy, then reached into his pocket and bit

US troops occupy Indianola. *Frank Leslie's Illustrated Newspaper.*

off a large chaw. "Fall in boys," Taylor ordered. The dismounted Texans obeyed. "The war's been going on for three years, and we have not had a chance to smell gunpowder," he yelled to his troops as his nervous horse paced to and fro. "Over in San Antonio they say we ain't anxious to meet the enemy." He paused. "We will show them that it's a durn lie," the captain growled.[32]

His assembled troops looked on in horror as the Federals deployed. "The long black line, composed of Federal infantry, was becoming every moment a more prominent feature in the landscape," Sweet remembered. A four-cannon Union battery trundled forward, its limbers moving into action as gunners deployed their pieces.[33]

"I am not going to sacrifice life, or wade in human gore," the captain assured his company, "but we will stay right here, and stand a few shells, anyhow. There ain't much danger until they get the range." The forty Texans obediently, if nervously, took cover behind a rail fence. "Don't leave until we have a shot, anyhow," the Captain repeated. "We cannot expect to defeat the enemy, but we can let 'em shell us a while." To make his point, Captain Taylor rode behind his men. "I'll shoot down the first man who starts to run before I do!"[34]

The Federal cannon deployed, as expected, "on a slight elevation four hundred yards distant, and wheeled around to bring the guns to bear on us," Sweet wrote. One of the young Texans, a red-haired cowboy who had never seen artillery in action, assumed the Federals were veering away in the face of this line of skirmishers. The soldier let out a hurrah for Jeff Davis, one for the Confederacy, and another for his captain. Just as the youngster was in full bellow and swinging his hat over his head, "there was a puff of smoke in front of the battery," Sweet continued, "and a shell went screaming, like a demon with a cold in his head, about four feet above Sam's red head."[35]

The other pieces fired in quick succession in an eruption of smoke and fire. "A cloud of dust appeared in the rear, and simultaneously about twenty feet of fence was spread over the adjacent country," Sweet wrote. A Texan sergeant braced his Enfield on the remaining rails, took aim, and picked off a mounted Federal officer.[36]

Captain Taylor addressed his men once again. "That will do, durn you!" he shouted. "Get up and git, now!"[37]

Relieved, the Texans scampered for their mounts and scattered across the prairie to spread the alarm the Federals were on the move. The Confederates abandoned Port Lavaca and the road to Victoria without a struggle.

Later that day, December 26, Warren marched his Federals into Port Lavaca, and his troops plundered the town and burned the business district. By the time they returned to Indianola on December 29, Warren had gained the measure of his Texan adversaries and had a good idea of the lay of the land along the western margins of Matagorda Bay.[38]

The most the Confederates could do in response was to keep the enemy under surveillance. The Union position at Decros Point on the tip of the Matagorda Peninsula remained under the scrutiny of a company of "exempts," state troops too old or young to be liable for conscription. These few dozen mounted citizen-volunteers, aided by scouts from the 1st Texas Cavalry, kept tabs on the movements of the Federal forces and sent periodic dispatches up the coast to officers at Caney Creek or by boat across the bay to the town of Matagorda. The Yankees appeared reanimated—they had burned Port Lavaca and held Indianola—but yet not launched a serious offensive.

Now . . . Tom Green was on his way, and the Federals would undoubtedly take a licking.

TWENTY   **MATAGORDA**

It is my desire, if possible, to get possession of Galveston.
—Major General Nathaniel P. Banks
Army of the Gulf

While Union troops raised hell in Indianola and Port Lavaca, Major General Cadwallader C. Washburn used the distraction to scout the Matagorda Peninsula as an approach to capturing Houston. A more modest Union expedition would leave Decros Point not only to get the lay of the land but also to pick off the enemy pickets and bring in a few as prisoners.

The Federal plan was to send out a two-pronged reconnaisance to traverse the entire length of the Matagorda Peninsula. In the early daylight hours of December 29, the gunboats USS *Sciota* and USS *Granite City* put Lieutenant Colonel Francis S. Hesseltine and one hundred troops from Companies C, H, and K of the 13th Maine ashore at Smith's Landing, about seven miles from where the peninsula joined the mainland, sealing the peninsula and cutting off enemy scouts from their friends at Caney Creek.

The USS *Granite City* stayed on station that morning to cover the expedition, but the USS *Sciota* continued northeast, allowing Brigadier General Thomas E. G. Ransom—who had been a surveyor before the war—to scout the Confederate positions at Caney Creek, at the mouth of the Saint Bernard River, and at Quintana and Velasco.

With the catchers in place, next came the beaters. Washburn ordered his only mounted troops, Company C, 4th Indiana Cavalry, to head up the peninsula from Decros Point. They would flush any coveys of Texans toward the New Englanders that had landed up the peninsula. On the trip back, the Hoosiers could drive any livestock they encountered into Union lines.[1]

The men from Maine came ashore without incident. Lieutenant Colonel Hesseltine, assembling his men, sent a detachment commanded by Lieutenant John S. P. Ham of Company C northeast, up the peninsula, to discover the whereabouts of the main Texan picket line with instructions to find where this God-forsaken sand spit rejoined the mainland. Meanwhile, Hesseltine led the rest of his troops southwest, down the peninsula, to drive any isolated Confederate snoopers toward Decros Point and the oncoming cavalry. When he had taken the measure of the terrain, he would signal for the USS *Granite City* to send ashore its boats and withdraw the expedition.

The peninsula's sand and scrub terrain made the task difficult. The thin strip of land was often only a mile wide in places but more than fifty miles long. Rugged dunes topped with scrub brush and cactus and cut by frequent creeks and washouts from the Matagorda Bay side backed the thin beach on the Gulf of Mexico side. A few isolated driftwood-and-brush corrals dotted the land where enterprising Texans had attempted a hardscrabble ranching existence by raising tough cattle in this dry wilderness of sand and thorns. The water approaches, too, were difficult. A channel a few hundred yards from shore on the Matagorda Bay side offered a scant four or five feet of water, too shallow for gunboats; the Gulf approach offered only three feet of water and often vicious surf.

Then, the weather turned. Strong winds from the south whipped up an angry sea and churned the surf into froth. No surfboats would survive the wild water; the Yankee infantry were now marooned. Still, all seemed safe and calm ashore, and Lieutenant Ham's returning detachment reported no trouble from the direction of the Confederate lines. The men of the 13th Maine, assured that all was well, spread out over the width of the peninsula and continued toward the southwest.[2]

After Hessletine's men had marched for about seven miles through thick brush and around troublesome sloughs, the long, deep alto notes of the USS *Granite City's* horn hooted from sea. Trying to understand the signal, Hesseltine realized the captain's urgency when the warship fired a thirty-pounder Parrot over his position toward the north. Turning his telescope in that direction, the lieutenant colonel discovered the cause for concern. "I was able to discern the head of a body of cavalry moving down the peninsula," he reported. The

Some of the crew aboard USS *Sciota*. *The Photographic History of the Civil War*.

USS *Granite City*, rolling wildly in the rough Gulf waters, shelled the oncoming Confederates but with little effect. "Their line stretched steadily for us . . . in half an hour their skirmishers were swarming up close to mine." Around sunset Hesseltine gathered his troops, and they took shelter in a wrecked driftwood-and-brush corral on the edge of the dunes.[3]

The Confederate riders, who were from Colonel August Buchel's 1st Texas Cavalry and Lieutenant Colonel Reuben Brown's 35th Texas Cavalry reined in and formed up to assess the situation. A scattering of pickets rode out to test the Yankee resolve, but a staccato of rifle shots and loud cheers convinced the Texans the effort of reducing the Federals positioned in their driftwood fort, fronted as it was by a swampy mire, would not be worth the casualties. In addition, the Confederates realized, while the gunboat that had been annoying them all evening—the USS *Granite City*—was withdrawing to the southwest, a new vessel—the USS *Sciota*—was coming in fast from the north. The Texans fell back under the cover of the rising darkness. Couriers slipped past the Union position, found the Texas scouts down the peninsula, and informed them they risked being cut off.[4]

The soldiers of the 13th Maine Infantry, who had set fires to mark each end of their position to identify themselves to the gunboats offshore, kept up a brave front at their driftwood barricade throughout the night. The Union troops feared they faced Green's notorious brigade, which was known to have recently left Louisiana. A heavy mist settled over the position that night, turning the landscape eerie.

Nervous pickets, peering through the fog, reported Rebels moving around the Union position on the Matagorda Bay shore, probably the returning couriers and their rescued pickets, and rifle fire flashed from the makeshift fort as the Federals challenged the phantom threat. Alerted by the gunfire, the USS *Sciota* slipped its anchors and, taking a hazardous and unstable position parallel to the beach and its crashing surf, fired several broadsides into the darkness. Shell fragments wounded two Texans and two mounts before the Rebels slipped away.[5]

The next morning, December 30, dawned misty, cold, and miserable. Lieutenant Colonel Hesseltine held his men in position but his covering gunboat, the USS *Sciota*, had disappeared from sight in weather described as "thick and hazy, with passing showers of rain." Other gunboats, including the USS *Granite City*—having reloaded its magazines at Fort Esperanza—and the USS *Monongahela*, probed in the soupy weather but could not locate the stranded infantrymen. By late afternoon, the ships gave up the hunt and dropped anchor to keep a lookout for the missing men from Maine. In the distance, heavy cannon fire from the Gulf indicated the USS *Sciota* had seen something worth shooting at, but the ship's exact location remained hidden in the gloomy weather.[6]

On land, the situation remained confused. Around noon, when the fog lifted and a drizzle began, Hesseltine spied a steamboat in the distance, but it was to his left, in Matagorda Bay, and heading down from the direction of the Confederate lines. His hopes for rescue vanished as 20-pounder rounds roared toward his Yankee outpost, scattering driftwood and sand over its defenders. The *John F. Carr* fired dozens of long-ranged shots but could not get a good angle on the low fort and caused no casualties.[7]

Commander John R. Marmion, the skipper of the *John F. Carr*, formulated a plan for dislodging the Yankees. He had earlier left word with the garrison at Matagorda: If they heard cannon fire, they were to load troops aboard the steamer *Cora* and make a dash across the bay to join the fight. Following this directive, about forty men from Company D, 35th Texas Cavalry, rattled across the gangplank, and the *Cora* was soon underway.[8]

The Rebel reinforcements would not arrive in time. By 3:00 PM, as the *Cora* churned the five miles of muddy saltwater separating it from the *John F. Carr,* Hesseltine stealthily abandoned his ersatz fort and led his command, now short of food and water, to their right and down the Gulf beach and away from the Rebel pounding. The detachment of the 13th Maine of the 13th Maine spent the rest of the day hurrying toward friendly lines, hoping to catch sight of any gunboats— which they did not. Occasionally they glimpsed Texas state troops, their original quarry, moving several hundred yards in the distance.[9]

The USS *Sciota*, meanwhile, had spotted the Maine soldiers moving along the beach but could not get their attention. The rest of the day, the ship steamed alongside the beach, a silent escort obscured from sight by the haze of the sea and sky. By evening, the USS *Sciota* joined a growing flotilla of vessels sent to retrieve the lost patrol. The USS *Penobscot* and the USS *Estrella* joined the USS *Monongahela* and the USS *Granite City*. The USS *Sciota*, thus relieved, "ran down the coast and came to anchor," logged the ship's skipper, Lieutenant Commander George H. Perkins. He then rowed over to speak to the commanders aboard the USS *Granite City* and the USS *Monongahela* and work out how to deal with the Rebel steamer prowling about on the inside of the bay.[10]

Unaware the enemy had slipped away, the Confederates prepared to strike. The *Cora* arrived at the *John F. Carr's* position around sunset, and the commanders decided to use the steamer's small boats to land the raiding party from Matagorda and fifteen men from the crews of the *Cora* and the *John F. Carr* that night. If they found the Federal position, and could surprise them, they would overrun their driftwood bulwark. The Texans loaded the boats sometime after 9:00 PM and pulled hard for the shore, 1,200 yards distant.[11]

By now, the Federals were several miles away, heading for safety. Having successfully slipped away from the enemy, Hesseltine kept his exhausted men moving down the beach amid another blanketing fog. At 10:00 PM, the wind shifted abruptly to the north. "The severest norther of the winter struck us," Hesseltine lamented. Just after midnight, he ordered his men to hunker down as the freezing wind whipped over them.[12]

The same wind also lashed the Rebels. "After running halfway to shore a most terrific norther began to blow," reported Captain E. S. Rugley of the 35th

Texas Cavalry, "which induced us to abandon the attack and order a return to the steamers." As the Texans turned about, wind-whipped whitecaps swamped two of the five overloaded boats. Fighting the wind, the steamers weighed anchor and tried to save the floundering men, but the tides shoved the *John F. Carr* out of the channel and into shallow water where it went aground. Eighteen of the Rebel raiders either drowned or died of hypothermia in the chaos. At first light, the *Cora* returned to Matagorda packed with survivors, leaving the *John F. Carr*, heeled over in the shallows, to its fate.[13]

The Mainers, unaware of the Confederate calamity occurring well to their rear, continued moving down the coast in the gloomy darkness and made it to the Dutch Settlement unmolested. Charlie Siringo, an eight-year-old lad at the time, wrote about the Yankee troops' arrival. "They camped one night close to our house and filled me up with hard-tack," he remembered, "which was quite a treat to a fellow living on mush and milk." The next morning, the soldiers had gone.[14]

On December 31 lookouts from the Federal flotilla finally spotted the Rebel steamers on the Matagorda Bay side of the peninsula and pounced. At 9 AM the USS *Sciota* opened fire on its enemy, and the USS *Estrella* soon followed suit. When one Rebel ship fled and the other failed to return fire, the USS *Sciota* decided they were not a threat and headed along the beach to retrieve Hesseltine's column

USS *Estrella* credited with destroying the Rebel gunboat
John F. Carr. U.S. Naval History and Heritage Command.

while the USS *Estrella* methodically pounded the stranded Rebel gunboat into wreckage. A lookout from one of the USS *Monongahela's* fighting tops reported a heavy column of smoke rising from the *John F. Carr's* last position, followed by flames. The Confederate vessel burned until nearly midnight on that New Year's Eve. The Federal gunners aboard the USS *Estrella* had made an easy kill.[15]

The USS *Sciota* once again sighted the men of the 13th Maine at 2 PM, dropped anchor in two and a half fathoms of water, lowered its boats into the pounding surf, and offered the weary troops a ride. Meanwhile, the Texan militiamen who had been the original target of the expedition had fled, many abandoning their mounts to take a sailing skiff across the bay to safety in the village of Matagorda. Hesseltine, warm and dry for the first time in two days, marveled at his command's ordeal. "In this report," he penned to Brigadier General Ransom, "you may understand exactly how 100 Yankees baffled, beat back, and eluded a large body of rebels and rebel gunboat without loss."[16]

For the inhabitants of the Matagorda Peninsula, the passage of the Union troops brought them into the vortex of war. Young Siringo, while wandering the sand hills near his home, came upon a casualty from the bungled Confederate landing, washed up on the beach. "His clothes were gone, and his wrist was marked 'J. T.' in India ink," the boy remembered. A neighbor, John Williams,

Charlie Siringo was a young eyewitness to the Civil War on the Texas coast. Here he is in 1912 as a much-admired author and chronicler of the Old West. Charles A. Siringo. *A Cowboy Detective: A True Story of Twenty-Two Years with a World Famous Detective Agency* (1912).

brought home a souvenir of the battle—an unexploded cannonball—to his eleven children. He took out the fuse, emptied the shell, and took it into his yard. He sent a son inside the house to fetch an ember from the fireplace with some tongs so that he could flash the remaining powder to delight his kids. "I was present, and not liking the looks of it, crept out behind the picket gate, a few yards away, and peeped between the pickets," Siringo remebered. Williams took the ember from his son and dropped it into the open artillery round.

It exploded. "For a few seconds everything was enveloped in smoke," Siringo recalled. "When the smoke disappeared sufficiently for me to see, the whole sky seemed to be a blaze of fire, and finally Mr. Williams emerged . . . hopping on one leg." The shell had carried away his foot, mangled his right leg, and torn away an ear. His daughter, who had been sitting nearby behind the family dog, emerged unscathed, but the pooch lost a leg. "Several pieces went through the house, and one piece went through the picket gate right over my head," Siringo continued. "The next day . . . I found a large piece sticking in the wall of an old vacant house a mile from where it exploded." Williams lingered a few days, but died from his injuries, leaving a widow and nearly a dozen orphans from his stupidity.[17]

The scouting expeditions around the rim of Matagorda Bay drew the same conclusions: to conquer Texas, Banks would have to send more men. The Army of the Gulf had too many missions. Banks attempted to defend his Texas campaign against Halleck's anxieties about Louisiana. "The orders of the Government seemed to be peremptory that I was to occupy a position in Texas," Banks reminded Halleck in the last week of December. Besides, the rivers in Louisiana remained too shallow to supply his forces by steamboats, long trains of wagons would be vulnerable to the Confederate cavalry, and the route traversed a country already burned over and "without supplies of any kind," Banks wrote. Instead, the Army of the Gulf, at least most of the 13th Army Corps, should finish their work in Texas. "It is my desire, if possible, to get possession of Galveston," he once again declared.[18]

Banks again pointed out Galveston Island and Brownsville would be the easiest positions to hold in Texas. The harvest would be ample enough to justify the swift completion of his campaign. "To this fact may be added that there are supplies and recruits which cannot be found in any other portion of this department," Banks noted. Once accomplished, the Union army in Texas could pivot back to Louisiana, leaving small garrisons on Galveston Island and at Brownsville on the Rio Grande.[19]

Banks and his army could then make Halleck happy and destroy or disperse the Confederate forces on the Red River in cooperation with Major General Frederick Steele operating out of Arkansas. "It was in this manner that we captured Port Hudson," Banks reminded Halleck. "It would have been impracticable to proceed against Port Hudson from the Mississippi without having first dispersed the army of Texas and Louisiana on the west of that river."[20]

Banks, having already made his mind to finish the chore in Texas, argued the state could only be conquered from its coastline. The overland route from southern Louisiana had proven problematic, mostly because of the poor roads and the difficulty in maintaining a supply line. Banks again suggested Union troops fall back behind the Atchafalaya River, from the Red River to Brashear City, and assume a defensive position while he finished the job in Texas. Even so, Banks reminded Halleck, he would need more men. "I recognize the embarrassments under which the Government labor in regard to reinforcements in this department," he wrote, "yet as my lines are continually extending, I thought it to be my duty to renew the suggestion."[21]

Halleck, warming somewhat to the idea of finishing off Texas first, cast about for more troops. He believed he might have some to spare in the Department of the South. Perhaps some of the regiments in North and South Carolina could head to Texas. Halleck also promised more cavalry, starting with the 3rd Maryland then forming in Baltimore.[22]

Texas first—then the Red River Valley. The matter was at last settled. Or, so Banks thought.

Like Lincoln, Halleck had been meddling in the affairs of the Department of the Gulf, trying to untangle the military mess he believed Banks had created. Considering the current state of affairs, Halleck now agreed the best line of defense west of the Mississippi was Berwick Bay and the Atchafalaya River. "It is the line which I advised you from the beginning to adopt," Halleck wrote, carefully forgetting some of the exchanges he had with Banks the previous summer. Despite what Governor Shepley and his cronies had wanted, everything north of that natural barrier could be given up without loss to the national cause. Halleck even retreated, temporarily, from his fixation on Shreveport. Besides, two campaigns through that region had captured or used up anything useful to the Union cause, including food, livestock, and emancipated slaves.[23]

As to Banks and his amphibious operations against the Texas coast in September and November, "no notice of your intention to make them was received here till they were actually undertaken," Halleck complained. "The danger . . . of dividing your army, with the enemy between the two parts, ready to fall on either with his entire force, was pointed out from the first." The only way to have made Banks's plan work would have been for him to receive large numbers of reinforcements so that he could whip Taylor and Magruder, simultaneously, on battlefields three hundred miles apart. The loss of manpower at Chickamauga and Chattanooga meant that could never happen.[24]

The image of the commander of the Department of the Gulf playing the role of a common brigadier by personally supervising the invasion of Texas seemed ludicrous to Halleck as well. While Banks had been away, Major General Franklin had been roughed up near Opelousas, and the Rebels infested the Mississippi yet again.

Brigadier General Joseph J. Reynolds was sent to New Orleans to keep an eye on things. Library of Congress.

Halleck imposed a solution, brought to him by Secretary of War Edwin M. Stanton, to compensate for Banks's frequent absences from his headquarters. He ordered Major General Joseph J. Reynolds to head to New Orleans to assume command of the garrison. This Kentucky-born, West Point–trained soldier had been one of the bright lights emerging from the disasters that befell the Army of the Cumberland at Chattanooga. Stanton and Halleck thought he might be just the right counterbalance, or spy perhaps, to a Massachusetts political general with back-door ties to the president.[25]

Halleck also took it upon himself to explain, and then correct, what he considered to be the ill-advised Texas Campaign. He wrote to the commander of the Department of Missouri, Major General John M. Schofield, in St. Louis and asked if perhaps the army at Little Rock under Major General Frederick Steele might mobilize for an expedition to Louisiana and thus reanimate Franklin's advance to form a junction in the Red River Valley. This scheme was an echo of the original plan from the previous summer—before the Chickamauga Campaign

Major General John M. Schofield, commander of the Department of Missouri. *Library of Congress.*

in Georgia had paralyzed operations in the Mississippi Valley and monopolized the attention of the nation. Shreveport could fall before Christmas, Halleck believed, and with it, Rebel resistance in Louisiana.

Schofield agreed, eager to be helpful, and offered a variation on the plan. An army from Arkansas under Major General Steele might indeed threaten the Red River Valley and draw Confederate attention, and troops, in the direction of Shreveport. Since Franklin had fallen back from Opelousas and clearly given up on attacking Alexandria, perhaps Steele might act alone. He could "at least hold that river while you operate in Texas. . . . No doubt this will also strengthen you and aid you to carry out your plans."[26]

Schofield, though, had misinterpreted Halleck's intentions in writing him. The general in chief no longer wanted anything to do with the Lone Star State. Instead, Halleck still wanted Shreveport. For the next month, he would write all of his officers in the west and create a network of support for his view of the war in the Trans-Mississippi, Banks be damned.

TWENTY ONE   **1864**

I dare not stir now.

—Major General Napoleon Jackson Tecumseh Dana
Commander, 13th Army Corps

On January 5, 1864, General François Achille Bazaine of France marched into Guadalajara, Mexico, at the head of more than six thousand French troops. He was greeted by local officials who claimed allegiance to the Mexican Empire, and citizens brought sweets and drinks to the Europeans as a show of welcome. This triumph, the capstone of a brilliant offensive conducted in the last weeks of 1863, saw the *Tricolour* floating over the important cities of Querétaro, Morelia, and Guanajuato. Franco-Mexican armies had also shoved President Benito Juárez out of his stronghold at San Luis Potosí.

The Imperial armies now held the major populations centers in the heartland of Mexico, and Juárez was a fugitive in Saltillo. Within a few weeks, Imperialists might hold a plebiscite, which would, predictably, demonstrate to a hesitant Ferdinand Maximilian Joseph, formerly of Austria, that the people of his new country loved him. The natives themselves—*el pueblo de México*—would likely offer him the Cactus Throne. Failing that, "the Archduke has been ready to take the progress of the French arms," a piece in the *London Daily News* explained, "as an index of the submission of the Mexicans to his rule."[1]

While the French successes ran counter to U.S. interests, there was hopeful news for President Abraham Lincoln and his government. "The towns that have declared for the French intervention acknowledge their adherence only so long as the French occupied them," Major General Nathaniel P. Banks wrote to General-in-Chief Henry Halleck. "The moment they left, the people resumed their allegiance to the Mexican authorities."[2]

The French captured Guadalajara amid the triumphant roar of a welcoming Mexican citizenry. But was it sincere? Godfrey Durand, *Expédition du Mexique. — La population de Guadalajara se portant au devant du corps du général Bazaine à son entrée dans la ville. (D'après un croquis de M. S. Barbier)*, *Le Monde Illustré* No. 360, March 5, 1864.

The Republican government in Mexico, though, seemed to be near collapse. Juárez, at Saltillo, considered retreating farther still, this time west into Durango. Major General Napoleon J. T. Dana, from his headquarters at Brownsville, advised against the move when asked. "It would be tantamount to a notice to the world that he had abandoned his cause and was about to fly," Dana scoffed. If he proceeded westward, Juárez would also be surrendering the Rio Grande Valley to the French. Instead, Dana urged Juárez to fall back through the mountains of the Sierra Madre Oriental and head northeast into Tamaulipas. "He would then have . . . his friends at his back."[3]

At the time, Mexican Republicans were having a hard time telling who their friends were. The Lincoln Administration seemed to have cut some deal with the French. Marshal Élie Frédéric Forey had arrived in Washington. "It is understood," declared a *New York Times* piece citing the *London Daily News*, "that

Senator James A. McDougall of California. He was ready for war with France. Library of Congress.

the extraordinary mission of Marshal FOREY to Washington had for its result an undertaking on the part of the United States Government not to dispute the new Mexican monarchy. In return it is believed that promises were made by France with regard to the attitude of that country toward the Confederate States."[4]

This assurance of mutual non-intervention by the United States and France nudged Maximilian toward a decision. He would accept the crown of Mexico.

Therefore, planting the U.S. flag in Texas had created the kind of success for which President Abraham Lincoln had hoped. Major General Banks had seen to it and on orders of his government, had landed thousands of troops in the state to make sure the French would not meddle in America's Civil War. The ploy had worked, but now the United States promised to not hassle the French as they remade Mexico. This agreement appeared to be a new, and hopeful, Franco-American accord. The Confederates, and Juarez, were now on the outside looking in.

One of the most relieved was the former French foreign minister, Édourard Antoine de Thouvenel. He had opposed his sovereign's flirtations with the Confederates and had actively worked against an alliance. When Napoleon III sacked him, Thouvenel's replacement, Édouard Drouyn de Lhuys, also pushed back against Confederate overtures. Even if "direct hostilities" with the United States did not occur, the Lincoln administration would ignore, if not encourage "departure of bands of volunteers for Mexico" seeking adventure in the ranks of Juárez's army, de Lhuys argued.[5]

In Washington, D.C., the U.S. Congress lagged behind these diplomatic developments and did not follow the script of this new American *entente cordiale*. Later in January, vitriolic Senator James A. McDougall of California introduced a resolution in the Senate declaring it the duty of the United States to demand a French withdrawal from Mexico. If they refused to go, he asserted, "it will become the duty of the Congress of the United States of America to declare war against the Government of France." Representative John Adam Kasson of Iowa put forward a similar bill in the house; Representative Henry Winter Davis of Maryland, chairman of the House Foreign Affairs Committee, took it up.[6]

The house measure passed unanimously, for which Senator Charles Sumner of Massachusetts, chairman of the Senate Foreign Relations Committee, chided his colleagues. "Have we not war enough already on our hands, without needlessly

Representative John Adam Kasson of Iowa was also ready for a showdown with the French. *Library of Congress.*

and wantonly provoking another?" McDougall's senate version died in committee under Sumner's gavel and saved the United States from an unnecessary showdown with France.[7]

While this international drama rolled along, the armies of the United States on the margins of the western Gulf of Mexico tended to more mundane matters. Fear of epidemic, not Rebel soldiers, rousted Major General William B. Franklin and his army from their fortifications in New Iberia. On January 6, 1864, a smallpox outbreak forced out the remnant of the Union army, now just a cavalry division and most of the 19th Army Corps. The men left their comfortable encampments and retreated southeastward, along Bayou Teche, into a winter storm that slashed at the column.[8]

"The English language is inadequate, the powers of rhetoric too feeble, to describe the march," Dr. Harris Beecher, assistant surgeon of the 114th New York remembered. "A confused mass of struggling, wallowing, dirty, half-concealed-in-the-mud humanity, all day slowly labored along the roads and across the fields." The regiments left behind a litter of abandoned gear, bogged wagons, and exhausted men and animals. After a couple of days and thirty miles of marching

Representative Henry Winter Davis promised to take up the issue of war with France in the House Committee on Foreign Affairs. *Library of Congress.*

in the miserable weather, this sodden portion of the Army of the Gulf went once again into winter camps, this time around the town of Franklin.[9]

An understanding with the Confederates of the 2nd Louisiana Cavalry allowed for invalid Federals to remain in hospitals at New Iberia, providing they behaved themselves. Some of the Federal medical staff stayed behind as well to deal with the disease. The Rebels avoided the town, keeping the balance of their command camped near St. Martinville while picketing the Union lines near Jeanerette.

U.S. troops also changed bases in Texas. Major General Dana, comfortable and capable in Brownsville, moved the headquarters of the 13th Army Corps north to wind-swept Fort Esperanza to take command at Matagorda Bay, leaving Major General Francis J. Herron, once again in serviceable health, in command on the Rio Grande frontier. Clearly the emphasis of the campaign had changed and intervening in Mexican affairs had become less important than conquering Texas.[10]

Mexico, though, continued to have deadly squabbles within sight of US troops in Brownsville. Across the Rio Grande, Mexican Republicans who were planning to liberate French-held Tampico first had to concentrate two armies

Senator Charles Sumner thought all of the talk of war with France to be ridiculous and worked to suppress it. *Library of Congress.*

at Matamoros. Governor Jesús de la Serna of Tamaulipas controlled the local garrison of about six hundred troops and six cannon commanded by the unpredictable local warlord Colonel Juan Cortina. In early January, President Juárez, in a bid to to maintain his authority on the border, ordered General Manuel Ruiz to move eight hundred troops and four cannon to the Rio Grande and assume command of all the Republican troops as the military governor of Tamaulipas.[11]

As had become routine, however, confusion and professional jealousy led to a bitter dispute among the Mexican Republican factions. Cortina and Serna eyed Ruiz's arrival suspiciously. Soon, insults—real and imagined—resulted in gunplay. Just after dark on January 12, "we were startled by rapid cannonading and musketry," Herron wrote, "evidently going on in the streets of Matamoros, just across the Rio Grande, which continued without cessation and spread over the greater portion of the town." The Union general dispatched an officer to make contact with Leonard Pierce Jr., the U.S. consul in Matamoros, to assess the danger. The message Pierce returned burned with urgency. "My person and my family are in great danger," he wrote. "From the well-known character of Cortina and his followers, I fear the city would be plundered." Not only would his residence be ransacked and his family threatened, but Pierce also faced the possible loss of $1 million in U.S. specie and other valuable property.[12]

Herron had to act quickly. He ordered Colonel Henry Bertram to turn out his 20th Wisconsin, secure the Rio Grande ferry, and lead four companies through Matamoras to rescue Pierce, his family, and the gold. The 10th Iowa, the 94th Illinois, and a battery of artillery stood ready to move into town and settle the brawl if circumstances required. As the U.S. troops double-timed through the streets of Matamoros, the firing ceased between the feuding Mexicans.

When Colonel Bertram arrived at Pierce's house, he reported, the consul "was very happy to see us." Officers from Cortina's command arrived as well to ask about American intentions. Once convinced the Wisconsin men would not interfere with their battle, the Mexicans resumed fighting. The U.S. troops escorted the consul and his family to safety the next morning while the internecine battle in Matamoras continued until midday. Cortina's forces were victorious, and Ruiz and

Colonel Henry Bertram, 20th Wisconsin, sparked an international incident by invading Mexico. emedals.com.

scores of his men fled into Texas for safety and protection under the American flag. Both Mexican Republicans and Franco-Mexican Imperialists expressed outrage over this American violation of Mexican sovereignty—US troops in the streets of Matamoros. It certainly damaged the new Franco-American amity.[13]

At Matagorda Bay, far up the Texas coast from the chaos on the Rio Grande, other developments were underway. The 4th Division, 13th Army Corps, arrived to join the 1st and 3rd Divisions as well as Brigadier General Thomas E. G. Ransom's 3rd Brigade, 2nd Division. These troops, nearly the entire 13th Army Corps, would finish the drive to Houston. To add some noise to the coming campaign and to keep the Confederates on edge, the navy initiated a routine of nearly daily bombardments of their works along the coast. The Union campaign for Texas would begin in earnest in the coming weeks.[14]

The political and international winds had shifted, though, and they would not fill every sail. Major General Cadwallader C. Washburn, the staunch advocate of capturing Houston, would be denied his laurels, and instead sailed away from Texas via New Orleans to Washington, D.C., at Lincoln's personal request. A veteran officer who had earned his spurs at Vicksburg leading men of the 16th Army

Corps, Washburn had never felt comfortable assigned to the 13th Army Corps in the Department of the Gulf. Superseded in command first by Major General Edward Otho Cresap Ord and later by Major General Dana, and presently stuck in the sands of the Texas coast without permission to defeat the enemy, Washburn found himself frustrated and in a professional cul-de-sac. Now, with Lincoln's help, he had found a way out.[15]

Banks hoped Washburn would serve as his personal envoy in the capital. "Major General C. C. Washburn, who visits Washington upon leave of absence, given by you, will be able to state to you more fully than it can be presented in dispatches, the condition of affairs in Texas," Banks wrote Lincoln on January 15. Washburn, though, was a poor choice of advocate or courier; he was the younger brother of Representative Elihu B. Washburne of Illinois, perhaps the greatest congressional supporter of Major General Ulysses S. Grant. The brothers instead plotted for Grant's ascension—and Banks's downfall.[16]

War Department policies also complicated the lives of Union commanders in the field. The previous June the adjutant general had arrived at a solution to handle Union regiments whose three-year enlistments were expiring. The Veteran Volunteer Order, or General Orders No. 191, recognized that in 1861 many of the Union's best regiments had enlisted for only three years. The new initiative would

Representative Elihu B. Washburne of Illinois (who unlike his soldier brother, added an "e" to his last name), was a powerful kingmaker in Congress, and an active backer of Ullyses S. Grant. He was rewarded—he became secretary of state under President Grant. *Library of Congress.*

incentivize these well-used units to reenlist for another three years. The first enticement was cash: a bonus of $402 to each soldier who stayed in the army. Each man who reenlisted would also receive a month's furlough. If three-quarters of a company or regiment opted to stay, they would receive furlough as a group before their enlistment expired, allowing the men to return home as a unit, see their families, and recruit new men to fill the ranks. As a point of pride, these regiments would also retain their unit name and number with the addition of "Veteran Volunteers." While their regiments were on furlough, soldiers who had opted to leave the army would serve out their enlistment with other units. This reshuffling meant commanders in the field would have to find a way to rotate home their best and most-seasoned regiments.[17]

The opportunity caused a moment of soul-searching for many soldiers. One unit was swayed by their colonel. "We were asked to reenlist for three years," remembered James Butler of Company E, 33rd Illinois. "The proposition was rather unpopular at first." Officers led the men away from Indianola, where they were quartered, and formed them into a hollow square on the Texas prairie. Colonel Isaac Elliott allowed his men to sit comfortably, then he addressed them. "Jeff Davis says that 'the Yanks are only in for three years, at the end of that time they will go home and stay,'" he roared. "Now I propose that we crowd that lie right down Jeff Davis's throat, and I don't care if it kills him." The soldiers roared their approval, and enough of the 33rd Illinois reenlisted to earn a trip home together.[18]

Major changes were also coming for those with higher ranks. At just the moment when Major General Banks and Halleck had reached a consensus about how to finish the Texas campaign, the presence of so many U.S. troops in the Lone Star State became obnoxious to the French *and* the Americans—especially after the Matamoros incident. Now, the Lincoln Administration had to find a way to maneuver Banks out of Texas.

Major General Banks, to his surprise, lost control of the Department of the Gulf. Although he was still the titular head, other men were making decisions on his behalf. Halleck, without informing Banks, had once again changed his mind and made arrangement to refocus the efforts of the Army of the Gulf exclusively on Louisiana. Halleck had already communicated with leaders in Arkansas and on the Mississippi to prepare for a general campaign supported by the powerful Mississippi Squadron of ironclads, tinclads, gunboats, and transports. Banks, the architect of the grand strategy in Louisiana and Texas, had been subtly cast into a supporting role.

Banks had argued against a move up the Red River for a variety of reasons, most notably low water levels. He also persisted in believing Houston, not Shreveport, was the most important point in the Trans-Mississippi. Halleck, tired of his contrary general, took issues into his own hands. He renewed previous conversations with his western generals.

A dispatch from Steele to Banks offered little enthusiasm for such a raid. The roads in Arkansas were in bad shape, and little could be done for months. When he could get his army under way, they would probably proceed down the Ouachita River valley in the direction of Monroe while Banks moved up the Red River toward Alexandria. "Sufficient forces moving up the two rivers could drive the rebels into Texas, which would probably cause many of the Missouri and Arkansas men to desert, and perhaps," he mused, "of the Texans also." Banks should not expect Steele to help much, however. "My troops are scattered," the commander in Little Rock wrote. "I shall endeavor to keep up communications with you through emissaries and shall be glad to receive any suggestions from you and to co-operate with you in any of your movements," Steele continued vaguely, "if possible."[19]

To gather support for his views, Halleck enlisted the aid of Major General William Tecumseh Sherman, a man whose opinion now clearly mattered. "Generals Sherman and Steele agree with me in opinion that the Red River is the shortest and best line of defense for Louisiana and Arkansas and as a base of operations against Texas," Halleck wrote Banks. Steele could not act alone, however, in moving on Shreveport. "His movements must . . . be dependent in a great measure upon yours." If Banks persisted with his operations on the coast of Texas, Steele would remain on the defensive along the Arkansas River and Sherman would continue to be plagued by Confederate raiders vexing the Mississippi.[20]

Halleck came directly to his point. "So long as your plans are not positively decided upon, no definite instructions can be given to Sherman and Steele. The best thing, it would seem," Halleck continued, "is for you to communicate with them, and also with Admiral Porter, in regard to some general co-operation, and all agree upon what is the best plan of operations." Banks would have to abide the judgment of officers in the Mississippi Valley. "The best military opinions of the generals in the West seem to favor operations on Red River, provided the stage of water will enable the gun-boats to co-operate," Halleck assured him a few days later. "It would open to us the cotton and stores in Northeastern Louisiana and Southern Arkansas." As a sign of his good intentions, Halleck would send Banks a cavalry and infantry regiment from Maine. He offered more field artillery if Banks needed it. In his January dispatches, however, Halleck implied no one but Banks had a passion for operations on the Texas coast.[21]

Banks, once again undercut by his superiors, did as he was told and wrote the officers Halleck mentioned to ask their opinions. Sherman replied first, having just returned from the Army of the Tennessee in northern Alabama. He had a more savage plan in mind. Instead of chasing every Rebel command that harassed the Mississippi River, perhaps it would be better to push them back aggressively—burn them down—to eliminate them as a threat. If Union armies rampaged for one hundred miles on both sides of the river, removing anything of use to the army including livestock and commodities while also liberating the slaves, the fighting spirit of the Confederacy would collapse.[22]

Sherman would initiate the process by mounting a destructive, two-pronged raid across Mississippi from Vicksburg and Memphis to destroy all means of sustaining Confederate forces in the region. His men would ravage a swath as far east as Demopolis, Alabama. This attack on the countryside of the Confederacy would draw Rebel troops toward Alabama, and Banks could mount a feint along the Mississippi Gulf Coast to convince the enemy Mobile was the true target of the campaign. In short, he wanted to revive the plans of the previous summer, but only as raids and not as occupations. By the end of the month-long march through Mississippi, "Mobile will have no communication with the interior," Sherman assured Banks, "save by the Alabama River." There would also be no hogs, chickens, corn, wheat, cattle, horses, mules, or slaves to sustain the Rebel war effort.[23]

The tactics of this Mississippi raid should then be applied to western Louisiana. "I think this movement and one similar on Shreveport, as soon as the Red River rises, would pretty well settle the main question in the Southwest,"

Sherman assured Banks. The Army of the Gulf could finish wrecking Louisiana, strip its last productive region of anything of value, and then with the assistance of troops from Arkansas and black regiments from the Mississippi Valley, hold the line along the Red River with outposts at Shreveport and Alexandria. Sherman, however, could not wait around to lend a hand. "I would like nothing better than to unite with you in such a movement, but I expect soon to be required by General Grant to hasten back to Huntsville, where I left the Army of the Tennessee."[24]

The promise of more muscle for the Army of the Gulf to accomplish these objectives was persuasive, and Halleck instructed the forces serving on the Mississippi to help with Sherman's proposed Louisiana project. If Grant did not summon him, Sherman might help in person; at the very least, he would lend some of his troops to reinforce Banks and his Red River raid.

What, then, would become of the offensive on the Texas coast, already stirring back to life? From the vantage point of the Yankee troops camped out around Franklin, Louisiana, the whole effort had been wasted. "In the previous July," observed Lieutenant Colonel Richard B. Irwin, "the occupation of some point in Texas had been put forward by Halleck as an object of paramount importance." How and where this occupation occurred had been left to Banks. When he landed troops on the Rio Grande, Secretary of State William H. Seward was delighted. "Halleck," Irwin noted, "was as frankly disgusted. Finally, when not one foothold but many footholds had been gained along the coast of Texas, Halleck wound up the long correspondence by renewing his instructions of the previous summer."[25]

Banks, undermined, became a forced convert to Halleck's directions, and agreed the Red River made sense after all. "With our united forces," Banks conceded, "the success of movements on that line will be certain and important." He never had enough troops, he believed, to achieve all his government had asked of him in the Trans-Mississippi. Now, he might. Texas, "as well as Arkansas and Louisiana, will be ours," he agreed, "and their people will gladly renew their allegiance to the Government." The fall of Shreveport would break the back of the rebellion in this part of the Confederacy. The railroad connecting Vicksburg, Mississippi, to Delhi, Louisiana, could be extended through Monroe to Shreveport, providing a year-round supply line. Union troops could then invade Texas through the agriculturally rich northeast—but this was unlikely to ever happen.[26]

Banks still grasped for a way to keep his Texas project alive. "I do not think it expedient to give up the occupation of Matagorda Bay, which is a key point in Texas, and may be of great service hereafter in communication with the coast from the interior," he noted. Union troops from New Mexico had reached the Pecos River and camped at Fort Lancaster. They might still press forward toward San Antonio. Banks would reduce the number of men in Texas, "to the lowest number consistent with the safe occupation of Matagorda Island."[27]

The men of the 13th Army Corps had no inkling their efforts in Texas had just been betrayed. Major General Dana had wasted little time after his arrival to learn the strategic situation at Matagorda Bay. He believed, as had Washburn, a march up the narrow peninsula toward Caney Creek made the most sense but also offered the greatest advantages to the defenders. A very narrow battlefield would leverage the Texans' smaller numbers, which he estimated at around four thousand to five thousand, while denying the Federals any room to maneuver. The U.S. navy would play a role, but Dana believed them to be noisier than they were lethal.

On January 16, Dana and his staff boarded the USS *Monongahela* and scouted the Texas coast as far north as the mouth of the Brazos River. The general encountered the other warships on station and watched as gunners tried unsuccessfully to hit a Rebel steamer, probably the *Cora*, far away on the other side of Matagorda Peninsula. He also surveyed the Confederate defenses at Caney Creek and the mouth of the St. Bernard River while the heavy guns of the USS *Monongahela* stirred up the enemy garrisons. His inspection tour ended with a glimpse of the forts at Quitana and Velasco. He transferred to the USS *Granite City* for a ride back to Fort Esperanza.[28]

What Major General Dana observed left him wanting more precise intelligence, and he ordered a reconnaissance in force. Following the same plan as Washburn had three weeks before, he ordered Lieutenant Colonel Francis S. Hesseltine and his entire regiment—four hundred men of the 13th Maine—to board the USS

Granite City and once again take the beach at Smith's Landing. On January 21 these troops, a shore party, and boat howitzers from the USS *Monongahela* and the USS *Sciota* waded ashore. Hesseltine's force would back down the Matagorda Peninsula toward Pass Cavallo and Decros Point, escorted by the USS *Queen* and the USS *Sciota*. With any luck, Confederates would sense an easy kill and once again pursue them from Caney Creek.[29]

Dana planned for this outcome to be different; he had sent the 13th Maine as bait for a trap. Brigadier General Ransom was moving up the peninsula with the 1st Brigade, 4th Division, 13th Army Corps, along with a rifled gun from the Chicago Mercantile Battery and fifty artillerymen serving as mounted scouts. If any Rebels came out, they would soon be overmatched. Ransom's force left the works at Decros Point at noon on January 21 and marched fourteen miles up the coast. The following day, they pushed another twenty-five miles up the coast, scattering isolated Rebel pickets who were now cut off from their own lines by Hesseltine's troops. The Yankees picked up three horses but all of the Texans fled by skiff across the bay to the town of Matagorda. Hesseltine and Ransom had come up empty.

The combined Federal force then continued up the beach to Smith's Landing. From here, Ransom ordered his mounted troops to ride on as far as the Rebel defenses at Caney Creek, four miles beyond where Matagorda Peninsula joined the mainland. Meanwhile, the general went aboard the USS *Sciota* for a scouting expedition of his own. From the top of the mainmast, Ransom had a clear picture of not only the Confederate fortifications but also the troops gathering to repel what appeared to be a Union offensive. A brigade of cavalry, estimated at about three thousand men, and a one-thousand-man brigade of infantry seemed game for a fight. A canal connecting Matagorda Bay to Caney Creek made enemy gunboats a factor as well.

The fort itself did not impress him. "His works are not formidable," Ransom reported, "and seem to consist of two or three detached field works, the one on the coast being the most extensive." The terrain, though, presented a bottleneck to any attack. Ransom had seen enough. He returned to his command and ordered the expedition back to Decros Point.[30]

Had he been able to see farther inland, Ransom would have been even more impressed by the strength of the Confederate position. Word of the Yankee advance had rocketed up Caney Creek, and Texans turned out in every camp that night. "A bugler sounded the alarm at 2 o'clock," Private Rudolph Coreth wrote his family. The 36th Texas Cavalry rode toward the coast, about two-dozen miles away. After delays and confused orders, his regiment and the rest of Brigadier General Hamilton P. Bee's Division gathered on the prairies between Caney Creek and Cedar Lake about midnight. "It made a remarkable impression to see cavalry converging together from all directions," he continued. "The moon was shining so full that one could see everything well."[31]

As the Federals marched back down the coast, scouts saw the steamers *Cora* and *Lucy Gwin* keeping pace with them out in the bay near the town of Matagorda and escorting the schooners *Lady of the Lake*, *Annie Dale* and *George Buckhart*. Even though this flotilla paled compared to the might of the Union ships on station, they were in shallow water and out of reach of navy guns. With their ability to flank Matagorda Peninsula, they would be a headache for any Union advance. The footsore troops arrived back at their base on January 25, discouraged.[32]

Behind them was one sign of their passing. In a lonely grave in the dunes of Matagorda Peninsula lay the body of Captain Charles R. March of Company F, 13th Maine. The Portland native died from a sailor's careless bullet. While shooting at cattle on the beach, the Yankee tar missed and instead sent his round through March's head and into another soldier. These two Maine soldiers, one dead and one wounded, were the only two casualties from the expedition.

When Ransom reported to headquarters, Major General Dana bore troubling news. Word had arrived from Major General Banks in New Orleans suspending the campaign in Texas—indefinitely. Dana and Ransom had learned U.S. forces would be abandoning Texas, not marching toward Houston and Galveston as they had supposed.

Major General Banks and the Army of the Gulf had been mere pawns in a much larger game. President Lincoln and General-in-Chief Halleck had originally ordered them into Texas to intimidate the French; now the government ordered them to avoid antagonizing the French. Instead, they would become instruments of total war as envisioned by the emerging leadership of the nation's military machine, Grant and Sherman. Halleck, like Banks, would soon be a relic of an earlier iteration of the war.

Dana shot back at his commander. "Believe me, chances are being thrown away, which are seriously to be regretted," Dana snarled in response to the news. Hoping to revive his offensive, Dana asked for just two regiments of cavalry and, with the forces he had at hand, he would prevail against the Texans and conclude the campaign decisively. "I can use them profitably; well, gloriously," he argued.[33]

But the veteran soldier also understood the implications of the changed circumstances. "I dare not stir now," Dana admitted, "under the information of your last letter."[34]

Men like Joseph Freeborn Rowley, a teamster who had dodged Confederate conscription, had welcomed the Federal presence in Texas and now expected the U.S. army to complete its conquest of the state. The Yankees' arrival, though, had stoked an atmosphere of suspicion. Rowley wanted out of the state and wanted to protect the life of his teenage stepson, Fred, but who could he trust? He had attempted to purchase passage to New Orleans from Brownsville, but the inflated prices proved prohibitively expensive. He cast about for some other way. "I applied for a pass," he wrote, "to go to Port Lavaca which was said to be in the hands of the Federals." Rowley, his charge, and another man left the relative safety of Brownsville to try their luck on Matagorda Bay.[35]

With the Rebels cleaned out of region by regular patrols from the 1st Texas Cavalry (Union), the journey passed uneventfully. When the trio approached Richard King's ranch, Rowley's companion began acting strangely. "The man that was along tore up his Federal papers, which I did not like," he continued. "I thought we was sold." He would not be betrayed without a fight, and he prepared to kill the man should his suspicions prove correct. The traveling party passed through the ranch unmolested and even unchallenged.[36]

They avoided Corpus Christi and passed through San Patricio, about twenty miles inland, and crossed the Nueces River. Now, Rowley faced real danger. "The town was full of Rebel troops," he noted. "They cried out to halt." The trio instead left the road and headed around this garrison, bushwhacking through dozens of miles of brush to bypass this Confederate outpost. "We went on without trouble." Clearly, getting to Port Lavaca would involve sneaking through the enemy lines, and Rowley gave up the plan.[37]

Instead, he went home to Hays County to fetch some belongings, intending to leave the tensions in Texas behind, forever. Perhaps head to Mexico.

It would not be as easy as he hoped.

TWENTY TWO   **A CONFEDERATE NATION**

They would rather have mules than Negroes and Confeder-
ate money.

—Private Rudolph Coreth
36th Texas Cavalry

❝ C hristmas has come and gone and old Winter has wept his snows upon the grave of the departed year—a 'Merry Christmas' would sound somewhat misty and ghostlike in the midst of January but it is not too late for a 'happy New Year,'" eighteen-year-old belle Mollie E. Moore of Tyler, Texas, wrote to Captain Elijah P. Petty, commander of Company F, 17th Texas Infantry. A lawyer in Bastrop before the war, the well-educated and sophisticated Petty had struck up a friendship with the girl, whose cousin was in his company. In a series of letters, the captain discussed literature and world affairs with her and picked up news from home. "From our coast we hear but little," Moore wrote, "we only know that Tom Green and his gallant command are there, and *we are content!*"[1]

Captain Petty, from his muddy encampment in the earthworks at Yellow Bayou liked the way Moore wrote and forwarded Moore's letter and another to his daughter as an example of good prose. "They are fine in sentiment, chaste and select in language and elegant in style," Petty wrote to his fourteen-year-old, Ella. "Study hard and read everything that is useful and ornamental and store your mind well with facts and well as language and fancy and you will have no trouble to excel in writing. Your mind is a rich and rare diamond," the homesick officer continued, "and I wish by polishing it to bring forth its beauties." Near the banks of Bayou des Glaise, Petty wondered where fate would take him while he neglected his family back at Bastrop.[2]

Petty, Lieutenant General Edmund Kirby Smith, and thousands of other Confederates, shivering in camps from Monroe to Port Lavaca, from Yellow Bayou to Chocolate Bayou, tried to make sense of the enemy strategy. Kirby

Smith had to consider where to distribute his meager forces. He kept Brigadier General Alfred Mouton's Division in Monroe to defend against an offensive from Federal troops at Natchez, Vicksburg and Little Rock. More importantly, knowing the Army of the Gulf was split between the 13th Army Corps in Texas and the 19th Army Corps on Bayou Teche, Kirby Smith assigned Major General John G. Walker's beefier forces to man an extensive earthworks about three miles west of Simmesport, along the west bank of Yellow Bayou stretching to its confluence with Bayou des Glaise, to protect the Red River Valley. Others in the division rebuilt and expanded Fort DeRussy, near the town of Marksville.

The weather—cold, wet, and miserable for nearly two months—kept the Rebel infantry in Louisiana hunkered down for the winter. Despite this, many soldiers like Captain Petty remained determined to see the cause through. "I am a soldier for the war," Petty wrote to his brother. "Never expect to cease hostilities until our country is free, and if I outlive the Confederacy, will not remain in the Union. Will beg my bread and drag my family out of the country in poverty. Have . . . sworn my children to eternal hostility to the Yankee race."[3]

The captain would have a chance to prove his Rebel ardor. Both Major General Richard Taylor and Kirby Smith believed the spring would bring a vicious campaign in the Red River valley. "The Federals do not speak hopefully of accomplishing much more in Texas," Taylor conceded. "Operations there will be confined to the coast." As a further sign the Federals had given up on holding Texas, the state's Union governor, Brigadier General Andrew Jackson Hamilton, had left Brownsville and returned to New Orleans.[4]

Lieutenant General Kirby Smith agreed with Taylor's assessment and added his strategic insight. If the Federals tried to move on San Antonio from Matagorda Bay, Major General John Bankhead Magruder's highly mobile force of two cavalry divisions, Brigadier General Hamilton P. Bee's and the recently promoted Major General Tom Green's, would savage their flank and their lines of communications. Kirby Smith explained the situation to President Jefferson Davis with clarity. "If [Major General Nathaniel P. Banks] operates directly on Houston he will encounter great natural obstacles, with little hope of success," the lieutenant general assured the president. Although Magruder had given up Matagorda Island, Fort Esperanza, and Decros Point, he had successfully trapped the Federals by amassing an army of some fifteen thousand men—and making good use of the Texas geography—to bar their way forward.[5]

The Confederates had left Banks only one route into the heart of the Confederate Trans-Mississippi. "The only true line of operations by which the enemy can penetrate the department is the valley of Red River, rich in supplies; with steam-boat navigation for six months in the year, it offers facilities for the co-operation of the army and navy, and enables them to shift their base as they advance into the interior," Kirby Smith wrote Davis. Major General Taylor concurred. He understood the implications: "We shall all be put on our mettle during the spring."[6]

Therefore, Major General Taylor readied his army for battle. The tactics of Major General Green's Texans had impressed him, and the mobility of this mounted force convinced him to create additional regiments of Louisiana cavalry that might serve a similar purpose and stretch his military reach. For the next three months, independent "conscript hunter" companies, like the Prairie Rangers of St. Landry Parish, found themselves shuffled into the regular roster of the Confederacy, along with conscripts they had rounded up and soldiers who had been exchanged from the armies captured at Vicksburg and Port Hudson.

Using these gleaned resources, Colonel Isaac Harrison oversaw the expansions of his 15th Louisiana Cavalry Battalion into the 3rd Louisiana Cavalry while officers gathered other troops from the vicinity of Monroe and formed them into the 4th Louisiana Cavalry. Officers crammed men into the 13th Louisiana Cavalry Battalion until it blossomed as the 5th Louisiana Cavalry. Harrison would command this tatterdemalion brigade as it operated north of the Red River and patrolled the west bank of the Mississippi.

Taylor scoured the population for even more men. One unit, including a battalion of notorious home guard companies from southwestern Louisiana, arrived in Shreveport to provide provost duty. Taylor organized the 7th Louisiana Cavalry at Moundville specifically to combat the growing strength of Ozémé Carrière's Clan but called on state militia units, the 1st and 2nd Louisiana State Guard, to serve as pickets near Federal positions.

Dismal civilian morale plagued Confederate Louisiana. In 1861 Pelican State secessionists had refused to accept the election of Abraham Lincoln as legitimate and had done all in their power to oppose him. By 1864 many of these same hot-blooded Louisiana revolutionaries had cooled. They realized they had traded the feared despotism of Republican rule for the actual despotism of Confederate rule.

As a result, this disaffected population actively sought a reconnection with their erstwhile enemy. This included trading cotton to Yankee agents—sometimes with the assistance of Rebel officers. Taylor sacked these profiteers, but the "temptation was too strong," he lamented, "and their successors did the same." One Louisiana soldier, exchanged after his capture at Port Hudson, was surprised by what he found at home, which he described as "a great change in the ideas and sentiments of the people." It was a shock to find "they were trading liberally with the Yankees and hauling cotton to them."[7]

Propping up the failing Confederacy had become too large of a burden for the average family trying to breast the storm of war. Civilians defied authorities and their Home Guard muscle by hiding corn, cotton, and chickens when the Confederate taxman arrived. Collection patrols had also become hazardous duty. By 1864 an estimated eight thousand Louisiana soldiers had shirked their commands and had no intention of returning to military service. Instead, they would protect their families from the grasping hand of the Confederacy.[8]

Taylor gave up and ordered the citizens of Louisiana south of Alexandria to abandon their homes in the face of the tempest about to break upon them. Most refused.

Meanwhile, piles of Confederate cotton, seized as tax-in-kind but with no outlet to Mexico, lay at the mercy of a Union advance up the Red River. Taylor suggested the government sell it to anyone who would have it. "Even if we sell for Confederate currency, it is much better than to destroy it," he admitted. The transactions might also help tamp down rampant inflation. "By so doing we would withdraw currency from circulation, and to that extent improve its credit," Taylor continued. It was likely most of this cotton would fall into the hands of speculators, who would sell it to northern customers. This made no difference now. "In the beginning of the struggle a great political influence was attributed to cotton. . . . Experience has shown the fallacy of these opinions," he wrote. King Cotton was dead.[9]

In the early days of the war, ardent secessionists had horded their cotton crops to keep them off the market as a way of leveraging the Confederate position internationally. These farmers and planters had shown their loyalty to the cause by essentially sacrificing their incomes. Some, following a government directive, had even burned their cotton to keep it from falling into enemy hands. The ploy had not worked. Now, three years into the war, the ability of southern families to sell their cotton—even to the Yankees—might save some from starvation. "Now the people see in the destruction of their cotton a mere sacrifice of property," Taylor observed, "useless to the cause, but ruinous to individuals."[10]

Soldiers in Louisiana sought any means to make money for their suffering families. A thriving black market flourished after the fall of Vicksburg. With the fate of the Confederacy in doubt, unscrupulous men made what money they could. "Some stole slaves from Louisiana and sold them in Texas. We fear many of our citizens have been badly swindled by buying slaves thus stolen from Louisiana," a correspondent wrote to the *Galveston Daily News*.[11]

Even goods captured from the Federals in battle made their way across the Sabine River. "A secret I have to tell you, but it is no secret here in the army," wrote Captain Petty. "After the capture of Brashear City . . . the officers generally began to steal and run off negroes and mules to Texas." One colonel, Petty claimed, took as many as twenty-five enslaved people along with mules and wagons. Another Texas officer, Captain Jerry C. Wilkins of Bastrop, sold two purloined slaves and twenty government mules to buyers at Niblett's Bluff for $8,000 in Confederate script. This officer, commander of Company D, 2nd Arizona Cavalry, invested his earnings in cattle then deserted. "How can our cause prosper," Petty asked, "when those in high places, have turned out to downright and open stealing?"[12]

The departure of so many Rebel troops from the Louisiana hinterlands during this period provided hope for Unionists still trying to make it to Federal lines in Louisiana. West of Opelousas, the much-abused Unionist Dennis Haynes, who had been holed up with sympathizers of the Clan, prepared for his final dash to freedom. He had been a refugee for nine months and had suffered profound hardships. An unhealed bullet wound festered in his upper arm, and an unset arm fracture caused additional pain. Soon, Haynes hoped, these horrors would be behind him.[13]

On January 12, 1864, equipped with an ersatz bit and bridle and a corn sack stuffed with Spanish moss as a saddle, Haynes mounted a "poor prairie pony" for what he hoped would be an end to his ordeal. He had thirty dollars in Confederate money and a local African American man as a guide. Haynes spoke no French; his guide spoke no English. "So we rode along like two dummies, and traveled all night," Haynes wrote. The pair made it halfway to New Iberia before Haynes's mount gave out. The men found refuge at a sympathetic home, where they waited for three days for the horse to recover and the weather to improve.[14]

They learned the Federals had abandoned New Iberia and retreated to Franklin. This would extend his trip another thirty miles; but still, Haynes was close. His guide swapped horses with him, escorted him to the main road along the eastern bank of Bayou Teche, then left, having pocketed the thirty dollars in Confederate script.

The Unionist refugee pressed on alone into the cold night. He swam his horse across Bayou Teche—Federals had burned the St. Martinville Bridge weeks ago—and made his way to a tavern operated by a freedman. Here Haynes learned the Rebels maintained a post just outside of town, but a Union hospital remained in smallpox-stricken New Iberia. Freedom and competent treatment for his injuries were only ten miles away. He just needed to slip past the Rebels.

Haynes worked out what he hoped would be the last steps of his journey. Boarding at the tavern overnight and remaining hidden throughout the day, he left the owner his horse in consideration for his kindness and discretion and headed once again into the Louisiana gloom, now afoot. Having been inoculated against smallpox, he did not fear the disease as much as the Rebel pistols.

On January 15, at an hour before midnight, he knocked softly at the door of the Union hospital. A soldier of the 114th New York Infantry opened it. "I told him what was the matter, and wished to see a doctor," Haynes wrote. The soldier showed him in. "My reason for wishing to stay in the hospital being that there was no chance of detection." Certainly, Haynes believed, even the most zealous of Confederates would steer clear of smallpox.[15]

The medical staff was away, working among the Federal troops at Franklin, but the fugitive rested easy knowing they would return soon. Perhaps by the next evening he could also make his way to those Union lines. The next afternoon,

Dr. George Hubbard of the 165th New York returned. He was shocked to find this gunshot stranger among his invalids. The doctor inspected Haynes and treated his wounds, but he declared, "This is no place for you." Haynes, assuming he was referring to the presence of smallpox, gave Dr. Hubbard's comment no credence. He had already been vaccinated against the disease.

An hour later, one of the Federals approached him. "You are betrayed," the soldier said. "Here come six of the devils now, with their carbines, right for the hospital." Troopers of the 2nd Louisiana Cavalry surrounded the building. A Rebel sergeant called out, demanding the Yankees turn over the person who had recently reported with a gunshot wound. "Seeing all hopes of escape cut off," Haynes sighed, "I went out, and was greeted with a salutation that was anything but pleasant or gentlemanly."[16]

A prisoner once again, but with his injuries now properly dressed, Haynes shuffled ahead of the Confederates toward a very dark future. "One offered me fifty dollars if I would run," he wrote, understanding he would be instantly shot if he tried to escape. Instead, Haynes continued to profess his innocence as the troopers hurried him along with the butts of their guns. Arriving at St. Martinville, the Rebels presented him to their commander, Major J. D. Blair, who was headquartered in an abandoned livery stable. The skeptical Confederates interrogated Haynes, even ordering his bandaged arm unwrapped.

When asked about his bullet wound, the Unionist answered vaguely: "My arm was broken in an affray." Haynes expanded the story, claiming he had been searching for his daughter, who had left home to try and find the where- abouts of her husband, reported killed at Port Hudson. "When last she wrote me she was at St. Martinsville," he lied. When he arrived there, Haynes said, "I was informed . . . that she came to New Iberia as a laundress to some Federal officer." Haynes explained he had only wound up among the Yankees because theirs was the only light on when he came to town. He was ill and injured and had sought treatment.[17]

The Confederates remained skeptical. Why had he not reported to their headquarters first? The Louisianans gave Haynes a blanket and placed him under guard. The next morning, soldiers from the 2nd Louisiana escorted Haynes fifteen miles to the provost marshal at Vermilionville, where he once again faced stern interrogation. The authorities, satisfied he posed no immediate danger, showed him to a pile of corn for his bed. "I was now for the third time cribbed, if not caged," Haynes wrote. He was sick with a severe cold, and his wounds throbbed. Confederate doctors treated Haynes for several days but eventually confined him to a cell.[18]

Outside of the Rebel lines, a growing battalion of bandits and jayhawkers rapidly filled the political void in southern Louisiana, despite the efforts of Confederate officials to prune them back. At the time Haynes arrived, they were on a rampage. Riders with the Clan swept the prairies of St. Landry Parish and even pushed close to Alexandria.[19]

Numerous incidents of brigandry were reported. Joseph B. Young, who lived ten miles west of Opelousas, walked onto his porch to find four men facing him with their rifles leveled and hammers cocked. This bunch stole his horse. A while later, they returned with a dozen friends who emptied his place of anything useful. One of the raiders told Young's wife "he wanted to kill every damned Confederate he could find."[20]

Terence Jeansanne, on a mission to round up beef cattle in Vermilion Parish, found himself, his five drovers, and five hundred head of cattle surrounded by jayhawkers who claimed they were protecting their property from Confederate impressment. They took the men's sidearms, mounts, and livestock. Before the raiders left, they told the hapless Jeansanne "their intention was to starve out the Confederate forces and thus bring the war to a close."[21]

Another drover, Francoise Savoy, faced a similar band on his way to round up cattle. The marauders identified themselves as some of Captain Carrière's Clan men, who had instructions "to arrest every man they found on the prairies." They let Savoy go, though, after he promised to keep quiet about the incident. They left him his horse, too, because "they considered him worthless."[22]

Confederate officials rang the alarm. Captain H. C. Monell, the conscription officer in Opelousas, wrote Taylor "the jayhawkers, having collected their forces, swept over the country . . . robbing the inhabitants in many instances of everything of value they possessed, but taking particularly all the fine horses and good arms they could find." Unlike in the past, these raids occurred at all hours, light or dark. "These lawless bands are daily increasing in numbers; not only are they collecting the discontented whites and free negroes, but the slaves, already demoralized by the Yankees, are going to them every day." Anyone loyal to the Confederacy in the area would have to leave or face a brutal end. Confederate conscription, Monell advised, "may be said to be suspended."[23]

Nearby, a camp for paroled prisoners awaiting exchange found itself under siege. Most of the men housed there quit the Confederate cause and headed for the Clan. "Those prisoners of Vicksburg and Port Hudson, of which there are

ATTENTION 28TH LOUISIANA!

The Officers and men of Company A and K, will report at once to the Commanding Officer of the 28th Louisiana, at Opelousas. Soldiers! the Secretary of War has ordered that you be put immediately in Camp to be declared exchanged, when two thirds of the command have been reassembled. Your comrades in arms East of the Mississippi River are in the field; and the men of North Louisiana belonging to the 3d, 17th, 27th and 31st have, with few exceptions, already reported at Camp. You have been at home for nearly six months. Do you mean to barter away the hard earned reputation you have won on every field for a few more unmanly days of ease? I cannot believe it. I have therefore, visited this Parish for the purpose of reassembling you. Report without delay as I will collect with Cavalry all Officers and men who have not reported by the 27th inst., to be afterwards dealt with as deserters.

ALLEN THOMAS,
Colonel 28th La. Regiment.

Opelousas, December 17, 1863.

A circular issued by Confederate authorities urging men captured and paroled to return to service. *Library of Congress.*

large numbers in the parish, have, in many instances, gone inside the jayhawkers' lines and cannot be got out," reported Captain M. L. Lyons. "Should this thing be allowed to go on any length of time, you can depend upon it a most fearful state of things will exist."[24]

The erosion of Confederate patriotism had a partial antidote farther north in Louisiana. Governor Thomas O. Moore, who had dragged the state out of the Union in 1861 and led its Confederate iteration through the punishing campaigns of 1862 and 1863, left office in early 1864. His successor was Henry Watkins Allen, a highly regarded and twice-wounded Confederate general who proved decidedly more sympathetic to the plight of Louisiana's civilians. He passed laws restricting the illegal pressing of private property into Confederate service, then moved aggressively to establish public hospitals, government stores, foundries, and factories to produce goods for his citizens and to succor the poor. He also established badly needed chemical facilities to craft medicines, turpentine, castor oil, medicinal alcohol, and carbonate of soda—for distribution to the suffering population of his state. He also protected their civil liberties. While this brought relief to the population north of Alexandria, it did little to alleviate the suffering of those living in the Jayhawker-infested and war-torn southern part of the state.[25]

After spending more than a year trying to advance the Confederate cause in his native Louisiana, Taylor, too, had finally reached the limit of his endurance. The strain of battle, the burden of maintaining a clearly failing cause, and the pressures of his position broke him down. He suffered from rheumatoid arthritis, and his joints ached all the time. He was also so very tired—body and soul. He asked Kirby Smith to let him rest for a couple of months. "You know there is no one to take your place, even temporarily without great injury to the cause," Kirby Smith replied. "The Department cannot do without you." Taylor, enslaved by the war he had so craftily waged for two year, had to press on through the pain toward a doubtful future.[26]

Perhaps the most potent part of Taylor's Louisiana army was now in Texas. Major General Green's cavalry division had arrived in camps around Houston during the last week of 1863. Since then the soldiers had done little but shiver, freeze, and grumble amid a series of harsh winter storms.

Private William Randolph Howell, a stalwart from the 5th Texas Cavalry, received orders to go home to Grimes County and gather up socks for his company to help combat the miserable weather. He scribbled in his diary: "Glorious detail!"[27]

On his way back to his command, the veteran noticed rooms were scarce along his route. The state troops Major General Magruder had called up were going home. He found one boarding house where he had stayed many times before "greatly crowded by militia on their return." To him, this appeared to be a sign the danger from Union invasion had passed.[28]

The Confederates, nevertheless, behaved as though Texas remained under threat. Still chasing the potential of an invasion, Green's cavalry division had camped at Sandy Point southwest of Houston and halfway between Velasco and Galveston Island. From there the command rode to San Felipe, put their horses to pasture, and took the train to Virginia Point to serve as part of the Galveston garrison. "I don't think we will have a fight here," Sergeant John W. Watkins wrote his wife on January 25. "But Magruder thinks they will try this place first, which I hope they will do, as I am tired of running around to hunt up a fight. I would rather fight them here than anywhere else."[29]

Lieutenant General Kirby Smith came to Texas in late January. He met with Governor Pendleton Murrah and Major General Magruder in Houston to discuss items of interest to the state, including the use of its militia as a pool of recruits for Confederate units, the financial and material requirements of the Confederate government, and the strategic situation on the Texas coast. He also wanted to look around.[30]

Soon afterward, Green's men rode a train into Galveston on February 5 and assembled at the town cemetery. Kirby Smith, Magruder, and Green reviewed the troops the following day. Satisfied this division remained as deadly as ever, the officers ordered the men back to a month of quiet duty at Virginia Point.[31]

Green's veterans resumed old campaign habits. "Wood and water very scarce, oysters abundant," Howell noted blandly about the camps. The source of the shellfish, though, was not the ocean but a railway car near the picket posts. Before long, Rebel sentinels were busily shucking and gobbling the mollusks.

After spending one evening ransacking this bounty, Private Fred Wade of the 4th Texas Cavalry returned to camp and told his comrades in the company about the seafood. His news unleashed a tempest of plundering. When Wade returned to his guard post the next morning, he found nothing but wreckage. "When I got to the car, it was empty, but piles of shells were all around. I began to hunt for oysters among the shells." During his rummaging, he saw the owner of the freight, a well-dressed foreigner, approaching along the railroad tracks. "He ran up to the empty car, then yelled, 'you tam tieves, you stole my isters.'" The Rebel soldiers would not tolerate such rudeness in a man and began bombarding the merchant with oyster shells. "We . . . told him not to call us thieves. Away he went up the track, dropping his hat, cane, and big cigar."[32]

After their restful month, Green's Texans moved their camps. On February 27, the rough and ready troops at Virginia Point received orders to relocate to the Brazos River line where they would recover their horses, now well rested after two months at pasture. The brigade loaded onto railroad flat cars and chugged up the line to Houston, where they disembarked, awaiting a new train for Columbia. Officers ordered the men into line, marched them into a side street, and then had them face in toward the railway platform. The troops waited in formation for additional orders.

Idle soldiers always find diversions. Private Wade of the 4th Texas Cavalry now turned his greedy palate away from seafood and toward bigger game. "I looked under the platform and there lay two big white hogs. I leveled my pistol and fired." The squealing of the stricken pig, the discharge of the weapon, and the hurrahs of the troops brought regimental officers running. "Colonel Hampton came running up demanding, 'Where's the man that shot that hog." None of the soldiers seemed to know.[33]

Later that night, Wade and some comrades returned to downtown Houston and recovered his victim. "We found a negro family who agreed to clean and cook the meat on shares." Soon the oinker was simmering in a variety of pots and skillets while company officers organized a collection to buy bread and amenities to go with the feast. "All chipped in and made enough money to buy forty loaves of bread while the negros cleaned the hog, put some on to boil, some to stew, some to fry, and some to bake. We sopped the bread in the grease and stowed away all the pork we could hold, giving the rest to the darkies, going to our [blankets] happy and full. We were always happy when we got enough to eat, and mad when hungry."[34]

Green's Division finally boarded the train and joined the rest of Magruder's Texas army on the lower Brazos River. The weeks of waiting for the Federals to advance from Matagorda Bay continued. Green used the time to drill his troops four hours a day, getting them ready for whatever lay in store. The only excitement came from the Federal navy's frequent bombardments of the Confederate works on the coast, "driving the Negroes and militia from the earthworks," according to Private Augustus V. Ball of McMahan's Battery. He could hear the far-off rumblings from his camp more than twenty miles inland on Caney Creek at the crossing of the road to Victoria.[35]

The fortifications were not the only target. While the Federal navy did lob shells at the Rebel works, they only wasted a few before continuing up the coast on the prowl for any musket-laden schooners trying to enter Texas rivers and bays. "It may be at vessels running the blockade, several have come in lately," wrote Edward Arall Pye, a doctor serving in the 4th Infantry, Texas State Troops. "This is about all we have to enliven us." Bored, men of the 2nd Texas Infantry tried to goad the Yankee tars into sending a round or two toward shore. "These . . . boys are perfect dare-devils," Pye noted, "and are doubtless causing the firing by exposing themselves on the beach."[36]

For the most part, the Texans on the coast were relaxed and confident despite the occasional shelling. "We are living as well as we can desire and having a good time generally," Private Ball wrote his wife. The Federals would never break the Brazos line, Ball believed. "We are determined by the help of God, to whip them back to their own country and teach them the lessons that our forefathers taught Great Britain, that we ourselves are rich and fully competent to defend our rights against the north and if it need be the balance of mankind."[37]

Outside these camps, Confederate conscription laws swept every military age man into the ranks. With most liable for service already mustered in, it fell to the home guard—men too old or young to be enlisted for service—to enforce this law, as well as to collect Confederate tax-in-kind produce like corn, wool, and cotton from the area's farmers and ranchers. "It may be said that the old men who belonged to these companies were nearly always laid up with rheumatism, or other ailments, real or feigned, and were seldom on duty, thus leaving the burden of service to rest on these embryo heroes of rustic chivalry," observed John Warren Hunter, a young Unionist from northeast Texas. "Subordinate officers from captain down, were usually beardless youths. These rawhide soldiers soon became a terror to the people among whom they were thrown."[38]

Hunter had a close call with the home guard near Columbus, Texas. He had taken refuge in Mexico—but he had ventured back into Texas on an errand for friends in Matamoros. He nearly got caught. "We passed by their quarters . . . and I took care to count all in sight—twenty-two only, and only five or six of these men who seemed to be over twenty-five or thirty years old. The rest were mere boys, swaggering young bullies." The loitering guards, kids his age, carried outdated hunting or squirrel rifles, single barrel shotguns, pepperbox pistols, an occasional Enfield, and a smattering of revolvers, all of which they displayed prominently. Hunter did his best to steer clear of them.[39]

Confederate authorities knew better than to allow unsupervised teenaged thugs to serve in their home county. The power they wielded could clearly be abused, so Home Guard commands served a good distance from their friends and family, ostensibly so they could administer their duties without reservation or bias. As a result, they often used their position to rob, cheat, and steal from people who were essentially strangers. They also harassed travelers, accusing many of real or probable Unionist sympathies—even combat veterans home on furlough. "The unfortunate soldiers who had passed through the carnage of battle at the front had to remain in the guard house until their papers came back unless willing to part with horse, arms, or a moiety of cash, in the event of which he was allowed to escape," Hunter spat. These outrages led to locals referring to these youths as "heel-flies," after pesky livestock parasites. "No class of men, or rather striplings, in our great state has ever been the recipient of more righteous contempt heaped upon them."[40]

Joseph Freeborn Rowley, also dodging Confederate conscription, resumed his journey to freedom. He and his stepson Fred again left their home in Hays County and made their way back toward Port Lavaca, hoping to enter the

Union lines there. Traveling at night, they navigated past Confederate camps and posts along Garcitas Creek. When they reached Port Lavaca, they found it deserted.[41]

Frustrated, Rowley changed his plans yet again, hoping now to reach Indianola. He learned Norris's Bridge over Big Chocolate Bayou had burned, blocking his route. They approached a nearby home, hoping for sympathy and directions. They proceeded with caution and soon were invited into the house. Instead of hospitality, the woman at home alerted other men staying in another room. "We drew our six-shooters and waited and so four men made their appearance and spoke very polite," Rowley remembered. "I returned the compliment as polite as them." The men told him nothing useful, so he and Fred turned to go. Before they could leave, the four men drew pistols. "Gentlemen, I will take you prisoner," their leader said.[42]

"We will see about that," Rowley replied. A close-range shootout occurred, and Rowley and Fred dashed out the door, caught their horses, and spurred away. Flashes of pistol fire came from the cabin as they fled. They rode for a mile but, fearing they would blunder into Confederate pickets, decided to stop, "supposing

A scene from the diary of Joseph F. Rowley, showing his attempt to reach Union lines at Lavaca but running afoul of Confederate pickets. J. F. *Rowley Diary, Ragan* MSS 00118, Box 1, *Cushing Memorial Library and Archives, Texas A&M University.*

the Federals would send troops in the morning to our assistance knowing they must have seen the flash of their guns." His prudence proved fortuitous. When dawn broke, Rowley saw enemy sentinels only three hundred yards away.[43]

Now he and Fred were boxed in, but they got on their horses and looked for a way out. Within minutes three riders approached, colts and Enfield ablaze. Unable to outride their pursuers, Rowley told Fred, "we will stop and whip them." When they dismounted, so did the posse. Rowley believed they were waiting for reinforcements. He was right. Three more men arrived, and the Confederates cautiously walked their horses toward the refugees. The six soldiers told Rowley to surrender. "Kiss my ass, God damn you," Rowley responded.[44]

The soldiers opened fire. Rowley and Fred remounted and galloped as hard as they could, making sure to ditch their Union passes. After a sixteen-mile chase, during which their pursuers had shot away most of their ammunition, Rowley flinched as a bullet cut his thigh.

Bleeding heavily, Rowley was ready to surrender. His stepson, however, was not. Rowley agreed to hold off the Rebels while Fred made his escape. "I thought I would bleed to death in a few minutes," Rowley wrote later. The pair bade each other a quick farewell, and Rowley turned to face the attackers.[45]

Rowley holds off his Confederate pursuers, hoping his stepson Fred will escape. Niether did. A scene from his diary. J. F. *Rowley Diary*, Ragan MSS 00118, Box 1, *Cushing Memorial Library and Archives, Texas A&M University.*

The Confederates again demanded that Rowley surrender. "I told them I would if they gave me assurances of a fair trial," he wrote. They agreed and continued toward him. When they were within pistol range, Rowley told the six to halt. "I told them that I would not surrender for them to kill unarmed." Again, the Rebels gave assurances and advanced. Rowley stopped them a third time, at nearly point-blank range, and again they promised a fair trial. Faint from blood loss, Rowley dropped his pistol. He was now a prisoner of the 33rd Texas Cavalry. The Confederates pursued Fred another four miles before they caught him.[46]

Hauled in a mule wagon across "the roughest hogwaller prairie," the prisoners passed from camp to camp for the next few weeks. They were charged with desertion, spying, and being traitors and Confederate officers referred the case to trial in Houston. Rowley and Fred headed for Columbia, Texas.

Confederates tossed Rowley into a jail cell in the county courthouse. "Green's brigade was there," he noted. That night, a band struck up some lively airs and marched toward the town square. "I thought our time had come," Rowley wrote, "for hanging was in fashion here." Instead, the band played, and troops marched, but no one came for him. He realized he was safe. "It was old Green, on a drunk." The next day, Rowley was bound on a train for Houston.

Eventually, judges released Rowley and Fred on the condition they serve in the 1st Texas Heavy Artillery in the forts on Galveston Island. Rowley was a Confederate after all.[47]

The Confederacy had become oppressive for its citizens in other ways as well. Not only did officials control people's lives, livestock, crops, and equipment, but they also commanded their slaves. Black hands built the Rebel fortifications. "The last Negro is taken from some places," complained Dr. Pye, "I don't think Magruder cares if the people of Texas starve." He hoped his field hands remained at home. "Do keep the plough going," he admonished his wife back on the farm near Hempstead, "so that if you should happen to be spared, we may have something to eat next year."[48]

Amid the brutality of the Confederate regime, morale among the militia sank. "Poor fellows, they are mighty gloomy and out of spirits," Pye noted. "Most of them abuse old Magruder and the war, each one considering himself the worst off of any man in the Confederacy." Despite the grousing, the doctor believed he

This sketch from J. F. Rowley's diary shows the conditions under which he was kept while a prisoner of the Confederates of the 33rd Texas Cavalry. He was chained to a tree. *J. F. Rowley Diary, Ragan MSS 00118, Box 1, Cushing Memorial Library and Archives, Texas A&M University*

and his comrades would soon be heading home. "I have no idea that the state is in danger of invasion this spring," he assured his wife. "I believe the Yankees are trying to keep us from making anything to eat next year—so far they are succeeding admirably. They have pulled the wool over Magruder's eyes I am afraid."[49]

Even soldiers enlisted in the Confederate army sensed the despair. Austrian-born Private Rudolph Coreth agreed the situation on the Texas coast seemed low. Major General Magruder had ordered planters on the Texas coastal plains to move their slaves and livestock well inland—at least seventy-five miles—to keep them out of Yankee hands. Since then, a swath of agricultural territory stretching from the Gulf of Mexico nearly to the old town of Gonzales lay abandoned. "Thus the fields are remaining uncultivated, and furthermore," Coreth added, "the Negroes . . . eat up a lot of provisions too which until now have been for the army's benefit." The farms of Texans who held no slaves also fell fallow, because Magruder's mobilization of state troops had taken farmers away from their plows. "Confidence in this war has now sunken very much," Coreth confided to his family, "even among the Americans. I talked yesterday with several and they were all in accord with one another that they would rather have mules than Negroes and Confederate money."[50]

Yet something else was stirring in this part of the decomposing Confederacy. Travelers on Texan roads might have noticed heavily laden freight wagons heading northeast toward Shreveport. The decision of the Lincoln administration to abide the French intervention in Mexican affairs—for the time being—and to abandon Texas to the Confederates had military implications. In the summer and fall of 1863, French warships had seized the vessels *Love Bird, Caroline Goodyear,* and *Nancy Dawson* and their loads of thousands of British Enfield rifled-muskets bound for Confederate buyers. At the time the move had pleased U.S. authorities and angered the Confederates. Now that France was neutral in the American Civil War, French authorities released the weapons and allowed them to continue on to their destinations. This war matrial passed through the interior of Texas by the wagonload, bound for Rebel soldiers operating in Arkansas and Louisiana.

The firearms, percussion caps, and cartridges would come in handy for the spring campaigns of 1864.[51]

EPILOGUE   **AGAIN**

"Ordered to Louisiana—again."
—Private William Randolph Howell
5th Texas Cavalry

ajor General Nathaniel P. Banks was a politician. Born to working-class parents serving the textile industry in Massachusetts, his gift for oratory had propelled him above his plebian origins and into a political career. He had climbed the ladder from the state legislature, to Congress, and into the governor's seat at the Massachusetts State House on Beacon Hill. He successfully navigated the roiling partisan waters of the 1850s to emerge as a prominent national figure and a standard-bearer of the newly formed Republican Party. Some believed he would eventually win the White House. More than most, Banks understood what it meant to be politically undermined. He knew exactly what had happened to him in Louisiana.

Before the war Banks had been a moderate, and it had cost him. As radicals in his party beat the drums of war, he had found himself out of step with the political mood. He left politics for a position with an Illinois railroad in 1860, in a development many interpreted as a professional exile. This move indeed damaged his reputation, and newly elected President Abraham Lincoln eschewed Banks for a cabinet appointment, probably because his political connections in Massachusetts had grown stale.

When war erupted, however, Lincoln appointed Banks as one the first major generals of the rapidly expanding Union army—in essence, a way of enlisting what was left of Banks's political capital. Banks demonstrated merit in the early part of the war. Maryland remained in the Union largely through the political skill he brought to his new command. Assigned first to Baltimore, then to the western reaches of the state, his suppression of secessionists' sentiments and assignment of Unionists to key administrative positions was a winning formula. With Maryland trending toward loyalty to the Union by early 1862 and with his bona fides established, Banks looked forward to demonstrating his skills in battle. Every American politician understood the buoying effect gunpowder brought to political ambitions.

War, however, is a chancy proposition. Cannon and muskets are not as easily manipulated as voters. In May 1862 the Massachusetts politician had been outfoxed by General Thomas J. "Stonewall" Jackson in the Shenandoah Valley and had earned the sobriquet "Commissary Banks," a label which would follow him into posterity. He rehabilitated his reputation somewhat by being conveniently injured in combat at Cedar Mountain at the beginning of the Second Manassas Campaign. While convalescing, he spent some time using his administrative skills to organize the defenses of Washington, D.C. In that capacity he developed a cordial relationship with President Lincoln.

His status refreshed and his body restored, Banks went to New Orleans at the head of a special mission at the behest of the White House. He was given an army of thirty thousand men, half of whom were essentially militia loaned for nine months from governors in New England. Here was the perfect combination of political connections and a military campaign in a theater considered less hazardous than others. Banks, as the commander of this people's army in the Department of the Gulf, was to restore Federal control to Louisiana, bring the state back into the Union, aid in the capture of the Mississippi, and make a loyal enclave in Texas. Success in this broad venture, Banks understood, would cement his reputation as the premier citizen-soldier of the republic. He would be a hero back home in New England.

In Louisiana, the Confederates boasted no Stonewall Jackson to bedevil Banks. There was instead a fallen angel, Richard, President Zachary Taylor's boy gone wrong, now an enemy major general. His minions, Alfred Mouton and Tom Green, should have been no match for the power and resources of the national effort to suppress them. Yet, these enemies proved to be a source of constant annoyance for a commander with borrowed troops and limited time. Banks spent the first half of 1863 trying to break the back of the rebellion in Louisiana.

He successfully captured Port Hudson in the process, but he only gathered political plaudits from his New England base. To his surprise, his Army of the Gulf was eclipsed by the exploits of the mudsill Midwesterners of the Army of the Tennessee. He also witnessed his own reputation recede into the shadow of Major General Ulysses S. Grant. How could this be? He outranked Grant!

Aggravations came not only from the Confederates but also from Banks's own government. His orders and his priorities kept changing. One of the most complicated, and most mentally consuming, was the directive to militarize the enslaved population of Louisiana and help raise an army of one hundred thousand black troops. This order complicated his transportation and logistics network, distracted his field commanders, and caused a manpower and talent drain as veteran Yankees transferred to these new regiments to turn raw recruits, most fresh from the sugarcane and cotton fields, and many who spoke only French, into a useful fighting force.

The government demanded more from Banks. General-in-Chief Henry Halleck, driven by Lincoln's demands, ordered Banks to vanquish the Rebel troops in western Louisiana. This meant the Army of the Gulf needed to destroy Taylor's command and prevent it from regenerating. Banks knew this would not be easy. The geography of western Louisiana made campaigning difficult. The Army of the Gulf was also at the farthest end of the Union logistics line, and mundane but vital items like wagons, bridging equipment, and the animals to haul them seemed always in short supply. Based on sheer numbers, the Confederates in western Louisiana should have been easy to overcome, but Louisiana itself multiplied the strength of the enemy in ways few in Washington appreciated.

In addition, the Confederates had embarrassed Banks. Taylor, who had been a student of war under the tutelage of Stonewall Jackson, had become an aggressive field commander. He could be counted on to strike whenever possible and to contest any ground he could. His most capable lieutenant, Green, led a highly mobile strike force of mounted Texans like a rattlesnake at any trespass. Banks may have feared him.

Then, Lincoln assigned Banks another Sisyphean task. The Army of the Gulf would be the hammer of the republic in an international faceoff. The French, meddling in Mexico, needed to see an American flag over Texas, and Banks and his command were the closest at hand. So, while simultaneously destroying the Confederate army in Louisiana, raising an army of black troops, and reorganizing and reconstructing Louisiana, Banks also had to "plant the flag in Texas."

To accomplish all of this, Banks had an ever-shifting army. Half of Banks's original command—the New England nine-month's men—went home, their short tenure in the army expired. The soldiers who had become veterans in the trenches at Port Hudson left. To assuage this loss, Grant sent Banks the seasoned fifteen-thousand-man 13th Army Corps. This gave Banks, he believed, nearly enough, but not all, the men he needed to accomplish his ever-growing chore list.

The fickle nature of the Lincoln administration compounded Banks's problems. Banks had successfully designed and implemented a quick invasion of Texas that had yielded promising diplomatic dividends. French shenanigans on the Gulf Coast seemed to be curtailed, and the illicit cotton trade, which was financing the Rebel cause west of the Mississippi, seemed on the verge of collapse. Halleck, resenting Banks for his success, ordered him out of Texas and back into Louisiana to pursue a campaign Banks did not want.

In the eyes of many Union officers in the Department of the Gulf, Banks seemed to be out of his depth. "Seven months has thus been spent in desultory adventures and multitudinous preparations without a serious military object," complained Lieutenant Colonel Richard B. Irwin of the 19th Army Corps.[1]

As winter faded into spring, Banks found a clarity of purpose. No longer burdened by active campaigns or the need to design his next offensive, he could return to his natural gift, politics. He would focus on restoring Louisiana to the Union, as a free state, with its capital in New Orleans. To facilitate the reconstruction of the Pelican State, Banks would impose a new racial order, as Lincoln had asked.

Banks's efforts were described and debated throughout New Orleans and beyond. Charles Prosper Fauconnet, a French diplomat in the Crescent City, described the political landscape to the foreign office in Paris. "In the city, the great questions of the day, the ones that presently dominate everyone's thoughts, are the elections and the reestablishment of the state government," he reported. "Meetings take place almost daily, and speeches are made by Unionists of every stripe." He described three principal factions: those for preserving the Louisiana constitution as it was, including the preservation of slavery; another, which wanted to scrap the document and remake it to abolish slavery. There was a third, an "ultra-abolitionist faction under the leadership of Mr. Thomas Durant, a former lawyer of this city and presently the attorney general of the United States," Fauconnet wrote. "The group that Mr. Durant represents is not only abolitionist, but they also seek to elevate Negroes to the same legal status as whites. In a word, they clamor for them to have the same rights, privileges, and social and political immunities attached to the status of citizen of the United States."[2]

The Frenchman did not trust Durant's motives. The faction claimed a devotion to the universal principles of human rights, but Fauconnet suggested there was "more ambition than genuine beneficence . . . the Negro is merely the means by which it hopes to take uncontested control over the state and become master of its destiny."[3]

The other abolitionist faction held a lower opinion of black people. "While accepting emancipation under the terms set out by President Lincoln," Fauconnet pointed out, this group "formally rejects the extension of political rights to Negroes." He believed this faction, too, believed liberated slaves transitioning into freedmen were merely tools giving politicians leverage to redraw the state constitution to their benefit. Their position "specifically claims that Congress abolished slavery in the territories and that Louisiana, having become a territory as a result of the rebellion, cannot reenter the Union and be restored to the ranks of the states except by means of a free constitution." Clearly, slavery would never survive readmission to the Union.[4]

In early February 1864, Banks issued General Orders 23, a set of twenty-five rules in which he regulated paid plantation labor. For example, press gangs could no longer force laborers on plantations into the army. Banks imposed measures to keep black families from harm, including establishing hospitals and recognizing the legal status of marriages. Unauthorized trade in liquor and clothing would be prohibited, and firearm ownership would be forbidden. Planters employing black laborers had obligations to protect, manage, and encourage their hands with adequate food, lodging, medical care, and education. Planters also had to treat them fairly.[5]

Against this backdrop, Banks sought a new order for Louisiana, especially for freedmen and freedwomen. "General Banks intends not only to regulate labor and make it obligatory for both farmers and blacks, but he seems to be making preparatory steps to make the latter future farmers, even landowners," the New York Times reported. "Far from encouraging the immigration of Negroes to other countries, he wishes to attach them more than ever to the land, and he invites other military departments to send him their superfluous black families."[6]

Black laborers also had responsibilities. "*Wages will be deducted in case of sickness, and rations, also, when sickness is feigned. Indolence, insolence, disobedience of orders, and crime, will be suppressed by forfeiture of pay, and such punishments as are provided for similar offences by Army Regulations.*"[7]

Having implemented a system of paid labor on southern Louisiana plantations, Banks would proceed to manage the campaign he had been assigned, powerful and punitive, that would scourge secessionists and annihilate the Confederate menace once and for all. His soldiers would once again take Alexandria and this time press on to Shreveport and finish the job started in the spring of 1863. The Rebels would be driven into Texas, and the Red River Valley would become the edge of Freedom. The enemy would be driven two hundred miles away from the Mississippi River, and Banks would once again be a hero. His message to the people of Louisiana was simple: take the oath of allegiance, conform to the new order, or lose your place. "All who contribute to this restoration project," Banks attested, at least according to Fauconnet, "render the government a service as great as those who have endured the terrible sacrifices of war."[8]

The reconstruction of Louisiana, one compatible with an abolitionist and Republican vision of the country, would surge forward. For the people of Louisiana who would be subjected to this latest Union effort to reverse the rebellion, life would remain a daily struggle—a strange existence between a failed insurgent government and a remote, yet looming, punitive response. For these simple folk—Unionists or Secessionist—there were no meetings around maps in headquarters, no discussions of grand strategy or movements of men, and no ceremonies and speeches. There was only the reality of their misery brought about by the war.

In mid-February, a Confederate jailer in Vermilionville jabbed a key into the lock at the parish hoosegow, turned it until it clicked, then swung open the creaking iron door. Dennis Haynes, the much-abused Texas Unionist, was once again free. Slightly bewildered, he did the only thing he knew to do—he returned to the shelter of Ozémé Carrière's Clan. Once again in the home of the prairie poor, northwest of Opelousas, Haynes rested, bathed, and got new clothing. A new man, he once again plotted his route into Union lines.[9]

This time Haynes had a better plan. He determined to make his way to the Federal outposts at Morganza or Port Hudson. He had met a man in jail who had convinced him east, rather than south, was the way to freedom in Louisiana. Restored and healthy, Haynes headed toward Washington, Louisiana, intending to ride a cotton barge down Bayou Courtableau to the Atchafalaya River. Arriving in Washington, he learned Confederate agents controlled all the traffic on the bayou and all of the cotton trade in the region. This part of his scheme would not do. He came up with another plan.

On February 16, Haynes left Washington on foot amid an unusual snowfall, this time posing as an itinerate teacher in search of a school. Once again, his wiles and guile served him well. He slipped through Confederate lines, crossed the Atchafalaya just below Morgan's Ferry, walked across the battleground of Sterling's plantation, and headed south to Bayou Grosse Tête, narrowly avoiding Rebel patrols. With the assistance of slaves and freedmen along the way, he at last emerged at False River near New Roads in Pointe Coupee Parish. He eventually reached the banks of the Mississippi, saw the U.S. flag floating above the earthworks at Port Hudson, and was soon across the river to liberty.[10]

"I here subscribed to the 'Iron-clad' [oath] and got transportation to New Orleans," Haynes boasted. "I was anxious to get to Franklin and inform the commanding officer there of the 'situation' in his front." Arriving at the Crescent

City, he fell in with the growing Texas refugee community and met with Brigadier General Andrew Jackson Hamilton, the Texas governor.[11]

Haynes found New Orleans to be a hive of activity. Elections for a new government were afoot, and the contest was heated. Michael Hahn, a German immigrant who had risen to serve as one of Louisiana's representatives to Congress in 1862, now ran to be its first Union governor since secession. Politicians were eager to meet Haynes, hoping to use his tales of hardship and suffering to bolster their anti-Confederate position. After meeting a number of eager candidates, officials, and soldiers—including Major General Banks—Haynes wrote an account of his travails and had it published in the *New Orleans Times*. Then he returned to his personal quest.

A meeting with Brigadier General Charles Pomeroy Stone, the chief of staff for the Department of the Gulf, launched Haynes toward his ultimate goal: revenge. Armed with an officer's commission, he found himself once again heading toward danger, this time with orders to report for duty at Franklin, Louisiana, as a scout for the Federal 19th Army Corps. Traveling by railroad and steamboat, he arrived rested and ready. He presented his credentials to the headquarters of an army readying for a spring campaign. For the moment, he was safe.[12]

An army underway, heading to war in late February 1864. The Mississippi Gunboat Flotilla escorts transports carrying Brigadier General Andrew Jackson Smith and elements of the XVI and XVII Army Corps, leaving Vicksburg and bound for the Red River to reinforce the Army of the Gulf. Francis H. Schell and Thomas Hogan, illustrators. From *Battles and Leaders of the Civil War* (New York: The Century Company, 1888).

About three hundred miles away, on the banks of the Brazos River, the weather was growing fresh, the air was warm, and the grass was turning green. Miles of encampments stretched across the Texas prairies, and the motions and sounds of military routines showed the sap rising in this far-away Confederate army.

Private William Randolph Howell, one of Green's Texans, had regained his fighting strength, if not his Confederate ardor, over the winter. A veteran of nearly three years of war—he had fought in New Mexico, at Galveston, in the Teche Campaign, on Bayou Lafourche, and around Opelousas—he knew something was brewing. A telegraph key had clattered at the end of the line on the Texas and New Orleans railroad, and dispatch riders carried the news across the Brazos River to Columbia. Howell, the veteran campaigner, watched the buzz ripple through the tent cities and down the well-rutted roads between bivouacs.[13]

He knew instinctively what was on the wind. When an excited comrade confirmed his suspicions, Howell took the news stoically. He pulled out his well-thumbed diary, fingered a field-grimed pencil, and scribbled a new entry for March 7, 1864.

"Ordered to Louisiana—again."[14]

ENDNOTES

CHAPTER ONE

1   Ignacio Zaragoza, *Cartas y Documentos, selección, introducción y notas de Jorge L. Tamayo* (Mexico: Fondo de Cultura Económica, 2006), 90–93.

2   For a more thorough discussion of this effort, see Nancy N. Barker, "Monarchy in Mexico: Hairbrained Scheme or Well-Considered Prospect?" *Journal of Modern History* 48 (March 1976): 51–68. See also Thomas Schoonover, "Napoleon is Coming! Maximilian is Coming? The International History of the Civil War in the Caribbean Basin," in Robert E. May, ed., *The Union, The Confederacy, and the Atlantic Rim* (West Lafayette, IN: Purdue University Press, 1995), 101–30.

3   U.S. Congress, Senate, *Message from the President of the United States*, 38th Cong., 2d. sess., Senate Ex. Doc. No. 11:281.

4   Dubois de Saligny to Edouard Antoine de Thouvenel, July 27, 1861, in Barker, "Monarchy in Mexico," 63. Dubois de Saligny had, a decade and a half before, represented French interests in Austin, Texas, as envoy to the Republic of Texas, before leaving in a huff over what he considered poor treatment related to an incident involving pigs that had ransacked his quarters.

5   *Chicago Tribune*, June 13, 1867, quoted in Thomas Schoonover, *Dollars over Dominion: The Triumph of Liberalism in Mexican–United States Relations, 1861–1867* (Baton Rouge: Louisiana State University Press, 1978), 280; *Charleston Mercury*, February 3, 1862. This thesis is excellently expanded to a great extent in Patrick J. Kelly, "The North American Crisis of the 1860s," *Journal of the Civil War Era* 2, No. 3 (September 2012): 337–68.

6   John Slidell to James Mason, June 6, 1862, quoted in Louis Martin Sears, *John Slidell* (Durham, North Carolina: Duke University Press, 1925), 300.

7   Justo Sierra, *The Political Evolution of the Mexican People*, with notes and introduction by Edmundo O'Gorman, trans. Charles Ramsdell (Austin: University of Texas Press, 1969), 312.

8   As published in Percy F. Martin, *Maximillian in Mexico: The Story of the French Intervention, 1861–1867* (New York: Charles Scribner's Sons, 1914), 107–108.

9   Ibid.

10 A sister ship to the more famous *Gloire* and *Invincible*.

11 The French needed a base where they could gather cattle and mules to supply their army farther south. Other vessels in the French squadron included the *Messéna*, the mortar vessel *Grenade*, and the transport *Dryade*. See David Marley, ed., *Wars of the Americas: Chronology of Armed Conflict in the Western Hemisphere, 1492 to the Present* (Denver: ABC Clio, 2008), 2:830; Jack Greene and Alessandro Massignani, *Ironclads at War: The Origin and Development of the Armored Battleship* (New York: Da Capo, 1998), 110.

12   H. P. Bee to S. S. Anderson, November 30, 1862, in U.S. War Department, *The War of the Rebellion, A Compilation of the Official Records of the Union and Confederate Armies* (Washington, DC: Government Printing Office, 1880–1901), Series I, vol. 15, 881. Hereafter cited as OR, with all references to Series I unless otherwise specified.

13   Delaney, Robert W., "Matamoros, Port for Texas during the Civil War," *The Southwestern Historical Quarterly* 58, no. 4 (1955): 473-87. *http://www.jstor.org/stable/30241907.*

14   H. P. Bee to S. S. Anderson, November 30, 1862, OR, vol. 15, 881.

15   *Papers Relative to Mexican Affairs, Communicated to the Senate June 16, 1864* (Washington, DC: Government Printing Office, 1865), 86, 97. Colonel Rafael de la Garza and Republican troops swept back into town and pounced upon the French as they withdrew, forcing them to burn the grounded warship *Lance* and the sidewheel lighter *Reforma* to prevent their capture. Republicans also seized three supply vessels that had also failed to reach the open ocean, including an American registered vessel, *Eugenia*, laden with munitions; the *Indus*, loaded with provisions; and the coal vessel *Britain and France.*

16   Thomas D. Schoonover, *Mexican Lobby: Matías Romero in Washington, 1861–1867* (Lexington: University Press of Kentucky, 2008), 28–32; Jason H. Silverman, "A Most Unlikely Friendship: Abraham Lincoln and Matias Romero," the website for President Lincoln's Cottage, January 26, 2017, *http://www.lincolncottage.org/a-most-unlikely-friendship-abraham-lincoln-and-matias-romero/#_ednref26.*

17   Robert Ryal Miller, "The American Legion of Honor in Mexico," *Pacific Historical Review* 30, no. 3 (August 1961): 231.

18   James Schouler, *History of the United States of America under the Constitution*, vol. 6, 1861-1865 (New York: Dodd, Mead, 1899), 428-29.

19   Richard B. Irwin, *History of the Nineteenth Army Corps* (New York: G. P. Putnam's Sons, 1893), 265.

20   Irwin, *Nineteenth Army Corps*, 266.

CHAPTER TWO

1   Edwin M. Stanton to Thurlow Weed, July 15, 1863, OR, vol. 27, pt. 2: 921.

2   Henry W. Halleck to Nathaniel P. Banks, July 24, 1863, OR, vol 26, pt. 1: 652–53.

3   Ulysses S. Grant, *Personal Memoirs of U. S. Grant* (New York: Century Company, 1895), 1:578–80.

4   Ibid.

5   Abraham Lincoln to Stanton, July 29, 1863, in *The Collected Works of Abraham Lincoln*, ed. Roy P. Basler (New Brunswick, NJ: Rutgers University Press, 1953), 6:354.

6   Banks to Halleck, July 30, 1863, OR, vol. 26, pt. 1: 663–64; "Abstract from returns of the Department of the Gulf, Major General Dabney H. Maury, C.S. Army, commanding, for September 30, 1863, headquarters, Mobile, Alabama," OR, vol. 26, pt. 2: 280.

7   Banks to Halleck, July 30, 1863, OR, vol. 26, pt. 1: 663–64; Grant, *Personal Memoirs*, 1:578–80.

8   Grant, *Personal Memoirs*, 1:578–80.

9   Irwin, *Nineteenth Army Corps*, 264–65.

10   Lincoln, Abraham, *Abraham Lincoln papers: Series 1. General Correspondence. 1833 to 1916: Leslie Combs to Abraham Lincoln, Tuesday, March 18,1862. Military advice.* Manuscript/Mixed Material. *https://www.loc.gov/item/mal1512500/.*

11   Banks to Halleck, July 30, 1863, OR, vol. 26, pt. 1: 663–64.

12   Lincoln to Stanton, July 29, 1863, OR, vol. 26, pt. 1: 659; Grant, *Personal Memoirs*, 1:484.

13   Grant, *Personal Memoirs*, 1: 578–80.

14   Ibid.

15   William Royston Geise, "The Confederate Military Forces in the Trans-Mississippi, 1861–1865: A Study in Command," (Ph.D. dissertation, University of Texas at Austin, 1974), 158.

16 David Dixon Porter to Gideon Welles, August 16, 1863, U.S. Naval War Records Office, *Official Records of the Union and Confederate Navies in the War of the Rebellion*, 27 vols. (Washington, DC: Government Printing Office, 1894–1922), (hereafter cited as ORN) vol. 25: 370; Banks to Porter, October 17, 1863, ORN, vol. 25: 502.

17 Lincoln to Grant, August 9, 1863, *Collected Works*, 6:374.

18 Grant, *Personal Memoirs*, 1:341.

19 Grant, *Personal Memoirs*, 1:578–80; Irwin, *Nineteenth Army Corps*, 258.

20 Lincoln to Banks, August 5, 1863, *Collected Works*, 6:364–65; Halleck to Banks, August 6, 1863, OR, vol. 26, pt. 1: 672.

21 "The Capture of Tampico by the French," *New York Times*, September 17, 1863.

22 Ibid.

23 Halleck to Banks, July 24, 1863, OR, vol. 26, pt. 1: 652–53.

24 Robert S. Weddell, *Plow-Horse Cavalry: The Caney Creek Boys of the Thirty-Fourth Texas* (Austin, Texas: Madrona Press, 1974), 94.

25 George L. Andrews to Richard Irwin, August 6, 1863, OR, vol. 26, pt. 1: 238; William H. Dobak, *Freedom by the Sword: The U.S. Colored Troops, 1862–1867* (Washington, DC: Center of Military History, 2011), 110; H. Soule to My Darling Mary, September 24, 1863, H. Soule Papers, Bentley Historical Library, University of Michigan.

26 Carl A. Brasseaux and Catherine Carmines Mooney, eds., *Ruined by this Miserable War: The Dispatches of Charles Prosper Fauconnet, a French Diplomat in New Orleans, 1863–1868* (Knoxville: University of Tennessee Press, 2012), 12–13.

27 Banks to Lincoln, August 17, 1863, Abraham Lincoln Papers, Library of Congress, Washington, DC, transcribed and annotated by the Lincoln Studies Center, Knox College, Galesburg, IL.

28 Banks to Halleck, August 26, 1863, OR, vol. 26, pt. 1: 697.

29 Christopher Peña, *Scarred by War: Civil War in Southeast Louisiana* (Bloomington, IN: Authorhouse, 2004), 339.

30 Edwin M. Stanton to George Shepley, August 24, 1863, OR, Ser. 3, vol. 3: 711.

31 Lincoln, *Collected Works*, 6:365.

32 Banks to Halleck, August 26, 1863, OR, vol. 26, pt. 1: 696; Banks to Edwin M. Stanton, April 6, 1865, OR, vol. 26, pt. 1: 18.

33 Banks to Halleck, August 26, 1863, OR, vol. 26, pt. 1: 696.

34 Ibid.

35 Ibid.

36 Banks to Halleck, September 21, 1863, OR, vol. 26, pt. 1: 729; Banks to Halleck, August 26, 1863, OR, vol. 26, pt. 1: 696.

37 Banks to Stanton, April 6, 1865, OR, vol. 26, pt. 1: 18.

38 Grant to Lincoln, August 23, 1863, *Collected Works*, 6:374–75.

39 P. H. Fowler, *Memorial of William Fowler* (New York: Anson D. F. Randolph, 1875), 65; Orton S. Clark, *The One Hundred and Sixteenth Regiment of New York State Volunteers* (Buffalo: Matthews and Warren, 1868), 124.

40 Lincoln, August 26, 1863, *Collected Works*, 6:406–7.

41 Ibid., 6:410.

42 Ibid.

CHAPTER THREE
1 William R. Bradfute to E. P. Turner, July 15, 1863, and Bradfute to Turner, November 27, 1863, *Compiled Service Records of Confederate Soldiers Who Served in Organizations from the State of Texas*, W. R. Bradfute, RG 109, M323, National Archives and Records Administration, hereafter cited as CSR-T W. R. Bradfute.

2 As quoted in Bruce S. Allardice, *Confederate Colonels: A Biographical Register* (Columbia: University of Missouri Press, 2008), 72; CSR-T W. R. Bradfute.

3   The Texans in Bradfute's Brigade were the 20th, 22nd, 31st, and 34th Texas Cavalry, two of which became part of Brigadier General Camille Polignac's Brigade. See Alwyn Barr, *Polignac's Texas Brigade* (College Station: Texas A & M University Press, 1998), 8–9.

4   Frank E. Vandiver, ed., *The Civil War Diary of General Josiah Gorgas* (Tuscaloosa: University of Alabama Press, 1947), 39.

5   "Abstract from returns of the Trans-Mississippi Department, Lieutenant General E. Kirby Smith, C. S. Army, commanding, for September, 1863," OR, vol. 26, pt. 2: 280–82.

6   Robert L. Kerby, *Kirby Smith's Confederacy: The Trans-Mississippi South, 1863–1865* (Tuscaloosa: University of Alabama Press, 1972), 137; John B. Magruder, "Proclamation," July 16, 1863, OR, vol. 26, pt. 2: 114–15.

7   Kerby, *Kirby Smith's Confederacy*, 144.

8   *Richmond Examiner*, July 21, 1863.

9   See Ronnie C. Tyler, "Cotton on the Border, 1861–1865," *Southwestern Historical Quarterly* 73, no. 4 (April 1970): 456–77. A thorough and more recent discussion of the Mexican cotton trade is James W. Daddysman, *The Matamoros Trade: Confederate Commerce, Diplomacy, and Intrigue* (Newark: University of Delaware Press, 1984).

10   *New York Herald*, July 29, 1865.

11   Richard King played a key role in Confederate commerce in South Texas. See Don Graham, *Kings of Texas: The 150-Year Ranching Saga of an American Ranching Empire* (Hoboken, NJ: John Wiley, 2003), 96–110.

12   Sir Arthur James Lyon Fremantle, *Three Months in the Southern States: April–June, 1863* (Mobile, AL: S. H. Goetzel, 1864), 16; John Warren Hunter, *The Fall of Brownsville on the Rio Grande, November 1863* (Brownsville, TX: printed by the author, 1950), 6; Daddysman, *Matamoros Trade*, 109.

13   E. B. Cox to E. McIlhenny, August 15, 1863, Sarah Avery McIlhenny Collection, McIlhenny Company Archives, McIlhenny Company, Avery Island, LA.

14   William Frederick Weeks to Judge John Moore, October 31, 1863, David Weeks and Family Papers, Louisiana and Lower Mississippi Valley Collection, Hill Memorial Library, Louisiana State University.

15   John Q. Anderson, ed., *Brokenburn: The Journal of Kate Stone, 1861–1868* (Baton Rouge: Louisiana State University Press, 1955), 191.

16   Mary Eliza Avery McIlhenny to Sister Anna, August 23, 1863, McIlhenny Collection.

17   Anderson, *Brokenburn*, 230; Mary Eliza Avery McIlhenny to Sister Anna, August 23, 1863, McIlhenny Collection.

18   Anderson, *Brokenburn*, 23.

19   W. L. Robards to Editor, July 27, 1863, *Houston Tri-Weekly Telegraph*, August 10, 1863, p. 2.

20   Ibid.

21   F. S. Wade, "Hog Eye Stories," 43, typescript in possession of the author, originally published in the Elgin (Texas) *Courier*.

22   Jerry Bryan Lincecum, Edward Hake Phillips, and Peggy A. Redshaw, eds., *Gideon Lincecum's Sword: Civil War Letters from the Texas Home Front* (Denton: University of North Texas Press, 2001), 225.

23   Ibid., 242–43.

24   Sarah Corothers to William Corothers, n.d., Duncan Corothers Collection, Texas State Library and Archives, Austin, Texas.

25   Confederate States Army, Department of the Trans-Mississippi, Headquarters, Bureau of Conscripts, Elkanah Greer and William Stedman, "General Orders Number 7," August 4, 1863, Confederate Imprints, Confederate Pamphlet 394, Manuscript Department, William R. Perkins Library, Duke University.

26   J. F. Rowley Diary, 1, August 27, 1863, Ragan MSS 00118, Box 1, Cushing Memorial Library and Archives, Texas A & M University.

27   Rowley Diary, 2, August 27, 1863.

28 Abram Sells in Work Progress Administration, *Slave Narratives: A Folk History of Slavery in the United States from Interviews with Former Slaves*, vol. 16, *Texas Narratives* (Washington, DC: Government Printing Office, 1941), pt. 4:44–46.

29 H. T. Douglas, "Circular, Department of the Trans-Mississippi, Headquarters Engineering Department, Shreveport, Louisiana, August 3, 1863," Confederate Imprints, Confederate Pamphlet 306, Manuscript Department, William R. Perkins Library, Duke University, Durham, North Carolina.

30 Edmund Kirby Smith to Sterling Price, September 5, 1863, OR, vol. 27, pt. 2: 994–95.

31 Kirby Smith to John Slidell, September 2, 1863, OR, vol. 27, pt. 2: 993.

32 Ibid.

33 Ibid.

CHAPTER FOUR

1 Edmund Kirby Smith to John Slidell, September 2, 1863, OR, vol. 27, pt. 2.

2 U. S. Grant to Henry Halleck, September 19, 1863, OR, vol. 30, pt. 3: 733.

3 Edwin C. Bearss, ed., *A Louisiana Confederate: The Diary of Felix Pierre Poché*, Eugenie Watson Somdel, trans. (Natchitoches: Louisiana Studies Institute, Northwestern State University, 1972), 15; Arthur Hyatt Dairy, August 20, 1863, Arthur W. Hyatt Papers, Mss. 180, Louisiana and Lower Mississippi Valley Collection, Hill Memorial Library, Louisiana State University.

4 Carl A. Brasseaux, "Ozeme Carriere and the St. Landry Jayhawkers," *Attakapas Gazette* 13, no. 4 (Winter 1978): 185–86; Gercie Daigle, "The Robin Hood of Mallet Woods," *La Voix des Prairies* 11, no. 41 (April 1990): 33–34; John Coleman Sibley to Nancy Elizabeth Sibley, August 16, 1863, in Donald Ray Parker, ed., "Civil War Diary and Letters of Lieutenant John Coleman Sibley, 2nd Louisiana Cavalry, Company E, Confederate States of America," 24–25, 124, bound typescript, John Coleman Sibley Collection, Box 2, Cammie G. Henry Research Center, Watson Memorial Library, Northwestern State University, Natchitoches, LA; Dennis E. Haynes, *A Thrilling Narrative: A Memoir of a Southern Unionist*, ed. Arthur W. Bergeron Jr. (Fayetteville: University of Arkansas Press, 2006), 134.

5 John Coleman Sibley to Nancy Elizabeth Sibley, August 16, 1863, in Parker, ed., "Civil War Diary and Letters," 24–25, 124, Sibley Collection.

6 William Randolph Howell to Editor, August 17, 1863, *Houston Tri-Weekly Telegraph*, August 31, 1863, p. 2.

7 Ibid.

8 John W. Watkins to Irene Watkins, August 18, 1863, Watkins Letters, Harold B. Simpson Confederate Research Center, Hillsboro, Texas.

9 Ibid.

10 Howell to Editor, August 17, 1863, *Houston Tri-Weekly Telegraph*, August 31, 1863, p. 2; John W. Watkins to Irene Watkins, August 18, 1863, Watkins Letters; John Coleman Sibley to Nancy Elizabeth Sibley, August 16, 1863, in Parker, ed., "Civil War Diary and Letters," 24–25, 124, Sibley Collection.

11 John Coleman Sibley to Nancy Elizabeth Sibley, August 16, 1863, in Parker, ed., "Civil War Diary and Letters," 24–25, 124, Sibley Collection.

12 Howell to Editor, August 17, 1863, *Houston Tri-Weekly Telegraph*, August 31, 1863, p. 2; John Coleman Sibley to Nancy Elizabeth Sibley, August 16, 1863, in Parker, ed., "Civil War Diary and Letters," 24–25, 124, Sibley Collection; Haynes, *Thrilling Narrative*, 10.

13 Howell to Editor, August 17, 1863, *Houston Tri-Weekly Telegraph*, August 31, 1863, p. 2; Haynes, *Thrilling Narrative*, 10.

14 Haynes, *Thrilling Narrative*, 10.

15 Haynes, *Thrilling Narrative*, 11. For more on Wells and the political turmoil in Louisiana, see Frank J. Wetta, *The Louisiana Scalawags: Politics, Race, and Terrorism during the Civil War and Reconstruction* (Baton Rouge: Louisiana State University Press, 2013).

16 Keet McDade to Ann McDade, July 22, 1863, Keet McDade Letters, private collection, typescript courtesy of Vernon Williams, Abilene Christian University; Thomas Jefferson League to Mary D. League, August 8, 1863, Thomas Jefferson League Papers, 1855–63, Rosenberg Library, Galveston, Texas.

17 Keet McDade to Ann McDade, July 22, 1863, McDade Letters; Thomas Jefferson League to Mary D. League, August 8, 1863, League Papers.

18 Samuel Amsler to "My Dear Parents," August 3, 1863, Amsler Family Papers, Texas Collection, Baylor University.

19 E. B. Cox to E. McIlhenny, August 15, 1863, McIlhenny Collection.

20 Eliza Robertson to Sarah Craig Marsh Avery, August 30, 1863, McIlhenny Collection.

21 Oscar Hass, ed., "The Diary of Julius Giesecke, 1863–1865," Military History of the Southwest 18, no. 3 (1988): 66–68; Annie Jeter Camouche, The Life of Annie Jeter Carmouche (New Roads, LA: Pointe Coupee Historical Society, n.d.), 32.

22 Hass, "Diary of Julius Giesecke," 68.

23 William Jeter to "My Darling Sis" [Anne Jeter], June 5, 1863, in Camouche, Life of Annie Jeter Carmouche, 109; Hass, "Diary of Julius Giesecke," 69.

24 Camouche, Life of Annie Jeter Carmouche, 33; Hass, "Diary of Julius Giesecke," 69.

25 Hass, "Diary of Julius Giesecke," 69; William Jeter to Lizzie W. Shepherd, March 22, 1864, in Camouche, Life of Annie Jeter Carmouche, 112.

26 Willam Jeter to Lizzie W. Shepherd, March 22, 1864, in Camouche, Life of Annie Jeter Carmouche, 112; Hass, "Diary of Julius Giesecke," 69.

27 William Jeter to Lizzie W. Shepherd, March 22, 1864, in Camouche, Life of Annie Jeter Carmouche, 112–18; Hass, "Diary of Julius Giesecke," 69–72.

28 Hass, "Diary of Julius Giesecke," 73.

29 Ibid., 73–74.

30 [Leila Robertson] to [Margaret Henshaw Avery], August 30, 1863, McIlhenny Collection.

31 O. M. A., August 1, 1863, to Editor, Houston Tri-Weekly Telegraph, August 21, 1863.

32 Eliza [Robertson] to [Sarah Craig Marsh Avery], August 31, 1863, McIlhenny Collection; Hyatt Diary, August 29, 1863.

33 Arthur W. Bergeron, ed., The Civil War Reminiscences of Major Silas T. Grisamore, C.S.A. (Baton Rouge: Louisiana State University Press, 1993), 126.

34 George Guess, August 22, 1863, to S. H. Cockrell, (George W.) Guess Letters, Mss. 793, Louisiana and Lower Mississippi Valley Collections, Hill Memorial Library, Louisiana State University.

35 Barr, Polignac's Texas Brigade, 22; Corothers Diary, August 20–22, 1863.

36 Corothers Diary, August 23, 1863; Bearss, Louisiana Confederate, 23; Hyatt Diary, August 23–24, 1863.

37 Robert Thomas Williams, August 16, September 7, "The Diary of Robert Thomas Williams: Marches, Skirmishes, and Battles of the Fourth Regiment, Texas Mounted Volunteers, October 1861 to November 1865," trans. Connie O'Donnell, Harold B. Simpson Confederate Research Center, Hill College, Hillsboro, TX. See Donald S. Frazier, Thunder Across the Swamp: The Fight for the Lower Mississippi, February 1863–May 1863 (Buffalo Gap, TX: State House Press, 2011). The charges and outcomes of this trial are contained in "General Orders No. 47," September 25, 1863, OR, vol. 15, part II, 1093–95.

38 Theophilus Noel, A Campaign from Santa Fe to the Mississippi: Being a History of the Old Sibley Brigade from Its First Organization to the Present Time; Its Campaigns in New Mexico, Arizona, Texas, Louisiana and Arkansas in the Years 1861-2-3-4(Shreveport, LA: Shreveport News, 1865), 51; Arizonan, July 5, 1863 to Editor, Houston Tri-Weekly Telegraph, July 17, 1863.

39 Sibley Diary, August 30, 1863, Sibley Collection.

40 George Guess to S. H. Cockrell, September 22, 1863, Guess Letters; John W. Watkins to Irene Watkins, August 26, 1863, Watkins Letters; Keet McDade to Ann McDade, August 12, 1863, McDade Letters.

41 John W. Watkins to Irene Watkins, July 27, 1863, Watkins Letters; John Coleman Sibley to his wife, July 31, 1863, Sibley Collection; Keet McDade to Ann McDade, August 12, 1863, McDade Letters; Sallie Patrick to William Randolph Howell, August 31, 1863, W. Randolph Howell Papers, 1861–79, Dolph Briscoe Center for American History, University of Texas, Austin.

CHAPTER FIVE

1   John W. Watkins to Irene Watkins, August 18, 1863, Watkins Letters.
2   Keet McDade to Ann McDade, August 12, 1863, McDade Letters; Michael J. Martin, A History of the 4th Wisconsin Infantry and Cavalry in the Civil War (New York: Savas Beatie, 2006), 212–13; D. H. Hanaburgh, History of the One Hundred and Twenty-Eighth Regiment, New York Volunteers [U.S. Infantry] in the Late Civil War (Pokeepsie [Poughkeepsie], NY: Enterprise, 1894) 83–85; Parker, ed., "Civil War Diary and Letters," 28.
3   Alfred P. Petticolas Diary, Volume III, August 30, 1863, p. 181, private collection, courtesy of Don Alberts, Rio Rancho, NM, typescript in possession of the author.
4   John D. Stevenson to J. B. McPherson, September 3, 1863, OR, vol. 26, pt. 1: 248–49; Anne J. Bailey, Between the Enemy and Texas: Parsons's Texas Cavalry in the Civil War (Fort Worth: Texas Christian University Press, 1989), 144–45.
5   Stevenson to McPherson, September 3, 1863, OR, vol. 26, pt. 1: 248–49; Henry L. Ingram, comp., Civil War Letters of George W. and Martha F. Ingram, 1861–1865 (College Station: Texas A & M University Press, 1973), 60–61.
6   Stephen A. Hurlbut to Frederick Steele, September 9, 1863, OR, vol. 22, pt. 2: 519–20.
7   Hurlbut to Henry Halleck, September 9, 1863, OR, vol. 22, pt. 2: 518–19.
8   Keet McDade to Ann McDade, August 26, 1863, McDade Letters.
9   Nathaniel P. Banks to H. H. Bell, August 27, 1863, ORN, vol. 25: 391; Robert Townsend to David Porter, September 2, 1863, ORN, vol. 25: 395; Townsend to Bell, August 30, 1863, ORN, vol. 22: 494–95; Porter to Gideon Welles, September 15, 1863, ORN, vol. 25: 413.
10 E. K. Owen to Porter, August 8, 1863, ORN, vol. 25: 346.
11 Howell Diary, September 2, 1863.
12 M. M. Crocker to William T. Clark, September 10, 1863, OR, vol. 26, pt. 1: 273–75.
13 Charles E. Furlong to editor, Madison Wisconsin Daily Patriot, September 21, 1863, in Quiner Scrapbooks, Correspondence of the Wisconsin Volunteers, 1861–1865, Volume 9, Mss 600, Wisconsin Historical Society, Madison, Wisconsin.
14 A. G. Malloy to W. H. F. Randall, September 9, 1863, OR, vol. 26, pt. 1: 278; Furlong to editor, Madison Wisconsin Daily Patriot, September 21, 1863.
15 W. Q. Gresham to Randall, September 7, 1863, OR, vol. 26, pt. 1: 277; Malloy to W. H. F. Randall, September 9, 1863, OR, vol. 26, pt. 1: 279.
16 Ibid.
17 Malloy to W. H. F. Randall, September 9, 1863, OR, vol. 26, pt. 1: 279.
18 George William Logan to Isaac N. Dennis, September 6, 1863, OR, vol. 26, pt. 1: 281–83.
19 M. M. Crocker to William T. Clark, September 10, 1863, OR, vol. 26, pt. 1: 273–75; Furlong to editor, Madison Wisconsin Daily Patriot, September 21, 1863.
20 Richard Taylor to Edward Surget, September 1863, OR, vol. 26, pt. 1: 281; Bergeron, Civil War Reminiscences of Major Silas T. Grisamore, 126.
21 George Guess to S. H. Cockrell, August 22, 1863, Guess Letters.
22 Ibid.
23 Richard Taylor, Destruction and Reconstruction: Personal Experiences of the Late War (New York: D. Appleton, 1879), 192.

CHAPTER SIX

1   Nathaniel P. Banks to Abraham Lincoln, October 22, 1863, OR, vol. 26, pt. 1: 290.
2   James Grant Wilson, "Horserace Changed a War," Kansas City Star, June 6, 1910.

3   Randal B. Gilbert, ed., "The Civil War Diary of Lt. Col. J. B. Leake," *Chronicles of Smith County, Texas* 41, no. 1 (1996): 46; Carlos Colby to his sister Sallie, September 10, 1863, Carlos W. Colby Papers, 1821–1937, Vault Case, MS 10014, Newberry Library, Chicago.
4   Carlos Colby to his sister Sallie, September 10, 1863, Colby Papers.
5   See Benjamin P. Thomas, ed., *Three Years with Grant as Recalled by War Correspondent Sylvanus Cadwallader* (New York: Alfred A. Knopf, 1955), 117; Gilbert, "Civil War Diary of Lt. Col. J. B. Leake," 46.
6   Banks to Henry W. Halleck, September 5, 1863, OR, vol. 26, pt. 1: 286.
7   H. P. Bee to Edmund P. Turner, September 14, 1863, OR, vol. 26, pt. 2: 228.
8   No author, "Miscellaneous," *The Literary Digest* XIV 11 (January 16, 1897): 347; Rick Beard, "General Grant Takes a Spill," *New York Times* "Opinionator," September 4, 2013, http://opinionator.blogs.nytimes.com/2013/09/04/general-grant-takes-a-spill/, accessed November 20, 2013. Private Henry Whipple of the 29th Wisconsin said the accident occurred at the corner of Grand and River Streets, but the actual location remains a mystery. See Henry P. Whipple, *The Diary of a Private Soldier: The Exact Copy of a Record kept Day by Day During the Civil War by Henry P. Whipple, late a Private in the Twenty-Ninth Wisconsin Volunteer Infantry* (Waterloo, WI: printed by the author, 1906), 26.
9   The review took place at the Champ d'Mars, which is now Audubon Park and the grounds of Tulane University. The location of the "nearby hotel" may indicate the famous resort Carrollton Gardens. See John Kendall, *History of New Orleans* (Chicago: Lewis Publishing Company, 1922), 752. Based on the evidence at hand, I believe Grant probably took his spill on the river road on his way back from lunch at a planter's house and inspecting the camps of the *Corps d'Afrique* at Camp Parapet. This puts the wreck near the intersection of St. Charles Street and Carrollton Avenue, and he was hauled to the Carrollton Gardens. See Lorenzo Thomas to Edward M. Stanton, September 5, 1863, OR, series 3, vol. 3: 769–70.
10 Beard, "General Grant Takes a Spill." See also Thomas, *Three Years with Grant*, 117, and Bruce Catton, *Grant Takes Command: 1863–1865* (Boston: Little, Brown, 1969), 26; see John Y. Simon, ed., *The Papers of Ulysses S. Grant*, vol. 9, July 7–December 31, 1863 (Carbondale: Southern Illinois University Press, 1982), 222–23. In Ron Chernow's masterful biography, *Grant* (New York: Penguin Press, 2017), 301-304, the author discusses General Grant's accident, without taking sides on whether he was drunk or not. He errs, however, in claiming Grant missed no battles because of his injury. Quite the contrary, it likely cost him the chance of taking Shreveport and being a major contributor to the collapse of the Confederate Trans-Mississippi.
11 Banks to Halleck, September 5, 1863, OR, vol. 26, pt. 1: 286.
12 Frederick Crocker to H. H. Bell, September 12, 1863, OR, vol. 26, pt. 1: 301.
13 Banks to Halleck, September 5, 1863, OR, vol. 26, pt. 1: 286.
14 Orton S. Clark, *The One Hundred and Sixteenth Regiment of New York State Volunteers* (Buffalo, NY: Matthews and Warren, 1868), 125.
15 Godfrey Weitzel to Wickham Hoffman, September 11, 1863, OR, vol. 26, pt. 1: 298.
16 Richard Dowling to F. H. Odlum, September 9, 1863, OR, vol. 26, pt. 1: 311.
17 Crocker to Bell, September 12, 1863, OR, vol. 26, pt. 1: 301; Clark, *One Hundred and Sixteenth Regiment*, 126; William B. Franklin to Banks, September 11, 1863, OR, vol. 26, pt. 1: 294–95.
18 Clark, *One Hundred and Sixteenth Regiment*, 126.
19 Crocker to Bell, September 12, 1863, OR, vol. 26, pt. 1: 301; Clark, *One Hundred and Sixteenth Regiment*, 126; Harris Beecher, *Record of the 114th Regiment, N.Y.S.V.: Where It Went, What It Saw, and What It Did* (Norwich, NY: J. F. Hubbard, Jr., 1866), 248.
20 Odlum to A. N. Mills, September 8, 1863, OR, vol. 26, pt. 1: 309.
21 Ibid.
22 Leon Smith to Edmund P. Turner, September 10, 1863, OR, vol. 26, pt. 1: 307.
23 John B. Magruder to William R. Boggs, September 9, 1863, OR, vol. 26, pt. 1: 303.

24 Elias P. Pellet, *History of the 114th Regiment, New York State Volunteers* (Norwich, NY: Telegraph and Chronicle, 1866), 149, 151; Franklin to Banks, September 14, 1863, OR, vol. 26, pt. 1: 298.

25 Franklin to Banks, September 11, 1863, OR, vol. 26, pt. 1: 295; Edward T. Cotham, Jr., ed., *The Southern Journey of a Civil War Marine: The Illustrated Notebook of Henry O. Gusley* (Austin: University of Texas Press, 2006), 173; Anonymous Civil War Diary, [Company C, 28th Massachusetts], Mss. 3328, Louisiana and Lower Mississippi Valley Collection, Hill Memorial Library, Louisiana State University.

26 Franklin to Banks, September 11, 1863, OR, vol. 26, pt. 1: 295; Cotham, *Journey of a Civil War Marine*, 173; Crocker to Gideon Welles, April 21, 1865, ORN, vol. 20: 545.

27 Crocker to Bell, September 12, 1863, OR, vol. 26, pt. 1: 301.

28 Ibid.

29 Smith to Turner, September 10, 1863, OR, vol. 26, pt. 1: 308.

30 Cotham, *Journey of a Civil War Marine*, 173.

31 Beecher, *Record of the 114th Regiment*, 248.

32 Crocker to Bell, September 12, 1863, OR, vol. 26, pt. 1: 301.

33 Dowling to Odlum, OR, vol. 26, pt. 1: 311; Beecher, *Record of the 114th Regiment*, 248.

34 Dowling to Odlum, OR, vol. 26, pt. 1: 311; Beecher, *Record of the 114th Regiment*, 249; Crocker to Welles, April 21, 1865, ORN, vol. 20: 544.

35 Ibid.

36 Howard Tibbits to Bell, September 10, 1863, ORN, vol. 20: 523; Crocker to Bell, September 12, 1863, OR, vol. 26, pt. 1: 301; Cotham, *Journey of a Civil War Marine*, 174.

37 Crocker to Bell, September 12, 1863, OR, vol. 26, pt. 1: 301; Crocker to Welles, April 21, 1865, ORN, vol. 20: 544.

38 Dowling to Odlum, OR, vol. 26, pt. 1: 311; Crocker to Gideon Welles, April 21, 1865, ORN, vol. 20: 547; Crocker to Bell, September 12, 1863, OR, vol. 26, pt. 1: 301; John B. Magruder to Samuel Cooper, September 27, 1863, OR, vol. 26, pt. 1: 306.

39 Crocker to Welles, April 21, 1865, ORN, vol. 20: 547.

40 Cotham, *Journey of a Civil War Marine*, 174.

41 Crocker to Welles, April 21, 1865, ORN, vol. 20: 547.

42 Ibid.; Dowling to Odlum, OR, vol. 26, pt. 1: 311.

43 Crocker to Welles, April 21, 1865, ORN, vol. 20: 547.

44 Godfrey Weitzel to Wickham Hoffman, September 11, 1863, OR, vol. 26, pt. 1: 299.

45 Crocker to Bell, September 12, 1863, OR, vol. 26, pt. 1: 301; Weitzel to Hoffman, September 11, 1863, OR, vol. 26, pt. 1: 299; Crocker to Welles, April 21, 1865, ORN, vol. 20: 547.

46 Odlum to Mills, September 8, 1863, OR, vol. 26, pt. 1: 309; Smith to Turner, September 10, 1863, OR, vol. 26, pt. 1: 307.

47 Pellet, *History of the 114th Regiment*, 152; Clark, *One Hundred and Sixteenth Regiment*, 126; Beecher, *Record of the 114th Regiment*, 249.

48 Franklin to Banks, September 11, 1863, OR, vol. 26, pt. 1: 297; Clark, *One Hundred and Sixteenth Regiment*, 127; Beecher, *Record of the 114th Regiment*, 249.

49 Beecher, *Record of the 114th Regiment*, 249; Pellet, *History of the 114th Regiment*, 152; Clark, *One Hundred and Sixteenth Regiment*, 127.

50 Cotham, *Journey of a Civil War Marine*, 6, 175.

51 Magruder, General Order No. 154, September 9, 1863, OR, vol. 26, pt. 1: 306.

52 Magruder, "To the Men of Texas," September 10, 1863, OR, vol. 26, pt. 1: 307.

53 Ibid.

54 Stanley S. McGowen, *Horse Sweat and Powder Smoke: The First Texas Cavalry in the Civil War* (College Station: Texas A & M University Press, 1999), 105; Donald S. Frazier and Andrew Hillhouse, eds., *Love and War: The Civil War Letters and Medicinal Book of Augustus V. Ball* (Buffalo Gap, TX: State House Press, 2010), 115.

55 Works Progress Administration, *Slave Narratives*, vol. 16, *Texas Narratives*, part 3: 191.

56 Ibid.
57 Beecher, *Record of the 114th Regiment*, 249.
58 Pellet, *History of the 114th Regiment*, 153.

CHAPTER SEVEN

1   James P. Foster to D. D. Porter, September 20, 1863, ORN, vol. 25, 422–24.
2   Gilbert, "Civil War Diary of Lt. Col. J. B. Leake," 46; Francis J. Herron to Charles P. Stone, September 8, 1863, OR, vol. 26, pt. 1: 312–13; J. Irvine Dungan, *History of the Nineteenth Regiment, Iowa Volunteer Infantry* (Davenport, IA: Luse and Griggs, 1865), 82.
3   Gilbert, "Civil War Diary of Lt. Col. J. B. Leake," 46; Herron to Stone, September 8, 1863, OR, vol. 26, pt. 1: 312–13; Dungan, *History of the Nineteenth Regiment*, 82. The batteries in Herron's Division included Battery F, 1st Missouri, with four 12-pounder Blakely rifles and two 12-pounder James rifles; Battery E, 1st Missouri, with two 12-pound Blakely rifles and four 10-pound Parrott rifles; and Battery B, 1st Missouri, with four 12-pounder howitzers and two 12-pounder Napoleons.
4   Keet McDade to Ann McDade, September 11, 1863, McDade Letters; Alwyn Barr, *Polignac's Texas Brigade* (College Station: Texas A & M University Press, 1998), 24.
5   Gilbert, "Civil War Diary of Lt. Col. J. B. Leake," 46; Herron to Stone, September 8, 1863, OR, vol. 26, pt. 1: 312–13; Dungan, *History of the Nineteenth Regiment*, 82.
6   Keet McDade to Ann McDade, September 11, 1863, McDade Letters; Joseph Faust to Hermann Seele, October 26, 1863, Oscar Haas Papers, 1844–1955, Dolph Briscoe Center for American History, University of Texas, Austin.
7   Keet McDade to Ann McDade, September 11, 1863, McDade Letters; Edward Hartly to "Em," October 3, [1863], Civil War Collection, Missouri History Museum, St. Louis.
8   Keet McDade to Ann McDade, September 11, 1863, McDade Letters.
9   Hartly Letter.
10 Ibid.
11 Ibid.
12 Ibid.
13 Ibid.
14 Herron to Stone, September 8, 1863, OR, vol. 26, pt. 1: 312–13; Gilbert, "Civil War Diary of Lt. Col. J. B. Leake," 46.
15 Gilbert, "Civil War Diary of Lt. Col. J. B. Leake," 46.
16 Herron to Stone, September 8, 1863, OR, vol. 26, pt. 1: 313.
17 Howell Diary, September 9, 1863.
18 James P. Foster to D. D. Porter, September 20, 1863, ORN, vol. 25, 422–24.
19 Dungan, *History of the Nineteenth Regiment*, 82–83.
20 Ibid., 82.
21 Howell Diary, September 10, 1863.
22 Gilbert, "Civil War Diary of Lt. Col. J. B. Leake," 46; Dungan, *History of the Nineteenth Regiment*, 83.
23 Howell Diary, September 12–13, 1863; Gilbert, "Civil War Diary of Lt. Col. J. B. Leake," 46.
24 Dungan, *History of the Nineteenth Regiment*, 83.
25 James A. Greer to D. D. Porter, September 14, 1863, ORN, vol. 25, 405.
26 Gilbert, "Civil War Diary of Lt. Col. J. B. Leake," 46.
27 Donald C. Elder III, ed., *A Damned Iowa Greyhound: The Civil War Letters of William Henry Harrison Clayton* (Iowa City: University of Iowa Press, 1998), 99.
28 Michael E. Banasik, ed., *Duty, Honor, Country: The Civil War Experiences of Captain William P. Black, Thirty-Seventh Illinois Infantry* (Iowa City: Camp Pope Bookshop, 2006), 255.
29 Gilbert, "Civil War Diary of Lt. Col. J. B. Leake," 46; Dungan, *History of the Nineteenth Regiment*, 83.

30   Edmund Kirby Smith to Richard Taylor, September 10, 1863, OR, vol. 26, pt. 2: 218.

31   M. M. Crocker to W. T. Clark, September 15, 1863, OR, vol. 26, pt. 1: 314–15; B. F. Price to his sister, September 9, 1863, Mary Martha Hackney Transcriptions of Price Family Papers, Special Collections, University of Texas, Arlington.

32   Ibid.; Frank Moore, ed., *The Rebellion Record: A Diary of American Events, with Documents, Narratives, Illustrative Incidents, Poetry, etc.* 12 vols. (New York: D. Van Nostrand, 1864) 7:53. Lieutenant William M. Skinner of the 3rd Arizona was captured.

33   Crocker to Clark, September 15, 1863, OR, vol. 26, pt. 1: 314–15.

34   Sibley to his wife, September 15, 1863, Sibley Collection.

35   W. T. Sherman to James McPherson, September 14, 1863, OR, vol. 30, pt. 3: 620.

36   Ibid.

37   Nathaniel P. Banks to Henry W. Halleck, September 13, 1863, OR, vol. 26, pt. 1: 289–90.

38   George Guess to S. H. Cockrell, September 9, 1863, Guess Letters.

CHAPTER EIGHT

1   George Guess to S. H. Cockrell, September 15, 1863, Guess Letters.

2   Clark, *One Hundred and Sixteenth Regiment*, 128.

3   Ibid.

4   Henry P. Whipple, *The Diary of a Private Soldier: The Exact Copy of a Record kept Day by Day during the Civil War by Henry P. Whipple, Late a Private in the Twenty-Ninth Wisconsin Volunteer Infantry* (Waterloo, WI: printed by the author, 1906), 26.

5   Charles P. Stone to William B. Franklin, September 24, 1863, OR, vol. 26, pt. 1: 734.

6   Nathaniel P. Banks to Henry Halleck, September 21, 1863, OR, vol. 26, pt. 1: 729; E. O. C. Ord to Charles P. Stone, September 26, 1863, OR, vol. 26, pt. 1: 738.

7   Ord to Stone, September 26, 1863, OR, vol. 26, pt. 1: 738.

8   Connor, H. N., "The Diary of 1st Sergeant H. N. Connor," September 17–21, 1863, edited by W. T. Block, http://www.wtblock.com/wtblockjr/diaryof.htm.

9   John W. Watkins to Irene Watkins, September 19, 1863, Watkins Letters.

10   Ibid.

11   Cooper K. Ragan, ed., "Diary of Captain George W. O'Brien," *Southwestern Historical Quarterly* 67 no. 2 (April 1964): 51.

12   Hyatt Diary, September 18, 1863.

13   Alfred Mouton to William Levy, October 4, 1863, OR, vol. 26, pt. 1: 328–29.

14   Ragan, "Diary of Captain George W. O'Brien," 51–52; Bergeron, *Civil War Reminiscences of Major Silas T. Grisamore*, 126–27.

15   Ibid.

16   Gilbert, "Civil War Diary of Lt. Col. J. B. Leake," 46; Dungan, *History of the Nineteenth Regiment*, 83; Oliver Gooding to Charles P. Stone, September 29, OR, vol. 26, pt. 1: 320.

17   Gilbert, "Civil War Diary of Lt. Col. J. B. Leake," 46; Gooding to Stone, September 29, OR, vol. 26, pt. 1: 320; R. B. Scott, *The History of the 67th Regiment Indiana Infantry Volunteers: War of the Rebellion* (Bedford, IN: Herald, 1892), 46–47.

18   Connor Diary, September 25–26, 1863.

19   Blessington, Joseph Palmer, 1841-1898. *The Campaigns of Walker's Texas Division: Containing a Complete Record of the Campaigns In Texas, Louisiana And Arkansas . . .* (New York: Lang, Little and Company, 1875; reprint Austin: State House Press, 1994), 132–33.

20   Tom Green to Louis Bush, October 2, 1863, OR, vol. 26, pt. 1: 329–32.

21   Connor Diary, September 25–26, 1863.

22   William Tecumseh Sherman, *Memoirs of General W. T. Sherman* (New York: D. Appleton, 1875), 1:346.

23   Banks to Halleck, September 26, 1863, OR, vol. 26, pt. 1: 735.

24   Hyatt Diary, September 27, 1863.

25   Rodman L. Underwood, *Waters of Discord: The Union Blockade of Texas during the Civil War* (Jefferson, NC: McFarland, 2003), 122; Patrick J. Kelly, "The North American Crisis of the 1860s," *Journal of the Civil War Era* 2, no. 3 (September 2012): 354–55. According to the 1863 edition of *Lloyd's Register of British and Foreign Shipping*, the 120-ton steamer *Love Bird* was built in Baltimore in 1857, was nearly seventy feet long, and drew just under eleven feet of water when loaded. Ironically, it had entered service as the *President Benson* and had been involved in the trade with Liberia.

26   Underwood, *Waters of Discord*, 122.

27   H. H. Bell to John Madigan, September 2, 1863, ORN, vol. 20: 514–15; Henry Rolando to H. H. Bell, October 13, 1863, ORN, vol. 20: 626.

CHAPTER NINE

1   Thomas Green to Louis Bush, October 2, 1863, OR, vol. 26, pt. 1: 329–31.

2   Hyatt Diary, September 29, 1863; Ragan, "Diary of Captain George W. O'Brien," 236.

3   Thomas Green to Louis Bush, October 2, 1863, OR, vol. 26, pt. 1: 329–31.

4   Ragan, "Diary of Captain George W. O'Brien," 236.

5   John W. Watkins to Irene Watkins, October 2, 1863, Watkins Letters.

6   Ibid.

7   Ragan, "Diary of Captain George W. O'Brien," 236; Hartley Letter.

8   Ragan, "Diary of Captain George W. O'Brien," 237.

9   N. J. T. Dana to Walter B. Scates, September 30, 1863, OR, vol. 26, pt. 1: 321.

10   Dungan, *History of the Nineteenth Regiment*, 87; Joseph Faust to Hermann Seele, October 26, 1863, Oscar Haas Papers.

11   Dungan, *History of the Nineteenth Regiment*, 87.

12   Ibid., 87–88.

13   Ragan, "Diary of Captain George W. O'Brien," 237.

14   Gilbert, "Civil War Diary of Lt. Col. J. B. Leake," 47.

15   Dana to Scates, September 30, 1863, OR, vol. 26, pt. 1: 322.

16   Ragan, "Diary of Captain George W. O'Brien," 237–38.

17   Lurton Dunham Ingersoll, *Iowa and the Rebellion: A History of the Troops Furnished by the State of Iowa to the Volunteer Armies of the Union, Which Conquered the Great Southern Rebellion of 1861–5* (Philadelphia: J. B. Lippincott, 1867), 351.

18   Hyatt Diary, September 29, 1863.

19   Hartley Letter.

20   Ragan, "Diary of Captain George W. O'Brien," 238; Barr, *Polignac's Texas Brigade*, 26.

21   Thomas Green to Louis Bush, October 2, 1863, OR, vol. 26, pt. 1: 329–31; Dungan, *History of the Nineteenth Regiment*, 90.

22   Hyatt Diary, September 29, 1863.

23   Ragan, "Diary of Captain George W. O'Brien," 238.

24   Ibid., 242.

25   Ibid.

26   Dungan, *History of the Nineteenth Regiment*, 88.

27   Dana to Scates, September 30, 1863, OR, vol. 26, pt. 1: 322.

28   Ragan, "Diary of Captain George W. O'Brien," 239.

29   Ibid.

30   Ibid.

31   Ragan, "Diary of Captain George W. O'Brien," 239.

32   Dungan, *History of the Nineteenth Regiment*, 88.

33   Ragan, "Diary of Captain George W. O'Brien," 240–41; Hartley Letter; Thomas Green to Louis Bush, October 2, 1863, OR, vol. 26, pt. 1: 329–31.

34   Hartley Letter.

35   Dungan, *History of the Nineteenth Regiment*, 88.

36   Hartley Letter; Augustine Robinette Diary, September 29, 1863, Iowa in the Civil War: Regiment Data *http://iagenweb.org/civilwar/regiment/infantry/19th/robinetted2a.htm*.
37   Green to Bush, October 2, 1863, OR, vol. 26, pt. 1: 329–31.
38   Hyatt Diary, September 29, 1863.
39   Ibid.
40   Dana to Scates, September 30, 1863, OR, vol. 26, pt.1: 322.
41   Hyatt Diary, September 29, 1863; Joseph Faust to Hermann Seele, October 26, 1863, Haas Papers.
42   Hyatt Diary, September 29, 1863.
43   Hartley Letter.
44   Dana to Scates, September 30, 1863, OR, vol. 26, pt.1: 322; Hartley Letter.
45   Hartley Letter.
46   Hyatt Diary, September 29, 1863.

CHAPTER TEN
1   Hyatt Diary, October 1, 1863; Ragan, "Diary of Captain George W. O'Brien," 243.
2   Sallie Patrick to W. R. Howell, October 14, 1863, Howell Papers.
3   Thomas Green, "Battle of Atchafalaya River—Letter from General Thomas Green to My Dear Wife [Molly Green]," October 1, 1863, *Southern Historical Society Papers*, edited by John William Jones (Richmond: Southern Historical Society, 1877), 3: 62–63.
4   Ibid.
5   Ibid.
6   Ibid.
7   N. J. T. Dana to Walter B. Scates, October 2, 1863, OR, vol. 26, pt. 1: 324.
8   Edmund Kirby Smith, "To the People of Arkansas, Louisiana, and Texas," OR, vol. 26, pt. 2: 581; Moore, *Rebellion Record*, 56.
9   Sallie Patrick to W. R. Howell, October 14, 1863, Howell Papers.
10   U. S. Grant to Nathaniel P. Banks, October 3, 1863, OR, vol. 26, pt. 1: 752.
11   David Dixon Porter to Gideon Welles, October 1, 1863, ORN, vol. 25: 440.
12   Connor Diary, October 4, 1863. This may describe a "Woodruff Gun," and if so would be the only evidence of its use by Confederate forces. It could have been a 1-pounder "Williams Gun." Both of these pieces, though, appear to be shorter ranged than described. Other possibilities are the Confederate Mountain Rifle, four of which were known to be in the Trans-Mississippi, and the Hugh's Breech-loading Rifle. Another candidate is the British 1-pounder Whitworth muzzle-loader, also rare in Confederate service. The term "Aunt Jane" may have been slang for a black woman, usually a slave, known to be obsequious in her service to white masters, much like the male counterpart, "Uncle Tom."
13   Connor Diary, October 4–6, 1863.
14   Ibid.
15   Ibid.
16   Howell Diary, October 4, 1863.
17   Ibid.
18   Connor Diary, October 4–6, 1863. Richard Taylor converted the steamboat *Hart* into the ironclad CSS *Stevens* in the spring of 1863 but scuttled the unfinished vessel upon his retreat in April. After reoccupying the area in May, crews raised the boat, started to repair and rebuild it, but sank it again when Federals had threatened in July.
19   Connor Diary, October 4–6, 1863.
20   Ibid.
21   Scott, *History of the 67th Regiment Indiana Infantry*, 48.
22   Bearss, *Louisiana Confederate*, 36–37.
23   Hyatt Diary, October 8, 1863.
24   Carlos Colby to his sister, October 11, 1863, Colby Papers.

25 Ibid.
26 William M. Levy to John Marsh Avery, October 2, 1863, ORN, vol. 25: 458; Porter to Welles, October 17, 1863, ORN, vol. 25: 450; Hyatt Diary, October 8, 1863.
27 Hyatt Diary, October 8, 1863.
28 Ibid.
29 Ibid.
30 Alfred Mouton to Richard Taylor, October 4, 1863, OR, vol. 26, pt. 1: 393; Connor Diary, October 7–14, 1863.
31 David C. Edmonds, *Yankee Autumn in Acadiana: A Narrative of the Great Texas Overland Expedition through Southwestern Louisiana, October-December 1863* (Lafayette, LA: Acadiana Press, 1979), 67–77.
32 William Frederick Weeks to Judge John Moore, October 31, 1863, Weeks Papers.
33 Edmonds, *Yankee Autumn*, 67–77.
34 Edmonds, *Yankee Autumn*, 81–85. Charles P. Stone, "Daily Memoranda for Adjutant-General's Officer, Department of the Gulf, October 9–14 [1863], OR, vol. 26, pt. 1: 382.
35 Stone, "Daily Memoranda," OR, vol. 26, pt. 1: 382.
36 Samuel H. Fletcher, *History of Company A, Second Illinois Cavalry* (Chicago: Samuel H. Fletcher and D. H. Fletcher, 1912), 125.
37 Ibid., 124.
38 Ibid.
39 Ibid., 125.
40 Connor Diary, October 7–14, 1863; Hass, "Diary of Julius Giesecke," 49–92; Howell Diary, October 4–15, 1863; Taylor to Boggs, October 11, 1863, OR, vol. 26, pt. 1: 386–87.
41 Stone, "Daily Memoranda," OR, vol. 26, pt. 1: 382.
42 Whipple, *Diary of a Private Soldier*, 29.
43 Stone, "Daily Memoranda," OR, vol. 26, pt. 1: 382.
44 Lincoln, *Collected Works*, 7:90.
45 Ibid.

CHAPTER ELEVEN
1   Moundville no longer exists. Bayou Beouf flows into Bayou Courtableau, and Bayou Teche splits off just below Washington, Louisiana.
2   Connor Diary, October 7–14, 1863; Hass, "Diary of Julius Giesecke," 49–92; Howell Diary, October 4–15, 1863; Richard Taylor to W. R. Boggs, October 11, 1863, OR, vol. 26, pt. 1: 386–87.
3   Taylor to Boggs, October 11, 1863, OR, vol. 26, pt. 1: 386–87.
4   McGowen, *Horse Sweat and Powder Smoke*, 106–11.
5   W. B. Franklin to N. P. Banks, October 14, 1863, OR, vol. 26, pt. 1: 338.
6   Howell Diary, October 4–15, 1863; Connor Diary, October 7–14, 1863; Hass, "Diary of Julius Giesecke," 75.
7   E. Kirby Smith to Richard Taylor, October 15, 1863, OR, vol. 26, pt. 2: 323.
8   W. B. Franklin to N. P. Banks, October 14, 1863, OR, vol. 26, pt. 1: 338.
9   *New York Herald*, November 8, 1863; Carl A. Brasseaux, "Ozeme Carriere and the St. Landry Jayhawkers," *Attakapas Gazette* 13, no. 4 (Winter 1978): 185–86; Gercie Daigle, "The Robin Hood of Mallet Woods," *La Voix des Prairies* 11, no. 41 (April 1990): 33–34; Edmonds, *Yankee Autumn*, 113–14.
10 Edmonds, *Yankee Autumn*, 155–56; Howell Diary, October 13, 1863; Taylor to Boggs, October 22, 1863, OR, vol. 26, pt. 1: 389.
11 Edmonds, *Yankee Autumn*, 156.
12 Howell Diary, October 14, 1863.
13 Edmonds, *Yankee Autumn*, 164.

14   Hass, "Diary of Julius Giesecke," 75; Caroline E. Whitcomb, *History of the Second Massachusetts Battery (Nims' Battery) of Light Artillery, 1861–1865: Compiled from the Records of the Rebellion, Official Reports, Diaries, and Rosters* (Concord, NH: Rumford, 1912), 56.

15   Anonymous Civil War Diary, October 15, 1863; J. T. Woods, *Services of the Ninety-Sixth Ohio* (Toledo, OH: Blade, 1874), 39.

16   Woods, *Services of the Ninety-Sixth Ohio*, 39.

17   Howell Diary, October 16, 1863.

18   Anonymous Civil War Diary, October 15, 1863; Woods, *Services of the Ninety-Sixth Ohio*, 39.

19   Howell Diary, October 16, 1863.

20   William B. Franklin to Nathaniel P. Banks, October 16, 1863, OR, vol. 26, pt. 1: 338–39.

21   Ragan, "Diary of Captain George W. O'Brien," 413–33; Bearrs, *Louisiana Confederate*, 38.

22   Ragan, "Diary of Captain George W. O'Brien," 419.

23   "Presentation of the Portrait of General Tom Green," 12, Miscellaneous Manuscripts and Addresses, Archives and Information Division, Texas State Library and Archives Commission, Austin, Texas.

24   Blessington, *Campaigns of Walker's Texas Division*, 134–35.

25   Ibid.

26   Bearss, *Louisiana Confederate*, 37.

27   Richard Taylor to W. R. Boggs, October 20, 1863, OR, vol. 26, pt. 1: 388.

28   Franklin to Charles P. Stone, OR, vol. 26, pt. 1: 772–73; Stone to Franklin, OR, vol. 26, pt. 1: 772–73.

29   Edmonds, *Yankee Autumn*, 193.

30   Connor Diary, October 19–21, 1863; Howell Diary, October 19, 1863.

31   Hass, "Diary of Julius Giesecke," 76; Thomas E. Mix, *Civil War Journal of Thomas E. Mix, Company B, 118th Illinois Volunteers* (Kenosha, WI: E. M. Earley, 1992), 24.

32   Hass, "Diary of Julius Giesecke," 76; Connor Diary, October 19–21, 1863; Howell Diary, October 19, 1863; John G. Fonda to W. Hoffman, October 21, 1863, OR, 53: 474.

33   Haas, "Diary of Julius Giesecke," 76; Connor Diary, October 19–21, 1863.

34   Minister quoted in Edmonds, *Yankee Autumn*, 193; Haynes, *Thrilling Narrative*, 15.

35   Connor Diary, October 21, 1863; Bearss, *Louisiana Confederate*, 42; T. B. Marshall, *History of the Eighty-Third Ohio Volunteer Infantry: The Greyhound Regiment* (Cincinnati: Eighty-Third Ohio Volunteer Infantry Association, 1912), 112.

36   Hyatt Diary, October 21, 1863; Blessington, *Campaigns of Walker's Texas Division*, 135.

37   Joseph Faust to Hermann Seele, October 26, 1863, Haas Papers.

38   Marshall, *History of the Eighty-Third Ohio*, 111–12.

39   Bearss, *Louisiana Confederate*, 32; Connor Diary, October 21–November 3, 1863; Hass, "Diary of Julius Giesecke," 76; Howell Diary, October 21, 1863; Taylor to Boggs, October 22, 1863, OR, vol. 26, pt. 1: 389.

40   Hyatt Diary, October 21, 1863; Connor Diary, October 21–November 3, 1863; Hass, "Diary of Julius Giesecke," 76; Howell Diary, October 21, 1863; Joseph Faust to Hermann Seele, October 26, 1863, Haas Papers; Blessington, *Campaigns of Walker's Texas Division*, 135.

41   Richard Taylor to William R. Boggs, October 22, 1863, OR, vol. 26, pt. 1: 389–90.

42   Blessington, *Campaigns of Walker's Texas Division*, 138; Jeffery S. Prushankin, *A Crisis in Confederate Command: Edmund Kirby Smith, Richard Taylor, and the Army of the Trans-Mississippi* (Baton Rouge: Louisiana State University Press, 2005), 56–58.

43   Ibid.

44   William B. Franklin to Charles P. Stone, October 23, 1863, OR, vol. 26, pt. 1: 340.

45   Ibid., 340–41.

46   Woods, *Services of the Ninety-Sixth Ohio*, 39; Marshall, *History of the Eighty-Third Ohio*, 112.

47   Mix, *Civil War Journal*, 25.

CHAPTER TWELVE

1   For a discussion of the interrelationship of Louisiana and Texas during the war, see James A. Padgett, ed., "Some Letters of George Stanton Denison, 1854–1866: Observations of a Yankee on Conditions in Louisiana and Texas," *Louisiana Historical Quarterly* 23, no. 4 (October 1940): 132–240.

2   "Civil War Diary of Henry Carl Ketzle, 37th Illinois Volunteer Infantry, Company A, 1861–1866, October 1863," accessed February 6, 2014, *http://www.ketzle.com/diary/fullcwdiary.htm*.

3   J. B. Magruder to William R. Boggs, October 27, 1863, OR, vol. 26, pt. 2: 360.

4   William B. Franklin to Charles P. Stone, October 24, 1863, OR, vol. 26, pt. 1: 340.

5   Richard Taylor to W. R. Boggs, October 25, 1863, OR, vol. 26, pt. 1: 390.

6   Blessington, *Campaigns of Walker's Texas Division*, 138; Prushankin, *Crisis in Confederate Command*, 56–58; Richard Taylor to W. R. Boggs, October 25, 1863, OR, vol. 26, pt. 1: 390.

7   Kirby Smith to Theophilus Holmes, October 25, 1863, OR, vol. 26, pt. 2: 1049; Kirby Smith to John B. Magruder, October 25, 1863, OR, vol. 26, pt. 2: 353–54.

8   Kirby Smith to Taylor, October 28, 1863, OR, vol. 26, pt. 2: 364.

9   Franklin to Stone, October 26, 1863, OR, vol. 26, pt. 1: 341.

10 Ibid.

11 Hass, "Diary of Julius Giesecke," 76; Hyatt Diary, October 26, 1863; Joseph Faust to Hermann Seele, October 26, 1863, Haas Papers.

12 Howell Diary, October 27, 1863; Hass, "Diary of Julius Giesecke," 76; Williams Diary, October 27, 1863.

13 Franklin to Stone, October 23, 1863, OR, vol. 26, pt. 1: 340.

14 As quoted in Edmonds, *Yankee Autumn*, 242, 248.

15 Edmonds, *Yankee Autumn*, 253–55; James E. Bradley Diary, October 19–November 3, 1863, Bradley (James E.) Papers, Mss. 1259, Louisiana and Lower Mississippi Valley Collection, Hill Memorial Library, Louisiana State University; Richard J. Fulfer, *A History of the Trials and Hardships of the Twenty-Fourth Indiana Volunteer Infantry* (Indianapolis: Indianapolis Printing, 1913), 91; *History of the Second Battalion Duryee Zouaves: One Hundred and Sixty-Fifth Regiment New York Volunteer Infantry, Mustered in the United States Service at Camp Washington, Staten Island, New York* (Salem, MA: Higginson, 1905), 22; Whitcomb, *History of the Second Massachusetts*, 56; "Return of the First Brigade," November 24, OR, vol. 26, pt. 1: 379.

16 Franklin to Stone, November 2, 1863, OR, vol. 26, pt. 1: 342; Franklin to Stone, November 3, 1863, OR, vol. 26, pt. 1: 342.

17 Howell Diary, October 31, 1863; Hass, "Diary of Julius Giesecke," 77.

18 Charles B. Stone to William Franklin, October 28, 1863, OR, vol. 26, pt. 1: 778.

19 Franklin to Stone, November 2, 1863, OR, vol. 26, pt. 1: 342.

20 Haynes, *Thrilling Narrative*, 14.

21 Ibid.

22 Ibid., 14–15.

23 As quoted in Edmonds, *Yankee Autumn*, 193; Haynes, *Thrilling Narrative*, 15.

24 Haynes, *Thrilling Narrative*, 16.

25 Ibid.

26 Ibid., 19–20.

27 Ibid., 24.

28 Ibid., 28–29.

29 Ibid., 27–28.

30 Stone to Franklin, October 28, 1863, OR, vol. 26, pt. 1: 779.

31 Ibid.

32 Ibid.

33 Stone to Philip St. George Cooke, October 28, 1863, OR, vol. 26, pt. 1: 779–80; Stone to David Dixon Porter, October 28, 1863, OR, vol. 26, pt. 1: 779.

34 Franklin to Stone, November 2, 1863, OR, vol. 26, pt. 1: 342.

[35] Ketzle Diary, October 1863.

[36] Donald S. Frazier and Andrew Hillhouse, eds., *Love and War: The Civil War Letters and Medicinal Book of Augustus V. Ball* (Buffalo Gap, Texas: State House Press, 2010), 146–47; "Abstract from returns of the District of Texas, New Mexico, and Arizona, Major John Bankhead Magruder, C. S. Army, commanding, for the month of October 1863," OR, vol. 26, pt. 2: 376.

[37] Frazier and Hillhouse, *Love and War*, 146–47.

[38] Ibid., 146–49.

[39] Magruder to Boggs, November 6, 1863, OR, vol. 26, pt. 2: 393.

[40] Unknown to Wade R. Boggs, November 1, 1863, OR, vol. 26, pt. 2: 377; Magruder to Boggs, November 6, 1863, OR, vol. 26, pt. 2: 393.

[41] Henry McCulloch to E. P. Turner, November 1, 1863, OR, vol. 26, pt. 2: 379.

[42] Ibid.

[43] Ibid.

[44] Frazier and Hillhouse, *Love and War*, 149–54.

CHAPTER THIRTEEN

[1] Hass, "Diary of Julius Giesecke," 77.

[2] Richard Taylor to W. R. Boggs, November 2, 1863, OR, vol. 26, pt. 2: 392

[3] Ibid.

[4] Tom Green to Edward Surget, October 4, 1863, OR, vol. 26, pt. 1: 393–95.

[5] C. C. Washburn to Wickham Hoffman, November 2, 1863, OR, vol. 26, pt. 1: 356; Hass, "Diary of Julius Giesecke," 77.

[6] Edmonds, *Yankee Autumn*, 269–70.

[7] Washburn to Hoffman, November 2, 1863, OR, vol. 26, pt. 1: 356.

[8] Ibid.

[9] Ibid.

[10] Ibid., 359.

[11] Woods, *Services of the Ninety-Sixth Ohio*, 39; Stephen Burbridge to William Morgan, November 7, 1863, OR, vol. 26, pt. 1: 360.

[12] Woods, *Services of the Ninety-Sixth Ohio*, 44.

[13] Woods, *Services of the Ninety-Sixth Ohio*, 44; Edwin B. Quiner Scrapbooks: Correspondence of the Wisconsin Volunteers, 1861–1865, mss 600, vol. 10: 270, Wisconsin Historical Society, Madison.

[14] Quiner Scrapbooks, vol. 10: 270; Marshall, *History of the Eighty-Third Ohio*, 113.

[15] Quiner Scrapbooks, vol. 10: 270.

[16] Alwyn Barr, ed., "The Battle of Bayou Bourbeau, November 3, 1863: Colonel Oran M. Roberts Report," *Louisiana History* 6, No. 1 (Winter 1965): 87.

[17] Ibid.

[18] Ibid.

[19] Ibid.

[20] Scott, *History of the 67th Regiment Indiana Infantry*, 50; Quiner Scrapbooks, vol. 10: 271; Woods, *Services of the Ninety-Sixth Ohio*, 43; Marshall, *History of the Eighty-Third Ohio*, 112.

[21] Ibid.

[22] Mix, *Civil War Journal*, 26.

[23] Washburn to Hoffman, November 7, 1863, OR, vol. 26, pt. 1: 357; Mix, *Civil War Journal*, 26.

[24] Barr, "Battle of Bayou Bourbeau," 87.

[25] Ibid.

[26] Ibid.

[27] Woods, *Services of the Ninety-Sixth Ohio*, 42.

[28] Stephen Burbridge to William Morgan, November 7, 1863, OR, vol. 26, pt. 1: 360; J. J. Guppey to A. B. Sharpe, OR, vol. 26, pt. 1: 364–66.

[29] Woods, *Services of the Ninety-Sixth Ohio*, 42–43.

30 As quoted in Barr, "Battle of Bayou Bourbeau," 88.
31 Woods, *Services of the Ninety-Sixth Ohio*, 42–43.
32 J. J. Guppey to A. B. Sharpe, OR, vol. 26, pt. 1: 364–66.
33 As quoted in Barr, "Battle of Bayou Bourbeau," 88.
34 Woods, *Services of the Ninety-Sixth Ohio*, 43.
35 Ibid.
36 Marshall, *History of the Eighty-Third Ohio*, 113.
37 *Overton (TX) Sharp Shooter*, August 2, 1888.
38 Woods, *Services of the Ninety-Sixth Ohio*, 44.
39 Ibid.
40 Barr, "Battle of Bayou Bourbeau," 88.
41 Quiner Scrapbook, vol. 10: 271.
42 Guppey to Sharpe, OR, vol. 26, pt. 1: 364–66.
43 Marshall, *History of the Eighty-Third Ohio*, 113.
44 An interesting discussion of the battle can be found in David C. Edmonds, "Surrender on the Bourbeux: Honorable Defeat or Incompetency Under Fire," *Louisiana History*, 18 (Winter 1977), 63-85.
45 Scott, *History of the 67th Regiment Indiana Infantry*, 52.
46 Washburn to Hoffman, November 2, 1863, OR, vol. 26, pt. 1: 357.
47 Woods, *Services of the Ninety-Sixth Ohio*, 43–44.
48 Quiner Scrapbook, vol. 10: 271; Whitcomb, *History of the Second Massachusetts*, 57.
49 Barr, "Battle of Bayou Bourbeau," 89.
50 Quiner Scrapbook, vol. 10: 271; Guppey to Sharpe, OR, vol. 26, pt. 1: 364–66.
51 Woods, *Services of the Ninety-Sixth Ohio*, 46.
52 Marshall, *History of the Eighty-Third Ohio*, 113.
53 Quiner Scrapbook, vol. 10: 271; Whitcomb, *History of the Second Massachusetts*, 57; Tom Green to Edward Surget, October 4, 1863, OR, vol. 26, pt. 1: 393–95; Washburn to Hoffman, November 7, 1863, OR, vol. 26, pt. 1: 358.
54 Woods, *Services of the Ninety-Sixth Ohio*, 45.
55 Ibid., 47.
56 Marshall, *History of the Eighty-Third Ohio*, 114.
57 Connor Diary, November 3, 1863.
58 As quoted in Barr, "Battle of Bayou Bourbeau," 90.
59 Woods, *Services of the Ninety-Sixth Ohio*, 47.
60 Marshall, *History of the Eighty-Third Ohio*, 114–15.
61 Green to Surget, October 4, 1863, OR, vol. 26, pt. 1: 393–95; *Overton (TX) Sharp-Shooter*, August 2, 1888; Barr, "Battle of Bayou Bourbeau," 90.
62 Marshall, *History of the Eighty-Third Ohio*, 115; *Overton (TX) Sharp-Shooter*, August 2, 1888.
63 Washburn to Hoffman, November 2, 1863, OR, vol. 26, pt. 1: 359; Stephen Burbridge to William Morgan, November 7, 1863, OR, vol. 26, pt. 1: 361.
64 Green to Surget, October 4, 1863, OR, vol. 26, pt. 1: 393–95.
65 Whipple, *Diary of a Private Soldier*, 31.
66 Hass, "Diary of Julius Giesecke," 77.
67 Richard Taylor to John B. Magruder, November 4, 1863, OR, vol. 26, pt. 1: 391.
68 Guppey to Sharpe, OR, vol. 26, pt. 1: 364–66.
69 Taylor, *Destruction and Reconstruction*, 151.

CHAPTER FOURTEEN
1 Edwin R. Lufkin, *History of the Thirteenth Maine Regiment: From its Organization in 1861 to its Muster-Out in 1865* (Bridgeton, ME: H. A. Shorey, 1898), 27.
2 Dungan, *History of the Nineteenth Regiment*, 117.

3   Henry A. Shorey, *The Story of the Maine Fifteenth: Being a Brief Narrative of the More Important Events in the History of the Fifteenth Maine Regiment* (Bridgeton, ME: Bridgeton News, 1890), 56–57.
4   Dungan, *History of the Nineteenth Regiment*, 118.
5   Shorey, *The Story of the Maine Fifteenth*, 57-58.
6   Henry T. Davis to George Caldwell, November 11, 1863, OR, vol. 26, pt. 2: 444–45.
7   Hamilton P. Bee to Edmund P. Turner, November 11, 1863, OR, vol. 26, pt. 2: 405–6; Bee to J. A. Quintero, November 9, 1863, OR, vol. 26, pt. 2: 399–400; Jerry Thompson, *Cortina: Defending the Mexican Name in Texas* (College Station: Texas A & M University Press, 2007), 112–14.
8   Richard Taylor to James Duff, November 3, 1863, OR, vol. 26, pt. 2: 444.
9   Nathaniel P. Banks to Henry W. Halleck, November 4, 1863, OR, vol. 26, pt. 1: 397.
10   Ibid., 398.
11   Charles P. Stone to William B. Franklin, November 5, 1863, OR, vol. 26, pt. 1: 788.
12   Banks to Halleck, November 4, 1863, OR, vol. 26, pt. 1: 398; George S. Boutwell to Abraham Lincoln, November 20, 1863, transcribed and annotated by the Lincoln Studies Center, Knox College, Galesburg, Illinois. Available at Abraham Lincoln Papers at the Library of Congress, Manuscript Division (Washington, DC: American Memory Project, [2000–02]), *http://memory.loc.gov/ammem/alhtml/alhome.html*, accessed February 8, 2014.
13   Thompson, *Cortina*, 113–14.
14   Banks to Halleck, November 6, 1863, OR, vol. 26, pt. 1: 399.
15   Ketzle Diary, November 6, 1864; Dungan, *History of the Nineteenth Regiment*, 118.
16   Lufkin, *History of the Thirteenth Maine Regiment*, 27.
17   Ibid.
18   Banks to Carleton, November 5, 1863, OR, vol. 26, pt. 1: 788.
19   Lufkin, *History of the Thirteenth Maine Regiment*, 28; Banks to Halleck, November 6, 1863, OR, vol. 26, pt. 1: 399–401.
20   Lufkin, *History of the Thirteenth Maine Regiment*, 28; Banks to Halleck, November 6, 1863, OR, vol. 26, pt. 1: 399–401; Banks to Lincoln, November 9, 1863, OR, vol. 26, pt. 1: 405; Banks to Halleck, November 9, 1863, OR, vol. 26, pt. 1: 405–6.
21   Banks to Lincoln, November 9, 1863, OR, vol. 26, pt. 1: 405; Banks to Halleck, November 9, 1863, OR, vol. 26, pt. 1: 405–6.
22   John Slidell to Napoleon III, December 4, 1863, ORN, series 2, vol. 3: 978.
23   Ibid.
24   Schoonover, *Mexican Lobby*, 29–30.
25   Ibid., 30.
26   Stephen A. Townsend, *The Yankee Invasion of Texas* (College Station: Texas A & M University Press, 2006), 34; Bee to Turner, November 8, 1863, OR, vol. 26, pt. 1: 434.
27   Bee to Turner, November 8, 1863, OR, vol. 26, pt. 1: 434.
28   Bee to Turner, November 11, 1863, OR, vol. 26, pt. 2: 405–6; Bee to J. A. Quintero, November 9, 1863, OR, vol. 26, pt. 2: 399–400; Thompson, *Cortina*, 112–14.
29   Bee to Turner, November 11, 1863, OR, vol. 26, pt. 2: 405–6; Bee to J. A. Quintero, November 9, 1863, OR, vol. 26, pt. 2: 399–400.
30   Bee to Turner, November 11, 1863, OR, vol. 26, pt. 2: 406; Bee to Turner, November 16, 1863, OR, vol. 26, pt. 1: 419–20.
31   Townsend, *Yankee Invasion of Texas*, 51.

CHAPTER FIFTEEN
1   *New York Times*, November 8, 1863, p.4.
2   Hass, "Diary of Julius Giesecke," 77; Edmonds, *Yankee Autumn*, 311.
3   Richard Taylor to Edmund Kirby Smith, November 7, 1863, OR, vol. 26, pt. 1: 392. Green commanded at Kock's plantation and Sterling's plantation and at Bayou Bourbeau.

4   Charles P. Stone to William B. Franklin, November 5, 1863, OR, vol. 26, pt. 1: 788.

5   Ibid.

6   Franklin to Stone, November 10, 1863, OR, vol. 26, pt. 1: 344.

7   Charles P. Stone to William B. Franklin, November 5, 1863, OR, vol. 26, pt. 1: 788.

8   Edmonds, *Yankee Autumn*, 319–21; Franklin to Stone, November 14, 1863, OR, vol. 26, pt. 1: 845–46.

9   Howell Diary, November 9, 1863.

10 Franklin to Stone, November 10, 1863, OR, vol. 26, pt. 1: 344.

11 John W. Watkins to Irene Watkins, November 12, 1863, Watkins Letters.

12 Edmonds, *Yankee Autumn*, 325–26.

13 John W. Watkins to Irene Watkins, November 12, 1863, Watkins Letters; Hass, "Diary of Julius Giesecke," 78.

14 Edmonds, *Yankee Autumn*, 325–26; Franklin to Stone, November 11, 1863, OR, vol. 26, pt. 1: 345.

15 Franklin to Stone, November 11, 1863, OR, vol. 26, pt. 1: 344.

16 John W. Watkins to Irene Watkins, November 12, 1863, Watkins Letters.

17 Blessington, *Campaigns of Walker's Texas Division*, 150–51; Brasseaux and Mooney, *Ruined by this Miserable War*, 28.

18 Blessington, *Campaigns of Walker's Texas Division*, 150–51; Brasseaux and Mooney, *Ruined by this Miserable War*, 28.

19 Franklin to Stone, November 13, 1863, OR, vol. 26, pt. 1: 345; Hass, "Diary of Julius Giesecke," 78; Howell Diary, November 16, 1863.

20 Stone to Nathaniel P. Banks, November 15, 1863, OR, vol. 26, pt. 1: 801; Edmonds, *Yankee Autumn*, 338–39; Lawrence Van Alstyne, *Diary of an Enlisted Man* (New Haven, CT: Tuttle, Morehouse, and Taylor, 1910), 225.

21 Edmonds, *Yankee Autumn*, 339–41.

22 Franklin to Stone, November 13, 1863, OR, vol. 26, pt. 1: 345; Hass, "Diary of Julius Giesecke," 78; Howell Diary, November 16, 1863.

23 As quoted in Bearss, *Louisiana Confederate*, 60.

24 T. A. Faries to T. B. French, November 18, 1863, ORN, vol. 20: 849; Bearss, *Louisiana Confederate*, 56, 60.

25 George C. Harding, *The Miscellaneous Writings of George C. Harding* (Indianapolis: Carlon and Hollenbeck, 1882), 330; Blessington, *Campaigns of Walker's Texas Division*, 151.

26 Harding, *Miscellaneous Writings*, 331.

27 Blessington, *Campaigns of Walker's Texas Division*, 151.

28 Harding, *Miscellaneous Writings*, 331.

29 Harding, *Miscellaneous Writings*, 331; Blessington, *Campaigns of Walker's Texas Division*, 151.

30 Frank M. Ramsay to David Porter, November 20, 1863, ORN, vol 20: 570; C. Dominy to James P. Foster, November 18, 1863, ORN, vol. 25: 571; Faries to French, November 18, 1863, OR, vol. 26, pt. 1: 454.

31 Ramsay to Porter, November 20, 1863, ORN, vol. 25: 570; Dominy to Foster, November 18, 1863, ORN, vol. 25, 571.

32 Foster to Porter, November 21, 1863, ORN, vol. 25: 572.

33 Ibid., 573; Ramsay to Porter, November 20, 1863, ORN, vol. 25: 570; Blessington, *Campaigns of Walker's Texas Division*, 153.

34 Henry Birge to G. Norman Lieber, November 19, 1863, OR, vol. 26, pt. 1: 806; Robert Townsend to Henry Bell, November 18, 1863, ORN, vol. 20: 687.

35 Townsend to Bell, November 18, 1863, ORN, vol. 20: 687.

36 Ramsay to Porter, November 23, 1863, ORN, vol. 25: 574.

37 Richard Lowe, *Walker's Texas Division CSA: Greyhounds of the Trans-Mississippi* (Baton Rouge: Louisiana State University Press, 2004), 152.

[38]   Faries to O. J. Semmes, November 21, 1863, OR, vol. 26, pt. 1: 455; "Extract from the log of the USS *Choctaw*, Lieutenant Commander Frank M. Ramsay, Commanding," ORN, vol. 25: 575; "Extract from the log of the USS *Neosho*, Acting Volunteer Lieutenant Samuel Howard, Commanding," ORN, vol. 25: 575.

[39]   *New York Herald*, December 7, 1863, as quoted in Lowe, *Walker's Texas Division*, 153; Brasseaux and Mooney, *Ruined by this Miserable War*, 28.

[40]   Brasseaux and Mooney, *Ruined by this Miserable War*, 28; *New York Herald*, December 7, 1863, as quoted in Lowe, *Walker's Texas Division*, 153.

[31]   Bearss, *Louisiana Confederate*, 56.

CHAPTER SIXTEEN

[1]   William H. Seward to Banks, November 23, 1863, OR, vol. 26, pt. 1: 815.

[2]   Henry W. Halleck to Banks, November 19, 1863, OR, vol. 26, pt. 1: 806.

[3]   Ibid.

[4]   W. T. Sherman, "The Vermont Boy Who Volunteered in 1861, Served Bravely, was Wounded Grievously, and Died for the Union: Eulogy of General T. E. G. Ransom Given before Ransom Post No. 131, Grand Army of the Republic (GAR), St. Louis, Missouri," *Washington National Tribune*, June 20, 1884; see also Jim Huffstodt, *Hard Dying Men: The Story of General W. H. L. Wallace, General T. E. G. Ransom, and their "Old Eleventh" Illinois Infantry in the American Civil War, 1861–1865* (Bowie, MD: Heritage Books, 1991).

[5]   Banks to Halleck, November 18, 1863, OR, vol. 26, pt. 1: 409–10; Shorey, *Story of the Maine Fifteenth*, 59; OR, vol. 26, pt. 1: 426–27, 409.

[6]   Shorey, *Story of the Maine Fifteenth*, 60; Townsend, *Yankee Invasion of Texas*, 17–27; Chester Barney, *Recollections of Field Service with the Twentieth Iowa Infantry Volunteers* (Davenport, IA: Gazette, 1862), 248.

[7]   *Corpus Christi Ranchero*, December 17, 1863; Barney, *Recollections of Field Service*, 247–48.

[8]   Shorey, *Story of the Maine Fifteenth*, 60; Lufkin, *History of the Thirteenth Maine Regiment*, 29. The story of the 15th Maine illustrates the particular strength of Federal forces in the Civil War and their embarrassment of riches, as far as manpower was concerned. Organized in January 1862, the 15th Maine saw service in a number of major theaters. It was first in Louisiana, then the Rio Grande and mid-coast invasion, then it returned to take part in the Red River Campaign. Afterwards the regiment took part in the Bermuda Hundred Campaign and was then sent to counter Jubal Early's Washington raid, followed by service in the Shenandoah Valley. After the Confederate surrender, the 15th Maine was part of the Union occupation forces in South Carolina, before the regiment was mustered out on July 5, 1866. Yet despite extensive service, the 15th Maine must have seen almost no fighting. In the course of the entire war, only five enlisted men and zero officers were killed in combat! But as a result of the regiment being stationed extensively in the sub-tropical regions of the South, three officers and 350 enlisted men died from disease, more deaths from disease than any other Maine unit. Frederick H. Dyer, *A Compendium of the War of the Rebellion* (Des Moines, IA: Dyer, 1908), 152; William F. Fox, *Regimental Losses in the Civil War, 1861–1865* (Albany, NY: Brandow, 1898), 467–68.

[9]   Bee to Turner, November 19, 1863, OR, vol. 26, pt. 1: 436–37; Bee to Turner, November 21, 1863, OR, vol. 26, pt. 1: 437–38.

[10]   Bee to Turner, November 19, 1863, OR, vol. 26, pt. 1: 436–37; Bee to Turner, November 21, 1863, OR, vol. 26, pt. 1: 437–38; Lester N. Fitzhugh, "Saluria, Fort Esperanza, and Military Operations on the Texas Coast, 1861–1864," *Southwestern Historical Quarterly* 61 (July 1957): 96. Bee's troops at this point consisted of only 355 men—five companies of the 33rd Texas Cavalry, one company of the 8th Texas, and a company of cadets. W. R. Bradfute and his command, of course, had no hope of succoring the Confederate fort. They were quickly driven off by cannon fire and fled to Matagorda, where Bradfute took over the command of the Fort Esperanza garrison from Major Ireland.

11 Bee to Turner, November 19, 1863, OR, vol. 26, pt. 1: 436–37; Bee to Turner, November 21, 1863, OR, vol. 26, pt. 1: 437–38.
12 John B. Magruder to W. R. Boggs, November 21, 1863, OR, vol. 26, pt. 1: 431–32.
13 Ibid.
14 Turner to W. R. Bradfute, November 26, 1863, ORN, vol. 20: 852; Turner to Bee, November 26, 1863, OR, vol. 26, pt. 2: 444.
15 Lufkin, History of the Thirteenth Maine, 29.
16 Townsend, Yankee Invasion of Texas, 51; T. E. G. Ransom to Augustus Sexton, August 18, 1863, OR, vol. 26, pt. 1: 426–27.
17 James Samuel Clark, Life in the Middle West: Reminiscences of J. S. Clark (Chicago: Advance, 1916), 106.
18 Kenneth Wayne Howell, ed., The Seventh Star of the Confederacy: Texas During the Civil War (Denton: University of North Texas Press, 2011), 155–56; Shorey, Story of the Maine Fifteenth, 61–62; John Ireland to Bradfute, November 23, 1863, OR, vol. 26, pt. 1: 447.
19 Bee to Turner, November 19, 1863, OR, vol. 26, pt. 1: 436–37; Bee to Turner, November 21, 1863, OR, vol. 26, pt. 1: 437–38; Fitzhugh, "Saluria," 96.
20 Kirby Smith to Magruder, November 26, 1863, OR, vol. 26, pt. 2: 444.
21 "Organization of the Commands of Colonels Augustus Buchel, Xavier DeBray, A. T. Rainey, and P. N. Luckett," November 11, 1863, OR, vol. 26, pt. 2: 407.
22 Minette Algelt Goyne, ed., Lone Star and Double Eagle: Civil War Letters of a German-Texas Family (Fort Worth: Texas Christian University Press, 1982), 110.
23 Frazier and Hillhouse, Love and War, 171.
24 After the fall of the fort, one Union soldier claimed the armament as Dahlgren pattern gun, six 32-pounders of late manufacture, and a 24-pounder; Jerry Thompson, ed., "A Chicken for Breakfast at the Expense of Mr. Rebel: The Journal of Sergeant Nelson Howard, Company E, 13th Maine Infantry on the Texas Coast, 1863-1864," Southwestern Historical Quarterly 123, no. 3 (January 2020), 329.
25 Fitzhugh, "Saluria," 97; OR, vol. 26, pt. 2: 446.
26 Shorey, Story of the Maine Fifteenth, 62.
27 T. E. G. Ransom to William H. Morgan, December 6, 1863, OR, vol. 26, pt. 1: 427-28; Jno. Ireland to Bradfute, November 23, 1863, OR, vol. 26, pt. 1: 447.
28 Shorey, Story of the Maine Fifteenth, 63; Isaac H. Elliott, History of the Thirty-Third Regiment Illinois Veteran Volunteer Infantry in the Civil War (Gibson City, IL: Regimental Association, 1902), 16; Ransom to Morgan, December 6, 1863, OR, vol. 26, pt. 1: 427-28.
29 Ibid.
30 C. C. Washburn to Nathaniel P. Banks, December 6, 1863, OR, vol. 26, pt. 1: 418–20; Shorey, Story of the Maine Fifteenth, 56–57.
31 Albert O. Marshall, Army Life, From a Soldier's Journal: Incidents, Sketches and Record of a Union Soldier's Army Life in Camp and Field, 1861–64, (Joliet, IL: Chicago Legal News, 1884), 335; Washburn to Banks, December 3, 1863, OR, vol. 26, pt. 1: 421.
32 Bradfute to Turner, July 15, 1863, and Bradfute to Turner, November 27, 1863, Bradfute CSR-T.
33 Marshall, Army Life, 328–29.
34 Henry D. Washburn to C. C. Washburn, December 3, 1863, OR, vol. 26, pt. 1: 421–22; Ransom to William H. Morgan, December 6, 1863, OR, vol. 26, pt. 1: 427–28.
35 Marshall, Army Life, 328-329; Washburn, December 3, 1863, OR, vol. 26, pt. 1: 422.
36 Marshall, Army Life, 326–27.
37 Henry D. Washburn to C. C. Washburn, December 3, 1863, OR, vol. 26, pt. 1: 421–22.
38 Leon Smith to Magruder, November 30, 1863, ORN, vol. 20: 853; Bradfute to Turner, November 27, 1863, Bradfute CSR-T.
39 Marshall, Army Life, 333.
40 Henry D. Washburn to C. C. Washburn, December 3, 1863, OR, vol. 26, pt. 1: 421–22; Elliott, History of the Thirty-Third, 48.

41   Dudley J. Wooten, ed. A *Comprehensive History of Texas* (Dallas, TX: Scarff, 1898), I: 542; Henry D. Washburn to C. C. Washburn, December 3, 1863, OR, vol. 26, pt. 1: 421–22.

42   Henry D. Washburn to C. C. Washburn, December 3, 1863, OR, vol. 26, pt. 1: 421–22; Shorey, *Story of the Maine Fifteenth*, 60.

43   Leon Smith to Magruder, November 30, 1863, ORN, vol. 20: 853; Goyne, *Lone Star and Double Eagle*, 112.

44   Leon Smith to John B. Magruder, December 1, 1863, ORN, vol. 20: 853–54.

CHAPTER SEVENTEEN

1   Tom Green to J. B. Magruder, December 4, 1863, OR, vol. 26, pt. 2: 477.

2   Augustus Buchel to E. P. Turner, November 9, 1863, OR, vol. 26, pt. 2: 400.

3   N. J. T. Dana to Nathaniel P. Banks, November 15, 1863, OR, vol. 26, pt. 1: 412–13.

4   Edmonds, *Yankee Autumn*, 336–37; Hass, "Diary of Julius Giesecke," 78–79.

5   William Frederick Weeks to Judge John Moore, February 1, 1864, Weeks Papers.

6   Botkin, *Slave Narratives*, vol. 16, pt. 4: 44–46.

7   Janet Allured, Judith F. Gentry, Mary Farmer-Kaiser, and Shannon Frystak, eds., *Louisiana Women: Their Life and Times* (Athens: University of Georgia Press, 2015), 103; as quoted in Edmonds, *Yankee Autumn*, 355–57.

8   Howell Diary, November 17, 1863; Edmonds, *Yankee Autumn*, 353–54.

9   Edmonds, *Yankee Autumn*, 358–60; Howell Diary, November 20, 1863; Hass, "Diary of Julius Giesecke," 79.

10   Charles P. Stone to Banks, November 19, 1863, OR, vol. 26, pt. 1: 810; Edmonds, *Yankee Autumn*, 358–60; Howell Diary, November 20, 1863; Hass, "Diary of Julius Giesecke."

11   Edmonds, *Yankee Autumn*, 364–70; Hass, "Diary of Julius Giesecke," 79; Howell Diary, November 21–23, 1863.

12   Howell Diary, November 20–22, 1863.

13   H. C. Wright, "Reminiscences of H. C. Wright of Austin," Wright, H. C., Reminiscences, 1840–1865, Dolph Briscoe Center for American History, University of Texas, Austin, 64.

14   Ibid.

15   Ibid. The Texan picket line was positioned near present-day Cade, Louisiana.

16   Ibid.

17   Ibid.

18   Ibid.

19   Ibid.

20   John W. Watkins to Irene Watkins, November 28, 1863, Watkins Letters.

21   Wright, "Reminiscences," 67.

22   Hass, "Diary of Julius Giesecke," 79.

23   Ibid., 79–80.

24   Sibley Diary, November 27, 1863.

25   Mix, *Civil War Journal*, 27–28.

26   Howell Diary, November 30, 1863.

27   Mix, *Civil War Journal*, 28.

28   "Department of the Gulf: The Banks Expedition, Return of General Banks," *New York Times*, December 4, 1863.

29   Ibid.

30   Ibid.

31   "S" to "Dear Bro.," November 9, 1863, Union Sailor Civil War Letter, Mss. 4890, Louisiana and Lower Mississippi Valley Collection, Hill Memorial Library, Louisiana State University.

32   See Fred Harvey Harrington, "The Fort Jackson Mutiny," *Journal of Negro History* 27, no. 4 (October 1942): 420–31.

33   Abraham Lincoln papers http://www.loc.gov/resource/mal.2842600State.

34   Ibid.

35 Ibid.
36 Lincoln to Nathaniel P. Banks, November 5, 1863, *Collected Works* 7: 91–92.
37 Ibid.
38 Banks to Lincoln, December 3, 1863, *Collected Works* 7: 90-91.
39 Ibid.
40 Ibid.
41 Lincoln to Banks, December 24, 1863, *Collected Works* 7: 89-90.
42 *The Statutes at Large, Treaties, and Proclamations of the United States of America, from December 1863 to December 1865*, vol. 13 (Boston: Little, Brown, 1866), 737–39.
43 Halleck to Banks, December 7, 1863, OR, vol. 26, pt. 1: 834–35.
44 Blessington, *Campaigns of Walker's Texas Division*, 153.
45 Ragan, "Diary of Captain George W. O'Brien," 429.
46 Jane Chinn, "The Burning of the Barns," 8, Chinn (Jane McCausland) Reminiscence, Mss. 2647, Louisiana and Lower Mississippi Valley Collection, Hill Memorial Library Louisiana State University; Blessington, *Campaigns of Walker's Texas Division*, 153.
47 Ragan, "Diary of Captain George W. O'Brien," 430.
48 Blessington, *Campaigns of Walker's Texas Division*, 155–56.
49 Lowe, *Walker's Texas Division*, 155–56.
50 Thomas W. Knox, *Camp-Fire and Cotton-Field: Southern Adventure in Time of War, Life with the Union Armies, and Residence on a Louisiana Plantation* (New York: Blelock, 1865), 471.
51 Ibid.
52 Ibid., 472–73.
53 Ibid.; Lowe, *Walker's Texas Division*, 155–56.
54 Knox, *Camp Fire and Cotton Field*, 472–73.
55 Ibid., 477.
56 Bearss, *Louisiana Confederate*, 61.
57 Lowe, *Walker's Texas Division*, 157–59; Hyatt Diary, December 12–13, 1863.
58 Bearss, *Louisiana Confederate*, 66–67.

CHAPTER EIGHTEEN
1   C. C. Washburn to Banks, December 1, 1863, OR, vol. 26, pt. 1: 417.
2   C. C. Washburn to Banks, December 1, 1863, OR, vol. 26, pt. 1: 418.
3   Elliott, *History of the Thirty-Third*, 249.
4   C. C. Washburn to Banks, November 30, 1863, OR, vol. 26, pt. 1: 417; C. C. Washburn to Banks, December 1, 1863, OR, vol. 26, pt. 1: 417.
5   C. C. Washburn to Banks, December 1, 1863, OR, vol. 26, pt. 1: 418.
6   Charles Stone to Washburn, December 5, 1863, OR, vol. 26, pt. 1: 420.
7   Ibid.
8   While Edmund J. Davis and the 1st Texas Cavalry (Union) moved up the river road, elements of the 37th Illinois Infantry followed, accompanied by the steamer *Mustang* loaded with supplies. August Santleben, *A Texas Pioneer: Early Staging and Overland Freighting Days on the Frontiers of Texas and Mexico*, ed. I. D. Affleck (New York: Neale, 1910), 32; Townsend, *Yankee Invasion of Texas*, 31.
9   J. F. Rowley Diary, Ragan MSS 00118, Box 1, Cushing Memorial Library and Archives, Texas A&M University, 3.
10 A. J. Hamilton to E. M. Stanton, December 19, 1863, OR, vol. 26, pt. 1: 865–66.
11 Townsend, *Yankee Invasion of Texas*, 43.
12 C. P. Stone to C. C. Washburn, December 10, 1863, OR, vol. 26, pt. 1: 837–38.
13 Frazier and Hillhouse, *Love and War*, 187.
14 Ibid., 188.
15 Goyne, *Lone Star and Double Eagle*, 113.
16 Ibid., 114.

17 Ibid., 114–15.
18 Frazier and Hillhouse, *Love and War*, 190.
19 Ibid., 190.
20 Green to Magruder, December 4, 1863, OR, vol. 26, pt. 2: 477.
21 Ibid.
22 Ibid.
23 Ibid. Tom Green faced a smear campaign in Texas during the summer and fall of 1862, and rumors flew around the state that he was a drunk, had been drinking with Sibley instead of managing the campaign, and was generally unfit for command. See Frazier, *Thunder Across the Swamp*.
24 Richard Taylor to Magruder, December 4, 1863, OR, vol. 26, pt. 2: 476.
25 Green to Magruder, December 4, 1863, OR, vol. 26, pt. 2: 477.

CHAPTER NINETEEN
1   Haynes, *Thrilling Narrative*, 30.
2   Ibid.
3   Ibid., 36.
4   Ibid., 32–35.
5   Howell Diary, November 30–June 14, 1863.
6   Ibid.
7   Howell Diary, November 30–June 14, 1863; "Return of the Fourth Division," OR, vol. 26, pt. 1: 431; E. Cunningham to John B. Magruder, December 2, 1863, OR, vol. 26, pt. 2: 468.
8   "Presentation of the Portrait of General Tom Green," 9, Miscellaneous Manuscripts and Addresses, Texas State Library and Archives Commission
9   Taylor, *Destruction and Reconstruction*, 178.
10 William Randolph Howell to Sallie Patrick, May 21, 1864, Howell Papers.
11 Thomas Green to Magruder, December 17, 1863, OR, vol. 26, pt. 2: 512.
12 Edmonds, *Yankee Autumn*, 392–93. This translates as "We Go. We go to Texas!"
13 Charles Stone to C. C. Washburn, December 5, 1863, OR, vol. 26, pt. 1: 420. Townsend, *Yankee Invasion of Texas*, 33–34.
14 Elliott, *History of the Thirty-Third*, 54; Alexander Edwin Sweet and John Armoy Knox, *On a Mexican Mustang, through Texas, from the Gulf to the Rio Grande* (Hartford, CT: S. S. Scranton, 1883), 476-477.
15 Townsend, *Yankee Invasion of Texas*, 35; C. C. Washburn to Charles P. Stone, December 14, 1863, OR, vol. 26, pt. 1: 853; Elliott, *History of the Thirty-Third*, 53–54.
16 Bobby J. McKinney, *Confederates on the Caney: An Illustrated Account of the Civil War on the Texas Gulf Coast* (Rosenberg, TX: Mouth of the Caney Publication, 1994), 2.
17 N. P. Banks to H. W. Halleck, December 12, 1863, OR, vol. 26, pt. 1: 847.
18 Ibid.
19 Kurt Hackemer, "Strategic Dilemma: Civil-Military Friction and the Texas Coastal Campaign of 1863," *Military History of the West* 26 (Fall 1996): 209.
20 C. C. Washburn to Stone, December 13, 1863, OR, vol. 26, pt. 1: 849; C. C. Washburn to Stone, December 15, 1863, OR, vol. 26, pt. 1: 859.
21 Townsend, *Yankee Invasion of Texas*, 34; N. J. T. Dana to N. P. Banks, December 24, 1863, OR, vol. 26, pt. 1: 876.
22 Townsend, *Yankee Invasion of Texas*, 35.
23 Frazier and Hillhouse, *Love and War*, 196.
24 Karen Gerhardt Fort, ed., *A Feast of Reason: The Civil War Journal of James Madison Hall* (Abilene, TX: State House Press, 2017), 139–40.
25 Sweet and Knox, *On a Mexican Mustang*, 479.
26 Ibid., 490–91.

27 Ibid., 491.

28 Ibid.

29 Ibid.

30 Ibid.

31 Ibid.

32 Ibid.

33 Ibid.

34 Ibid.

35 Ibid.

36 Ibid.

37 Ibid., 497.

38 Townsend, *Yankee Invasion of Texas*, 35–36.

CHAPTER TWENTY

1   Townsend, *Yankee Invasion of Texas*, 36; Lufkin, *History of the Thirteenth Maine*, 62. The USS *Sciota*, a ninety-day gunboat, had already seen hard service on the coast of Texas and Mexico. Finally relieved in the summer of 1863, the *Sciota* was steaming up the Mississippi River toward New Orleans when the gunboat USS *Antona* accidently rammed it and sank the vessel in twelve feet of water. Refloated, the *Sciota* proceeded to New Orleans for a complete overhaul. The ship returned to the coast of Texas in early December 1863.

2   Townsend, *Yankee Invasion of Texas*, 36.

3   Frank S. Hesseltine to T. E. G. Ransom, January 1, 1864, OR, vol. 26, pt. 1: 747.

4   E. P. Turner to William Alston, December 30, 1863, ORN, vol. 20: 749.

5   Hesseltine to Ransom, January 1, 1864, OR, vol. 26, pt. 1: 747; Augustus Buchel to L. G. Aldrich, December 31, 1863, ORN, vol. 20: 750.

6   Log of USS *Monongahela*, ORN, vol. 20: 745; Log of USS *Sciota*, ORN, vol. 20: 745.

7   Hesseltine to Ransom, January 1, 1864, OR, vol. 26, pt. 1: 747.

8   E. S. Rugeley to James Perry Bryan, ORN, vol. 21: 857–58; Hesseltine to Ransom, January 1, 1864, OR, vol. 26, pt. 1: 747.

9   Hesseltine to Ransom, January 1, 1864, OR, vol. 26, pt. 1: 747.

10 Log of USS *Sciota*, ORN, vol. 20: 745.

11 Rugeley to Bryan, ORN, vol. 21: 857–58.

12 Hesseltine to Ransom, January 1, 1864, OR, vol. 26, pt. 1: 747.

13 Rugeley to Bryan, ORN, vol. 21: 857–58; Hesseltine to Ransom, January 1, 1864, OR, vol. 26, pt. 1: 748.

14 Charles A. Siringo, *A Texas Cow Boy, or Fifteen Years on the Hurricane Deck of a Spanish Pony* (Chicago: Siringo and Dobson, 1886), 1, 17, 24.

15 Log of USS *Monongahela*, ORN, vol. 20: 745; Log of USS *Sciota*, ORN, vol. 20: 745.

16 Log of USS *Sciota*, ORN, vol. 20: 746; Hesseltine to Ransom, January 1, 1864, OR, vol. 26, pt. 1: 748.

17 Siringo, *Texas Cow Boy*, 26–27.

18 Banks to Halleck, December 30, 1863, OR, vol. 26, pt. 1: 889.

19 Ibid.

20 Ibid.

21 Banks to Halleck, December 23, 1863, OR, vol. 26, pt. 1: 871–72; Banks to Halleck, December 30, 1863, OR, vol. 26, pt. 1: 890; Halleck to Banks, January 4, 1864, OR, vol. 34, pt. 2: 15.

22 Ibid.

23 Halleck to Banks, December 7, 1863, OR, vol. 26, pt. 1: 834–35.

24 Ibid.

25 Ibid.

26 J. M. Schofield to Banks, November 19, 1863, OR, vol. 26, pt. 1: 807.

CHAPTER TWENTY ONE

[1] Schoonover, *Mexican Lobby*, 33; *London Daily News*, January 4, 1864; N. P. Banks to H. Halleck, December 11, 1863, OR, vol. 26, pt. 1: 840.

[2] Banks to Halleck, December 11, 1863, OR, vol. 26, pt. 1: 840–41.

[3] N. J. T. Dana to Banks, December 24, 1863, OR, vol. 26, pt. 1: 876.

[4] "Two Days Later from Europe; the Columbia at St. John's N.F. Maximilian Preparing to Go to Mexico. Marshal Forey's Visit to Washington," *New York Times*, January 17, 1864.

[5] Lynn Marshall Case and Warren F. Spencer, *The United States and France: Civil War Diplomacy* (Philadelphia: University of Pennsylvania Press, 1970), 308, 312, 508–9; Patrick J. Kelly, "The North American Crisis of the 1860s," *Journal of the Civil War Era* 2, no. 3 (September 2012): 351–52.

[6] Schoonover, *Mexican Lobby*, 33–35; John G. Nicolay and John Hay, *Abraham Lincoln: A History* (10 vols., New York: Century, 1890), 7:407; Silverman, Jason H., "A Most Unlikely Friendship: Abraham Lincoln and Matias Romero," the website for President Lincoln's Cottage, January 26, 2017, http://www.lincolncottage.org/a-most-unlikely-friendship-abraham-lincoln-and-matias-romero/#_ednref26.

[7] Schoonover, *Mexican Lobby*, 33–35; Nicolay and Hay, *Abraham Lincoln*, 7:407; Silverman, "Most Unlikely Friendship."

[8] Beecher, *Record of the 114th Regiment*, 284–85.

[9] Ibid.

[10] G. Norman Lieber, "Special Orders, No. 322," December 24, 1863, OR, vol. 26, pt. 1: 879.

[11] Thompson, *Cortina*, 168.

[12] L. Pierce, Jr., to F. J. Herron, January 12, 1864, in *Papers Relative to Mexican Affairs, Communicated to the Senate June 16, 1864* (Washington, DC: Government Printing Office, 1865), 62–63.

[13] Matias Romero to William H. Seward, February 4, 1864, in *Papers Relative to Mexican Affairs*, 58–59; Henry Bertram to F. J. Herron, January 12, 1864, in *Papers Relative to Mexican Affairs*, 64; Herron to C. P. Stone, February 4, 1864, in *Papers Relative to Mexican Affairs*, 65.

[14] ORN, series 1, vol. 21: 39–40. The 1st and 2nd Brigades, 2nd Division, were on the Rio Grande, while the 3rd Brigade served at Matagorda Bay. The 1st and 3rd Divisions were also at Matagorda Bay.

[15] Lincoln, January 23, 1864, *Collected Works*, 7:148.

[16] Notes to Lincoln, January 23, 1864, *Collected Works*, 7:148.

[17] General Orders No. 101, "For Recruiting Veteran Volunteers," June 25, 1863, OR, series 3, vol. 3: 414–15.

[18] Elliott, *History of the Thirty-Third*, 136.

[19] Steele to Banks, February 5, 1864, OR, vol. 34, pt. 2: 246–47.

[20] John M. Schofield to Halleck, November 10, 1863, OR, vol. 22, pt. 2: 701; William Steele to Schofield, November 9, 1863, OR, vol. 22, pt. 2: 700; *New York Times*, November 7, 1863; Schofield to Banks, November 19, 1863, OR, vol. 26, pt. 1: 807; Halleck to Banks, November 19, 1863, OR, vol. 26, pt. 1: 806; Halleck to Banks, January 4, 1864, OR, vol. 34, pt. 2: 15.

[21] Halleck to Banks, January 4, 1864, OR, vol. 34, pt. 2: 16; Halleck to Banks, January 11, 1864, OR, vol. 34, pt. 2: 55–56.

[22] Halleck to Banks, January 4, 1864, OR, vol. 34, pt. 2: 16; Halleck to Banks, January 11, 1864, OR, vol. 34, pt. 2: 55–56.

[23] Sherman to Banks, January 16, 1864, OR, vol. 34, pt. 2: 431.

[24] Ibid.

[25] Irwin, *Nineteenth Army Corps*, 282.

[26] Banks to Halleck, January 23, 1864, OR, vol. 34, pt. 2: 133–34.

[27] Ibid.

[28] Log of USS *Monongahela*, January 16, 1864, ORN, vol. 21: 39–40.

29 Log of USS *Sciota*, January 20–21, 1864, ORN, vol. 21: 48–49; Log of USS *Monongahela*, January 20–22, 1864, ORN, vol. 21: 48–49.

30 T. E. G. Ransom to Hugh G. Brown, January 25, 1864, OR, vol. 34, pt. 1: 100.

31 Goyne, *Lone Star and Double Eagle*, 117.

32 Ransom to Brown, January 25, 1864, OR, vol. 34, pt. 1: 50–51.

33 Dana to W. B. Scates, January 28, 1864, OR, vol. 34, pt. 1: 99.

34 Ibid.

35 Rowley Diary, 3–4.

36 Rowley Diary, 4.

37 Rowley Diary, 5–6.

CHAPTER TWENTY TWO

1 Norman Brown, ed., *Journey to Pleasant Hill: The Civil War Letters of Captain Elijah P. Petty, Walker's Texas Division, CSA* (Austin: University of Texas Press, 1982), 313.

2 Brown, *Journey to Pleasant Hill*, 312.

3 Ibid., 325.

4 Richard Taylor to William R. Boggs, January 16, 1864, OR, vol. 34, pt. 2: 879; Edmund Kirby Smith to Jefferson Davis, January 20, 1864, OR, vol. 34, pt. 2: 895–96.

5 Taylor to Boggs, January 16, 1864, OR, vol. 34, pt. 2: 879; Kirby Smith to Davis, January 20, 1864, OR, vol. 34, pt. 2: 895–96.

6 Kirby Smith to Davis, January 20, 1864, OR, vol. 34, pt. 2: 895–96; Taylor to Boggs, January 16, 1864, OR, vol. 34, pt. 2: 879.

7 Taylor, *Destruction and Reconstruction*, 235; F. Jay Taylor, ed., *Reluctant Rebel: The Secret Diary of Robert Patrick, 1861–1865* (Baton Rouge: Louisiana State University Press, 1959), 21; Ethel Taylor, "Discontent in Confederate Louisiana," *Louisiana History* 2, no. 4 (Autumn 1861): 419.

8 Taylor, "Discontent in Confederate Louisiana," 420.

9 Taylor to Boggs, January 11, 1864, OR, vol. 34, pt. 2: 852–53.

10 Taylor o Boggs, January 11, 1864, OR, vol. 34, pt. 2: 852–53; Taylor, *Destruction and Reconstruction*, 182; T. Michael Parrish, *Richard Taylor: Soldier Prince of Dixie* (Chapel Hill: University of North Carolina Press, 1992), 317–20.

11 "State of Things in Lower Louisiana," *Galveston Weekly News*, September 2, 1863.

12 Brown, *Journey to Pleasant Hill*, 262.

13 Haynes, *Thrilling Narrative*, 32-35.

14 Ibid.

15 Ibid.

16 Ibid.

17 Ibid.

18 Ibid.

19 Ibid.

20 Joseph B. Young, "Sworn Affidavit," February 13, 1864, OR, vol. 34, pt. 2: 964; Taylor, "Discontent in Confederate Louisiana," 425–28.

21 Terence Jeansanne, "Sworn Affidavit," February 13, 1864, OR, vol. 34, pt. 2: 964; Taylor, "Discontent in Confederate Louisiana," 425–28.

22 Francois Savoy, "Sworn Affidavit," February 13, 1864, OR, vol. 34, pt. 2: 965; Taylor, "Discontent in Confederate Louisiana," 425–28.

23 H. C. Monell to Taylor, February 13, 1864, OR, vol. 34, pt. 2: 965–66.

24 Lyons to Richard Taylor, February 13, 1864, OR, vol. 34, pt. 2: 966–67.

25 John D. Winters, *The Civil War in Louisiana* (Baton Rouge: Louisiana State University Press, 1963), 318–19.

26 As quoted in Parrish, *Richard Taylor*, 319.

27 Howell Diary, January 9, 1864.

28 Ibid., January 19, 1864.

TEMPEST OVER TEXAS   479

29 John W. Watkins to Irene Watkins, January 25, 1864, Watkins Letters.
30 Kerby, *Kirby Smith's Confederacy*, 177.
31 Howell Diary, February 6–27, 1864.
32 F. S. Wade, "Reconstruction Days," in *Hog Eye Stories*, 22.
33 Ibid., 23.
34 Ibid., 23–24.
35 Frazier and Hillhouse, *Love and War*, 203. Ball was east of the present-day town of Bay City, Texas.
36 Frank E. Vandiver, ed., "Letters from the Confederate Medical Service," *Southwestern Historical Quarterly* 55, no. 3 (January 1952): 384.
37 Frazier and Hillhouse, *Love and War*, 203.
38 John Warren Hunter, *Heel-Fly Times in Texas: A Story of the Civil War Period in Texas* (Bandera, TX: Frontier Times, 1931), 7–8.
39 Ibid.
40 Ibid.
41 Rowley Diary, 6–7.
42 Ibid.
43 Ibid., 8–11.
44 Ibid.
45 Ibid., 11–14.
46 Ibid.
47 Ibid., 14–29.
48 Vandiver, "Letters from the Confederate Medical Service," 381.
49 Ibid., 384, 387.
50 Goyne, *Lone Star and Double Eagle*, 113.
51 Kelly, "North American Crisis of the 1860s," 357.

EPILOGUE
1   Irwin, *Nineteenth Army Corps*, 282.
2   Brasseaux and Mooney, *Ruined by the Miserable War*, 56.
3   Ibid.
4   Ibid., 54–56.
5   General Orders No. 23, February 3, 1864, OR, vol. 34, pt. 2: 231.
6   *New York Times*, February 15, 1864, p. 55.
7   General Orders No. 23, February 3, 1864, OR, vol. 34, pt. 2: 231.
8   Banks quoted by Fauconnet in Brasseaux and Mooney, *Ruined by the Miserable War*, 56; *New York Times*, February 15, 1864, p. 55.
9   Haynes, *Thrilling Narrative*, 50–51.
10 Ibid.
11 Ibid.
12 Ibid., 53–54.
13 S. S. Anderson to John B. Magruder, March 5, 1864, OR, vol. 34, pt. 2: 1027.
14 Howell Diary, March 7, 1864.

BIBLIOGRAPHY

MANUSCRIPT COLLECTIONS

Aimer Collection. Watson Memorial Library. Cammie G. Watson Research Center. Northwestern State University, Natchitoches, LA.

Amsler Family Papers, 1848–1939. The Texas Collection. Baylor University.

Anonymous Civil War Diary. [Company C, 28th Massachusetts], Mss. 3328. Louisiana and Lower Mississippi Valley Collection. Hill Memorial Library. Louisiana State University.

Bradley, James E. Papers, Mss. 1259. Louisiana and Lower Mississippi Valley Collection. Hill Memorial Library. Louisiana State University.

Burrud, John B. Papers, 1862–1870, Mss Hm 75115-75334. Huntington Library.

Chinn, Jane McCausland. Reminiscence, Mss. 2647. Louisiana and Lower Mississippi Valley Collection. Hill Memorial Library. Louisiana State University.

Civil War Letters, 1863. MSS 3188, Misc: C. Louisiana and Lower Mississippi Valley Collection. Hill Memorial Library. Louisiana State University.

Colby, Carlos W. Papers, 1821–1937. Vault Case, MS 10014. Newberry Library. Chicago.

Collard, Felix Robert. "Reminiscences of a Private, Co. G, 7th Texas Cavalry, Sibley Brigade, C.S.A." Private collection. Typescript in possession of the author and used with permission of Dr. Felix Robert Collard, Silver City, New Mexico.

Confederate Imprints, Confederate Pamphlets 306, 394. Manuscript Department. William R. Perkins Library. Duke University.

Connor, H. N. "The Diary of 1st Sergeant H. N. Connor." W. T. Block, editor. *http://www.wtblock.com/wtblockjr/diaryof.htm*.

Corothers, William. Diary and Letters. Duncan C. Corothers Collection. Archives and Information Division. Texas State Library and Archives Commission.

Fortier, Alcee trans., Heléne Dupuy, *Memorable Days and Various Notable Circumstances During the Civil War in the United States in the State of Louisiana from 1861 to 1865*. Private collection. Typescript in the possession of the author.

Guess, George W. Letters. Mss. 793. Louisiana and Lower Mississippi Valley Collection. Hill Memorial Library. Louisiana State University.

Haas, Oscar. Papers, 1844–1955. Dolph Briscoe Center for American History. University of Texas, Austin.

Harding, Miss Sidney. Diaries, July 1863. U-230. Mss. 721. Louisiana and Lower Mississippi Valley Collection. Hill Memorial Library. Louisiana State University.

Hartly, Edward. Civil War Collection. Missouri History Museum, St. Louis.

Howell, W. Randolph. Papers, 1861–79. Eugene C. Barker Texas History Collection. Dolph Briscoe Center for American History, University of Texas, Austin.

Hyatt, Arthur W. Papers, Mss. 180. Louisiana and Lower Mississippi Valley Collection. Hill Memorial Library. Louisiana State University.

Ketzle, Henry Carl. "Civil War Diary of Henry Carl Ketzle, 37th Illinois Volunteer Infantry, Company A, 1861–1866." *http://www.ketzle.com/diary/fullcwdiary.htm*, accessed February 7, 2014.

Klein, Joseph. "Civil War Memories," *http://marilyndoyle.com/Klein/klein.html*.

Kopke, H. F. Letters. Private collection. Manuscript in possession of Randy Mallory, Tyler, Texas.

Lauve, Gustave. Letter. Mss. 893. Louisiana and Lower Mississippi Valley Collection. Hill Memorial Library. Louisiana State University.

League, Thomas Jefferson. Papers, 1855–1863. Rosenberg Library. Galveston, Texas.

Lincoln, Abraham. Papers. Library of Congress, Washington, DC. American Memory Project. Transcribed and annotated by the Lincoln Studies Center. Knox College, Galesburg, IL. *http://memory.loc.gov/ammem/alhtml/alhome.html*.

Machen, Henry L. Collection. Watson Memorial Library. Cammie G. Watson Research Center. Northwestern State University, Natchitoches, LA.

McDade, Keet. Letters. Private collection. Typescript courtesy of Vernon Williams, Abilene Christian University.

McIlhenny, Sarah Avery. Collection. McIlhenny Company Archives. McIlhenny Company. Avery Island, LA.Rowley, J. F. Diary. Ragan MSS 00118, Box 1. Cushing Memorial Library and Archives. Texas A & M University.

Shelly, William. Diary. Mss. 3604. Louisiana and Lower Mississippi Valley Collection. Hill Memorial Library. Louisiana State University.

Sibley, John Coleman. "Civil War Diary and Letters of Lieutenant John Coleman Sibley, 2nd Louisiana Cavalry, Company E, Confederate States of America." Donald Ray Parker, ed. Bound typescript. John Coleman Sibley Collection. Box 2. Cammie G. Henry Research Center, Watson Memorial Library, Northwestern State University, Natchitoches, LA.

Soule, H. Papers. Bentley Historical Library. University of Michigan.

Stoker, William E. Papers. National Civil War Museum. Harrisburg, PA.

Union Sailor Civil War Letter, Mss. 4890. Louisiana and Lower Mississippi Valley Collection. Hill Memorial Library. Louisiana State University.

Wade, F. S. "Hog Eye Stories." Originally published in the *Elgin (Texas) Courier*.

Watkins, John W. Letters. Harold B. Simpson Confederate Research Center. Hill College. Hillsboro, TX.

Weeks, David. Family Papers. Louisiana and Lower Mississippi Valley Collection. Hill Memorial Library. Louisiana State University.

Wharton, Edward Clifton. Family Papers. Mss. 1553, 1575, 1594, 1610, 1613, 1663, 1714, 1736. Louisiana and Lower Mississippi Valley Collection. Hill Memorial Library. Louisiana State University.

Williams, Robert Thomas. "The Diary of Robert Thomas Williams: Marches, Skirmishes, and Battles of the Fourth Regiment, Texas Mounted Volunteers, October 1861 to November 1865." Connie O'Donnell, transcriber. Harold B. Simpson Confederate Research Center. Hill College, Hillsboro, TX.

Wright, H. C. "Reminiscences of H. C. Wright of Austin." Wright, H. C., 1840–1865. Eugene C. Barker Texas History Collection. Dolph Briscoe Center for American History, University of Texas, Austin.

GOVERNMENT DOCUMENTS

National Archives and Records Administration. *Compiled Military Service Records of Confederate Soldiers*. Record Group 109.

National Archives and Records Administration. *Compiled Service Records of Confederate Soldiers Who Served in Organizations from the State of Texas*.

National Archives and Records Administration. *Compiled Military Service Records of Volunteer Soldiers Who Served the United States*. Record Group 94. RG 109, M323.

National Archives and Records Administration. *Orders and Circulars, 1797–1910. Records of the Adjutant General's Office, 1780s–1917*. Record Group 94.

Naval Historical Center, Department of the Navy. *Dictionary of American Fighting Ships*. 8 vols. Washington, DC: Government Printing Office, 1975–81.

Papers Relative to Mexican Affairs, Communicated to the Senate June 16, 1864. Washington, DC: Government Printing Office, 1865.

Report of the Joint Committee on the Conduct of the War at the Second Session Thirty-Eighth Congress. Washington, DC: Government Printing Office, 1865.

The Statutes at Large, Treaties, and Proclamations of the United States of America, from December 1863 to December 1865. Vol. 13. Boston: Little, Brown, 1866.

U.S. Congress, Senate, *Message from the President of the United States*. 38th Congress, 2d. session. Senate Ex. Doc. No. 11:281.

U.S. Department of the Navy. *Report of the Secretary of the Navy, December 1863*. Washington, DC: Government Printing Office, 1863.

U.S. Naval War Records Office. *Official Records of the Union and Confederate Navies in the War of the Rebellion*. 27 vols. Washington, DC: Government Printing Office, 1894–1922.

U.S. War Department. *How to Feed an Army*. Washington, DC: Government Printing Office, 1901.

U.S. War Department. *The War of the Rebellion: A Compilation of the Official Records of the Union and Confederate Armies*. 128 vols. Washington, DC: Government Printing Office, 1880–1901.

Work Progress Administration. *Slave Narratives: A Folk History of Slavery in the United States from Interviews with Former Slaves*. Vol. 16, *Texas Narratives*. Washington, DC: Government Printing Office, 1941.

NEWSPAPERS

Amesbury (MA) Villager
Bellville (TX) Countryman
Boston Herald
Boston Morning Journal
Boston Traveler
Charleston Mercury
Chattanooga Rebel
Chicago Tribune
Cincinnati Daily Commercial
Corpus Christi Ranchero
Dallas Herald
Fitchburg (MA) Dailey Sentinel
Franklin (LA) Planters' Banner
Galveston Weekly News
Houston Tri-Weekly Telegraph
Kansas City Star
London Daily News
New Orleans Delta
New York Herald
New York Irish American
New York Times
Overton (TX) Sharp Shooter
Richmond Examiner
Wheeling (WV) Daily Intelligencer

PUBLISHED PRIMARY SOURCES

Anderson, John Q., ed., *Brokenburn: The Journal of Kate Stone, 1861–1868*. Baton Rouge: Louisiana State University Press, 1955.

Banasik, Michael E., ed. *Duty, Honor, Country: The Civil War Experiences of Captain William P. Black, Thirty-Seventh Illinois Infantry.* Iowa City: Camp Pope Bookshop, 2006.

Bangs, I. S. "The Ullman Brigade." *War Papers Read Before the Commandery of the State of Maine, Military Order of the Loyal Legion of the United States.* 4 volumes. Portland: Lefavor-Tower Company, 1898–1915.

Barney, Chester. *Recollections of Field Service with the Twentieth Iowa Infantry Volunteers.* Davenport, IA: Gazette, 1862.

Bauer, Craig, and Todd Mefford. "Eyewitness Report on the Battle of Fort Butler, Donaldsonville, Louisiana, June 27–28, 1863, and a Review of African-American Participation in the Fight." *Louisiana History* 45, No. 2 (Spring 2004): 201–8.

Bearss, Edwin C., ed. *A Louisiana Confederate: The Diary of Felix Pierre Poché.* Eugenie Watson Somdel, trans. Natchitoches: Louisiana Studies Institute, Northwestern State University, 1972.

Beecher, Harris H. *Record of the 114th Regiment, N.Y.S.V.: Where it Went, What it Saw, and What it Did.* Norwich, NY: J. F. Hubbard, Jr., 1866.

Bergeron, Arthur W., Jr., ed. *The Civil War Reminiscences of Major Silas T. Grisamore, C.S.A.* Baton Rouge: Louisiana State University Press, 1993.

Berlin, Ira, Joseph P. Reidy, Leslie S. Rowland, eds. *Freedom's Soldiers: The Black Military Experience in the Civil War.* New York: Cambridge University Press, 1998.

Berlin, Ira, Thavolia Glymph, Steven F. Miller, Joseph P. Reidy, Leslie S. Rowland, and Julie Saville, eds. *Freedom: A Documentary History of Emancipation, 1861–1867, Selected from the Holdings of the National Archives of the United States.* Series 1, Volume 3: *The Wartime Genesis of Free Labor: The Lower South.* New York: Cambridge University Press, 1990.

Blessington, Joseph Palmer. *The Campaigns of Walker's Texas Division: Containing a Complete Record of the Campaigns In Texas, Louisiana And Arkansas . . .* New York: Lang, Little and Company, 1875; reprint Austin: State House Press, 1994.

Bosson, Charles F. *History of the Forty-Second Regiment Infantry, Massachusetts Volunteers, 1862, 1863, 1864.* Boston: Mills, Knight, 1886.

Brasseaux, Carl A., and Katherine Carmines Mooney, eds. *Ruined by This Miserable War: The Dispatches of Charles Prosper Fauconnet, a French Diplomat in New Orleans, 1863–1868.* Translated by Carl A. Brasseaux. Knoxville: University of Tennessee Press, 2012.

Brown, Norman, ed. *Journey to Pleasant Hill: The Civil War Letters of Captain Elijah P. Petty, Walker's Texas Division, CSA.* Austin: University of Texas Press, 1982.

Bryan, Jimmy L., ed. "Whip Them Like the Mischief: The Civil War Letters of Frank and Mintie Price." *East Texas Historical Journal* 36, no. 2 (1998).

Butler, Benjamin. *Private and Official Correspondence of General Benjamin F. Butler.* Jesse Aimes Marshall, ed. Norwood, MA: Plimpton Press, 1917.

Camouche, Annie Jeter. *The Life of Annie Jeter Carmouche.* New Roads, LA: Pointe Coupee Historical Society, n.d.

Case, Theodore S. *The Quartermaster's Guide: Being a Summary of Those Portions of the Army Regulations of 1863 and General Orders from the War Department from May 1, 1861 to April 10, 1865, which affect the Quartermaster Department.* St. Louis: P. M. Pinkard, 1865.

Clark, James Samuel. *Life in the Middle West, Reminiscences of J. S. Clark.* Chicago: Advance, 1916.

Clark, Orton S. *The One Hundred and Sixteenth Regiment of New York State Volunteers.* Buffalo, NY: Mathews and Warren, 1868.

Clarke, James Freeman. *Memorial and Biographical Sketches.* Boston: Houghton, Osgood, 1878.

Cotham, Edward T., Jr., ed. *The Southern Journey of a Civil War Marine: The Illustrated Notebook of Henry O. Gusley.* Austin: University of Texas Press, 2006.

De Forest, John William. *A Volunteer's Adventures: A Union Captain's Record of the Civil War.* Baton Rouge: Louisiana State University Press, 1996.

Duganne, Augustine Joseph Hickey. *Camps and Prisons: Twenty Months in the Department of the Gulf.* New York: J. P. Robens, 1865.

Dungan, J. Irvine. *History of the Nineteenth Regiment, Iowa Volunteer Infantry.* Davenport, IA: Luse and Griggs, 1865.

Eaton, John. *Grant, Lincoln, and the Freedmen: Reminiscences of the Civil War with Special Reference to the Work for Contrabands and Freedmen of the Mississippi Valley.* New York: Longmans, Green, 1907.

Edmonds, David C., ed. *The Conduct of Federal Troops in Louisiana during the Invasions of 1863 and 1864: Official Report Compiled from the Sworn Testimony under Direction of Governor Henry W. Allen, Shreveport, April, 1865.* Lafayette, LA: Acadiana Press, 1988.

Elder, Donald C., III, ed. *A Damned Iowa Greyhound: The Civil War Letters of William Henry Harrison Clayton.* Iowa City: University of Iowa Press, 1998.

Elliott, Isaac H. *History of the Thirty-Third Regiment Illinois Veteran Volunteer Infantry in the Civil War.* Gibson City, IL: Regimental Association, 1902.

Ewer, James K. *The Third Massachusetts Cavalry in the War for the Union.* Historical Committee of the Regimental Association, 1903.

Fletcher, Samuel H. *History of Company A, Second Illinois Cavalry.* Chicago: Samuel H. Fletcher and D. H. Fletcher, 1912.

Fort, Karen Gerhardt, ed. *A Feast of Reason: The Civil War Journal of James Madison Hall.* Abilene, TX: State House Press, 2017.

Frazier, Donald S., and Andrew Hillhouse, eds. *Love and War: The Civil War Letter and Medicinal Book of Augustus V. Ball.* Buffalo Gap, TX: State House Press, 2010.

Fremantle, Sir Arthur James Lyon. *Three Months in the Southern States: April–June, 1863.* Mobile, AL: S. H. Goetzel, 1864.

Fulfer, Richard J. *A History of the Trials and Hardships of the Twenty-Fourth Indiana Volunteer Infantry.* Indianapolis: Indianapolis Printing, 1913.

Gilbert, Randal B., ed. "The Civil War Diary of Lt. Col. J. B. Leake." *Chronicles of Smith County, Texas* 42, no. 1 (1996).

Goyne, Minette Algelt, ed. *Lone Star and Double Eagle: Civil War Letters of a German-Texas Family.* Fort Worth: Texas Christian University Press, 1982.

Grant, Ulysses S. *The Papers of Ulysses S. Grant.* Edited by John Y. Simon. Vol. 9, *July 7–December 31, 1863.* Carbondale: Southern Illinois University Press, 1982.

Grant, Ulysses S. *Personal Memoirs of U. S. Grant.* 2 vols. New York: Century Company, 1895.

Hanaburgh, D. H. *History of the One Hundred and Twenty-Eighth Regiment, New York Volunteers [U.S. Infantry] in the Late Civil War.* Pokeepsie [Poughkeepsie], NY: Enterprise, 1894.

Harding, George C. *The Miscellaneous Writings of George C. Harding.* Indianapolis: Carlon and Hollenbeck, 1882.

Hass, Oscar, ed. "The Diary of Julius Giesecke, 1863–1865." *Military History of the Southwest* 18, no. 3 (1988): 49–92.

Haynes, Dennis E. *A Thrilling Narrative: A Memoir of a Southern Unionist.* Edited by Arthur Bergeron, Jr. Fayetteville: University of Arkansas Press, 2006.

Hepworth, George H. *The Whip, the Hoe, and Sword; or, the Gulf-Department in '63.* Boston: Walker, Wise, 1864.

Hewitt, Clarissa Grant. *Diary of a Refugee.* Edited by Frances Fern. New York: Moffat, Yard, 1910.

Howard, R. L. *History of the 124th Regiment Illinois Infantry Volunteers: Otherwise known as the Hundred and Two Dozen from August 1862–August 1865.* Springfield, IL: H. W. Rokker, 1880.

Howe, Henry Warren. *Passages from the Life of Henry Warren Howe Consisting of Diary and Letters Written During the Civil War, 1861–1865.* Lowell, MA: Courier-Citizen Company, 1899.

Ingram, Henry L., ed. *Civil War Letters of George W. and Martha Ingram, 1861–1865.* College Station: Texas A & M University Press, 1973.

Irwin, Richard B. *History of the Nineteenth Army Corps*. New York: G. P. Putnam's Sons, 1893.

Johns, Henry T. *Life with the Forty-Ninth Massachusetts Volunteers*. Pittsfield, MA: C. A. Alvord, 1864.

Jones, John William, ed. "Battle of Atchafalaya River—Letter from General Thomas Green to My Dear Wife [Molly Green]." October 1, 1863. In vol. 3 of *Southern Historical Society Papers*. Richmond: Southern Historical Society, 1877.

Jordan-Bychkov, Terry G., et al., eds. "The Boesel Letters: Two Germans in Sibley's Brigade." Translated by Irma Oglendorf Schwarz. *Southwestern Historical Quarterly* 102, no. 4 (April 1999), 457–86.

Knox, Thomas W. *Camp-Fire and Cotton-Field: Southern Adventure in Time of War, Life with the Union Armies, and Residence on a Louisiana Plantation*. New York: Blelock, 1865.

Lane, Walter P. *The Adventures and Recollections of General Walter P. Lane: A San Jacinto Veteran, Containing Sketches of the Texian, Mexican, and Late Wars, with Several Indian Fights Thrown In*. Edited by Jimmy L. Bryan, Jr. Dallas: William P. Clements Center for Southwest Studies, 2000.

LeGrand, Julia. *The Diary of Julia LeGrand, New Orleans 1862–1863*. Edited by Kate Mason Rowland and Mrs. Morris L. Croxall. Richmond, VA: Everett Wadley, 1911.

Lincecum, Jerry Bryan, Edward Hake Phillips, and Peggy A. Redshaw, eds. *Gideon Lincecum's Sword: Civil War Letters from the Texas Home Front*. Denton: University of North Texas Press, 2001.

Lincoln, Abraham. *The Collected Works of Abraham Lincoln*. Edited by Roy P. Basler. 9 vols. New Brunswick, NJ: Rutgers University Press, 1953–55.

Lufkin, Edwin B. *History of the Thirteenth Maine Regiment: From its Organization in 1861 to its Muster-Out in 1865*. Bridgeton, ME: H. A. Shorey, 1898.

Maddocks, Elden B. *History of the Twenty-Sixth Maine Regiment*. Bangor, ME: Charles H. Glass, 1899.

Marshall, Albert O. *Army Life, from a Soldier's Journal: Incidents, Sketches and Record of a Union Soldier's Army Life in Camp and Field, 1861–64*. Joliet, IL: Chicago Legal News, 1884.

Marshall, T. B. *History of the Eighty-Third Ohio Volunteer Infantry: The Greyhound Regiment*. Cincinnati: Eighty-Third Ohio Volunteer Infantry Association, 1912.

Massachusetts Adjutant General's Office. *Massachusetts Soldiers, Sailors, and Marines in the Civil War*. 8 volumes. Norwood, MA: Norwood Press, 1931–1937.

McCann, Thomas H. *The Campaigns of the Civil War in the United States of America*. Hudson County, NJ: Hudson Observer, 1915.

McKinnon, Annie S. "Escape from New Orleans Prison." *Confederate Veteran* 13, no. 1 (January 1905).

McLeary, J. H. "History of Green's Brigade." In Wooten, Dudley G., ed. *A Comprehensive History of Texas*. 2 vols. Dallas: Scarff, 1898.

Mix, Thomas E. *Civil War Journal of Thomas E. Mix, Company B, 118th Illinois Volunteers*. Kenosha, WI: E. M. Earley, 1992.

Moore, Frank, ed. *The Rebellion Record: A Diary of American Events, with Documents, Narratives, Illustrative Incidents, Poetry, etc.* 12 vols. New York: G. P. Putnam, 1861–1863; D. Van Nostrand, 1864–1868.

Moors, John Farwell. *History of the Fifty-Second Regiment, Massachusetts Volunteers*. Boston: G. H. Ellis, 1893.

Muenster, Emily Frazier, and Fred W. Edwards, eds. *From Tallow Candle to Television: An Autobiography of Dr. J. M. Frazier*. Belton, TX: Mary Hardin-Baylor University, 1981.

Murray, Thomas Hamilton. *History of the Ninth Regiment, Connecticut Volunteer Infantry, "The Irish Regiment," in the War of the Rebellion: The Record of a Gallant Command on the March, in Battle, and in Bivouac*. New Haven: Price, Lee, and Adkins, 1908.

New York State Military Museum and Veterans Research Center, NYS Division of Military and Naval Affairs. Unit History Project. "161st Regiment New York Volunteer Infantry

Civil War News Paper Clippings." URL: *http://www.dmna.state.ny.us/historic/reghist/civil/infantry/161stInf/161stInfCWN.htm*. accessed October 15, 2013.

Nicolay, John G., and John Hay. *Abraham Lincoln: A History*. 10 vols. New York: Century, 1890.

Martin Hardwick Hall and Edwin Adams Davis, eds., Noel, Theophilus. *A Campaign from Santa Fe to the Mississippi: Being a History of the Old Sibley Brigade from Its First Organization to the Present Time; Its Campaigns in New Mexico, Arizona, Texas, Louisiana and Arkansas in the Years 1861–2–3–4*. Houston: Stagecoach Press, 1961.

Nott, Charles C. *Sketches in Prison Camps: A Continuation of Sketches of the War*. New York: A. D. F. Randolph, 1865.

Padgett, James A., ed. "Some Letters of George Stanton Denison, 1854–1866: Observations of a Yankee on Conditions in Louisiana and Texas." *Louisiana Historical Quarterly* 23, no. 4 (October 1940): 1132–240.

Parton, James. *History of the Administration of the Department of the Gulf in the Year 1862*. New York: Mason Brothers, 1864.

Pellet, Elias P. *History of the 114th Regiment, New York State Volunteers*. Norwich, NY: Telegraph and Chronicle, 1866.

Plummer, Albert. *History of the Forty-Eighth Regiment M. V. M. During the Civil War*. Boston: New England Druggist, 1907.

Powers, George W. *The Story of the Thirty-eight Regiment of Massachusetts Volunteers*. Cambridge: Dakin and Metcalf, 1866.

Putnam, George Haven. *Memories of My Youth, 1844–1865*. New York: G. P. Putnam's Sons, 1914.

Quien, George. *Reminiscences of the Services and Experience of Lieutenant George Quien of Company K, 23rd Connecticut Volunteers*. Waterbury, CT: 1906.

Rankin, David C., ed. *Diary of a Christian Soldier: Rufus Kinsey and the Civil War*. New York: Cambridge University Press, 2004.

Santleben, August. *A Texas Pioneer: Early Staging and Overland Freighting Days on the Frontiers of Texas and Mexico*. Edited by I. D. Affleck. New York: Neale, 1910.

Scott, R. B. *The History of the 67th Regiment Indiana Infantry Volunteers: War of the Rebellion*. Bedford, IN: Herald, 1892.

Sherman, Andrew M. *In the Lowlands of Louisiana in 1863: An Address Delivered by Andrew M. Sherman at the Forty-Second Reunion of the Twenty-Third Connecticut*. Morristown, NJ: Howard Publishing, 1908.

Sherman, W. T. "The Vermont Boy Who Volunteered in 1861, Served Bravely, was Wounded Grievously, and Died for the Union: Eulogy of General T. E. G. Ransom given before Ransom Post No. 131, Grand Army of the Republic (GAR), St. Louis, Missouri." *Washington National Tribune*, June 20, 1884.

Sherman, William Tecumseh. *Memoirs of General W. T. Sherman*. 2 vols. New York: D. Appleton, 1875.

Shorey, Henry A. *The Story of the Maine Fifteenth: Being a Brief Narrative of the More Important Events in the History of the Fifteenth Maine Regiment*. Bridgeton, ME: Bridgeton News, 1890.

Simpson, Brooks D., ed. *The Civil War: The Third Year Told by Those Who Lived It*. New York: Library of America, 2013.

Siringo, Charles A. *A Texas Cow Boy, or Fifteen Years on the Hurricane Deck of a Spanish Pony*. Chicago: Siringo and Dobson, 1886.

Smith, George G. *Leaves from a Soldier's Diary: The Personal Record of Lieutenant George G. Smith, Co. C, 1st Louisiana Regiment Infantry Volunteers [White] During the War of Rebellion*. Putnam, CT: n.p., 1906.

Stanyan, John M. *A History of the Eighth Regiment of New Hampshire Volunteers*. Concord, NH: Ira C. Evans, 1892.

Stearns, Albert. *Reminiscences of the Late War*. Brooklyn: printed by the author, 1881.

Sweet, Alexander Edwin, and John Armoy Knox. *On a Mexican Mustang, through Texas, from the Gulf to the Rio Grande*. Hartford, CT: S. S. Scranton, 1883.

Taylor, F. Jay, ed. *Reluctant Rebel: The Secret Diary of Robert Patrick, 1861–1865.* Baton Rouge: Louisiana State University Press, 1959.

Taylor, Richard. *Destruction and Reconstruction: Personal Experiences of the Late War.* New York: D. Appleton, 1879.

Thompson, Jerry, ed. *From Desert to Bayou: The Civil War Journal and Sketches of Morgan Wolfe Merrick.* El Paso: Texas Western Press, 1991.

Thompson, Jerry, ed. "A Chicken for Breakfast at the Expense of Mr. Rebel: The Journal of Sergeant Nelson Howard, Company E, 13th Maine Infantry on the Texas Coast, 1863-1864," *Southwestern Historical Quarterly* 123, no. 3 (January 2020), 317-343.

Townsend, Luther Tracy. *History of the Sixteenth Regiment, New Hampshire Volunteers.* Washington, DC, Norman T. Elliot, 1897.

Van Alstyne, Lawrence. *Diary of an Enlisted Man.* New Haven, CT: Tuttle, Morehouse, and Taylor, 1910.

Vandiver, Frank E., ed. *The Civil War Diary of General Josiah Gorgas.* Tuscaloosa: University of Alabama Press, 1947.

Vandiver, Frank E., ed. "Letters from the Confederate Medical Service." *Southwestern Historical Quarterly* 55, no. 3 (January 1952).

Whipple, Henry P. *The Diary of a Private Soldier: The Exact Copy of a Record kept Day by Day During the Civil War by Henry P. Whipple, late a Private in the Twenty-Ninth Wisconsin Volunteer Infantry.* Waterloo, WI: printed by the author, 1906.

Woods, J. T. *Services of the Ninety-Sixth Ohio.* Toledo, OH: Blade, 1874.

Zaragoza, Ignacio. *Cartas y Documentos, selección, introducción y notas de Jorge L. Tamayo.* Mexico: Fondo de Cultura Económica, 2006.

SECONDARY SOURCES

Allardice, Bruce S. *Confederate Colonels: A Biographical Register.* Columbia: University of Missouri Press, 2008.

Allured, Janet, Judith F. Gentry, Mary Farmer-Kaiser, and Shannon Frystak, eds. *Louisiana Women: Their Life and Times.* Athens: University of Georgia Press, 2015.

Arceneaux, William. *Acadian General: Alfred Mouton and the Civil War.* Lafayette: Center for Louisiana Studies, University of Southwestern Louisiana, 1981.

Bailey, Anne J. *Between the Enemy and Texas: Parsons's Texas Cavalry in the Civil War.* Fort Worth: Texas Christian University Press, 1989.

Ballard, Michael. *Vicksburg: The Campaign that Opened the Mississippi.* Chapel Hill: University of North Carolina Press, 2004.

Barker, Nancy N. "Monarchy in Mexico: Hairbrained Scheme or Well-Considered Prospect?" *Journal of Modern History* 48 (March 1976): 51–68.

Barnickle, Linda. *Milliken's Bend: A Civil War Battle in History and Memory.* Baton Rouge: Louisiana State University Press, 2013.

Barr, Alwyn, ed. "The Battle of Bayou Bourbeau, November 3, 1863: Colonel Oran M. Roberts' Report." *Louisiana History* 6, no. 1 (Winter 1965): 83–91.

Barr, Alwyn. *Polignac's Texas Brigade.* College Station: Texas A & M University Press, 1998.

Barringer, William E. *A House Dividing: Lincoln as President Elect.* Springfield, IL: Abraham Lincoln Association, 1945.

Bauer, Craig. *Creole Genesis: The Bringier Family and Antebellum Life in Louisiana.* Lafayette: University of Louisiana at Lafayette Press, 2011.

Bauer, Craig. "The Last Effort: The Secret Mission of the Confederate Diplomat, Duncan F. Kenner." *Louisiana History* 22, No. 1 (Winter 1981): 67–95.

Beard, Rick. "General Grant Takes a Spill." *Opinionator* (blog). *New York Times,* September 4, 2013. *http://opinionator.blogs.nytimes.com/2013/09/04/general-grant-takes-a-spill/.*

Bearss, Edwin Cole. *The Vicksburg Campaign: Grant Strikes a Fatal Blow.* Volume 2. Dayton, OH: Morningside Press, 1986.

Bearss, Edwin Cole. *The Vicksburg Campaign: Unvexed to the Sea*, Volume 3. Dayton, OH: Morningside Press, 1986.

Bearss, Edwin Cole. *The Vicksburg Campaign: Vicksburg is the Key*. Volume 1. Dayton, OH: Morningside Press, 1985.

Bell, Andrew McIlwaine. *Mosquito Soldiers: Malaria, Yellow Fever, and the Course of the American Civil War*. Baton Rouge: Louisiana State University Press, 2010.

Bergeron, Arthur W., Jr. "Fort Berwick and Fort Chêne: Guardians of the Attakapas." *Louisiana History* 47, no. 4 (Autumn 2006): 435–50.

Bergeron, Arthur W., Jr. *Guide to Louisiana Confederate Military Units, 1861–1865*. Baton Rouge: Louisiana State University Press, 1989.

Block, W. T. "Calasieu Parish, La: Hotbed of the Civil War Jayhawkers." *http://www.wtblock.com/wtblockjr/calcasie1.htm.*

Bragg, Jefferson Davis. *Louisiana in the Confederacy*. Baton Rouge: Louisiana State University Press, 1941.

Brasseaux, Carl A. "Ozeme Carriere and the St. Landry Jayhawkers." *Attakapas Gazette* 13, no. 4 (Winter 1978): 185–89.

Brasseaux, Carl A., and Keith P. Fontenot. *Steamboats on Louisiana's Bayous: A History and Directory.* Baton Rouge: Louisiana State University Press, 2004.

Case, Lynn Marshall, and Warren F. Spencer. *The United States and France: Civil War Diplomacy.* Philadelphia: University of Pennsylvania Press, 1970.

Catton, Bruce. *Grant Takes Command: 1863–1865*. Boston: Little, Brown, 1969.

Cornish, Dudley Taylor. *The Sable Arm: Black Troops in the Union Army, 1861–1865*. University of Kansas Press, 1987.

Costello, Brian J., Murray G. LeBeau. *A History of Pointe Coupée Parish, Louisiana*. Donaldsonville, LA: Margaret Media, 2010.

Cotham, Edward T. Jr. *Battle on the Bay: The Civil War Struggle for Galveston*. Austin: University of Texas Press, 1998.

Current, Richard Nelson. *Lincoln's Loyalists: Union Soldiers from the Confederacy*. Boston: Northeastern University Press, 1992.

Daddysman, James W. *The Matamoros Trade: Confederate Commerce, Diplomacy, and Intrigue*. Newark: University of Delaware Press, 1984.

Daigle, Gercie. "The Robin Hood of Mallet Woods." *La Voix des Prairies* 11, no. 41 (April 1990): 33–35.

Delaney, Robert W. "Matamoros, Port for Texas during the Civil War." *Southwestern Historical Quarterly* 58, no. 4 (1955): 473-87.

Dobak, William H. *Freedom by the Sword: The U.S. Colored Troops, 1862–1867*. Washington, DC: Center of Military History, 2011.

Downs, Jim. *Sick from Freedom: African American Illness and Suffering during the Civil War and Reconstruction*. New York: Oxford University Press, 2012.

Durel, Lionel C. "Creole Civilization in Donaldsonville, 1850, According to 'Le Vigilant.'" *Louisiana Historical Quarterly* 31 (October 1948), 981-994.

Edmonds, David C. "Surrender on the Bourbeux: Honorable Defeat or Incompetency Under Fire," *Louisiana History* 18 (Winter 1977), 63-85.

Edmonds, David C. *The Guns of Port Hudson*. 2 vols. Lafayette, LA: Acadiana Press, 1984.

Edmonds, David C. *Yankee Autumn in Acadiana: A Narrative of the Great Texas Overland Expedition through Southwestern Louisiana, October–December 1863*. Lafayette, LA: Acadiana Press, 1979.

Finch, L. Boyd. *Confederate Pathway to the Pacific: Major Sherod Hunter and Arizona Territory, C.S.A.* Tucson: Arizona Historical Society, 1996.

Finch, L. Boyd. "Surprise at Brashear City: Sherod Hunter's Sugar Cooler Cavalry." *Louisiana History* 25, no. 4 (Fall 1984): 403–34.

Fitzhugh, Lester N. "Saluria, Fort Esperanza, and Military Operations on the Texas Coast, 1861–1864." *Southwestern Historical Quarterly* 61 (July 1957): 66–100.

Foner, Eric. *Free Soil, Free Labor, Free Men: The Ideology of the Republican Party before the Civil War.* New York: Oxford University Press, 1970.

Fowler, P. H. *Memorial of William Fowler.* New York: Anson D. F. Randolph, 1875.

Fox, William F. *Regimental Losses in the Civil War, 1861–1865.* Albany, NY: Brandow, 1898.

Frazier, Donald S. "'The Battles of Texas will be Fought in Louisiana:' The Assault of Fort Butler, June 28, 1863." *Southwestern Historical Quarterly* 104 (January 2001): 333–63.Frazier, Donald S. *Blood and Treasure: Confederate Empire in the Southwest.* College Station: Texas A & M University Press, 1995.

Frazier, Donald S. *Blood on the Bayou: Vicksburg, Port Hudson, and the Trans-Mississippi.* Buffalo Gap, TX: State House Press, 2015.

Frazier, Donald S. *Fire in the Cane Field: The Federal Invasion of Louisiana and Texas, January 1861–January 1863.* Buffalo Gap, TX: State House Press, 2009.

Frazier, Donald S. *Thunder Across the Swamp: The Fight for the Lower Mississippi, February 1863–May 1863.* Buffalo Gap, TX: State House Press, 2011.

Freeman, Douglas Southall. *Lee's Lieutenants: A Study in Command.* 3 vols. New York: Charles Scribner's Sons, 1942-1944.

Geise, William Royston. "The Confederate Military Forces in the Trans-Mississippi, 1861–1865: A Study in Command." Ph.D. Dissertation. University of Texas, Austin, 1974.

Graham, Don. *Kings of Texas: The 150-Year Ranching Saga of an American Ranching Empire.* Hoboken, NJ: John Wiley, 2003.

Greene, Jack, and Alessandro Massignani. *Ironclads at War: The Origin and Development of the Armored Battleship.* New York: Da Capo, 1998.

Hackemer, Kurt. "Strategic Dilemma: Civil-Military Friction and the Texas Coastal Campaign of 1863." *Military History of the West* 26 (Fall 1996): 187–214.

Herrington, Fred Harvey. "The Fort Jackson Mutiny." *Journal of Negro History* 27, no. 4 (October 1942): 420–31.

Herrington, Fred Harvey, ed. "A Peace Mission of 1863." *American Historical Review* 46, no. 1 (October 1940): 76–86.

Hewitt, Lawrence. *Port Hudson: Confederate Bastion on the Mississippi.* Baton Rouge: Louisiana State University Press, 1994.

History of the Second Battalion Duryee Zouaves: One Hundred and Sixty-Fifth Regiment New York Volunteer Infantry, Mustered in the United States service at Camp Washington, Staten Island, New York. Salem, MA: Higginson, 1905.

Hollandsworth, James G., Jr. *The Louisiana Native Guards: The Black Military Experience During the Civil War.* Baton Rouge: Louisiana State University Press, 1995.

Hollandsworth, James G., Jr. *Pretense of Glory: The Life of General Nathaniel P. Banks.* Baton Rouge: Louisiana State University Press, 1998.

Howell, Kenneth Wayne, ed. *The Seventh Star of the Confederacy: Texas During the Civil War.* Denton: University of North Texas Press, 2011.

Huffstodt, Jim. *Hard Dying Men: The Story of General W. H. L. Wallace, General T. E. G. Ransom, and their "Old Eleventh" Illinois Infantry in the American Civil War, 1861–1865.* Bowie, MD: Heritage Books, 1991.

Hunter, John Warren. *The Fall of Brownsville on the Rio Grande, November 1863.* Brownsville, TX: printed by the author, 1950.

Hunter, John Warren. *Heel-Fly Times in Texas: A Story of the Civil War Period in Texas.* Bandera, TX: Frontier Times, 1931.

Ingersoll, Lurton Dunham. *Iowa and the Rebellion: A History of the Troops Furnished by the State of Iowa to the Volunteer Armies of the Union, Which Conquered the Great Southern Rebellion of 1861–5.* Philadelphia: J. B. Lippincott, 1867.

Kelly, Patrick J. "The North American Crisis of the 1860s." *Journal of the Civil War Era* 2, no. 3 (September 2012): 337–68.

Kendall, John. *History of New Orleans*. Chicago: Lewis Publishing Company, 1922.

Kerby, Robert L. *Kirby Smith's Confederacy: The Trans-Mississippi South, 1863–1865*. Tuscaloosa: University of Alabama Press, 1991.

Levine, Bruce. *Confederate Emancipation: Southern Plans to Free and Arm Slaves During the Civil War*. New York: Oxford University Press, 2005.

Lowe, Richard. *Walker's Texas Division CSA: Greyhounds of the Trans-Mississippi*. Baton Rouge: Louisiana State University Press, 2004.

Malone, Ann Patton. *Sweet Chariot: Slave Family and Household Structure in Nineteenth-Century Louisiana*. Chapel Hill: University of North Carolina Press, 1996.

Marks, Paula Mitchell. *Hands to the Spindle: Texas Women and Home Textile Production, 1822–1880*. College Station: Texas A & M University Press, 1996.

Marley, David, ed. *Wars of the Americas: Chronology of Armed Conflict in the Western Hemisphere, 1492 to the Present*. 2 vols. Denver: ABC Clio, 2008.

Marshall, Michael. *Gallant Creoles: A History of the Donaldsonville Canonniers*. Lafayette: University of Louisiana at Lafayette Press, 2013.

Marten, James. "Drawing the Line: Dissent and Disloyalty in Texas, 1856–1874." Ph.D. dissertation. University of Texas, 1986.

Marten, James. "A Wearying Existence: Texas Refugees in New Orleans, 1862–1865." *Louisiana History* 28, No. 4 (Autumn 1987): 343–56.

Martin, Michael J. *A History of the 4th Wisconsin Infantry and Cavalry in the Civil War*. New York: Savas Beatie, 2006.

Martin, Percy F. *Maximilian in Mexico: The Story of the French Intervention, 1861–1867*. New York: Charles Scribner's Sons, 1914.

Mathews, James T. "A Time for Desperate Valor: The Confederate Attack on Fort Butler, Louisiana, 1863." *Military History of the West* 26 (Spring 1996): 23–34.

McGowen, Stanley S. *Horse Sweat and Powder Smoke: The First Texas Cavalry in the Civil War*. College Station: Texas A & M University Press, 1999.

McKinney, Bobby J. *Confederates on the Caney: An Illustrated Account of the Civil War on the Texas Gulf Coast*. Rosenberg, TX: Mouth of the Caney Publication, 1994.

Messner, William F. *Freedmen and the Ideology of Free Labor: Louisiana, 1862–1865*. Lafayette: Center for Louisiana Studies, 1978.

Miller, Robert Ryal. "The American Legion of Honor in Mexico." *Pacific Historical Review* 30, no. 3 (August 1961): 229–41.

"Miscellaneous." *The Literary Digest* 14, no. 11 (January 16, 1897): 347.

Moore, Albert Burton. *Conscription and Conflict in the Confederacy*. Columbia: University of South Carolina Press, 1996.

Murray, R. L., ed. *Madison County Troops in the Civil War*. Wolcott, NY: Benedum Books, 2004.

Oakes, James. *Freedom National: The Destruction of Slavery in the United States, 1861–1865*. New York: W. W. Norton, 2012.

Odom, Van D. "The Political Career of Thomas Overton Moore, Secession Governor of Louisiana." *Louisiana Historical Quarterly* 26 (October 1943): 975–1054.

Parrish, T. Michael. *Richard Taylor: Soldier Prince of Dixie*. Chapel Hill: University of North Carolina Press, 1992.

Peña, Christopher G. *Scarred by War: Civil War in Southeast Louisiana*. Bloomington, IN: Authorhouse, 2004.

Peña, Christopher G. *Touched by War: Battles Fought in the Lafourche District*. Thibodaux, LA: C. G. P. Press, 1998.

Phisterer, Frederick. *New York in the War of the Rebellion, 1861–1865*. Albany: Weed, Parsons, 1890.

Pound, DaNean Olene. "Slave to the Ex-Slave Narratives." M.A. Thesis. Northwestern State University, Natchitoches, LA, 2005.

Prichard, Walter. "The Effects of the Civil War on the Louisiana Sugar Industry." *The Journal of Southern History* 5 (August 1939): 315–32.

Prushankin, Jeffery S. *A Crisis in Confederate Command: Edmund Kirby Smith, Richard Taylor, and the Army of the Trans-Mississippi*. Baton Rouge: Louisiana State University Press, 2005.

Ragan, Cooper K., ed. "Diary of Captain George W. O'Brien." *Southwestern Historical Quarterly* 67, no. 2 (October 1963): 235–46.

Ragan, Cooper K., ed. "Diary of Captain George W. O'Brien." *Southwestern Historical Quarterly* 67, no. 3 (January 1964): 413–33.

Raines, C. W. *The Year Book for Texas*. 2 vols. Austin: Gammel Book Company, 1902.

Rein, Christopher Michael. *Trans-Mississippi Southerners in the Union Army, 1862–1865*, M.A. Thesis. Louisiana State University, May 2001.

Ripley, C. Peter. *Slaves and Freedmen in Civil War Louisiana*. Baton Rouge: Louisiana State University Press, 1976.

Roberts, Oran M. "The Battle of Bayou Bourbeau, November 3, 1863: Colonel Oran M. Roberts' Report." *Louisiana History* 6, no. 1 (Winter 1965): 83–91.

Roland, Charles P. *Louisiana Sugar Plantations During the Civil War*. 1957. Reprint. Baton Rouge: Louisiana State University Press, 1997.

Rothman, Adam. "The Horrors '12 Years a Slave' Couldn't Tell: What a Civil War Soldier's Diary Tells Us about Solomon Northrup's Ordeal." The website for Aljazeera America. January 18, 2014. *http://america.aljazeera.com/opinions/2014/1/the-horrors-a-12yearsaslaveacouldnattell0.html*. Accessed June 22, 2014.

Schoonover, Thomas. "Napoleon is Coming! Maximilian is Coming? The International History of the Civil War in the Caribbean Basin." In Robert E. May, ed., *The Union, The Confederacy, and the Atlantic Rim*. West Lafayette, IN: Purdue University Press, 1995.

Schoonover, Thomas D. *Dollars over Dominion: The Triumph of Liberalism in Mexican–United States Relations, 1861–1867*. Baton Rouge: Louisiana State University Press, 1978.

Schoonover, Thomas D. *Mexican Lobby: Matías Romero in Washington, 1861–1867*. Lexington: University Press of Kentucky, 2008.

Schouler, James. *History of the United States of America under the Constitution*. Vol. 6, 1861–1865. New York: Dodd, Mead, 1899.

Sears, Louis Martin. *John Slidell*. Durham, NC: Duke University Press, 1925.

Sierra, Justo. *The Political Evolution of the Mexican People*. Edited by Edmundo O'Gorman. Translated by Charles Ramsdell. Austin: University of Texas Press, 1969.

Silverman, Jason H. "A Most Unlikely Friendship: Abraham Lincoln and Matias Romero." The website for President Lincoln's Cottage. January 26, 2017. *http://www.lincolncottage.org/a-most-unlikely-friendship-abraham-lincoln-and-matias-romero/#_ednref26*.

Smith, George Winston. "Some Northern Wartime Attitudes Toward the Post–Civil War South." *Journal of Southern History* 10, no. 3 (August 1944): 253–74.

Stone, Edwin M. *Rhode Island in the Rebellion*. Providence: George H. Whitney, 1865.

Sutherland, Daniel E. "Abraham Lincoln, John Pope, and the Origins of Total War." *Journal of Military History* 56, no. 4 (October 1992): 568–74.

Sutherland, Daniel E. "Looking for a Home: Louisiana Emigrants during the Civil War and Reconstruction." *Louisiana History* 21, No. 4 (Autumn 1980): 341–61.

Taylor, Ethel. "Discontent in Confederate Louisiana." *Louisiana History* 2, no. 4 (Autumn 1961): 410–28.

Thomas, Benjamin P., ed. *Three Years with Grant as Recalled by War Correspondent Sylvanus Cadwallader*. New York: Alfred A. Knopf, 1955.

Thompson, Jerry. *Cortina: Defending the Mexican Name in Texas*. College Station: Texas A & M University Press, 2007.

Townsend, Stephen A. *The Yankee Invasion of Texas*. College Station: Texas A & M University Press, 2006.

Tsapina, Olga. "Where Solomon Northrup was a Slave." *Verso*, the blog of the Huntington Library. March 3, 2014. *http://huntingtonblogs.org/2014/03/where-solomon-northup-was-a-slave/*.

Tunnell, Ted. *Crucible of Reconstruction: War, Radicalism, and Race in Louisiana, 1862–1877.* Baton Rouge: Louisiana State University Press, 1984.

Tyler, Ronnie C. "Cotton on the Border, 1861–1865." *Southwestern Historical Quarterly* 73, no. 4 (April 1970): 456–77.

Ullman, Daniel. *Organization of Colored Troops and the Regeneration of the South.* Washington, DC: Great Republic, 1868.

Underwood, Rodman L. *Waters of Discord: The Union Blockade of Texas during the Civil War.* Jefferson, NC: McFarland, 2003.

Vandiver, Frank. "Texas and the Confederate Army's Meat Problem." *Southwestern Historical Quarterly* 47, no. 3 (January 1944): 225–33.

Ward, Susan Hayes. *George H. Hepworth: Preacher, Journalist, Friend of the People, the Story of His Life Told to Susan Hayes Ward.* New York: E. P. Dutton, 1903.

Way, Frederick, Jr. *Way's Packet Directory, 1848–1994.* Athens: Ohio University Press, 1982.

Weddell, Robert S. *Plow-Horse Cavalry: The Caney Creek Boys of the Thirty-Fourth Texas.* Austin, TX: Madrona Press, 1974.

Wetta, Frank J. *The Louisiana Scalawags: Politics, Race, and Terrorism During the Civil War and Reconstruction.* Baton Rouge: Louisiana State University Press, 2013.

Whitcomb, Caroline E. *History of the Second Massachusetts Battery (Nims' Battery) of Light Artillery, 1861–1865: Compiled from Records of the Rebellion, Official Reports, Diaries, and Rosters.* Concord, NH: Rumford, 1912.

Whitman, William S., and Charles H. True. *War for the Union: A History of the Part Borne by Maine Troops in the Suppression of the American Rebellion.* Lewiston, ME: Nelson Dingley Jr., 1865.

Williams, George Washington. *A History of the Negro Troops in the War of the Rebellion, 1861–1865.* New York: Harper, 1888.

Wilson, Joseph Thomas. *The Black Phalanx: A History of the Negro Soldiers of the United States in the Wars of 1775–1812, 1861–'65.* Hartford, CT: American Publishing Company, 1890.

Winschel, Terrence J. *Triumph and Defeat: The Vicksburg Campaign.* Campbell, CA: Savas Publishing, 1999.

Winschel, Terrence J. *Vicksburg: Fall of the Confederate Gibraltar.* Abilene, TX: McWhiney Foundation Press, 1999.

Winters, John D. *The Civil War in Louisiana.* Baton Rouge: Louisiana State University Press, 1963.

Wood, C. E. *Mud: A Military History.* Potomac Books, 2007.

Wooten, Dudley J., ed. *A Comprehensive History of Texas.* 2 vols. Dallas, TX: Scarff, 1898.

INDEX

9th Army Corps, 24

13th Army Corps, 32–33, 44, 46–49, 108–110, 138, 151, 160–162, 165–166, 168, 194, 205, 210–211, 213–214, 223, 225, 227–228, 233, 241, 243–244, 248–249, 257, 265, 270, 296, 297, 299, 307, 315, 320, 325, 336, 345, 348, 350, 374, 384, 387, 401, 406, 411, 413–414, 419–420, 425, 446

15th Army Corps, 24, 33, 49, 166, 171

16th Army Corps, 34, 100, 387

17th Army Corps, 33–34, 49, 98, 154–155, 157, 159

19th Army Corps, 21, 24, 47–48, 107, 109–110, 115, 131, 135, 156, 160–163, 165, 167, 170–171, 205–206, 211, 213–214, 217–218, 225–226, 249, 270, 296, 307, 348, 387, 410, 425, 446, 450

A

A.G. *Brown* (steamboat), 182, 210, 313

Abbeville, Louisiana, 92, 93, 206, 213

Acadians (including Cajuns and "Kajans"), 60, 253, 352, 382

African American troops (see individual units; see also slaves), 22, 25, 27–28, 37–38, 39–40, 75, 152, 154, 199, 232, 297, 348, 370

Alamo City (see also San Antonio, Texas), 321, 332, 344

Alamo City Guards (see Texas troops: Edgar's Texas Battery)

Alamo, The Battle of, 20, 57

Alexandria (steamer), 114, 118, 131

Alexandria, Louisiana, 3, 24, 27, 38, 42, 43–45, 49, 56, 63, 76, 79, 89, 91, 102, 104–107, 152, 154, 157–158, 164–167, 170–171, 200, 205, 207, 208, 218, 221, 227, 230–232, 237, 238, 244–246, 251, 254, 257, 260–261, 291, 356, 358, 360, 368, 372, 405, 416, 418, 427, 431, 433, 448

Allen, Henry Watkins, 433

Almonte, Juan, 20–21

Alvarado, Francisco, 388

Antelope (blockade runner), 309

Antietam, Battle of, 173, 182

Arago (steamboat), 138

Argus (steamboat), 163, 170, 207-208

Arizona troops (see individual units), 56, 93, 105, 153, 170, 209, 278–280, 290
Mounted troops
1st Arizona Cavalry, 262, 377,
2nd Arizona Cavalry, 69, 91, 93, 152, 286, 428
3rd Arizona Cavalry, 91, 152–153, 176, 193
4th Arizona Cavalry, 262
Philip's Regiment (see 2nd Arizona Cavalry)
Stone's Regiment (see 3rd Arizona Cavalry)

Arkansas River, 154, 416

Armant, Leopold L., 90–92

Armstrong, Frank, 34

Army of Arkansas, 31, 44, 154

Army of Northern Virginia, 21, 157, 252

Army of the Cumberland, 26, 404

Army of the Gulf, 33, 45–48, 85, 108, 133, 136, 156–157, 159, 167, 171, 182, 200, 202, 210, 215, 217, 220, 224, 227–228, 232, 238, 247, 249, 268, 311–312, 325,

347, 369, 394, 401, 411, 415, 418, 421, 425, 445, 450

Army of the Ohio, 26

Army of the Potomac, 47–48, 173, 182, 258

Army of the Tennessee, 24–25, 34, 97, 102, 154–156, 171, 228, 417–418, 445

Army of the Trans-Mississippi, 55, 171, 245

Atchafalaya River, 25, 27, 56, 91, 93, 97–98, 102, 106, 110, 138–140, 143–146, 148–152, 157, 163–168, 170, 173, 175–177, 179, 193–197, 200, 202–203, 205, 207–208, 211, 228, 233, 238, 246–247, 312, 313–314, 321, 363, 367, 383, 402, 449

Austin, Texas, 29, 65, 69, 71, 80–81, 306, 333, 342, 372–373

Avery Island, 3, 57

Avery, John Marsh, 207–208

Avery, Margaret Henshaw, 90

Avery, Sarah Marsh, 65, 85

Avoyelles Parish, 253

B

Bagby, Arthur Pendleton, 217, 226, 237, 266, 272, 279, 288, 290, 354

Bagdad, Town of (also Playa Bagdad), 16, 61, 62, 295, 300,

Ball, Augustus V., 260, 261, 263, 333, 375, 376, 377, 388, 436,

Banks, Nathaniel P., 2–3, 24–28, 30, 33, 35, 37–48, 75, 85, 93, 95, 97, 107–111, 113–115, 117, 136–137, 155–162, 164, 171, 182, 199–200, 210–211, 213–216, 218, 221–222, 225, 227–229, 232–233, 237, 239, 241–244, 246, 248, 251, 256, 257–258, 262, 265, 273, 291, 293–294, 296–298, 300–302, 304, 306, 308, 309, 312, 323–326, 331–332, 345–346, 355–362, 369–371, 374, 377–378, 381–382, 384, 386, 387, 394, 401–406, 408, 414–419, 421–422, 425–426, 443–448, 450

Bastrop, Texas, 67, 426, 428

Bates, Joseph (see also 13th Texas Volunteers), 56

Baton Rouge, Louisiana, 41, 43, 47, 50, 92, 114, 149, 170, 258, 285, 319, 356

Baylor, George Wythe (see also 2nd Arizona Cavalry), 285, 286, 288

Bayou Beouf, 168, 231, 232, 236, 238–239, 244

Bayou Bourbeau, 217, 221, 224–227, 234–235, 250, 266–271, 273–276, 279, 281–290

Bayou Bourbeau, Battle of, 265, 273, 291, 293, 296, 297, 308, 378, 382

Bayou Carencro, 163–164, 207, 211–212, 214, 217–218, 220–225, 233, 240, 248–251, 256, 266, 268–270, 274, 276, 280, 283, 286, 290–291, 310–311, 331

Bayou Courtableau, 217, 221, 224, 228, 237–238, 247, 249, 449,

Bayou des Glaise, 424–425,

Bayou Fordoche, 140, 143, 145, 148, 151–152, 168–169, 177, 180–181, 185–187, 194, 363

Bayou Fordoche, Battle of (see Sterling's Plantation, Battle of), 308, 368, 378

Bayou Gross Tête, 139–140, 149–150, 170, 176, 193, 258, 319, 363–364, 449,

Bayou Lafourche, 66, 89, 232, 312

Bayou Macon, 31, 98

Bayou Mallet, 77, 81

Bayou Sara, Louisiana, 137–138, 147, 315, 318, 364

Bayou Teche Campaign (see also Teche Campaign), 42, 85, 86, 93, 94, 125, 159, 161, 164, 171, 194, 352, 380–382, 451

Bayou Teche, 24, 56, 79, 84, 86, 89, 105, 157–159, 161, 163, 169–170, 198, 200, 202–203, 205, 209–210, 228, 231–232, 239, 243, 246, 295, 312–313, 348, 351, 355, 358, 372, 383, 410, 425, 429

Bayou Vermilion, 209, 210, 211, 214, 218, 232, 251, 309, 314, 349, 350, 352–353

Bazaine, François Achille, 19, 20, 21, 264, 406, 407

Beaumont, Texas, 44, 48, 107–108, 114, 118–120, 132, 134, 218, 220, 260–261, 263, 330, 333, 345–346

Bee, Hamilton P., 17–18, 57, 173, 297–298, 304–306, 329, 332, 345, 376–377

Beecher, Harris, 125–126, 131, 135, 410

Benavides, Santos, 305

Berwick Bay, 44, 49, 84, 91, 113, 117, 157, 159, 161–162, 165–166, 167, 170, 198, 200, 222, 228, 232, 240, 243, 251, 256, 257, 265, 311, 312, 314, 320, 402

Big Cane, Louisiana, 168, 207–208, 231, 237–238, 239, 266

Black Hawk (steamboat), 321–322

Black River, 102, 103

Black, John C., 185, 186, 189

Blessington, J. P., 232, 237, 317, 319, 363,

Boca Chica, Texas, 173, 293, 295, 299, 300

Boggs, William R., 73, 213, 265

Bonham, Texas, 74, 262
Boone, Hannibal Honestus, 139, 142, 176–178, 180–181, 187, 193, 197
Botany Bay Plantation (also see Sterling's Plantation), 140, 142, 146, 150–151, 169, 176–183, 185–186, 188–189, 192, 194–195, 198
Boutwell, Charles, 213, 215, 298
Bradfute, William R., 52, 53, 328–329, 336, 339, 341, 342
Bragg, Braxton, 26, 172
Brashear City (Morgan City), Louisiana, 27, 28, 43, 91, 106, 156, 158–159, 160, 181, 210, 218, 243, 259, 267, 312–313, 330, 370, 374, 402
Brashear City, Battle of, 43, 181, 267, 382, 428
Brazoria, Texas, 377, 385–386
Brazos Island (see also Brazos Santiago), 293, 296
Brazos River, 243, 306, 329, 333–369, 371, 374–376, 378, 385–388, 419, 435–436, 451
Brazos Santiago Island, 241, 265, 293–297, 358
Brown, Albert H., 295, 287
Brownsville, Texas, 17, 29–30, 45, 57, 61–64, 244, 257, 260, 295–296, 298–302, 304–305, 307, 324–326, 333, 358, 372–373, 376, 378, 380, 384, 386–387, 401–402, 407, 411, 422, 425
Buchel, Augustus, 220, 261, 333, 346
Buehler, Theodore, 278, 282
Burbridge, Stephen, 225, 227, 250, 267–290, 292
Bureau of Conscription, Confederate (see also conscription), 70
Butler, Benjamin F., 12, 40
Buzzard Prairie (Louisiana), 211, 217, 221, 225, 227, 266–268, 272–273, 276, 279, 280–281, 286, 288–289, 313

C
Cactus Throne, The, 13, 23, 263, 303, 406
Cahawba (steamer), 86, 121, 125–126, 131
Cajuns (see Acadians)
Calcasieu bottoms (see Calcasieu River)
Calcasieu Jayhawkers (see Jayhawkers)
Calcasieu Pass, 117,
Calcasieu River (including Calcasieu bottoms), 27, 79, 84, 206, 218, 238, 245, 255, 380

California, 19, 47, 103, 408–409
Camp Hubbard, 41
Camp Pratt, Louisiana, 349–350
Caraway, Nathaniel Jackson, 272–273, 276
Carbajal, José María Jesús (also spelled Carvajal), 61, 67
Carleton, James Henry, 300
Carmouche, Emile, 86, 178
Carol Jones's Store, 253
Caroline Goodyear (steamer), 302, 442
Carrière, Ozémé (see also the Clan), 80, 222, 235, 251–252, 380–381, 426, 431, 449
Carrollton, Louisiana, 108, 112, 210, 241
Catahoula Lake (also Catahoula basin), 104, 154
Cedar Bayou, 331, 336
Champ d'Mars (see also Carrollton, New Orleans), 114
Charlie (N. P. Banks's horse), 108, 110, 112
Chattanooga, Tennessee, 26, 136, 157, 171, 199, 266, 324, 357, 387, 403–404
Cheneyville, Louisiana, 236, 252–253
Cherokee Nation (also Cherokees), 55, 262
Chickamauga, Battle of, 171, 173, 221, 403–404
Chihuahua, Mexico, 15, 300
Chocolate Bayou, 342, 345, 389, 391, 424, 438
Chretien Point Plantation, 225–227, 266–268, 271–272, 276, 279, 289
Cinco de Mayo, (see also Puebla, Battle of), 6–7, 11
Clack, Franklin (see also Louisiana troops: Confederate Guards Response Battalion), 91, 178, 187–188
Claiborne Plantation, 315
Clan, the (see also Carrière, Ozémé), 80–84, 95, 222, 235, 251, 380–381, 426, 428, 431–432, 449
Clark, Orton, 49, 114, 115, 118, 131–132, 159–160
Clarksville, Texas (near Brownsville), 300
Clayton, William Henry Harrison, 150–151
Clinton (steamer), 331
Coahuila, Mexico, 15, 17, 68, 303
Cobos, José Maria, 300–302
Colby, Carlos, 109, 207
Colorado River, 29, 243, 306, 373
Columbus, Texas, 437
Columbus, Wisconsin, 292
Comanche Nation, 262
"Commissary" Banks (see Banks, Nathaniel P.)

Confederate Army of the Trans-Mississippi, 55, 171, 245

Confederate Impressment Act (March 26, 1863), 58, 75, 431

Confederate tax-in-kind, 58, 427, 436,

Connor, H. N., 163, 201, 202, 204, 234, 235, 236, 237, 288,

Conscription (see also Bureau of Conscription, Enrollment Act), 38–39, 41, 55, 59, 67–68, 70–71, 76–77, 82, 252, 375, 393, 422, 426, 431–432, 436–437

Conservatives (Mexican political faction), 8, 9, 10, 263, 264, 303

Coreth, Rudolph, 333, 343, 376, 377, 421, 424, 441

Corinth, Battle of, 47, 92, 103

Corothers, Sarah, 69–70

Corothers, William N., 69, 93

Corps d'Afrique, 37–39, 101, 138, 156, 181, 232, 236, 297, 313, 318, 349

Corps d'Afrique troops
Infantry
4th Infantry, 357
16th Infantry, 297
22nd Infantry, 313
25th Infantry, 347
Engineers
1st Engineers, 326
2nd Engineers, 370–371

Corpus Christi, Texas, 57, 260, 306, 326, 328–329, 332, 387, 422

Cortina, Juan Nepomuceno "Cheno," 17, 19, 61, 66, 295, 298, 300–301, 412

Cotton (including cotton trade), 12–14, 17–18, 42, 59–65, 70, 79, 98, 100, 163, 208, 232, 242, 296, 298–300, 304–305, 321, 332, 341, 343, 352, 358, 372, 384, 387, 388, 417, 427–428, 437, 445–446, 449

Cow Head Bayou, 177–178

Cox, E. B., 63, 85

Creek Nation, 55, 262

Crescent (steamer), 121

Crescent City, (see also New Orleans), 446, 449

Crocker, Frederick, 117–118, 121, 123–130

Crocker, Marcellus, 102, 104–105, 155

CSS *Cotton*, 86

CSS *Diana*, 86

CSS *Hunley*, 73

CSS *Missouri*, 73

CSS *Queen of the West*, 86

CSS *Stevens*, 203, 209, 210

D

Dan G. Taylor (steamboat), 138

Dana, Napoleon Jackson Tecumseh, 173, 182–183, 185–186, 193–194, 197, 198, 211, 205, 210, 222, 233, 241–243, 245, 248, 256–257, 265, 299, 309, 325, 331, 346–347, 372–373, 378, 384, 387, 406–407, 411, 414, 419–422

Davis Guards (see also Texas troops: Company F, 1st Texas Heavy Artillery), 118, 130

Davis, Edmund J., 203, 241, 307, 388

Davis, Henry Winter, 19, 409–410

Davis, Jefferson, 61, 392, 415, 425–426

Day, Henry, 139, 143–145

Debray, Xavier, 333

Decros Point, 334, 369–370, 384, 387, 393–395, 420, 425

DeCrow, Thomas, 370

Defenders of the Monroe Doctrine (see also filibusters), 19

Delhi, Louisiana, 98, 418

Demopolis, Alabama, 89, 417

Department of the Gulf (Union), 24, 44, 108, 121, 156, 199–200, 241, 257, 259, 293, 296, 308, 324, 331, 355–356, 358, 362, 402–403, 414–415, 444, 446, 450

Department of the Trans-Mississippi (Confederate), 45, 52, 54, 59, 71, 120, 157, 158, 198, 200, 208, 218, 383

Derby (blockade runner), 309,

desertion (and deserters), 70, 84, 91, 95, 208–209, 253, 261, 375, 416, 440

Dime (steamboat), 220

District of Texas, New Mexico, and Arizona, 132, 307

District of West Louisiana, 218, 308

Donaldsonville, Louisiana, 24, 66, 137, 169, 312, 315, 319–320

Dowling, Richard "Dick," 115, 117–119, 120, 125–127

Duperier, St. Leon, 313, 351

Durango, Mexico, 15, 407

Durant, Thomas J., 41, 215, 361, 447

Dutch Settlement (Matagorda Peninsula), 370, 399

E

Eagle Pass, Texas, 45, 61–62, 306, 345, 372, 384

Eastern Sub-District of Texas, 220

El Sal del Rey (saltworks), 304, 387

Elliott, Isaac, 341, 415,
emancipated slaves (freedmen), 2, 22, 37, 39, 45, 75, 200, 308, 351, 403, 447
Emancipation Proclamation, 21, 41
Emerald (steamboat), 315, 317–319
Emory, William H., 48, 108, 110
Empire Parish (steamboat),
Enrollment Act of March 3, 1863, 67
Evergreen, Louisiana, 205, 207, 238, 251, 265–266

F

False River, Louisiana, 449
Farrar, Bernard G., 153, 154
Fauconnet, Charles Prosper, 38–39, 322, 446–448
Faust, Joseph, 194, 236, 247
Filibusters (see also 1st Mexican Volunteers, Defenders of the Monroe Doctrine, Mexican Aid Society, Mexico Club, Monroe Doctrine Committee, and Monroe League), 295
Flanders, Benjamin F., 215–216
Fletcher, Samuel H., 212
Florilda (steamboat), 120, 125
Flournoy, George, 236
Fonda, John G., 233, 250, 274, 276
Ford, John Salmon "Rip," 71
Forey, Élie Frédéric, 13, 15, 18, 20, 21, 264, 307, 407
Fort Adams, Mississippi, 146, 150
Fort Beauregard, Louisiana, 102, 104, 105, 108, 152, 155
Fort Bliss, Texas, 300
Fort Brown, Texas, 298
Fort Butler, Louisiana, 3, 22, 166, 320, 382
Fort Delaware, Delaware, 87, 88
Fort DeRussy, Louisiana, 425
Fort *Esperanza*, Texas, 52, 306, 324, 329, 331, 334–336, 339–341, 343, 369–370, 384, 386, 397, 411, 419, 425
Fort Griffin, Texas (see also Sabine Pass), 115, 117, 119–121, 124–127, 129–130
Fort Jackson, Louisiana, 66, 357
Fort Lancaster, Texas, 419
Fort Ringgold, Texas, 372
Fort Semmes, Texas (see also Mustang Island) 326–329, 331,
Foster, James P., 137, 318,
France, 7, 9–12, 59–60, 264, 303, 307, 406, 408, 409–411, 442

Franklin, Louisiana, 86, 163, 165–167, 169–170, 198, 200, 205, 207, 239, 411, 418, 429, 449, 450
Franklin, William B., 47–48, 107, 113–114, 117–118, 121, 123–125, 131–132, 156–157, 161–162, 165–167, 170, 205, 213–214, 220–222, 224, 229, 233, 235, 239–241, 243–249, 251–252, 255–259, 265, 268, 295, 307, 308–310, 311–314, 321, 348–351, 356, 371, 379, 403, 405, 410
Fuller, Edward Wood, 86, 88
Fulton, Arkansas, 72

G

Galveston Island (see Galveston, Texas)
Galveston, Battle of (see Galveston, Texas)
Galveston, Texas (and Galveston Island), 15, 18, 35, 40, 44–45, 48, 52, 56, 65, 85, 107, 114, 118, 125, 194, 260, 263, 330, 342, 345–346, 358, 370, 372, 375, 385–386, 394, 401–402, 421, 434, 440, 451
General Banks (steamer), 124–125, 130
General Orders 23, 447
George Buckhart (schooner), 421
George Peabody (steamer), 259–260
Georgia, 22, 25–26, 89, 134, 157, 171–172, 199, 221, 238, 325, 357, 375, 405
Gettysburg, Battle of, 2, 22–24, 27
Giesecke, Julius, 86–89, 226, 235, 247, 251, 265–266, 291, 307, 311, 354
Goodrich's Landing, 31, 98
Gould, N.P. (see also Texas troops: 23rd Texas Cavalry), 333
Grand Bois, The, 314, 351
Grand Coteau, Louisiana, 222–223, 266, 271, 273
Grand Ecore, Louisiana, 72, 90, 230
Grand Lake, 86, 91
Grant, Ulysses S., 24–28, 30, 32–35, 40, 42, 45–49, 75, 85, 107–113, 136, 154–157, 171, 199, 228, 265, 357, 360, 414, 418, 422, 445–446
Gray, Henry, 163, 168, 178, 182, 192
Great Britain, 7, 21, 436
Green, Tom, 2, 58, 68, 93, 97–98, 101–102, 106, 133, 139, 145–147, 159, 164–170, 175–181, 187, 191–194, 196–198, 202–203, 207–208, 211, 217–218, 221–222, 224–228, 230–231, 234, 236–237, 247, 260, 265–266, 270–272, 279, 289, 291,

308, 310, 312–313, 321, 345, 349, 353–354, 364, 377–379, 382–385, 393, 424, 434, 436, 440, 444–445
Griffin, W. H., 118
Grimes County, Texas, 434
Grover, Cuvier, 211, 225
Guadalajara, Mexico, 15, 406–407
Guanajuato, Mexico, 15, 406
guerilla warfare (see also Jayhawkers), 7, 32, 34
Guerra de la Reforma (War of the Reform), 7
Guess, George, 92–93, 95, 101, 106, 158–159
Guppey, Joshua James, 277, 280–281, 284, 290, 291–292
Gusley, Henry O., 125, 127, 128, 132

H

Hahn, Michael, 214–215, 450
Halleck, Henry, 24–26, 30, 33, 35, 37, 40–46, 100, 111, 113–114, 156–157, 159, 171, 199, 242, 294, 296–298, 304, 324–325, 357–359, 362, 374, 386–387, 401–406, 415–418, 421, 445–446
Hamilton, Andrew Jackson, 373–374, 425, 450
Hancox (steamboat), 209,
Hankamer, Charles, 287, 288
Harrison, James, 186, 187, 188, 192, 230
Harrisonburg, Louisiana, 102, 104, 105, 106, 155
Hart (steamboat, see also CSS *Stevens*), 209
Hartley, Ed (Edwin), 143, 144, 145, 187, 191, 192, 194
Haynes, Dennis, 84, 252–255, 380–381, 428–431, 449–450
Hays County, Texas, 372, 423, 437
Heel-flies (includes conscript hunter; see also Home Guard), 426, 437
Helena, Arkansas, 31, 158, 199
Henry Von Phul (steamboat), 364–367
Herron, Francis J., 32–33, 97, 110–111, 136–140, 145–152, 157, 164–170, 173, 177, 182, 411–412
Hesseltine, Francis, 394–400, 419–420
Hill Country of Texas, 74, 376
Hineston, Louisiana, 84, 252, 254–255
Hog Point (Pointe Coupee Parish), 315, 317, 365
Holmesville, Louisiana, 168, 205, 231, 238, 247, 259, 265, 270, 291
Home Guard (see also heel-flies), 80, 84, 252, 253, 255, 426, 427, 436–437

Houston, Sam, Jr., 376
Houston, Texas, 44–45, 48, 49, 52, 61–62, 64–65, 72, 74, 85, 90, 107, 111, 119–120, 126, 132, 199, 230, 241, 243–244, 261–263, 306, 329, 332–333, 342–343, 345, 358, 369–372, 386, 389, 394, 413, 416, 421, 425, 433–435, 440
Howell, William Randolph, 81, 82, 83, 96, 146, 148, 196, 203, 221, 223, 224, 225, 227, 229, 248, 251, 301, 349, 352, 355, 381, 382, 383, 434, 443, 451
Hunter, John Warren, 437
Hurlbut, Stephen A., 34, 100
Hussar (steamer), 370
Hyatt, Arthur W., 79, 164–165, 172, 176, 187–188, 192–196, 207–209, 236–237, 247, 367

I

Iberville, steamboat, 101, 114, 138
Ike Hammit (steamboat), 321
Ile Copal Plantation, 210, 213, 251, 381
Illinois, 3, 50, 104, 160, 161, 162, 199, 331, 414, 443
Illinois troops
  Mounted Troops
  2nd Illinois Cavalry, 212, 310
  3rd Illinois Cavalry, 310
  118th Illinois Mounted Infantry, 233, 234, 235, 240, 249, 274, 310, 355
  Infantry
  33rd Illinois, 324, 331, 336, 338, 339, 341, 342, 370, 384, 389, 415
  37th Illinois, 151, 185, 186, 187, 189, 242, 260, 299, 372
  91st Illinois, 140, 387
  94th Illinois, 140, 143, 144, 195, 187, 299, 412
  97th Illinois, 109, 207
  99th Illinois, 389
  Artillery
  Chicago Mercantile Battery, 420
Imperialists (Mexican), 15, 17, 29, 264, 300, 303, 304, 406, 413
Indian Nations (Indian Territory), 158
Indiana, 3, 104, 160–162, 287, 337
Indiana troops
  Mounted troops
  4th Indiana Cavalry, 266, 394
  Infantry
  8th Indiana, 165, 326, 339, 389

11th Indiana Infantry, 160, 166, 286
18th Indiana, 331, 339–389
26th Indiana Infantry, 148–149, 183, 184, 188–192
32nd Indiana, 233
46th Indiana, 288
47th Indiana, 160
60th Indiana, 269, 274–277, 280, 281, 283–285, 287, 289–290
67th Indiana, 205, 269, 273, 276–279, 281–282, 289–290
Artillery
1st Battery, Indiana Light Artillery, 320
1st Indiana Heavy Artillery, 311, 315
Indianola, Texas, 15–16, 35, 44, 52, 55–56, 73, 330, 342, 344–345, 369–371, 376, 384, 389, 391, 393–394, 415, 438
Iowa, 3, 19, 160, 168, 385, 409
Iowa troops
Infantry
10th Iowa Infantry, 412
19th Iowa, 140, 148–150, 183–294, 299
20th Iowa, 109, 326
23rd Iowa, 370
24th Iowa, 286
34th Iowa, 326
Ireland, John, 336
Irish Bend, Battle of, 89
Irwin, Richard B., 21, 23, 28, 418, 446

J

Jackson, Battle of, 342
Jackson, Mississippi, 24, 34, 89
Jayhawkers, 77, 84, 95, 235, 253, 346, 431, 433
Jeanerette, Louisiana, 169, 201, 203, 349, 411
Jefferson, Texas, 74, 158
Jeter, William, 86–88
Johnson, Amos, 126, 129
Jones, John B., 188, 190
Joseph, Ferdinand Maximilian (Austrian Archduke), 8–9, 23, 263, 406, 408
Juárez, Benito, 6–8, 10, 17–18, 20, 35, 67, 111, 300–304, 324, 373, 406–409, 412

K

Kansas, 158, 262,
Keary, Hugh, 253
Keary, Patrick, 252
Keary, W. E., 253
Kentucky, 29, 33, 34, 162, 267, 404

Kentucky troops
Infantry
17th Kentucky, 317
19th Kentucy, 168
22nd Kentucky, 320
7th Kentucky, 320
Ketzle, Henry Carl, 242, 260, 299
King Ranch, 62, 304, 305, 306, 329, 387, 422
King, Richard, 62, 304, 387, 388, 422,
Kiowa Nation, 262
Kirby Smith, Edmund, 49, 52–61, 63, 70–76, 81, 85, 93, 100, 106, 108, 120, 152, 154, 157, 173, 198–199, 208, 213, 218, 221, 232, 238, 242, 245–246, 261, 265, 305, 308, 325, 329–330, 332–333, 368, 377–378, 424–426, 433–434
Knox, Thomas W., 365–367
Kock's Plantation, Battle of, 24, 43, 89, 226, 282

L

Lafourche Campaign, 194, 308, 321, 451
Lafourche District, 27, 41, 42, 259, 321, 362, 363, 364
Lake Charles, Louisiana, 79, 218
Lake Fausse Pointe, 314, 351
Lake Providence, Louisiana, 31
Lane, Walter P., 133, 169
Laredo, Texas, 61, 62, 260, 304, 305, 306, 345, 384
Latrille, Charles Ferdinand, Comte de Lorencez, 10
Lawler, Michael K., 297, 320, 364
Le Gloire (French ironclad frigate), 16
League, Thomas Jefferson, 84
Leake, Joseph B., 109–110, 148–152, 169, 180, 183–191
Lee, Albert, 244, 310–313
Lhuys, Édouard Drouyn de, 408, 409
Liberals (Mexican), 7–8, 17–18
liberated slaves (see emancipated slaves)
Liberty, Texas, 56, 107, 389
Likens, James B., 345
Lincecum, Gideon, 68–69
Lincoln, Abraham, 18, 21–22, 26–30, 32–35, 39–41, 45, 48, 50, 156, 216, 228, 242, 298, 302, 304, 323, 357, 359–362, 373, 389, 402, 406–409, 413–415, 421, 426, 442–447

Little River, 102, 104
Little Rock, Arkansas, 45–46, 48, 55, 100, 106–107, 136, 153–154, 157, 167, 368, 404, 416, 425
Livonia, Louisiana, 170, 193, 363–364
Logan, George, 105
Logan, John L., 101, 147–146, 150, 169, 175
Los Algodones (The Cotton Time, see also cotton), 62
Louisiana troops, Confederate
    Mounted troops
    2nd Louisiana Cavalry, 79, 82–83, 91, 95, 97, 106, 154, 163, 200, 203, 210, 214, 222–223, 247, 249, 266, 354, 383, 411, 430
    3rd Louisiana Cavalry, 426
    4th Louisiana Cavalry, 426
    5th Louisiana Cavalry, 426
    7th Louisiana Cavalry, 426
    The Mounted Zouaves, 214, 313, 351
    13th Louisiana Cavalry Battalion, 90, 426
    15th Louisiana Cavalry Battalion, 90, 102–103, 105, 152, 426
    Prairie Rangers, 80, 426
    Infantry
    1st Louisiana State Guard, 426
    2nd Louisiana State Guard, 426
    4th Louisiana Infantry, 86
    10th Louisiana "Yellow Jacket" Infantry Battalion, 351
    18th Louisiana Infantry (Creole Regiment), 90, 92, 178, 181, 185
    24th Louisiana Infantry (Crescent Regiment), 178, 181, 185
    28th Louisiana Infantry, 105, 178, 181, 185
    Confederate Guards Response Battalion (Clack's Battalion), 79, 176–178, 186–187, 192, 207, 236
    Consolidated Crescent Regiment, 367
    Mouton's (Gray's) Brigade, 56, 91, 164, 181, 183, 186
    Mouton's Division, 166, 207, 237, 312, 313, 363, 364, 368, 425
    Artillery
    1st Regular Battery, 86, 139, 176–177, 180, 181, 222–223, 226, 366,
    Benton's Louisiana Battery, 105
    Pelican Artillery, 176, 315, 366
    St. Mary's Cannoneers, 315

Louisiana troops (see also Corps d'Afrique), Union
    1st Louisiana Cavalry (Union), 160, 217, 233, 247, 249, 266, 270, 350
Love Bird (steamer), 173, 174, 302, 442
Lubbock, Francis R. (Governor of Texas), 59,
Luckett, Philip N., 345, 263
Lufkin, Edwin B., 293, 300, 301, 331
Lyon's Ferry, 170, 176

M
Magruder, John B., 45, 52–53, 56, 57–58, 91, 93, 119–120, 132–134, 218, 220–221, 243, 245–246, 261–263, 291, 296, 305–307, 309, 310, 325, 329, 330, 332–334, 344–346, 375–378, 382, 384, 385, 387, 403, 425, 434, 436, 440, 441
Maine troops,
    13th Maine Infantry, 300, 327, 331, 394–396, 398, 400, 419– 421
    15th Maine Infantry, 294, 296, 326–328, 331, 336
Major, James P., 56–57, 91, 93, 105, 152, 167, 170, 176, 197, 202, 205, 211, 217, 234, 235, 237, 266, 272, 278, 279–280, 287–290, 308, 321, 378
Maltby, William "Captain Jeff," 328, 331
Manhasset (collier), 174–175, 195
Maple Leaf (steamer), 85, 87–90, 178
Marshall, Albert, 338–341
Marshall, T. B., 237, 240, 274, 279, 286, 289, 324
Marshall, Texas, 43, 45, 58, 59, 74, 158,
Martin (enslaved man), 134
Martin, Robert M. "Bloody Bob," 80, 83–84, 253
Maryland troops: 3rd Maryland Cavalry, 402
Maryland, 19, 102, 228, 303, 402, 409, 443, 444
Massachusetts troops
    Infantry
    28th Massachusetts, 226
    54th Massachusetts, 22
    Artillery
    2nd Massachusetts Battery (Nims's), 226, 369, 274, 285–286
Matagorda Bay, 18, 29, 52, 243, 329–330, 332–334, 336, 343–344, 358, 370, 372, 374, 380, 384–386, 388–389, 393, 395, 397, 399–401, 411, 413, 419–420, 422, 425, 436

Matagorda Island, 52, 306, 331, 334, 336, 337, 341, 387, 419, 425
Matagorda Peninsula, 334, 344, 369–371, 374–375, 385, 387, 393–394, 400, 419–421
Matamoros (steamboat), 326, 384
Matamoros, Tamaulipas, Mexico, 16–17, 61–63, 71, 173, 295, 298, 301–304, 307, 372, 412–413, 415, 437
Maximilian (see Joseph, Ferdinand Maximilian)
McCallum Plantation, 138, 151, 140, 146–147, 149, 169
McClellan (steamer), 294, 296, 326
McCulloch, Henry, 262
McDade, Keet, 85, 95, 97, 101
McDougall, James A. (Senator from California), 19, 408–409,
McIlhenny, Edmund, 65
McIlhenny, Marshall, 65
McIlhenny, Mary Eliza Avery, 65
McKernan, Michael, 126
McLane, Robert M., 302–303
McMillan, James W., 170
McNeil, Henry C., 222
McNelly, Leander, 247
McNulta, John, 144, 145
McPherson, James B., 33–34, 49, 155, 157–158, 166
Mejia, Henry A., 36
Memphis, Tennessee, 34, 100, 156, 417
Meridian, Mississippi, 89
Mermentau River, 79, 206, 218, 220, 232, 246, 259, 309, 311, 330
Mexican Aid Society (see also filibusters), 19
Mexican Republican troops: 1st Mexican Volunteers, 20
Mexican War, 48, 52, 62, 295
Mexico City, 2, 7, 10, 15, 19–21, 264, 301
Mexico Club, the (see also filibusters), 19,
Michigan troops
  Artillery
  6th Michigan Heavy Artillery, 38
  7th Michigan Battery, 339, 389,
Milliken's Bend, Louisiana, 22, 31
Mississippi troops, Union
  Artillery
  2nd Mississippi Artillery (African Descent), 153
Missouri troops, Union
  Mounted troops
  6th Missouri Cavalry, 140, 142, 150, 177, 180, 187, 191, 197, 233, 274, 281, 350
  Infantry
  30th Missouri, 152–153
  Artillery
  Battery F, 1st Missouri Artillery, 339
Mobile, Alabama, 25, 26, 28, 30–33, 35, 40, 45, 46, 48, 73, 85, 96, 151, 291, 332, 417
Monroe Doctrine Committee, the (see also filibusters), 19
Monroe Doctrine, 8, 11, 19
Monroe League, the (see also filibusters), 19
Monroe, Louisiana, 45, 46, 49, 56, 76, 86–87, 88, 98, 100, 368, 416, 418, 424, 426,
Montgomery, Bacon, 150, 180, 187
Moore, John, 348
Moore, Mary, 348
Moore, Thomas O. (Governor of Louisiana), 59, 348, 433
Morgan Bend, 365
Morgan's Ferry, 91, 97, 139–140, 145, 148–149, 154, 159, 163, 168, 170, 172, 175, 177, 194–195, 205, 207, 247, 364, 449
Morganza, Louisiana, 28, 101, 138, 140, 142, 145–147, 152, 165, 167, 169, 177–178, 180–182, 185–186, 188–189, 192–193, 198, 246–247, 315, 319, 322–323, 364–365, 378, 449
Moundville, Louisiana, 217, 230, 234, 236, 237, 238, 249, 270, 272, 426
Mouton, Alfred, 56, 91, 139, 164–167, 170, 202, 205, 207, 209–210, 237, 312–313, 363–364, 368, 382, 425, 444
Murrah, Pendleton (Texas Governor), 59, 434
Mustang Island, 56, 326, 330, 331, 358

N
Nacogdoches, Texas, 253
Nancy Dawson (steamer), 442
Napoleon III (Emperor of France), 10–14, 21, 23, 27, 29, 39, 43, 46, 59, 60, 173, 264, 302–303, 322, 408
Natchez, Mississippi, 31, 33–34, 43, 49, 89, 102, 105–107, 137, 150, 152–153, 158, 166–167, 170–171, 199, 238, 425
Natchitoches, Louisiana, 42, 63, 73, 90, 238, 245, 254
Nebraska (steamboat), 319
New Braunfels, Texas, 194, 376
New England, 28, 48, 159, 195, 297–298, 327, 444–446
New Iberia, Louisiana, 64, 65, 85, 89, 91, 163, 165–166, 168, 200, 203, 206, 209–210, 213, 222, 233, 239, 240, 243, 245–246,

249, 257, 310, 312–314, 321, 325, 346, 347–356, 369, 380–382, 410–411, 429–430

New Mexico Territory (and New Mexico Campaign), 29, 86, 93, 132, 194, 300, 378, 382, 419, 451

New Orleans, Louisiana, 12–13, 17–18, 20, 27–28, 30, 33, 36, 38–39, 41–43, 45, 47–48, 50, 61, 65, 67, 86–87, 89–90, 93, 97, 101, 108–109, 111, 113, 125, 132, 134, 138, 147, 151, 154–156, 159–160, 169, 171, 173, 175, 183, 210, 214, 221, 227, 229, 231–233, 241, 243, 248, 251, 255, 258, 291, 294–297, 308–309, 311, 321–322, 324–325, 331, 333, 347, 355–357, 360, 362, 371, 373, 404, 413, 421–422, 425, 444, 446, 449–450

New Roads, Louisiana, 138, 315, 449

New Texas Landing, Louisiana, 149, 151

New York City, 19, 222, 307, 322, 355, 356, 365, 407, 448

New York (state), 19, 28, 48

New York Troops
Mounted troops
14th New York Cavalry, 233, 266
75th New York (mounted) Infantry, 124, 313
Infantry
6th New York Infantry, 86
114th New York Infantry, 121, 125, 131, 410, 429
116th New York Infantry, 49, 114, 118, 131, 159
128th New York Infantry, 97
160th New York Infantry, 121
161st New York Infantry, 124
165th New York Infantry (Duryea's Zouaves), 160, 170, 430
173rd New York Infantry, 49

Niblett's Bluff, Louisiana, 63, 83, 95, 114, 120, 159, 164, 220, 245, 260–261, 263, 265, 428

Normandie (French ironclad frigate), 16

North Star (steamer), 114, 356

Northern Sub-District of Texas, 262

Norwood Plantation, 140, 142, 148–150, 177–181, 183, 189

Nuevo Léon, Mexican state of, 15, 17, 68, 303

O

O'Brien, George W., 164, 168, 177–178, 184–185, 188–191, 230, 363–364

Odlum, Frank F., 118–120, 124, 130

Ohio, State of, 160, 162, 286

Ohio Troops
Infantry
42nd Ohio, 320
83rd Ohio, 236–237, 269, 271, 274–275, 279, 281–282, 284, 286–287, 289–290
96th Ohio, 227, 240, 265, 269, 271, 276–278, 280–285, 287, 289–290
120th Ohio Infantry, 320
Artillery
17th Ohio Battery, 268–269, 278–279, 281–282, 285–286, 289–290

Old Spanish Lake, 73

Olivier Plantation, 313

Olivier's Landing, 290, 210

Opelousas Road, 140, 146, 148–149, 150, 177–178, 227

Opelousas, Louisiana, 77, 79–80, 82, 86, 91, 93–94, 140, 149, 164, 177–178, 213, 217, 220–222, 224, 227–239, 244–245, 247–252, 259, 265–269, 271–272, 276–280, 283, 290–291, 308, 380–381, 403, 405, 428, 431, 449, 451

Orange, Texas, 44, 120

Ord, Edward O. C., 46, 47, 162, 166, 210, 220, 222, 228, 229, 414

Ouachita River, 49, 100, 102, 103, 104, 108, 152, 153, 155, 368, 416

P

Padre Island, 57, 293, 295, 358

Palacios, Texas, 371

Palmetto Ranch, 296

Panama (French warship), 173, 302, 307

Pass Cavallo, 52, 334, 343, 369, 420

Patout Plantation, 349,

Pea Ridge, Battle of, 32, 342

Pellet, Elias P., 121, 131, 131, 132, 135

Pennsylvania troops
Artillery
3rd Pennsylvania Heavy Artillery, 87

Petite Anse Island, 63, 355

Pineville, Louisiana, 152, 154

Planter (steamboat), 326, 384

Plaquemine, Louisiana, 97, 100, 139, 170, 258–259, 319–320, 362, 364

Poché, Felix Pierre, 77, 79, 230, 232, 315, 322–323, 367–368

Point Isabel, Texas, 293–295,

Pointe Coupee Parish, 86, 138, 150–152, 164, 173, 178, 198, 205, 210, 231, 237, 293,

313, 315, 322, 325, 347, 349, 355, 364, 367, 369, 449
Polignac, Prince Camille Armand Jules Marie de, 93, 229–230
Port Barré, Louisiana, 224, 228, 230, 233, 236–238, 240, 244, 247–249, 266
Port Hudson, Louisiana (including battle of), 20, 22–24, 26–27, 29–30, 33, 38, 42, 47, 49, 52, 58, 85–87, 97, 101, 106, 137–138, 146, 156, 297, 315, 318–319, 356, 379, 385, 402, 426–427, 430, 432, 445–446, 449
Port Lavaca, Texas, 125, 260, 342–345, 376, 389, 391, 393–394, 422–424, 347, 438
Porter, David Dixon, 31–32, 136, 155, 200, 259, 417
Powderhorn, Texas (see also Indianola), 376
Price, Sterling, 55, 106, 154, 245
Proclamation of Amnesty and Reconstruction, 362
Puebla, Battle of 7, 11–13, 28
Puebla, Mexico, 5, 7, 10, 20

Q

Quartermaster Department, Confederate, 74
Quintero, José Agustín, 61
Quitana, Texas, 344, 369, 375, 419

R

Rainey, Alexis T., 345, 347,
Randal, Horace, 103, 105, 106
Ransom, Thomas E. G., 325–328, 330, 337, 339, 341, 394, 400, 420, 421
Rapides Parish, Louisiana, 80, 84
Red Chief (steamboat), 209, 233, 240
Red River (and Red River Valley), 42–43, 45, 47, 49, 56, 73, 90, 92, 100, 106–107, 110, 137–138, 146, 154–155, 157–158, 164, 166–167, 169, 205, 207–208, 221, 231–232, 238–239, 241, 245–246, 248, 258, 265, 312, 315, 318–319, 321–332, 358, 368, 402, 404–405, 416–418, 425, 448, 450
Red River Campaign, 425–427, 448, 450
Refugees, 65
Reynolds, Joseph J., 404
Richmond, Texas, 376, 386
Richmond, Virginia, 54, 58, 60, 89, 94, 157, 308
Rinaldo, steamboat, 103
Rio Grande City, Texas, 61, 372,

Rio Grande Valley, 30, 61, 295, 300, 304, 346, 372, 407
Rio Grande, 10, 17, 29–30, 57, 59, 61–62, 66, 70, 75, 111, 173–174, 241–242, 257, 260, 331, 333, 346, 357, 359, 361, 372–373, 384, 386–387, 402, 407, 411–413, 418
Robert Fulton (steamboat), 163, 170, 207–208
Roberts, Oran M., 238, 249, 271, 272, 273, 275, 276, 277, 278, 280, 284, 288, 290
Robertson, Eliza, 85, 91
Robertson, Leila, 89–90
Romero Avendaño, Matías, 18, 35, 302–303
Rosecrans, William, 25, 26, 34, 136, 157, 171
Rosedale, Louisiana, 364
Rountree, Leonidas "Lee," 101, 139, 142, 176, 177, 178, 180, 181, 187
Rowley, Joseph Freeborn, 70–71, 372–373, 422–423, 437–441
Ruiz, Manuel, 301, 412–413
Rusk, Texas, 57

S

Sabine City, Texas, 44, 118, 120, 133, 263,
Sabine Lake, 114, 115, 124, 125
Sabine Pass Expedition (including the Battle of Sabine Pass), 113–114, 119–120, 123, 129, 130, 132–133, 135, 152, 155–156, 159, 175, 198, 237–238, 295, 358, 375
Sabine Pass, 18, 52, 56, 107, 113, 115–120, 123, 125, 129–132, 152, 174, 195, 220, 260, 263, 330, 333, 358
Sabine River, 40, 43, 64, 71, 79, 95, 106, 115, 120, 125, 203, 206, 218, 220, 243, 245, 253, 257, 260, 261, 296, 305, 309, 332, 346, 358, 380, 386, 428
Saligny, Alphonse Dubois de, 10–11
Sallie Robinson (steamboat), 138
salt, 63, 64, 85, 304, 355, 364
Saluria, Texas, 56, 260, 306, 329, 334, 337, 343, 369
San Antonio River, 332
San Antonio, Texas, 17, 29, 52, 57, 62, 72, 74, 300, 306, 332–333, 342, 344–345, 369, 374, 376, 384, 386, 389, 392, 419, 425
San Bernard River (defenses), 385
San Felipe, Texas, 434
San Luis Potosi, 15, 20, 111, 406
San Patricio, Texas, 422
Sandy Point, Texas, 434
Santa Gertrudis Creek, 62, 304, 387
Santleben, August, 372

Sayers, Joseph Draper, 383
Schofield, John M., 404–405
Scurry, William Read, 93
Second Mexican Empire, 23
Sells, Abram (enslaved man), 71
Semmes, Oliver J. (see also Louisiana
    troops: 1st Regular Battery), 86, 176
Serna, Jesús de la, 412
Shadows, The, 348
Shepley, George F., 40–41, 215, 216, 360–361,
    403
Sherman, William Tecumseh, 24, 33, 49,
    154–158, 166–167, 171, 325, 357, 387,
    416–418, 422
Shreveport, Louisiana, 42–43, 45, 49, 53–54,
    58–59, 61–62, 70–74, 98, 100, 106–107,
    120, 152, 154, 158–159, 166, 168, 199,
    203, 221, 238, 245, 253–254, 267, 305,
    329, 332, 358, 403, 405, 416–418, 426,
    442, 448
Sibley, Henry Hopkins, 93–95
Sibley, John Coleman, 79–80, 83, 95, 154,
    354, 355, 382
Sierra Méndez, Justo (Mexican Historian), 11
Simmesport, Louisiana, 138, 145, 170, 177,
    205, 208, 238, 246–247, 313, 368, 425
Singer contact mines, 73
Siringo, Charlie, 399–401
Slaughter, James E., 332–334, 376
slavery, 6, 21–23, 39, 41, 179, 183–187, 307,
    362–363, 447
slaves, 22, 29, 38–39, 41–42, 45, 53, 57–58,
    64, 66–67, 72, 75, 100, 134, 192, 195, 200,
    208, 232, 235, 253, 308, 362–363, 403,
    417, 428, 432, 440–441, 447, 449
Slidell, John, 11, 74–75, 302
Smith, Leon, 118, 120, 124, 138, 130, 330, 343
Smith, Susan (enslaved woman), 348–349
Smith's Landing (Matagorda Peninsula),
    370, 394, 420
Sneed and Cottier Plantation, 315, 365–366
Sonora, Mexico, 15
South Carolina troops: 2nd South Carolina
    (Union), 22
Southerner (steamboat), 313
Spaight, Ashley W., 91, 106, 118, 124, 345
Spain, 7, 10, 303
Spanish Lake (see also Old Spanish Lake),
    209, 349, 350, 352
Speed, James, 387–388
Speight, Joseph, 56

Springfield Landing, Louisiana, 138
Squires, Miles T., 202
St. Charles (steamboat), 209,
St. Charles Hotel (New Orleans), 41, 112, 215
St. Joseph Island, 331, 336, 358
St. Landry Parish, Louisiana, 80, 426, 431
St. Louis, Missouri, 30, 364, 404
St. Martinville, Louisiana, 214, 314, 351, 411,
    429–430
St. Mary's (steamboat), 370
Stanton Edwin M. (Secretary of War), 24–25,
    27, 41, 199, 373, 404
Steele, Frederick, 31, 44–48, 52, 100, 102,
    106, 154, 157–158, 402, 404–405, 416
Steele, William S., 262
Sterling, M. C., 140,
Sterling's Plantation (see also Botany Bay
    Plantation), 143, 145–146, 149–150, 152,
    177–178, 184–187, 189, 191, 193, 363
Sterling's Plantation, Battle of, 196, 198, 230,
    238, 241, 270, 279, 293, 297, 363, 367,
    382, 449
Stevenson, John Dunlap, 48, 98, 100, 155,
    157
Stone, Charles Pomeroy, 161, 239, 241, 244,
    256–257, 259, 308–309, 313, 350, 369,
    371, 374–375, 450
Stone, Kate, 64–65
Sumner, Charles (Senator from
    Massachusetts), 19, 409, 411
Sweet, Alexander Edwin, 380, 389–392

T
Tamaulipas, Mexico, 15, 306, 347, 407, 412
Tampico, Mexico, 15–16, 18, 36–37, 346, 411
Taylor, Richard (Captain, Company A, 33rd
    Texas Cavalry), 296, 391
Taylor, Richard, 24, 25, 41–43, 47, 56, 80,
    84, 90–95, 98, 100, 105–106, 108, 152,
    154, 157–158, 161, 163–164, 166–167,
    169–171, 200, 205–208, 212–214,
    217–218, 221, 224, 226–227, 230–239,
    241, 243–247, 251, 253, 259, 265–266,
    270, 272, 291–292, 296, 308–310, 312,
    315, 325, 330, 332, 351, 356, 364, 368,
    377–379, 382–383, 392, 403, 425–428,
    431, 433, 444–445
Taylor, Zachary, 232, 444
Teche Campaign (April–May 1863), 42,
    85–86, 93–94, 125, 159, 161, 164, 171,
    194, 205, 352, 380–382

Teche Region, 24, 56, 79, 84, 89, 105, 157–
158, 161, 163, 169–170, 198, 200–203,
205, 209–210, 228, 231–232, 239, 243,
246, 295, 312–313, 348, 351, 355, 358,
372, 383, 410, 425, 429
Tejanos, 295
Ten Percent Plan, see Proclamation of
Amnesty and Reconstruction
Tensas River, 31, 56, 102
Terrell, Alexander, 333
Texas Coast Command, 52
Texas Hill Country, see Hill Country of Texas
Texas Marine Department vessels
Cora (steamboat), 329, 330, 336, 343,
397–399, 419, 421
Annie Dale (schooner), 421
John F. Carr (steamboat), 330, 343,
397–400
Josiah H. Bell (steamboat), 115, 330,
Lady of the Lake (schooner), 330, 421
Lucy Gwin (steamboat), 330, 421
Neptune (steamboat), 330
Uncle Ben (steamboat), 115, 120, 124,
129, 330
Bayou City (steamboat), 330
**Texas troops (see also Arizona troops),
Confederate**
Mounted troops
1st Texas Partisan Rangers, 91, 152, 169,
200, 203
1st Texas Cavalry, 120, 133, 134, 218, 220,
393, 396
2nd Texas Cavalry, 56, 91, 333, 342
2nd Texas Partisan Rangers, 91, 152
4th Cavalry, Texas State Troops, 345,
4th Texas Cavalry, 85, 86, 91, 94, 98, 139,
181, 226, 235, 237, 265, 272, 291, 307,
311, 352, 354, 382, 435,
5th Texas Cavalry, 76, 80–82, 91, 95–97,
139, 146, 159, 181, 196, 203, 221–222,
229, 237, 248, 272, 289, 301, 309–310,
313, 344, 349, 353, 381–382, 434, 443
5th Texas Partisan Rangers, 262
7th Texas Cavalry, 91, 139, 181, 194,
236–237, 247, 271, 273, 284, 350,
352, 354
12th Texas Cavalry Battalion, 134
12th Texas Cavalry, 90, 100
13th Texas Cavalry Battalion (Waller's
Battalion), 85, 91, 97, 139, 237, 272,
282–283, 290, 313, 364, 383
19th Texas Cavalry, 90

20th Texas Cavalry, 262
23rd Texas Cavalry, 120, 134, 260, 333,
375
26th Texas Cavalry, 333
29th Texas Cavalry, 262
30th Texas Cavalry, 262
33rd Texas Cavalry, 295–296, 299, 305,
345, 380, 384, 389, 440–441
35th Texas Cavalry (Brown's), 333,
396–398
35th Texas Cavalry (Liken's), 345
36th Texas Cavalry, 333, 339, 343, 376,
421, 424
37th Texas Cavalry, 333
Border Regiment, 262
Rountree's (Texas) Battalion, 91, 97, 139,
177, 319, 333
Texas Squadron (see also 11th Texas
Volunteers), 163, 166, 200, 203, 235,
287
Waller's Battalion (see 13th Texas
Cavalry Battalion)
Infantry
2nd Texas Infantry, 345, 376, 436
3rd Infantry, Texas State Troops, 327
3rd Texas Infantry, 120, 345,
4th Infantry, Texas State Troops, 436
8th Texas Infantry, 327, 329, 332, 334
11th Texas Infantry, 272, 275, 278, 284,
290,
11th Texas Volunteers Battalion (see
also, Texas squadron), 91, 124,
163–164, 178, 184–186, 230, 345, 363
13th Texas Cavalry (Dismounted), 231
13th Texas Volunteers, 56, 91
15th Texas Infantry, 178, 186, 188, 197,
272, 275, 278, 284, 289–290
16th Texas Infantry, 232, 236, 237, 315,
317, 364,
17th Texas Infantry, 424
18th Texas Infantry, 238, 271, 275, 278,
284, 290
19th Texas Infantry, 319
20th Texas Infantry, 125, 134, 345
21st Texas Infantry Battalion, 118, 120,
124, 345
22nd Texas Cavalry (Dismounted), 90,
22nd Texas Infantry, 230
31st Texas Cavalry (Dismounted), 91, 92,
158, 178, 186
34th Texas Cavalry (Dismounted), 38, 90
Waul's Texas Legion, 345–346

Harrison's (Speight's and Polignac's) Brigade, 56, 164, 168, 178, 181, 182, 187, 186, 189, 192, 230

Walker's Texas Division, 56, 90, 102, 104, 106, 152, 166, 170, 205, 207, 230, 237, 312, 313, 319, 321, 363, 364, 368, 383, 425

Artillery

1st Texas Heavy Artillery, 134, 440

Austin (Texas) Light Artillery, 333, 345

Creuzbaur's Texas Battery, 346

Daniel's Texas Battery (The Lamar Artillery), 272, 279, 315, 319, 323,

Edgar's Battery, (Alamo City Guards), 321

Fox's Texas Battery, 345

Gibson's Battery, 91, 345

Gonzales's (Texas) Battery, 56, 120

Hugh's Texas Battery, 346

Jone's Texas Battery (The Dixie Grays), 120, 346

McMahan's Battery, 333, 375–376, 436

Moseley's Battery, 333

Nichols's (Texas) Battery, 56, 120, 346

Pratt's Texas Battery, 90

Val Verde Battery, 139, 149, 226, 272, 279

Texas troops, Union

Mounted troops

1st Texas Cavalry (Union), 201, 203, 210–211, 217, 222, 226–227, 241, 295–296, 299, 304, 307, 309, 333, 372, 376, 422

2nd Texas Cavalry (Union), 387

Thibodaux, Louisiana, 41, 66, 319, 322

Thirteenth Amendment, 41

Thomas (steamer), 124–125

Thomas, Lorenzo, 108, 112

Thouvenel, Édourard Antoine de, 408

Tiger Island, 159

Todd, Samuel M., 80

Trinity River, 389

Trinity, Louisiana, 89, 102, 103, 104, 106, 152, 153, 154, 167

Tunica Bend, 146

Tyler, Texas, 65, 424

U

U.S. Constitution, 6, 41, 362

U.S. Navy, 31, 74, 118, 123, 243, 245

Unionism, Unionists, and Unionist dissent, 17, 41–42, 76–77, 83–84, 111, 201, 203–204, 222, 241, 247, 252–256, 295, 298,

346, 360–362, 372–373, 376, 380–381, 390, 428–430, 437, 444, 447, 449

US Enrollment Act of March 3, 1863 (see also conscription), 67

USS *Alabama*, 384

USS *Argosy*, 320

USS *Arizona*, 113, 124–127, 129

USS *Cayuga*, 121, 174

USS *Champion* (Gunboat No. 24), 101

USS *Choctaw*, 318–319, 321–322

USS *Clifton*, 113, 118–121, 124–132, 375

USS *Essex*, 320

USS *Estrella*, 398–400

USS *Granite City*, 113, 116–117, 124, 130, 340, 394–398, 419–420

USS *Indianola*, 73

USS *Kenwood*, 137, 193, 319

USS *Lafayette*, 136–137, 193, 318–319, 321, 364, 366

USS *Louisville*, 101

USS *Monongahela*, 326–327, 329, 397–398, 400, 419–420

USS *Morning Light*, 115

USS *Neosho*, 137–138, 193, 322, 364–367

USS *Osage*, 137–139, 208

USS *Penobscot*, 398

USS *Queen*, 420

USS *Rattler*, 149–150

USS *Richmond*, 356

USS *Sachem*, 113, 124–127, 129, 131, 375

USS *Sciota*, 394, 396–400, 420

USS *Seminole*, 174

USS *Signal*, 137, 317–319, 321–322,

USS *St. Claire*, 319-320

USS *Velocity*, 115

Utica (steamer), 86–87

V

Val Verde, Battle of, 196,

Van Buren, Arkansas, 72

Van Dorn, Earl, 52

Vandever, William, 168

Velasco, Texas, 56, 243, 260, 329, 344–345, 369–370, 374–375, 385–386, 388, 394, 419, 434

Veracruz, Mexico, 8, 10, 15, 20, 264

Vermilion Bayou, Vermilion River (see Bayou Vermilion)

Vermilion Parish, 431

Vermilionville (Lafayette), Louisiana, 79, 85, 91–92, 95, 114, 158–159, 163–164, 166, 205, 207–209, 211, 213, 220–223, 239,

243, 248–249, 251, 257, 268, 291, 293, 297, 307–311, 313, 330, 351–352, 377, 381, 383, 430, 449

Vermont troops
Infantry
8th Vermont Infantry, 121
Veteran Volunteer Order (General Orders No. 191), 414
Vicksburg Campaign, 20, 22, 23, 24, 25, 26, 29, 30, 31, 32, 48, 52, 58, 66, 85, 87, 89, 106, 110, 113, 145, 154, 156, 161, 199, 228, 282, 293, 325, 337, 340, 342, 345, 356–357, 359, 379, 387, 413, 426, 428, 432, 450
Vicksburg, Battle of, see Vicksburg Campaign)
Vicksburg, Mississippi, 34–35, 43, 45, 48–49, 98, 107–108, 152, 154–156, 158, 167, 171, 238, 385, 417–418, 425
Victoria, Texas, 62, 98, 134, 306, 332, 339, 369, 371, 374, 376, 386, 389, 393, 436
Vidal, Adrían J., 295
Vidalia, Louisiana, 31, 89, 102, 152–154, 164, 167
Vidaurri, Santiago, 17, 61, 68, 303, 306
Vienna, Louisiana, 98
Ville Platte, Louisiana, 235–238, 266
Vincent, William G., 200, 203, 204, 205, 209, 223, 383
Virginia Point, Texas, 375, 385, 434, 435

W

Wade, Fred, 68, 435
Walker, John G., 56, 59, 90, 93, 102, 152, 166, 205, 230, 312, 315, 347, 362, 364, 367, 368, 425
Warren, Fitz Henry, 384, 389, 391, 393
Washburn, Cadwallader C., 213, 228, 248, 267–270, 272, 274–276, 283, 288–291, 297, 331, 336–337, 339–340, 342, 369–372, 374–375, 377–378, 382, 385–387, 394, 413–414, 419
Washburn, Elihu B., 414
Washburn, Henry D., 336–337, 339, 341–342, 384
Washington County, Texas, 68
Washington, Arkansas, 45
Washington, D. C., 18, 27, 30, 35, 45, 47, 171, 215, 298, 302, 362, 373–374, 407–409, 413–414, 444–445

Washington, Louisiana, 81, 91, 164–165, 168, 170, 197, 202, 205, 214, 217, 228, 230–232, 236–238, 244, 247–249, 265–266, 449
Waterloo, Louisiana, 365
Watkins, John W., 76, 80, 82–83, 95, 97, 159, 163–164, 181, 310–311, 344, 353, 434
Waul, Thomas, 345,
Weeks, Charles Conrad, 348–349
Weeks, William Frederick, 64, 209, 210, 348
Weisinger, Reed, 178
Weitzel, Godfrey, 41, 48, 107, 109–111, 114, 117–118, 121, 123–124, 130, 211, 225–227, 233
Wells, James Madison, 84
West, Charles Shannon, 81–82
West, J. W., 93
Western Sub-District of Texas, 260
Whitaker, John Smith, 215
White Cloud (steamboat), 319
White River, 31
Whitley, Sharp R., 354
Wilkins, Jerry C., 428
Williams, John, 400–401,
Winn Parish, Louisiana, 76
Wisconsin, 103, 162, 228, 271, 292,
Wisconsin troops
Mounted troops
4th Wisconsin Cavalry, 97
17th Wisconsin Mounted Infantry, 97, 104, 105, 153
Infantry
20th Wisconsin Infantry, 140, 412–413
23rd Wisconsin Infantry, 233, 269, 271, 274, 276–277, 280–281, 283–284, 287, 289–291,
29th Wisconsin Infantry, 160, 214, 286, 291
Artillery
1st Independent Battery Wisconsin Light Artillery, 370
Woods, Peter C., 333, 343

Y

Young's Point, Louisiana, 31

Z

Zaragoza, Ignacio Seguín, 5–7, 11, 20

CPSIA information can be obtained
at www.ICGtesting.com
Printed in the USA
JSHW011407030423
39758JS00003B/3